BROTHERS IN ARMS

BROTHERS IN ARMS

The Kennedys, the Castros, and
the Politics of Murder

Gus Russo and Stephen Molton

BLOOMSBURY

New York   Berlin   London

Published by Bloomsbury USA, New York

All papers used by Bloomsbury USA are natural, recyclable products made from wood grown in well-managed forests. The manufacturing processes conform to the environmental regulations of the country of origin.

LIBRARY OF CONGRESS CATALOGING-IN-PUBLICATION DATA

Russo, Gus.
   Brothers in arms : the Kennedys, the Castros, and the politics of murder / Gus Russo and Stephen Molton.—1st U.S. ed.
      p.   cm.
   Includes bibliographical references
   ISBN-13: 978-1-59691-532-9 (hardcover)
   ISBN-10: 1-59691-532-3 (hardcover)
   1. Kennedy, John F. (John Fitzgerald), 1917–1963—Assassination.   2. Kennedy, Robert F., 1925–1968—Assassination.   3. Kennedy, John F. (John Fitzgerald), 1917–1963.   4. Kennedy, Robert F., 1925–1968.   5. Castro, Fidel, 1926–
6. Castro Ruz, Raúl, 1930– 7. Assassination—Political aspects—United States—History—20th century.   8. Assassination—Political aspects—Cuba—History—20th century.   9. United States—Foreign relations—Cuba.   10. Cuba—Foreign relations—United States.   I. Molton, Stephen.   II. Title.

   E842.9.R873   2008
   973.922092—dc22

                                                                          2008023589

First U.S. Edition 2008

1 3 5 7 9 10 8 6 4 2

Typeset by Westchester Book Group
Printed in the United States of America by Quebecor World Fairfield

Contents

Cast of Characters

American Politicians and Officials

James Jesus Angleton (1917–1987) — Long-serving chief of the CIA's counterintelligence (CI) staff (1954–1975). (CIA crypto: KU/MOTHER.*)

Richard Mervin Bissell, Jr. (1909–1994) — CIA Deputy Director for Plans (1958–1961), directed the overthrows of foreign leaders Jacobo Árbenz Guzmán (Guatemala), Patrice Lumumba (Congo), Rafael Leónidas Trujillo (Dominican Republic), Abd al-Karim Qasim (Iraq), Ngo Dinh Diêm (Vietnam), Fidel Castro (Cuba), and others.

Joseph Anthony Califano Jr. (b. 1931) — General Counsel for the U.S. Army during the Kennedy administration, aide on the Pentagon's Cuban Coordinating Committee.

Allen Welsh Dulles (1893–1969) — longest-serving CIA Director (1953–1961). Longtime Kennedy family friend who served on the Warren Commission.

Jack Edward Dunlap (1928–1963) — Employee of the National Security Agency (NSA) and liaison to CIA's interagency "Staff D," which controlled the Castro assassination plots. Sold Staff D files to KGB.

Desmond FitzGerald (1910–1967) (pseudo "James Clark") — Headed CIA's Far East Division in the 1950s, later the Cuba Desk, then named Chief of

---

*Other relevant CIA cryptos include: KUBARK (CIA Headquarters), ODENVY (FBI), ODYOKE (U.S. Government), PBRUMEN (Cuba), PBPRIME (United States), LCFLUTTER (Polygraph), LIENVOY (Wiretap).

the Western Hemisphere (1964) before becoming Deputy Director for Plans (1965–1967).

General Alexander Haig Jr. (b. 1924) — During the Kennedy years, Haig served in the Office of the Deputy Chief of Staff for Operations (DCSOPS) at the Pentagon (1962–1964) and the Cuban Coordinating Committee. He later served as Military Assistant to the Presidential Assistant for National Security Affairs, Henry Kissinger. In 1970, President Richard Nixon promoted Haig to Deputy Assistant to the President for National Security Affairs. He served as White House Chief of Staff under Presidents Nixon and Gerald Ford. From 1974 to 1979, Haig served as the Supreme Allied Commander Europe.

Samuel Halpern (1923–2005) — After serving in the OSS, became a career CIA officer (1948–1974); became Deputy Chief for Operations and Executive Officer at the CIA's Tokyo Station, then Des FitzGerald's Executive Assistant on the Cuba Desk. In the early 1970s he was Deputy Chief of the CIA's Division of Domestic Collections. He retired in 1974 after receiving the Intelligence Medal of Merit.

Richard McGarrah Helms (1913–2002) — CIA Director of Plans (1962–1964), became CIA Director (1966–1973).

James Hosty (b. 1927) — FBI Special Agent in Dallas who monitored Oswald in 1963.

John Fitzgerald Kennedy (1917–1963) — Thirty-fifth President of the United States (1961–1963). (GP/IDEAL.)

Robert Francis Kennedy (1925–1968) — Attorney General of the United States (1961–1964), Senator from New York (1965–1968). (GP/FOCUS.)

Lyndon Baines Johnson (1908–1973) — Thirty-sixth President of the United States (1963–1969).

Laurence Keenan (b. 1925) — FBI Special Agent sent by J. Edgar Hoover to Mexico immediately after the assassination.

John Alexander McCone (1902–1991) — CIA Director (1961–1965).

David Atlee Phillips (1922–1988) ("Orville Horsfall") — CIA Officer (1950–1975) involved in clandestine operations in Guatemala, Cuba, and Chile from the 1950s to the early 1970s. Head of Cuban Operations in 1963 while stationed in Mexico City. Became head of Covert Ops, and later Chief of Western Hemisphere.

Winston Mackinley Scott (1909–1971) ("Willard C. Curtis") — After working as FBI agent in Havana during World War II, became CIA Mexico City Station Chief (1956–1969).

Theodore "Ted" Shackley (1927–2002) — CIA Station Chief in Miami (JM/WAVE) during Kennedy administration. He later oversaw "Operation Phoenix" in Vietnam, before being named to head all CIA worldwide covert ops in 1976.

Martin Underwood (1915–2003) — Public relations man for Mayor Richard J. Daley in Chicago in the fifties; brought to Washington by Joseph Kennedy to assist in the 1960 presidential election. Later hired full-time by President Johnson as his top advance man for foreign trips.

Cubans (Including Exiles)

Luis Alberu Souto (b. 1915) — Spanish-born Cuban artist working in the Cultural Attaché Office of the Cuban embassy in Mexico City in the 1960s. The entire time, he was a paid informant (LI-RING-3) for Win Scott.

Sergio Vicente Arcacha Smith (1923–2000) — Cuban Ambassador to India under Batista's predecessor, Cuban president Carlos Prío Socorras. He fled Cuba after Castro's victory and became the New Orleans delegate of the Cuban Revolutionary Council.

Fulgencio Batista y Zaldivar (1901–1973) — Cuban President (1940–1944) and "Military Leader" (1954–1959).

Luisa Rodríguez Carrelero Calderón (b. 1940) — Cuban DGI agent working in the Commercial Office of the Cuban embassy in Mexico City in 1963.

Fidel Alejandro Castro Ruz (b. 1926) — Cuba's Military Leader and twenty-second President (1959–2008). (CIA crypto: AM/THUG.)

Raúl Modesto Castro Ruz (b. 1931) — Cuba's twenty-third President (2008–), previously Second Secretary of Central Committee of the Communist Party of Cuba, First Vice President of the Cuban Council of State, and Minister of the Revolutionary Armed Forces from 1959 until 2008.

Dr. Rolando Cubela Secades (AM/LASH) (b. 1933) — High-ranking Cuban revolutionary and physician enlisted by the Kennedy administration to murder Fidel after Cubela became disillusioned with Castro and his brand of Communism.

Osvaldo Dorticós Torrado (1919–1983) — Twenty-first President of Cuba (1959–1976).

Fabian Escalante Font (b. 1940) — Senior Cuban G2 officer, became head of the Department of State Security (DSE) in 1976, and in 1982 became a senior official in the Interior Ministry. He became the regime's official expert and spokesman on the Kennedy assassination. War name "Roberto."

Ernesto "Che" Guevara (1928–1967) — Argentine-born Marxist who became a Castro "compadre" in the Cuban revolution as a commander in the 26th of July Movement. Became president of the Cuban National Bank and "supreme prosecutor" over the revolutionary tribunals and countless firing squad executions. (CIA crypto: AM/QUACK.)

Carlos Lechuga Hevia (b. 1918) — Cuban Ambassador to the United Nations (1962–1964) when that office provided cover for the 1962 Cuban terrorist New York bomb plot; previously was Cuban Ambassador to Mexico (early 1962), where sources say he had an affair with Silvia Durán—which Durán herself has admitted. He was a contact of New Orleans–based G2 spy Fernando Fernández.

Ramiro Valdés Menéndez (b. 1932) — Founding member of the 26th of July Movement and a member of the Politburo of the Communist Party of Cuba; has held many important governmental posts, including Interior Minister and Vice Prime Minister.

Maria Teresa Proenza (b. 1908) — Cuban intelligence propagandist working in the Cuban Mexico City embassy under the cover of Cultural Attaché.

Oscar, Antonio, Reynoso, et al. — Cuban intelligence officers who broke their silence in 2004–2005 regarding Cuba's year-long relationship with Oswald and their foreknowledge of his deadly intent. In 2005, they were persuaded to tell their story for German network WDR, albeit without use of their images.

Vladimir Rodríguez Lahera (1937–1986) (AM/MUG-1) — High-ranking member of Castro's DGI intelligence service, defected to the U.S. in 1964 and began working for the CIA.

Soviets

Nikita Sergeyevich Khrushchev (1894–1971) — Soviet Premier and First Secretary of the Communist Party of the Soviet Union (1953–1964). After his removal by bloodless coup in 1964, Khrushchev was monitored by the KGB, forcing him to smuggle his memoirs out to the West in 1970.

Vladimir Alexandrovich Kryuchkov (1924–2007) — Communist Central Committee Party member starting in the 1950s, later KGB First Directorate Chief (1978–1988) and KGB Chairman (1988–1991).

Nikolai Sergeyevich Leonov (b. 1928) — Senior KGB officer responsible for liaison with Cuba; became early mentor of Che Guevara and Raúl Castro. KGB Mexico City Station Chief in the 1960s.

Vasili Nikitich Mitrokhin (1922–2004) — Archivist for the KGB's First Directorate (1956–1985). In 1992, he smuggled out over 25,000 pages of key documents he had copied by hand, giving them to England's MI6 intelligence service.

Marina Alexandrovna Medvedeva Nikolayevna Prusakova Oswald-Porter (b. 1941) — Russian-born wife/widow of Lee Harvey Oswald.

Col. Ilya Vasilyevich Prusakov (1910–1992) — Marina's uncle with whom she lived in Minsk; senior engineering official in the Ministry of Internal Affairs (MVD), the parent of the KGB.

Vladimir Yefimovich Semichastny (1924–2001) — Head of the KGB from 1961 to 1967.

Aleksandr Nikolaevich Shelepin (1918–1994) — Head of the KGB from 1958 to 1961.

Major General Igor Demyanovich Statsenko (1918–1987) — Senior Soviet Military Commander in Cuba in the 1960s. Observed the interrogation of Rolando Cubela after his arrest.

Mexicans

Fernando Gutiérrez Barrios (1927–2000) — Chief of the brutal Dirección Federal de Seguridad (DFS), or Mexican secret police (1964–1970); governor of Veracruz (1986–1988) and Secretary of the Interior (1988–1994). Worked undercover for Win Scott (as LI-TEMPO-4).

Silvia Tirado de Durán (b. 1937) — Mexican national, employee of the Visa Section of the Cuban consulate in Mexico City in 1963. Castro supporter.

Pedro Gutiérrez Valencia (b. 1904) — Mexican credit investigator for El Palacio de Herriro department store; investigated many employees of the Mexican Cuban consulate, including Luisa Calderón.

Elena Garro de Paz (1916–1998) — Considered one of the most important Mexican writers ever, she was married to Mexican Nobel Prize winner in literature Octavio Paz. With her teenaged daughter Elenita, Elena was a regular on the cultural and diplomatic party circuit in Mexico City.

Oscar Contreras Lartigue (b. 1939) — 1963 law student at Mexico City's National Autonomous University. He belonged to a left-wing student group that supported the Castro revolution and had contacts in the Cuban embassy.

Others

George de Mohrenschildt (1911–1977) — Dallas petroleum geologist who befriended Oswald and his wife Marina in 1962 and 1963.

Lee Harvey Oswald (1939–1963) (GP/FLOOR) — New Orleans–born Marxist and Castro sympathizer who murdered President Kennedy and Dallas policeman J. D. Tippit, and gravely wounded Texas Governor John Connally, on November 22, 1963.

Jack Ruby (*né* Jacob Rubenstein) (1911–1967) — Dallas nightclub owner who murdered Lee Harvey Oswald on November 24, 1963, after his emotional devastation resulting from Kennedy's death two days prior.

Antulio Ramírez Ortiz (1926) — Puerto Rican who hijacked a U.S. commercial plane to Cuba in 1961. He worked inside G2 headquarters for the next few years and then came to the U.S. in 1975, where he served time in federal prison for the hijacking.

Maj. Gen. Edwin Anderson Walker (1909–1993) — Career Army officer (1928–1961). Upon retirement, became a spokesman for arch right-wing extremists, bigots, and anti-Communists. Missed being killed by Lee Harvey Oswald by a millimeter on April 10, 1963.

New Year's Day parade in Havana, 1962

Introduction

JOHN FITZGERALD KENNEDY assumed the presidency at a remarkable moment in history. The ferocity of World War II was past, and the generation that had fought that war—not the senior officers, but the people in the trenches—felt it was their turn to assume command of America. So when the old warhorse Eisenhower passed the torch to Kennedy, this dashing young political actor was already a symbol as much as he was a man—an emblem of post-apocalyptic resurgence, of a victorious America ready to take responsibility for rebuilding a shattered world.

With the help of television, which made him all the more accessible, John Kennedy was the embodiment of the new, modernist America. It was as if this rich, glamorous Navy veteran had been born for the part. He was the youngest man ever elected to the office, and his beautiful wife and children completed the picture of a president ready-built to provide hope for a postwar world.

The sense of near-predestination that attended Kennedy made his assassination that much more shocking. The man had survived World War II only to be gunned down, in full view, riding in a convertible on a sunny American street. That last Kennedy footage, that portrait of youth, beauty, charm, power, and death, was part of the reason his murder would be so instantly fictionalized; why the truth of it would take almost half a century to know. It was simply beyond reason, beyond comprehension.

Kennedy personified America's victorious philosophy, its complex democratic ideals, its mighty capitalism, and its unstinting belief in liberation through personal initiative. Wall Street had given the Kennedys their fortune, and Wall Street had given the country its new warriors. The world conflict had dwindled to a cold war between social theories, and the new breed of warrior-spies were mostly men from the gentry, men who had lived the American Dream at its material best and had the most to lose if the nation faltered under the weight of its victory.

There was another wildly charismatic political actor of the day, Fidel Castro, a guardian of the other virtue—collective freedom from the depredations of capitalism. He was the personification of a new socialism, post-Nazism. In his military garb, calling for liberation from imperialism and exploitation, he too brought a sense of hope and justice in the wake of devastation.

These two leaders prevailed over the Western Hemisphere in the early 1960s, having risen to power with two fundamentally different visions of freedom. Initially, some saw a natural kinship between them, but politics would prevent it; they were each in the grip of the new war's paradigm, one of strictly defined opposites. Kennedy and Castro and their indispensable brothers in arms, Robert and Raúl, forged in conflict and conditioned to court it, would become each other's nemeses.

Two would be killed. Two would make it to old age. And only one among them, Robert, would ever really force himself beyond those times and seek some reconciliation of the opposites. Locked in their corners, frozen in their political personas, the brothers' war almost became a world war, more than once, and it lives on as few other war stories ever have.

As of 2003, a convincing argument could be made that there was no reason to add to the ocean of ink devoted to "the Kennedy assassination." By that time, the conclusion that Lee Harvey Oswald committed the deed had long been sealed, except in the minds of those unfamiliar with the ballistics evidence, or those few who would never accept his guilt under any circumstances. But even for those who know that Oswald pulled the trigger, there still existed thorny questions within the story.

The central questions, for the authors of this book at least, had always been: did Oswald commit the act *for* Castro; and did Castro or his agents play any role in the tragedy? The killer was well known for his support of the Castro revolution, and Fidel himself, unbeknownst to the Warren Commission appointed to investigate the crime, had been the object of numerous murder plots orchestrated by agents of Oswald's victim, John Kennedy. Who could have a stronger motive than Castro and his agents? They hated the Kennedys, and the feeling was mutual. Oswald had visited the Cuban and Soviet embassies in Mexico City shortly before he killed the president; there was impressive anecdotal evidence that a deeper, more ominous relationship with those consuls had resulted. But those routes to the truth had long been blocked, even to government insiders who were searching for it.

Nonetheless, the notion that this murder was the result of Cuban "blowback," the unintended consequence of a foreign policy decision, was much more than just an idle theory to those insiders; indeed, it has been considered seriously by many of America's most informed government and law enforcement officials. From presidents and their aides to senior FBI and CIA officers, there has been a quietly voiced opinion that the hand of Fidel Castro may have touched this crime. Some claimed it as simple fact. None of the more popular conspiracy theories have this kind of support inside the D.C. Beltway, because none of those other theories have ever made believable connections between Oswald and his supposed clients, the mob, the CIA, oil magnates, Lyndon Johnson, etc.

Kennedy assassination researchers disagree, often rabidly, on many aspects of the event, but there is consensus on one thing: there were huge and intentional gaps in the official investigations. For the authors, those gaps were at their widest on the topic of Oswald's possible Cuban motives, rumored since before the echoes of those three shots in Dealey Plaza had entirely receded. Yet after the disinformed Warren Commission closed the case, no official agency, no deep-pocketed network felt compelled to spend serious money to look into it further, and few single authors could mount such an investment either. Their reasoning was understandable: not only would such an undertaking be expensive, but, more important, there was no guarantee of success. The most that one might be able to obtain was far-off-the-record testimony; persuading foreign spies to go public is one of the most difficult tasks the journalist can face. Thus, the Cuban angle, always the most compelling, seemed certain to fall through the cracks of history.

Meanwhile, the truth was being buried by other factors as well.

Assassinations pose the same mysteries as ordinary homicides, but multiplied by the infinite exponents of political intrigue. In a democratic society, freedom of information includes the freedom to reach outrageous conclusions. Myths can become reality almost as easily as they do in highly controlled propaganda states.

The murder of John Kennedy became the material of an entire generation's myths and legends. After Dallas, America's open culture became the seedbed for anti-government propaganda sent from Moscow and Havana, much of which is now taken as fact. They even tampered with the one and only legal indictment ever brought in the case, against Clay Shaw and his so-called conspirators in New Orleans. But the truth of Dallas, or as much of the truth as we are ever apt to know, was simpler, more human, and thus more classically tragic than any of the stories concocted by the Kremlin or the New Orleans district attorney, or a host of other conspiracy hunters. It was a story of American and Cuban virtue gone awry; of great talent, ideal-ism, intellect, and precocity met squarely by the forces of hubris, machismo, recklessness, and hate.

Before the scientific analyses of the House investigation in 1979, there were legitimate reasons to question whether Oswald was even the shooter. But even after Oswald's guilt was resolved, the authors of this book remained haunted by the lack of a meaningful inquiry into his sojourn in Mexico City, then the heart of Western Hemisphere espionage, where unvetted reports of Oswald's contacts were rampant and often credible.

As the years went on, coauthor Russo began interviewing officers of the Dallas Police, FBI, CIA, and the Secret Service, along with presidential ad-visers, U.S. official congressional investigators, and numerous foreign intelli-gence services. Although one might expect all these agents' disparate agendas to cloud the issue, in fact the opposite was true. A pattern reflecting the true essence of the Kennedy story began to emerge. Among this hierar-chy, there is a startling amount of agreement. When trying to ferret out the facts of history, there is nothing more impressive than this sort of unanimity by agents with traditionally opposing agendas. Thus, the only remaining questions are: why did Castro-supporter Oswald do it; and what corrobo-rating evidence would prove it enough to put the case to rest?

At long last we have those answers.

But to understand Oswald's crime fully, it must be seen within the wider scope of assassination as a political instrument of the 1960s. Internationally, it was a time full of assassins. In the years leading up to President Kennedy's death, leaders would be killed in the Congo, the Dominican Republic, and Vietnam, to name but a few. Assassination was experiencing a resurgence.

This was partly a response to the immense death tolls in the "total war-fare" of World War II. The dictatorships that had sparked that war had raised a host of urgent moral and political questions in its aftermath, particularly with the emergence of new weapons capable of such mass destruction.

Faced with the choice between a resumption of total war and some more contained option, why *wouldn't* the U.S. government, or any government, consider assassination as an alternative? No wonder the option became com-monplace in the thinking of the founders of the Central Intelligence Agency. The new agency's best and brightest, men like Frank Wisner, Desmond FitzGerald, Tracy Barnes, Allen Dulles, Kermit Roosevelt, and Richard Bissell, were veterans of World War II. The memories of Hitler and Stalin we carved in their psyches. The choice of homicide over genocide seemed to be a clear one—assassination was simply a particularly extreme "psychological operation" to remove a leader with perceived personality disorders before his problems spilled into the world. By the time John Kennedy took office, it was fast becoming a prerequisite for any standard military coup.

But the problem with assassination as an instrument of change, of course, was that anyone could use it. It could cut both ways. The relationship between *sane* charismatic leaders and their populations could also be severed, just as conclusively. In the wake of Dallas, fearing an international meltdown, Lyndon Johnson halted all attempts to kill or overthrow Castro and conspired—with Robert Kennedy—to cover the assassin's ideological tracks. Johnson made an executive decision to break the personalized cycle of violence; but, although he averted an international firestorm, the damage to America's internal life had just begun.

Lee Harvey Oswald's murder of the president was a perfectly aimed act of terrorism, destroying the nation's sense of security and undermining its social contract. It ushered assassination into the American domestic experience as a seemingly perennial event: these were the years of Malcolm X, Dr. Martin Luther King, Harvey Milk, Ronald Reagan, Andy Warhol, John Lennon. Worse, it set in motion a "psychological operation" on a national scale, one that continues to this day.

The two-part question of Oswald's deepest motive and modus operandi have haunted American life for forty-five years, but the last few witnesses who could lay this case to rest have finally come forward.

In 2003, coauthor Gus Russo received a phone call from his friend Wilfried Huismann, a documentary filmmaker and investigative reporter[1] from Bremen, Germany. Willi was calling to say that he had persuaded the German network WDR (Westdeutscher Rundfunk Köln) to underwrite new research into the labyrinth of foreign intrigue surrounding the Kennedy case, enabling him and Russo to make a documentary film about it. The timing was perfect. Russo had recently received a tip from the National Archives that thousands of unredacted versions of previously released documents and recordings had been re-released well ahead of schedule. Russo signed on to collaborate on the film.

Brothers in Arms was largely inspired by the interviews acquired for the resultant 2006 WDR television documentary, *Rendezvous with Death*, and

chive material. These reports have helped fill in many
mes—in the historical record, and there are additional
oughout.

importance of the new witnesses, most of whom, as
agents, chose, for good reason, to speak with their names
concealed, the reader is owed some explanation. (One witness, Marty
Underwood, is discussed in detail in the Appendix.) First, no one was paid
for their interviews; one key witness, "Oscar Marino," actually was angered
and humiliated when the authors offered to pay his taxi fare to the airport.
All were reluctant, and none sought fame or fortune; to the contrary, most
did not even seem to appreciate the importance of what they were revealing,
and had no knowledge that they were corroborating each other and the top-
secret documents we were receiving from the other end of the earth. "What
does it matter now?" was a refrain we heard repeatedly during these interviews. They had moved on, completely uninterested in why many Americans
hadn't. Although the witnesses were located surprisingly quickly, it took
many months—in one case, years—of patient cajoling to persuade them to
speak on film.

Most surprising, there was no sense of agenda or retribution involved in
what they were saying. These were not aggrieved or exiled agents hoping to
"get even." Although most were former Cuban intelligence agents now living outside Cuba, they nonetheless made it clear that their former bosses,
the Castros, had been well within their rights to defend themselves against
America by any means available. Furthermore, they agree among themselves that the Kennedys were aggressors and that the Cuban revolution was
initially a worthy undertaking. They have no qualms about their continued
hatred of the Kennedys, and are more saddened than angered by the turn
Castro's regime took in later years. Some had abandoned Cuba, not because
of disagreements with the revolution, but out of a desire to give their children better lives. Every interviewee's background was double-checked and
verified through reliable sources. Playing a key role in vetting these witnesses
was one of Mexico's leading private investigators, Maurico Laguna Berber.

That brings us to Nikolai, our source inside the Russian FSB (Federal Security Service), which had been formed in 1995 as a direct successor to the
KGB after the dissolution of the Soviet Union. He would unlock secrets that
the U.S. government itself could have unlocked years ago. As the *Rendezvous*
team was planning out the film, Russo learned that in the 1990s the Russian
government had offered to sell the KGB's previously unreleased "encrypted"
file on Oswald to U.S. authorities. Two commissioners from the Assassina-

tion Records Review Board (ARRB) traveled to Moscow to negotiate the deal, but came back empty-handed—not only was the price high, in the hundreds of thousands of dollars, but the offer was inconsistently offered, then withdrawn on a whim. The frustration at this lost opportunity is only multiplied when one considers that the ARRB suggested that the National Archives purchase the famous Zapruder film, which they did in 1998, paying the Zapruder family $16 million for the right to preserve, *but not own*, their silent, 26-second, 8 mm film of the assassination. This million-dollar storage adds nothing to our body of knowledge about the event, whereas we would have learned reams from the KGB file for a fraction of the price.

It occurred to Huismann that the team might gain access to the same material via a longtime reliable source within the FSB, an agent who, for obvious reasons, could be referred to only by a pseudonym, "Nikolai," in the film. "I have enlisted Nikolai on many occasions in the past for investigative projects," Willi said, and he had proved 100 percent reliable and accurate. At the time of the Kennedy assassination in 1963, Nikolai was a young officer in the KGB, and he would rise through the ranks to become a senior officer of the KGB and FSB. Consequently, Nikolai was tasked by Willi to try to get a look at the Oswalds' KGB/FSB headquarters files and report what he found. Later he was given one more name to research, "Cubela," whom he had never heard of. Beyond that, he was told nothing about our film, its hypothesis, or the details we were receiving from our Cuban contacts. The process was harrowing, for Nikolai could not enter the KGB sanctuary and its encrypted files at will—he needed a legitimate excuse to make an entry. Had he been caught observing files improperly, he would have spent the rest of his life in a Siberian prison camp. For this self-jeopardy, Nikolai was paid the grand total of $1,000.

Over the next two years, the film team waited for calls from Nikolai, calls that came out of the blue every four or five months. "I got in. We should meet," would be Nikolai's terse message. Through a roundabout process, Willi and Nikolai would meet in a neutral third country and conduct the debriefing. Although Nikolai dared not make off with documents, he made detailed notes of what he observed and read them to Willi at their meeting. Often the details were as disturbing to Nikolai as they were to the rest of the team. But, given his track record on previous projects over a ten-year period, we have no doubt about his truthfulness and accuracy in reporting.

Finally, it seemed, it might actually be possible to fully tell the story of those turbulent years. The story that resulted is not about *who* shot President Kennedy, nor is it about the motives of Jack Ruby, Oswald's assassin;

those issues have long been resolved. Instead, it is about the last remaining mysteries in the case—Oswald's deepest motive and the political repercussions of it. It is about when it was that the Cubans were aware of him and his plan, and how they abetted it. And finally, it is about how President Johnson and Robert Kennedy managed the resulting geopolitical crisis; and how the politics of murder changed their lives and ours in the aftermath.

So, is *Brothers in Arms* the final chapter to the story of Lee Harvey Oswald? We believe it is. But as Lincoln scholar Roy P. Basler wrote, "To know the truth of history is to realize its ultimate myth and its inevitable ambiguity." Put another way, historians rarely aspire to a courtroom, let alone a mathematical, standard of proof, because those standards are impossible to achieve; those who crave a "smoking gun" in any historical event will be frustrated.

Given the vicissitudes of human memory and the woeful incompleteness of the written record, not to mention the basic human propensity to exaggerate and dissemble, the best one can hope for is to understand the essence of an event, as related by the best sources available. One central player from the era remarked, about the 1962 Cuban Missile Crisis, "If you could interview Fidel, Raúl, JFK, and Bobby separately, you'd get four different versions of the story, guaranteed." Thus, a cynic could always point to the inconsistencies, personal agendas, and so forth, and dismiss the direct accounts of the people who *lived* these events. That would be a mistake; when such people are approached with an open but critical mind, at times a consensus begins to emerge; and through it, one can discern something previously unknown.

The authors are convinced that the conclusions herein finally explain the disparate actions of all the key players before, during, and after the events of that tragic November weekend in Dallas. We have labored to present them forthrightly, not as pawns on a historical game board but just as people who found themselves caught up in the chaotic aftermath of a world war.

Having reconstructed the roles of all these tragic actors, we have concluded with some sadness that the lessons of the politics of murder were lost on most of them, and lost on most of the body politic as well. An exception was Robert Kennedy. He, like Raúl on the Cuban side, was the most relentless advocate of no-holds-barred covert actions—including assassination—within his brother's inner circle. For Robert, after the Kennedys' humiliation at the Bay of Pigs, the personal *was* the political where Castro was concerned. He could easily rationalize his emotional reaction by merely citing the horrible brutality of the Castro regime toward its own people. The impulse for revenge and the political justifications for it were virtually inseparable until, as Lyndon Johnson secretly expressed it, Castro got Kennedy before Kennedy could get him.

The awful responsibility borne by Robert after John's death might have destroyed lesser men. In some sense, if one sees his post-Dallas life as a pilgrimage of atonement, completion, and responsibility, it did destroy him: it resulted in his assassination. But before it did, he applied the lessons of political violence as few leaders had done before or have done since. That is the full story of Robert Kennedy. His 1960s perfectly mirrored America's, from Cold War triumphalism to brinksmanship; from disaster and the end of innocence to a new covenant of peace and justice.

The greatest tragedy, the one that could compound those of the 1960s immeasurably, would be if nations continue to ignore what Bobby Kennedy learned in the hardest way imaginable: violence is never a straight line toward a predictable, cleansing result. Even when there is truly no alternative but to use it, it always comes back around with a vengeance.

CHAPTER 1
Living Through Another Cuba

IT WAS EARLY EVENING WHEN, after weeks of restless waiting, Dr. Rolando Cubela Secades was finally freed from his secure location in Paris and driven across town by his friend Carlos Tepedino. Cubela was among the most trusted members of Fidel Castro's inner circle, and Carlos, a Havana-based Italian, was his intermediary to the people with whom he was now dangerously allied. Tremendous forces were gathering around them, and the two barely spoke en route to their rendezvous.

A wolfishly handsome young man, Cubela still wore the full beard of a guerrilla; for him, the revolution had never really ended. Only five years earlier, he had been fighting alongside Fidel and Raúl Castro in the mountains of the Sierra Maestra, eating rats and lizards to survive in the fitful war against the Cuban dictator Fulgencio Batista. Together with their Argentine comrade Che Guevara and the men of their July 26th Movement, the Castros had finally straggled into Havana—alongside other factions—as the long-haired, emaciated heroes of the mountain war. Now Cubela was a seasoned veteran, an army major general and, like Che, a physician in strict service to the people.

But for all his devotion to principle, Cubela was a mercurial and complicated man, a doctor who could take a life as well as save one. He had proven himself as both assassin and soldier in the war; but when it ended, he soon realized that his revolutionary dream was not the one that had triumphed. The army that had overthrown Batista was a cross section of Cuban society: liberal urban professionals, shopworn laborers, and dispossessed peasants; reformist Catholics and intellectual atheists. But their moderate leftism had been hijacked by Fidel's hard-line socialism. As Castro's *barbudos* began to overrun the Cuban people, Cubela had reached out to the only force that could help him stop this new dictatorship: America, or specifically its surrogate, the Central Intelligence Agency. Now, barely thirty years old, he had convinced the Agency that he was deeply disillusioned with the leader he had helped bring to power—and capable of backing up his bitterness with mayhem.

It was overcast in the City of Light, but despite the chill, the sidewalk cafés were already aglow in the gathering dusk of a Friday night. The two men arrived at the luxury apartment building where, just a few weeks earlier, Cubela had met with a man who called himself James Clark. In fact, "Clark" was the alias used by the CIA's Cuba Desk chief, Desmond FitzGerald, when he was on covert operations. Even without knowing the man's real identity, Cubela had been convinced that he was a senior American official; he wore his blue-blooded authority well. The man known as Clark had given Cubela the assurances he demanded—that the operation under discussion had been approved at the highest levels of the United States government. And within days of that first meeting, Robert Kennedy, the president's brother, had contacted Cubela directly. Had it not been for those extraordinary guarantees, Cubela would not have returned to this place.

He and Tepedino were greeted this time by Cubela's CIA case officer, Nestor Sanchez, a ten-year Agency veteran known to the Cubans only by his alias, "Nicholas Sanson." Clark was not in attendance, but Cubela's other handler, a man he knew as Long, was. The spies had been absorbed into the most secret of secret CIA cells, "Staff D," the keepers of the Agency's nastiest dilemmas.

For almost three years now, the overseers of Staff D—men like Bill Harvey, Des FitzGerald, Sam Halpern, and Harold "Hal" Swenson—had siphoned a black budget from the actual purpose of the department, a joint NSA–CIA gathering of foreign signals intelligence. The money had gone into a secret project that had thus far been frustratingly unsuccessful. But Cubela's appearance that night gave them some hope. Cubela was there because he had promised to kill Fidel Castro.

The men exchanged pleasantries, then "Sanson" got down to business, handing Cubela a page from the *Miami Herald*. The article described a speech given by the U.S. president just four days before. Embedded in the speech were key phrases written by "James Clark," meant as a secret signal to Cubela.

"It is important," said John Kennedy, "to restate what now divides Cuba from my country and from all the American countries: it is the fact that a small band of conspirators has stripped the Cuban people of their freedom and handed over the independence and sovereignty of the Cuban nation to forces beyond the hemisphere . . . As long as this is true nothing is possible.

Without it everything is possible. Once this barrier is removed we will be ready and anxious to work with the Cuban people in pursuit of those progressive goals that, a few short years ago, stirred their hopes and the sympathy of many people throughout the entire hemisphere . . . For once Cuban sovereignty has been restored we will extend the hand of friendship and assistance to a Cuba whose political and economic institutions have been shaped by the will of the Cuban people."

Cubela read the pages and then set them aside.

Sanson placed a small black leather case on the table before him.

Inside, Cubela found a metal tube, encased in foam rubber. Sanson plucked it from its nest, unscrewed the cap, and produced a single brushed-chrome Paper Mate pen. Holding it up for closer observation, he pushed the depressor. In his other hand he held a tiny flashlight, and when he switched it on, a fluorescent beam revealed a microthin needle where the ballpoint would ordinarily be. The instrument was a finely tooled syringe, created at Langley for one purpose: it could be filled with a highly effective poison. Sanson suggested Black Leaf 40, a slow-acting pesticide, commercially available.

The Paper Mate weapon took Cubela off guard. This deadly little prop implied close quarters, one-on-one.

"I requested rifles and explosives," he said, querulous. Cubela had a house at Varadero Beach, right next door to one of Fidel's many domiciles; that seemed like the place for an easy strike.

Sanson placed the fake ballpoint back in its tube. He explained that if Cubela needed to get in close, he would be frisked and a dart-gun would give him away. The case officer promised once again that the rifles and explosives would be forthcoming, all the weapons Cubela and his fellow insurrectionists would need for both a palace coup and the widespread revolt that would ensue. These munitions were in fact already stockpiled at a secret location in rural Cuba that would be revealed at the last moment.

Cubela slipped the tube into an inside pocket, weighing his reply. Before he could give it, a telephone rang across the room. Tepedino answered and then passed the phone to Sanson. The call was urgent, he said.

Sanson listened, briefly, and then returned the phone to its cradle, pausing for a long moment before he relayed what he had been told.

The president of the United States had just been shot, he said, in Texas.

It was not certain whether the shots had been fatal, but Sanson had been instructed by the caller to end this meeting forthwith. The pen was suddenly forgotten, the ritual air of expectation gone. America's second Cuban coup attempt in two and a half years was over before it began.

The men stood to put on their coats.

"Why do such things happen to good people?" Cubela said. The question hung there.

Tepedino was the one to break the silence. He asked Cubela if he wanted to be taken back to his hotel or someplace else, but the young physician declined and left on his own, walking into a cold drizzle. It was dark by this time. The doctor wandered to a bridge and found himself staring into the River Seine. He reached into his pocket, removed the tube, and let it drop into the current. Already, people were yelling the news from their windows to passersby along the riverbank. Kennedy, the American president, was dead.

As Cubela's pen was drifting to the bottom of the Seine, Luisa Calderón was sitting at her desk at the Cuban embassy in Mexico City. A vivacious brown-haired woman, Calderón worked as a secretary but was in fact "DGI,"* a Cuban intelligence agent like everyone else in the embassy's employ there. At 2:00 P.M. on November 22, she received a phone call from a friend. It is not known who the caller was. The taped intercept indicates only a female, giddy with excitement.

"Luisa, Kennedy has been killed! Assassinated in Texas."

"No, really? When?"

"At one o'clock—"

"Fantastic! Wonderful." Luisa laughed, her thoughts racing ahead.

"Apparently, his wife and brother were also wounded—"

Their laughter overpowered them for a moment.

"Wonderful," Luisa gushed. "What good news!"

"The consequences?" the caller asked rhetorically. "Only good ones," she sang, succumbing to hysteria once again. Luisa tried to compose herself.

"He was a family man, yes," Luisa said, "but also a degenerate aggressor—"

"—Three shots in the face!"

"Perfect . . ."[1]

The call ended.

Luisa dialed a number on her phone console. An embassy colleague picked up, someone named Nico. They too had a laugh at Kennedy's expense, and then Nico asked her this:

---

* The General Intelligence Directorate (DGI), established under the Ministry of the Interior (MININT) in late 1961, was responsible for foreign intelligence collection, similar to America's CIA.

"Okay. What time will the plane arrive?"

"At four, and at four-thirty they must be at the airport."[2]

Shortly after Nico signed off, someone else phoned Luisa, another woman, also breathless.

"Luisa, have you heard about Kennedy yet?!"

"Yes," she replied. "I knew almost before Kennedy did."

"They've arrested the guy. He's president of a Fair Play for Cuba Committee."

"I already knew that. A gringo, right?"

"It seems he lived for a time in Russia, but they wouldn't grant him citizenship—"

"Damn it! How do they know that already?! Did they say his name?"

"Oswald—something like that. He hasn't confessed to anything . . ."[3]

Luisa hung up the phone, her mind reeling. She had just been investigated by her superiors for maintaining a prohibited relationship with the American known as Oswald.

Seven weeks before, he had shown up at her consulate, and, though she was likely unaware of it, he had been seen in meetings with DGI agents with much higher operational clearance than she. Had he been one of their "foreign collaborators"—one of the countless ones she had seen making contact with Cuban spies, making plans and arranging for false passports? If he was, then the revolution had struck a lightning blow for the oppressed masses, worldwide—and it had come through her office.

Fidel Castro was meeting with French journalist Jean Daniel in Havana when he received the news of Kennedy's death. Daniel had met with the American president just a month before and had come to Castro with a message from Kennedy, an overture of peace. When Fidel had taken a moment to ponder this latest news, he looked sharply at Daniel.

"This is an end to your mission of peace," he said.

The conversation labored on, both men no doubt mired in their own thoughts; as it drew to a close, Fidel returned to the implications of what had just happened.

"Now they will have to find the assassin quickly, very quickly, otherwise— you watch and see, I know them—they will try to put the blame on us for this thing." He told the Frenchman that in the late 1950s, as Fidel's revolution to unseat Fulgencio Batista was reaching its climax, he had decided not to authorize the Cuban dictator's murder.

"I have always been violently opposed to such methods," he said, without irony. "First of all from the viewpoint of political self-interest, because, so far as Cuba is concerned, if Batista had been killed he would have been replaced by some military figure who would have tried to make the revolutionists pay for the martyrdom of the dictator. But I was also opposed to it on personal grounds; assassination is repellent to me . . ."

Daniel would later remark that he was shocked that Fidel displayed no emotion when he heard the news, almost as if he had expected it.[4] Indeed, he had. Fidel had been well aware that a young American "foreign collaborator," in contact with his agents in the embassy in Mexico, was plotting this murder on his own initiative, a last resort to prove his devotion to Fidel's cause. The act was a prelude to his own recruitment into Fidel's intelligence corps, or so the man had been led to believe.

But Fidel knew even more. As one of his most senior intelligence officers would admit forty-three years after the fact, Dr. Rolando Cubela's every contact with agents of Castro's great adversaries, the Kennedy brothers, was being monitored and reported to Havana.

At the very moment Cubela had been taking possession of his poison pen in Paris, twenty-four-year-old Lee Harvey Oswald, in Texas, had been aiming a four-power rifle scope at the back of the head of the thirty-fifth president of the United States. When he squeezed the trigger seconds later, John Kennedy was gone. It would take four and a half more years for Bobby to be gone as well, but by the dark logic of violence, guilt, and desperate atonement, his own death began that night as well.

Early in the year 1956, Fidel would have done anything to fulfill his Cuban revolutionary dream. He had been in revolt for twenty-five of his thirty years, first from his father, Angel, then from his Jesuit mentors, then from his own gnawing obscurity, and finally from the forces of bourgeois capitalism. He had raised $29,000 by this time, $20,000 of it from within Cuba, and had pulled together a band of eighty-two men in Mexico City, but his plan required still more money. He needed capital to wage his war against capital, and where else to find it but across the border of the most powerful economy on earth.

Fidel had done it before, in 1949 and 1955, going hat in hand to Cuban exiles from New York to Miami and charming them with gales of outraged humanism. He had raised thousands of dollars. More recently, however, Batista had pressured the Eisenhower government not to let Fidel into the States anymore. He would have to get in through a back door, as legions of

Latinos had been doing since America stole its southwestern states from Mexico.

So, while his younger brother, Raúl, and their new Argentine comrade, Ernesto "Che" Guevara, were tending to the hearts, minds, and bodies of their cadre in Mexico City, Fidel squatted amid the cactus on the Mexican side of the Rio Grande and prepared to cross. It was a night run, in all likelihood. Perhaps only his driver and the coyotes and the tarantulas and javelinas were there to witness it, but eventually he waded in, and when he reached the other side, he trekked to a Texas border town a few miles away through the darkness. There, he made his rendezvous with Carlos Prío, the former Cuban president who had been ousted by Batista in March 1952. Prío thought Fidel's brigade intended to return him to the presidency when their revolution succeeded. In time, Prío would be disappointed, but for the moment Fidel left the meeting $50,000 richer. He wrapped up the cash, mounted it on his head, and returned through the currents. Fidel was back in business.[5]

They were a ragtag bunch, the small army awaiting him back in Mexico City. Most of them were not peasant soldiers; they were petit bourgeois idealists, intellectuals, and middle-class professionals, unschooled in the rigors of revolution. Fidel himself was a lawyer, a dandy with guerrilla pretensions. He and Raúl, a shy and bookish man, had seen battle only once before, and it had sent Raúl running for the hills. These greenhorns had taken to wearing beards, however, the better to prevent infiltrations by arrivistes, and it gave them a certain peasant air in common. They had been bunking in six rented houses, and their training so far consisted of rowing rented boats around Chapultepec Lake hour after hour, climbing mountains, and undergoing weapons training near the town of Chalco, twenty-five miles outside the capital. Che, a fire-breathing extremist where politics were concerned, had no such fire for physical regimens. A lifelong asthmatic, he spent his weekends laying siege to the mighty, extinct volcano Popocatépetl, but he never quite managed to reach its summit.

Three years earlier, on July 26, 1953, Fidel and Raúl had made their revolutionary debut in a 120-man assault on the Moncada army garrison at Santiago, Cuba, a city where Fidel had been sent as a child and corporally abused by his Haitian tutors.[6] That plan had been predicated on it being *carnaval* season; Batista's soldiers would either be away on R&R or too inebriated to fight. Neither proved to be true. The attack might have given the insurrection its name, the July 26th Movement, but militarily it was a fiasco, thanks to Fidel's weakness as a tactician. Jaime Costa, one of the surviving comrades, would later recall that Fidel "ran around screaming orders hysterically. The orders made no sense."[7] The only luck was that the lieutenant who captured Fidel did not kill him on sight. He was arrested instead, contrary to standing orders, and sent to stand trial.

The Castro brothers were sentenced to fifteen years on the Isle of Pines, a small island off the Cuban coast. "Condemn me," Fidel chided the court. "It does not matter. History will absolve me." The speech staked a claim to restore the 1940 constitution, never mentioned "socialism," and suggested a return to a "government of popular election." It was chock-full of many populist promises. By the end of the decade, they would dissolve into a cult of one-man legerdemain.

His term in prison was a young intellectual's daydream spent under minimum security, a virtual graduate school for revolutionaries. They read voluminously from a library they accumulated, kept in touch with the political machinations of the outside world, and gained weight on the prison food. Fidel created a studious regimen for his comrades, he and Raúl hosting revolutionary bull sessions, and Fidel nudging Raúl further along the path to Marxist-Leninism that the younger brother had embarked on in 1951.

Fidel kept the question of his own Communism under wraps. Raúl may have been his ideological beard, taking the hit while Fidel remained aloof; or Fidel's first allegiance may simply have been to Fidel until Raúl and Che forced him to the left. The Fidelist documents of that time don't mention socialism because the Cuban people were not predisposed to it.[8] It was not until he was the leader of Cuba and had become aware of the imminent Bay of Pigs invasion in 1961 that Fidel claimed his revolution to be a *socialist* one.

In a monumental blunder by Batista, the Castro brothers were released under a general amnesty after less than two years, thus giving them free rein to fight again. Raúl, the homebody, went straight back to the family estate in Birán as he had after the Moncada disaster. Fidel went underground, sleeping in different places each night and issuing his manifestos on the fly. While Fidel had avoided political labels, Raúl had been identified as a commie and was soon accused of plotting to bomb a cinema. He was the first to flee the country, exiling himself to Mexico. Indeed, Raúl was a true believer. He started doing advance work for the Castros' next revolutionary wave.

Fidel made his way to Havana to continue his plots against the government. There, he was protected by a spirited group of very young revolutionaries who stayed in constant communication with other fledgling units. Among them were student activists Rolando Cubela, twenty-two years of age, and an eighteen-year-old revolutionary who went by "Oscar Marino," an ally of another eighteen-year-old, Santiago-based underground leader Frank

País.* Marino would go on to become a founder of the revolution's G2 spy agency and later its chief recruiter in Mexico.† His sensitive executive positions would eventually give him a bird's-eye view of the dramas that would play out between Cubela, other sundry G2 agents, and a young Castro sympathizer in America, one Lee Oswald.

On July 8, 1955, six weeks after their release from prison, Fidel joined his younger brother in Mexico City, penniless and wearing a gray wool suit. Even as a student in the heat of Havana, Fidel had insisted on wool suits at the university, an affectation that must have made him seem either prone to chills, or curiously penitent, or both.

At first he and Raúl lived in a refuge for Cuban exiles, the apartment of an old friend, María Antonia González, who became the den mother of the revolution. They had no troops yet, but Fidel's yen for power kept them going, along with the monthly stipends from María, $40 for the younger brother, twice that for the older. Fidel began laying out his battle plan almost immediately upon his arrival, and it continued when the two of them moved on to a funky hotel, aptly located on Insurgentes Boulevard.

It was in Mexico City that the Castro brothers had first met Ernesto "Che" Guevara. Che was working as a poorly paid doctor at the General Hospital, specializing in allergies, and moonlighting as a news photographer. When Raúl entered Che's life, the Cuban had already been in battle (however dubiously) and been incarcerated for his politics (however comfortably). Che, by contrast, was an armchair revolutionary, living on the cheap with his fiancée, Hilda, and honing his rhetoric in the hot spots of the leftist café society. Young and clean-shaven, he was a talented writer of poetry and prose, and also spoke excellent French.[9] His English, by contrast, was halting, but he had seen Yankee capitalism's dark side up close, and his enmity for the United States was already intense. He had once been stranded in Miami for a month, and that experience alone had alienated him; but it was during his bohemian travels through South and Central America from 1952 to 1954 that his hatred was galvanized. He had witnessed the CIA-orchestrated overthrow of Guatemala's president Jacobo Árbenz, a democratically elected, moderate leftist who had sought to introduce basic land reform in his country and took exception to the high profits of America's United Fruit Company there.

---

*País would achieve revolutionary martyrdom status in 1957, while his Havana comrade, Marino, helped organize "revolutionary workers' brigades."
†G2 was Cuba's State Secret Police.

Raúl, according to Hilda, was already a fervent admirer of the Soviet Union. He saw the Marxist imperative as inherently transnational and anti-American, and was personally quite "merry, open, sure of himself, very clear in the exposition of his ideas, with an incredible capacity for analysis and synthesis."[10] None of these were traits that Raúl had exhibited as a child, but somehow his brother's tutelage, his travels, and his studies in prison had given the once-unremarkable young man an unlikely confidence. He was a man on a mission.

And he was the one who introduced Fidel to Che, on a cold night in Mexico City. Their first encounter was at María Antonia's apartment, and it went on for ten solid hours, the two of them comparing philosophies with such mutual excitement that by the next day, Che had joined Fidel's revolution, despite doubts about the unfolding plan of attack itself. From then on, the two met nearly every other day. Che's abhorrence of the United States began to rub off on Fidel. Hilda's best friend, the Venezuelan poet Lucila Velásquez, spent long nights with them, observing that "without Ernesto Guevara, Fidel Castro might never have become a Communist. Without Fidel Castro, Ernesto Guevara might never have been more than a Marxist theorist, an intellectual idealist."[11] As their combined energy began to express itself in more and more grandiose ways, members of the city's progressive community began to take notice. Fidel never missed a chance to make a speech that might win allies.

Among the influential people to whom the Castros and Che reached out were the erudite Mexican poet and critic Octavio Paz, and his wife, Elena Garro. They and their young daughter, Elenita, were the centers of a peripatetic literary salon that bound the Latin art world together: Vienna one week, New York the next, Havana here, Madrid there, and Mexico City as home base. Fidel and Raúl came and went, and among the regulars were such rising stars as Nicolás Guillén and Alejo Carpentier. Eight-year-old Elenita would become something of a literary mascot and got to know and love them all, but the fine-boned, soft-spoken, and still-obscure Che Guevara made as much an impression on her as the famous people did. He was becoming a force in his own right.

On August 18, Che married Hilda in Tepotzotlán, with Raúl in attendance. Fidel was supposed to have been the witness, but his presence was nixed as a security risk. He was convinced that various forces—including Batista's overseas operatives, the FBI, and the Mexican secret police—had him in their sights.[12]

He was right. Batista's Cuban agents had pursued Fidel from the moment he was released from prison, shutting down *La Calle*, the Havana newspaper he wrote his broadsides for, and keeping him on the move from one comrade's house to another each night.[13] They were soon on his trail in Mexico as well, and friends in Havana passed the word to Fidel that Batista had put a $20,000 bounty on his head.[14] For all Fidel's obsession with secrecy, very little was kept secret from Fulgencio Batista.

On June 20, 1956, the Cuban dictator succeeded in provoking the Mexicans into doing something about this little army of insurgents. These three musketeers, Fidel, Raúl, and Che; some of their stalwarts like Ramiro Valdés and Juan Almeida; and two dozen others were arrested by agents of Mexico's Federal Security Directorate (DFS). Batista immediately demanded that they be extradited back to Cuba and had one of his operatives torture a member of the brigade.

Here, the exact lines of conflict become blurred. The DFS leader of the raid, twenty-eight-year-old Mexican army officer Fernando Gutiérrez Barrios, was the man who captured Fidel's band. Fidel would have considered Barrios a typical tool of the oligarchy, but an unlikely respect quickly grew between himself and Fidel. When Barrios realized that he was dealing with a group of disciplined guerrillas (and not drug smugglers, as initially thought), the two became friends.[15] "He was a kind and gentlemanly policeman who conversed agreeably and even had some leftist ideas," Fidel would later say.[16] It would prove to be a profound understatement. Whatever the reason they were grabbed, Castro and Gutiérrez Barrios struck up a curious relationship that spring of 1956 and the Fidelistas were released by the end of July. "I sympathized with Fidel Castro," Gutiérrez Barrios would admit in 1995, "first, because we were of the same generation, and second, because of his ideals and conviction."[17]

Notwithstanding his sympathies, Gutiérrez Barrios would rise to head the DFS and become one of the most brutal antileftist authorities in all of Latin America. In time, he would serve as a liaison to both the CIA and to Fidel; over the years, he and Fidel came to an understanding. When Castro seized power in Havana, he agreed not to export revolution to Mexico. In return, the DFS agreed to shield the Cubans from other adversaries and feed useful intel to Castro's new intelligence agency, the G2. Whatever else they consented to may never be known—Gutiérrez Barrios died with his secrets—but it is certain that the two men became fast friends.

The moment Fidel was released, he asked Gutiérrez Barrios to keep him apprised of any other police operations that might be coming down the line.

Barrios agreed, even calling ahead to make certain that local authorities did not stand in the way as the young revolutionaries embarked on their voyage back to Cuba.

In the 1950s, according to a U.S. intelligence official (speaking on condition of anonymity), Mexico City (along with Vienna) had become known as a "spy trampoline," a prime jump point for Communists wishing to rendezvous with their U.S. informants, although the Mexicans were equally helpful to the United States at that time, assisting the CIA in spying on Communist countries as well.

Besides the Batista network and the DFS, another pair of eyes was trained on Castro's brigade in the Mexico of the 1950s, those of a sympathetic Russian.

Nikolai Sergeyevich Leonov had first come to Mexico City in 1953 when he was sent there as a member of the Soviet Foreign Service. Raúl had just made his first trip outside Cuba for the Soviet-sponsored international youth convocation in Vienna. The trip had taken him to three Communist capitals in Eastern Europe as well, and it cemented his interest in Marxist philosophy. The KGB had been monitoring the delegations, of course, scouting the young and the restless lefties for future reference.[18] Whether by accident or by design, the twenty-five-year-old Leonov met Raúl on his return trip to the Americas aboard a vintage Italian passenger ship, the *Andrea Gritti*, and the two became friends. Leonov would report that they "understood each other instantly, and were burning with desire to give our lives to the service of the people."[19]

Two years later, when Raúl was doing his Mexican advance work for Fidel, the friends met again and Raúl introduced the Russian to another new compadre, Che, and Leonov too became part of their burgeoning scene.

When pressed by historians years later, Leonov would insist that he was not yet a KGB operative when he reunited with Raúl and met the Castros' band of hairy men, but he would join the Soviet intelligence service in the summer of 1958, become its station chief in Mexico City, and eventually rise to the KGB's second most powerful position, deputy chief of the First Chief Directorate of the State Security Committee. In the summer of 1956, Leonov was keeping close contact with the Castros when they were arrested on that June day; and seven years later, on a bright September day in 1963, Leonov would still be KGB station chief in Mexico City when a tearful, agitated young American militant named Lee Oswald would barge into the Soviet and Cuban embassies, demand credentials to visit Cuba, and then threaten to kill President Kennedy.

And Barrios would be Leonov's counterpart in the Mexican DFS.

In mid-August of 1956, John F. Kennedy, a thirty-nine-year-old second-term senator from Massachusetts, was returning from the Democratic National Convention in Chicago. The erudite Adlai Stevenson from Illinois had received the nomination and then left it to the convention to choose his running mate. Jack had very nearly captured the banner, but finally lost it to Senator Estes Kefauver.

Kennedy was disappointed, but his appetite had been whetted. He was beginning to think that "it should be as easy to get the nomination for President as it was for Vice President,"[20] and his comment reflected the dazzling confidence that had caught the attention of the party bosses. They were suddenly seeing more in him than just the panache of intelligence, good looks, and great wealth. By this time, the toothy face and gangly frame had filled out; the voice had deepened. There had been something arresting about him onstage in Chicago, and something bold about the way he staked his positions. Young Jack Kennedy was a comer.

Yet even then he was a brilliant man whose instinct for power had a dangerous shadow, at least for a politician—indiscriminate lust, inherited from his father, Joe Kennedy Sr. As soon as the convention was over, Jack left the bosses begging for more and flew off to the south of France, where Joe Sr. was on holiday at the family villa. It was there that the two men decided that Jack should go straight for the presidency in 1960, if Eisenhower beat Stevenson and won a second term. His wife, Jackie, stayed behind, in the last trimester of a pregnancy. She would lose that baby, and when Jack opted not to race back to the States to be with her, it would nearly destroy their marriage.

It would also mark a turning point in his younger brother Bobby's relationship both with Jackie and with the family at large. It was Bobby who got her through the aftermath, and who shamed his brother into returning home. When Jack finally did come back, he managed to repair the damage, but then he hit the road again, spending that fall campaigning for Stevenson-Kefauver and currying favor with the party bosses by trading on his status as a decorated war veteran. When his pal Charlie Bartlett asked why he didn't just wait for a while, bide his time, Jack replied, "No, they will forget me. Others will come along."[21]

Bobby, fast becoming the family's most dogged political tactician, had seen how Kefauver had turned his chairmanship of the Kefauver Crime Commission into a publicity bonanza and gained himself a national reputation. The new medium of television was perfect for kindling a political career, and gangsters (and Communists) were the perfect antagonists for a nation that had run out of Hitlers and Mussolinis. Within a few months, Bob helped establish the McClellan Rackets Committee, with himself as the committee counsel and Jack as a Senate committeeman. Now the Kennedys had their own hoodlums to berate, just like Estes Kefauver, and they were bound for the presidency.

They had been "born Democrats," even though they were the sons of one of America's wealthiest self-made men, a man for whom power was an acquisition like any other. Jack had wanted to be a journalist at first, but his father had other plans. The oldest son, Joe Jr., had been his first choice for the presidency, but he was killed in World War II. Jack became the designated hitter, as if power were just another trophy he was simply expected to win. Some believed that Jack could as easily have been a Republican, if that had been the path laid out for him. Tony Gallucio, Jack's secretary in Boston, once remarked that the Kennedys "were master political technicians. They knew how to get elected," but "they had no philosophy."[22] Indeed, Jack grew impatient with nuanced political philosophies at that point in his career, particularly "prissy" liberalism.

In many ways, Jack Kennedy was not much different from the young Fidel Castro. Both had been dominated and manipulated by their fathers. Where Joe Sr. had acquired his millions as a scheming, streetwise Irish outsider, Ángel Castro lived as a gentrified peasant, self-made and considered rich on his own turf but still a lowly *guajiro* in the eyes of the Cuban aristocracy. Their talented and confident sons had leaped over decades, even centuries of class prejudice to become leaders by sheer force of personality. They were intellectually curious, articulate, easy in the company of men, and attracted to the spotlight.

Both Jack and Fidel came from large Catholic families, and both of their fathers made a sport of bedding women out of wedlock. Joe Sr. kept his mistresses out of sight, in hotel rooms, at the penthouses of trusted friends, or on his private yacht. Ángel took his lovers wherever he desired them, including his own home. Fidel, Raúl, and their siblings had been born to Ángel's housekeeper while she worked for his wife, and Ángel made no secret of the small shack full of his offspring who lived just out of sight of the *casa grande.* In the eyes of the Catholic Church, the Castro children were all illegitimate, a particular humiliation for the daughters, but one that Fidel and Raúl felt as well. It was not until Fidel was seventeen years old that Ángel recognized him as his legal offspring. Fidel loathed him.

Still, perhaps recognizing Fidel as exceptional—and therefore a good reflection on himself—Ángel would grant him special privileges, sending him to the country's best preparatory school, keeping him in natty clothes, and furnishing him with a car as he approached his college years. Fidel overcame his "rustic" upbringing to be reasonably well liked at Belen Prep. Although as a child he had famously assaulted a priest in retaliation for abuse, priests would later become the adults he respected most; a priest named Amado Llorente was his favorite teacher, and Fidel attended Mass daily.

Even then, though, some of the priests sensed a certain moral indifference in Fidel. His temper could be savage. He accepted leadership from no one, taking only the wise counsel of Llorente. He arrived at the University of Havana like a young lord. Dressed like a businessman, albeit with a lounge lizard's flair for excess, he hit campus in full possession of his powers of persuasion and intimidation, and quickly learned to negotiate the thuggish politics that thrived there. When asked by a schoolmate what his aspirations were, the nineteen-year-old Fidel said, without irony, "I want to win glory and fame!"[23] That was the sum of his ambition—he was a political chameleon, pursuing power for its own sake. His classmates were initially fond of him, but his loyalty and charm receded as power came closer within reach.

Years later, in 1961, the CIA did a psychological workup on him. Given its agenda at that time, one should take these speculations with a large grain of salt, but the Agency's description of him may have some validity:

"Fidel Castro is not 'crazy' but he is so highly neurotic and unstable a personality as to be quite vulnerable to certain kinds of psychological pressure. The outstanding neurotic elements in his personality are his hunger for power and his need for the recognition and adulation of the masses. He is unable to obtain complete emotional gratification from any other source . . ." Deeper in the text is a particularly telling passage, apropos of his relationship to Angel: "Castro's aggressiveness stems from constant attempts to achieve a special position that is denied him. When he achieves what he desires, he needs constant reassurance that he is justified in occupying this special position. . . . Currently he is wringing it from the Cuban masses . . . As long as the masses continue to support him, he will not suffer from anxiety, depression, or overt psychiatric symptoms." But the most disturbing conclusions

were yet to follow: "He is insatiably narcissistic . . . and has a wish for martyrdom . . . His first consideration is to maintain power control for himself.
He probably would destroy both himself and the Cuban people to preserve
this status."[24, 25]

The stately Harvard campus was not exactly the political trench warfare
that the University of Havana was, and Jack Kennedy's psychological issues
were certainly not as aggravated, but he too went through a transformation
as he made his way out of school, through the war, and into a campaign for
Congress in 1946. The unpretentious, and egalitarian PT-boat commander of
World War II gave way to a cooler peer of the realm whose once-disarming
charm had come to seem more calculating. He was capable of kindness and
understood, intellectually, that power could improve the lives of those less
fortunate; but one of his lovers of long standing noted his "tremendous
acceptance of inequality at every level . . . That was absolutely acceptable."
He seemed content to believe that "people who are different have different
responses. The pain of poor people is different from 'our' pain."[26]

Fidel, too, was an elitist, in his own sphere. On the Castro plantation,
Fidel's sister, Juanita, noted that he treated the peasants with the same cru-
elty that his father did. "There were a lot of employees working on the farm
and serving at the house," she reported—nearly a thousand people in all—
but, according to Juanita, "Fidel never took care of these people. On the contrary, I remember he criticized my father for being too generous with
them."[27] He made no public declaration on behalf of the poor until he joined
Cuba's leftward drift in his early twenties—right around the time that Jack
was first elected to Congress.

Fidel and Jack's younger brothers, Raúl and Bobby, started out with more
heart. Though raised under virtually the same circumstances as their older
brothers, they began their lives as introverted underdogs and were more attuned to injustice, more aggravated by it, as a result.

Robert Kennedy was the seventh child of Joe Sr. and Rose Kennedy, the
third son born after four girls. Like Raúl, he was the child closest to his
mother; he was considered by the self-consciously tough Kennedy men to be
a borderline "sissy." He was so devoutly religious that many family members expected him to enter the priesthood, and so sensitive to the teasing
and sparring of his two older brothers, Joe Jr. and Jack, that he was known
to burst into tears from the sheer intensity of the family's competitive climate. He was, to use his father's word, the runt, less handsome and outgoing than the older boys.

By the time he reached adulthood, he had diligently covered his heart with a tough-guy attitude. He surrounded himself with men from the middle and working class and affected their stance; but deep down Bobby was empathetic, the counter to Jack's aristocratic remove. Jack would claim that his mother never touched or soothed him as a child and that he himself didn't like to be touched as an adult. Bobby, on the other hand, had his mother's absolute devotion and was physically demonstrative, passionate, romantic. As an adult, he directed those traits into the ruthless practice of law and politics, outgunning the gunmen, finally, and becoming the family's tactical hit man.

Raúl was the empathetic one in his family, too. Five years younger than Fidel, Raúl had been the passive child, the frail mama's boy, soft, short, and easily intimidated, with none of his brother's braggadocio or verve. He didn't even look like a Castro, to some eyes, and was saddled as a child with the nickname *el Chino*, the Chinaman. As they reached manhood, Raúl's personal goals were always subordinate to the radical zeal Fidel instilled in him. But even later in life, Raúl the Terrible kept alive something of the soulful decency he had as a kid. No matter how callously, even murderously effective he proved to be as a leader, his reputation was built on the genuine respect, friendship, and loyalty of those in his command. He was a loving father and spouse, cared openly about those in his inner circle, invited and accepted honest feedback, and was comfortable with his intellectual equals and treated them as such. He could be mischievously funny, could drink like a man with a slit throat, and was known to party with hilarious abandon. Fidel, conversely, surrounded himself with his intellectual inferiors, was averse to being alone but trusted no one, did nothing with abandon, and would drive his few real peers into exile or have them executed. Raúl admired Fidel, but was not particularly loved by him.

Bobby Kennedy's most loved older brother was Joe Jr. When Joe died in battle, Bobby's attention shifted to the next oldest brother, Jack. He adored him, scuffling along in his glamorous shadow, becoming his fixer, his body man, and, in the end, the last keeper of the family's most miserable secrets. Jack teased and chided him, listened to his calculations and took his advice, but gave Bobby little back in way of overt affection.

As the older brothers rose to power in the late 1950s, it was the younger ones who did the heavy lifting. The older men were the trumpeters, the dazzlers, the personalities. The younger ones became the heavies, the ideologues, the ones who kept needling the older ones toward the darker realms of power.

In their formative years, it was the younger men's organizational skills and doggedness that finally gained their brothers' respect. In time, that respect became a dependency, a bond of trust the older ones could not easily make or keep with anyone else. One came to the geopolitical arena on wheels of fire, the other on wings of gold. But the cornermen, the ones who stayed in the shadows and kept the battle raging, selflessly devoting themselves every day to their families' political supremacy, were Raúl and Bobby.

Inside the ring of kinship, these bonds would become so fierce that, for the younger siblings, what offended the dignity of a brother offended the dignity of his entire nation. It was a recipe for the most dangerous kind of sibling rivalry, brothers against brothers.

The Castro brothers had come to Mexico in 1955 because, as Fidel would preach in Tuxpan thirty-two years later, "it was the common house of all Latin Americans . . . There were Peruvians because there was a tyrannic government there, there were Dominicans because there was a tyrannic government in Santo Domingo, there were Nicaraguans because the Somoza tyranny was already there, there were Guatemalans because the CIA had just defeated the Árbenz government with its attack."[28]

And there was Fulgencio Batista, a mulatto born in poverty who became the only Cuban man of his class to ever reach the presidency. He was elected with the help of the far left in 1940; his first term had been a mixed bag, authentically reformist in ways that won the support of the workers, but also brutal and repressive in equal measure. He lost the presidency in 1944, but regained it in 1952 in a coup three months before the scheduled elections. In 1954, he ran for reelection unopposed. By the time his second presidency collapsed at the end of 1958, the dictator's personal wealth would be estimated at between $60 and $300 million, most of it ill-gotten—either plundered from the Cuban people or received as payola from the American mob, who had built a gilded cage of vice in the capital city. But in the fall of 1956, Batista was still running Cuba as his personal police state. Initially, Fidel's ideology seems to have been one of simple repulsion. He might not yet have settled on a proactive philosophy, but he knew what he was against—the regime of Batista.

With the $50,000 that former president Prío had given Fidel on the north shore of the Rio Grande, and another five grand handed over by the poet Teresa Carillo, Fidel had raised enough money to buy the revolution's mother ship, the one that would launch his July 26th Movement across the Caribbean and on to the coast of the homeland. He had looked high and low for the right, affordable vessel, even venturing to the harbor at Baltimore, Maryland, before Eisenhower banned him from entering the country. He considered a PT boat at one point, but finally settled on a once-luxurious white yacht, the *Granma*. She had sunk in a hurricane in 1953 and was in need of repair, but when Fidel found her on the Tuxpan River, he bought the boat, along with a house from which to stage the voyage, from an American, Dr. Robert Erickson.

In early September, Gutiérrez Barrios tipped Fidel that Batista was once again putting the squeeze on the Mexicans to bust him. Fidel quietly moved his men into the Erickson house. The brigade had been hardening itself for the assault, but there was one last question that hung in Fidel's mind.

As final plans were being set for *Granma*'s voyage, he decided that he must test his brother's revolutionary will. Their father, Angel, was said to be a man who could kill with cold alacrity, and Fidel, too, had shown a talent for violent displays early on, earning the nickname *el loco*. But Fidel still felt that the gentle, generous, egalitarian side of Raúl had not yet been sufficiently tempered by violence. It was time for his baptism in blood. So shortly before they set out for Cuba, Fidel ordered his brother to kill—on scant evidence—a young comrade who he feared might be a traitor.

Raúl picked up a gun, cornered the man, and dispatched him without hesitation. By the end of the night, he would kill for the second time in his life, running over a peasant en route to the docks where the yacht was waiting to carry them to glory.

In the ensuing years, people have debated whether Fidel ever committed murder. Che wrote the only firsthand report of Fidel killing a soldier in the Sierra Maestra. Carlos Bringuier, a Cuban exile in the United States, would insist that Fidel killed his cousin at the University of Havana. But few debate either Raúl's baptism in blood or his ongoing ministry. Once he accepted it as one of his duties, he became known as the movement's executioner. One former comrade recounted that he and Che made a competitive sport of it, but it is not known precisely how many people Raúl has killed personally. Of the deaths he has overseen, some were street criminals, but the vast majority were political enemies, and estimates of the toll range as high as fourteen thousand, claimed in a Harvard University study.[29] The Cuba Archive Project concluded that some fifty-six hundred Cubans have died in front of firing squads and another twelve hundred in "extrajudicial assassinations." Apparently, Fidel delegated most executions to Raúl—and to Che, who was reported, by firsthand accounts from the Castros' political prisoners, to be a particularly "gleeful executioner" at the La Cabaña fortress prison. Minors and females were not spared. The Cuba Archive has documented 219 female deaths, including eleven by firing squad and twenty extrajudicial assassinations. No one knows exactly how many people Che personally killed or ordered killed, or who died as a result of his actions in foreign wars, but the archive places the number in Cuba alone at about four thousand. He took special pride in shooting people in the back of the head and was known to have considered hate to be something akin to a revolutionary sacrament.

"Hatred is an element in the struggle," he said, "unbending hatred for the enemy which pushes a human being beyond his natural limitations . . ." "A people without hate cannot triumph against an adversary."

Raúl's brutality would become equally legendary among the Cuban people. He first showed his penchant for bulk murder in 1958, in the Sierra Maestra, when he dispatched eleven peasants for refusing to serve as guides or otherwise cooperate with the rebel army. From January 1 to January 13, 1959, 272 executions directly attributed to Raúl were carried out in Santiago de Cuba, 90 without a prior trial, and 78 with Raúl Castro delivering the coup de grace. In 1959, 263 additional executions were carried out in Raúl Castro's line of command outside of Santiago, in the rest of the province of Oriente. In 1960, four executions were carried out in Havana under Raúl's line of command.*

But he would be haunted by it all. Ten years after his baptism in blood, he would order that the bones of many he had executed be dug up and dumped into the sea off the south coast of Oriente Province.[30]

While the Castros prepared to launch, October 1956 was a volatile month inside Cuba as well. The Socialist Youth Party of Cuba was trying to talk Fidel out of his insurrection and enlist him to align himself with them. But Havana was primed for revolt, and Fidel was not about to turn back. Plots against Batista's inner circle had accelerated within the country, and one of the principal conspirators was Dr. Rolando Cubela, who had first gained attention in 1953 as a twenty-year-old activist medical student at the University of Havana. He had helped organize the Directorio Revolucionario (DR), a more violent faction of the decades-old Federation of University Students (Federación de Estudiantes Universitarios, or FEU), and aim their ire against Batista.

On October 27, 1956, upon orders from Fidel in Mexico to "produce actions," Cubela participated in the execution of Antonio Blanco Rico, chief

---

*The regime's penchant for execution and assassination extended far beyond the geographical boundaries of Cuba. For a thorough discussion of Cuba's use of terror and assassination, please see our online essay at http://cuban-exile.com/brothersinarms.html.

of Batista's secret police. Cubela and his allies had set out to kill Batista cabinet member Santiago Rey Pernas, but when Rey failed to show at the Montmartre nightclub, they spotted Blanco exiting the lobby elevator and opened fire on him with machine guns, killing Blanco instantly and wounding another officer's wife. In the following days, Batista's forces killed ten revolutionaries in retaliation.

In Mexico, Fidel was furious about Cubela's improvisation. "I do not condemn assassination attempts as a revolutionary weapon if the circumstances require it," he intoned to the faithful. "But such acts must not be indiscriminate . . . the assault on Blanco Rico was not justified. Blanco Rico was not a Fascist executioner." It would not be the last point of conflict between himself and Cubela. The doctor would join the revolution soon enough, would even prove to be a wildly brave and relentless freedom fighter, but it would be Cubela's unit that would capture the Presidential Palace in Havana twenty-six months later, and Cubela who would initially refuse to surrender the building to Che. This confrontation presaged a long and complicated relationship between Cubela and the Castros, one that continues to this day.

There was one more piece of news that Fidel would meet with profoundly mixed emotions that month.

As the Castro boys were making the last preparations for their voyage, a comrade brought news that their father, Ángel, had died. Fidel—the bastard son who had threatened to burn Ángel's house down when he was not yet a teenager; the same house he grew up within sight of but was seldom allowed to enter—had almost no response, murmuring, simply, "What a shame." The estate was estimated at $1 million, enough money to finance twenty *Granmas*, but Fidel didn't ask for one detail of his father's death; he just pressed on for updates on the political situation in Havana. Raúl, on the other hand, stood up and left the company of his brother, and found a private place to weep.[31]

With the death of their father, the hour had come. Fidel had often sworn, "In 1956 we will be free or we will be martyrs." It was time to keep his pledge to the Cuban people.[32]

A sea captain he was not, however. After Barrios called ahead to Fidel, guaranteeing their safe travel, they set sail for Cuba's Oriente Province. The plan was to land at a town called Niquero in a reenactment of the assault by founding father José Martí that began the Cuban War of Independence in 1895. But once again, romantic symbolism would be undercut by much the same incompetence that had sunk them at Moncada. At 1:00 A.M. on November 25, 1956, the Castro brothers and their revolutionary sibling Che put out from Tuxpan, Veracruz, on the Mexican Gulf Coast, with an eighty-two-man brigade aboard a yacht that held twenty-six. One of its two engines was malfunctioning. The brigade had no navigational experience. They had no medicine, and they had barely enough food or fuel to make it to Cuba. Che, the brigade's doctor, was supposed to be ready to treat any wounded, but instead was cut down by a severe asthma attack just after they set sail.

A contingent of fifty compatriots awaited them on the east coast of Cuba with food, arms, and vehicles. But high winds blew them off course almost immediately and they missed their target site by fifteen miles, fearing that they might have veered off to Jamaica. Instead, they were forced into a swamp near the village of Las Coloradas, where they couldn't even unload most of their weapons in the boggy, crab-infested waters.

Nonetheless, they regrouped and headed for the Sierra Maestra, sustained by peasants on the route who gave them just enough provisions to survive. They were ambushed by a Batista force at Alegría de Pío, and most of the brigade was killed. On December 18, twenty-four days into the glorious invasion, twelve of the original eighty-two straggled into the dense mountains of the Sierra Maestra. Fidel and Raúl were among them, along with a wounded, bleeding Che.

On October 3, 1956, the same month that the Socialist Youth Party of Cuba had appealed to Fidel to drop his quest and join theirs, a pale, lonely teenager sat down in his mother's small apartment in Fort Worth, Texas, and wrote a letter to the Socialist Youth Party of America, also known as the Young People's Socialist League, or YPSL. The apartment at 4936 Collingwood was the nineteenth home this boy had known.

> I am sixteen years of age and would like more information about your youth League. I would like to know if there is a branch in my area, how to join, ect. [sic], I am a Marxist and have been studying socialist principles for well over fifteen months. I am very interested in your Y.P.S.L. Sincerely, /s/ Lee Oswald.

It's no wonder that he was aching for some sense of belonging. His father, Robert Edward Lee Oswald, had died two months before Lee was born in the fall of 1939. Years later, in a rambling, copiously misspelled manuscript titled "The Collective," Oswald would describe his childhood thus: "Lee Harvey Oswald was born in October, 1939 in New Orleans, La. the son of a Insuance Salesman whose early death left a far mean streak of independence brought on my negleck." Lee had an older brother, Robert, perhaps the only person he would ever truly love, and a half brother, John Pic. All three boys lived under the thumb of their mother, Marguerite, an engulfing, even grotesque woman. Money-crazed, self-pitying, overwhelmed by widowhood, and controlling by nature, she would invade her sons' lives, alternately doting on them and berating them until they were forced to reject her, even violently. When Lee was still an infant, she became so overwhelmed and unstable that she put the two older boys into an orphanage, and planned to put Lee there soon as well. To help herself cope, she allowed a couple to move into the apartment with them, but they took to slapping the baby and she kicked them out. In December 1942, she put Lee into the orphanage too, but a little over a year later she checked all three boys out again and resumed custody.

There is some evidence that Lee may have suffered brain damage at the age of five. Marguerite was, by most accounts, a paranoid personality, perhaps even borderline psychotic, who could not hold on to friends and was forever hitting the road. During one such quick exit, this one out of Fort Worth, one of the movers decided to repark the van. As he backed out of the drive, Robert cut behind the van on his bike, followed by his little brother on his tricycle. When the driver braked, a chest of drawers toppled over the back gate and fell right on top of Lee.

He was unconscious for eight days. Lee's doctor came to Marguerite, who was dithering on a bench in a hallway, and told her that "if the boy comes to at all, he's going to have a problem."

From then on, Lee would suffer occasional blackouts, doing things he couldn't remember, walking out in the middle of classes and wandering his school's hallways.[33]

When Lee was six, his mother married a man named Edwin Ekdahl, the only father he would know. He thrived for a time, but the marriage devolved quickly into harangues about money; when the divorce came to trial, young Lee was dragged into the proceedings. He refused to testify, insisting, even at eight years old, that he couldn't tell truth from fiction.

With Ekdahl gone, Lee withdrew and Marguerite pursued him, smothering him with attention if not affection, and encouraging him to stay home from school. He was an introvert who lived in books and fantasies. He had moderately high IQ scores, and she would tell him that that made him better than the other children, insisting that he could learn more from books than from teachers. Until he was ten, the two often slept in the same bed, and he would fall asleep listening to her rant against the United States in half-cocked, "anti-imperialist" diatribes. America had done her wrong at every turn, she would say, and the rants were sure signs that she would be preparing to move again. Off to Benbrook, Texas, or back to Fort Worth. It hardly mattered when the urge to move hit her. Lee was once elected president of his grade-school class, but that blush of popularity was brief. By the time he got to Benbrook, he was imploding, socially. Instead of finding friends among the neighborhood kids, he would position himself along their routes after school and ambush them with rocks. He took to brandishing knives, and one of his few new pals once watched as he chased John Pic around the apartment with a butcher knife, finally throwing it and sinking it into a wall. Marguerite shrugged it off.

The older boys escaped by joining the military, John Pic the Coast Guard, Robert the Marines, but even New York City wasn't far enough away for John. Mama found him, with his new wife and baby, in a cramped East Nineties apartment, and she and Lee moved in like mold. Lee and Marguerite would have screaming fights. When John's young wife asked Lee to turn down the TV one day, twelve-year-old Lee pulled a knife on her. When Marguerite tried to rein him in, Lee punched her right in the teeth.[34] John finally sent them packing, but Marguerite only got as far as an outer borough.

She found them a dank basement place in the Bronx. By that time, Lee was a latchkey kid, a loner in the most populous city in the land. He took to riding the subways for days at a time. (It was on the streets of New York that Lee first encountered true Communism, when an old lady handed him a pamphlet about the Rosenberg spy case.) When he wasn't riding, he was reading or losing himself in the novelty of the new TV shows; he particularly liked *I Led Three Lives*. His truancy brought the attention of the authorities. He was sent to the city's Youth Home for evaluation.

By this time, his mental illness was becoming obvious. He had a hair-trigger temper. Since brother Robert was the only person he looked up to, Lee lived in hopes of joining the military, but he refused to pledge allegiance to the flag. He was primed for a fight, almost any fight, and the colors of the banner hardly mattered. Caseworkers at the home described him as "intensely self-centered," cold, detached, "with schizoid features and passive-aggressive tendencies." The staff psychiatrist noted "intense anxiety, shyness," with "feelings of awkwardness and insecurity . . . emotional isolation and deprivation, lack of affection, absence of family life and rejection by a self-involved and conflicted mother." He further noted that Lee had "a vivid fantasy life, turning around topics of omnipotence and power."[35]

In November 1953, almost exactly ten years before Lee tasted omnipotence, a judge in the city's Domestic Relations Court remanded him to a home for troubled boys. America had done Marguerite wrong yet again. She packed up the household and skipped town for New Orleans, with Lee in hand.

His abuse of her increased in proportion to her neglect. He became a little dictator, holing up in his room with his books and classical records. He would go fishing with other boys but stay off by himself, leaving the fish he caught to die on the shore. At fourteen, he was enrolled in his tenth school and hatching a plan to steal a gun; he had his eyes on a Smith & Wesson on display in a local store. He had even bought a glasscutter, but a friend pointed out the alarm strip around the window's edge and he backed off of the plot. By this time, he identified himself as "a self-made communist," and the ferocity of his opinions was startling to other kids and adults alike. In his brother Robert's absence, he had bought and nearly memorized a Marine Corps handbook, and at fifteen he quit school and tried to join the Corps. The recruiters rejected him.

Marguerite moved them back to Texas. Lee returned to summer school briefly in July 1956, just as Senator John F. Kennedy was preparing to attend the Democratic Convention in Chicago. Lee didn't stay in school for long, however. When he dropped out again, he finally bought his first rifle, a bolt-action .22. At sixteen, he told a friend that if he got the chance he would kill President Eisenhower for "exploiting the working people."[36]

A week after his seventeenth birthday in October, the same month that Fidel learned of Angel's death, Lee was finally admitted to the United States Marine Corps. On the 26th of the month, he reached San Diego and reported for duty. In short order, he realized that he had made a gross error—indeed, he would come to hate the Corps and all it stood for. But at least he was free of his mother. From then on, he would rarely see or make contact with Marguerite.

He would also become known to his fellow Marines as a fervent supporter of the band of guerrillas now fighting in Cuba's Sierra Maestra.

Kennedy and Castro came to power atop the wasteland of two world wars, and an atomic bomb that had made such all-consuming wars obsolete. On the global, ecological scale there was no safe haven. The exponential effects of a nuclear exchange erased all borders. Smaller, proxy wars were the only way left to fight, wars in which big ideas could be fought over in small countries, lest the big countries engage directly and incinerate the planet. In effect, small nations became the killing fields wherein large nations would put their opposing philosophies to the test, and the Kennedys and Castros were among the first practitioners of this new way of warring.

There would be no lasting peace, but at least the Cold War had a way of consolidating and clarifying things, internationally, much as a two-party system does on a national scale. Fascism had been defeated. It was now down to just two competing ideologies, one on the left, and one that had been the center, a simple dichotomy that was easy to understand because it was so implicit in the individual human psyche.

If there is one psychological principle most analogous to the binary conditions of the Cold War era, it might be the axiom that human beings have two basic needs within which most other needs are subsumed: the need for basic survival inside a protective and supportive communal group, and the need to be valued and encouraged as a unique, individual part of that group. The fulfillment of one of those needs is the utilitarian basis of protective communism; the fulfillment of the other is the cornerstone of creative capitalism. One to the exclusion of another can only result, psychologically speaking, in "half a person," and yet the entire geopolitical landscape was divided along precisely those lines in the mid-1950s. The all-embracing solidarity of the commune and the competitive individualism of the marketplace had become *opposite* scenarios for the pursuit of happiness.

By the end of 1956, the Castro brothers and Che were fighting for their lives in the mountains of Cuba. The Kennedy brothers had set their sights on the most powerful office in the world. And young Lee Oswald had qualified as a "marksman" with the M-1 rifle. Seven short years later, Jack and Lee would be dead. A few years after that, Che would be killed in a Bolivian jungle, and Bobby in a Los Angeles hotel kitchen. For all Jack's absorption in toughness, he died having defied right-wingers on two continents to create a Western Hemisphere "Alliance for Progress," a bold coalition meant to moderate the brutal oligarchies of Latin America and the red utopia offered by Cuba. After Jack's death, Bobby Kennedy would also be searching, with the adamant humanism of a priest, for some Eden, some third way between dehumanizing communism and abject, end-game capitalism. In the years before *his* death, he would be fighting desperately for some return to balance, both within his own soul and in the world at large.

Lee Oswald was also groping for some relief from the "either/or" rigidities of his time when he wrote: "No man, having known, having lived, under the Russian Communist and American capitalist system, could possibly make a choice between them. There is no choice, one offers oppresstion [*sic*] the other poverty. Both offer imperialistic injustice, tinted with two brands of slavery . . ." On the left end of the spectrum, Lee imagined that Fidel was making something more populist, more free yet fair, and he would die on a quest for his own "third way," imagining it to exist in Cuba, where his "both/and" salvation awaited him.

Even Fidel himself seemed to hover for a time between democratic and hard-core communist ideas; that is, until his brother reeled him back in. Raúl was the one who seems never to have wavered; never to have sought out any sort of reconciliation between opposites. At every chance to moderate and negotiate, he chose to provoke or retaliate; to destroy the center and all points between it and the hard left. Whether because of the new magnifying power of television or the existence of ultimate weapons or both, individual leaders suddenly had the power to take the whole world to the brink of destruction in an afternoon, and did. Marx and Aristotle had agreed on history's three-act structure. The end of World War II was the end of the modern world's Act Two. The election of John F. Kennedy was the beginning of Act Three: the time in which world conflict would resolve into some sort of synthesis, or one side would destroy the other, or all would be lost, forever.

CHAPTER 2
Revolution

ON APRIL 1, 1959, Jack and Bobby Kennedy presided over a strategy session at the family compound in Palm Beach, a meeting with their closest advisers to discuss how Jack might secure the Democratic nomination for president of the United States. If they could pull it off, Jack, at forty-one years old, stood to become the youngest man ever elected to the presidency. The day was bright with promise, the men in short sleeves and sunglasses arrayed in a circle on the veranda overlooking the sea.

But for all the candidate's well-aimed curiosity, all his dazzling flights of intellect, and his force of personality, there was something illusory about John Kennedy. He had the gift of being able to look like someone other than who he was. He appeared to be the picture of youthful vitality, but he was actually quite ill much of the time. He had an exquisite and sophisticated wife and a pretty, infant daughter, but he cheated on Jackie with the abandon of a man with a week to live. He had the air of a humanist intellectual but the reflexes of a merciless and calculating infighter. As he sat down that morning with half a dozen stellar men who had devoted themselves to helping him become president, he was secretly concerned that any one of his telephones might be tapped because of yet another ill-considered fling.[1]

His brother Bobby was particularly wired that day, pacing the wide front porch from one end to the other whenever he wasn't seated at Jack's right hand. Among the young team with them that day were their brother-in-law Steve Smith, Jack's Senate staffer Ted Sorensen, two Boston-bred political operatives named Kenny O'Donnell and Larry O'Brien, pollster Lou Harris, and Robert Wallace, another of Jack's legislative aides.[2]

Confidence was high, and they made quick work of assessing the relative threats posed by their rivals. Missouri senator Stuart Symington looked presidential, but wasn't. The Senate majority leader, Lyndon Johnson, resembled a towering basset hound, and although he certainly had the chops

Transaction Receipt

Teller transactions received after 2:00 p.m. will be posted on the next business day.
Teller transactions received on Saturdays and days before legal holidays, will be posted on the second business day.
The Trans. No. and Date, Bank Symbol, Account No. Teller No. & Amt. of Deposit are Shown Below. Subject to Provisions of the Uniform Commercial Code and to Detailed Verification.

```
ShoreBank Main
005 94 02/20/10          12:02
Savings Withdrawal       $50.00
Acct# 1400035802
```

....APPLY TODAY FOR A VISA DEBIT CARD....

1268-38

SHOREBANK
Let's change the world.®

7936 S. Cottage Grove
Chicago, Illinois 60619
773/288-1000

I.F.S. 4-122-63

to govern, he was a New Deal southerner and therefore would have few political prospects on either side of the Mason-Dixon line. "The Happy Warrior," archliberal Minnesotan Hubert Humphrey, was considered too far to the left to be right, and Adlai Stevenson was a write-off at that point, having run for the presidency twice and failed, the second time with Kefauver instead of Kennedy as his running mate. Adlai was still respected, however, and it was assumed that the old Illinois draft horse would have some place in the new cabinet if they were to win the White House.

As the meeting went on, Joe Sr. would chime in, accustomed to being listened to. He was, after all, said to be worth $400 million. Still, his influence was not quite as pervasive as it had been. Jack had wrested a bit of autonomy from the old man; he was the one conducting the state-by-state inventory that day, leaving Joe to editorialize from the margins as talk turned to who should be the primary spokesman in the various regions. They would have to deploy non-Catholics in some states, but the team was certain that they could overcome most of the resistance to Jack's age and religion.

Old Joe kept trying to get off the sidelines. "I'm going to tell you, we're going to win this thing. And I don't care if it takes every dime we've got!"

"Now wait a minute, Dad," Bobby teased him. "There are others in this family."[3]

It was a funny, passing reproach, but it was also a subtle expression of Bobby's newfound authority within the family, one that had begun when Bob called Jack to task for his sexual behavior after he lost his vice-presidential bid in 1956. More recently, Bob had gained additional stature as legal counsel to the McClellan Committee. In fact, just a week earlier, on March 24, he had made headlines by keelhauling gangsters Carlos Marcello and Sam Giancana as part of a larger pursuit of Teamsters Union boss Jimmy Hoffa. Bobby's prosecution of his duties had become so tireless and brazen that he had physically collared Hoffa in a Washington restaurant.

The labor king was being led to a table one noonday when a voice rang out across the restaurant. It was Bobby. He stalked up behind Jimmy, strong-armed the Detroit muscleman, and spun him around. Hoffa grabbed Bobby's suit coat and slammed him against a wall. "I'm only gonna tell you this one time," Jimmy said. "If you ever put your mitts on me again I'm gonna break you in half."[4] The battle spilled over to the afternoon session of the committee, where the men argued over whether Hoffa had threatened to break Bobby's back.

"Figure of speech," said Jimmy. ". . . I don't even know what I was talking about and I don't know what you're talking about."

"Uh . . . Mr. Hoffa, all I'm trying to find out, I'll tell you what I'm talking about. I'm trying to find out whose back you were going to break."

"Figure of speech . . . figure of speech."

But there was nothing figurative about it in the mind of Bob Kennedy. When he sensed the presence of evil in someone, he addressed it directly and often without tact. Where Jack came off as a man who wore his gravitas in easy balance with his wit and the air of entitlement, Bobby, on the loose in Washington for the first time, quickly became typecast as dogmatic, bellicose, and—the adjective that would stick—ruthless.

The truth, though, somewhat belied the appearance. In an interview five years after this meeting on the Palm Beach veranda, Kenny O'Donnell would say, "Jack was the tough one. Not Bobby. Jack would cut you off at the knees. Bobby would say, 'Why are we doing that to this guy?'"[5]

Jackie started calling him "Saint Bobby" in gratitude for his outbursts of chivalry. The journalist Murray Kempton thought of him as a "Catholic radical," and Alice Roosevelt Longworth, the doyenne of Washington society, would come to see him as less a politician at heart than as a "revolutionary priest."

It was precisely this aspect of Bobby, his zeal and his propensity for moral seizures, that drove Joe Sr. around the bend. The altar boy had grown up to become a Savonarola in a rumpled Brooks Brothers suit. A few months after Bob confronted Jack on Jackie's behalf in the summer of '56, he crossed swords at Christmas with his father over his assault on mob-infected unions. The McClellan Committee investigation was just getting up to speed. Bob was going at it hammer and tong, proud to be doing battle over something that mattered.

But Joe Sr. was no stranger to dealings with the underworld. His fortune—his family's fortune—would have been impossible without it, and he took a dim view of his own son's strident, public moralizing. A huge argument exploded between them. Joe believed that Bobby was insanely naive, that his quest for justice was about to turn the whole labor movement against the family, thus demolishing Jack's shot at the presidency. This in itself was an admission that working people, the Teamsters in particular, were in the grip of both management and their own mobbed-up labor leaders, nationwide. Joe's warnings rang like a practical admission of defeat and only inflamed Bob. He countered that his crusade would actually add luster to the family name by freeing the working class from an army of goons. Joe greeted this with disgust. He sensed that he might be losing his lifelong control over his boys, and he asked Supreme Court Justice William O. Douglas to explain the danger to Bobby, to try to rein him in, but Douglas had no luck. Robert Francis Kennedy was a man on a crusade, and not a very nuanced crusader.

Whether Bobby knew of the family's ties to organized crime at that time, he had demonstrated that he was quite willing to override his father's grand objections and act independently. If he *did* know, then it suggests that his crusade might have been a kind of oedipal unease with the family's precipitous rise to great wealth amid rumors of Joe's turpitude. Kennedy biographer Doris Kearns Goodwin suggested it was a necessary form of patricide. In fact, Bob must have known. Hoffa himself made reference to the Kennedy history of bootlegging as an example of how immigrants had to do business to get a leg up in the New World. Others had made public allusions to Joe's shady dealings on Wall Street and in Hollywood, dating back to those olden days of Prohibition. It could not have been a secret.

And because Bobby had not relented on that Christmas morning, he now found himself the unchallenged moral center of the family, reeling Jack in when he dallied too foolishly, and defying Joe Sr. in defense of political rectitude. In just two years, Bob's own sense of moral balance would be grossly compromised in pursuit of the Castro brothers, but as of then, on a torpid spring day in Florida, he had emerged from his father's shadow as his older brother never had.

And Joe understood the differences between his second and third sons. "Bobby feels more strongly for and against people than Jack—just as I do . . . He hates the same way I do." He saw the depths of Bob too, the places that went beyond his own ability to feel. "Bobby is soft—soft on people . . . he has the capacity to be emotionally involved, to feel things deeply, as compared to Jack and that amazing detachment of his."[6] In any case, Bob was utterly devoted to Jack's ascent, but it was as much the commitment of a mentor as it was of an adoring kid brother. Bob was already laboring to engage Jack more passionately in the ways of the world, in the very issues and ideals, in fact, that were about to define the coming decade and the generation that came of age within it.

Murray Kempton saw the two men as a contrast "between those who are properly oriented and those who are truly involved."[7] Jack was a political aesthete, cool to the touch and cerebrally calculating the odds in his favor. Bob was, in an analogy made by the British newspaper publisher Lord Beaverbrook, a kind of Richard the Lionheart, a man whose winning instinct was essentially not self-centered but driven by a need to right wrongs and to accomplish something of lasting benefit to people. His work on the

McClellan Committee became a book, *The Enemy Within*, about racketeering and its wider implications for America. "The paramount interest in self," Bobby wrote, "in material wealth, in security must be replaced by an actual, not just vocal, interest in our country, by a spirit of adventure, a will to fight what is evil, and a desire to serve."

His own best interests were almost always secondary to the crusade, the overarching agenda of changing the world, and what better way to change it than to gain the presidency. Joe Sr. may have been the campaign's bank, and Jack its brainy cause célèbre, but Bobby was its heart, from that morning on the porch in Palm Beach all the way through Jack's presidency and his own mad dash to the end of his life. As the family was about to embark on its ultimate voyage in search of power, the underlying dynamic was one of inexpressible love, impregnable loyalty, and a brass-knuckled will to alter the face of history, just because they could.

Jack Newfield, himself a radical but of the journalistic sort, would ask Bobby years later, "If you weren't born a Kennedy, what would you have been?" Bobby replied, "Either a juvenile delinquent or a revolutionary." He was a lawyer, however, and then attorney general and then a politician who became a senator and ran for president. As a Kennedy, he couldn't possibly have qualified as a revolutionary. "Still," said Newfield, "he had empathy with people who were revolutionaries, and he admired that role. If Kennedy had a Walter Mitty life, he would have been Che Guevara."[8]

In Cuba, Castro's nascent revolution was about to break out. Rolando Cubela had gone to Florida to further equip Castro's rebels, and when he returned from Miami, he and Castro's *Granma* group linked up with the forces under Frank País, Carlos Franqui, and Huber Matos, a total of about two hundred strong, to consolidate control of the Sierra Maestra region. They executed many Batista supporters along the way. Similar bloodletting was ordered on the four fronts in Oriente Province, directed by the Castro brothers and Juan Almeida Bosque. Politically diverse as the revolution was, the 26th of July Movement was already heavily populated by Communists.

By this time, the Eisenhower administration's tolerance for Batista's flagrant corruption had passed the breaking point. Consequently, the U.S. placed an embargo on Batista, which led to a crippling shortage of supplies and spare parts. Batista's forces were left completely dispirited and unable to put up a fight. Suddenly, the U.S. Navy in Guantánamo and the CIA had shifted their bets to the insurgents.

In late December 1958, the city of Santa Clara was captured by the combined forces of Che Guevara, Rolando Cubela, José "El Mexicano" Abrantes, and William Morgan. Batista panicked and fled Cuba for the Dominican Republic just hours later on January 1, 1959. On January 2, Guevara entered Havana, with Castro himself arriving six days later.

The transition was far from smooth. In January 1960, a group of 3,500 anti-Communist peasants went into the Escambray Mountains in the first open revolt against the new Castro regime. The resistance was ruthlessly suppressed. The Castros began maligning the peasants as "bandits" and would soon order the massive at-gunpoint relocation of thousands of them from the Escambray area. During this "pacification" operation, Fidel employed overwhelming force, at times consisting of 250,000 troops (against the 3,500 peasants). As in the purges of Hitler and Stalin, the peasants were herded into trains, where families were separated and banished. The men were sent to prisons and forced-labor camps throughout Cuba. Women and children were housed in expropriated houses converted into detention centers in faraway cities.

These displaced and broken families were held incommunicado in distant areas of the island; and when their children were six years old, they were forcibly removed from their mothers and interned in Communist indoctrination schools. The men were subjected to abusive and inhumane treatment in "closed towns." Eventually, the widely scattered family members were reunited in these closed towns, but they were prohibited from returning to their original land. Four decades later, the Escambray insurgents were still being treated as prisoners and hostages of Castro's regime.*

In April 1959, four months after the Cuban revolution was won, Che's comrade in arms Fidel Castro visited the United States, victorious, obstreperous, and resplendently populist in his olive drab fatigues. It was the first time he'd been back among the Yankees since his swim across the Rio Grande in 1956, and this time he arrived in style. Fidel had come at the in-

---

*Castro's war was concluded in 1965, after killing a total of 2,236, according to Dr. Armando Lago's research for an upcoming book. From this total, Dr. Lago says, 1,415 were executed on sight without trial. Castro's policy was to execute all prisoners by shooting or hanging after viciously torturing them. The losses by Castro's forces are also believed to have been staggering, but there is little documentation available to determine the actual numbers. According to the book *Cuba in Revolution: Escape from a Lost Paradise* by Miguel A. Faria Jr., M.D. (p. 113), Raúl Castro admitted that Castro's army suffered 6,000 deaths from the freedom fighters in the Escambray. The total cost in human lives of the Escambray revolt against Castro was far greater than in all the years of skirmishes against the Batista regime (1952–1958).

vitation of curious American news publishers. He was armed with every bit of charm he could deploy, including his little son, Fidelito, by his side. He and the Yankee press were still in their honeymoon period, fueled in part by reports in the *New York Times*, under Herbert L. Matthews's byline, that Fidel was not a Communist, was actually opposed by his Red countrymen, and was instead the champion of "a new deal for Cuba." His trip was unofficial, and—despite America's belated support for the revolution—President Eisenhower declined to meet him, but Fidel's guerrilla style served him well on the hustings. As Ike withdrew, Fidel advanced. As Ike regrouped, Fidel dispersed into the jungle of American celebrity. If he couldn't get the president's attention, he would go straight to the American people instead.

Since the great insurgent victory on New Year's Day, Fidel had consolidated his power and begun to dominate the multifaceted movement that had driven out Batista, largely by means of "special courts" and the execution of those officials whom the former dictator had left behind when he fled to the Dominican Republic. Under Fidel and Che's orders, at least 151 Cubans would be executed by firing squad in the first months of the revolution alone. By the second year, according to *Time*, the number had hit 587. Among these dangerous enemies of the state were some 94 minors, some as young as fourteen years old. And they were just getting started. *Time* magazine's February 3, 1961, issue reported: "The year 1961 was supposed to be 'The Year of Education' in Fidel Castro's Cuba. Last week the slogan was enlarged. It is now also 'The Year of the Firing Squad.' The announcement was made by Cuba's Agrarian Reform Chief Antonio Núñez Jiménez in a speech to a crowd of gun-toting militiamen. Added the Reformer: 'We will erect the most formidable execution wall in the history of humanity.' "

It must be remembered that America had never officially protested the brutalities of Batista, though thousands had been tortured and killed under his rule. And previous fallen Cuban regimes had been met with rampant vigilante justice on the streets. American politicians who had largely turned a blind eye to Batista and then abandoned him were now outraged: Fidel was equally outraged at what he considered rank hypocrisy. His supporters argued that at least the Castros' trials were a disciplined exertion of state justice and not a bloody free-for-all. In reality, though, they were an instrument for centralizing power and sending a message to the people that vigilantism was a privilege to be exercised only by their rulers. Those who could afford an escape from the island did so by any means possible. Those who had been exiled by Batista begun to return, but with them came both celebrations and rumors of a gathering counterrevolution.

By 1960, the honeymoon with America would be over, but in 1959 it was still mostly hearts and flowers. With his typically ferocious energy, Fidel demanded Cuban equality before the Senate Foreign Relations Committee, made the rounds of radio and television stations, mugged for cameras at the Cuba desk in the UN General Assembly, gave speeches before tens of thousands at Harvard, Princeton, and Columbia, and savored every chance to promote his revolution and himself. There was even talk that a Texas oilman and a Hollywood producer were brokering a deal for Marlon Brando to play him in a movie.[9]

Amid all the glad-handing, the question lingered: Was Fidel a Communist—that is, an ideological ally of America's greatest enemy? No one knew for sure, not even his inner circle. When squeezed on the Communist question, in private, by his finance minister, Lopez Fresquet, he assured him, "Look, Rufo, I am letting the Communists [in Cuba] stick their heads out so I will know who they are. And when I know them all, I'll do away with them with one sweep of my hat."[10]

Washington wasn't so sure, though. When the new, vaguely aligned leader got to D.C., President Eisenhower headed out of town to play golf. Fidel did take a lengthy Sunday meeting with Vice President Richard Nixon at his office, an encounter that lasted for two and a half hours, but the cordiality was forced and would have collapsed altogether if Fidel had known how hard the vice president was working to assassinate him and overthrow his regime. Brother Raúl would figure it out soon enough.

Clearly, the U.S. government was suffering from a certain schizophrenia about Fidel at this point, one that extended all the way into the labyrinth of the CIA. Former CIA analyst and Cuba expert Brian Latell recounts that Nixon's report to Ike would emphasize certain "indefinable qualities" of Fidel's, aspects that promised an ongoing impact on Cuba and the rest of Latin America,[11] but other, more deadly impulses were already loose in the executive branch. At their meeting, Nixon put on his game face and pressed Fidel rhetorically about democracy and dictatorship. Fidel's response was ambiguous. "Dictatorships are a shameful blot on America, and democracy is more than just a word."[12] He proceeded to lecture Nixon, scolding him that democracy was impossible as long as there was injustice in the world. After the meeting, Nixon concluded that Fidel was, if not a Communist himself, at least a philosophical captive of Communists. His follow-up memo to Ike had no clarifying effect on the national security apparatus, however. Fidel continued to be a subject of cautious debate, and Ike himself remained indecisive as to exactly what to do about him.

Fidel kept them guessing, too. In a meeting with United Nations reporters, he went out of his way to make it clear that he would not be exporting his up-start revolution, even if it did tend to inspire and instruct other populations living in the harness of oppression.

He played the beguiling tourist in the off-hours, visiting Mount Vernon and the Lincoln and Jefferson memorials. As his Washington visit drew to a close, he disappeared off the radar of his American surveillance contingent for hours, driving into the humbler parts of the city and catching a meal in a Chinese restaurant. He smiled for the cameras, gave extensive interviews, charmed reporters at the National Press Club, and promised good relations with the United States whenever the question was broached. At a mass rally of thirty-five thousand in New York's Central Park, his disquisition went on for two hours, but the public was warming to this seemingly modest yet elo-quent rebel.

At the Hotel Statler late one night, Cuban journalist Luis Conte Aguero brought a beautiful, blue-eyed American blonde named June Cobb to meet him. She was thirty-two and she had no claim to fame at that point, except that—six weeks earlier—she had brought a copy of Fidel's "History Will Ab-solve Me" speech (from his 1953 trial) back from Cuba and she and a friend had translated it for publication. June had dummied up a booklet, and Fidel was so pleased when he saw it that evening that he approved an initial print run of a thousand offset copies for distribution, city-wide.[13] The New York papers picked it up, as did a new organization of Cuba sympathizers—mostly well-known artists and journalists—known as the Fair Play for Cuba Committee (FPCC).[14] June didn't much care that they had purloined her translation (she would soon publish a second run of five thousand and yet another one of fifty thousand), but she was not impressed by the FPCC crowd. They seemed undiscerning to her, an odd combination of de rigueur and doctrinaire.[15]

Born in Oklahoma, June boasted a rebellious résumé, including a stint at the University of Mexico where she had fallen in love with a Colombian man, with whom she lived for six months in the Ecuadoran jungle. Her time there inspired a concern over coca addiction among the Indians. That was why she had been drawn to Fidel and Raúl in the first place: their campaign against the debilitating effects of vice under Batista.

Fidel's secretary, sister in arms, and sometime lover Celia Sánchez first took a shine to June in New York, and by September 1959 she would be headed to Havana as a translator of Fidel's speeches and all-round public relations assis-tant. They put her to work translating his new land-reform laws into English.

As the party swelled around them, no one could have foretold her controversial effect on Fidel and his inner circle over the next few years. In the heady atmosphere of April 1959, June Cobb was just another of the eager young guests who wanted to help Cuba and be close to the Maximum Leader. Later, she would say of herself, "I suppose you can call me a sucker for lost causes."

Fidel's American coming-out party would end in Texas, eleven days after his arrival. He had enjoyed it tremendously, it seemed. En route to his next swing, through Latin American, he was met in Houston by Raúl, who had just arrived from Havana—and who was furious. With the tacit backing of Che, Raúl spent his very first night in America in the Shamrock Hilton, spewing invective at the big brother who he thought had been soft-pedaling the true nature of the Revolution up and down the whole East Coast.

It is possible that Fidel was simply enjoying his moment too much to spoil it by declaring his true allegiances. But, it was during Fidel's tour that Raúl made his first secret and official contact with the Soviet Union. While Raúl had already chosen his path, Fidel was still pausing at the ideological fork in the road. On that night at the glittery Shamrock, eighteen stories above the street, their argument exploded into a full-blown sibling harangue that went on half the night. At one point they were heard accusing each other of being the sons of a whore,[16] and after it was over, Raúl withdrew and stayed out of sight, fuming in one of the fifty-six rooms the Cubans had taken.

The rift almost leaked out. The next morning they tried to make a show of solidarity, wheeling across the Texas landscape in a twenty-two-car motorcade. They stopped for food at a diner and then again for a barbecue at a spacious ranch. Fidel posed wearing a Stetson, toyed with a gold-platinum six-shooter he had been given, and fawned over a champion quarterhorse colt, another bit of largesse from the assembled oilmen who were their hosts. Raúl glowered beneath his proletarian beret and endured the rest of the junket until they got to the Houston airport that night. There was one more private explosion between them before they parted ways, Fidel bound for South America, Raúl headed back to Havana.

When Fidel returned home to the motherland in May, the rift between the brothers was now a rift across the country itself. The Cuban Communists had obviously advanced their position, with the blessings of Raúl and Che, but inside the 26th of July Movement the debate about Communism was raging, even in the party's house organ, *Revolución*. The Movement seemed to be cracking in half. On May 8, Fidel felt compelled to make a major address to the nation in order to distance himself from "Communist ideas."[17]

By this time, the first stage of the post-revolution exodus from Cuba was more or less over. The hard-line Batistianos had been the first to hightail it out of Cuba on New Year's Day, and, by the spring and summer, the scared oligarchs were leaving too. But it was the next wave of the exodus, in the coming year, that would have the most damning and decisive effect on the New Cuba. Fidel's grand tour of the hemisphere would prove to be his last flirtation with democracy. If his early Marxist tutorials of Raúl had been a tactical feint, leaving him free to be ideologically nimble, he would be forced to declare his socialism soon enough. Eisenhower and Nixon would soon be handing power to the Kennedys, who would soon be forced to make certain ominous declarations of their own.

At about the time that Fidel was finishing up his American tour, Marine buck private Lee Oswald had so trashed his service record in the Corps that he was spending his days cleaning latrines, mowing lawns, and swabbing the decks at the base at El Toro, California. No sooner had this small, meek, and bookish southern boy arrived at the Second Training Battalion in San Diego than his fellow Marines dubbed him "Ozzie the Rabbit." The teasing was merciless, and his initial defense was the usual one: hiding out in books—Whitman's *Leaves of Grass* and Orwell's *1984*. He liked to dream of fame and glory, but he had no rapport with other men, and when he was perfunctorily promoted to private first class in May, his arrogance presented itself. He started proclaiming the incompetence of his superiors just in time to be shipped out to Japan.

It didn't get better. Posted to Marine Air Control Squadron One at Atsugi, twenty miles out of Tokyo, he became the Boy in the Radar Bubble whom no one could stand.[18] (Although the airbase was also home to the CIA's top-secret U-2 spy plane, Oswald had nothing to do with that operation, as some have alleged.*) He had brought an unauthorized derringer with him to Japan,[19] but he accidentally shot himself in the left elbow with it. He spent two and a half weeks in the hospital, and when he got out, his unit was sent to the Philippines for a three-month stint at Subic Bay.

---

* A retired engineer and former junior commandant of a Marine Corps League detachment in Pennsylvania had this to say: "I was stationed with Lee Harvey Oswald in barracks 5 at Atsugi, Japan, Marine side . . . He was never an important factor in our squadron, MACS-1 as soon after he arrived, he was court-martialed and reduced in rank to the lowest enlisted grade of Private for fighting with two NCO's. He was also afforded a 'sand shower' by directive from our first Sgt. in order to motivate him into taking a shower every day of his life. He did after that. His total duties as a Pvt. in the radar hut, was to be on the

He passed a test for promotion to the rank of corporal, but the upgrade never came, scotched by the pistol incident. While waiting for court-martial proceedings to be brought against him for the derringer, he was punished with KP duty. His attitude went south. He became openly insubordinate. His performance rating dropped below the level needed to receive an honorable discharge, and, while stationed off the Indonesian coast during the internal war there in March of 1958, he began to speak and act like a full-blown Communist, at least out of sight of his superiors. Later, in a letter written from Russia to his brother, Robert, he would describe his Indonesian duty thus: "I remember well the days we stood offshore at Indonesia waiting to surpress [sic] yet another population, when they were having a revolution there . . . I can still see Japan and the Philippines and their puppet governments."[20]

Another strange incident involving firearms occurred before he left the Philippines. A private first class whom Lee knew well was found dead of a gunshot wound at his guard post outside an airplane hangar. The death was ruled accidental, a dropped gun that misfired, but after a Corps investigation there were rumors that Lee was involved and the hangar itself might have housed a U-2 spy plane. Rigorous investigations since that time have not altered the initial finding, but the incident is worth noting as a measure of his comrades' low esteem for the "pinko" Marine. This would have been an extremely serious accusation, and yet the other men discussed it openly.

Back in Atsugi, he was court-martialed and found guilty of the weapons charge. Demoted back to private and given twenty days at hard labor, he was enraged, and it was during his time in the brig that he first started fantasizing about defecting to the Soviet Union.

His contact with Japanese Communists, while on leave in the Orient, might also have contributed to the fantasies of flight into the arms of Mother Russia. Apparently, it was also during these leaves that his first sexual experiences

---

plotting board, taking directions from our controllers. He was not exposed to anything classified except the equipment he worked on which were our scopes that plotted all air activity within 250 to 300 miles of our station. He was classified as a 'yardbird' as we call screwups in the Corps, so very few if any hung around with him at all. I was in the security section, G-2 as a secondary MOS [Military Operational Specialty] to my original 6741 radar controller in charge of security clearances, applications etc. His temporary secret clearance was taken away after his court martial, so he was in the lowest category of service we had in the unit . . . [The CIA's U-2] maintenance crew were bunked out in our barracks 5, but had no intimate contact with our troops." See http://cr4.globalspec.com/blogentry/ 4899/The-Engineer-Who-Knew-Lee-Harvey-Oswald.

occurred, perhaps not all of them heterosexual in nature. According to Daniel Powers, a Marine officer with whom Lee served during basic training in Biloxi, Mississippi, the young Oswald "had a lot of feminine characteristics," and they tended to increase his isolation. Several of his fellow Marines in Japan claimed that he was familiar with a transvestite club in Yamato, and others said that he seemed to have been a regular at a gay bar called The Flamingo in Tijuana, Mexico, during his California stints.[21]

A portrait of intractable solitude begins to form in this series of cameos: the image of an existential stranger, untethered, unloved, and unloving of himself. His letters to Robert continued. His brother showed some caring for him, but Lee was fast becoming a man who inspired no trust in people and no sustained affection.

At a certain point, the loneliness prompted him to seek acceptance from those Marines who had been torturing him. He tried being funny, but the jokes misfired, and the failure drove him ever deeper into novels and Russian-language books. He started drinking heavily, baiting people into ugly debates, and telling his officers where to get off. When he got a chance to exact revenge on the guy who he blamed for getting him an inordinate amount of KP duty, he dumped a highball on him in a joint called The Bluebird Café and was promptly hit with another court-martial.

Not long after he came out of the brig, he was sent to Taiwan with his unit, and it was there that he finally lost it. His sense of imprisonment, his budding hatred for America, and the constant browbeating and denigration from other Marines pushed him over the edge. On guard duty one night he started firing his M1 at imaginary figures in the forest; he was in such a blithering state of despair that he was sent back to Japan for rest and recuperation.[22]

When he returned to duty once more, it was to the Marine squad at Iwakuni. By then, he was completely devoted to Communism and missed no opportunity to sing its virtues. By November of 1958, he was shipped back to the States and assigned to Air Control Squadron Nine, once again at the El Toro Marine base in Southern California.

At the same time, one of his great heroes, Fidel Castro, was marching toward his destiny, the Cuban Revolution reaching its apex. During the month's leave that Lee took before heading to El Toro, President Eisenhower sent another mixed message to Batista, urging him to go into exile and hoping that his absence would allow an American-backed force to head off the various revolutionary factions bearing down on Havana. Batista refused on December 9. Lee reached El Toro on January 1, 1959, just as the Castros were beginning their victory march into Havana.

Castro's victory put a new spring in Lee's step. He fancied himself a political intellectual by now, reading *Das Kapital*, *Mein Kampf*, and *Animal Farm*, and poring over the Russian-language newspaper he subscribed to, struggling to learn all he could. He played his Russian composers at rock 'n' roll volume, and insisted on using the red pieces whenever he played checkers. His fellow Corpsmen had a new nickname for him now, "Oswald-skovich," and Lee loved it so much that he began to insist on it as his name.[23]

But for all his comic, even pathetic, posturing, this marks the time when the monomania of Lee's adolescence gave way to a serious pursuit of real fame and glory through action. At El Toro, a Brooklyn-born Marine named Nelson Delgado was assigned to share duty with him in the radar bubble, and he became one of Lee's few friends, partly because they both admired Castro. By this time, Lee's Red fantasies had spurred him to make actual plans. Fidel was still parrying the accusations that he was a Marxist, but Lee appears to have already reached the conclusion that he was, or soon would be; and with that, he decided to pay a visit to the Cuban consulate in Los Angeles. In fact, he probably ventured even further into the Cuban community.

Gerry Hemming, an American mercenary who would later join *anti-Castro* forces, was a guard at the suburban home of Manuel Velásquez, the Cuban consul at that time.[24] According to Hemming, a young man of Lee's general description arrived at the house, gave his name as Oswald, and told the guard that he resided in Santa Ana, the town where El Toro was located. The man remarked that he wanted to board a flight to Cuba—the flight, he explained, that would deliver weapons he believed to be hidden in the consul's home. He hoped to join Fidel's revolution, he said. Hemming was suspicious. How could this odd American know of such a flight, much less its purpose? It suggested that he had already had more than a passing contact with members of the consular staff, but was he friend or foe? Hemming brushed him off and then tried to follow him out to the street to copy his license-plate number, but the man disappeared in an instant, apparently by car, whether alone or with a driver.[25]

When Lee let Delgado in on the extent of his forays into L.A., Delgado got scared and tried to put some distance between the two of them. He had seen a stack of "spotter" photos of a fighter plane among Lee's papers, pictures that he put into a duffel bag, along with other possessions, and asked Delgado to lock in a bus station locker for him.[26] And Delgado witnessed another odd scene while the two were on guard duty at the front gate, a civilian who arrived to pay a visit to Lee and engaged him in a heated discussion; Delgado assumed the man was connected to Lee's Cuban escapades.[27] Almost two decades later, the CIA would review Pfc. Oswald's shadowy Cuban connections and conclude: "Delgado's testimony says a lot more of possible operational significance than is reflected by the language of the [Warren Commission] report, and its implications do not appear to have been run down or developed by investigations. Thus, the record of the beginning of Oswald's relationship with Cubans starts with a question mark."[28]

After two courts-martial and a nervous breakdown, Lee was a washout as a Marine and, on August 17, he applied for a dependency discharge, putatively to help his mother, who he claimed had suffered an injury. In fact, he had no intention of going to Marguerite's aid. When he was finally discharged on September 11, 1959, he went straight to Fort Worth and told her he was taking a job at an import-export company. In fact, he was defecting to the Soviet Union.

The only thing he had excelled at during his tour of duty in the Marine Corps was his marksmanship. In 1956, he had qualified as a "sharpshooter," and even upon his release he was certified as a "marksman." The NCO in charge of his training, Sgt. James Zahm, reported that "In the Marine Corps he is a good shot, slightly above average . . . and as compared to the average male . . . throughout the United States, he is an excellent shot."[29] Contrary to the myths that flourished in the decades after Dallas, when Lee Oswald fled the Marines and set out for Moscow, he was taking with him at least one crucial skill; he was fully capable of the murder that would make him so infamous four years later.

In early August 1959, a young woman arrived at the railroad station in the eastern Soviet city of Minsk, nearly penniless and hoping to find safe haven with relatives there. Raised mostly by her mother, her grandmother, and her stepfather's aunt, a fearless and religious little woman full of love, Marina Prusakova had been effectively banished from Leningrad by family members who feared that her rebellious ways would bring shame upon herself and them.

She arrived at Minsk unexpectedly, and her aunt Musya was overjoyed to see her, but the reception was tinged with an undertone of mistrust. Her hated stepfather had sent a letter a year before, falsely claiming that Marina had become a prostitute.

Her female relatives seem to have withheld judgment, however, and, although Aunt Musya's apartment was too crowded with children already, her childless uncle Ilya and aunt Valya agreed to take her in. It was not without trepidation on Ilya's part. He was a high official in the Byelorussian Ministry of Internal Affairs, the MVD. He had a spacious apartment with a private telephone, and he carried the rank of colonel, which rendered him an powerful person in the city. Taking in a young woman with a rebellious streak could sink his career.

But she had some training as a pharmacist, so—perhaps at the urging of his childless wife, who began to think of Marina as a daughter—Ilya pulled some strings and landed her a job as an assistant at the Third Clinical Hospital. The girl was smart, a hungry reader of classic novels. She was outgoing—perhaps a little too outgoing—but she tried hard to live by Ilya's rules, happy for Valya's devotion and for a foster father who, if not openly kind or demonstrative, at least would not denigrate her.

She thrived in Minsk, though her girlfriends at work saw her precocity as something more akin to recklessness. There were many boys hovering about, and she played them off against each other with aplomb, but the rebel who was perhaps most like her was one Misha Smolsky, a stylish redhead who was the Soviet equivalent of the Carnaby Street "mods" about to sprout in London. Her biographer would later describe him coming to pick Marina up after work "wearing a hip-length overcoat, a pair of pointed English shoes, and a towering karakul cap."[30] He smoked a pipe, and he led a clique of bright young things who didn't put much stock in Communism and steeped themselves in Western ideas. They devoured Hemingway and Remarque as much for the explicit sex as for their world-weary attitude toward power. They passed around copies of banned books like Pasternak's *Dr. Zhivago*, swapped slang and cultural nuggets mined from the BBC and Voice of America, slept around, and bopped into the wee hours to the strains of American jazz and rock 'n' roll. "A thing had to be forbidden for us to get hold of it somehow," Marina would recall years later.

There were other boys too—a dark-eyed Jewish architect named Leonid Lonya whose religion Marina dared to ignore but with whom she refused to live out of wedlock, as he suggested. There was her lapdog, Sasha the med student, who plodded along behind her no matter how she treated him. And there was Anatoly Shpanko, another med student, whose curly blond hair, bright smile, and unerring honesty would have won her heart completely if she hadn't still been biding her time. For all his devotion to her, she kept him in limbo, kissing him with her eyes open to whoever else might walk by.

Just a few years later, when she was leading the life of an abused and neglected wife in Texas, she would stop what she was doing whenever the young American president would appear on television, and be reminded of

Anatoly. It would make her wonder how she had been so stupid in her choice of husbands. But back then, even in Communist Minsk, the great postwar youth movement of the 1960s was getting under way. A girl could make love when she wanted and not suffer the consequences that her unmarried mother had. If they were stealthy about it, a girl and her friends could read what they pleased and say what they thought and dance to the music that moved them, even in the Workers' Paradise. The youthquake was upon them. It knew no boundaries or borders, and Marina Prusakova was not going to miss a minute of it.

Two months after Marina arrived in Minsk and two days before his twentieth birthday, on October 16, 1959, Lee Oswald finally made it to Moscow. He would later tell his brother, Robert, that he had planned to defect for a year, and his journey bore all the marks of a pilgrim's progress: a renunciation of all ties to his former life, his family, his country, and what he considered to be the decadent privations of corporate capitalism. In his diary he wrote: "Arrive from Helskinki by train; am met by Intourist Representative and taken in car to Hotel Berlin. Register as student on a five-day Deluxe tourist ticket. Meet my Intourist guide Rimma Shirakova. (I explain to her I wish to apply for Russian citizenship.)"

When Rimma met Lee and discovered that he was traveling deluxe and had booked the same first-class accommodations at the hotel, she was astonished. It appears that Lee had saved nearly two thirds of the money he made as a Marine. Now, as if treating himself to one good petit bourgeois spree before ascending to the Workers' Paradise, he was hell-bent on spending all he had made; his indulgence was all the more surprising to her because he was no more than a boy dressed in a cheap overcoat and thick-soled military boots, probably his Marine-issue gear. He was pallid and skittish, and his Russian seemed nearly nonexistent. He didn't want to visit the cultural sites, so she took him on a morning spin through Moscow, ending with a stop at Red Square. He stood and stared and was perfectly polite, a decent sort, she thought; but he left all the talking to her, posing no questions, and when she dropped him back at the Berlin Hotel, he ate his lunch alone.[31]

An afternoon trip to the Kremlin was postponed. He just wanted to find a nice place to sit and talk. He may have simply been exhausted, and Rimma's account suggests that he was lonely and wanted to unburden himself. Although it was a minor breach of protocol to depart from the schedule, Rimma found them a bench near the hotel and gave him her full attention for the rest of the afternoon.

He spoke of battlefields, implying that he had been in combat and didn't want to fight in another unjust war. He shared a little information about his roots, his life. It was not urgent, just poignant. He wasn't yet implying that he had any important information to impart, just casual thoughts about life and more pointed, angry ones about America. It wasn't until late afternoon, when he told her that he wanted to stay in Russia, that she felt her position being compromised.

"I explain to her [Rimma] I wish to apply for Russian citizenship," he scribbled in his diary. "She is flabbergasted, but agrees to help. She Checks with her boss, main office Intourist, then helps me address a letter to Supreme Soviet asking for citizenship."

In the ensuing four days, the sympathetic Rimma broached his request with the boss of the Passport and Visa Office, Alexander Simchenko.[32] She and a colleague named Rosa brought Lee to the office, though Simchenko was not about to pass the request further. It was sure to be denied, so he humored the eager, smiling young man.

He seemed to be a bit of an actor, this Oswald, charming and adaptable, but he came off as a mama's boy in dire need of adult supervision; he had no idea what he was getting himself into. Underdressed, hatless, with a pendant bearing his name on a silver chain around his neck, he looked like someone's lost dog. Simchenko conducted a cursory interview and then politely ended the conversation. When Lee left, the officer suggested that the girls buy him a hat.[33]

Sunday was Lee's twentieth birthday and his third day in Russia. It's not known whether Rimma bought him a hat, but she did take him to Lenin's tomb in Red Square.[34] Vladimir Ilyich's ears were starting to turn black. Stalin, lying in a glass coffin side by side with Lenin's, looked waxen, his mustache dusty, but there they were, the Father of Bolshevism encased beside the absolute dictator. These were the literal embodiments of an ideology to which Lee had devoted himself, but he showed no particular reaction. He just stood in line, passed by the grandly mounted cadavers, and moved on.

On that Monday, October 19, 1959, in the Cuban province of Camagüey, a hero of the Cuban revolution was about to draw a line between himself and the Castros that would startle the populace and mark what Theodore Draper would call "the real point of no return in Cuba . . . long before any overt American action was taken against the Castro regime."[35]

Huber Matos, a schoolteacher who had saved Fidel's forces in the Sierra Maestra with a planeload of guns and ammo in March of 1958, was resigning as the military leader of Camagüey Province. Matos was the most powerful voice of protest yet to speak against the creeping Communist tide. Leaders of the 26th of July Movement were being cast aside in droves. Communist players were seizing control of the provincial government, and when they tried to seize the rebel army itself, Matos decided to confront the Castro brothers directly. Neither of them would grant their former savior an audience, however, and so he tendered his resignation, along with a host of other Camagüey military leaders.

By this time, Fidel had apparently fallen into line with Raúl and Che. On October 20, Fidel came to Camagüey and had Matos arrested in his home and charged with treason. This only escalated the crisis. Members of the Castros' cabinet were furious, and the former head of Havana's urban underground, Faustino Pérez, refused to sign the resolution against Matos. When an emergency meeting of other anti-Communist cabinet members was reported back to Fidel, he crashed the meeting and confronted them, face to face. Two of his most important members resigned, Pérez and the Minister of Public Works, Manuel Ray.

Huber Matos would stand trial on December 1. Fidel himself delivered a seven-hour harangue in which he claimed Matos had effectively conspired to split the military from the regime itself, thus betraying the Revolution to the Americans and all other opponents. Despite Matos's wide popularity and his undeniable importance to Fidel's victory the year before, he would be sentenced to twenty years in prison. No matter how long Fidel avoided a public declaration of himself as a Communist, the country was systematically being painted red one man at a time, from Pinar del Río to Santiago de Cuba.

During Lee Oswald's time in Moscow, he was such a rarity that he was sought out and interviewed by an American journalist stationed there named Aline Mosby. She would later remark on the same incurious aspect that Rimma had noticed. "He appeared totally disinterested in anything but himself. He talked almost non-stop like the type of semi-educated person of little experience who clutches at what he regards as some sort of unique truth."[36] He seemed to want to tell his tale to anyone who would listen. Another journalist, Priscilla McMillan, then a correspondent for the *Progressive*, interviewed him in her hotel room and wrote a feature story about him. "I thought he was very, very young and touching in his eagerness to stay in Russia, but afterwards I did not think a great deal about him. Except for one thing. Oswald said that he was a Marxist and was defecting because of his beliefs. In Moscow we thought we had seen everything, but we had never seen anyone like this . . . here was this boy who was prepared to take a very drastic step because of his political convictions."[37] She saw him as a soft-spoken, even gentle, boy, but during their talks he referred to himself as "unemotional," and years later she had difficulty reconciling him with the killer of a president. By coincidence, McMillan's first job out of college in the early fifties had been as a researcher for John F. Kennedy, just after he was elected to the Senate from Massachusetts. She had found Kennedy "de-lightful and eccentric," but felt that his ambition to become president had been forced on him by Joe Kennedy Sr. She wrote of Jack: ". . . I thought he had done it at a cost to his capacity for empathy and imagination. He had a candor and breathtaking detachment about himself, but I wondered how well he understood other people, especially those who lacked his kind of ambition, or those who happened to be failures."[38]

Lee failed on his first try at citizenship in the Soviet Union. He had begun to seed his conversations with hints that he was *afraid* to go back to the States and might have information that the Russian state could find useful. It was a fruitless ploy. On the day before his visa ran out, Rimma broke the news that his application had been rejected. He was stunned, and this time he *insisted* that he had important strategic information to give. Once again, Rimma tried to intercede for him; but when a female KGB officer inter-viewed him, he more or less repeated his mini-biography and restated his reasons for wanting to defect, but gave up little of substance. Rimma came away with the opinion that Lee "did not produce a good impression on the lady." The former head of the KGB and the man who oversaw Lee's case, Vladimir Semichasty, would recall decades later that "Oswald knew very little . . . He didn't have any operational knowledge." "He wasn't talking about anything that, as we say in Russia, 'the sparrows in the trees aren't al-ready singing about.' "[39]

On October 21, Lee bared his soul in his diary: "Evening 6:00. Receive word I must leave country at 8:00 PM tonight as visa expires. I am shocked! My dreams! I retire to my room. I have $100 left. I have waited for two years to be accepted. My fondest dreams are shattered because of a petty official, because of bad planning. I planned too much!"*

As Rimma waited to have dinner with him, to try to soothe his heart-break and see to it that he left the country, Lee took a razor to his left wrist,

---

*Lee Oswald was dyslexic. His pervasive misspellings have been corrected in this example.

cutting into the flesh and perhaps the tendons as well.[40] Lee documented the moment in his diary, perhaps later that night or in ensuing days, with his good hand: "7:00 PM. I decide to end it. Soak wrist in cold water to numb the pain. Then slash my left wrist. Then plunge wrist into bathtub of hot water. I think, 'when Rimma comes at 8 to find me dead it will be a great shock.' Somewhere a violin plays as I watch my life whirl away. I think to myself, 'how easy to die,' and 'a sweet death to violins.' About 8:00 Rimma finds me unconscious (bathtub water a rich red color). She screams (I remember that) and runs for help. Ambulance comes, am taken to hospital where five stitches are put in my wrist. Poor Rimma stays at my side as interpreter (my Russian is still very bad), far into the night. I tell her, 'go home.' My mood is bad, but she stays. She is my 'friend.' She has a strong will. Only at this moment I notice she is pretty."

In fact, when Lee didn't meet her as planned, she found his hotel room door locked from the inside and summoned Internal Security. A locksmith came, but when they couldn't open the door they broke it down with such force that they tumbled onto the floor of Lee's suite. It was the men who found Lee, not Rimma. She summoned the ambulance.[41]

After he was wheeled out, unconscious, Rimma went back into his room to gather some of his belongings, noticing how paltry his stack of clothing was. She retrieved a copy of *The Idiot* that she had given him for his birthday, and went on to Botkin Hospital.

He was treated for a gash five centimeters long and placed in the mental ward. The next day, he was up and around, yammering to the other patients in his broken Russian. The razor apparently had not opened a vein, and his psychiatrist, Dr. Lydia Mikhailina, believed "that this was a 'show suicide' attempt since he was refused political asylum, which he had been demanding."[42] Her verdict notwithstanding, Lee's claims that he was afraid to go back to America now found some sympathy within the Soviet bureaucracy. When he was released from Botkin on October 28, he returned to the Hotel Berlin and then moved to the Metropole to await their judgment.

Lee had emerged as the classic autodidact, just as Aline Mosby had quickly deduced. In popular parlance, he didn't know what he didn't know, but his paranoia, his flair for the dramatic, and his secrecy gave him the sort of mind that could project himself into intrigue and might actually have made him a good spy had he not been so awkward and mentally disturbed. As his childhood friend Allen Campbell put it after Lee had attained global infamy, "Lee was the biggest geek in the world. That the CIA or the KGB would hire him is ludicrous."[43]

The KGB was watching him, however, and while Lee bided his time at the Metropole, he decided to underscore his commitment to Soviet life by contacting the American embassy and revoking his U.S. citizenship. He went in person, probably on the assumption that the bugged embassy would permit Soviet spies to overhear his speech and be more likely to let him stay in the USSR. The American consular official, Richard Snyder, thought Lee was just a dumb kid without the faintest idea what Russia was about; he told Lee he'd grant his wish, but not without a few choice comments about Marxism. Lee was establishing a pattern where embassies were concerned, one he'd follow all the way to the Cuban and Russian embassies in Mexico City a few years later: seek asylum and make speeches on your behalf, with the assumption that you're under surveillance from all sides. If at first you don't succeed, offer some sort of secret information in trade, or express your fear of America in a loud or radical way, and solicit protection. Eventually, you will get what you want.

The KGB had first contacted Lee at Botkin Hospital and had considered recruiting him, either as an intelligence or counterintelligence agent. But the man who made the final decision many months later, Vasili Petrov, the head of the Belarus KGB, would conclude that Lee "didn't have the intellectual capacity to be a professional agent."[44] After Dallas, it was a decision that he was exceedingly glad to have made.

His suicide attempt was quickly diagnosed as "political blackmail," and once they figured out that he wasn't a CIA man, "We decided to send him further away from Moscow since we were not convinced that this would be his last effort at blackmail. We were sure that he would try something again, and we didn't want to deal with that in Moscow." They also sought to avoid an international scandal that might result from tossing him out of the country. So they decided to send him to Minsk, 450 miles away, deposit him in a decent apartment, and put him to work in a factory. If he was so hot to serve the Motherland, then he would have to do it in Minsk. If he was capable of blackmailing them again, then they would have to bribe him in advance.

The decade of the 1960s began, in Cuba, with Fidel's expropriation of seventy thousand acres of land owned by the American sugar industry, including thirty-five thousand acres of Oriente property that belonged to the United Fruit Company. It must have given Che a certain satisfaction that Fidel was taking aim at companies that had been instrumental in the overthrow of Árbenz in Guatemala. American secretary of state John Foster Dulles was a stockholder in United Fruit, and a legal adviser to the company.

His brother, Allen Dulles, the CIA director, had been a president of the company, and his predecessor at the Agency, Walter Bedell Smith, had been president of United Fruit after the Árbenz coup.[45] Fidel had messed with the biggest sugar daddies in Washington, and air attacks on Cuban sugarcane crops commenced almost immediately.

In that same month, on January 2, 1960, Senator John Kennedy announced his candidacy for president of the United States. Jack had carried a quote from Rousseau with him for many years: "As soon as any man says of the affairs of the state, What does it matter to me? The state may be given up as lost."[46] That summoning spirit was evinced in his announcement speech, made in a caucus room of the Old Senate Office Building, and it would echo throughout the campaign and on to the day of his inauguration. He cast himself as a challenger, a person who provoked others to join him on a new frontier, and for all of his outward charisma, his inner life was expanding as well. He was directing his substantial intellect and political imagination toward a new paradigm of power.

His oldest friend, Lem Billings, had first seen this transformation coming three years earlier, not long after the '56 convention. He and Jack and Joe Sr. were having dinner at Palm Beach one night when Lem made some reference to one of Jack's nastier sybaritic romps. The old man reacted sharply, slapping the table.

"You're not to speak like that anymore," he growled. "There are things that you just can't bring up anymore, private things. You've got to forget them. Forget the 'Jack' you once knew . . . Forget he ever existed . . . The day is coming, and it's coming soon, when he won't be 'Jack' anymore at all—not to you, and not to the rest of us either. He'll be 'Mr. President.' And you can't say or do anything that will jeopardize that."[47]

Jack would always be Jack, but he had been seasoned in the last few years. He knew that he loved politics as more than a game now. He sensed that what America had given the Kennedys required them to give something back, something that would ennoble the family and perhaps even the nation that it served. The enigma of Jack Kennedy hid much more than his sins; it hid a deeply reflective and searching aspect as well.

He preferred that it be hidden. The image he wanted to project was not Adlai Stevenson's homey midwestern intellectual, but an ultramodern, thinking man's war vet: part executive and part movie star. And thus armed, the Kennedy boys hit the ground running, heading off to do battle in the Wisconsin primary. Their main opponent in the dairy land would be Hubert Humphrey from the neighboring state of Minnesota, but Humphrey was actually a stalking horse for the ten-gallon Texan and majority leader of the Senate, Lyndon Johnson.

One of the first obstacles Jack would have to face was the issue of his Catholicism. His campaign happened to coincide with a slow-building earthquake within the church itself, triggered a year before by the new pope, John XXIII. He had called for an ecumenical council, Vatican II, to examine the mission of the church in the postwar world. An avuncular and beloved old man, Pope John had been grossly underestimated by the church's conservative elite, and they would be doubly shocked by what the Kennedy campaign was about to do.

As Jack set out for the presidency, Father John Courtney Murray, an American Jesuit, was among a host of daring Catholic thinkers who were considered dangerous at that time. Murray had been taking part in and advocating ecumenical gatherings with non-Catholics, and had been posing heretical questions about the separation of church and state,[48] his modernism hinting at a much wider unrest among younger priests, nuns, and theologians. Yet it was to clergymen like Murray and Bishop John Wright that Jack sent his speechwriter, Ted Sorensen, in search of ways to address "the Catholic issue" on the campaign trail.[49]

This, combined with John XXIII's full-court press in Rome, would soon become known as "the two Johns" effect. The church did not want to alienate its most stellar, up-and-coming politician, and thus Murray and his group regained their rightful place in the church leadership, thereby advancing the progressive trend.

The Catholic dimension of the 1960s, though not the cause of its most pivotal events, was nonetheless an undertone of those events, for better and for worse. At its best, the Kennedys' reformist influence on a new generation of Catholic clergy would become a secret weapon in the democratic center/left movement to fight Communism in Latin America. Cuban Catholic laity would be among the most forthright center/left members of the anti-Castro exile movement. The Kennedys would bring a new generation of American Latinos into the Democratic Party, and Bobby's late-sixties friendship with farm labor hero César Chávez would inform his later views on nonviolence and poverty, immeasurably. At its worst, however, an internecine power struggle would emerge, something reminiscent of the Borgias. A number of Catholic politicians would be violently driven from power just before or during the Kennedy administration, namely the Congo's Lumumba, the Dominican Republic's Trujillo, and Vietnam's Diêm. The Castro brothers were fallen Jesuits who both tried to vanquish and co-opt the church during their ascendancy, and the Chicago mobsters who had been dispatched to assassinate them were Catholic Italian-Americans. Those were but a few of the Catholic implications.

In the election year 1960, however, those undertones had yet to emerge. The American people were concerned only about whether Jack, as president, would be influenced by the Vatican. It had not occurred to them how much the Vatican—and the rest of the Catholic world—would be influenced by Jack.

Two days after John Kennedy announced his candidacy, Lee Oswald was granted temporary residency in the Soviet Union after spending months holed up in a dinky room at the Metropole.

He was almost out of money. He didn't even have adequate clothes to go out into the Moscow winter, so he took cheap meals in his room and pored over Russian-language books. He had written his brother Robert that he was defecting from the America he hated. There was a telegram from his half-brother, John Pic, on November 9, begging him to reconsider.[50] It appears that Lee may have met a few Russians here and there, possibly in the hotel. If he assumed they were KGB agents, quietly keeping tabs on him, it isn't known.

On November 16, he had been informed that he could stay in the country while the bureaucracy pondered his case, and it looked as if he might have succeeded in his quest, after all. Priscilla McMillan spoke with him that evening and, with some boyish pride, "he told me about his only expedition in Moscow alone. He had walked four blocks to Detsky Mir, the children's department store, and bought himself an ice cream cone. I could scarcely believe my ears," she recounted. "Here he was, coming to live in this country forever, and he had so far dared venture into only four blocks of it. I was astounded by his lack of curiosity and the utter absence of any joy or spirit of adventure in him. And yet I respected him. Here was this lonely, frightened boy taking on the bureaucracy of the second most powerful nation on earth, and doing it single-handedly . . . I was sorry for him, too, for I was certain he was making a mistake."[51] Richard Snyder, at the embassy, had opted to stall the revocation of his citizenship, since he was so young and wouldn't be allowed to leave Russia if the deal was done. Unaware of this, Lee remained determined. His suicide attempt had begun to pay off.

Just before New Year's, at the end of 1959, Rimma finally came to tell him that he would be allowed to stay in Russia, but would be moving to Minsk. Lee cried. He had had daydreams of becoming an important official in Moscow, or a spokesman, or some other public person. He knew nothing about Minsk.

But at bottom, he was relieved. His Red dream was coming true.

For all the myths that have collected around him, Lee Oswald was more or less what he appeared to be—a person whose grating sense of injustice and personal isolation drove him out of America in search of a Marxist utopia. He was an early personification of "the sixties generation," footloose and fed up with his nuclear family, defiant of authority, sexually tolerant, disdainful of formal education, indifferent to the work ethic, and fair-minded on the subject of race. He was drawn to the anti-celebrity of outlaws, which happened to include everyone from Jesse James and Jack Kerouac to the Castro brothers and Che Guevara, and he was very, very angry at his homeland.

Before Lee left for Minsk, he sent another letter to his brother, Robert: "I want you to understand what I say now, I do not say lightly or unknowingly, since I've been in the military," he wrote, ". . . in the event of war I would kill any American who put a uniform on in defense of the American Government—Any American."[52] In one of his diaries, Oswald added another telling detail: "I despise the representatives of both systems weather [sic] they be socialist or christan democrats, whether they be labor or conservative they are all products of the two systems."[53]

He was born on the cusp between the Beat Generation and the hippies, but to see Lee standing behind his humble working-class pad on Neely Street in Dallas a few years after the Russian episode, dressed in pre-punk black with a pistol on his hip, a rifle in one hand and copies of the *Militant* and the *Worker* in the other, is every bit as iconic of the sixties as the picture of Black Panther Party leader Huey Newton holding his rifle and spear and seated like an urban prince on a rattan chair. Lee made copies of his radical self-portrait, inscribing one of the photos with the words "Ready for anything." A friend of his wife's would later add: "Hunter of fascists, ha-ha-ha."[54]

And yet Lee became the face that the Baby Boom generation could not see in the mirror, the one who chose war, not love, but who was otherwise, in so many ways, as outraged, idealistic, as paranoid and sometimes delusional as the rest of that upstart generation.

It is in Minsk that Lee Harvey Oswald came of age as an avatar of the incipient radical youth culture that was about to burst forth worldwide. It was there that he would initially find company with the young hipsters of their day, the kids who read and debated, the kids who flaunted their independence of thought and danced the night away and reaped the sensual benefits of birth control. But then came the darkness that was also there in his personality, the impossibility of real intimacy for someone so trapped inside himself. It was in Minsk that he would begin in earnest to indulge his violent fantasy life, and there that he would first gain a rapport with Communist Cubans and the sinister side of utopia.

CHAPTER 3
The Patriot Game

L EE OSWALD ARRIVED at the old Minsk train station either late on the evening of January 7, 1960, or early in the morning of the eighth. He was met by a pair of Soviets identifying themselves as Red Cross workers, who escorted him to the Hotel Minsk, where he was checked in to room 453.[1]

The Belarus capital was considered to be a much more wholesome environment than Moscow, which was regarded by other Soviets as full of nasty, conniving people, lousy food, disgusting air, dirty streets, and unregenerate gangsters. Minsk was not blessed with as many cultural institutions, but, as one journalist put it, "its crowds were relatively friendly and sane." It was "one of the more positive centers in the Soviet Union and that is precisely why the Soviet authorities sent him there."[2]

The city had its skeletons, though. By World War II, 40 percent of the population was Jewish, and Minsk had thus become a concentration center for Jews on their way to the Nazi extermination camps in Poland and beyond. Minsk was mostly leveled in the war, but was rebuilt with the forced labor of German POWs. By the time Lee arrived, it was prospering as a Communist-utopian center full of universities, police and military academies, and thriving factories pumping out textiles, machines, processed foods, machine tools, cars, and tractors.

The moment Lee stepped off the train, a detail of KGB officers began shadowing him as case number 31451; his code name was Likhoy. His new street-Russian name would become "Alik," the closest thing to "Lee" in the Russian language. The KGB's chief of counterintelligence in Minsk, Colonel Golubtsov,[3] had already received a dossier on him from Moscow in which he was characterized as "a disgruntled former U.S. Marine private claiming to be a Marxist and seeking Soviet citizenship . . ."[4] Even then, he was thought of as a threat to the Soviet Union and probably useless as a source for intelligence about the West. He was absolutely not to be debriefed, and there were many reasons that he was not to be trusted. The KGB considered former members of the U.S. armed services to be likely candidates for recruitment by American intelligence. Lee claimed to be a Communist but had all the Marxist-Leninist proficiency of an "apple": red and tough-skinned on the outside, but white and soft on the inside. The KGB feared that he might be a better Russian speaker than he pretended to be, that he might be on a reconnaissance mission to test how the Soviets dealt with defectors, or that he might just be a mental case who would prove to be no more than a massive babysitting problem. The other confounding prospect was, of course, that he might be exactly what he said he was, a bona fide defector who wanted to start a new life in the USSR, in which case it was wise to treat him well until they could thoroughly vet him, and then use him as a propaganda prop. With all of these contingencies in mind, Colonel Golubtsov assigned to the case an officer named Alexander Fedorovich Kostikov.[5]

Soviet government policy was to set defectors up in a comfortable style, both to proselytize for the Russian Dream and to avoid complaints.[6] "Alik" received no special treatment by the Soviets. His accommodations were in no way exceptional, although the combined income from the job the Soviets got him and the Red Cross stipend he received was equal to that of the director at the factory he was assigned to work in. His new home, in an old five-story stone apartment block along the Svisloch River, had a columned balcony and broad views of the Minsk opera house and a government ministry building. He was living like a grown-up for the first time in his life. In fact, he was living like a middle-class bon vivant, right smack in the middle of utopia, an American scene-stealer who basked in his small celebrity and was considered so exotic by both the KGB and the common folk that he was quickly dubbed "the man from Mars."

He was such an anomaly for Soviet intelligence that at first they wondered whether the CIA had developed the long-wished-for "sleeper agent," a passively programmed spy who didn't quite know he was a spy. They would script conversations with agents posing as workers, who would try to lure him into conversations about secret matters, just to gauge his reactions. His phone was tapped and his bachelor pad bugged from nearly every angle, from the flat upstairs and the one below, and from microphones planted inside the apartment itself. Years later, the state police would be able to reconstruct not only Lee's political journey and his increasingly demented conversations about murder and mayhem, but the breathless progress of his amours as well. KGB officers photographed and kept him under surveillance night and day, from the moment he was given his visitor papers in Moscow and through the Byelorussian chapter to the instant when he left the country thirty months later. His co-workers and closest pals were all talking to the KGB, off-camera, and there seems to have been virtually nothing about his life that could be kept secret from the eyes and ears of the Soviet state. And—as would be evident in his later performances at the American embassy—he must have known it, on some level.

Oswald went to work in the Byelorussian Radio and Television Factory, a combine that had between five and ten thousand workers during that period. He was put in the Experimental Shop, which produced parts for cutting-edge technologies and new electronic components under development. It's not certain whether that shop required a high security clearance; but if so, he might have been purposely placed there to determine whether he was a spy.[7] After six weeks, during which he showed no signs of being covert, they transferred him to the metal lathe shop, where he proved to be as inept as he had in the Experimental Shop. It's likely that the KGB concluded that Lee was either too careful an agent to snoop around in the sensitive niches of the shop, or was a legitimate defector who was too clumsy, undereducated, and surly to be placed where he might break something. Some of his colleagues were reportedly shocked to find that he had had radar training in the Marine Corps, so electronically clueless was he on the job.

He had other priorities. He dated every woman he could get his hands on. He started dressing better to attract them, and his outlandish Americanism, the "ism" he was there to renounce, became his most conspicuous asset. He found a posse of male friends, perhaps for the first time in his life, and there were hunting trips with the boys. There were nights at the opera, at the movies. There were picnics on the weekend—and there were those Russian girls.

There were also young Cubans on the prowl. As the Castros continued to co-opt the Cuban revolution and Raúl flirted ever more heavily with the Soviet state, he was sending his youngest spies to Minsk for special training at the Russians' MVD (Ministry of Internal Affairs) academy on Ulyanov Street, a subsidiary of the KGB that was responsible for civil law enforcement and more shadowy pursuits as well. Within the school's hierarchy was Colonel Ilya Vasilyevna Prusakov, Marina's uncle.

Among the students there were José Abrantes, the personal assistant to the Cuban intelligence chief, Ramiro Valdés Menéndez; and one Fabian Escalante Font, a young agent of increasingly dangerous reputation who would soon rise to the top of the G2. There were approximately two hundred students at the MVD academy at the time Lee arrived in Minsk, and the place was well known to residents because of its one-way windows and the high stone wall that shielded it. The courses focused mainly on the CIA and FBI, on their methods and means of recruiting. The Cubans, who had quickly become proficient in spycraft, were not particularly impressed with the quality of information coming out of the school at that time, but after their training in Minsk they were usually sent to more thorough and specialized facilities of the GRU* (Soviet Military Intelligence) or STASI (East German Secret Police) in Prague and elsewhere.

As it happened, Lee was interested in studying German, and his KGB file describes how "friends" steered him to the Foreign Language Institute (FLI) located directly adjacent to the MVD academy on Ulyanov Street. Among those new friends was Ernst Titovets, who had taken it upon himself to introduce Lee to his circle of pals. Lee's linguistic curiosity was perhaps secondary to his ongoing search for women, of whom there were plenty at the FLI. Many of them spoke English; thus they were already on the KGB's radar, and they were soon particularly attentive to the young American with the subtle southern drawl. KGB Colonel Golubtsov elaborated in retrospect that "while Oswald had some increasing capacity in Russian, we had to connect him to people who could exchange intimate conversations with him in English. After all, how can you develop a person under suspicion without knowing his language? . . . You would have to assume that Foreign Language Institute girls were in a position to inform us how Oswald was behaving. Counterintelligence monitored this entire process and was kept informed."[8]

The KGB service reports created an astonishingly thorough narrative of Lee's activities. They chronicled his movie-going habits, every piece of cake and cup of coffee he consumed in public, his stinginess on dates with women he wasn't enthused about, his preference for blondes, his ignorance of Marxist-Leninist theory, the records and appliances he bought, the hardware stores he visited, and, of course, the friends with whom he consorted. The "official" record of his life in Minsk omitted only what reflected badly on the Soviet intelligence apparatus.

We now know for certain that Lee did make a connection to Cuban students in Minsk. There must be significant evidence of it in the KGB's files, if

---

*Glavnoje Razvedyvatel'noje Upravlenije, meaning Main Intelligence Directorate of the General Staff of the Armed Forces of the Russian Federation.

only because there were a dozen agents watching or listening to his every move, but the details remain sketchy—only fleeting glimpses of the KGB's most sensitive "encrypted" Oswald file have surfaced. It seems possible that Oswald befriended Fabian Escalante, among the most ambitious of those rising stars and the future head, according to some Cuban defectors, of Cuba's "wet operations." According to these same sources, they would certainly know each other once Lee got back to the West.

It was early enough in the Castro regime that these young spies-in-training were openly concerned about the fate of the Revolution, especially given the poor quality of life they saw in the Soviet Union. The Castros' staying power was by no means certain. By the spring of 1960, the rift in the 26th of July Movement had widened perilously. Politicians who had been waiting to see how Fidel performed were leaving, including former premier Manuel "Tony" Varona. The huge property expropriations of the summer would trigger the departure of many in the business community. On the heels of Huber Matos's conviction, the purges in the education system had sent hundreds of teachers into self-exile, and when the Communists took over the unions, many more of the Castros' former supporters saw the writing on the wall. By year's end, some hundred thousand Cuban politicos had emigrated to the United States.[9] Among them were some of the finest minds of the revolution, including Manuel Ray, Rufo López Fresquet, and Felipe Pazos.

The young Cubans in Minsk were a world away from all this, of course. They had been handpicked for their loyalty to the Castros; but all Cubans, no matter where on earth, had to be watchful of the situation in Havana, if only for survival's sake, and these were a particularly lively and daring lot. They spent most of their time in the MVD bunker; but when they were out and about, the voluble, outgoing islanders made a strong impression. Lee would later tell a friend: ". . . I am not interested, as you know, in stylish clothes. Of course, the Cubans dressed to kill." And when Marina Prusakova caught them in her sights, she would go into a fugue state of admiration. "They were outgoing and gay," she recalled. "Often they carried their guitars with them, and [with] their catchy Caribbean tunes, [they] danced so well. They were such fun!"[10] (She was so taken with the musicality of the Cubans that she would mention their guitar playing to former CIA director Allen Dulles during the investigation into the Kennedy assassination years later, adding that Lee had befriended "a Cuban family" when he was in Minsk.[11] In a later conversation about her attraction to American black men, she would tell a friend, "Neither Russians nor American whites can compare to such beautiful men"—although "maybe the Cubans I met in Minsk were just as attractive."[12])

So while the Cubans were lighting up the ladies of dolorous Minsk, Lee was studying German next door to their school and carousing with the English-speaking women of the FLI. According to the KGB, one of them, Galya, invited Lee up to her dorm room "often," and on one occasion he was seen surrounded on a bed by six girls, all chatting with him in his native tongue. He spent so much time on Ulyanov Street that he soon got acquainted with a number of the junior Cuban spies. Marina would tell the FBI about one of Lee's friends, Alfred, a "young man from Cuba [who] spoke Spanish"[13] and who would later attend the University of Moscow.[14] Lee would brag to Marina that he had gotten tight with some of the young future Cuban "ministers" and expected that he might be such a minister there himself, one day.

In the U.S., the election year had brought the question of Havana's true allegiance to a boil, and the debate had given rise to an organization that would be credited as the first sign of a "New Left" in American politics. Driven by younger minds, people who had been freed from the old Communist turf wars over Stalinism, Trotskyism, and the like, the New Left was comprised of a wider spectrum, more American and less doctrinaire. Pejoratively, they were labeled more "pink" than "red," and they were certainly sympathetic to anticapitalist arguments, but the New Left focused less on the union wars of the 1930s and more on social activism, on nuclear disarmament for the betterment of all, and on civil rights and liberties.

And Fidel was still playing fast and loose with the leftist labels of the time. No one had yet nailed him down. On January 23, 1960, Robert Taber, an American newsman who had been the first journalist Fidel had invited to Cuba, published an article sympathetic to the Revolution in the left-leaning *Nation* magazine. He had become increasingly convinced that a propaganda counteroffensive, abetted by the American journalistic establishment, had been launched against the leaders of the Cuban revolution.

One of the *Nation*'s readers, Alan Sagner, a real estate developer and well-connected Democrat from New Jersey, read the piece and decided that something had to be done.

Sagner contacted Bob Taber at CBS News, where he worked the night shift, alongside two other newsmen with a yen for social reform. One, Richard Gibson, was a trailblazer of the profession, an African-American journalist who had been the recipient of a Whitney fellowship. The other was a CBS vet named Ed Haddad, and their common passion was often the subject of conversation on predawn coffee breaks near the network's midtown news offices. Fidel was a man of the people, they still believed, a homegrown populist who simply wanted to end corruption and rein in the Cuban oligarchy.

The four—the three journalists and Sagner—were among a total of seven men who would soon found an organization called the Fair Play for Cuba Committee (FPCC). The idea, as Sagner announced in the organization's newsletter, was "one of simple humanitarianism for the Cuban people, who have suffered so long." They did not take "a position of unqualified support of Castro's government," but were "dedicated to the premise that small and underprivileged countries be allowed to solve their peculiar problems, both social and economic, without undue pressure." Sagner assured readers that "no money for this ad or our mailings was received from Cuba or the Cuban government or any other agency or institution."[15]

At the first meeting, it was decided that the formation of the organization should be heralded with an ad in the *New York Times*. The full-page ad appeared on April 6. Almost instantly, the FBI and CIA opened files on the new group; they suspected that Fidel had funded the ad and might even be putting up the bulk of the organization's cash. Nonetheless, the subsidiary FPCC chapters thrived with the help of its early "famous names," among them William Appleman Williams, Norman Mailer, Saul Landau, Helen Nearing, Allen Ginsberg, Lawrence Ferlinghetti, Martin Hall, Waldo Frank, and Carleton Beals.

Other sympathizers came forth as well, even as the Castros kept sliding further and further toward hard-line communism. An ex–merchant marine named Vincent "Ted" Lee, of Tampa, Florida, showed up in New York City and started hanging out with Taber and Griffin, gradually inheriting leadership of the organization as some of the founders sought other outlets for their political expression. Ted Lee was reputedly an expert in illegal travel to and from Cuba. A CIA source, Maria Snethlage, head of the Hague's Werkgroup Informatie Cuba, knew Ted from Havana and described him as "a man of violence and entirely full of hate." She reported these feelings to Richard Gibson,[16] and these weren't the only signs that the organization was drifting into darker waters.

Taber and Griffin left the committee, and many of the more famous names were leaving too, perhaps increasingly aware that the FPCC was becoming a wall-to-wall front for the Castro brothers' stateside intelligence operation. Still, there were others who were all the more attracted, precisely because of the group's increasing radicalism. Later, one of them would be Lee Harvey Oswald.

While Oswald and the FPCC sympathizers applauded the Revolution from afar, a handful of Americans actually made their way to Cuba to support the cause directly. June Cobb and William Morgan were among the standouts.

By the end of 1959, Cobb, the Latinophile from Oklahoma who had met Fidel on his tour of New York earlier that year, had become a part of the new political scene in Havana. At the invitation of his revolutionary muse, Celia Sánchez, June had come to Havana to work for the Revolution. By most accounts, June, in her youth, was a liberated woman ahead of her time, a person whose bohemian lifestyle and derring-do were very unusual in the early 1960s. Whether her reputation was earned or not, June was as smart as she was attractive, and she took a place very close to Fidel's top-floor suite at the Havana Hilton. She became so close to the Maximum Leader that she even lived for a time at Fidel and Celia's beach house while recuperating from surgery.

Within a short time, June was working down the hall from Fidel's office. A few doors away was the director general of the Office of the Prime Minister, Juan Orta Cordova,[17] whose grand title belied the fact that he was essentially an office manager. June saw him as a "right winger and a racist," a boob who had no contact with Fidel but liked to strut his stuff nonetheless.[18] The only thing June had in common with Orta was that both were quickly becoming disillusioned with the Castros and in a short time would offer their services to the CIA—Cobb to spy on Castro's supporters, and Orta to kill him.

And Cobb and Orta were far from alone in their apprehensions about the Castros. Rolando Cubela was having second thoughts about the revolutionary alliance he had struck with the brothers. During the revolution, Cubela had fled the island and sought haven briefly in the U.S., where he purchased arms and returned as Directorio Revolucionario Estudiantil (DRE) military leader to Cuba on February 1, 1958 with sixteen other students. For the remainder of that year, Cubela and his column fought in the Escambray in coordination with Castro and Guevara's guerrillas. After Batista's sudden departure in the early morning hours of January 1, 1959, Cubela and the DRE assumed control of the Presidential Palace and refused to hand it over to Guevara's troops—he refused to acknowledge the Communist Che—even though an agreement existed between Castro's forces and the students.* Despite the clash, Cubela enjoyed Castro's confidence.[19] Not long after Fidel's January 1, 1959, triumph, Cubela was elected president of the government-sponsored FEU,† although he still harbored great distrust of Fidel's increasing Communist leanings and indiscriminate use of the firing squad. Among those to whom he confided his misgivings was Carlos Tepedino, the owner of La Diadema Jewelers, located in the Havana Libre Hotel. Cubela, who had known Tepedino since 1953, didn't know it at the time, but his friend's receptivity was not all that surprising: he was secretly working for the CIA, code-named AM/WHIP.

Besides June Cobb, the only other American to have been so embraced by the revolution was a thirty-year-old adventurer from Ohio named William Alexander Morgan, the son of a corporate executive with a stormy, romantic, and nomadic personality who had started running guns to the embryonic July 26th Movement in 1958. He quickly distinguished himself in battle and was promoted to major in the rebel group known as the Second Front. But Morgan would run afoul of the revolution he had helped to win, and he would be among the thousands who would be executed, probably with Che as a witness.[20]

Meanwhile, in the spring of 1960, just a year after her virtual adoption by Fidel, June Cobb found herself swept up in a scandal. Castro made a second trip to New York, one that presented a stark contrast to the triumphal 1959 tour. Notably, Fidel and Soviet premier Khrushchev appeared as allies before the UN, haranguing the assembly about the crimes of capitalism. In the midst of the tour, the story of a seventeen-year-old German woman named Marita Lorenz hit the tabloids, a tale of rape and sexual bondage at the hands of Fidel. Lorenz claimed to have been impregnated by Castro. June would later claim that the father was Jesús Yánez Pelletier, Fidel's bodyguard, and also a friend of hers. But regardless of the patrimony, it was a public relations debacle. Just as Fidel was denouncing the decadent excesses of the West, he was being pilloried as a sex deviant. Che was so infuriated that he had Yanez locked up for counterrevolutionary activity and began casting about in search of Fidel's betrayers. His paranoid eye soon fell on the Yankee expatriates living in Havana, but they were not as easy to dispatch as Cuban citizens. June was exceedingly well connected by this time, and William Morgan had achieved the revolutionary status of something like a rock star.

---

*Both Guevara and Cubela signed the agreement.
†Federación Estudiantil Universitaria (International Federation of Students).

The CIA had been keeping tabs on June. She was a good candidate. She had hoped that the U.S. would stop bombing Cuban cane fields and thus pushing Fidel to the left, but when the Communist influence on him became obvious, her anger became evident too. She had openly disagreed with his turn toward Marxism and authoritarian rule. In fact, she later admitted that she'd been tempted at one point to read his own words back to him: "Be it dictatorship to the left or dictatorship to the right, a dictatorship is a dictatorship." News of her rage seeped into the underground; before long, the CIA reached out to her. On the pretext of needing medical treatment, she arranged to go to New York for her first rendezvous with them.[21]

But she returned to Cuba seemingly unfazed by this first overture, even though Che's "investigation" was ongoing. Finally, as the American election was heating up, he ordered a roundup of anyone suspected in the Marita Lorenz buzz, including June Cobb and William Morgan.

The accusations against June Cobb were far more amorphous than those against Morgan, and Fidel and Celia were able to protect her; but they had cooled to her, and June's access to them dwindled away. (That too was probably Che's doing, with the help of Raúl. Luís Conte Aguero, the journalist who had introduced Cobb to the Cuban delegation in New York, would later tell the Agency that Fidel's two watchdogs had come to fear June's influence on Fidel.)

Still, given her friendship with him, June had narrowly escaped a long imprisonment, or worse. Two months before the U.S. presidential election, she finally saw fit to leave Cuba for good. As 1960 played out, the strange story of the wild Oklahoma girl turned gringa-in-residence of the Castros' inner circle would only get stranger.

The Agency's courtship of her had turned to more serious talks. On November 3, five days before Jack Kennedy won the presidency, her recruiter sat her down and asked, "Would you consider going to bed with a man for the good of your country?"

"Not if Nixon gets elected," she replied.

June was nothing if not frank. She became a CIA operative, making a verbal agreement with the Agency in June 1960 that was formalized on September 12, stipulating a $200-per-month salary for an initial one-year contract. Her mission, as spelled out in her CIA contract: "To penetrate the Cuban government in an effort to obtain information on present and planned activities of the Castro regime." It was called Operation JMARC. Her first crypto was AMUPAS, her pseudonym "Jean Pierson." (Future pseudonyms would be "Clarinda E. Sharpe" and "Joyce Pineinch.") Cobb would soon gain direct access to the White House through Kennedy Latin expert Richard Goodwin.

"I was delighted with Mr. Kennedy," she later said. "My acquaintance with Mr. Goodwin . . . was a result of my interest in contributing to the Kennedy campaign by [contributing] some notes on Cuba."[22]

By the summer of 1960, the first phase of the plan devised by Joe Sr. and Jack after the Democratic convention four years earlier had been realized. Kennedy had won seven presidential primaries since January. The road to the upcoming party convocation in Los Angeles looked golden.

Jack was forty-three years old. Bobby was thirty-five, and he had served his brother's interests with such buzz-saw determination that many within their circle had come to dislike him considerably. Even still, it was Bobby who had been the most shocked at the mindless, aching poverty they had seen on the road, suffered by black and white, red and brown alike. It was mostly Bobby who had noticed the listless appraisals of the candidate from the dark doorways of West Virginia, seen the faint sneers on such young faces in the ghettos of Milwaukee. What was even more shocking than the degradation was the profound resignation, the attitude that hope was a luxury not available to the poor. This worldly-wise rich man, Bobby Kennedy, had finally seen America for what it was worth and what it wasn't, and it had sobered him, sharpened him. Whether or not any of this registered with Jack, it was clear that the campaign had given him the utmost respect for his younger brother. "I don't know what Bobby does," Jack had told his friend Charles Bartlett, "but it always seems to turn out right."

What Bobby did, eighteen to twenty hours a day, ranged from bringing on "media experts," a brand-new conceit in 1960, to quashing blackmailers trying to trade on rumors of Jack's erotic escapades. With the seven primary wins in his pocket, the nomination was in sight. And with Jack's newfound prestige and prospect, there was an ever-wider path to his door. The world had come knocking.

Among those knocking were two Cuban patriots who were invited to visit Jack at his Washington Senate office sometime in July, a secret meeting arranged by the CIA. Manuel Artime was in his late twenties and had been in the country for only seven months, but he had an intuitive grasp of power and what to do with it. Much like Jack, Manuel was a smart and cagey fighter with a movie-star sheen. Artime hoped to use that killer combination to lead Cuba one day, or a least ensure that Fidel did not.

Artime had served as a lieutenant in the Castro brothers' army until he was imprisoned in 1959 for using his Movimiento de Recuperación Revolucionario (Movement for Revolutionary Recovery, or MRR) as a front to attempt to topple Fidel. He had managed to escape and finally fled the country for Miami on December 11, the same month that Huber Matos went on trial in Havana for treason. But Artime loved his country too much to simply leave her behind. He was ready to do battle against Fidel.

Dr. José Miró Cardona was with Artime in the car en route to the Senate Office Building that day. Cardona had been Fidel's first prime minister, but he too had been radically disillusioned. Now, as the men were chauffeured toward the Hill by Col. Fletcher Prouty, the Air Force liaison to the CIA, the Cubans carried high hopes that whoever won the presidency, be it Kennedy or Nixon, he would take the counterrevolutionary struggle to heart.[23]

Fidel was in the midst of what historians would call his "second civil war," the first having been fought against Batista in defense of democracy, the second against the democratic elements of his own 26th of July Movement. The first wave of exiles, the oligarchs, were vocal and well connected, but their position was one of simple opposition to the Castro regime rather than support for any particular successor. At their insistence, President Eisenhower had authorized "exploratory plans" for some sort of coup, but the pressing question was—as always—which of the emergent factions to work with, now that the second wave was hitting American shores.

The first choice was Artime's moderate leftist group, MRR, which was still comparatively small and couldn't yet unite the exile community, but could most readily enlist the Cuban people. Artime himself was also the most experienced military man. The second choice, created just a month before, in June, was known as the Frente Revolucionario Democrático, the FRD, comprised of five exile factions, of which Artime's was only one. The other four were led by Manuel Antonio de Varona, José Ignacio Rasco, Aureliano Sánchez Arango, and Justo Carrillo. In effect, "the Frente" was the closest thing to a centrist coalition available, since the greatest number of emigrants thus far had been right-wingers; but there was mistrust between groups.

No record survives of what Artime and Cardona discussed with Senator Kennedy that afternoon, or whether Bobby was with them. But what is certain is that when the two Cubans entered the senator's private sanctum, a suite full of seafaring charm and Yankee entitlement, their mission was to acquaint the likely Democrat nominee with the CIA's plans, already afoot, to take down the Castro regime.

It would be the first of perhaps half a dozen meetings Jack would take with Agency leaders and their proxies that summer and fall, meetings that appear to have constituted an effort on the part of the CIA's director, Allen Dulles, and his deputy, Richard Bissell, to manipulate political events.

By June 1960, Vice President Nixon's plot to remove the Castros was at full throttle. In fact, the plans had first been rolled out at least eighteen months earlier. Some reports provided only unverifiable hints. Cuban intelligence asserts that in December 1958, Indiana native Alan Robert Nye landed in Cuba with the goal of shooting Fidel with a "long rifle." Nye, who always maintained his innocence, was tried and sentenced to death, but released on the promise that he leave Cuba within twenty-four hours. Another unverified tale alleges a January 1960 attempt by Marita Lorenz, the German woman who Fidel was alleged to have abducted the year before. Lorenz claimed that after she escaped Castro's clutches, landing in New York in late 1959, she was "turned around" by CIA operatives and sent back to poison Fidel. Her claims, however, cannot be verified.* What's certain is that when Lorenz fled Havana, her mother Alice reported that June Cobb called her from Castro's headquarters and offered Alice a job in Cuba if she would return with her daughter. Playing "bad cop," another Castro agent, Olga Blanco, called Alice and threatened that "if Marita went out with another man, Fidel would have her shot."

But along with these contested allegations came more concrete action. In June 1960, a Kennedy family acquaintance at the CIA, Richard Bissell, had put both "Staff D" and the Technical Services Staff to work to find the right means to murder Castro. Since the Agency was not yet geared up to actually do the deed themselves, someone came up with the dazzling idea of enlisting the highly motivated American Mafia to "whack" Castro. (Florida mob boss Meyer Lansky had already put a million-dollar bounty on The Beard in hopes of rolling back the revolution and reviving the billion-dollar gambling and vice rackets they had lost in Cuba when Castro's *barbudos* took power.) The murder would be integral to the invasion plans.

The Chicago crime cartel known as the Outfit, with Johnny Rosselli and Sam "Mo Mo"/"Mooney" Giancana in the lead, finally agreed to do it—for "patriotic" reasons, according to Rosselli.

The plan was to have geared up in November of 1960, according to an FBI "bug" that picked up Giancana at a Chicago tailor shop discussing a scheme

---

*Furthermore, the CIA's internal review of her story determined that the Agency had no relationship with her. Her alleged CIA "contact," Frank Sturgis, also vigorously denied her involvement with his anti-Castro group.

to deliver poison to one of Fidel's mistresses.[24] That would be the month of the presidential election. Was it planned in order to give the Democratic challengers a "November surprise," or to simply force the continuity of a Cuban coup on whoever won? Or was "Mooney" just talking out of his Panama hat?

Whatever the case, the assassin in charge was to be Richard Cain, the Outfit's mole inside the Chicago Police Department, and the idea was to hit Fidel when he showed up for sexual maintenance with one of his favorites who operated out of the Nacional Hotel in Havana. Under orders from Giancana, Cain opened an office in Chicago at Rush and Oak streets, to prepare for the second phase of the CIA's coup. Cain was recruiting Cuban insurgents and soldiers of fortune to go down to South Florida to train as guerrilla warriors. They were to be foot soldiers in the invasion that would take back Cuba from Fidel.

On the night of July 20, within days or weeks of Jack's first meeting with Artime and Cardona, word came to the Agency's Miami station from a Cubana Airlines pilot working undercover for the CIA that a rare opportunity was about to present itself. Raúl Castro was in Prague, and the pilot was due to fly there from Cuba on the twenty-first to pick him up and bring him back to Havana. The pilot had offered to crash the plane "three hours outside of Havana"; and if he was killed in the crash, he asked only that the Americans pay for his young son's college education. Richard Bissell was off sailing his yacht. The players needed an answer immediately, and the task fell to Bissell's deputy, Tracy Barnes, a gutsy war veteran and founder of the Agency who was known for his uninhibited machismo. His choice—short-lived as it would be—marked a turning point in the history of the Agency.[25] For the first time, the CIA was in a position to sanction the imminent murder of a foreign leader, and that is precisely what Barnes did—without consulting Bissell or the DCI, Allen Dulles. He gave the go to the case officer and authorized a payment of $10,000 if the pilot was successful.[26]

Immediately, he knew he had overstepped. Whether Dulles interceded or Barnes gave the order, the pilot's case officer got back to his post after giving the green light and found a cabled countermand from Barnes. "DO NOT PURSUE," it read. "WOULD LIKE TO DROP MATTER." It was too late. The plane had already departed for Prague. Bissell would later speculate that it was Dulles who had canceled the operation, considering it too risky, too likely to result in too many innocent deaths, and, worse, too likely to leave Fidel still at the helm in Cuba.[27]

Fortunately for Barnes (and Raúl), the plan fell apart. The pilot got cold feet on the return, and the plane landed safely in Havana. But such were the stupefying options in play as Jack prepared to accept the nomination in Los Angeles. Two days later, on July 23, Dulles beat a path to the Kennedy compound in Hyannis Port for a lengthy meeting with Jack. According to Agency files, the purpose of the huddle was to discuss updates on the Russians' missile capability, but chances are that Cuba was a sidebar, at the very least.

Jack had taken the nomination in L.A. on the first ballot. On a balmy California night in July, he stood before the convention and delivered his first clarion call for the New Frontier:

"The American people expect more from us than cries of indignation and attack . . . For the world is changing. The old era is ending. The old ways will not do. Abroad, the balance of power is shifting. There are new and more terrible weapons, new and uncertain nations, new pressures of population and deprivation . . . More energy is released by the awakening of these new nations than by the fission of the atom itself . . .

"The new frontier of which I speak is not a set of promises—it is a set of challenges. It sums up not what I intend to *offer* the American people, but what I intend to *ask* of them . . . It holds out the promise of more sacrifice instead of more security . . . Beyond that frontier are uncharted areas of science and space, unsolved problems of peace and war, unconquered pockets of ignorance and prejudice, unanswered questions of poverty and surplus . . . For the harsh facts of the matter are that we stand on this frontier at a turning point in history . . ."

There was another secret meeting between Kennedy and the exile leaders during the campaign, this one in Florida, at the Palm Beach mansion.

Sergio Arcacha Smith had been Cuba's ambassador to India under Carlos Prío Socarrás, in the period between Batista's two terms as leader. That would be but one of a number of careers in his life, all of them built on his warm, extroverted, and almost cherubic presence. He was pleasantly stocky, of medium height, and wore a pencil-thin mustache to give himself a more serious appearance, the sort of man who disarms almost immediately. The new career he was embarking on with this meeting in Palm Beach was as one of Bobby Kennedy's most trusted and pivotal exile allies, those men who would soon refer to themselves as Los Amigos de Roberto.

Smith had known of Fidel from his college days. By 1954, he had left the diplomatic corps and was working as assistant manager of the Lago Hotel in Caracas, Venezuela, and it was then that he first became aware that his schoolmate was the same man who was in prison for leading the Moncada attack the year before. *El loco* had become the face of the anti-Batista movement, but in those early years Sergio did not vest much in the outcome.

"I was neither for Batista nor against him," the former diplomat would say, years later. Much like Fidel, Batista had almost no discernible political program beyond his own advancement, having gone from President Ramón Grau's army chief of staff in the forties, to left-supported, democratic president, to right-wing dupe of American organized crime. "He made himself." Sergio would shrug. "He was the president . . . and he needed somebody to teach him how to eat, how to sit down with people. He was a man who really just wanted to be something."[28] Sergio didn't expect much better from *el loco*, but when the Castros' revolution was won, he, like many other members of the Cuban establishment, took a wait-and-see attitude.

But as they waited and saw disenchantment harden into outrage, the idea for the Frente took shape, and Sergio found himself finally invested in Cuba's future. He went down to progressive Venezuela to help set up the FRD coalition. The organization would soon move its base to Mexico City, and in August of 1960 he headed to Miami to await further instructions. By his recollection, it was probably either in late September or early October that he and other leaders of the Frente went to pay a call on Jack Kennedy in Palm Beach.

By some accounts, Jack was still wrestling with the Cuba question. Prior to his presidential campaign, Jack had been hard-pressed to judge Fidel Castro harshly, still convinced that domineering American companies had handed Fidel his revolution on a silver platter. In his book *The Strategy of Peace*, written for the 1960 campaign, he had likened Fidel to Simón Bolívar, the champion of Latin American anticolonialism, and referred to him as the "George Washington of South America."[29] In conversations with friends, he reinforced the point, telling one of them: "I don't know why we didn't embrace Castro when he was in this country in 1959, pleading for help . . . Instead of that, we made an enemy of him, and then we get upset because the Russians are giving them money, doing for them what we wouldn't do."[30] Even shortly before he was killed, in the conversations with French journalist Jean Daniel, Jack would plainly state that he believed America bore some responsibility for the excesses of the Batista regime. "I believe that we created, built, and manufactured the Cuban movement, without realizing it," he told Daniel.[31] Jack and Joe Sr. were at odds on the question. The father had even teased him lately that if Jack hadn't been running for president, he would be voting for Nixon. Now, Joe reminded Jack that the men on their way to the mansion that day would be taking his measure; but Jack and Bobby would be taking theirs too, Jack reminded his father. Two pastel-colored Cadillacs rolled up to the Kennedy mansion, their passengers similarly arrayed in pale business suits of conservative cut and floral hue. Sergio recalled that nearly a half dozen of the exiles' representatives were with him when they arrived, including Manuel Artime, one or both of the San Roman brothers (Pepe and Roberto), Miró Cardona, and perhaps Erneido Oliva. Joe Sr. was there to greet them, along with the candidate and Bobby.

As the men settled in, Artime reprised the position that he had presented in the July meeting with Jack in Washington. Cuba's political corruption was seeping up through Fidel's ranks, said Artime, and now it definitely wore a Communist face. Sergio chimed in. The Revolution had been stolen from the people. He called Fidel "a bowl of dirt," both for reasons of ethics and hygiene, and Jack laughed along, gibing at the Castros for continuing to wear their uniforms even though the fighting had stopped almost two years before.

That, of course, was the point the Cubans were stressing. Fidel was a professional revolutionary, not a political leader. He ruled by theatrics and violence. Jack expressed his best intentions, promising a deep and thorough examination of the issues, but when there was no direct indication of what those intentions were, one of the exiles made it more blunt. He said that if the plans to overthrow Castro were to proceed, then they would certainly spread the word to the overwhelmingly Catholic Cuban voters of South Florida. So much for secrecy, Jack and Bobby must have thought. Trading votes for promises of a covert attack was not exactly presidential; the plan seemed doomed to fail on both the political and military fronts.

But Sergio implied that New Orleans's Cubans could be similarly enlisted. He was about to open a chapter of the Cuban Revolutionary Council (CRC) there, he said.

"Rumors are that the U.S. will embargo Cuba," he told the brothers. "Thousands of Cubans are streaming into New Orleans every week, just as they are into Miami. With the help of certain American organizations and the Catholic Church, we are uniting their rage."

And they were not just right-wing organizations, the Frente men attested. The anti-Castro movement was becoming as polymorphic as Cuba's political culture had been before Fidel.[32]

Sergio and Bobby did not speak directly that day, but they did meet each other's gaze at a couple of points, Bobby listening intently. The Cubans' passion and courage impressed the Kennedy men. Their reports also seemed to confirm what the Agency had been implying—if an invasion before the election was imminent, then the Cubans would probably not have paid them a visit. In the short run, therefore, the brothers could rest easy.

If they won the election, however, the longer term was not so comforting. The invasion plan already had a certain life of its own.

The meetings continued. CIA files indicate that there was another Dulles/Kennedy confab on September 19, when the campaign was in full throttle. And another occurred between Jack and someone who may have been Bissell at a safe house in northwest Washington, near CIA headquarters, perhaps a month before the election. This one, according to Clarence B. Sprouse, an Army sergeant who helped to prepare documentation for the meeting, was focused on what had become known as "the Trinidad landing," the incipient plot to overthrow the Castros that Ike had set in motion the preceding spring. Both Nixon and Kennedy were briefed in that time frame, though Nixon was the sitting vice president and Jack was still just a candidate. As the campaign reached its climax, the deputy CIA director, General Charles P. Cabell, gave Jack a final update on November 2, just six days before the election.

Another Kennedy pal, John M. Patterson, the Democratic governor of Alabama, also gave Jack a heads-up in October. The CIA, he said, was already sending elements of the Alabama National Guard to train pilots in Nicaragua for what was still being positioned by the Cuban democratic left as an operation to infiltrate small guerrilla units into Cuba to support the underground and foment internal upheaval. Patterson suspected that a foreign policy coup and an electoral one might be in the offing, all in a single bold stroke that would put Nixon in office on the knife-edge of what was likely to be a very close election.

As Patterson would later tell Hersh, he had brought $10,000 in cash with him to the meeting. "Contributions. In a paper bag . . . That's the way we did things then," he said, grinning sheepishly. Kennedy registered no emotion as the Nicaraguan story was told; and when Patterson was done, Jack tucked the money away, thanked him, and left.[33]

Jack, with his newfound insight, decided to position himself as tougher on Cuba than Ike and Nixon. In the short haul it was a shrewd move; Nixon had helped to build the plan, but he couldn't counter Jack's rightward shift without compromising the entire operation. In the presidential debate on foreign policy that soon followed, Nixon tried to imply that Kennedy had heard about the Cuba plans, but finally he was flummoxed by Jack's sudden hawkishness.

The candidates were coming to the end of a 68-day marathon, the Kennedys putting tens of thousands of miles on the *Caroline*, the family's twin-engine prop plane. On one such hop over Seattle, one of Jack's aides looked out over a naval armada bobbing in the glassy harbor.

"Just think, Senator," he said impulsively, "in a few months they'll all be yours."

"Thanks a lot," Jack winced, knowing better.[34]

The flip remark would have its prophetic overtones, though. The problems that would flow from a misappropriation of military power the following spring were being planted right then and there.

As he had in his 1952 Senate run against incumbent Henry Cabot Lodge, he dodged to the right, this time claiming that Eisenhower and Nixon had allowed a "missile gap" to develop between the U.S. and the USSR. There was no such gap. The Soviets were outgunned by nearly every measure, and, once elected, Jack would be forced to admit that the bogus claim could have emboldened the Soviets into thinking that they were stronger than they in fact were, and thus embark on nuclear misadventures.

He also elected to dodge to the right on Cuba. By stirring up an untoward fear of Fidel, he ran the risk that can turn a leader into a follower, a servant to the fear they've made; he had forced himself to keep the terror alive and real, or appear to be a cynical fear-*monger*. So with Jack's feint right, Nixon was being chumped on a grand scale—and on national television, no less. No wonder he was in a sweat.

With the election possibly slipping through his fingers, Nixon began badgering the CIA to go forward with the plan immediately. Rumors mounted that Dick might have succeeded, and Jack was quietly aghast, making several probes at the CIA to find out if they were true. (This may explain the quick sit-down with General Cabell on the eve of the election.) In any case, he was apparently reassured. The Kennedy campaign had out-righted the right.

Years later, in his memoir, *RN*, Dick Nixon wrote: "Kennedy conveyed the image—to 60 million people—that he was tougher on Castro than I was." It was a lesson in political gamesmanship that Nixon would never forget—indeed, one that would lure him to the brink of his own political disaster. It was a fatal watershed in the careers of both men, figuratively for Dick, literally for Jack. The trumping of Nixon on Cuba would encourage his lesser traits later on, setting him on a path to impeachment at the end of his own presidency. And that gambit would backfire on Jack too. He had put himself in a trick bag. He had locked himself into a deal with the devil that would ultimately get him killed.

When Lee wasn't partying the night away on Ulyanov Street, he was at the factory. Once his initial celebrity wore off, though, he began to slough off, dawdling over magazines in the commissary and even proposing a sit-down strike at one point. He became known less as a worker than a shirker; and, as the first anniversary of Lee's arrival in Russia approached, his disenchantment was already growing. In an October diary entry, he wrote: "The coming of fall, my dread of a new Russian winter, mellowed in splendid golds and reds of fall in Byelorussia. Plums, peaches, apricots and cherries abound for these last fall weeks. I have a healthy brown color and am stuffed with fresh fruit, at other times of the year unobtainable."[35]

His first serious girlfriend was a beautiful young Jewish woman named Ella Germann, probably his first real love. They met at the factory, and Lee courted her passionately. But Ella, a virgin who maintained an exacting view of both sex and the truth, soon became skeptical of his stories. He had always enjoyed lying, but he hadn't yet learned to do it well. By Lee's twenty-first birthday on October 18, his romancing of Ella had become troublesome. His lies dampened her attraction to him. She would claim, years later, that she was not in love with him, and when he took to satisfying his needs with another young woman, the relationship foundered.

"November finds the approach of winter now," Lee wrote, aspiring to something Chekhovian, perhaps. "A growing loneliness overtakes me. In spite of my conquest of Inna Tachina, a girl from Riga, studying at the Music Conservatory in Minsk. After an affair which lasts a few weeks, we part." An extra page, not part of the formal diary, elaborates on the affair: "Inna Tachina . . . I met her in 1960 at the Zigers', her family (who sent her to Minsk) apparently well off. Inna likes fancy clothes, well-made shoes and underthings. In October 1960 we begin to get very close culminating in intercourse on October 21. She was a virgin and very interesting. We met in such fashion on 4 or 5 occasions ending November 4, 1960. Upon completion of her last year at Minsk Conservatory she left Minsk for Riga."[36]

Four days after Lee's last fling with Inna, the American people went to the polls to cast their vote for a new president of the United States by the smallest vote margin in American history.

That evening, November 8, 1960, Bobby Kennedy's cottage at the family's Hyannis Port, Massachusetts, compound had been turned into Mission

Control for the climax of Jack's campaign. The place was thronged with Kennedys, staffers, friends, phone operators, and their resident pollster, Lou Harris, who was tucked away upstairs with his slide rule. The new medium of television had played an unprecedented role in American politics this election, and the compound was ablaze with klieg lights. But no amount of heat or light could hasten the process. It would be a long night.

They won Pennsylvania and, to Jack's surprise, it looked like he might take California. But the Farm Belt seemed to be sliding into the Nixon column. Ohio slipped away. Joe Sr. was anchored at the center of the storm, and at one point Jack walked over to him and raised his clenched fist, and the old man covered it with his free hand, the family's handshake of solidarity. Bobby was mostly silent, riveted on the returns. A little after midnight, California was still in play, along with Michigan, Minnesota, and Illinois. It was time for Bobby to put in a call in to Illinois' political godfather, Chicago Mayor Richard J. Daley.

"Mayor, we don't have your vote," Bobby said flatly. Something about Bobby's tone—perhaps a hint of judgment, given Daley's renowned corruption—made Jack take the phone away from him. He and the mayor had a brief conversation, Jack starting with genial thanks for Daley's unstinting support throughout. What was Dick Daley's estimation of things in Illinois?

"Mr. President," the Mayor intoned, "with a little bit of luck and the help of a few close friends, you're going to carry Illinois."

Among those "friends" were the same wiseguys who had been trying to whack Fidel.

By the time CIA director Allen Dulles arrived at the Kennedys' Palm Beach compound on November 18, he and FBI director Hoover had just been assured of reappointment by the president-elect. Some would later claim that the ready continuation of Allen's eight-year stint as the DCI was a gesture of thanks for helping to secure Nixon's defeat. Though Dulles was uncomfortable with the idea of a president who was only half his age, there was still warm personal history here, between the Kennedy family and both Dulles and his deputy, Richard Bissell. Dulles was unaware that Jack planned to ease him out by July 1961 and promote Bissell to the job, so the atmosphere was cordial that day, even casual at first. Bobby was in attendance, as was Joe Sr. There was no need for secret talks anymore. It was time to get down to brass tacks about the Cuba plans.

But those plans were built on a faulty precedent, thanks to Richard Bissell. Bissell was brilliant, but he was prone to hubris and he was subjected to almost no oversight. His vast talent for systems analysis had put him in charge of all Allied shipping during World War II, and then he had made himself indispensable to the Marshall Plan and the Ford Foundation. But he was more than a formidable man behind a desk: he was drawn to action, to the application of intellect in real contests for tangible power. At a Georgetown dinner party at the end of 1953, CIA director Allen Dulles offered him a job as his special assistant. Bissell took it.

A few months later, in June 1954, he was trying to overthrow reformist Guatemalan president Jacobo Árbenz Guzmán, who had had the audacity to appropriate the vast plantations of the United Fruit Company and undertake significant land reform.

The summer before that, in August 1953, the Agency had unseated Iran's nationalist prime minister Mohammed Mosaddeq in defense of Great Britain's oil monopoly there. Crucial to the coup's success had been Kermit "Kim" Roosevelt, grandson of President Teddy, and a man of prodigious daring and brains. When the CIA decided to reprise its Iranian victory in Guatemala, they tapped Kim Roosevelt again.

Roosevelt declined. For such a coup to succeed, he told Dulles, both the military and the population must "want what we want." It was an observation that American spies would have done well to heed in coming years. Árbenz was overthrown by a combination of maneuvering and circumstance. Land reform made United Fruit nervous. A campaign was launched to paint Árbenz as a Commie. He overreacted to fears of the CIA and sought arms from the real Communists of the Eastern bloc, thus giving *Time* magazine and the *New York Times* fodder—with the overt encouragement of the Agency—to sell Árbenz as the new bogeyman. Then, lost in a circus of lame pyrotechnics, rumor-mongering on a pseudo–Voice of Liberation radio station, and a few real skirmishes, the addled Árbenz lost his grip, panicked, and was abandoned by his military. The CIA was stunned at its scattershot success; but once the shock wore off, they were convinced that they had nearly mastered a new kind of war, reliant on "PSYOP," or psychological operations.

These methods wouldn't be so easy to replicate in Cuba, and Bissell knew it when they arrived in Palm Beach that November day, even if Dulles didn't. Notes from the CIA's briefing meeting, three days before the two top spooks sat down with Jack, had put the difficulties in plain sight: "There will not be the internal unrest earlier believed possible, nor will [Castro's] defense permit the type [of] strike first planned . . . Our second concept (1,500–3,000) man force to secure a beach with airstrip is also now seen to be unachievable, except as a joint Agency/DOD [CIA/Pentagon] action."[37]

In other words, Bissell, as head of the invasion planning task force—known as Western Hemisphere Branch Four (WH/4)—knew that the mission as planned was doomed. He may not have told Dulles that, or the president-elect, either. But the WH/4 operation, as Bissell would say thirty years later, "had acquired a considerable momentum and could not just be turned off and on."[38]

It was a way of saying that Richard Bissell wouldn't take no for an answer.

The CIA men got started in the living room, a dim Moorish revival space a bit mildewed from long exposure to the sea. After some congratulatory talk and some kibitzing about the nasty work of the transition, the two spies began to detail the approach that was still being hammered out with the querulous Cubans. The exiles were in the process of forming yet another revolutionary council, and the various options were sketched out once more.

Bissell's presentation took less than an hour. Initially, he described various political actions that were already being undertaken inside and outside of Cuba. He went into the propaganda efforts, via radio and print, including broadcasts from the Swan Islands, located between Cuba and Central America. The CIA had been supporting a number of dissident groups inside the country to whom they were air-dropping supplies and equipment. In the scenario Bissell described, such a force might penetrate Cuba through a town like Trinidad in the central, tobacco-rich province of Las Villas. The people there were said to be extremely anti-Castro, and the rebels could gain cover and traction right away, arming the locals and encouraging an uprising that would spread quickly. Once the insurgent cells were in place, there would be an air-and-sea attack that would establish a staging base for the next wave of assaults. And then there was the kicker: If needed, all of that would be followed by an aerial bombardment of Havana to support the guerrillas who would be moving, in theory, to the capital.

As part of his pitch, it's likely that Dick Bissell also made some mention of overt U.S. military intervention as a contingency. The subtext seems to have been: "This might work, or this and that might work, but in a pinch we may ask you for American troops." Throughout Bissell's presentation, Dulles kept asserting that the Soviet military was moving into Cuba by leaps and bounds. There wasn't much time, he kept saying. In reality, time had already run out.

Jack hadn't prepared any questions in advance, but his focus and his few questions were piercing, focused on tactical detail and real prospects for success, and he revealed nothing of his inclinations.

It was a beautiful day, and when the Cuba presentation ended they decided to repair to the backyard swimming pool. Bissell drifted off to the far end of the terrace there. Dulles continued on with other matters that required Jack's attention. When the spooks left after about two hours and forty minutes, they had convinced themselves that Jack's reaction had been favorable. Jack's style was questioning, a journalistic instinct. He kept his own council, as did Bobby, offering few opinions along the way. The CIA men developed a habit of misinterpreting his silence as assent.

They heard what they wanted to hear and, in reality, these plans were already so far along that Dulles would soon be sharing them with corporate leaders in New York, including execs from Standard Oil of New Jersey, International Telephone and Telegraph, Texaco, the American Sugar Refining Company, and the American and Foreign Power Company. Some would advocate sabotaging the Cuban sugar crop, burning more of the cane fields and wrecking the refineries. Others were gung ho to place an embargo on food, drugs, and spare parts for machinery; Dulles vetoed the food and drugs idea.[39] The people shouldn't be made to suffer directly; but if things went as planned, all of the Cuban markets would be theirs again.

But, in fact, Fidel Castro was no Jacobo Árbenz. Thanks to his undercover operatives in Central America, Fidel already knew a great deal about these plans. He was not the sort of man to panic, and he had learned the smoke-and-mirrors lessons of the Guatemalan coup. It would take more than PSYOP to bring him down; and the more he knew, the more absurd the CIA's self-assurance became.

When Dulles and Bissell finally rolled up their maps and charts and left the Kennedy mansion that November night, Bobby watched the fatigue wash over his brother's face. Many historians have remarked on the transition period as emblematic of a new style of governance. Joe Sr. had been the campaign's bank. They weren't carrying a lot of IOUs when the prize was won, and those to whom they did owe some fealty, such as the American blacks who had rallied to their cause, they thought they could repay only minimally. When J. Edgar Hoover was reappointed as head of the FBI the day after the election, it was largely because he knew of Jack's sexual athleticism and might use it against him unless he was kept enthroned. Small matter that he was hostile to the civil rights movement; he was dangerous to Jack Kennedy's personal freedom of movement. Thirty-four million people had voted *against* the president-elect, but the Kennedys were freer to govern as they pleased than most politicians had been: their fortune allowed them to depart from the customs of quid pro quo. They were free to think for themselves, and it quickly became apparent that, in the words of John H. Davis, they were "impulsive and battle-prone," and were forming a government "that strove to circumvent bureaucracy, public opinion, and conventional channels, in favor of the shortcut, frequently the wholly secret shortcut, to the goal of the moment."[40]

Perhaps Bissell sensed that this would be their style, and was betting his hunch on Castro's downfall. It was a fairly safe bet at that point. Besides their father, the only other people to whom the Kennedys might owe their victory were the boys at the CIA.

On Sunday, December 11, a seventy-three-year-old former postal clerk named Richard Paul Pavlick was way out of his element. In fact, the New Hampshire native was driving his dilapidated 1950 Buick slowly through the swank streets of Palm Beach, Florida, looking for the Kennedy mansion. Mr. Pavlick hated Catholics. Mr. Pavlick hated the Kennedys. And Mr. Pavlick was going to do something with that hate.

A few months earlier, he had given his shack to a youth camp in his hometown of Belmont and then promptly disappeared. The local postmaster would occasionally get enigmatic postcards from the old guy, all of them written from the same cities and on the same days that John F. Kennedy was appearing in his bid for the presidency. The Secret Service was informed, and they tried to snare him, but at one point Pavlick got within ten feet of the senator in Hyannis Port, and on this bright Sunday he was still at large.

At midmorning, he found the stucco Mediterranean-style mansion and parked his car just up the street. He had taken care to write a suicide note to the people of the United States. "It is hoped by my actions that a better country . . . has resulted," he had written, and by way of ensuring it he now sat with one of his liver-spotted hands gripping a switch that was wired to seven sticks of dynamite. When the president-elect emerged on his way to that godforsaken Catholic church of his, Mr. Pavlick would do the world a favor and send the man sky-high. This was it. Today was the day.

The mansion's door opened. Kennedy came out. Pavlick prepared himself to ram the man's car as it came out of the driveway.

But then Mrs. Kennedy appeared behind him, their little girl prancing along beside her like a leprechaun and their new baby in her arms, all of them dressed up for Sunday. Kennedy took the girl's hand, laughing as she broke into song.

The family got into the car. The car and a backup crept down the driveway and turned onto the street; but just as it did, Pavlick let go of the trigger he was holding. The cars drove right past him. Right exactly past him. He could see them laughing through the windows, but they glided on by, leaving the old man trembling in his rage and confusion.[41]*

Kennedy's security hardly improved after he was sworn in. A motivated killer could get off a shot on almost any day, and, in just under three years, one would.

When nearly all of the positions in the Kennedy government had been filled, the most important one remaining in December 1960 was the position of attorney general. The new government would begin in roiling times. Organized crime was becoming a pressing concern—the FBI had never really touched it. The nuclear age posed new challenges to the planet at large, and to liberties at home. The civil rights movement was intent upon burying the legacy of slavery, and the complacencies of the Eisenhower era were already giving way to youthful demands for a new activism in government. The sixties had arrived. The chief legal officer of the United States would have to be someone of fitting experience, courage, and imagination.

Among those Jack offered the Justice Department job to was Connecticut's elegant, liberal governor, Abraham Ribicoff, who had delivered his state to the Kennedy column and served the campaign articulately and well. But Ribicoff demurred. "I don't want a Jew putting Negroes in Protestant schools in the South," he told Jack. By this time, Bobby knew something about religious bigotry and sensed that if Ribicoff took the slot and his name were put before Congress, he'd spark so much controversy that he'd never be confirmed in Protestant America. Ribicoff had suggested a place on the Supreme Court but agreed to become secretary of health, education and welfare instead.

Old Joe had a vested interest in the AG appointment, and he weighed in heavily with Jack on the beach at Hyannis Port. The job should go to Bobby, Joe said. The president would, in the parlance of the Secret Service, need a "body man," an absolutely trustworthy confidant who had his back, no matter what the political pressures. Jack would also need someone who could cover his ongoing indiscretions, run interference with J. Edgar Hoover

---

*Pavlick was arrested four days later, before he could make another attempt without Kennedy's family present. After his arrest, Pavlick, who had a hundred sticks of dynamite in his possession when nabbed, spent four years in a New Hampshire mental facility. When Kennedy heard of the would-be assassin, he was merely bemused, according to his speechwriter, Ted Sorensen. Pavlick died in 1975.

(who reported to the AG's office), and take the heat off him when tough decisions had to be made about the rule of law.

But Bobby refused to take the job, too. "In the first place, I thought nepotism was a problem," he would later explain. "Secondly, I had been chasing bad guys for three years and I didn't want to spend the rest of my life doing that."[42] He thought that "with the name the same, and brothers, I would be creating so many problems in civil rights. It would be 'the Kennedy brothers' by the time the year was up, and the President would be blamed for everything we had to do in civil rights . . . it was an unnecessary burden to undertake."[43]

When word of the offer to Bob leaked out, the press agreed with him, jeering at the suggestion from coast to coast. His friends agreed, too. Bob didn't want to be taking orders from Jack. He wanted to write, or perhaps run for governor of Massachusetts; but wherever he landed, he categorically was not interested in the Justice job. With his lines firmly drawn, he took off with wife Ethel for a vacation to Mexico, and Jack continued to stew.

The moral axis of the family may have shifted, but the power of persuasion remained with Joe Sr., and Jack was increasingly convinced. On December 13, the older brother called Bobby at home and pressed him once more to take the helm at Justice. Bobby started to decline, but Jack cut him off. "Don't tell me now," he said. "I want to have breakfast with you in the morning."

When Bobby hung up, he was still intractable, but he knew there would be a cost. He turned to Ethel and said, "This is going to kill my father."

December 14 was bitterly cold. Bob took his friend John Seigenthaler with him for moral support, and the two arrived at Jack's Georgetown house, only to be met by the now-constant gaggle of reporters, all shivering on the sidewalk with nothing but coffee and cigarettes to warm themselves with.

Jack's maid, Provi, was the only other person present that morning, a fitting irony; while the job of the sixties' attorney general was being discussed, the African-American Provi cooked breakfast in the kitchen. In the living room, small talk turned to joking about the new, straightlaced secretary of state designate, Dean Rusk. They went to the breakfast nook to eat what Provi had prepared, and finally Bob asked, "Well, Johnny, what about me?"

Jack addressed his answer to Seigenthaler, as if he were judge and jury.

Seigenthaler would recount Jack's final appeal this way: "I need someone I can completely and totally and absolutely rely on, somebody who's going to tell me what the best judgment is, my best interest. There's not a member of the cabinet I can trust in that way . . . Sure, I can call you on the telephone, but what I really need is someone who's there, available to meet with me. I have nobody. There is nobody . . . If I can ask Dean Rusk to give up a career; if I can ask Adlai Stevenson to make a sacrifice he does not want to make; if I can ask Bob McNamara to give up a job as head of that company . . . certainly I can expect my own brother to give me the same sort of contribution. And I need you in this government."

With that, Jack got up and went into the kitchen.

After all the childhood years in which Bob was chided as the soft one, the mama's boy, the altar boy, and after all the hard-fought times in which he defied that given role and proved himself to be among the strongest of the Kennedy men, this was perhaps the moment when Jack's respect for him, even perhaps his *love* for him, was most openly admitted. When Seigenthaler suggested that it was time to go, Bob retorted, "No, wait! I've got some points to make."

"There's no point to make," said his friend.[44]

And he was right. Jack's unparalleled vulnerability had rendered any such points moot. He came back into the nook, grinning in presupposed victory.

"So," he said, "that's it, gentlemen. Let's grab our balls and go."

Scattering whatever sentiment might still be hanging in the air, Jack told Bobby to go comb his hair before they went out to tell the chilled reporters the news. It might make them nervous if a job of such gravitas was about to be filled by a guy who looked like some prep-school junior just off a scrimmage line.

The next day, December 15, as Mr. Pavlick was crossing the Royal Poinciana Bridge back into Palm Beach, Officer Lester Free spotted the New Hampshire license plate, B1 606, and the old codger's car was surrounded. The Buick was still full of dynamite and Mr. Pavlick was still full of hate. After his initial hesitation the preceding Sunday, he had gone on to St. Edward Church while Kennedy and his family were inside. Since then he had cased the place again, but now he was in custody.

"I felt the Kennedy money was how he got the White House," he explained. "I wanted to teach the United States the presidency is not for sale . . . I did not wish to harm [Mrs. Kennedy] or the children . . . I decided to get him at the church or someplace later," he said from jail, admitting that too many people—albeit Catholics—would have died at the church. He had reconnoitered the mansion repeatedly. "The security is lousy there," he added helpfully.

When Bobby's appointment to the DOJ was announced, the press was incredulous. The Chicago Outfit was enraged. Bobby's law-school mates at the University of Virginia were speechless. Jack rode it out like the Yankee prince he was, and when Christmas came, he reverted to his ironic ways and signed Bobby's gift, a leather-bound edition of Bobby's book about the mob, in typical fashion. Where Jackie inscribed it, "To Bobby—who made the impossible possible and changed all our lives," Jack took acid pen to paper and wrote, "For Bobby—The Brother Within—who made the easy difficult. Jack, Christmas 1960."

A month later, just after Jack's inauguration, the two would be at a dinner party when Jack would joke, "I don't know why people are so mad at me for making Bobby attorney general. I just wanted to give him a little legal practice before he becomes a lawyer."

After dinner, Bobby cornered the new president of the United States, his fists pressed righteously to his sides.

"Jack, you shouldn't have said that about me!"

"Bobby, you don't understand. You've got to make fun of it, you've got to make fun of yourself in politics," Jack said.

"You weren't making fun of yourself," Bobby snarled. "You were making fun of me."[45]

There was something telling about Jack's Christmas inscription, something deep, after all. Bobby had indeed become "the brother within." In fact, as they set out across the dark and monstrous waters of the Cold War, each man would carry the other within himself, Jack holding Bobby as perhaps his moral compass, and Bobby holding Jack in his heart, at his worst and at his best, even long after Jack himself was gone.

June Cobb's first operation for the CIA was to go to New York City and use her charms to get acquainted with Richard Gibson, the CBS newsman who had cofounded the Fair Play for Cuba Committee. After a series of casual meetings, the Agency's initial suspicions were confirmed: the Castros were intimately involved with the FPCC's activities.

Gibson, Cobb already knew, had traveled to Cuba, perhaps with the aid of V. T. Lee's skills as a boundary jumper. He had met with both Fidel and Cuban president Osvaldo Dorticós, and had received a total of $15,000 to help finance the organization. Cobb later testified that when she was working with the Castros, she had firsthand knowledge that the FPCC was financially supported by Havana.

"I remember when they came begging for money," Cobb recalled. "They [Richard Gibson and others] went to the prime minister's office." Juan Orta turned them down, telling them that "they were too anti-American, as opposed to pro-Cuba, and they should be ashamed coming from a rich country and begging from a poor one." But Dorticós and Che, the "foreign relations" department, saw the value of sponsorship right away, and checks in the thousands were soon being sent to the FPCC through the Cuban UN Mission. Cobb's friend Teresa Cassuso saw the checks, but apparently the American lefties weren't all that grateful. Gibson later complained to Cobb that the Cubans were stingy.[46]

Before Gibson left the FPCC leadership to pursue other interests, the Cubans had tried to recruit him as their public relations officer at the United Nations, but the journalist declined that role.

In the coming year, June would be transferred to Mexico City and her cryptonym changed to LI COOKY. In that incarnation, she would once again be placed at the vortex of events that would have global implications.

Lee Oswald spent New Year's Eve of 1961 with Ella and the Germann family. Soon after, he asked her to marry him. She declined. His secrecy and indifference to the truth had had a killing effect. On January 2, 1961, he wrote: "She hesitates then refuses, my love is real but she has none for me . . . I am stunned she snickers at my awkwardness in turning to go (I am too stunned to think) I realize she was never serious with me . . . I am miserable."[47]

Across the world, Lee's mother was faring no better. His abrupt departure from the Marine Corps and his quick stopover to see his family en route to the Soviet Union had left Marguerite in an agitated state that still had not ended more than two years later. She had decided on drastic action to find him. Lee had written to his brother, Robert, from Moscow, and that must have been the first time that she had had any confirmation of his whereabouts.

So, a few days after John Kennedy was inaugurated as president of the United States, Marguerite Oswald boarded a train in Fort Worth, Texas, found a seat in coach, and set off for the nation's capital to plead her case to the new president. Perhaps the promise of the New Frontier had given her some hope that the young administration could help *every* American, even her. She had borrowed money on an insurance policy to make the trek, and had purchased a new pair of shoes for the occasion. In her testimony a few years later, she wasn't sure if the trip had taken two days and three nights, or three days and two nights; but in any case, she sat up most of the way and arrived at Union Station in Washington on January 26, six days after Jack had been sworn into office.

When she called the White House, "a Negro man was on the switchboard, and he said the offices were not open yet."[48] Calls from the public were not put through until 9:00 A.M., but when she did call back then and asked to speak to the president, Jack's secretary, Evelyn Lincoln, noted the call on her official call sheet and graciously informed Mrs. Oswald that President Kennedy was in a conference but that she would gladly take a message. One account suggested that Lincoln was fibbing, that she covered the receiver and passed the caller's request on to Jack, who happened to be flipping through his appointment book when the call was put through. In this version, Jack quipped that the woman should call her congressman, not the president, and went back into his office.

Since she couldn't speak with the president, Marguerite asked to speak with the new secretary of state, Dean Rusk, at which point her call was put through to Rusk's office. Rusk was in conference as well. Would the caller like to leave a message? Perhaps feeling that her opportunity was slipping away, Marguerite told his secretary what the nature of the call was. "Yes," she said. "I have come to town about a son of mine who is lost in Russia. I do not want to speak—I would like personally to speak to Secretary Rusk," she insisted.

The secretary put Marguerite on hold for a time. It's not known if she conveyed the message directly to Rusk; but when she returned, she put Marguerite through to D. E. Boster, a special officer in charge of Soviet affairs. He told her he was familiar with her son's case, though it's not known whether he referred to the broad strokes indicated by the secretary or to information gleaned from the American embassy in Moscow where Lee had renounced his U.S. citizenship. Boster suggested that they meet, referred Marguerite to the Washington Hotel near the State Department, and set an appointment time for 11:00.

After checking into the hotel, she took a bath, dressed, and then headed for the Department of State. But before she got to Boster's office, she stopped at a pay phone in a corridor, where she called Rusk's suite yet again and told the woman that she would rather speak with the secretary of state.

"Mrs. Oswald," Rusk's secretary urged her, "talk to Mr. Boster. At least it is a start."

So on she trundled to Boster's office. Along the way, she took pictures of the Department and years later would offer them to Warren Commission investigators as proof of her story.

Boster greeted her at his office. "Mrs. Oswald, I am awfully glad you came early," she recalled, "because we are going to have a terrible snowstorm, and we have orders to leave early in order to get home."

They were joined by another bureaucrat, and Marguerite had some official papers with her which she presented, probably having to do with Lee's discharge from the Marine Corps. "Now," she said, "I know you are not going to answer me, gentlemen, but I'm under the impression that my son is an agent."

"Do you mean a Russian agent?" one of the men asked.

"No, working for our government, a U.S. agent. And I want to say this: that if he is, I don't appreciate it too much, because I am destitute, and just getting over a sickness . . ." (She allowed, in her recounting, that she had "had the audacity to say that.") Furthermore, she had gone through all of this without medical care, without money, without compensation. She avowed that she was "a desperate woman."

They did not address her claim immediately. She went on to say that her son should not have gone into a foreign country and left her alone. She wanted her son at home with her.

"Now, he has been exploited all through the paper as a defector," she said, but she then seemed confused about whether or not he was, indeed, an agent of the U.S. government, and then admitted that if he was a bona fide defector, then "that is his privilege, as an individual."

One of the men, according to her, replied, "Mrs. Oswald, we want you to know that we feel the same way about it . . . We want him to do what he wants to do." The State Department men told her that there was no evidence to suggest that Lee had gone to the Soviet Union as an agent, and that she should dismiss the idea.

Marguerite Oswald got no more satisfaction than that. As she had done so many times before, during Lee's traumatic childhood, she was once more claiming an acute victimization at the hands of the American government. She left Washington soon after. Eight weeks later, on March 22, she received a letter from the State Department informing her of Lee's address in Minsk.[49]

When Jack met with Dulles and Bissell in mid-November, the first phase of the Cuban Revolution was over. Capitalism was finished in Cuba. Fidel had nationalized most of the foreign companies that had still flourished on the island when he took power. Sitting in his office, little more than a hundred miles from where the CIA men were sitting with the new president-to-be, Fidel was already braced for an American invasion, which he thought Eisenhower might attempt as his last hurrah. Much of his intelligence was coming from agents like Fabian Escalante, one of the young undercover agents whom the Castros had sent to Minsk for training, who was now based in Costa Rica, one of the staging areas for Cuban exiles prepping for the invasion. Years later, Rafael Nuñez, Fidel's diplomatic attaché in Costa Rica, allowed that Fabian's "main objective was to gather intelligence on the exile training camps." By early 1961, Escalante would zero in on the exact site where the invasion would come ashore. Even the last-minute switch to the Bay of Pigs was detected. "When the Bay of Pigs occurred, Castro was waiting for them," Nuñez continued.[50]

By late 1960, the porousness of the Guatemalan training camps was already undermining any hopes the Americans might have had for secrecy. According to Lyman Kirkpatrick, an inspector general of the CIA, Fidel "directed his security forces to round up all known or suspected members of the opposition. Nearly one hundred thousand were arrested and taken to detention camps all over the island."[51] This was the "hard core" of the opposition that Artime and the center/left faction of the Cuban exiles would be counting on in an internal uprising, but the longer the planning went on, the more doomed it was.

Six weeks after the Dulles and Bissell sit-down with the Kennedy brothers, on the last day of 1960, Fidel ordered a mass mobilization to repel what he thought was an imminent invasion. America was a useful prod to the revolutionary spirit. The Castro brothers had decimated the opposition by now. Not only had they purged the hard core of rightist oligarchs, but they had exiled most of the creative moderates who might have helped them come up with a coherent fiscal policy at that point. The economy was foundering, relying mainly on the advice of the autodidact Che and the improvisations of a handful of hacks from the Cuban Communist Party.

As Jack held court with the CIA and Fidel steeled himself for an American attack, the plan was unraveling and the planners didn't seem to know it. Had the Agency slowed its progress to ensure Jack's election? If so, had they consciously determined that it was worth the risk of exposing the operation through delay? Was Eisenhower reluctant to hand a new president an issue of "deniability" by taking a parting shot at the Cuban regime? Regardless, Bissell and Dulles seriously underestimated Cuban intelligence. True, the stateside exiles were still in ideological disarray. But by arguing the method of Fidel's removal, the Americans had lost the element of surprise. Where Mosaddeq and Árbenz had failed to anticipate a U.S.-sponsored coup, the Castros had not only done just that, they'd turned the threat to their advantage. In easing Jack Kennedy into the presidency, the CIA set into motion a Cuba crisis that would continue right up to Dallas; all at once, they helped grant Jack the ultimate prize and handed him the seeds of his own destruction.

And there was one more ill omen just before Jack took power on January 20, 1961. On the seventeenth, Patrice Lumumba, prime minister of the Republic of the Congo, was assassinated in a plot orchestrated by Belgium with the tacit approval of the CIA.

CHAPTER 4
On the Beach

A T ABOUT THE SAME TIME that Marguerite Oswald came to Washington to prod the Kennedy administration to help her rescue her son from Communist Russia, the new president was setting out to find a "third way" between the false promises of the Castros' neo-Marxism and the stranglehold of a centuries-old oligarchy.* But the pressure for action was building so rapidly that a highly polarized approach was taking shape, one that would make the closeted aggression of the Ike-Nixon years seem like a mere warmup.

It all started with a seemingly temperate directive.

In setting his course, the new president beckoned his young adviser and speechwriter, Richard Goodwin, to his office to help him. Goodwin had only been out of Harvard Law School since 1958, but he wrote and thought extremely well and had risen fast in Washington power circles. After a stint at the Supreme Court, he had taken on the TV quiz-show scandals as a staffer for the House Commerce Committee, and then assumed the job of speechwriter for a presidential candidate. He could write for Jack's voice and style and cadence better than anyone else but Ted Sorensen, and now here he was—putting words in the mouth of the president himself.

When Goodwin reported for duty, Jack was staring out through the glass doors at the White House garden and the grounds beyond, a solitary man at

---

*In the early 1960s, a centuries-old Latin American oligarchy stood on the backs of two hundred million poor people, two fifths of whom were under fifteen years old. One third of them would die before they turned forty. Half were illiterate. Two percent of the populace controlled fifty percent of the wealth, and over two thirds of the people existed in the most degrading kind of poverty. Most of the national governments of the continent considered themselves "free" republics, but in the thirty years leading up to the Kennedys' ascendancy, there had been ninety-three illegal changes of regime.

the crossroads of a hundred merging truths. The president turned from his musings and greeted Goodwin.

"Look at this, Dick," said the president, pointing at the floor beside his desk. "You know what that is?"

Goodwin peered closely at dozens of small holes in the floor as Jack answered his own question.

"It's from Ike's golf shoes. He put 'em on at this desk, then walked out here to practice his putting. Maybe we ought to put a rope around this piece of floor and leave it as an Eisenhower memorial."

Jack circled back to the business side of the desk. "Well, I guess we all have our way of relaxing from the burdens of office; at least I won't leave any marks on the floor."

There was a fat file on the desk. He picked it up. "Telegrams from Latin America . . . There's even one from that bastard Somoza saying my election has given him new hope for Nicaraguan democracy. Draft an answer saying that's my hope too—democracy for Nicaragua. That ought to scare him."

Talk turned to another telegram, this one from Rómulo Betancourt, the president of Venezuela who had overthrown a dictator, been freely elected in the aftermath, and was now considered the embodiment of the liberal democratic forces in South America. Betancourt had also sent congratulations, but his "great hopes" sprung from real progressive passion, and Jack read them aloud too, by way of putting Goodwin in charge of a brave new effort.

"I'd like to get a major statement on our Latin policy soon," Jack told him. "Next to Berlin it's the most critical area, and will be for a long time. The whole place could blow up on us. You remember those people who threw rocks at Nixon. I'd like to believe it was Nixon's personality, but they were sending us a message. We can't embrace every tinhorn dictator who tells us he's anticommunist while he's sitting on the necks of his own people. And the United States government is not the representative of private business. Do you know in Chile the American copper companies control about eighty percent of all the foreign exchange? We wouldn't stand for that here . . . There's a revolution going on down there, and I want to be on the right side of it . . . We have to let them know that things have changed."

Goodwin took the president's measure. No chief executive except Franklin Roosevelt had attempted to do anything for Latin America; all others had simply helped themselves *to* Latin America. The new administration would be bucking a tide that had been thundering against Latino shores since the Monroe Doctrine of 1823.

"If you want them to believe you, we'll have to back it up with action,"

Goodwin warned, "and that means a very large commitment. It's a big continent."

Jack assured him that that was exactly what he had in mind. "I don't know if Congress will give it to me. But now's the time, while they're all worried that Castro might take over the hemisphere." It was Goodwin who had helped inflame the anti-Castro language as the campaign heated up, and it would now be Goodwin who would be charged with creating a diplomatic bulwark against Castro in South America.

"I'm worried myself," the president went on. "Not about Castro particularly, although we do have to do something about him; but if people think they have to choose between Communism and not eating, they'll go for Communism. Wouldn't you? I would. Do you think we can have something ready in a month?"

Goodwin told him that, what with the template of Jack's campaign position papers and the Latin American task force that was already working, it shouldn't be too difficult. "If we can get everyone to agree," he hedged.

"I don't care if everyone agrees," Jack shot back. "You know what our thinking is. That's the only agreement you need—with me."

As the meeting ended and Goodwin was leaving, Jack added a chorus to the verses he'd been playing. "One more thing, I don't want this to be an anti-Castro speech. Just throw Castro in with the other dictators. I don't want them to think the only reason we're doing this is because of Cuba. Latin America's not like Asia or Africa. We can really accomplish something there."[1]

Goodwin's task force report would propose that upstart democratic-progressive movements in Latin America "should be known to have the co-operation and support of the United States, just as every Communist group in Latin America is known to have the support of Moscow or of Peiping." It went further, conceding that hard-core capitalism had a bad name among most Latino people; Latin Americans might want something softer, perhaps more in keeping with their ancient, tribal means of survival. "Our economic policy and aid need not be limited to countries in which private enterprise is the sole or predominant instrument of development," the task force report read.

Goodwin's group came foursquare up against others in the executive branch who held that kind of thinking in contempt. In their view, right-wing dictatorships were preferable to the Communist insurgence; to attempt to block revolution with reform would only estrange the oligarchs. It would allow liberals to bring on inflation, scare off investors, and undermine "social discipline," thus creating conditions for local Communists to cast them aside and take over. In other words, there were no alternatives to the Iron Fist at the one extreme or the Red Tide at the other. The oligarchy must retain its control, because the slightest relaxation of it would lead to a Red Flood. It was the same logic that American slaveholders had used to prohibit their human property from learning to read.

John Kennedy was trying to stake out something better. His first State of the Union address created Food for Peace, an Alliance for Progress, and a Peace Corps. On February 12, he sent George McGovern, the Food for Peace director, and historian Arthur M. Schlesinger to Latin America as the first envoys to that region from the new administration. McGovern was to find the best ways to spread America's huge food surplus around the world, to greatest effect, and Schlesinger's tacit mission was to probe attitudes about Castro among the Latino leadership. Their first stop was Buenos Aires.

Fidel, at this point, had still not admitted to the world that he was a Communist. But Argentina's president Arturo Frondizi had no doubts that he was. Castro was not the fundamental question, however, not in Frondizi's mind. "The elimination of Castro will not solve the underlying problem," he said. "What is required is an attack on the conditions that produced him. If he is eliminated and these conditions are left unchanged, new Castros will arise all over the continent." Besides, he later averred, four major countries of the region—Colombia, Brazil, Mexico, and Peru—wouldn't support an overthrow in Cuba for fear of domestic unrest of their own, in retaliation.

At the center of the sleek new architectural showcase of Brasilia, the president of Brazil, Jânio Quadros, looked like a portrait of the most severe modernism, his thick-framed glasses and black mustache giving him the air of a scholarly Groucho trapped inside a Latin version of *The Fountainhead*. He was not so confident, nor so jolly, however. In fact, he was soon telling his American friends that Brazil's finances were in desperate straits. The Americans decided not to torture him with questions about Fidel. He was in enough political pain already.[2]

Next stop, La Paz. Bolivia had undergone a middling revolutionary phase already, nationalizing the tin mines and some other industries, but Eisenhower had tried a more enlightened approach with President Paz Estenssoro than he had with Árbenz in Guatemala, subsidizing a third of the national budget and trying to muscle the economy nonviolently. There was still great poverty, and Bolivia's Communists had co-opted the poor, turning any swipe at the Communists into a swipe at all workers and peasants. Paz Estenssoro didn't miss a beat when Schlesinger asked him what should be done about Fidel. Castro should be "eliminated," no doubt about it, but the best weapons were probably economic sanctions and an educational campaign.

When they got to Lima, they found that Peru's radical democrats wanted the Organization of American States (OAS) to confine Fidel to Cuba; he could have his island as long as he didn't start exporting himself. Many of these Catholic progressive leaders were excited at Kennedy's victory, but optimism about Latin America was not quite so high.

In Caracas, assassination was Rómulo Betancourt's daily concern. He was hoping simply to be the first Venezuelan president to actually serve his entire term, and it wasn't even Venezuelans who were trying to kill him. It was Trujillo, the savage, fascist Dominican president. A year before, a car bomb had exploded as Betancourt's limo was passing. The flames had burned the backs of his hands when he put them over his face, and now he had to salve the scars every day. Nonetheless, it was plain to Schlesinger that his charisma was borne out in close quarters, along with his intelligence, command, and quiet, good-humored decency.

As the president and the historian talked in a fragrant garden late that evening, Betancourt asked his staff to project one of his favorite films, *The Blue Angel*, on an outdoor screen. The two men were smoking cigars and it was a full moon, and as all those streams of light and smoke wrapped the flickering icon of Marlene Dietrich, the talk turned to Cuba. Betancourt quoted Quadros, something he had said after visiting the island nation, post-revolution.

"Those people have no aim, no purpose, no doctrine, no ideology. It is government by epilepsy," Quadros had said.

Betancourt, however, thought the Castros and their *barbudos* were more focused than that. Fidel was a Communist and would soon declare himself so. The party was highly disciplined. In chaotic conditions, they were often the best prepared to stall entropy and provide purpose for new leaders trying to project fresh destinies. There at mid-century, the Communists were the new missionaries. The narrative they brought with them was simple: clear and clean and full of promises that suffering would soon be over, not through immersion in the transcendent waters of Christian love and forgiveness, but through the fire of revolutionary hate and exoneration.

As the night birds sang and Dietrich hovered before them, the historian asked the president if he thought Fidel should be toppled. Betancourt said that the OAS would have to take Trujillo down first. Only then might the countries of the south be united against Fidel.

The Communist Eastern bloc now thought of Cuba as its new little brother. While Raúl continued to build the G2, Che and his STASI advisers from East Germany had become the architects of the Ministerio del Interior, the MININT, and it now ran the government for all intents and purposes. Che was also overseeing the majority of the executions being performed at that time, from his office at La Cabaña, the old Spanish fortress that had been re-fitted as a prison. It was said that he often watched the death squads from his window while he ate lunch.

When he was not signing death sentences, Che was holding court in the house he had purloined from Cuba's wealthiest building contractor just after the revolution. The mansion was one of the most elegant on all of swank Tarara Beach, just fifteen miles outside Havana. According to Cuban journal-ist Antonio Llano Montes, who was personally threatened by Che for exposing the fact, the place had "a yacht harbor, a huge swimming pool, seven bath-rooms, a sauna, a massage salon and several television sets," which included a prototype wide-screen set with remote control. "The mansion's garden had a veritable jungle of imported plants, a pool with waterfall, ponds filled with ex-otic tropical fish and several bird houses filled with exotic tropical birds. The habitation was something out of *A Thousand and One Nights*."[3]

Che often hosted Angel Ciutat there, a Spanish-born member of the So-viet GRU (Main Intelligence Directorate) who had been tight with Trotsky's assassin, Ramón Mercader, and had fled Spain for the Soviet Union after Franco came to power. Ciutat was a practiced killer himself, having cut his teeth with Stalin's chief of police, and it was under his tutelage that Che learned how to direct Cuba's secret police. Ciutat insisted that all execu-tioners use live ammunition. There would be no shooting of blanks by morally queasy gunners. He called it *El Compromiso Sangriento*, or the Blood Covenant. It rendered everyone complicit in the killing, thus assuring their loyalty through bonds of guilt and promising remission through the grace of the Castros and Che. It was Ciutat who ordered that any cadet who wished to graduate from Cuba's military academy had to first join a firing squad; had to enter into *El Compromiso Sangriento* and help to make the revolution strong. It was the time of the assassins indeed.

Jack Kennedy and Dick Bissell saw the world in similar strategic terms, and their rapport was growing. In the first three months of the new presidency, they met some thirteen times, off the record, and by now it was a commonly held belief, within the Agency, that Bissell was the heir apparent at the CIA.

The schemes to kill Castro were expanding on a number of fronts. Tony Varona, one of the leaders of the Cuban exiles' Frente, had hatched a plan known as *El Rescate*—the Rescue—to prepare Fidel's murder. Varona had asked Rescue leaders to send somebody down to Miami to work with Johnny Rosselli, even as the G2 was busting Rescue collaborators in Havana. According to Fabian Escalante, who, since Minsk, had been advancing quickly up the G2 hierarchy, the chief of the Cuban intelligence "Attacks Bureau," Mario Morales Mesa, intercepted a number of plots against Fidel in the weeks and months that preceded the Bay of Pigs invasion. His G2 captain had "infiltrated an agent into the [*Rescate*] group: Alcibíades Bermúdez, also a captain of the Rebel Army, who had been instructed to recruit fighters for an uprising in the Pinar del Río mountains."[4] Bermúdez was among many Castro agents whose job was to lure anti-Castroites into the open, and he had also been told to prepare men for a coastal invasion that would probably come within weeks or months at most. Johnny Rosselli's murder operation—instigated by the Eisenhower administration—was seen as the heart of the scheme. And it was thoroughly penetrated by Escalante and the rest of Raúl Castro's guard.

But the mob gambit entered another phase when meetings were held in September 1960 between a CIA representative and Rosselli at the Plaza Hotel in New York for the purpose of planning another attempt on Fidel. Rosselli again enlisted Giancana and Florida boss Santo Trafficante. Subsequent meetings took place in Miami Beach's shiny new Fontainebleau Hotel, a favored mob hangout. One month before the Bay of Pigs invasion, the CIA delivered poison pills to Rosselli and Trafficante, who in turn delivered them to Castro's secretary, Juan Orta, who planned to poison Castro's food while he dined in his favorite Chinese restaurant.

In Central America, Manuel Artime and his compadres trained for the coming debacle in coordination with the island-based plots. But even this offshore maneuvering leaked like a sieve, with much of the raw intelligence analyzed by the likes of Escalante and fellow Cuban spy Juan Felaifel Canahan.[5] Escalante—working under the war name of "Roberto"—confided to a Cuban attaché in Costa Rica that his visits had only one purpose, to coordinate the infiltrations of Artime's operation.[6]

Felaifel also made key inroads into Operation Zapata, as the CIA called it, getting his own brother, Ánis, installed as Artime's intelligence chief.[7] Artime learned of the subversion far too late, accusing his own pilot of working for Cuban intelligence and betraying the operation.[8]

All this data only confirmed what had been flowing from far more intimate sources. Castro's minions hardly had to spy at all—a major percentage of their intelligence was gleaned by debriefing the prostitutes of the region. The poor "working girls" of the Central American barrios felt some solidarity with the Fidelistas and passed along the exiles' pillow talk.[9]

Juan Antonio Rodríguez Menier, a G2 founding officer, wrote that at least three intelligence officers had informed Fidel that the landing would take place at a "place known as Cochinos." When the Bay of Pigs invasion finally approached, Fidel and Raúl saw it coming as surely as if they had watched a tropical storm blow in slowly across the sea.

The mood at the White House was supremely confident, however, and, despite the doubts that the Agency had committed to paper, Richard Bissell remained outwardly buoyant. He wasn't alone. The new national security adviser, McGeorge Bundy, had been one of Bissell's star students at Yale and, soon after the inauguration, the two were spending long hours at the White House, extending their college study of economics to include the erasure of anticapitalist leaders. They hatched a plan, gave it the code name ZR/RIFLE, and put it under the control of William K. Harvey, a former FBI guy turned CIA operative who took a dim view of assassination but liked his flamboyant life enough to stanch his objections.

When the president asked Bill Harvey to a get-acquainted meeting at the White House, Harvey trundled up to the door of the Oval Office, pulled a .38 revolver from his pants, handed it over to a Secret Service man, and glided in to meet Jack.

"So"—the president smiled, perhaps disbelievingly—". . . you're our 'James Bond'?"

Physically, Harvey was no James Bond. With his thin mustache, his thinner hair, his dewy pate, his bulbous, mournful eyes, his pear-shaped body, his dapper dress, and his omnipresent cigarette, he resembled a squat Jackie Gleason.

Harvey was a player. He was the man who had exposed Kim Philby, the KGB "mole" who had burrowed into both British and American intelligence and remained there for years before Harvey nailed him. He had also masterminded the Berlin Tunnel, which was bored six hundred yards from West into East Berlin in order to tap Soviet military phones. The man began his lunches with two double martinis and a single one, a dosage that did nothing to cloud his brilliant mind, and he was known to stroll the halls with two pearl-handled pistols jutting out of his belt. He claimed to be a world-class Lothario, despite his girth, his gamy hygiene, and his alcoholic air, and was such a keeper of secrets that even the CIA was jealous. His fitness report for the period of 1960–62 characterized him as "less than outgiving of information about operational matters in which he is engaged."[10] This was par for the course for spies of that era. Unfettered by bureaucracy or the press, such men were their own centers of power, operating on the assumption that, unless the president forbade it, it was condoned.

The month of March was a loaded one.

Jack had still not been convinced of the imperative to attack Cuba. He was caught between his wariness of military solutions and his political certainty that the Republicans would excoriate him if he balked. If he had known everything that Bissell knew, he would have scrapped the operation completely. If he had known what Fidel knew, he might very well have scrapped the CIA and started from scratch.

In reality, the CIA of that time was still nearly as pluralized a community as was America itself, and there were at least two camps, philosophically, one essentially led by Bissell, the other by Richard Helms, the deputy chief of operations. Bissell's group backed the Cuban invasion to the fullest. Helms's group, however, believed that large, paramilitary operations like the Bay of Pigs idea "would destroy the CIA."[11] Helms and his fellow executives, largely from Ivy League backgrounds, saw the Agency as an intellectual's intelligence-gathering apparatus, not a dirty military training ground. Their talent was in their collective brain power, not their testosterone.

But Bissell and Dulles were adamantly pressing Jack forward, even though their reconnaissance had told them it was "unachievable." It is likely that they assumed that Jack knew the risks—that deniability might have to yield to the undeniable force of U.S. troops if things got dicey on the ground. The Iran and Guatemala coups had been finessed without the need for an overt incursion, so perhaps they figured that the third time was charmed as well. Whatever their assumptions, on the eleventh of March, Bissell sat down to brief the president in the Cabinet Room, along with the Joint Chiefs of Staff, the new defense secretary, Robert McNamara, Secretary of State Dean Rusk, and McGeorge Bundy.

The Trinidad plan had been slow-cooked and seasoned to a stew of contradictory ideas. It provided for a brigade of 750 men who would land on a beach near the port on the south coast of Cuba. Bissell had based the assault on the landing at Anzio in World War II (not incidentally, a disaster for the Allies); but as his lecture unfolded, Kennedy, who had been so studiously neutral in times past, suddenly stopped him, full of questions. The strategy, flawed though it was, actually made some sense: if the invaders could make their way into the mountains, where popular resentment of Castro was thought to be greatest, they might, over time, replicate Fidel's own Sierra Maestra success. The president, however, was more concerned with initial appearances than with the long-term (and probably incalculable) prospects for a successful guerrilla movement. He wanted a low-profile insertion, not an invasion per se.

"It's too spectacular," said Jack. "It sounds like D-day. You have to reduce the noise level of this thing."

The former Yale professor with the impeccable manners almost forgot presidential etiquette. "But you have to understand—" he began.

But the president understood him perfectly, and he still wasn't impressed; the political dimension had been left completely unconsidered. He preferred military risk to political risk, he insisted. There could be no open military action taken by the United States. There could be no discernible CIA footprint, and that was that.

Jack sent Dick back to the drawing board, demanding a more solitary landing site and much less racket, but the inherent contradiction would never be reconciled. Without the "noise," the tacit threat of the American fist, this pitifully small brigade would be to Fidel's two hundred thousand men what a minnow was to a barracuda. It would be a snack.

On March 13, the entire Latin American diplomatic corps was invited to assemble in the East Room of the White House, where the new First Lady greeted them in her impeccable Spanish. She led the diplomats and their spouses on an hour-long tour of the executive mansion; when they returned, the Marine band played, the crowd was seated, and the president commenced to christen the "Alliance for Progress."

"We meet together as firm and ancient friends," he declared, invoking a past that never really was. "Our continents are bound together by a common history, the endless exploration of new frontiers. Our nations are the product of common struggle, the revolt from colonial rule. And our people share a common heritage, the quest for the dignity and the freedom of man." It was a powerful speech, one of Goodwin's best, moving boldly and gracefully from an admission of America's sins in the region to a pointed indictment of the indigenous oligarchs for sins of their own, and ending with hope for absolution in the form of a Ten Year Plan for the Americas.

"With steps such as these," Jack went on, "we propose to complete the revolution of the Americas . . . To achieve this goal, political freedom must accompany material progress . . . Therefore let us express our special friendship to the people of Cuba and the Dominican Republic—and the hope they will soon rejoin the society of free men."

While the higher precepts of social change were being applied in the East Room, man's lower nature was running amok outside. Staff D's talent search for a Castro hit man was going global. Bissell, Bill Harvey, and the CIA's Dr. Sidney Gottlieb, from the Science and Technology Directorate, were still working on killing methods for Johnny Rosselli and the Outfit prospects. Harvey was trying to recruit one Jose Marie Andre Mankel, a dope smuggler and mercenary from Cologne, Germany, who had been a CIA gun in pursuit of Lumumba.

June Cobb's former boss Juan Orta Cordova, Fidel's private secretary, had agreed to slip him a poison pill; six pills had been given to the Rosselli/Giancana team to pass to Orta. The pills were designed to act slowly, giving Orta time to slip them into Fidel's espresso and then get away; but if pills and java and Fidel failed to meet, then there was an employee in the Pekin Chinese restaurant who had agreed to tuck some pills into a duck.

It was also sometime during that period that Rolando Cubela Secades, a major in the new Cuban Army, was in Mexico City for his first meeting with the CIA, a relationship that would continue until the day Jack Kennedy died. The wolf had shaved his beard. He looked almost collegiate, like a young fraternity man, but there remained something canine about him, as if his loyalty could go to whoever fed him. There was also an epicene aspect to Rolando Cubela. In the coming years it would be alleged that this man who professed hatred of Fidel was also Raúl's occasional lover. That alone might explain what would become of Cubela. No matter how recklessly he played the game between Fidel, Bobby, Raúl, and Jack, he would manage to live through it.

Even then, in March 1961, Cubela had already shown that he could stretch the bounds of Fidel's patience. He was well up in the Castro brothers' hierarchy, now the leader of Cuba's International Federation of Students, an organization that often served as cover for vetting potential pro-Fidel assets abroad. As such, he traveled at will and stayed away from Cuba for long, and apparently un-policed, stretches of time. Rolando had tasted the fruits of the Free World. He had lived in foreign capitals. He had seduced stewardesses on jet planes. He was a citizen of the planet, and it appears that he came and went as he pleased.

And when he met with the American spies, Cubela made it clear that he was itching to take "action" against Castro, the man who had stolen his revolution. He and comrade Juan Orta wanted to defect, he said, and Cubela must have been convincing because plans for a surgical "exfiltration" were apparently undertaken then and there.[12] Orta was still slated to try to kill Fidel; but in any case, they would be extracted. Those were the plans.

But as they were being implemented, it appeared that Fidel was becoming suspicious of his friend. The defection would have to be postponed, perhaps curtailed altogether. A pattern was being established. No matter how long Rolando's leash, no matter how much he kept saying that he wanted to oust Fidel, he never seemed to want to take things to the final phase. Whether it was because he was nervous about stepping straight into the power void when Fidel died, or because he was ultimately one of his most loyal spies, has been a subject of speculation for over forty years. The truth of his motivation would prove much more self-serving.

The Friday following the White House diplomatic reception for the Alliance for Progress, March 17, Marina Prusakova was dressing to go out for a dance at the Minsk Palace of Culture. She was still playing the field. On that night, she was toying with the affections of both Sasha and Anatoly, and as she languished in front of the mirror at her uncle Ilya's flat, sculpting her hair into this shape and that, both boys were already waiting for her outside the palace.

At 10 P.M., she arrived in a red Chinese brocade dress. Sasha, the lapdog, had been waiting outside for almost three hours. Anatoly was nowhere to be seen, not even in the overlit, cavernous hall that Sasha stiffly danced her around. She was bored to frozen tears, but another young man came along, one named Yury. He had a dusky-eyed stranger with him. Dressed in a gray suit and a white-on-white shirt and tie, the stranger seemed sure of himself. He introduced himself as "Alik" and quickly asked Sasha for permission to dance with her.

Alik impressed her immediately. He danced with a certain panache. He was well mannered and well groomed. She suspected from his accent that he was Estonian or Latvian, and when she told him her name, he said it was pretty. Yeah, she thought, the lamest line in the book, but his charms did gain some depth as they kept talking.

"It's not just your name that's pretty," Lee said. "You're pretty too. I saw you when you came in. I was trying to figure out how to meet you, but you had a crowd around you. I'm glad we finally met . . ."

He wouldn't dance with anyone else, even when poor Sasha managed to start her up again. She was combing the room for Anatoly, hoping to drive him to distraction, but she still couldn't find him, and by now she had a covey of men following her into the bar. Lee hung back. Much champagne was consumed, Marina reveling in the attention so much that when the self-possessed Anatoly finally appeared, she treated him like a puppy she was trying to shake off her leg. Lee was transfixed by her.

He had lost the affection of Ella Germann just ten weeks earlier. Women of such quality seldom latched on to him for long, and perhaps it was just as well. They might only disappoint each other. But tonight he had found another sort of woman, a minx, a libertine, a "matchstick" girl in a red dress with an incandescent sexuality that captured him immediately.

He kept his wits about him, however. They all repaired to Yury's house, and when she found out that he was American, he had her attention as certainly as she had grabbed his.

She "liked the way he talked. She especially liked the way he stuck up for his country. She asked him if he loved America. He did, he said, but he did not love everything about it."[13] There was unemployment and there was racism. Education and medical care were too expensive, but housing was better in America than in Russia. There was more space for the cost. After his incredible journey to leave the States, after circling the globe and slicing his wrist and moving alone to a city where he knew no one and could not speak the language, just to get away from the reviled country of his birth, he found himself telling this group of tipsy young bohemian Communists that America was probably a more democratic country because of free speech.

When he conversed with a few other boys in English, Marina was spellbound. She took him back to her aunt and uncle's flat. Aunt Valya let her in and then hurried back to bed when she realized her niece had brought some other kids home. Marina tiptoed along behind her, whispering excitedly.

"Sasha's here," she said, ". . . Sasha and another boy, an American. He's really nice. Come in and I'll introduce you—"

"Are you out of your mind?" Valya scolded. "Bringing an American here and the place in such a mess?! . . . I look awful," she muttered, shuffling back to bed. "Oh, my God, an American was the only thing lacking in your collection."[14]

Marina had always wanted to go to America. One of her beaus, Oleg Tarusin, said that she was always "desperate to leave the USSR."[15] Now she had a real live American boy in her sights, and they were so much alike— raised by their mothers, never having known their fathers, volatile and lonely and dying to break out of themselves. A month later, on the eve of the Cuban invasion, Lee would propose marriage.

In the weeks between Lee's first meeting with Marina and the day he proposed, Fidel Castro spent his days in preparation for John F. Kennedy's doomed brigade. But Fidel's would-be assassins were either losing his scent or losing their desire. Juan Orta, opting not to risk torture or a firing squad, sought refuge at the Venezuelan embassy on April 11. He would stay indoors for three and a half years, first there and then in the Mexican embassy, until, for some reason, Fidel allowed him to escape to Mexico City. He finally arrived in Miami in February 1965, where he became a highway toll collector. He died of diabetes in Miami in 1977 at age seventy-three.

Bobby, perhaps unaware of the unholy alliance between spies and gangsters at this point, or of the backroom deals his own father had cut to secure Jack's election, was bearing down on the very people who were bearing down on the Castros—the very ones who controlled a vast nationwide labor voting bloc. It seems that "Mooney" Giancana and Johnny Rosselli exacted their revenge by quietly ordering their people to "stand down" on the plots.

"Mooney's going to get even with the Kennedys."

So spoke the brains of the Outfit, Murray "Curly" Humphreys, to his wife, Jeanne. In a series of conversations shortly before her death in 2001, Curly's widow Jeanne said she was not a bit surprised that the mob felt betrayed. "Before Kennedy was elected," Jeanne said matter-of-factly, "from what I understand, [the assassination plot] was legitimate. But after the Kennedys started going after the Outfit, as they did after the election, Mooney decided to string them along to get even with them." Rosselli later admitted that after the word came down from Chicago, the plots "never got further than Santo" Trafficante. Trafficante himself told his lawyer that one batch of poison pills he received from the CIA were never even sent to Cuba. "I just flushed them down the toilet," he said.[16]

The Bearded One did not dwell on his own death much, or so it appears. In the weeks leading up to the invasion, given the yield of intelligence from G2, he was dwelling only on how to defend Cuba from the coming attack. A CIA memorandum written two years later would provide rich detail of those weeks, and of Fidel's new Cuba in general.

By the time Jack was in the White House, Cuba was awash in revolutionary propaganda. There was almost no advertising anymore, the billboards and buildings and newspapers festooned instead with government slogans

and inspirational verse. Sports events had seen a recent uptick in attendance, a sign to Fidel that the people were happy, and the streets were full of
the usual festive Cuban uproar on Saturday nights. On Sundays, or at least
on major religious holidays, the churches were still full, though any clergy
that resisted the Castros were no longer at their pulpits.[17] And Fidel made it
a point to be out among the people as often as possible, basking in their
attention and waving back when they called out to him.

He was invigorated by the pace of his life and the affection of those
Cubans who had avoided incarceration or worse. Despite his irregular hours,
the hurried or missed meals, and the stresses of governing and of avoiding assassination, Fidel was sleeping six hours a night and—when not absorbed in
work—he enjoyed the physical challenges of everything from underwater
spearfishing to baseball. He ate lightly and topped off most meals with a dish
of sour milk. Orange juice was his drink of choice, except for a couple of
scotch-and-sodas on Saturday nights, and his consumption of cigars was
fairly constant.[18] Given the purges that had been under way for two years,
Fidel was quite secure among crowds of ordinary Cubans, thinking of them
as insulation from any potential assassin. He learned from the people and
believed that moving among them increased their respect and affection for
him, even if they harbored silent grudges against his government.[19]

He was not an easy target. Eight to twelve men traveled with him in a
three-car caravan of late-fifties Oldsmobiles, Fidel's in the middle, often
with him at the wheel. One of the guards prepared all his meals and served
him, even when he was out at a restaurant, so any poisoning plots probably
wouldn't have worked anyway. All of his men were armed with stun guns,
automatic rifles, and machine guns. Their convoy whipped through the countryside and the city alike at top speed, and the rear car's driver was expert at
preventing any other vehicle from joining the motorcade.[20]

He had also taken great pains to change the relationship of the Cuban
people to their army. Under Batista, the militias had been considered little
more than plunderers. Whatever the reality in the countryside, the ideal Castro promulgated was that soldiers were to pay for whatever necessities they
appropriated, and that the people consider them to be in their humble service.[21] This too was thought to enhance his security.

He was already building low-cost housing, fifteen thousand apartments
planned for the road to Varadero alone. They were making pervasive use of
brightly painted cinderblock wherever homes were needed, and he wanted
vacation houses for workers, resorts and fisheries and state farms. Despite
the early stages of what would soon become a full-blown drought, he was

planting trees, millions of them up and down the country, and he had taken action to diversify the nation's agricultural base beyond what had been its mono-crop, sugar.

All of Cuba was there for him to re-create, and as he greeted the third spring of his reign, Fidel Castro was a veritable dervish of creation.

The Bay of Pigs, roughly ten by twenty miles, sits on Cuba's southern coast. (The name actually has nothing to do with a swimming porcine population— it is a mistranslation of Bahia de Cochinos, Bay of Triggerfish, an odd creature that grunts like a pig when hooked.) At the northern end lies Playa Larga, at the eastern side Playa Giron.

Fidel knew the Bay very well. It was one of his favorite fishing spots; he often spent weekends there at what became known to his bodyguards as "Fidel's key." Salt marshes extended around the bay, some five miles in width and virtually impassable except for two roads, a main one running through, which connected to another one cut from the eastern side. The surrounding countryside was flat. There were no hills nearby where invaders might vanish into a guerrilla mist. Whoever controlled the far ends of these roads controlled them in their entirety, everything from the solid ground, at the north end of the marshes, to the beach. The salt marshes were spongy. A man trying to hike through them would quickly sink to midcalf and, if he lingered, was apt to trap himself in viscous muck. Thus, the roads had been constructed by laying a sandwich of pulverized rock and packed dirt on top of the rock base, reached only by arduous digging deep under the marshes. It would prove to have been a fortuitous piece of engineering.

Fidel already knew that the invading brigade was being led by "military minds," regular officers with the usual methods. He did not hold "the military mind" in very high regard. His revolutionary experience and guerrilla temperament had convinced him that the methods and movements of military regulars were predictable and lacking in contingency plans. Along with monitoring the training camps in Guatemala, Fidel's G2 and DGI had been combing through American press coverage in the weeks leading up to the assault. The imminent invasion was obvious from the intelligence Escalante and company were providing. The only thing that could not be easily discerned was the exact date of the charge, and whether it would come in the form of a unified front or a number of coastal landing parties that would attack at multiple points. Fidel claimed, two years afterward, that he had been confident that the site would be the Bay of Pigs. First, he reasoned, they would try to decimate his air force, so he spread his planes all over the island

and had them camouflaged.[22] He would need more men trained in artillery, including antiaircraft weapons, so he put his team of Czech experts (a gift from the Eastern bloc) to work teaching droves of Cuban soldiers in the mornings. Those students, in turn, would then train the next crowd that afternoon, day after day, until his fifty-four 20-millimeter antiaircraft guns were fully manned. As far as he was concerned, nothing short of massive air support would break the back of his artillery.

A few months earlier, in early January, Sergio Arcacha Smith stood up to address the New Orleans Junior Chamber of Commerce, declaring that "Cubans will launch an invasion sometime in 1961 to overthrow the regime." The actual invasion wouldn't be launched from America, he said, "but Cubans are being recruited by the front [Frente/FRD] in this country and sent elsewhere to train." It was anticipated that the counterrevolution would take some six months to achieve its victory, and Sergio turned the speech into a fund-raiser to help in combating Communist propaganda "all over Latin America." He shared the dais that day with Oscar Higgenbotham, a former executive of the Central Espana Sugar Mills in central Cuba, and with Carlos Márquez Díaz, another former Cuban consul who was removed when the Castros took power. Both men were helping to finance the New Orleans–based resistance.[23]

The next day, another of their colleagues announced the opening of offices for the Friends of Democratic Cuba, Inc., at 402 St. Charles Street, in the Balter Building. Money would be raised, a charter would be forthcoming; the FDC membership was already building rapidly.

By April, Sergio still couldn't provide any funds of his own yet, but he had maintained his disciplined habits and he was still a natural, avuncular leader. He arose early each day and would go first to the shortwave radio he kept near at hand, making note of any coded messages that might be bringing fresh information from the rapidly expanding network of insurgents, both inside Cuba and in the States. There was chatter on this April morning, but nothing he had time to decipher.

He and Shelia and the children had been living in New Orleans for six months, but the transition to American life had been disorienting and still they were struggling. At age thirty-eight, he was feeding his family on donations from a Cuban charity group and looking for work, hopefully back in hotel management. A proud man, he would spend nearly an hour every morning grooming himself and preparing his clothes so that no one he met would suspect the true state of their lives, and his only solace was to get ever more deeply engaged in the exile plots. Sergio may have been struggling in private, but in public he had quickly become the face of local resistance to the Castros.

By now, the FDC was working at fever pitch—trying to procure six ambulances, create a field hospital, and air-drop medical aid to Frente-supported guerrillas already fighting Castro in eastern Cuba. What's more, they were endeavoring to help get an estimated fifty-two thousand dissident Cubans out of the country. They had also enlisted a former FBI man, now a local detective, to conduct background checks on Cuban students who wanted to join Sergio's group, making sure that none of them were actually pro-Castro sympathizers.[24] These students were actually bound for more than office work at the FDC; they were looking to be trained as part of Brigade 2506.

A week before the invasion, Sergio told the New Orleans press, "Preparations are almost complete for an anti-Castro invasion . . . [it] could begin this afternoon, tomorrow, anytime. We are just waiting for the signal."[25]

So much for secrecy. Sergio would later admit that "Cubans talk too much," himself included, and Fidel had his eyes and ears in New Orleans as well as Miami.

By this time, the Soviet Union itself had advance word of the attack. Even though Khrushchev was dubious of the reports, thinking Kennedy more purposeful than that, the Kremlin knew a week in advance. What's worse is that the CIA *knew* that Moscow had pierced the veil of secrecy, knew in fact that the Cubans had at least four double agents inside the Guatemalan camps. No one on the anti-Castro side knew the exact date of the invasion except people at the highest levels of the operational planning, not the exiles, nor members of the cabinet. And yet not only had the Soviets pinpointed the exact date, April 17, but there would be no official indication that Bissell or Dulles told President Kennedy this piece of news.[26]

In hindsight, the Agency's lies of omission would come to seem nearly equal to what truths they did report. A fiction was being created for the president, a narrative with less and less resemblance to the truth, and it was way too late to stop it now.

At 11:00 P.M. on the Sunday before the invasion, Sergio received a coded message from the invasion force on his shortwave radio at his home: "Look to the rainbow. The sky is clear. The fish are ready."

This was it. The liberation of his homeland was imminent. He believed it with all his heart and soul.

Some of the more discerning exiled Cubans, among them Ernest Betancourt (no relation to Rómulo in Venezuela), a former supporter of the Castros who had defected, thought the invasion plan was a pure example of late-colonialist ignorance. When he tried to warn the White House, he was rebuffed. He went then to Charlie Bartlett, Jack's longtime confidant, and tried to reason with him. Betancourt insisted that the Kennedys were seeing the Castros purely through the Cold War context and were not realistic about Fidel's popularity. He told Bartlett "that the operation was anti-historical. There was a total lack of understanding [in Washington] of what Fidel had done." Bartlett didn't convey it to Jack, and instead warned the Cuban Cassandra that he was putting himself in political jeopardy to keep harping on it.[27]

It might have been anti-historical, but it was now inevitable.

Two days before the invasion was scheduled to commence, the president approved an attack of six B-26 bombers against what they could find of Fidel's air force. They hit less than half of it, and his bombers and the training jets that had been armed with rockets came through unscathed. The first bombing sortie was deemed inadequate. All it did was prompt Cuban and Russian protests.[28]

At this point, Cuba was festooned with warnings of an invasion. Posters showing troops with RPD light machine guns read "*Alerta! Alerta!*" and now it was confirmed: the United States had drawn the first blood in this not-so-secret war. With this confirmation that the big guns had him in their sights, Fidel finally admitted to the world, in a portentous speech to his people, that he was a "socialist." If he was about to be preemptively attacked by the most powerful army in history, he would at least declare his true colors and go down fighting.

A second bombing raid had been planned for April 16, the day before the invasion, but Jack canceled it, removing himself to his newly leased country retreat, Glen Ora, forty miles west of the White House in Virginia, and leaving Secretary of State Rusk to run interference. Given his stated preference for the Agency's style over the State Department's, Jack's remove suggests that his instincts were already on alert, that he may have sensed a fait accompli by the Agency and realized that he needed State in the mix after all. Rusk was considered cautious in the extreme, even timid, but suddenly the Agency was having to go through him to get answers.

In fact, the president was trying to have it both ways, caught, as usual, between the international left and the American right. The first raid had sounded an alarm in the Communist world, just as Jack was on the brink of a coveted summit with Soviet premier Khrushchev. If Fidel's air force was still viable, it imperiled the exile invaders. But a second air raid would point straight back to Washington, thus imperiling the Khrushchev summit and Jack's chance for an early foreign policy bonanza. He would rather take political heat for a failed invasion (should it fail) than balk and have his own right wing on the rampage. Politics prevailed.[29]

Bissell was alarmed. He had assumed that he and Jack were in total synch, so when he was suddenly refused access to a president he had been increasingly close to in recent months, he and Deputy Director Cabell went straight to Foggy Bottom to confront the secretary. They were certain that if the second air raid did not commence at once, the entire invasion plan would crumble. It was vital to take out more aircraft, Cabell said, because the invasion's ships and troops would be so highly exposed to bombardment as the men came ashore. Rusk, who had earned his stripes as a colonel in the Burma theater of World War II, was less than convinced. He shared Jack's suspicion that the Agency was hyping the risks and luring the Pentagon into the fray. And it appears now that this was precisely what Bissell was doing. That was, after all, the striking caveat of the CIA's internal memo five months before: "Our second concept (1,500–3,000) man force to secure a beach with airstrip is also now seen to be unachievable, *except as a joint Agency/DOD action*" [emphasis added].

The plan had been adulterated, probably fatally. The original plot was to have been a landing at Trinidad, an anticommunist stronghold near the Escambray Mountains, which had a good airstrip, a mountain sanctuary where fighters could disappear if their invasion failed, and a local population ready to either protect or fight alongside them. The White House, however, aspiring to "plausible deniability," a newfangled and subjective realm of strategic thinking, had moved the site to a place that would prove disastrous. A group of between 1,400 and 1,500 men, now named Brigade 2506, would land in a secluded swamp hoping to spark a counterinsurgency, then cross the island to Havana, topple Fidel, and insert a provisional government. To do it, they had chartered four transport vessels, the *Río Escondido*, the *Houston*, the *Caribe*, and the *Atlántico*. Two CIA-owned infantry landing craft were also part of the armada, the *Blagar* and the *Barbara J.*

Rusk suggested that the ships that carried the men and materiel be offloaded by night. He also held that, as in Burma, air attacks were less of a real danger than an irritation. Military arguments had held sway with the first day's bombing, but now the political ones were foremost. The Agency men wouldn't relent, however, and, as they sat in Rusk's office, the secretary called Jack at Glen Ora. If Kennedy was not going to authorize offensive strikes against Castro's air force, then, Cabell begged, he should at least allow for defensive action from planes aboard the aircraft carrier USS *Boxer*, waiting fifty miles off Cuba as they spoke. He wanted that squad to be able to cover the fleet as it withdrew, but again Jack refused.[30]

Fidel was asleep in Havana when he was awakened with the news that the invasion had begun. According to him, within minutes of his arrival at the Bay of Pigs, he concluded that this attack was a diversion. In all likelihood, he simply couldn't imagine that the *brigadistas* would try to seize the country from such a boggy corner of the southwest side of the island. He believed that the main wave would hit at Pinar del Río, where Che was in command of several thousand troops, primed for battle. It was three hundred miles away, but Fidel set out for it straight away.

Pinar del Río was the closest spot in Cuba to the United States, which explains Fidel and Che's assumption. But in fact, the only army coming ashore there was a fake one, a miniature facsimile of the force that had driven Árbenz out of office in Guatemala City seven years earlier. The only threat to Pinar del Río was a CIA team with three rowboats full of mirrors, bottle rockets, Roman candles, sparklers, smoke bombs, and tape-recorded battle sounds. When Fidel arrived there and the ruse became apparent, he immediately headed back to the site he had originally suspected, the Bay of Pigs.[31]

No sooner had Fidel left than Che gave himself a subcutaneous wound with his own gun, probably a misfire. The bullet ripped through his chin and made its exit just above his temple, sparing his brain but taking him out of the fray for the next three days. The scars would be clear in every photo taken thereafter, but they were not the scars of battle.

The exiles were making an amphibious landing while something close to forty-one thousand Cuban troops and militia were already moving to greet them. The Brigade, most of whom had been trained for no more than a month, were carrying light weapons and had only a day's ammunition. Fidel's forces had been well stocked by the Soviets with heavy artillery, planes, and tanks.

For all of Jack's efforts not to leave a Yankee footprint, the first shot fired was from the gun of an American CIA agent as he led the Brigade's frogmen ashore. His bullets hit a Cuban army jeep.[32] Soon the battle was in full fever.

By Castro's account, it was obvious that he already had the air advantage, and he immediately ordered his planes to ignore the insurgent troops on the beach and proceed straight to the landing vessels in the distance. The insurgents advanced without much initial resistance. The militia, trained by Che, was almost immediately in chaotic flight from the exiles' first volley. (This may have been due to the same psychological domination that had prevailed in the Guatemalan coup. Fidel's confidence may have been high, but his troops, assuming it was essentially an American attack, were braced for D-day.) Batteries of Soviet 122-mm howitzers were wheeled into place. Two thousand rounds of fire filled the air and still the Brigade advanced, their meager airborne assets directed straight at the Cuban troops as they fanned out to engage paratroopers at the road head. Nilo Messer, an exile survivor, would recount that as the first blood-match exploded, "the *milicianos* surrendered in droves. One entire battalion . . . surrendered en masse. So a couple of our guys are sitting there guarding a few hundred *milicianos*! But finally the Castro troops caught on. They saw we'd been abandoned, saw nothing else was coming, and realized how badly they outnumbered us."[33]

Fidel's planes were bombarding the ships without much return fire, and once he gained the upper hand, he wouldn't stop dominating the battle in the air.

Meanwhile, many of the Brigade's amphibious launches were being caught on the heavy coral reefs across the entrance to the Bay. Fidel assumed that the exiles' provisional government was aboard the ships, waiting for a signal to come ashore. It was apparent that the Brigade was not in a position to seize much turf, much less stir the masses to join the revolt. They were bogged down in the hostile terrain, and Fidel moved to assure that any such provisional leadership would not make it to the beach behind them, unleashing wave after wave of Cuban regulars against the Brigade.[34] In that first day, the *brigadistas* sustained more casualties, man for man, than the U.S. forces at Normandy had in June 1944; but, under repeated strafings and a rain of Soviet artillery shells, they held firm.

Fidel's fear that his counterrevolutionary successors might be aboard the ships was logical but incorrect. In fact, the Cuban Revolutionary Council (CRC), held together now by Agency spit and baling wire, was being kept incommunicado in a house in Opa-locka, Florida. Once it was clear that the invasion was under way, their leaders, who knew less in advance of the landing than Fidel himself did, were begging to be flown to the front, but they remained sequestered.

In their stead, the CIA's PR man, Howard Hunt, released a bulletin, putatively from the CRC, which opened: "Before dawn, Cuban patriots in the cities and hills began the battle to liberate our homeland from the despotic rule of Fidel Castro." The ruse worked, at least initially; the story was that a small landing had occurred for the purposes of sparking and supplying an indigenous uprising, and the American press ran with it.

On the beaches, chaos reigned. Fidel's troops were using runners to communicate, not radios, and this led to a number of bungled messages. That in turn sparked flashes of friendly fire among the Cuban regulars, and the battle burned on into the night.[35]

By dawn of day two, the CIA informed Jack that the Brigade was surrounded and would be slaughtered unless he ordered a direct intervention by the U.S. Navy. At the CIA command post, an unshaven, indignant, and rattled Richard Bissell demanded that the president authorize an American air strike to fend off the encircling Cuban regulars. He was dumbstruck that the president would let the operation crash and burn when he had such extraordinary power to prevent it; but at the White House, when the admiral in charge of the Navy off the Cuban coast pleaded with Jack to let him retaliate, the president took one of the magnetized ship models from the war map and slid it farther into the blue expanse of open sea. He wanted the American ships moved far beyond the Cuban horizon, as if his authorship of the attack could still be denied.

The *Houston* was sunk, the men aboard either drowning or being eaten by sharks. Then the *Río Escondido* started taking fire. It was the only supply line left, loaded for ten days of fighting, but it was ordered to withdraw. The *Blagar* did what it could to fend off the air attacks.

On the beach, Pepe San Roman, the Brigade's commander, was madly signaling headquarters: DO YOU PEOPLE REALIZE HOW DESPERATE THE SITUATION IS? DO YOU BACK US OR QUIT? ALL WE WANT IS LOW JET COVER. ENEMY HAS THIS SUPPORT. I NEED IT BADLY OR CANNOT SURVIVE. PEPE.

On the second night of the battle, the annual congressional reception was under way at the White House, a white-tie affair hosted primarily by the First Lady, since Jack kept leaving to get updates on the battle. At one point, Jackie was on the dance floor with Jack's crony, Senator George Smathers of Florida, when Bobby cut in and took Smathers by the arm, leading him away.

Vice President Johnson followed them out of the reception.

"What the hell's goin' on, Bob?!" Lyndon asked.

"The shit has hit the fan," Bobby seethed, leading the way through the mansion. "The thing has turned sour in a way you wouldn't believe!"

Along with Bobby and Lyndon, Jack had summoned from the party the

Joint Chiefs in their full dress uniforms, along with Secretary of Defense Bob McNamara, Secretary Rusk, Admiral Arleigh Burke, and General Lyman Lemnitzer. Some accounts place Richard Goodwin, McGeorge Bundy, and General Maxwell Taylor there as well. Bissell was most certainly there, looking haunted and pale with rage. Brigade members were dying on the beach, he said. In Miami, the confined CRC leaders had discerned the crisis, and, as Bissell went on, his voice trembling with restraint, he made it clear that only if jets were launched from the U.S.S. *Essex* could victory be snatched from almost certain defeat.

But Jack was livid and reminded Bissell that he had warned him "over and over again" that he would not send American troops into combat to save the operation.

Someone referred to sketchy reports that mass arrests were under way in Havana. In fact, several hundred thousand potential freedom fighters had been rounded up in recent weeks, including throughout the battle. Rebels in the Escambray Mountains had been contained by the Cuban militia, thus couldn't have made it to support the Brigade in the Bay of Pigs region; and the two most capable officers suspected of being their leaders, William Morgan and Humberto Sori Marin, had been shot.

Goodwin demanded to know why the internal Cuban opposition wasn't warned, but Bissell cut him off. The problem was far more desperate now. Whatever the internal political conditions were—and no one really knew, of course—the resupply wasn't making it to shore. Bissell had planes searching the swamps for survivors, but—

Jack interjected. It appeared that the Russians were threatening to seize West Berlin if the U.S. made an open move on Cuba. There were also updated reports that one member of the Cuban Revolutionary Council, enraged at being sequestered in Florida, was threatening to commit suicide. All were furious at having been sidelined by the gringo masterminds. Some of them had sons on that beach.

And Richard Bissell was at full throttle. They were facing the complete destruction of forces they had sponsored, he ranted. All sabotage and propaganda broadcasts had broken down and, with the cancellation of the second bombing raid, the brigade was without 80 percent of the air support they had expected.

Bobby was equally enraged. What if additional air cover didn't make the difference? What if it just meant a delay before collapse, and the U.S. was exposed with no hope of victory? Bissell snarled back at him that the situation could still be redeemed, but only with air cover. It was the nadir of John Kennedy's public life. Shaking his head, rubbing his hands repeatedly over his eyes, he made a choice, an awful, perhaps futile choice, but one that Bissell could accept, if only as a stopgap measure. At 3:30 A.M. he authorized six unmarked Navy fighters to provide air cover for a bombing run by the B-26s, which in turn would allow the exiles' ammunition resupply from the ships. With that bit of cover, the warships and the LCUs could unload at Giron, but the jets were not to attack ground targets under any circumstances.

Rusk warned that Jack had already promised there would be no American intervention. He would be proven a liar if he went in now.

"Dean," Jack snapped, his hand raised to his chin, "we're already in it up to here."

Jack seemed close to tears of rage and dread, and Bob was unnerved by it. He went to his brother, put his hands on Jack's shoulders.

"They can't do this to you, Johnny," he murmured. "These fucking black-bearded Commies cannot do this to you."[36]

Jack just turned, pushed open the French doors behind his desk, and walked onto the dark lawn of the South Grounds. He trudged back and forth through the wet grass, the Secret Service detail keeping watch on his white-gray silhouette for well over an hour as he paced, his first great crisis at hand.

Dawn at Opa-locka Air Base in Florida found the leaders of the CRC sprawled on cots in a dilapidated barracks. When they were awakened, by a presidential delegation of Adolph Berle, the assistant secretary of state for Latin America, and Arthur Schlesinger, they looked heartsick and drained. The men from Washington brought little in the way of news. Miró Cardona, the president of the Cuban Revolutionary Council, wept at the sight of Kennedy's men, and it seemed to Schlesinger that he had aged ten years in a week. If the White House would not send in air cover, the battle would be lost, and if that was to be, then the CRC wanted to die with their forces on the beach. "It is this which I request," said Miró. "This which I beg."[37]

Tony Varona was so enraged that he could barely speak, spitting invective. Manuel Ray was much calmer, but he too took aim at the Agency. True, Fidel had been locking up indigenous rebel forces, but the CIA had not even made use of the sabotage operations those forces *had* put in place.

"For over a month, we've had a tunnel under the Havana electric-power installation," he reminded Kennedy's people. "We were told that ten to fifteen thousand men would be available." He claimed to still trust the president but implied that "those who really run things" were the ones who should take immediate responsibility to prevent a massacre, let the council drop the illusion that they were the leaders, and fly them to the battleground so they could fight as soldiers.[38]

When Varona threatened to go public if no air support was forthcoming and they weren't taken to the bay, Schlesinger frantically called the White House. Only a meeting with the president might prevent them from making years of secret planning horribly public. Late in the morning of Wednesday, April 19, the exhausted and infuriated members of the Cuban Revolutionary Council were released from their virtual house arrest at Opa-locka and flown, at Arthur Schlesinger's insistence, to Washington.

When Jack came back inside from his walk across the grounds, there was only more bad news. He slept briefly but woke up in his bedroom, weeping, heartsick at the horrors that had been unleashed. When he arrived downstairs in the Oval Office, his hair was askew and his tie was crooked, but he pulled himself together for the next emergency meeting in the Cabinet Room.[39]

After dawn, the Navy jets Jack had approved took flight from the USS *Essex*, but—because of confusion over time zones, the jets from the *Essex*, nearby, arrived an hour too early. They never found the B-26s lumbering in from Nicaragua. Two of the old bombers were shot down. A third dropped a load of napalm, hitting perhaps a thousand Cubans, but was hit by anti-aircraft fire. He made it back to base; but after the other two were hit, some of the supply ships had not dared to unload. Of the munitions that were released, most went into the sea.

On the Bahia de Cochinos, at 6:42 A.M., Pepe San Roman's next frantic message ended: . . . SEND MORE. At 7:12, his next one came: ENEMY ON TRUCKS ARE RIGHT NOW 3 KMS. FROM BLUE BEACH. The last one was: AM DESTROYING ALL MY EQUIPMENT AND COMMUNICATIONS. TANKS ARE IN SIGHT. I HAVE NOTHING TO FIGHT WITH. AM TAKING TO THE JUNGLE. I CANNOT WAIT FOR YOU. PEPE.

By the end of the third day, the *brigadistas* were out of food, out of ammunition. Scores of them lay dead, and hundreds had been wounded. Their mortar and machine-gun barrels had melted in the relentless combat. They had been abandoned. On the blood-soaked sand or half buried in the smoldering marshes lay thousands of dead and wounded from both sides. Estimates of exile casualties range from 100 to 120 *brigadistas* killed or wounded, and between 2,200 and 5,000 of the Castros' loyalists. The brigade's survivors would put the number at 114 exile casualties and 3,100 *Fidelistas*.[40]

Jack accepted defeat with statesmanlike grace. Dulles was asked to fall on his sword, and left the Agency. Bissell got himself a medal but would not ascend to the CIA director's position, and would never regain the Kennedys' trust any more than they would regain his.

There was evidence that the Agency had told the Brigade that, had the White House tried to call off the invasion, the CIA would have gone on anyway. Jack and his cabinet had gone forward with the assurance that an internal uprising was imminent, that the exiles were merely a fuse for widespread counterinsurgency. But the CIA had already admitted, internally, before Jack even took office, that there was little evidence of "a critical shift of popular opinion away from Castro"; by the end of 1960, it was already conceding the ruthless political efficiency of the Cuban regime, saying that any dissent would probably be "offset by the growing effectiveness of the state's instrumentalities of control."[41]

Less than three months into Jack's first term, the worst had happened—the immense apparatus of the American government had slipped from his control. As the scale of the calamity became clear, Jack's dependency on Bobby would increase exponentially. Jack would later bemoan the fact that he had not pulled Bobby into the Cuban plans from the start. Joe Sr.'s insistence on putting Bobby in the cabinet had never seemed more prescient. Given his host of enemies, both foreign and domestic, Jack could ill afford to lose his grip again.

He would try to get Bobby to take over the CIA, but Bobby convinced him that it would be more prudent if he simply became Jack's personal eyes and ears there. One of Jack's closest, lifelong friends, Lem Billings, would reflect, "Up until that time, Jack more or less dismissed the reasons his father had given for wanting Bobby in the cabinet as more of that tribal Irish thing. But now he realized how right the old man had been. When the crunch came . . . Bobby was the only person he could rely on to be absolutely dedicated. Jack would never have admitted it, but from that moment on the Kennedy presidency became a sort of collaboration between them."[42]

As Jack waited in the Oval Office for the CRC members to arrive from Opa-locka, looking drawn and wasted in his rocking chair, Walt Rostow sat across from him, watching him scan the front page of the *Washington News*. It was over, screamed the headlines. All hopes for a counterrevolution had collapsed. The Brigade had been defeated, and its members were now facing an uncertain fate.

While Rostow looked on, Jack "let the paper crumple onto the floor without a word."[43]

The Brigade members themselves knew that the sudden switch from Trinidad to the Bay had doomed the mission. "The Trinidad site was 400 percent better," said Erneido Oliva. "We have a big airstrip . . . We have a huge bay. We have a population that could have joined us. We were close to the Escambray Mountains . . . so there you have a source of reinforcement . . . from the population, from the guerrillas that were at that time in the Escambray. But they [the Kennedy administration] considered that it was too spectacular, that it would show the involvement of the United States, and that's something that they wanted always to hide. It was naive to try and hide something like that. How could the Cubans ever have been able to mount that type of operation? I don't know what those people were thinking at the time. It was more than naive. It was stupid to think that you can hide the hands of the Americans in something like that."

Nonetheless, Oliva refused to disparage the president—at least he tried, unlike his successors. "The others made a lot of promises during their respective political campaigns while running for the presidency, but did nothing when they attained it," he said.[44]

For the Castros, such a victory was almost unimaginable. Fidel was ecstatic, even as he wondered whether the botched attack by the Brigade would be followed by a direct assault by the U.S. military. When it didn't come, he helped to round up the *brigadistas* personally. Coming upon one group of twenty or so, bloodied and stunned but still armed, he had no fear of them. According to him, they simply confirmed his theory that regular military forces lost all initiative when their well-laid plans collapsed. The insurgents were quickly disarmed and herded into trucks. He would also claim that the death toll of the *milicianos* was not much greater than that of their enemy, no more than 150 to 180 dead.

But Castro had seen the battle at its most horrific. By some accounts, he was sniping at the invaders from a helicopter with his own rifle. He understood their valor, and in the coming days, he would quietly admit to one of the Brigade's men that he wished he had thousands like them in his own army.

The CRC's Manuel Artime was among those who fought on the beach; but, as the battle waned, he was not among the dead and could not be tracked. Another *brigadista*, Enrique "Harry" Ruiz-Williams, lay gravely wounded in an empty house on the shore, along with a few other men too mangled to do more than hide and wait for death. Harry had seventy wounds, he would later learn, and he was drifting into shock when a figure suddenly appeared in the rectangle of twilight where the door had been.

It was Fidel Castro. Harry knew it as soon as he could focus, and he groped for a .45 pistol he had stashed under the blood-drenched mattress he was lying on. He may even have grabbed and aimed it. He would never be able to remember for sure, years later, but Fidel knew what he intended.

"What are you trying to do, kill me?" he said. There was no particular anger in his voice. He might even have been amused.

"That's what I came here for," Harry gasped. "We've been trying to do that for three days."

One of Fidel's captains took the gun away and patted Harry softly. "Take it easy," he said. "Take it easy. You're in bad shape."

"Is there an American here?" Fidel wanted to know, shining a flashlight across the war-torn faces. When he could not readily identify one, he stepped back and lifted the shattered door off a body. It was the corpse of Oscar Vila, who had been beside Harry when a shell had exploded before them.

"This man is dead," said Fidel, dropping the door to the side. "These men can't stay here. Take them to Covadonga and put them in the hospital."[45]

On April 26, revolutionary guards herded the 1,189 surviving brigade members (114 had been killed) into the Sports Palace, where Fidel then lectured them for three and a half hours. Che had arrived at the Bay of Pigs just in time for the action to be over. His self-inflicted wound begs various explanations, though it does not seem like a simple attempt to avoid battle or he wouldn't have shot so close to his brain. Whatever the psychology of it, he swaggered into a roomful of captives upon his arrival and told them that they were all about to die. Fidel had already opted for a more cunning plan, however. He was not going to execute them, he said, not unless they were among Batista's war criminals.

During the public harangue of these traitors, these worms, these *gusanos*, one of the Brigade members asked him if he was a Communist. Fidel disregarded him, preferring instead to zero in on a black man among the prisoners, a man named Tomas Cruz.

"You," he scolded Cruz, "a Negro, what are you doing here?" Negroes lived free under his regime, he said. They were even allowed to go swimming alongside white people.

"I don't have any complex about my color or my race," Cruz murmured. "I have always been among white people, and I have always been as a brother to them. And I did not come here to go swimming."[46]

When the Brigade's commander, Pepe San Roman, was brought to the palace, it was not to the arena but to an office tucked high in the rafters. He was given a cup of coffee and a cigar, and then Fidel trudged in with the Cuban president, Osvaldo Dorticós, at his heels, along with a few other officials.

He treated Pepe to a rant about John Kennedy, what a madman he was, what a betrayer of the Brigade he was, what a pig.

"How is it that you are involved in this, San Roman?" Fidel wanted to know, with nagging astonishment. All Pepe would give him was his name, rank, and serial number. "How in the hell can you come here attacking our own country, helped by our enemies?! You are a traitor to your country. You have gone against all the rules and all the laws of the world. And now you say you are not going to talk?"

Fidel had Pepe locked in a small cell in a nearby building, returning days later to excoriate him again. During those long days and nights, Pepe became ever more enraged at what had happened on the beach. He was sure that his brother, Roberto, was dead, that Artime and Oliva and Ferrer were dead. Sometimes, amid fantasies of revenge and nightmares of execution, he would wonder if the Americans had not changed their minds at the last moment, had been unable to draw them back in time. But mostly, Pepe San Roman simply prepared himself for a long life in captivity.

His friend Manuel Artime managed to survive in the swamps for fourteen days, he and a few of his men living on little birds and whatever else they could catch. Early on, they found some fresh water; but as the days in the swamps dragged on, their thirst became so intense that they couldn't move their tongues, could not talk.

In the aftermath, Fidel moved constantly, charged up and craving the gratitude of the masses. He told a funeral crowd of ten thousand, "The United States sponsored the attack because it cannot forgive us for achieving a Socialist revolution under their noses!" A few days later, he delivered a four-hour victory speech to millions, on TV, saying: "Imperialism examines geography, analyzes the number of cannons, of planes, of tanks, the positions . . . The revolutionary examines the social composition of the population. The imperialists don't give a damn about how the population . . . thinks or feels."

There was nationwide applause, according to some accounts, and there was jubilation in the streets that night, despite the remaining chance that a greater attack was on its way.

At about the time that the invasion was being launched against Cuba, Lee and Marina were beginning a new phase of their romance. She had toyed with him after the first night of dancing, but he kept coming on. There were little gifts. He gave her other small signs that he was serious about her. When Uncle Ilya and Aunt Valya had him over to dinner, Ilya had made a toast to "the health and happiness of Americans in the USSR," and, as he stood up to leave the table, Lee had stood as well, a gesture of respect that Ilya liked. He pulled Lee aside as he repaired to his living room, saying, "Take care of this girl. She has plenty of breezes in her brain." And when the women cleared the table, Lee followed them into the kitchen and started giving them a hand, another bit of good manners her surrogate parents noticed.[47] He was very careful not to scare Marina away.

One night at his apartment, he caught her, eye-to-eye, and swore that she had to leave immediately or he would not be able to let her go all night. She left, delighted at having had such an effect. When he crept to the edge of a full-blown proposal a few days later, she skipped away for a bit, her friends aghast that she could dabble with an American boy that way. When he got carried away again with her one night, she distanced herself once more, keening that he was just another nasty boy with itchy fingers. But she kept coming back.

He told her he was an orphan. It drew her nearer. She too was an orphan. He had an apartment of his own. She had never had so much privacy with a boy before—a place like that was heaven to the matchstick girl. Okay, so she was not in love with him; but when he took her hand and strolled down the street with her, people noticed. The American was someone people noticed, someone who they knew about, and when he staked his claim to her she was more than just someone who was easy on the eyes: she was suddenly someone special.

He was not in love with her either. He admitted to his trusty diary that he was putting the rush on Marina to get back at Ella for jilting him in January. Ella must have given him some sense that he could be better, that he could transcend his past, that he might even belong somewhere, with someone of conscience and substance. Marina, one suspects, was a hot young pistol of a girl who churned up his hormones, who he could make do with but who would not really take him anywhere beyond the confines of himself.

When word leaked out that he had proposed marriage, Anatoly cornered her, accused her of falling for Lee because he was a foreigner with privileges. She tried to contain her true feelings. She already sensed that Lee might not stay in the motherland forever; and if he left, where else would he go but back to America? America.

On Sunday, April 30, she put on a simple, short wedding gown, white with some small, grassy flourishes, and accompanied Lee downtown to the government registry office, along with a neighbor in tow as a witness. There they were married by a kindly old man who warned them with a weary smile to "make allowances for each other's characters" and admonished her to be a good wife and not look at other boys.[48]

The marriage was a mistake. While riding its brief arc, she would try to console herself with fantasies of Anatoly Shpanko, the one who she left for Lee; the one with the wide smile and the insouciant air that would remind her of America's young president; the one she once described as "a rare person . . . honest in everything he did." With Lee, honesty was in short supply, and so was patience. Did she provoke his jealousy? A Communist Party archivist who would read their file years later would refer to Marina as a "complete slag." Others who were still monitoring Lee confirm that their relationship was a classic *amour fou*. He tried to strangle her once, but she gave as good as she got, according to the KGB. Discussions of divorce followed soon after the marriage ceremony, but the interim had left them pregnant.[49]

So it would only get stranger. For reasons she would never fully understand, he would be transformed over the next two and a half years into a person in gravitational collapse. In her diary, she would keep a poem tucked away:

> *I may curse you later*
> *Your features;*
> *To love you is like a disaster*
> *To which there is no end*
> *There is no friend, no comrade*
> *Who could drag me out of this conflagration*
> *In the broad light of day.*
> *Despairing of salvation*
> *I dream in the daytime*
> *And live near you*
> *As near an earthquake.*

CHAPTER 5

Meet the Boys on the Battlefront

M IRÓ CARDONA AND TWO of the others had sons on the beach at the Bay of Pigs, but only Antonio "Tony" Varona knew that his boy was dead, and none were yet aware of the ghastly extent of the failure when they arrived at the White House that afternoon. Jack, looking wasted in his rocking chair, sat between the six men who flanked him on the couches and apologized for their sequestration in Florida, which he claimed not to have known about. He reflected briefly on the death of his brother, Joe Jr., in World War II, but Tony Varona was not consoled.

Some say he actually addressed Jack as a "son-of-a-bitch"; it's commonly accepted that he said, "You've been taken for a ride, Mr. President, and this council has been taken for a ride."

With the slightest gesture, Jack seemed to concur. He *had* been taken for a ride: by Lemnitzer of the Joint Chiefs (whom Jack had concluded was a fool), and by the key men at the CIA. On balance, however, given the demands on the nation's security, he still could not authorize a follow-up invasion by U.S. troops. All he could do was to send in ships to try to rescue survivors that night. Through the conversation, there was the implicit threat that the CRC members would go public with their anguish. Jack reminded them that they were free to conduct themselves as they wished, but he made it plain that he would not give up on Cuba. That was enough to quiet their indignation, and the secrets were ultimately kept.

Schlesinger had been alarmed at the president's appearance when he came into the meeting, but by the end of it was stunned at how much he had rallied, wan demoralization turning to vigorous candor. It was a good thing he had regained himself.

Within hours, Dick Nixon was there with Kennedy in the Oval Office, called in as part of a "unity" offensive.

"[The Cuban debacle] was the worst experience of my life," Jack told Nixon, but he believed that the CRC would stand by him. "They're ready to go out and fight again, if we will give them the word and the support." Nixon took this in. He too must have been studying the new president, as had Schlesinger. It was more than professional courtesy that made Jack ask the next question—he was genuinely seeking Nixon's counsel.

"What would you do now?"

"I would find a proper legal cover and I would go in," Dick said. "The most important thing at this point is that we do whatever is necessary to get Castro and Communism out."

But Jack told him that he believed the risks to be too great. His best Kremlin experts were warning that Khrushchev might move on Berlin if the U.S. tried to take Cuba. For the next hour, the men talked of power dynamics from the Caribbean to Germany and Asia. South Vietnam's President Diêm, who was about to stand for reelection, was nervous that the U.S. might leave him in the lurch with *his* Communist threat. Assurances would have to be made, probably in the form of more American military advisers.[1]

Nixon pledged his support "to the hilt" that afternoon, but his party was already on the offensive, hitting hard at the inability of "the boys" to deal with the Havana regime. With Fidel openly admitting his Marxist allegiances, the Red Tide was now—as the Republicans kept repeating—just fifteen minutes off Miami Beach. And, although Kennedy might not have known it yet and would never have let Nixon know it, doubts about him were even creeping into the White House staff.

Talk turned to politics, their stock-in-trade. "The way things are going, and with all the problems we have," said Jack, "if I do the right kind of job, I don't know whether I'm going to be here in 1964." In that climate of fear, with toughness a political necessity but war an unpopular proposition, Kennedy's best instincts as president might be precisely the ones that would keep him from reelection.

"It really is true that foreign affairs is the only important issue for a president to handle, isn't it?" he said to Dick. "I mean, who gives a shit if the minimum wage is $1.15 or $1.25, in comparison to something like this?"

Depressed, embittered, and shaken, Jack Kennedy was learning all too quickly just how right Harry Truman had been about the office in which he sat. All the questions of right and wrong, of good and evil, were not only permissible here, they were essential. If there was any place on earth that was the fulcrum of human life or death in the mid-twentieth century, it was the

Oval Office of the White House. The buck stopped there, inside the president's own mind.

Across town, Bobby was transforming the once-stately Department of Justice into a three-ring circus of can-do activism. The youngest attorney general in the country's history took his mandate everywhere, thrusting the long arm of the law into corrupt labor unions, into the machinations of the mob, into the calculated disobedience of civil rights tacticians, and into the bloody secrets of the Ku Klux Klan. There was no place he seemed unwilling to venture in pursuit of a cleansed and purged and strengthened America. His pugnaciousness and entitlement were off-putting at first for many of the old hands at Justice, but they were balanced by equal measures of consideration and kindness. The place was suddenly imbued with a spirited sense of urgency and excellence which some had thought unlikely in the extreme. The radical priest was now the highest lawyer in the land.

Unbeknownst to official Washington or the American people, he had also become, in the wake of the Bay of Pigs, the virtual head of the CIA's counterinsurgency operations, if not of the Agency itself. Overnight, a thirty-six-year-old man with no experience in the intelligence field had become the eyes and ears of the president, his spy in the house of spies, and his covert field marshal. And, as Bobby expressed it soon after his appointment, his top priority was to "Get rid of that bastard Castro!"

The first part of Bobby's new sub-rosa appointment was to have him, along with his great friend (and Jack's military adviser) General Maxwell Taylor,* added to the powerful Special Group.† This White House committee, first formed in 1954 by President Eisenhower, was largely responsible for reviewing and approving covert action programs initiated by the CIA. Now, the new Special Group (Augmented) would oversee programs of aggressive sabotage against the Castro brothers.

When Bobby's day ended at Justice, he had his driver drop him off at the CIA, initially at its District headquarters on E Street and later that year at the spanking new central facility in Langley, Virginia, a ten-minute walk from his

---

*So close were Bobby and Taylor that in 1965 Bobby would name the ninth of his eleven children Maxwell Taylor Kennedy.
†The Special Group was chaired by President's Special Assistant for National Security Affairs McGeorge Bundy, and included Deputy Under Secretary of State U. Alexis Johnson, Deputy Secretary of Defense Roswell Gilpatric, Director of Central Intelligence Allen Dulles, and Chairman of the Joint Chiefs of Staff General Lyman Lemnitzer.

family's nineteenth-century manse, Hickory Hill, in McLean. He was there to do battle. Bobby had a nearly obsessive mistrust of career spies, a feeling obviously exacerbated by the Bay of Pigs fiasco. Many within the Agency still referred to Fidel as "the little guy" and thought he didn't warrant the attention he was being given. The Soviets had Western military forces at *their* back door, after all. Tactically speaking, the overwhelming power of nuclear weapons made an enemy's physical proximity a parochial concern. Politically, however, Cuba's Marxist tilt was another matter. Eisenhower had decided that Fidel was scary, therefore—despite disagreement within the CIA—he *was* scary, and the Kennedys had been set up for continuity. Politics seemed to dictate that Fidel had to go.

In matters of espionage, the president was all-powerful; the CIA had been structured as his "unseen hand," and those who ran the Agency in 1963 had no choice but to obey Bobby's directives. CIA veteran Ralph McGehee has written: "The CIA is not now nor has it ever been a central intelligence agency. It is the covert action arm of the President's foreign policy advisers. In that capacity, it overthrows or supports foreign governments while reporting 'intelligence' justifying those activities. It shapes its intelligence . . . to support presidential policy."[2]

At the new CIA building, Wild Bill Harvey and his wry, diminutive assistant, Sam Halpern, had been made the point men in what was becoming known as the Cuba Project. Working away in a basement office (with Bill's liquor bottles and pearl-handled pistols within reach), they had been tasked with the development of a new Cuba attack strategy. But long before they presented their ideas later that year, they had come to disagree strongly with the "boom and bang" notions that Bob's new front man, Brigadier General Edward Lansdale, was proposing. Lansdale, a champion of the new theories of counterinsurgency, was considered a maverick by the Pentagon. In his view, political dexterity, sabotage, and selective elimination were the best approaches, instead of overt military subjugation of large populations. Bobby chose him as his Cuba Project coordinator, and the CIA had to accept him.

Bill Harvey, however, held that assassination as a strategy was a tactic of last resort. He believed in professional tradecraft, methodical infiltration and the creation of an infrastructure that empowered dissident populations and enabled effective coups. From their windowless cave, Bill and Sam had managed to place some agents in Havana, but—contrary to the optimistic promises of the exiles—their coordinated efforts throughout the summer failed to create a network that could support an incursion. Of the Cuban citizens who had not been jailed, slaughtered, or run off the island, the overwhelming majority seemed to support Fidel. In Harvey's view, any hope of a popular uprising there looked like a pipe dream.

By his mid-thirties, Bobby was already adept at covering his brother's mistakes and indiscretions. Problems arose and were dispensed with aggressively. You had your own network of fixers, and so you fixed things. You didn't go through channels, you made your own. The whole exercise built Bobby's confidence in small-scale conspiracies of silence.

As if to goad the professional spies, Bobby assembled his parallel Agency of exiles, making no great attempt to hide these freelance operations from Langley. Down in Miami and the sleepier shadows of New Orleans, he assembled a posse that became known as Los Amigos de Roberto. Some of these operatives were men he had met in Florida before Jack took office, men like Manuel Artime and Sergio Arcacha Smith, men who Bobby assumed would rule Cuba when Fidel was driven from power. These "Amigos" in turn enlisted their own coterie of true believers. They would be Bobby's most trusted and confidential exile advisers/operatives.

To one of these men, Rafael "Chi-Chi" Quintero, Bobby once said that his deep-seated antagonism for Fidel had nothing to do with ideology—it was simply a matter of avenging the Kennedy name. This was probably bluster. Bobby knew the political advantages of a Castro ouster. With the toppling of Fidel, the Kennedys' closest nemesis would be gone, the Red-baiting opposition would be beaten at their own game, and the White House would very likely be secured for another four-year term.

On May 1, 1961, a thirty-five-year-old Puerto Rican man named Antulio Ramírez Ortiz boarded a National Airlines commercial jet in Miami, armed with a gun. He took his seat and waited for takeoff.

A rebel with a flair for the dramatic, Antulio had had his imagination captured by tales of the Cuban Revolution, and he had made the short trip from Puerto Rico to see it for himself in the late 1950s. Once there, though, he had been arrested by Batista's police for plotting an urban insurrection, and was chained to a wall on the day that the capital fell to the *barbudos*. The Castro brothers set him free and eventually asked him to work as a low-echelon operative in New York, spying on activities inside the Dominican Republic's consulate. They too were trying to kill President Trujillo, just as the Americans were.

From New York, Antulio went to California for a time; when diplomatic relations between the United States and Cuba were severed, he found himself stranded. All commercial flights between the U.S. and the island nation were suspended. This was a nervy young man, however. He was not about to remain in indolent America just as the Castro brothers were refining their new Marxist state.

Shortly after the big jet was airborne, Antulio got up, walked into the cockpit, put his gun to the pilot's head, and directed him to drop him off in Cuba. The pilot did as he was told, and the action would go down as the first Havana-bound hijacking of the era. But it was not well received in the upper echelons of Cuba, much as they thought it was brave and radical. Antulio had never quite had the stuff to become either a DGI or G2 agent, and this stunt might have demonstrated why. It was so wildly theatrical, attracting so much untoward attention that his old friends in Havana had to grill him for days to determine to their satisfaction that he had not been "turned" by the CIA.

When the interrogations were over, however, Antulio was welcomed back into the fold, accepted as a hero, and allowed to live in the G2's three-building compound, apparently as an errand boy and mascot of sorts, and eventually as a trusted chef to Cuba's intelligence elite. In time, he would meet them all. "Everyone knew and liked me," he would recall, "[including] also the commanders. I chatted with Fidel, with Che Guevara. Mostly, however, with Commandante Ramiro Valdés, who was the boss of the secret services."[3]

Valdés would also be named secretary of the interior, and it was when Valdés's guard was down that Antulio would one day discover, by sheer accident, the depth of Cuba's interest in one Lee Harvey Oswald.

In late May, while the president and First Lady were on a state visit to Paris, Dominican Republic president Rafael Trujillo was driving a Chevy Bel Air down Avenida George Washington, headed out of the Dominican city that bore his name, when he was assassinated.

Richard Goodwin would later assert that Kennedy had asked him to thwart the CIA's plans to terminate the bloodthirsty Dominican dictator, quoting Jack as saying, "Tell them no more weapons. The United States is not to get involved in any assassinations. I'd like to get rid of Trujillo, but not that way."

When Secretary of State Rusk called Jack in Paris to tell him the news, the president's first question was: "Were we involved?"

"I don't think so," said the secretary. "There's some confusion."[4]

But the CIA was involved. The assassins had used weapons supplied by the Agency in two separate caches sent via diplomatic pouch, and now rumors were rife that Trujillo's son, Ramfis, in Paris to deposit some of his father's plunder, might be gunning for the American president in retaliation.

Rusk was winging his way to Paris, and his undersecretary, Chester Bowles, had been left in control of the operations center in Washington. But in reality, this was Bob's first appearance on the world stage as the head of covert actions. "Let Bobby play around," Jack had told Rusk. "If he gets in your way, let me know."

Bob and Secretary of Defense McNamara were on the case immediately, marching into the ops center, shoulder to shoulder, to recommend preemptive action against the Dominican Republic to prevent any reprisal. Chet Bowles had opposed the Bay of Pigs operation, and he was just as opposed to an invasion now. He didn't even want to make any threatening gestures by ordering U.S. warships to hug the Dominican coast.

Bobby screamed at him, "You're a gutless bastard!"

Bowles, in disgust, refused to engage him, but kept on making furious phone calls to the White House staffers in Paris, trying to get to Jack. Finally, Bowles reached him in the middle of the night.

"They want to send in the Marines," Bowles told him.

The president was not about to leap into another Caribbean fiasco so soon, and he said so.

"Well, I'm glad to hear it," said Chet Bowles, "and in that case, would you clarify who's in charge here?"

"You are," Jack assured him.

"Good," Chet replied. "Would you mind explaining that to your brother?"[5]

It is hard now to picture the Lee Harvey Oswald who sang "Moscow Evenings" and "Chattanooga Choo Choo" to his new bride on their wedding night, who carried her up the stairs to their apartment and across the threshold, American style, who was tender with her the first time they made love. He was surprised that the "matchstick girl" had saved herself, but apparently she had, and he knew enough to thank her for giving him the gift of her virginity. As the light of dawn poured through the curtains, someone knocked sharply on the apartment door, startling them awake. Lee answered. Aunt Valya greeted him, and then proceeded to drop a white plate on the floor, shattering it to bits, for luck.[6]

They were tentative lovers, the young man unable to control his ejaculations at first, the young woman terribly shy about her thin body, her awkward approaches. But he was nothing but admiring of her in bed, and they both gained confidence with each other.

It was true that Ella Germann was still lurking in his heart; Marina even claimed to have seen her crying on the street outside their apartment on their wedding day. Yes, she had been distressed to find him reading a recent letter from his mother, whom she had thought was dead. Sometimes when she came home, she would find him writing things that he would then shove out of sight and lock away. She didn't like the oily shotgun he had hung on the wall over the couch, but she figured that was just what men did. The courtship had been so short that in the days immediately following the wedding, a few of the young adults within her circle tried to make her feel like a political opportunist, looking for a ticket to America. An old boyfriend tried to defame her, and some of her girlfriends openly questioned her motives, but she held on to him.

He held on to her too, but he was preoccupied during those weeks. He had seen all he needed to see of Minsk. He was a married man now. It was time for his life to advance, and so he had applied for acceptance to Patrice Lumumba University in Moscow, an arduous process given his dyslexia. He was no longer a person of interest around town, just the American shirker with the parrotlike smile. He had some friends, Ernst Titovets the best of them. He still liked to attend the local dances and concerts, the occasional movie. When he burst into a Harry Belafonte song, or hummed Russian folk tunes, or reached for a Rachmaninoff arpeggio, he felt momentarily light-hearted and optimistic, but Lee was homesick. The factory work was wearing on him. The regimentation of the Soviet system, the tedium of party meetings, the little slights he felt from co-workers, all had begun to sour him on the Red Utopia. And then, when Patrice Lumumba University rejected his application, what was left of his comradely resolve crumbled to powder. The school's decision effectively destroyed any hope that he could attend college in Russia. If he didn't take some sort of action, he would be consigned to the workers' purgatory for the rest of his days.

In the spring of 1961, Cuba was in a state of full alchemical transformation. Fidel was turning all the base metals of post-revolutionary chaos into political gold. Juan Antonio Rodríguez Menier, a prince of the DGI until his defection in 1987, was there to witness the fusion of Cuban sentiment in the spring of 1961. "Though the Cuban people were not at all disposed toward communism, Fidel used the anti-American feeling to insist that Cuba needed a powerful ally and he established firm ties to the Soviet Union. The Bay of Pigs gave him the opportunity to proclaim himself a Communist and become a popularly accepted anti-American tyrant backed by the power of the Soviet Union, though he never became a Soviet puppet."[7]

Most of the Communist world analyzed the attempted invasion broadly, as just another symptom of capitalist imperialism, but Fidel took to humiliating the Kennedy brothers personally, calling them "cretins" and "ignorant beardless kids." Kennedy was disparaged even in the Castro home, according to Fidel's daughter, Alina, who remembered how Kennedy was referred to as "Kennedy Frog Eyes Monroe, Master of Imperialism."[8]

But this was more than just an exchange of insults. Fidel wanted confrontation. "War against the United States is my true destiny," Fidel snarled in a letter to Celia Sánchez before coming to power. "When this war is over I'll start that much bigger and wider war." This screed is now one of the major exhibits in Havana's Museo de la Revolución.[9] In 1964, Fidel's sister, Juanita, would defect to the States and buy a pharmacy in Miami. In 1965, she was asked to testify before the U.S. House Committee on Un-American Activities, where she stated that: "Fidel's feeling of hatred for this country cannot even be imagined by Americans . . . His intention—his *obsession*—is to destroy the U.S.!"[10] Well before the Kennedy attack, in 1959, Fidel's Air Force chief, Major Pedro Díaz Lanz, testified, "[Castro] is always telling us we are going to have to fight the Americans—the Marines—and harping all the time on this theme. He wants war with the U.S."[11]

Raúl's bloodlust was even more apparent: "My dream is to drop three atomic bombs on New York." U.S. ambassador to Cuba Philip Bonsal related this 1960 quote in a telegram, declassified in 2002, to then-President Eisenhower's Secretary of State Christian Herter. Bonsal heard Raúl say it, in confidence, to his interior minister, José Naranjo, when Raúl was in the Soviet Union, hoping to acquire nuclear weapons from Khrushchev.[12] One would expect that the Russians heard it too, and it might explain Moscow's attitude toward the Castros in coming crises.

But until they got those weapons, the Castro brothers' war against the U.S. would have to be fought in the intelligence trenches. In testimony before a U.S. Senate subcommittee two decades later, G2 defector Gerardo Peraza made clear that "the principal function of the [Cuban] Directorate of Intelligence was penetration and recruitment in the United States of America. The Cuban intelligence service has always been against the United States. Exclusively. All the other countries where they work, they do it to direct the activity against the United States . . . This is the reason for being of the Cuban intelligence service."

In the spring of 1961, the Castros' intelligence directorate was just two and a half years old. Captain Manuel "Barba Roja" (Red Beard) Piñeiro Lozada had been recently appointed to head up the DGI (the General Intelligence

Directorate, or Dirección General de Inteligencia). Born in Matanzas, the son of a Bacardi executive, Piñeiro had left his business studies at Columbia University early to join the 1959 Cuban Revolution. His official DGI title had become general inspector of the Department of Operations.

Ramiro Valdés Menéndez, the new head of the Department of Intelligence of the Red Army (Departamento de Inteligencia del Ejercito Rebelde, or DIER, later referred to as the "G2"), had moved his headquarters from in front of La Bahía de Habana tunnel to an immense compound at the end of Fifth Avenue, near Fourteenth Street in the Miramar district where the road to Jaimanitas Beach began. The grand old building, surrounded by mamoncillo trees and royal palms, had been used by Batista as a federal bank. In 1961, it was a chaotic place, the revolution's international nerve center, armed to the walls with Russian-made artillery and staffed by thirty hard-pressed functionaries and officials, all but three of them men and most of them in their early twenties.

Decades later, living on the U.S. West Coast, the aging former G2 gofer, Antulio Ramírez Ortiz, would recall overhearing many conversations at G2 headquarters that spring, angry exchanges about John Kennedy. "The G2 had an agent with the cover name 'The Professor,' in Washington," he recalled. (The true identity of "The Professor" remains unknown.) "He had been placed in the direct vicinity of Kennedy. Shortly after the Bay of Pigs invasion this agent reported that Kennedy was planning a new invasion of Cuba, this time better prepared than the first time. The best people of the G2 leadership got together and considered how one could eliminate Kennedy. [He] was much hated in the Cuban secret service."[13]

In late spring, it was decided that a Ministry of Interior was needed that would encompass the G2 and the DGI, and all intelligence agencies would ultimately answer to Raúl, who would borrow MININT agents (especially such officers as Fabian Escalante Font) to work with him on international operations, particularly "wet" operations.

Raúl was on his way to becoming a master spy. This largely self-educated, slinking, shy, and unimpressive man was already one step ahead of the CIA on almost every front, from the Bay of Pigs plan to its overtures to Rolando Cubela. From its humble beginnings in Havana's Military Hospital of Colombia, the brothers' total intelligence operation had swelled to five thousand staffers by this time, and their overwhelming priority was to plant as many operatives and agents as possible inside the U.S., especially within the ranks of the exile "traitors." In the words of former CIA Cuba analyst Brian Latell, today Cuban intelligence ranks "among the four or five best anywhere in the world." Asked to comment on Raúl's hands-on style, Latell added: "He's good. He's really, really good." Indeed, Latell insists that Fidel owes his life to Raúl, many times over.

By mid-1961, there had already been a dozen American plots against Fidel. Bissell had put Bill Harvey in charge of ZR/RIFLE, a busy contingency operation that was open to every imaginable scenario, from the sublime to the ridiculous.

Initially, Cuban intelligence used such men as William Morgan in ad hoc spy missions. Just after the revolution, before his own anti-Castro conversion came, Morgan entrapped over two hundred local Cubans who were working the assassination-and-coup angles with the network of counter-revolutionaries based in Miami. But that was just a reactive strategy. It soon became clear that the attempts to kill Fidel would be constant, and therefore the Castro brothers' spies would have to penetrate every single American plot if he was to survive.

In 1983, Jesús Méndez, a former DGI agent, boldly insisted that during an extended period of the 1960s, Cuban intelligence had turned every last one of the suspected U.S. agents inside Cuba, had "doubled" them and placed them back into the U.S. to report on anti-Castro activities. They were either turned after they were infiltrated to Cuba, or they successfully pretended to have been turned by the Agency. In either case, all owed their final allegiance to Fidel, and the vast majority of them were pure ideologues, neither bought nor blackmailed into service. "Nearly all the agents recruited by the CIA, back to the early sixties, were . . . plants taking instructions from Cuban premier Fidel Castro," Méndez said. Maj. Florentino Aspillaga Lombard, who defected in 1987, specifically identified thirty-eight Cubans recruited by the CIA who were doubles working for Fidel, this despite their having passed CIA lie detector tests. According to Rodríguez Menier, the Cubans had received extensive training in beating the polygraph machine. In fact, the Cuban doubles were so adept and so bold that they were instructed to make personal appeals to their case officers if there was a problem with the test results. As their Cuban trainers had predicted, the double agents' case officers were usually manipulated into believing their Cuban sources over the machines.*

---

*Rodríguez Menier produced two internal documentaries for MININT, wherein about forty penetration agents explained precisely how they had convinced the CIA that they'd been successfully recruited.

Once inside, these phony U.S. operatives were able to feed a mass of mis-information to the CIA that is probably still stored in the computers of American intelligence. And while the files of the G2 fairly bulged with a con-stant flow of information from the American side, they had also set up shop in the heart of New York City. G2 defector Peraza noted that the Castro brothers' United Nations diplomats were moonlighting for the new DGI as a basic job qualification: "The rules of the DGI are that all the diplomats who come to the United States or to New York have to be members of the intelli-gence service."[14] The Federation of American Scientists confirmed Peraza's claim: "The Cuban mission to the United Nations is the third largest UN del-egation, and it has been alleged that almost half the personnel assigned to the mission are DGI officers. The DGI actively recruits within the Cuban émigré community and has used refugee flows into the United States to place agents."

South Florida was where the CIA was constructing JM/WAVE, its single largest office outside of Langley. Miami's Dade County was where Fidel and Raúl's spies were most pervasive and penetrating. By the summer of 1961, more than 140,000 Cubans had fled the island, the vast majority of them mi-grating to Miami-Dade.

On the second day of July, in the Idaho resort town of Ketchum, a man who had been a literary hero to John F. Kennedy, to Fidel Castro, and to Lee Har-vey Oswald finally succumbed to his despair and took his own life with a shotgun. Ernest Hemingway had been suffering from various maladies for a number of years: most unbearably, depression. His illness had prevented him from attending John Kennedy's inaugural, in fact, and thus the two men had never met, despite their mutual esteem.

His widow, Mary, maintained that his suicide was a gun accident, and she would grieve him for years to come. His decline had been harrowing, a kind of emotional dementia that set in while the rest of his mind remained clear. In the weeks following his death, when she wasn't inconsolably lost, she was preparing herself to make the last, long journey to say good-bye to the home they had shared in Cuba.

In 1937, at about the same time that he had begun to question his conver-sion to Catholicism, Hemingway traveled to Spain to cover the civil war there, and it was then that his infatuation with Spanish culture began. His partner on the story was Herbert Matthews, the same man who had chronicled Fidel's revolutionary days in the Sierra Maestra for the *New York Times*, and whether it was Matthews or some other influence that drew him to Cuba,

Hemingway visited there in 1939. Soon after, he found Finca Vigia ("lookout farm") in San Francisco de Paula outside of Havana, and promptly bought it. He would come and go over the years, but when the Castro brothers came to power, he stayed on, even after the oligarchs had departed and thousands of his leftist democratic brethren had followed them into exile. It was at the *finca* that he wrote two of his greatest works, *The Old Man and the Sea* and *For Whom the Bell Tolls*, the book that Fidel would claim—perhaps only in tribute—had taught him guerrilla warfare.

They met at least twice, the first time in 1960 at the Tenth Annual Hemingway Fishing Tournament at the Barlovento Yacht Club, a contest that Fidel was to have judged but wound up entering and then winning with the biggest marlin specimen of the day. On another occasion, the Hemingways invited the Cuban leader to the farm for a night of food and spirits and conversation. A real camaraderie seemed to be developing. But then a friend of the author's was killed by the regime, and the rapport between the two men dissolved. Ernest finally suffered his own personal disenchantment, as so many thousands of others already had, and he and Mary left the island for Idaho on July 25, 1960. He spent the last year of his life in and out of the Mayo Clinic, trying desperately to kill the beast of his depression.

In order for Mary to go to Cuba legally, she had to gain permission from the United States government. The embargo prevented travel there, but through an intermediary, William Walton, who went straight to the president, she was able to start planning her trip.

As a result of Jack Kennedy's helping gesture, the *finca* would become one of the most unlikely settings for a plot to assassinate Fidel. It would also provide the only written evidence of what has been denied by the Kennedy family to this day—that Jack and Bobby knew of the murder plots, and condoned them.

On July 8, Lee and Marina, now pregnant, spent the early morning waiting for his flight to be called at the Minsk airport. They had ordered breakfast, but both were too anxious to actually sit down to a meal; the trip was unauthorized. He had come to a decision: he had realized the limits of his prospects here, and he wanted to go back to the United States and take his new wife with him. Rather than tip the KGB that this was his hope, he had decided to go straight to the American embassy in Moscow and test the waters. He had renounced his U.S. citizenship, and the Americans might arrest him if he tried to return there, but he was determined to risk it.

The flight was announced. As they said their good-byes, it had occurred to both of them that he might not return, since he was not authorized to travel such a distance. When his plane took off, Marina hurried back to work at the hospital pharmacy, full of trepidation and knowing full well that their secret could not be kept for long. She was afraid to go to America, not only because she might never be allowed to return to Russia and her family, but because— since learning of her pregnancy—she had felt strangely repulsed by Lee's body and unsure of her feelings for him. In brief flashes, he could be plaintive to the point of becoming menacing. In other moments that should have been fond and fetching, her love sometimes seemed like a concoction to her, a way to force change upon herself, not a spontaneous adoration that had arisen from within her. Perhaps her marriage was a bit opportunistic, but she was in it now, for better or for worse.

Lee, for his part, had made his peace with Marina, excited that he'd soon be a father, and committed enough to his repatriation effort that even the prospect of a jail term didn't deter him. July 8 was a Saturday, but he arrived at the U.S. embassy on Moscow's Sadovoye Ring, unannounced, and rang up to the living quarters of the American Foreign Service officer, Richard Snyder, who had processed Lee's case when he arrived in the fall of 1959.

Snyder didn't much like this young guy, and he greeted him with diplomatic detachment. But Lee was in luck. It was State Department policy to delay the processing of defections by agitated or otherwise unstable people, not to mention suicidal ones such as Lee. Renunciation of citizenship was irreversible, after all, and Snyder sensed Lee's immaturity, so the officer had stalled the young man's paperwork. The delay meant that Lee was still, officially, a citizen of the United States. Whether or not Lee realized that he owed this piece of good fortune to Snyder, the officer noticed that he was considerably less belligerent than he had been a year and a half before, perhaps even contrite.[15]

Snyder told him to come back to the embassy on Monday.

That night, in a misbegotten test of her feelings for her husband, Marina allowed herself a last-minute date with an old boyfriend: not Anatoly, but poor Leonid Gelfant.

He had procured an empty apartment. He brought a bottle of something sweet. He was, she soon realized, trying to lose his virginity with her that night and had somehow been convinced that she was so unsure of her new status as wife and mother-to-be that she might be game. Leonid made Lee seem like a Casanova by comparison. The date ended in a lurid little tangle of misgivings, and she ran home in the middle of the night.[16]

Compounding her guilt, Lee called her the next day, relieved that he hadn't been arrested and flush with a half-cocked idea that she should follow him to Moscow, the better to make him appear a mature, reasoned American family man who deserved to be readmitted to his homeland. She complied on the morning that he was scheduled to meet with Snyder. She had never flown before, and in all the excitement, she vomited during the flight and landed at the Moscow airport disheveled and disoriented, carried along in a kind of vertigo between one world and another one.

But he had filled their hotel room with blue cornflowers. She made love with him before their appointment in order to erase the misadventure with Leonid, and when she arrived later at the American embassy, stepping across its threshold in her English-made wedding shoes, she might have been a Russian Dorothy first setting foot in Oz. A roomful of Russian secretaries put her at ease. Maybe they would save her if she was clapped into American handcuffs. Then again, maybe they were KGB. She snuffed out the thought and took in her surroundings. The air conditioning was a revelation. The offices seemed to be miracles of clean, modern efficiency. This was her entrée to the world of her country's mortal enemy, but it seemed calm and bright and soothing.

This was the day that would catapult her from her home, through the elusive joys of an immigrant coming to America, and straight into a nightmare.

According to her biographer, Priscilla Johnson McMillan, while Lee was meeting with embassy officials, "Marina had to go to the toilet. On the way she paused at the water cooler and had only to press a knob and cold water came cascading out. But the washroom itself—that was a work of art! It was immaculate and as fragrant as a garden. There was even real toilet paper. Marina had seen that, instead of small squares of newspaper, only once in her life before, at the Hotel Metropole in Leningrad. There were paper towels, too, and green liquid soap. Again, she had only to press a knob."[17]

For the rest of the day, it was all simply wondrous. The troubles would soon begin, however. Before they would actually set sail for America, she would become an outcast in Minsk. Her friends would ostracize her. She would be expelled from the Komsomol. She would jeopardize the well-being of her aunt and uncle, and she would be forced to win her freedom to emigrate only by meeting with the KGB directly.

By midsummer, thousands of Cuban exiles had landed in New Orleans, and Sergio Arcacha Smith was part of the unofficial welcoming committee. The newcomers did not readily assimilate, and they rejected the term "refugees," insisting that they were "exiles," soon to return to their homeland.

Sergio made the most of this defiant spirit, speaking at any public event he could to trumpet the anti-Castro cause, and setting up a temporary Cuban Revolutionary Council office. He had his eyes on another space in the Newman Building, a weary, three-story white stone and brick edifice at 544 Camp Street. It wouldn't be available until fall, but it was exactly the right place for the CRC. On the ground floor was a restaurant, Mancuso's, fast becoming a haven for anti-Fidelistas. Across the street was Place Lafayette, a park commemorating the site where the flag of a free Cuba was first flown in 1850, fifty-two years before it became an independent republic.

At the end of the workday, the park would swell with Cubans, mostly men, but a young wife here, an old widow there; a gallery of faces under the streetlamps, wreathed in cigar smoke. They would play dominoes and talk politics into the wee hours, the lilt of *son* music wafting from transistor radios, conga drums bubbling up from a circle of players on the stone benches. Others joined the evening confabs, young gringos of a military mind. Very soon, the Big Easy was second only to Miami as a bastion of Cuban counterinsurgency, and Place Lafayette was the heart of it, a green crossroads for patriots, mercenaries, and politicos.

There were other young men in their midst, no doubt, men who were there to spy, not to join with their fight. Foremost among those moles in the coming years would be one who was then still languishing in Russia, Lee Harvey Oswald.

In July 1961, David Ferrie was still crestfallen about the Bay of Pigs debacle. He had helped Sergio with the recruitment of the landing force, Brigade 2506, and with the coordination of supply shipments to the training camps in Latin America. On the eve of the invasion, he and one of his young recruits, Layton Martens, were at the home of another friend, Al Landry, squeezed into a tiny room listening to shortwave radio broadcasts of the action. As it became clear that it was all going bad, Ferrie slipped into a mean funk that lasted for months.

At a luncheon speech before the New Orleans chapter of the Order of World Wars, he became so exercised in his criticism of President Kennedy's conduct of the invasion that he was asked to curtail his remarks. It was an incident that would later be used against him by the city's DA, Jim Garrison, but it was a momentary aberration. In reality, David Ferrie was a devout Irish Catholic and former seminarian, the well-bred son of a Cleveland police official, who idolized Jack Kennedy. He had voted for him. He was adamant that his election to the presidency was nothing short of "fabulous," according to Martens, and he was certainly not alone in his condemnation of the invasion's execution. The president was among his own fiercest critics at this point.

Gradually, Ferrie's anger cooled and he returned to the business of working for the Castro brothers' ouster.

He had first gotten involved with the exiles in early 1961, as part of his work with the Catholic Charities.[18] Catholic reformers had been well represented in the 26th of July Movement, and Ferrie had initially been a supporter of "the bearded one"; but, as with so many millions of others, he was infuriated when Fidel's "second revolution" began. It was through his connections to the church that he was able to make use of certain properties along Lake Pontchartrain, remote parcels of land that would eventually become training camps for the continuous Cuban plots. The CRC soon moved into Camp Street. From his sparely furnished office on the second floor, Sergio and his people were deeply involved in smuggling refugees out of Cuba and smuggling spies in. New plans were being issued almost daily. Through the CRC's New Orleans network, working directly with the underground, Cuban crops were being set afire. Bombs were being planted around Havana harbor.[19] Ferrie was prepared to bomb refineries along the harbor himself. He created designs for two-man submarines that could do it from positions offshore, even building two prototypes.[20] He made them out of B-47 wing tanks, and when he and the Cubans were prevented from actually deploying them, he kept one of them in his yard as insurgent lawn art.

By the summer, word in Place Lafayette was that the CIA was "under a presidential hammer." One of the CIA's regional front operations, Southern Airways, had been abolished, and local mercenary operations were scrambling to retool their paramilitary operations to make them look more autonomous of the Agency. As the Kennedy brothers' post–Bay of Pigs policy was coalescing in Washington, auxiliary units not directly under the control of the CIA were being attached. Sergio was already making direct reports to Bobby Kennedy by then, though he wouldn't say so explicitly until 1967.

Ferrie became indispensable. At six feet tall, he was a cinder-eyed, fuzzy-browed man with a carpetlike hairpiece whose odd appearance took some people aback. But he had a practiced radio announcer's voice, a commanding speaking style, and the courage to back up his furious stump speeches against Fidel with action. On July 18, Sergio wrote a letter to Ferrie's boss at Eastern Airlines, Eddie Rickenbacker, asking that he be allowed to take ninety days off with pay so he could continue to help revitalize the anti-Castro effort. The letter attested to how invaluable Ferrie was becoming on every front, politically, economically, and militarily. In fact, such a deep well of passion was David Ferrie that Sergio attributed the entire revival of local Cuban-exile morale to him.

Always on the lookout for new recruits, Ferrie contacted Layton Martens, a thin and feral kid whom he had taught to fly years before in the Civil Air Patrol program. The two had great respect for each other, despite their age difference. Layton affected a tough attitude, but he was precociously bright and politically savvy, a natural-born operative. Ferrie had already let on that he was allied with some of the Cubans around Place Lafayette. The tough guy was not yet out of his teens, but Ferrie sensed that he was anxious for more hard-core intrigue.

Ferrie buttonholed him at a restaurant one night and began to make his pitch. Rumors from Cuba had given him a certain prescience.

"Look, I really need to know if you're willing to stand up for your country and do some things that are extraordinary," he suddenly said, "if I can count on you to do these things and keep it between us . . ."

Layton was struck by the evangelical tone in Ferrie's voice.

"I'm gonna introduce you to some things that are extraordinary indeed," he went on. "Are you willing to do that?"

"Like what?" said Layton.

"It has to do with the Cubans," Ferrie replied, "a possible missile crisis . . . perhaps even war with the Russians."[21]

With an apocalyptic come-on like that, Layton could not resist. He signed on and was soon at work at the CRC office as another of Sergio's assistants.

Even by the summer of 1961, nearly a year and half before the Cuban missile crisis, the expatriate community was receiving intelligence from the underground that there were Soviet missiles in Cuba. Layton soon heard talk of it around the office. Through an elaborate communications method (including coded messages in the cancellation marks on stamped letters from Cuba), rumors of such weapons were being relayed with some regularity.

Then, one very hot night, Layton was sweating through paperwork with Sergio when Ferrie ran in the door, his hairpiece askew.

"They've got missiles!" he gasped. The underground had seen at least ten portable tactical weapons, possibly nuclear, in various locations around the island. They were reporting them fully deployed around Mariel Harbor, the port where the missiles had first arrived. Ferrie said they'd be getting maps of the sites in the morning, perhaps even photos. He had already reported the information to their New Orleans FBI contact, Warren DeBrueys.

Sitting in the Versailles Restaurant in Miami's Little Havana more than thirty-five years later, Sergio would recall that no sooner had DeBrueys passed the Cuban reconnaissance on to his superiors, than Bobby Kennedy was calling from Washington.[22]

Sergio's first impulse was to express his regrets—he was sorry to be the bearer of bad tidings. But Bobby was enthused at the quality of the intelligence. He'd be sending geodetic survey maps down to them, he said, and he wanted Sergio's informants to mark them where they thought the Soviet launchers, nuclear or otherwise, might be.

Just keep the stuff coming through DeBrueys, Bobby told him. "We're not getting anything like this from the CIA."[23]

Late in July, Mary Hemingway and her companion, Valerie Danby-Smith, arrived in Cuba to pack up family treasures and turn Finca Vigia over to the regime, which was making plans to convert it into a museum.

The couple had departed Cuba abruptly, and the house was as they had left it, Hemingway's shelves full of books buttressing the walls, paintings everywhere, manuscripts in varying states of completion neatly stacked here and there. A skeleton staff had opened the house in anticipation of their arrival, and there was a huge fruit basket waiting for them, a gift from Premier Castro. With it was a note offering his condolences and his assistance, should any be required. He had been a great admirer of Ernest and wished to be of service.

A few nights later, on short notice, Fidel paid the women a visit, arriving in his jeep with only a retinue of aides following in another nondescript vehicle, no bodyguards. Mary had assembled the servants to greet him on the porch and, once they had all shaken the hand of the Maximum Leader, he was led to a parlor for coffee and refreshments. The talk was easygoing. They discussed the transfer of the home to the people of Cuba, and Fidel reminisced about the day of fishing with Ernest at Barlovento. He admired the mounted animal heads on the walls, trophies that the women had been trying to document the origins of for the museum. If there was any mention of the ugly circumstances that had prompted the author's self-exile the year before, they were not recorded by the participants.

Fidel wanted to see where Hemingway had written his stories, so Mary took him outside to a three-story tower she had had built for him, a writing roost. In truth, Ernest hated the thing; he preferred to write in the bedroom. But Fidel was charmed by the tower, and to her astonishment, he propelled himself straight up the stairs, completely heedless of any possible threat at the top. That apparent lack of concern for his own safety made an impression on Mary that afternoon, and she would share it, most innocently, upon recounting the visit to others. He and his entourage left soon after, Fidel encouraging her once more to call on him if there was anything else she required.

The last of her memories of the place were packed into crates, the paintings by friends Paul Klee, Juan Gris, Masson, the raft of stories left unfinished. She and Valerie were required to carry only hand luggage off the isle, but she was not about to leave half his legacy behind. She procured the services of a shrimp boat that was headed for Tampa for repairs, and had the crates secreted aboard for safe transport across the sea, leaving only the *finca*, its furniture, and a few objects of interest to signify the spirit of the husband she had lost.[24]

Fidel would soon make it a shrine.

There was a maxim of the time among young adults in Russia. You were born. You went to school. You became a young Pioneer, you became Komsomol, and then you died. Joining Komsomol, the civic society that conferred good citizenship and reinforced correct behavior, was the surest sign that you had embraced futility; that you were resigned to your socialist fate, and a member in good standing. You might defy Komsomol in your youth, and they might forgive you (unlike the Communist Party), but you would probably never leave it.

And yet here was Marina, sitting at a table in a big, stark room atop the hospital like a defendant, facing a row of her peers. She had made an unauthorized trip to Moscow with a man, with the American, and he had applied for an exit visa. It was July 26. The air was warm and smoky, even with the windows open and a sluggish breeze coming off the river.

Her main interrogator was a big, square female nurse from the pediatric ward.

"You're being rude, Marina Prusakova—"

"Oswald—"

"There's no reason to be rude," the nurse winced, as if she were sympathetic. "You will get a bad reference if—"

"I don't need a reference. I'll go with a bad reference if necessary. I'm not such a criminal. I love the pharmacy girls, I love them a lot as girlfriends, and I'm not a bad friend! I would give everything for the girls because they are simple, good girls . . . If you don't like me, I don't like you—no skin off my back."

"People like you don't belong in Komsomol," said the nurse. "You should be expelled."

"That's fine. I'm very happy—"

"Why don't you want to be in Komsomol?" a petite red-haired girl asked, a sweet-faced kid who Marina had smiled at on the stairs.

"Because I don't like it. Because it's boring."

"Then why didn't you say so earlier?"

"Because I didn't want people to think I was different."

The nurse broke in again. "What do you think of Komsomol?"

"Komsomol is Komsomol . . . Maybe I'm 'an anti-Soviet element,' " she said in a spooky voice. "That would make it easy for you."

The nurse leaned back, supercilious now. "What's your relationship to this man you went to Moscow with?"

The redhead spoke up. "It's her husband."

The nurse paused, then tried to cover it. "What sort of person is he?"

"You better ask the MVD," Marina shot back.

"Why MVD if we can ask you?"

"Because I might not tell you." As the nurse was about to go on the attack, Marina rolled over her. "He longs for his homeland—"

"But didn't you try to persuade him to stay here?"

"No. I don't think it'll be better there. I'm not going because I'm looking for something better; I'm just going with my husband. It's possible that it will be worse there. I haven't been there, and you haven't been there, so how can we express an opinion?"

For a moment, she had them all tongue-tied. She dove back in. "I will not leave my husband. He's a good person and I'm satisfied with him. He's more dear to me than your opinions. What are you going to do, confront people who gave me good references and yell at them? Don't persecute them. Better to reprimand me—"

"But we respect you," cried the little redhead. "We love you!"

The others got in on it then.

"Yes," they said. "We respect you, don't you see? We love you. You won't have friends like us there—"

"I don't want to have friends like that," Marina volleyed, chin up, tears in her eyes. "I see how much you love me."

That night, as she recounted it all to Lee, he said, "Don't worry, everything will be fine."

She paused over that, wondering. "The most important thing now is leaving," she murmured. It would take months for them to know their fate, but now they'd be cast to the edges.

"I know that." He started rubbing her shoulders from behind. "We're leaving," he said, as if he could be certain. "No need for scandals."

"Don't look for the truth, you'll never find it anyway," she replied, as if the main conversation was with herself at that moment. "I was told that by my mother."

"Everything will be fine."

"You think so? . . . Why do I feel sad? My husband isn't throwing me out of the house."

"I love you."

"That's what you say now, but afterward you'll say that you don't love me."

"Your husband loves you," he repeated, nuzzling her hair.[25]

A few weeks later, in early August, Jack Kennedy's Latin American hand, Dick Goodwin, landed in Montevideo, Uruguay, with a U.S. delegation of thirty-two others to advance the cause of the Alliance for Progress. From there, they were carried to Punta del Este, a seaside resort that had been all but vacated for the arrival of the economic ministerial elite of the Americas.

The delegations came to only a few hundred people, but every American republic was represented and, by Goodwin's rich account of twenty-seven years later, they "represented a staggering diversity of political and economic structures—dictatorships and democracies, entrenched privilege and populist aspiration . . . From the beginning attention was focused on the dramatic conjunction of the men who led the delegations from the United States and Cuba,"[26] Treasury Secretary C. Douglas Dillon and revolutionary icon Che Guevara, the millionaire and the guerrilla.

According to Arthur Schlesinger's account a few years later, some joked that there were only "two left-wing governments present—the United States and Cuba."[27] A few of the delegations would argue for Cuba's inclusion in the still-forming Alliance. Others disputed it, upholding center-left principles of democratic rule. Che, whose jungle fatigues were the only clothes well suited to the heat, was courtly and polished. He made it clear that he agreed with many of the Alliance's goals but considered its program an attempt to impede natural revolutionary processes, an imperialist Band-Aid applied only out of fear of Fidel and Raúl. Cuba would not be a part of this sad exercise.

Nonetheless, the twenty delegations set to work on a stunning set of goals, including land reform, eradication of illiteracy, and reduction of child mortality rates. Fourteen of such goals would become the Charter of Punta del Este, "a summons to a democratic revolution."[28] In Dillon's hotel room the night before the conference opened, he had put the State Department boys in a dither by spontaneously pledging a billion dollars a year to the effort of hemispheric, liberal reform. When State's Ed Martin claimed that Dillon couldn't do that, Dillon overruled him. He was Jack Kennedy's plenipotentiary, and that was that. The administration's aim was clear—to hammer out a Third Way for Latin America before it was too late.[29]

As it happened, Goodwin was a cigar smoker. (Che's bodyguards were turning a cool profit selling Cuban cigars to delegates whose tastes had been whetted by the American embargo.) When Che noted Dick's habit, he made him a gift of a beautiful mahogany box full of Havanas, replete with the Cuban national seal. There was a note attached: "Since I have no greeting card, I have to write. Since to write to an enemy is difficult, I limit myself to extending my hand."[30]

The gesture was meant as an entrée to informal talks before the conference ended. The Americans thought it could probably do no harm; but when Che protested the "imperialist" nature of the Alliance in subsequent days, it set off a flurry of jabs and feints that gave both Dillon and Goodwin second thoughts.

A "chance" meeting did happen despite it, however; Che surprised Goodwin at a party in a small apartment in Montevideo just before the Americans flew back to Washington. He entered like a pirate in olive drab between two of his bodyguards, and, after another round of sparring, the two men sat down with two translators. A three-hour discussion ensued.

Guevara, whose public bearing was always so staunch and *macho*, appeared almost "feminine" by Goodwin's account. He started by thanking the Americans for the Bay of Pigs.

Goodwin said he was welcome.

The invasion had enabled the revolution to unite the people behind them, Che elaborated.

Given the public discord in the U.S. as a result of the debacle, Goodwin suggested that perhaps the Cubans could attack American-held Guantánamo at the eastern tip of the island, and thereby lend some of their unity to John Kennedy.

The joke wasn't lost on Guevara, but there were more serious matters at hand. Che made it clear that he was, indeed, a Communist, as was Fidel; that they believed their regime to be strong and impenetrable; and that their victory proved that socialist revolution could be spread throughout the region.

True, he allowed, there were still counterrevolutionaries afoot. Sabotage remained a problem. The Catholic Church was recalcitrant, and the Cuban economy was still too dependent on sugar alone. But the point that Che eventually reached came in the form of a modus vivendi: Cuba would pay for expropriated properties in trade, it would avoid any military or political partnerships with the Eastern bloc, and it would desist in exporting its revolution to other desperate nations—but on two conditions. In exchange, the United States must agree not to overthrow the Cuban regime, and it would have to discontinue the trade embargo.[31]

Jack Kennedy greeted this news by lighting up one of the cigars from the mahogany box and instructing Goodwin to circulate a memorandum of his impressions to key people in the White House, at State, and over at the Pentagon. It seemed that the Cubans were sincerely seeking a rapprochement, and Jack was initially intrigued.

The right wing, however, was hovering. Although Goodwin asserted that the meeting was accidental, that the Kennedy administration had not initiated "secret talks" with the Cubans, Republicans insisted that the meeting was deliberate and that young Goodwin was "a kid playing with fire."[32] As political detractors suddenly cornered Goodwin and Kennedy, accusing them of appeasing the Castro regime, Che himself had run afoul of the Russians for his handling of the Cuban economy. Both men thus momentarily weakened on their home turf, Goodwin advised a cool, unhurried response to Che's overture that amounted to benign neglect. The Kennedys looked for political cover and opted to let Che's offer drop.

The opportunity spun away like a passing planet seen from a hurtling rocket ship, fading into the infinite darkness.

By September, the East/West stakes had risen dangerously. In the wake of the ill-fated invasion of Cuba, Kennedy had met with Khrushchev in Vienna and their talks had devolved into threats and counterthreats over divided Germany. When the Soviet leader warned that he would cut off Allied access to Berlin, Jack called up his reserve forces, Nikita built a wall dividing the city, and the USSR resumed its atmospheric nuclear testing in Central Asia, unleashing three hydrogen bombs of unparalleled power.

One evening that summer, as he was preparing to speak to the nation about his recent trip to Europe, Jack asked an aide to produce some statistics of an alarming nature: The president asked the statistician what the American death count would be after a "nuclear exchange" with the Soviets.

The Pentagon's morbidity expert reported that seventy million human beings would perish, roughly 40 percent of the population of the United States, if such a war broke out.

And how many, he asked, if just one Russian nuke got through and struck close to an American city? How many then?

The word came back: "Six hundred thousand."

"That's the total number of casualties in the Civil War," said the president, who obviously meant to say *fatalities*. "And we haven't gotten over that in a hundred years."[33]

Such were the questions that plagued the American president in the summer of 1961. But when Jack told a group of Republican congressmen that he would need an increased expenditure for civil defense if the country had a hope of limiting its nuclear casualties, a few of the leaders had balked, telling the president that it would probably be too expensive.

On the evening of September 25, 1961, Lee Oswald rushed home to his pregnant wife, closed the doors to the balcony for discretion's sake, and turned on the radio.

"President Kennedy is going to speak tonight," he said, spinning the dial in search of the Voice of America.

They had heard the young president speak before, and this was an especially important address, one that would be broadcast live before the UN General Assembly, addressing the east/west crisis in Berlin.

The Kremlin did its best to jam the Voice, but broadcasts still made it through the filter, albeit in ghostly, warbling form. Lee was rapt throughout the hour-long speech. Marina had noted his intense interest in politics, of course, and she sat by him silently for a while before heading off to the kitchen to prepare dinner. When it was over and Lee came out of his trance, she asked him what it had been about.

"About war and peace," he said before translating pieces of the speech for her.

"That's funny," she said, "everybody wants peace here. They want peace there, too. So why do they talk about war?"

"Politics," was Lee's smiling response.[34]

She wasn't sure what that meant, in his view, but a few days later he was defending both Kennedy's speech and the U.S. in general in a kitchen debate with her uncle Ilya. Lee's KGB watchers had dubbed him "the radish," red on the outside, white on the inside. Increasingly, as his disenchantment with Russia grew, he had added a bit of blue to the array. He sounded almost patriotic, Marina thought, and she liked the way he rose to America's defense.

Ilya had been furious about Lee's decision to take his new family back to the States, insisting that he never would have given Marina's hand in marriage if he had known. Given Ilya's position in the MVD, he must have had to do some fancy maneuvering in the wake of Lee's choice; indeed, he may already have been working to strike a bargain with the KGB, even then, in order to save his job, hold on to his privileges, and keep his niece out of trouble.

Since July, he had made a certain peace with Lee, however, or perhaps he was just putting the best face on his anger. As they jousted over the Kennedy speech, Ilya defended Russia just as stoutly as Lee defended the U.S. The only thing the two men could agree on was the dastardly nature of the Bay of Pigs invasion. Lee was still furious about America's treatment of Cuba, and of Fidel in particular. He had even told Marina, only half in jest, that if their first child was a boy he wanted to name it Fidel.

A few weeks after Kennedy's speech, Lee took her to a movie about Castro by Russian director Roman Karmen, a heroic portrait that only deepened his infatuation with Fidel. This Caribbean form of Communism seemed more familiar, somehow. From his romantic perspective, it felt fresher, more rustic and tangible, more in synch with his ideals. As it took hold in his imagination, he returned to the spirited subculture of the three hundred Cuban students on Ulyanov Street, and forged deeper into that world.[35] He thought they had tremendous verve. They were irrepressible in ways that Lee may have associated with the West, perhaps with the people of New Orleans. They dressed in actual colors. They dated Russian girls in defiance of the rules. They played music and danced, and no sooner did the Soviet militia crack down on their recreations than they devised others. Their greatest fear about America was that if it succeeded in toppling Fidel, they would be stranded in the great gray deep freeze of dour Mother Russia. This was a proletariat that knew how to party. This was Lee's kind of Communism.

And, at the very least, it was a bright distraction while he waited for the birth of his child and for news from the U.S. embassy in Moscow.

In November 1961, Bill Harvey and Sam Halpern had a plan, the next phase in the ongoing attempt to "Get rid of that bastard, Castro!" Halpern came up with a name for it: Operation Mongoose, named after a carnivorous predator that kills its prey after stealing its eggs. It dispatches its enemy and removes its progeny, thereby preventing any line of succession—exactly what the Kennedy White House and the CIA had in mind for the Castros and their political descendants.

The plans were to continue fomenting revolution. The aim was to see them to completion by October of 1962. The specific policies would be formulated by Bob's coordinator, Ed Lansdale, a trailblazer of such a divided nature that he had served as the inpiration for characters in both *The Quiet American* and *The Ugly American*. He was as earnest in his anti-totalitarian zeal as any man in Christendom, and he was as stealthy and thorough in its application, as—perhaps—a mongoose.

By most estimates, the operation had somewhere between $50 million and $150 million to spend on its endeavor. The logistics would be implemented by the CIA's Bill Harvey and his "Task Force W." The White House had taken the Cuban operation out of the purview of the Agency's Western Hemisphere Division and placed it directly in the control of Bobby and the White House staff. A twenty-by-forty-foot room in the West Wing of the Executive Mansion had been dubbed the Situation Room. McGeorge Bundy was buried in there every morning, pawing through raw electronic intelligence reports, thousands of them a day. The Agency could only play catch-up. The president had direct oversight now. The Kennedys had become so distrustful of Langley that they insisted on reading "the narrative" straight off the teletypes and the scrambler phones.

It was impossible, of course, to sideline the Agency completely, nor did they want to. The Cuba Project was still officially an Agency operation, focused on its single goal, to depose Fidel (whose cryptonym was now AM/THUG), along with his brother, Raúl, and their minions, from Dr. Che Guevara (AM/QUACK) on down. To achieve this end, Lansdale brought aboard the same CIA team that had, by the skin of its teeth, brought down Árbenz in Guatemala in 1954: Tracy Barnes, David Atlee Phillips, David Morales, William "Rip" Robertson, and E. Howard Hunt.

By the end of the year 1961, Operation Mongoose had been officially in existence for a month, and all it had done was to infuriate the Castro brothers. The Cuban G2 and the DGI depended on the Soviets for technical support and training, as in Minsk. They received all the best Soviet "widgets and gadgets" that Moscow could supply, state-of-the-art stuff, but the Castros had insisted on their independence in matters of spycraft. They determined their own targets, particularly those in Florida which the Russians wanted nothing to do with. As the secret war intensified, the Soviets, in fact, were increasingly impressed, even unnerved, by the brash way the Cubans engaged the enemy.

General Oleg Kalugin was the KGB's head of operations against the United States at the time, a spy based in New York and Washington who would eventually be promoted to Chief of Foreign Counterintelligence ("K Branch"). He would later recall ". . . that Cubans did not play by the rules that we considered absolutely mandatory. With their revolutionary spirit, with their zeal to damage the United States, they would often ignore some of the elementary regulations, which we abided by. I even admired the Cubans for lack of discipline. They would go ahead and surge forward because they knew they had to do something, well, . . . to hurt the United States. The Soviets were much more cautious. They knew the implications."[36]

Given Cuba's rogue tendencies, Nikita Khrushchev had made it the KGB's business to stay on top of U.S. efforts, and they too had learned of Mongoose. To deter it, Khrushchev sent his island ally 40,000 Russian troops, 1,300 field pieces, 700 antiaircraft guns, 350 tanks, and 150 fighter jets. Fidel and Raúl were soon wonderfully well protected.

Fidel's personal safety was—and still is—assured by the General Directorate of Personal Security (DGSP), the only division of the MININT that exists without any intrusion from the MININT, the MINFAR, or the Communist Party of Cuba. Background investigations of DGSP guards were extraordinary and would only become more so after 1963. Those who were chosen received the most special of privileges.[37] As its first success, the DGSP captured a would-be assassin named Eutimio Guerra, a bodyguard who had been bunking in the same room with Fidel until his plans were discovered.

Fidel has had personal bodyguards since a price was put on his head by Batista and some of his rich supporters before the revolution. After the victory, when internal dissidents and the CIA were both hunting them, the Castro brothers expanded their team of bodyguards, initially protecting all the key players; but in 1961, they subdivided that force into individual cells that operated independently.

From the beginning, most of Fidel's team were veterans of the 26th of July Movement; but as a counterrevolution began to take shape, Ramiro Valdés Menéndez replaced the vets with members of the People's Socialist Party (PSP), who owed their allegiance solely to Castro. By 1963, they in turn would be purged when Fidel felt it necessary to do battle with what would be termed the first "Microfraction" of the PSP, which he believed the Soviets had incited to oust him. Besieged as he was, he would remain one step ahead of his would-be assassins, whether they were coming from his left or his right.

By the fall of 1961, Fidel was well into the process of acquiring his six domiciles, all under the protection of the Department of Frequent and Permanent Residences. He soon had a home in the Cubanacán district, on 164th Street; another in Santiago de Cuba; a mansion on Varadero that had once belonged to the Dupont family; an apartment in the Vedado district on Eleventh Street; a country estate in the San Andrés Valley of Pinar del Río Province; and a place on Santa María del Mar beach inside the Havana city limits. There was also a house in each of the Cuban provinces that the department guarded and could be used by other high officials when Fidel was not in need of it.

Beyond the inner circle of protectors was the Security Brigade (Bon), a second perimeter in the form of a battalion of soldiers, and beyond that, a third and fourth concentric ring that surrounded him when he was in public or at any other special venue.

The man who was placed in charge of penetrating the plots against him was Fabian Escalante Font. He "had eyes everywhere," all the way to the depths of the most intimate conspiracy.[38] Many even allege that he went on to become the regime's star assassin in uncounted foreign and domestic hits. So successful and so renowned did "Roberto" Escalante become that he would one day inspire a hit Cuban TV show, based on his exploits.

And so confident of that reputation did Fidel become that he regarded himself as invincible. According to Marita Lorenz, the young woman whom the New York tabloids had claimed was Fidel's sex slave in 1959, she escaped his clutches—Fidel sent her to New York after a botched Cuban abortion—only to be sent back by the CIA to poison him. Fidel knew exactly what she had come to do.

"I know you have come to kill me," he sneered, confronting her in the hotel room to which she had been brought by Fidel's aides. "Here." He handed her a gun and lay down on the bed.

Marita pointed it at his head, the barrel trembling at the end of her arm. Finally, she just burst into tears.

"I can't do it," she moaned, dropping the weapon in the sheets.

"Of course you can't," said he. "No one can."

The last elements of the Trujillo family were driven out of the Dominican Republic by the end of November. Trujillo's son, Ramfis, had personally executed six of his father's assassins, then skipped back to Paris to exile himself. It was never proved that he had been hunting Kennedy when both were in the French capital, but two of Ramfis's uncles, Petan and Hector, were lying in wait to oust the new, U.S.-backed president of the "D.R.," Joaquín Balaguer. When the sun rose over the National Palace on the nineteenth of the month, however, there were two American aircraft carriers and a guided-missile cruiser parked three miles offshore. The U.S. consul passed President Kennedy's latest ultimatum on to the Trujillo brothers: get off the island that day, or prepare for the United States Marines to come ashore. They were soon whisked away on a Pan American aircraft and taken to the place that had served as Latin America's political triage and recovery unit for nearly a century, Miami.

On November 30, Operation Mongoose was officially put into motion, with Ed Lansdale as the head of the Cuba Project's Special Group (Augmented), or SGA. Tracy Barnes's old Árbenz team was already busy shuffling through the deck of ideas. Among the most colorfully absurd was one to convince Cuba's Catholic population that if Fidel were purged, Jesus Christ would soon return to the world and would do so by way of Cuba.

In December, Kennedy embarked on a swing through South America—over the objections of the Secret Service. Nixon had been pelted with rocks there just two years earlier, but Nixon was Nixon. Jack took the gamble and went to Bogotá to see Alberto Lleras Camargo, then on to Venezuela to show his support for his charismatic Latin equivalent, Betancourt. He was there to promote the goals of the newfound Alliance for Progress, and the crowds were ten deep along the avenues, an unprecedented reception for an American president. As Richard Reeves put it, "The most powerful man in the world was young; he was Catholic; he had a dark and beautiful wife who spoke Spanish to the crowds. And he was there. Anything seemed possible."[39]

As Jack's limo eased through the rapturous masses in Bogotá, President Lleras turned to him and asked, "Do you know why those workers and *campesinos* are cheering you like that?" Jack smiled and waved and cocked his ear closer for the answer. "It's because they believe you are on their side," Lleras continued.

On the way back to Washington, the First Couple spent a day with Joe Sr. in Palm Beach. The next day, the nineteenth, Jack returned to the White House and was about halfway through his day when Bobby called with some difficult news. Their father had suffered a massive stroke on the golf course. Jack went straight back to Florida.

Old Joe would never again reign supreme. At St. Mary's Hospital, it took the old man two days to recognize Jack, and, by then, the president was on the move once more. He had to meet with British Prime Minister Harold Macmillan to discuss Christmas Island, a site that Jack needed the Brits to cede for atmospheric nuclear tests.

They met in Bermuda just before Christmas, a productive day-long huddle on the white sands. Macmillan's habit was to write in his diary at the end of the evening. He liked Jack, and he made note of his wit and charm. He was concerned for his obvious physical discomfort, too. The president's back gave him nearly constant pain and made him unable to sit for lengths of time. The man was usually in motion, if only because stillness was often agonizing. Bundy, his national security adviser, had once admonished him about the White House staff's "problem of management. We can't get you to sit still."

But the British PM expressed concern for the deeper implications of that restlessness, something that went to the heart of the young man's capacities in an incredibly dangerous time:

"There is a marked contrast between President Kennedy 'in action' on a specific issue (e.g. Congo, West Irian [Indonesia], Ghana), and his attitude to larger issues (nuclear war, the struggle between East and West, Capitalism and Communism, etc.). In the first he is an extraordinarily quick and effective operator . . . On the wider issues, he seems rather lost . . ."

On Christmas Day, Lee Oswald was granted exit visas for himself and Marina, now seven months pregnant, a veritable nativity scene of return from exile.

She had come to see his dark side more and more plainly by this time. He had taken to helping his friend Ernst Titovets learn English by improvising dialogues with him at the kitchen table and recording them on a reel-to-reel. One night, he improvised in the role of a serial killer.

"Tell us about your last killing," Ernst prodded.

"Well, it was a young girl under a bridge. She came in carrying a loaf of bread and I just cut her throat from ear to ear."

"What for?" Ernst asked Lee's imaginary self.

"Well, I just wanted the loaf of bread, of course."

"What do you take to be your most famous, uhh . . . in your life?"

"Well," said Lee, "the time I killed, uhh, eight men on the Bowery that were on the sidewalk there. They were just standing there loafing around. I didn't like their faces so I just shot them with a machine gun. It [the murder] was very famous. All the newspapers carried the story."[40]

There was more to this than just macabre play. It was a symptom of more active fantasies. Lee was still under constant observation. It's likely that the KGB even entered his apartment from time to time when he and Marina were out. By whatever means, one of his KGB overseers, Oleg Nechiporenko, was informed just before the new year that the American had started building bombs. "He had already built two iron casings, one box-shaped and the other cylindrical. Each contained two compartments; one filled with shot and the other with explosives. He had also prepared paper-tube fuses, 4–5 centimeters long and 2 millimeters in diameter. They were to be filled with gunpowder, with the fuse designed to last approximately two seconds."[41] How and where he constructed them isn't known, but he hid them from Marina, in the apartment. He couldn't have built them at the factory, because it would have been noticed. The implications were all the more sinister because Khrushchev was due to visit Minsk in January, but there was disagreement about how advanced Lee's experiments were. Another KGB man reported that Lee soon disposed of the amateur devices in the apartment house's trash bin and, upon closer examination, they were deemed to be little more than "toys."[42]

There was another unnerving episode. On January 2, 1962, Lee alarmed his KGB shadows again by hoisting his shotgun off the living room wall, carrying it down to the street, and boarding a streetcar with it. Such things were unheard of in the Soviet Union at that time. His secret police tails kept him in their sights all the way across the city, but he ended up at the pawnshop where he had purchased the gun the year before, and he came out a few moments later, empty-handed and eighteen rubles richer.[43]

By this time, the Minsk KGB was fed up with Lee. His was a "primitive, basic" case, according to one of his handlers.[44] He was a person who never showed the slightest sign of being an operative, a person of relatively simple behavior and only mild intelligence who nonetheless devoured many intelligence resources while producing zero yield. They would recommend that Moscow do nothing to impede his repatriation to America. Their attitude was "good riddance to bad rubbish."

On February 15, Marina Oswald gave birth to a daughter, June, and it would not be until early June 1962 that the young family would finally be allowed to depart for the United States of America.

The day that Marina was released from the hospital, February 23, 1962, was also the day that Uncle Ilya was summoned to the office of Captain Alexander Federovich Kostikov to report on his briefings of his niece, Marina, talks meant to guide her behavior once she reached America. Kostikov's top-secret memo makes it clear that there had been two conversations between them, that "P" (Prusakov) would "continue to have educational conversations" with her and with Lee, and that her uncle Ilya was concerned that Lee might be "a dubious personality," that his niece might be in danger. She had protested that he was nothing of the sort.[45]

Decades later, in a mountain village in Austria in 2005, a current FSB (successor to the KGB) agent would meet with one of the authors' investigative partners at a secret rendezvous. A man with access to the most sensitive records of Soviet history, "Nikolai" (as he chose to be referred to) had agreed to search one of the most subterranean of KGB archives—the "encrypted" files—for anything pertinent to the Kennedy assassination.* Among the discoveries he made was that—in addition to the heart-to-heart talks with her uncle—KGB agents had met directly with Marina at least once before she emigrated. According to Nikolai, who had read the file and scribbled notes, she was allowed to go only if she would agree to their plan to use her as a sleeper agent. Before their departure, the KGB told her that in return for letting her go to the States, they would activate her after a couple of years, if need be, as an asset inside the U.S. That was the trade.[46] When and if they asked for it, she would provide information or conduct an action from abroad. It was understood that to refuse to cooperate would jeopardize those left behind in the homeland.

In Dallas, Texas, where the Oswalds would be living nearly two years later, and where Lee would die, FBI agent Jim Hosty would be the second agent assigned to Lee after his re-entry interview, and Hosty would have such suspicions from the beginning. Everything he had learned in his training told him that Marina would never have been allowed to leave Minsk without making a deal with the KGB. Not only was Hosty aware of her uncle Ilya's status as an MVD colonel, he was also well versed in the FBI's criteria for suspicion, an eight-point checklist that Marina filled as though it had been written with her in mind.[47]

What's more, Hosty knew that since every one of Oswald's friends was reporting to the KGB, that since his closest friend, Marina, was a member of the Komsomol (the Communist Youth Party) and the niece of Ilya Prusakov,

---

*Nikolai was a trusted longtime source for the award-winning Willi Huismann (see Introduction), and, throughout their partnership on many projects, had never delivered anything but accurate information.

it was absurd to think that she would not have been approached. Additionally, almost immediately after her arrival in the U.S., Marina dutifully reported her new address to KGB case officer Vitaly A. Gerasimov, stationed at the Soviet embassy in Washington. Gerasimov's responsibilities included paying U.S. contacts for intelligence data.[48] *

Hosty would beseech his superiors to open an investigation of Marina immediately upon her arrival from Russia, but he was reminded that FBI protocols prevented it: at that time, pre-9/11, foreigners could not be investigated until six months after their arrival, unless there was some evidence that they had committed a crime.

---

*Given the KGB's desperation to plant eyes and ears in the West, her "arrangement" was a no-brainer. As a field agent with a near-photographic memory, Hosty would also recall the experience of another young American, James Mintkenbaugh, who lived in the USSR until 1959, when he too decided he had seen enough of the Red Utopia. Upon his return to Boston, he told FBI agents that the KGB had asked him if he would marry a young Soviet woman and take her back to the U.S. with him, but he had declined.

CHAPTER 6
Both Sides Now

IF 1961 ENDED on a tense note, the new year would commence with eerie foreshadowing as the Cubans ratcheted up the propaganda effort inside their capital city. On New Year's Day, 1962, Fidel and Raúl celebrated the beginning of the revolution's fourth year with a *carnaval* and parade that would begin on Havana's Malecon and then pour into the side streets, a mass of hot rhetoric and patriotic song oozing through the capital like a lava flow. The propaganda ministry had recently approved a cartoon of the American president injecting a child with heroin, which was run in the magazine *Mella*, and poster-sized reproductions were visible on that day, bobbing above the heads of the crowd. Except for open depictions of "perverted" sex, there were no fantasies of American decadence that would be off-limits to the mouthpieces of the regime, and the retribution they dreamed of was now being enacted before thousands of Cuba's citizens.

Attendance at the parade was mandatory for all but the oldest and youngest Cubans, and hundreds of buses brought more people in from the countryside. On the parade route, fried fish, pork rind, and *plátanos* sizzled on barbecues. Fresh *líquidos* spilled from the vendors' big glass jugs, furtively spiked with rum. The live music of the neighborhoods tangled with the martial tunes broadcast for the occasion from hundreds of transistor radios. Kids hawked fruits and sugar pastries from doorways, and the sidewalk booths were bursting with revolutionary gimcracks, on sale to the people for pennies.

The centerpiece of the procession was an oversize casket bearing an effigy of President Kennedy, with the words MR. KENNEDY LIES HERE. CUBAN REVOLUTION KILLED HIM painted in bold white letters in English.[1]

Smiling from the presidential reviewing box were Raúl, Fidel, Che, Blas Roca, and President Dorticós, as tens of thousands lined the streets, cheered from the windows, and jeered from the rooftops. *"Kenn-e-dee, muerte! Kenn-e-dee, muerte!!"*

Early in February, Fidel received a copy of a Soviet report that he interpreted as another sign—this one straight from Kennedy's mouth—that a new Cuban invasion plan was under construction in Washington. That report would provide yet another bit of kindling for the crisis that would ignite in the coming year.

At the end of January, President Kennedy met with Aleksei Adzhubei, the editor in chief of the Kremlin house organ, *Izvestia*, and the son-in-law of Soviet premier Khrushchev. With him was Georgi Bolshakov, putatively an information apparatchik at the Soviet embassy and the editor of Russia's English-language magazine, *USSR*, but in fact an intelligence officer in the Red Army. He was wily, a man to watch with eyes wide open, but he was affable and well regarded, a reliable conduit between Kennedy and Khrushchev in crucial moments. The group sat down to lunch, along with Mrs. Kennedy and Adzhubei's wife, Rada, a striking blonde in a sable coat. At one point, little Caroline careened into the room, her face wet with tears. She had awakened, unhappily, from a nap; and as Jackie picked her up and took her back to her room, Jack used her entrance to make a poetic point, telling the Russians that Caroline had both a crucifix and a Russian doll in her bedroom.

"Your father-in-law said that our children should live under Communism," Jack remarked. "But I prefer to put these two objects in front of her bed for her to choose—a present from Khrushchev and a present from the Pope. Let her decide."[2]

After lunch, Jack led the men into the upstairs Oval Room. There was much to discuss, given the tensions of the preceding year, and Jack and Adzhubei did most of the talking. Kennedy began by warning that the Kremlin should not underestimate his resolve on Berlin. The previous summer, the Soviets had erected a wall through Berlin to prevent residents of Communist East Germany from emigrating to the West through free West Berlin. Now there was a standoff between the U.S. and East German armies to prevent a Communist takeover of the whole city, a strategic loss for the Western powers.

The president and his guest circled each other on the volatile subject of Cuba as well, and when Adzhubei asked the president, point-blank, if another invasion was being planned, the president replied, just as bluntly, "No." But then things got murky.

"If I run for reelection," he said, "and the Cuban question remains as it is—then Cuba will be the main problem of the campaign, [and] we will have to do something."

It had to have made Adzhubei sit up and take notice; and, as Jack went on, it only got murkier.

He told the Russians that after the Bay of Pigs shambles, he had hauled Allen Dulles onto the carpet "and dressed him down. I told him: 'You should learn a lesson from the Russians. When they had difficulties in Hungary, they liquidated the conflict in three days."[3]

Within hours of the meeting, Adzhubei fired a secret communiqué off to his father-in-law in the Kremlin, and Fidel was copied with some version of that report almost immediately. Castro believed that the word "intolerable" had been used by the president in describing Russia's increasing influence in Cuba, and he took the comment about Hungary to be a warning to Moscow. Jack, by Fidel's estimation, was saying that because the U.S. did not intervene when Russia occupied Hungary, the United States would expect the same restraint if they invaded Cuba.[4]

McGeorge Bundy, who was apparently present as well, would recall the conversation differently. Bundy believed that Jack did not use the word "intolerable," but rather said that it was difficult for the U.S. He also insisted that Jack had simply equated Hungary and Cuba as similarly important to the Russia and the U.S., respectively.

But the vagaries of the meeting did significant damage: in the following days, Fidel would use the report to garner a much larger infusion of Soviet military assistance.

Within a week of Adzhubei's communiqué, the Soviet Presidium approved a Cuban military aid package of $133 million, one that had been sidelined for months. Thirteen days after that, the KGB confirmed that "an [American] operational plan against Cuba" was in the works, with the president's approval, and that its air support would likely be based in Texas and Florida.[5]

As the perceived threats to Cuba triggered Russian countermeasures, Operation Mongoose was actually foundering. In fact, it was having so little impact on the Cuban infrastructure that its leaders were considering ways to create a phony provocation from Fidel's end, thereby justifying an all-out military assault. That was what the Cubans were expecting this time, anyway: no half-measures using exiled proxies, but a full-tilt attack with the signature of the Pentagon firmly emblazoned across its face.

Mary Hemingway had been mourning her husband for seven months. The winter solitude of Idaho was wearing on her, so in February, just as the Presidium was sowing the seeds of the Cuban missile crisis, Mary was setting off to spend the rest of the season in her New York City apartment.

Even winter can't dampen the sheer sociability of the city. A blizzard may muffle the screech and rumble of the subways through the sidewalk grates, but it only fills the bars and restaurants, the museums and the concert halls even fuller, and she knew the town would do her good.

As her traveling companion to Cuba, Valerie Danby-Smith, put it, Mary would not consciously have aided or abetted any scheme against the person of Fidel Castro. But the artistic and political circles of the East had a way of bleeding together, and her recent encounter with the premier was soon the stuff of cocktail chat from Manhattan to Georgetown.

Once she was settled into her flat, the city called her out, and she made the rounds to the homes of friends, hungry for liveliness and good cheer. Her afternoon with Castro became a favorite yarn in the salons of the lit crowd, topped off as it was by the little smuggling operation on the shrimp boat, the old man's crates of stories being spirited out to sea. She had been so struck by Fidel's heedless charge up the stairs of the tower, she kept saying; so keenly aware that he was still a guerrilla with an almost ghostlike freedom to appear and disappear on the landscape; and so struck by how few trappings of power he surrounded himself with. Whatever his ugly secrets, to her he had seemed like an embodiment of his ideals, a man among the people, protected by his very rapport with them and their apparent faith in him. She was hardly a naive woman. She saw him clearly, but his charismatic aura could not be denied.

And in many American households, Fidel still held a certain fascination. New Yorkers were as hungry for stories about him in the winter of 1962 as they had been when he came through in 1959, and Mary fed hers to anyone who was interested. Among them were writers and journalists, of course. By the second week of March, the *New York Times* and *Post* had picked up a newsy version of the story, though neither of the papers mentioned Fidel's light security. Mary's friend Clifton Daniel, an assistant managing editor of the *Times* (and Harry Truman's son-in-law), thought that Edward R. Murrow should talk to Mary. Murrow, the legendary newsman who was now heading up the United States Information Agency (the USIA), agreed.

On March 20, Murrow dropped Daniel a follow-up letter.

"Mary Hemingway did call," he wrote. "We had an interesting and useful conversation and I passed her remarks on to one or two interested parties down here."

The USIA was, after all, a player inside Operation Mongoose.

Those interested parties proved to be the members of the Special Group (Augmented), the SGA, which met in the Oval Office on March 16, 1962, four days before Murrow's casual letter to Daniel. The purpose of the meeting was to set presidential guidelines for Operation Mongoose, just then getting up to speed, and it was attended by the president; Bobby; Mac Bundy; the newly sworn director of the CIA, John McCone; General Maxwell Taylor, military adviser to the president (and the only member of the top brass whom Jack actually liked); the chair of the Joint Chiefs, General Lyman Lemnitzer; U. Alexis Johnson, a deputy undersecretary of state; Roswell Gilpatric, deputy secretary of defense; and Ed Lansdale. Lansdale would write a memorandum of this meeting that would become the only known piece of documentary evidence that Jack and Bobby ever endorsed or authorized a hit on Fidel.

The meeting commenced with a briefing from Lansdale about the training of Cuban exile insurgents in the fine points of guerrilla warfare. The president then reiterated that he was not yet ready to approve any direct American military involvement in such plans. Lately, he had made many speeches warning against the new insurrectionary forms of war and calling for improved countermeasures. The history of warfare had reached the point in which conflict was either catastrophically global, or secreted in the supposed "backwaters" of civilization. It was all or nothing.

According to Lansdale, it was Bobby who opened the discussion about Mary Hemingway. She had apparently conveyed that Castro was drinking heavily, disgruntled by the way things were going in Cuba. What this specifically referred to was anyone's guess, but certainly his economic woes and the stress of being constantly hunted might have had something to do with it.

Bobby then briefly described "the opportunities offered by the shrine" to Hemingway. Fidel's movements had proved very hard to track, and when he was seen, he was usually protected by a phalanx of guards. The *finca* implication was that he held the place in some personal esteem and his retreats there were relatively vulnerable. If he was known to visit the *finca*, however unpredictably, it might still present an opportunity for a stakeout by the Cuban underground. Mary's conversation with Murrow had been mirrored by other sources, and Lansdale's memo, written later that same afternoon, called the plan "worth assessing firmly and pursuing vigorously. If there were grounds for action, the CIA had some invaluable assets which might well be committed for such an effort."[6] There were hints in his text that the CIA was not at its usual place at the hub of such discussions but was just another spoke. "McCone asked if his operational people were aware of this; I told him that we had discussed this, that they agreed the subject was worth vigorous development, and that we were in agreement that the matter was so delicate and sensitive that it shouldn't be surfaced to the Special Group until we are ready to go, and then not in detail." Lansdale went on: "I pointed out that this all pertained to fractioning the regime. If it happened, it could develop like a brush-fire, much as in Hungary, and we must be prepared to help it win our goal of Cuba freed of a Communist government."

According to Peter Kornbluh, a senior analyst at the National Security Archive, the Special Group at that time "routinely planned sabotage, violence and chaos to undermine Castro." The only plan that would be taboo to the SG—at least until it was a fait accompli—would have been the murder of a foreign head of state. In the words of a former CIA director, "The language of the memo speaks for itself. The only thing that Robert Kennedy can be referring to is the assassination of Castro. This paragraph should never have been written."[7]

There are no records, however, to show that the Finca Vigía scenario was ever put into action. The next month, other CIA murder plots were reactivated (after a hiatus while the Cuba Project was being built), but none of the players of that era would recall any further action being taken there. Its greatest significance is in establishing the long-obscured Kennedy record on that count, but the Hemingway option would go down as just another on a list of hundreds of others and only serves, in retrospect, to emphasize what an impossible task it was proving to be.

John Sherwood, a CIA case officer for the Cuba Task Force, reflected on it years later: "We didn't have any assets that could do anything with this information then. We had a few agents in Cuba who could send us secret-writing intelligence reports. That was it. All kinds of things bubbled up then . . . No one knew anything. Any information about Castro was exciting. We never penetrated the entourage. We never knew where he was."

The March 16 SGA confab provides convincing evidence that the Kennedys were directing the assassination probes; other insiders have since confirmed it. A year later, Joseph Califano (who would become an aide to President Lyndon Johnson) was working as an assistant to Cyrus Vance, the general counsel of the Department of Defense. Joe was also on Bobby's Cuban Coordinating Committee with Alexander Haig Jr. and others when, at a meeting attended by the attorney general, Bobby "talked about knocking off Castro. I was stunned. He [RFK] was talking so openly, and there were other people in the room." The phrase "knock off" was clear. It meant kill, "no ifs, ands, or buts. No doubt."[8]

"Bobby was always for that kind of thing," Undersecretary of State George Ball later said. "He was fascinated by all that covert stuff, counter-insurgency and all the garbage that went with it."[9] When asked recently about the assassination plotting, Thomas Parrott, the CIA officer assigned to act as secretary to the SGA when such things were discussed, replied, "I'm convinced that Bobby knew plenty about it and was the engine behind it to a considerable extent . . . saying, 'We don't care what you do.' He knew perfectly well, I'm convinced . . ."[10] In his autobiography, Richard Bissell added his perspective, writing: "To understand the Kennedy administration's obsession with Cuba, it is important to understand the Kennedys, especially Robert. From their perspective, Castro won the first round at the Bay of Pigs . . . He had defeated the Kennedy team; they were bitter and could not tolerate his getting away with it. The president and his brother were ready to avenge their personal embarrassment by overthrowing their enemy at any cost."[11]

Lastly, when the CIA conducted its own "after action" report of the assassination plots during this period, it concluded: "We cannot overemphasize the extent to which responsible Agency officers felt themselves subject to the Kennedy administration's severe pressures to do something about Castro and his regime. The fruitless, and in retrospect, often unrealistic plotting should be viewed in that light."[12] Most observers agree that what Bobby knew, Jack knew. For the doubters, Thomas Parrott himself would finally concede that "We weren't supposed to admit that our decisions went to the president, but they did."[13] In the case of the Hemingway option, the president, in adition to Parrott, was in the room.

One month after the SGA meeting, Mary Hemingway was the honored guest at a White House dinner to celebrate the life of her husband. By this time, she may have surmised that her cheerful account of Fidel's charm and bravery might have been misapplied toward ugly ends. During the course of the evening, she managed to get the president's attention long enough to express her considered opinion that his confrontational posture toward Cuba was "stupid, unrealistic and worse, ineffective."

Jack was mightily displeased at her insolence, it was said, but not in the least bit deterred. The secret war between the Kennedy and Castro brothers was just hitting its stride.

In April, Bill Harvey finally got around to reestablishing contact with Johnny Rosselli, the CIA's original point man in the mob-driven scheme to hit Castro. Harvey and his new boss, Directorate of Plans chief Richard Helms, continued to take a dim view of this plan, especially since the 1961 plots had been so neatly x-rayed by the Castro brothers. Still, Harvey was a

Company man, and much as he grumbled, he did rendezvous with Rosselli, handed him some more poison pills, and left a van for him in a Miami parking lot, stacked to the roof with bomb detonators and guns of every description.

But the relationship between Harvey and the Kennedys degenerated rapidly, even as Mongoose was ramping up. Harvey felt that Bobby's direct relationship with the anti-Castro exiles was ludicrously transparent. It was suicide for a person in Bob's position to be known to operatives in the field, to be seen coming and going, but Bobby was either oblivious to the risk or willfully indifferent.

Reporter-author David C. Martin once witnessed an encounter that became typical of the Bobby/Harvey relationship: "During one meeting, Kennedy rattled off a series of questions to Harvey, finishing with, 'and I've got ten minutes to hear the answer.' When Harvey exceeded his time limit, Kennedy walked out. Harvey kept talking."[14]

Sam Halpern, Harvey's assistant on the Cuba Project, was sitting across from his boss in the Mongoose operations center one afternoon when Bobby called and started haranguing him. Bobby wanted to know why it was that when the Cuba Desk did things "secretly," news of it kept ending up in the press. Harvey, who by now considered Bobby clueless about the conduct of "unattributable" operations, started to explain "in words of one syllable" that when the Cuban underground managed to blow something up, it was going to make headlines, somewhere, somehow. It was Bobby and his brother who were "demanding the 'boom and bang' all over the island," Harvey reminded him.[15]

At this point in the Cold War, the CIA's largest outposts were no longer in places like Berlin or Cairo, but in Miami and Mexico City. The Miami JM/WAVE Base was mission control for the ouster of Fidel and Raúl. Functioning under the cover of Zenith Technical Enterprises, JM/WAVE operated from Building 25, a two-story clapboard box at the University of Miami's secluded South Campus, formerly the Richmond Naval Air Base. The west face of the building itself bore a curious resemblance to the porte cochere of the north front of the White House, replete with the raking cornice and pediment. But it was not a lush lawn that surrounded it—just stringy ground cover and tattered banana palms poking from white, sandy soil. Inside, it was more or less an enormous barracks cut into offices, communications bays, and eating and sleeping areas.

Ted Shackley, a rising CIA star (and Bill Harvey's former number two in

Berlin), was JM/WAVE station chief from early 1962 through the middle of 1965; and some three to four hundred agents toiled under his leadership, making JM/WAVE the largest CIA station in the world, second only to the headquarters in Langley, Virginia.[16]

One day, while Harvey was on one of his periodic operational forays to the base, he heard the unmistakable rumble of a helicopter landing on the hardened turf outside the building. He peered out to see Bobby alighting from the chopper. Apparently, he had shuttled over from the family compound at Palm Beach, another blatant breach of secrecy. Harvey took a long pull from one of the liquor bottles he kept in a drawer and braced himself.

Bobby was soon inside, shouting out orders. When he found Harvey's office, there was no greeting. He just kept up his barrage. Harvey engaged him, as usual, and Bobby only grew more angry, insisting that the men on the CIA side were not being aggressive enough, that not enough men were dying for the cause, if dying was what it took. Crossing to a teletype machine from which new orders from Langley were spewing, Bobby ripped the paper from the machine, a skein of highly sensitive, coded material, and was heading out the door with it when Harvey rose from his chair.

"Hey!" he barked. "Where are you going with that?!" He snatched the paper from Bobby's hand, folded it into a wad, and shoved it in his pocket, staring at the hawk-faced attorney general eyeball-to-eyeball.

It is not known who blinked first, but that was probably the beginning of Harvey's end at the Cuba desk. Harvey was too disgusted to care, at that point.[17]

And tensions only escalated between Bobby and the Agency at large. CIA director John McCone witnessed another blistering verbal assault between Bobby and Harvey, not once arising to Harvey's defense. Still, the relationship dragged on and would not come crashing down until the climactic missile crisis, later that year.

People under such terrible, complex mental strain were apt to resort to the worst kinds of behavior. Bobby was trying in vain to spark a counter-revolution among people whose forces had been radically depleted—not least by the effects of the Bay of Pigs invasion. The Republican right was constantly positioning itself as tougher than the Kennedys, more willing to brandish "the nuclear option." It was a kind of schoolyard baiting, reiterated every morning from Capitol Hill and half the newspapers in the nation. Bob believed, in his soul, that his brother had to be the carrot, and he the stick, if they were to remain in office, vanquish the perceived threat from the Castros, and offer the desperate populations of Latin America an alternative to Communism before the whole continent tipped into anarchy.

What Bobby did not know, because it was not fully revealed until years later, was that Bill Harvey was trying to save him from himself. Harvey's notes, scrawled in cursive and left for historians to discover after his death, would vouch for it. To the end, he continued to believe that assassination was "the last resort beyond last resort," a tactic of desperation and weakness. He said as much to the plot's designated fixer, mobster Johnny Rosselli, admitting that there wasn't "much likelihood of this going anyplace."[18] Rosselli already knew that. The wiseguys themselves had pulled back, once it became clear that the new and improved Justice Department was coming for them. What serious assassination plotting that did continue, inside and outside the purview of the CIA, did so without the concerted effort of Harvey. Indeed, Bill Harvey may be the single greatest reason that Fidel and Raúl Castro were still walking the earth in 2008.

As the Oswalds' departure from Minsk drew near, their friends stopped coming by to visit. Lee's pal Ernst Titovets recalled that the marriage and June's birth had its way of easing single friends out of the picture, but there was another reason: people stopped dropping by because they were sure that KGB surveillance would have been stepped up. The couple saw less and less of their old gang, but a few, like Lee's best friends, Titovets and Pavel Golovachev, stuck around in the last few months.

Pavel didn't give Marina much thought. He probably knew her reputation. Whether she had fooled Lee into thinking she was a virgin when they married, or had simply revealed her extracurricular frolics after they were wed, Marina got around in that first year, at least according to some of her male friends. It didn't much matter to Pavel. He would surreptitiously share a cigarette with her on the balcony, since Lee hated to see her smoke, but beyond that little intimacy he didn't relate to her much.

He was focused mainly on Lee, partly under duress. Pavel was not much of a patriot. The only reason he started giving information to "the Organs," the KGB, was that he had been strong-armed into it. He had made it a point to give Lee subtle hints that his life was not private, and he tried to give up very little to the Organs, but over time he had been forced to meet regularly with Alexander Kostikov like some real-life spy, one time on a street corner, the next time in a park, another time at a kiosk. On one occasion, Alexander urged Pavel to tell Lee that his father was a hotshot in the Soviet Air Force, just to see if it captured any special interest.

It didn't. Lee had known that General Golovachev was a war hero and commander of Northwestern Siberia since he and Pavel had met in the radio plant a few months after his arrival. It never seemed to matter to him. When Pavel did as Alexander had instructed him, Marina put him on the spot. She knew how to read the tea leaves.

"Why are you saying that to him?" she challenged Lee's buddy.

Or was it a challenge? Pavel couldn't be sure if she was really savvy enough to suspect him of trying to lure Lee into trouble, or if she was just asking why he didn't address the information to her.[19]

Unbeknownst to Pavel, Lee and Marina were well aware of the surveillance. "We'd become like two kids," Marina would recall. When she and Lee wanted to keep anything private, they would go to the balcony or turn on a radio, mostly to protect the interests of friends or, more important, Uncle Ilya and Aunt Valya. "I was his ally all the way through. Just for the damn principle of it."[20]

Lee desisted from making too many incendiary comments about Russia, though he was more disillusioned by the day. The second thoughts had begun soon after he got there in October of 1959. The first American official who grilled him on why he wanted to defect, just six days after setting foot in Moscow, had told him, "USSR [is] only great in Literature."[21] Snyder at the American embassy had tried to warn him off his plan, had even saved his American citizenship for him. When Lee made note of his first encounter with the engineer who ran his department in the Minsk plant, a Jewish-Argentinian immigrant named Alexander Ziger, he wrote that "he seems to want to tell me something," and five months later his new friend had advised him "to go back to the USA." It was the first voice of direct opposition Lee had heard. "I respect Ziger; he has seen the world. He says many things and relates many things I do not know about the USSR. I begin to feel uneasy inside, it's true!"[22] The factory's party secretary, Lebizen—"fat, fortyish, and jovial on the outside"—started making him paranoid. The omniscient portrait of Lenin, keeping watch over Lee and his co-workers during morning calisthenics each day, gave him the creeps. "Shades of H. G. Wells!" he wrote.

But there was no surge of American patriotism in him. There was just the unease; the absence of a true sense of belonging anywhere; the corrosive dissatisfaction with "society," in all its forms; the yearning for some perfect world.

Now, when he made positive comments about the United States, they were apt to touch on the bizarre. One evening when the two men were just sitting around the apartment, Pavel asked how Lee would sate Marina's sudden desire for earthly goods when she first caught sight of the Land of the Free.

Out of the blue, Lee told Pavel that he didn't quite get what life in the United States was like, and then added: "You could always make a lot of money by shooting the president," he said.[23] Not since 1955, when he'd told a friend that he would like to kill Eisenhower for exploiting the poor, had Lee shown any predilection for assassination, and the comment instantly sprung to Pavel's mind when he learned of Lee's arrest eighteen months later.[24]

Lee had been writing a manuscript about life in the USSR. It was called *The Collective*, and it was one of those surreptitious projects of his that undermined Marina's trust in him. In the preface, he had written: ". . . full of optimism and hope he stood in Red Square in the fall of 1959 vowing to see his chosen course through, after, however, two years and a lot of growing up I decided to return to the USA."[25]

By this time, the KGB had come to realize that Marina didn't think much of her partner. It's not known if the secret police were aware of her indiscretions, but they were definitely interested in the degree of his sincerity as a husband. He had gotten married rather abruptly, but their sex life seemed adequate from his end, his moments of tenderness and humor legitimate. When she became pregnant and it appeared that he was sincere about taking his family with him to the States, it put to rest any last suspicions that he might be CIA.[26] If he had cut his wife and child loose before bounding out of the country, it would have alarmed them; but as their departure approached, Kostikov and his contacts became convinced that he was exactly what he appeared to be, a confused kid who had gone off on a brave adventure, become dispirited and homesick, and just wanted to take his little family back to his homeland.

That's not to say that there weren't still troubling passions afoot. The marriage was already subject to the strains of his weird secrecy, her ability to bait him with comments about other men, and his ever more frequent screaming fits. There had been more physical confrontations between them, if only tussles that usually ended in stalemate. His pornography collection kept growing. He now had a separate diary with entries about his activities made in an indecipherable code. Some investigators have assumed that it was a "blue" chronicle of extramarital amours, if indeed there were any in Minsk. But given his secrecy and Marina's later claims that Lee had friendships with resident Cubans, it is just as possible that this other diary contained details of those encounters. In any case, as with so many other relationships in his life—with his mother, the Marines, his new wife, or his country of choice—when disillusionment set in, he tended to exhibit the psychological problems first diagnosed when he was an adolescent. He became schizoid, by turns manic and passive-aggressive. His delusion—that he was a great man and would soon be appreciated as such—intensified.

As the last, lonely days approached, they sold all their furniture, the baby's crib included.

When the apartment was nearly stripped, Lee and Marina had one more ritual to perform: There was a very small device on a wall of the apartment, a thing of no discernible purpose that made a faint ticking sound, day and night. The couple had concluded that it was some sort of monitoring device, courtesy of the KGB. After the embassy trip, it had remained unclear whether they'd ever be allowed to leave. She had always been a renegade, outspoken and given to a certain wildness. And over time, perhaps since her visit to the American embassy, or since she was expelled from the Komsomol, Marina had found it harder to suppress her political rebelliousness.

And so they made a pact between them. They vowed that on the day of their departure—if that day ever came—they would stand in front of the little thing and tell the truth, express their true feelings about everyone they knew, everyone they suspected of being a KGB mole, all of it, if only to let the secret police know that they had always been well aware of their game.

On their last day in the apartment, they spilled out all their worst suspicions to the tiny "ear" on the wall.[27]

Even then, there was no great relief. As they crossed the threshold on May 22, the last words the KGB would record would be hers to him.

"You fucking guy," she said to her husband, "you can't even carry a baby."

At the Minsk train station, they were observed by a man behind a column but tried to ignore him. There was a tearful farewell to Uncle Ilya and Aunt Valya, who seemed to be trying to avoid being seen, and then the little family was off to Moscow for processing. There were a few days spent there, lighthearted ones as the reality set in, and then they took another train, westward bound.

A few hours later, the couple crossed the border into Poland. Warsaw looked just as forlorn as Russia had; but later that night, Marina awoke as they entered Berlin and she realized that there were two cities, the dark socialist one and the brightly lit capitalist one.[28] She tumbled back into sleep, rocked gently by the glide of the train, and when she awoke once more she found herself in what seemed to be a fairy tale. It was Holland. As her biographer would later describe it, "They rattled through village after village, each one prettier than the last and so clean that they looked as if they must be inhabited by dolls."[29]

On June 4, they boarded a ship of the Holland-America line, the *Maasdam*, and set out from Rotterdam. It was on this voyage that Lee began to change forever in her eyes.

Marina spent most of the journey in their cabin with the baby. Lee, however, would take stacks of the ship stationery to the library and scribble away there for hours. Marina did not know it, but her husband anticipated being met on the New York docks by reporters and pictured himself holding a press conference. Between bouts of seasickness, he wrote draft upon draft of imagined questions and answers, preparing a script for the defector-celebrity. He suspected that the FBI would be questioning him as well.

The duologues he wrote, and then the sprawling, one-sided diatribes they became, read now like a manifesto addressed to himself.

"The biggest and key fault . . . of our era is of course the fight for markets between the imperialist powers . . . which lead to wars, crises and oppressive friction which you have all come to regard as part of your lives. And it is this prominent factor of the capitalist system which will undoubtedly eventually lead to the common destruction of all the imperialistic powers . . ." But then, after bizarre lists were made of Marx and Engel's "mistakes," he departed from Communist cant, berated himself for the "immature" attitude that put a "curse on both your houses," and then ventured out to the waters of utter isolation. "Where can I turn? To factional mutants of both systems [Communism and capitalism], to oddball Hegelian revisionists out of touch with reality, [to] religious groups, to revisionists or to absurd anarchism? No!" In the middle of the sea, he clung to a library table amidships and wrote and wrote, reaching a kind of psychopolitical weightlessness, his identity momentarily suspended: "I have lived under both systems. I have sought the answers and, although it would be very easy to dupe myself into believing one system is better than the other, I know they are not."[30]

"I despise the representatives of both systems, whether they be socialist or Christian democracies," he went on. Other pages barely survived the crossing, smeared and gouged, scratched out and torn as he tried to write through his dyslexia. What remained readable included scrawled warnings of Armageddon, which he seemed to expect within weeks, perhaps even days. It could come at any moment, he railed, and if there was anything left, he promised himself that he would set up a peace organization, something beyond the two systems which "have now at this moment led the world in unsurpassed danger . . . into a dark generation of tension and fear . . ."[31]

The avatar of the sixties was bringing it all back home.

On June 13, the *Maasdam* docked in Hoboken, New Jersey, across the Hudson from the gleam of the New York City skyline. Marina, pleased that the date happened to be her lucky number, was excited to finally be coming ashore in America, but Lee was wound tight, still expecting to be met by Feds, cops, or reporters—or all three.

But the pier was abuzz with ordinary citizens and immigrants, no cops, no press. The absence of the latter was his first disappointment. He had craved the attention, but, as if to deny it, he said to her, "Thank God there are no reporters!" Marina could hear the lie beneath his exclamation, and he lied some more to the one person who *had* come to greet them, Spas T. Raikin, a rep from the Travelers Aid Society, there at the behest of the State Department.

He told Raikin that he had been a Marine stationed at the U.S. embassy in Moscow. He lied that he had landed with only $63 in his pocket, and he made it clear that he was taking his family to his brother's home in Texas, although brother Robert wouldn't be able to chip in for the fare to bring them there. When Raikin suggested that there might be a solution and urged them to accompany him to the Department of Welfare, Lee accepted the invitation.

Raikin took them into the city, via the Port Authority Bus Terminal at Forty-first Street, and on downtown to Franklin Street, to the New York City Department of Welfare. Lee was escorted into an office and seated before a desk. Marina and the baby waited in a private area of the reception room, the young mother breast-feeding the child.[32]

A few minutes passed, and then a caseworker came in and informed Lee that his brother's wife, Vada, had been called in Texas. The Department had asked her for $200 for the family's airfare to Dallas–Fort Worth. She promised to call her husband and make the arrangements.

Lee was furious. He sprang to his feet. He had told them not to do that!

He was told that it was routine in cases of indigents.

He was not indigent, he protested.

The caseworker reminded him that he had told Raikin he had no funds. Had they asked Marina, she would have dodged the question. She had been instructed by Lee not to talk about how much money they carried, though she believed he had just under $200 on his person.

Lee made a scene, thrashing around the office and demanding that the Department of Welfare pay for their tickets. The caseworker icily explained that, although it was standard procedure to give returnees a small amount of resettlement money, the law required them to seek travel expenses from friends or family, if he himself had no means.

Lee finally relented, and with that, he was on his way to Texas. But Marina was keen to new changes in her husband's temperament. Years later, she would observe that "immediately after coming to the United States, Lee changed. I did not know him as such a man in Russia . . . He helped me as before, but he became a little more of a recluse . . . He was very irritable, sometimes for a trifle."

The circumstances of his debriefing by the CIA are sketchy, but whether it was done in New York or in Texas, there is strong evidence that it was conducted by a Major Andy Anderson from the Agency's Domestic Contacts Division.

There were others with peripheral involvement. Thomas Casasin was the deputy chief of the Agency's "6 Research Section" at that time, the division that routinely debriefed defectors from Russia. He had been informed of Lee Oswald's return to the States, and a month after he got to Texas, Casasin sent a memorandum to the chief of the Soviet Section in Paris, Walter P. Haltigan, suggesting that someone from the Office of Operations should debrief him. Casasin wrote that Oswald looked "odd," and might have been sent out of Russia by the KGB. Casasin and Haltigan did not follow up and would not be sure, in later years, whether such a repatriation interview ever took place.[33]

Another Agency man named Donald Deneselya would provide further evidence, however, that a CIA officer with the last name Anderson had debriefed Lee. Deneselya, who worked under legendary "spycatcher" James Angleton, received a memo about the interview shortly after it occurred; it was four or five pages long, devoted mainly to descriptions of the Minsk radio plant.[34] Lee had spent almost no time in sensitive areas of the plant, so he would have had nothing of interest to reveal, apart from quotidian details of factory life, the quality of the food, and the like. The KGB had made sure of that.

In 1993, author John Newman found trace evidence in Lee's CIA file that the debriefing took place, an imprint of one document that had bled through to another. It contained the name Anderson and what looked like the first name Andy, beside the "OO" code for the Domestic Contacts Division, but the actual debriefing report was not in the file.[35]

The Agency was almost always working at cross-purposes with the FBI, and—in hindsight—it certainly did not apply enough resources to Oswald upon his return, whether it was in Texas, New Orleans, or Mexico. Even the recordings of him, picked up by bugs in the Cuban and Soviet embassies in Mexico City a month before Dallas, were not listened to in time to prevent what happened. They were routinely logged and shelved, to be listened to at a later date. Given the vast reach of the CIA, the numbers of assets and operatives it employed, and the number of enemies it watched, the failure to adequately profile and track one returned defector would have gone unnoticed—had he not shot the president.

With his pathological secrecy, the rich and yet luminously disturbed nature of his inner life, Lee is a man who resists historical attempts to describe him. Faced with the task of unpacking Oswald's psyche, Norman Mailer emerged with only this overarching question: ". . . Oswald was a secret agent. There is no doubt of that. The only matter unsettled is whether he was working for any service larger than the power centers in the privacy of his mind."[36]

As recent evidence suggests, he was both: at once a man in service to his own subjective agency, and a "patsy" for larger clandestine elements. Lee Oswald was never an operative for the American CIA, or for the Mafia. No evidence has arisen, from friends, family, associates, or authorities in either the United States or the old Soviet Union, that Lee was an agent of the American government. Nor was he, as Casasin feared, "sent out" by the KGB to spy on the United States. They had seen enough of him to know that he was neither smart enough nor mentally reliable enough to be trusted. What he was, within weeks of his arrival, was a Cuban-aligned sleeper agent, a potential asset who might prove useful to Havana one day. This was his greatest dream, one that he had auditioned for perhaps as early as his visits to the Cuban embassy in L.A. before he defected to Russia—to convince his heroes that he was one of them: that he believed as they believed, and that he could deliver on his violent promises. He would try his best to become a "self-recruited" Cuban spy, all the while ignorant of the fact that G2 already had its sights fixed on him.

The Feds did a slightly better job than the CIA in documenting Oswald's return. On June 26, FBI agent John Fain met and debriefed him in Fort Worth shortly after he and Marina got there. Unbeknownst to Lee, it was Fain who had been charged with conducting the pro forma investigation stateside, when Lee first defected to Moscow.

With Fain now was his assistant, B. Tom Carter. They wanted to know two things. Why had Lee gone to Russia? And had the KGB conscripted him? On hearing the first question, Lee was irascible, telling them first that he didn't want "to relive the past," and then that he went to the Soviet Union simply because he wanted to do so.[37] To the second question, he answered in the negative, repeatedly, vowing that it had been nearly impossible to get Marina out of the country, that the pain and heartache had been enormous for her, and that he wouldn't tell them names or addresses of her relatives for fear of reprisal by the Soviets.

He lied. He bobbed and weaved, as he so often did, almost for sport. He did promise to contact the Feds if Soviet intelligence tried to contact him, but when Fain wrote up his notes of the meeting, his overriding impression was that the guy was chilly, "evasive," and "arrogant." It was possible, he conceded, that Lee's arrogance might have been a cover for simply being afraid, but Fain felt that he should be interviewed again.

When Lee got home, he lied to his older brother, Robert, too, asserting that the FBI had asked him if he was a spy for the U.S. government.

"Don't you know?" Lee quoted himself as saying, with a smirk.[38]

In the late spring of 1962, presidential advance man Marty Underwood was asked to reconnoiter a Kennedy visit to Mexico City. Marty had been doing the advance work for Mayor Richard Daley in Chicago when the Kennedy patriarch, Joe Sr., conscripted him for the presidential campaign. When Jack was elected, the Kennedy White House pulled him into service on especially important junkets, putting him on the payroll as an employee of the Department of Commerce. "It was a cover job," Marty would later explain. "The White House did it all the time because of budget restraints on the president's staff. That way they could have more employees and hide the fact from Capitol Hill. I was with Commerce for eight years and never worked for them a day in my life."

The man could whip up a crowd from thin air, it seemed. John P. Roche, a presidential speechwriter for both Jack and his successor, would say, "The Kennedy honchos struck me as good in a mechanical way, but the genius of the tribe was Marty Underwood . . . After watching Marty for four years, I was convinced he could turn out a huge crowd in the middle of the Kalahari Desert on 24-hour notice."[39]*

Marty's power lay partly in his utterly innocuous appearance. He was as nondescript, balding, rumpled, and unfashionable a gray-flannel man as you could find in the bar car of any commuter train. But by some sixth sense about crowds and power, he could summon a mass of individuals and aim their attention like the best herding dog. He also had a disarming knack for coordinating presidential security between the notoriously turf-obsessed soldiers of the Secret Service, the FBI, and the CIA, and as a result he had made many friends among the senior officers of those agencies.

Jackie accompanied the president on the Mexican trip that began on June 29 and would end on July 2. Every trip that Jack made south of the border was for the purpose of extolling his new dream for a "democratic revolution" in Latin America. When he arrived, his first speech reiterated that theme, paying tribute to the Mexican Revolution and emphasizing that the wider revolution he hoped for would not be finished "until every child has a meal and every student has an opportunity to study, and everyone who wishes to work can find a job, and everyone who wishes a home can find one, and everyone who is old can have security."[40] The First Couple was received with open arms.

But even as the motorcade snaked its way from the airport and into the concrete canyons of the city, even as the throngs cheered "Viva Kennedy," and a blizzard of serpentine and confetti spilled from the rooftops, someone was stalking the president. The CIA's Mexico City station chief, Win Scott, had alerted the advance team and hundreds of police were fanning out across the city.

Win's team had uncovered a Cuban plot to assassinate the president. A Cuban with a concealed weapon was arrested, and it is not known why he was later released, except that Mexico had a special tolerance for Cuban desperados. Little else came to light about the incident.[41] Win's agents had dismantled the plot, and for Marty, it just went with the territory.

---

*Roche was far from alone in his praise of Underwood: presidential aide Jack Valenti, Secret Service agent Clint Hill (assigned to the First Lady), and Washington columnist Marianne Means were among the chorus that sang Marty's praises.

In the tense hours before the plot was foiled, however, a fast friendship formed between Marty and Win Scott. The two men would die, years later, with many of their secrets still intact, but the trust that was built in June 1962 would provide the next president, Lyndon Johnson, with vital links in the historic chain of evidence between Fidel Castro and Lee Oswald.

The Cubans responded to the First Couple's wildly enthusiastic Mexican welcome by doctoring one of the news photos of them and running it in the official Havana press—a perfectly false portrait of Jack and Jackie, staggering, drunk, down a Mexico City street.[42]

By the time the FBI's John Fain had conducted his follow-up interview with Lee in August, he was convinced that the Oswalds had made no contact with the Dallas–Fort Worth Communist Party and appeared to pose no security risk. Lee's file was closed. Marina's case file was kept open, but hers was one of dozens and not particularly important to anyone in the field office.

On the other side of the world, there was a breathtaking development that would have entirely contradicted Fain's assumption, had it become known then. No one would hear of it for forty-three years, in fact, and it was only because of FSB (former KGB) officer Nikolai that we know of it now.

A former general of the KGB/FSB, who had examined the Kennedy dossier in the most restricted sanctum of Soviet intelligence, told Nikolai in 2005 that in the summer of 1962, the Soviets recommended Lee Harvey Oswald to its Cuban equivalents, G2 and the DGI.

Nikolai did not want to believe that. Even forty-two years removed from the bloody events of 1963, the thought was utterly paralyzing. If his conscience had not gotten him moving again, he might never have spoken of it or allowed a thought of it again for the rest of his life. But he had to see for himself, so, under the pretext of working on an urgent and current intelligence matter, and only after months of planning, Nikolai stole into that inner sanctum and pulled the file that his friend had spoken of, if only for a few moments.

"On a microfilm, I saw then with own eyes that there is actually an information [about] the Cuban country security," Nikolai marveled. "It is a secret telegram to Havana of 18 July 1962. It was signed by General Major Vladimir Kryuchkov, of the Communist Party Central Committee [CCCP]. I tried to memorize the wording of the telegram. For there is no way I can make copies of records in the archive. The risk [to me] would be too high."[43]

It should be noted that, as KGB historian Christopher Andrew points out, the CCCP held dominion over the KGB archives.[44] Kryuchkov, at the time a thirty-eight-year-old protégé of the soon-to-be KGB chief, Ambassador Yuri Andropov, was a hawkish, virulent anti-American, who himself would go on to head up the First Directorate of the KGB (foreign operations) in 1967, before becoming KGB chairman in 1989.[*]

On July 18, 1962, just over a month after Lee, Marina, and the baby arrived in New Jersey, the KGB's encrypted Oswald file was sent by Kryuchkov to G2 headquarters in Havana, to the attention of Ramiro Valdés Menéndez.

According to Nikolai, it read: "Lee Harvey Oswald left the Soviet Union in order to establish himself with his Soviet wife Marina in the U.S.A. He is ideologically unsound and psychically unstable." Nevertheless, Kryuchkov asked his Cuban counterpart, Valdés, "to observe Oswald in the US."[†]

This report would soon be corroborated by actors from the Cuban side—aging Cold Warriors still alive in the Americas. One of them, who went by the name "Oscar Marino," had been a senior Cuban spy, a founder of G2, a revolutionary companero of Fidel's, and "an old weapons companion and colleague"[45] of Fabian Escalante Font. It took over a year of negotiations for him to agree to sit for interviews. He lived, and perhaps still lives, in a Latin American metropolis, once a revolutionary, now a businessman; and when asked about his politics in 2005, he sighed that he had "had enough" of ideology and bloody intrigue. When the subject of "Oswald" was first broached with the old spymaster, he said, "it was too 'delicate' to discuss."[46] There was no way that he would consent to a meeting, but there was a little echo behind his words, an after-tone that was free of constraints.

---

[*] The hard-liner Kryuchkov would be an enthusiastic proponent of the Soviet invasion of Afghanistan. Under his stewardship, the KGB recruited two of its best U.S. turncoats, Aldrich Ames (CIA) and Robert Hanssen (FBI). So hawkish was Kryuchkov that he was fired as KGB chief in 1991 for taking part in the failed coup against Soviet president Mikhail Gorbachev, after years of opposition to perestroika and Gorbachev's overtures to the West. He died on November 23, 2007.

[†] Some, such as CIA counterintelligence czar James Angleton, believed that the hard-liners had recommended Oswald to the Cubans precisely to have *them* work with him to kill Kennedy instead of the KGB. The theory goes that the hard-liners hoped to use the killing to depose Khrushchev in an internal coup (Angleton interviews in Trento, *The Secret History of the CIA*, 255–263). However, it is now clear that the Soviets weren't recommending Oswald as much as they were asking the Cubans to keep an eye on him. Additionally, there is no evidence that the KGB had ever targeted Kennedy—it is only a theory. The coup, led by KGB chief Semichastny and Party Presidium president Leonid Brezhnev, was successful one year after Kennedy's death.

Finally, after being courted and cajoled for another stretch of months, Oscar agreed to a brief tête-à-tête in a home near Mexico City.

He was old and ill by that time, his movements painstaking. But his eyes were still young, curious, clear, and radiant with power and authority. Oscar let it be known immediately that he did not "want to strain himself before the propaganda cart of the U.S. government."[47] He had been a leftist his whole life and would remain so, but he was saddened by the "moral decline" of the revolution in Havana, the way that Fidel had degraded the ideals, had made the revolution his personal whore. He simply wanted future generations to know what had really happened, and it was not in order to cleanse the CIA's image or let the American mobsters off the hook. "The CIA is a snake and it bites by nature . . . We believed in the revolution and we must defend it," he said with an urgency that denied his age. "The USA and President Kennedy personally were determined to destroy our revolution. He was not for many Latin Americans a hero, a progressive man, and not for us Cubans. For us, . . . he was the counterrevolution personified. When Kennedy died, I cried no tears."[48]

Oscar joined the anti-Batista resistance as a nineteen-year-old kid, fighting in Havana for the urban guerrilla faction championed by the legendary Frank País in Santiago. When the revolution was won, he helped to create the revolutionary workers' brigade, and then went on to join the secret service in 1961 and become a founding member of G2. His position in the strategic leadership meant that he was regularly apprised of all the operations in progress: this is why he was in a position to know of the Oswald overtures.

He had nothing to do with Oswald directly. His field of operation was the containment of internal counterrevolutionaries. He had no knowledge of the man known as Nikolai, nor of an encrypted "Oswald file," nor of how G2 became aware of the American. When he was asked when the Cuban secret service first made contact with Lee, Oscar flinched and gave a long pause, gazing out a window at the tops of some mimosa trees.

"It was in the fall of 1962," Oscar said with certainty.

He had seen Lee Oswald's name on a "foreign collaborators" list, he said. Oscar had been present during high-level discussions on how to make contact with him, perhaps by drawing him to Mexico City.

He would tell more, eventually, but that was enough for the moment.

There was another source, too, and despite credibility issues regarding other matters in his life, what this man has said about the Cubans and Oswald warrants new consideration, especially when considering the eerie symmetry of his assertions with those of other new witnesses, none of whom he has ever met. Antulio Ramírez Ortiz, the Puerto Rican–born man who, as a young revolutionary, had spied for the Cubans at the Dominican consulate in New York, then hijacked a jet to Havana, is now elderly. He cannot recall whether it was the summer of 1962, or in the fall, that he too came upon the Oswald file, but he knew that he was still working as a chef and errand boy for G2 at its Havana headquarters.

Despite his felonious past, Antulio had been allowed, after serving a tenyear prison term for the hijacking, to defect back to the United States a decade later. His wife, Cora, was present in 2005 when he recounted the experience from the safety of his home in California. She was unable to sit still at the outset and pressured Antulio to hold himself back. The subject was still too dangerous, she insisted.

"After so long time, nothing more will happen to me." Antulio shrugged. "Moreover"—he smiled shyly—"I forgot most of it."

When he first hijacked his way back to Cuba, it had taken him a while to regain G2's trust. A prying, impetuously brave man by nature, he was dying to know where he really stood with them, and he said as much to a female G2 agent named Niurka, whom Antulio had always showered with gifts from his travels. Antulio's curiosity seemed harmless enough, and it was Niurka who eventually told him, in passing, that contact files of G2 boss Valdés were kept in the office of his assistant, an agent Munos. She added that Valdés had a lover, a woman named Migdalia, with whom he would tryst on Saturdays at a nearby hotel. Munos would accompany Valdés to stand by during his love-fests, as bodyguard.

So one Saturday, when Valdés and his bodyguard were out, Antulio decided to satisfy his curiosity about what his mentors thought of him. He had been interrogated harshly after the hijacking and, despite the acceptance he enjoyed by 1962, he still had doubts about whether or not he was completely trusted. So he took his chance, slipping into Munos's office for a quick recon.

"In my file were two copies of the interrogations that one [G2 agent] had carried out with me," he said. "On one of the copies, photos were fastened." That was apparently the full extent of his dossier; there was nothing he didn't already know.

But as Antulio Ramírez Ortiz was putting his file away, his attention fell on the dossier after his, labeled "Oswaldo-Kennedy." "The name 'Oswald,' I had heard never previously." According to his unpublished 564-page memoir, *Castro's Red Hot Hell*, the file contained a summary report from senior

G2 official Abelardo Colomé Ibarra (war name "Furry") to Valdés concerning the Kryuchkov-Oswald transmittal, which Antulio recalled as saying: "The KGB has recommended this individual, Lee Harvey Oswald, to us, not pressing it much. He is a North American, married to an agent of the Soviet Organism [Communist Party] who has orders to go and settle in the United States. Oswald is an emotional adventurer. Our embassy in Mexico has been instructed to get in contact with him. Be very careful."[49]

Paperclipped to the dossier was a photo of Kennedy's future assassin.

Ramirez had read this only twelve to eighteen months before "Oswaldo" was busted for killing Kennedy, thus the clarity of his recall. It sprang from his memory the moment he saw Oswald's face on TV.

The only other thing Antulio remembers about the document itself was that it was printed on yellow paper. At the time of his discovery, another female G2 employee named Pastora explained the color scheme to Antulio: If a personnel document was issued on yellow stock, it had only one meaning—if that individual was deployed in an operation, he would have to be eliminated immediately after completion of the mission.

In July 1962, another link was forged. On the thirtieth of the month, the CIA formalized its contact with Rolando Cubela Secades, then seen as their best bet to slay Fidel and take back Cuba. The Cubela project was given the CIA code name AM/LASH.

By all appearances, Dr. Cubela's reservations about Fidel had begun with simple disaffection over how he was treated after the revolution—he believed that he had been given neither proper respect nor reward. But that soon gave way to another, much deeper disenchantment. The ways in which the Castros were fashioning their new government seemed less and less inclusive, more and more homogenous, and the people who were being invited into the core of power were not people who Cubela trusted.

It was sometime early in the summer of 1962 that he voiced those misgivings to Carlos Tepedino, an Italian jeweler who operated stores in the Havana Libre Hotel and in New York City. CIA officers working within the U.S. embassy in Havana had recruited Tepedino, and he befriended the doctor, even helping him financially at one point. It was Tepedino who ultimately convinced Cubela that what he was sensing between the Castro brothers was a deliberate turn toward Marxism.

The doctor's term as head of the student organization, FEU, was coming to an end, and he would return to the Cuban Army that summer; but the more that events in the Cuban government proved Tepedino right, the more

Cubela wanted to simply defect. The Italian was right, he decided. The Castro brothers had performed a nationwide "bait and switch" on half the intelligentsia of the country.

The CIA had other plans for the doctor, however. At their urging, Tepedino convinced Cubela that he could be much more effective if he stayed inside the country and used his insider status to take the measure of other officers in the Army who might help him to foment a coup.

When Cubela eventually agreed, it was time to discuss logistics. Cubela had significant freedom of movement as the leader of FEU, and he had been conducting an affair with an airline stewardess based in France, so his ongoing amours provided a good cover for the commencement of his training. He was taken to St. Andres Air Force base in the south of France, and there his instruction in the clandestine arts of "secret writing" and the use of plastic explosives began.

At St. Andres, he made it clear that "if he could do something really significant for the creation of a new Cuba, he was interested in returning to carry on the fight there," the CIA's inspector general later summarized. "He said he was not interested in risking his life for any small undertaking, but that if he could be given a really large part to play, he would use himself and several others in Cuba whom he could rely upon . . . He said he had plans to blow up an oil refinery, as he felt that the continuing . . . semblance of normal functioning in Cuba depended upon a continuing supply of petroleum . . . He also wanted to plan the execution of Carlos Rodríguez, a top-ranking Castro subordinate."[50]

But during the following month, a glitch appeared in the relationship. Cubela was asked to take a polygraph test, a standard request made at the time of all anti-Castro "assets." Cubela refused to take the test, and that set off a wave of second-guessing at CIA headquarters. Was AM/LASH a double agent? (Ironically, the Agency in the summer of 1962 was already rife with Cuban double agents.) On August 18, Langley sent a cable to St. Andres, an order "that no physical elimination missions be given Cubela."[51] But the negotiations with Cubela would continue. He might not have been a double in the summer of 1962, but he was one by the summer of 1963. In that interregnum, as the courtship began and halted and then resumed again, the sly Dr. Cubela would not only remain an asset in waiting with the CIA, but—according to Oscar Marino and others—he would also become the first member of the Cuban regime to make contact with Lee Harvey Oswald. Oscar Marino was in a position to know: at the time, one of his assignments was the monitoring of Dr. Cubela.

"Cubela was a traitor," Oscar would attest in 2005, "and [he] wanted to murder Fidel on behalf [of] the CIA. Correct. [But] we did not know that yet when he was delegated to make contact with Oswald. We trusted him at this time, fully and entirely. He was an important man in the revolution, a very capable commander."[52]

By the summer of 1962, the Fair Play for Cuba Committee had been deeply infiltrated by agents of the Castro regime. Without the knowledge of the FPCC's founders and their supporters, the organization was already being used as a front by which to plot a devastating attack on New York City, scheduled for late November, at the height of the holiday season.

At the FPCC headquarters, the unsuspecting office staff was involved in more prosaic tasks. One late-summer afternoon, Richard Gibson, the CBS News man who had cofounded the committee, was putting in some time at the office when he opened a letter from a Lee Bowmont in Fort Worth, Texas. Enclosed were some photos and a newspaper clipping of local activities similar to those extolled by the FPCC. Gibson sent a routine reply to the pro-Castro Bowmont and included along with it some literature about the organization's stated aims of increased diplomacy and peaceful coexistence.

Sixteen months later, the events of 1962 would come roaring back to haunt Richard Gibson—among them, the letter from Lee Bowmont. The reporter had moved to France by then and was no longer an active member of the disgraced organization he had helped to create. As details of the assassin's life saturated the news, Gibson would quietly deduce that the man who had sent the letter from Fort Worth was the killer who loved to use aliases, Lee Harvey Oswald.[53]

CHAPTER 7
Talking Cuba Crisis

IN JULY OF 1962, Lee and Marina moved out of Robert and Vada Oswald's house and into an apartment with Marguerite. The mother had left her job in Crowell, Texas, and swooped down into Fort Worth to ingratiate herself with Marina and force her way back into Lee's life. Lee went along with it, at least for the moment. He may still have been suffering from the dull shock of his reentry into American life. He was only halfheartedly looking for a job. He didn't have a high school diploma and had spent three years "behind enemy lines," a fact that he omitted from employment applications. He was depressed at the thought of taking another unexceptional job like the one he had worked at in Minsk; even with his utter lack of qualifications, he still thought he should be an official of some kind. He had said, from time to time, that he expected that his kids would work in the White House someday.

With those unmet expectations itching at him, it must have been only the more humiliating to find himself living in the funky Rotary Apartments at 1501 West Seventh Street with a mother he reviled.

But Marguerite covered the rent. She slept on a sagging divan in the living room. She insisted on doing the cooking and most of the cleaning. Marina felt sorry that Lee was so cold to her, and she and Marguerite created a decent facsimile of a mother/daughter relationship during the brief time they lived together, despite the huge language barrier. The only pleasure Lee took from this living arrangement was at the dinner table. Generally, he was fussy about his food, even Marina's painstaking efforts; but much as he detested Marguerite, he loved her cooking. It was their one mutually satisfying form of communication.

Still, even the cuisine wasn't enough to keep him there once he found a job: working as a sheet metal lackey at the Louv-R-Pak division of the Leslie Welding Company. It was a hard-labor, blue-collar gig, but it afforded them a renewed independence from Marguerite.

Life at home was getting worse, though. There had been a couple of hysterical scenes and much screaming and slamming of doors, with Marguerite railing that Marina had taken her son away from her. On August 10, Lee, Marina, and the baby moved out.

He found them something that the landlord called a duplex at 2703 Mercedes Street, actually just half of a rundown, one-story clapboard house across from a Montgomery Ward store.

Call it the American equivalent of a workers' row house. The paint was peeling. It hugged the edge of a dusty road, albeit one that led straight to Lee's workplace. The furniture was minimal and threadbare, and the neighborhood was depressed.

To Marina, though, it was finer than anything she might ever have had in Russia. The place had rooms, each with its own special function. There was a private patch of ground out back, with real grass. And more inspiring than that, there was that "Monkey Wards" across the street; the welcoming smells of cotton candy and cardboard and creosote; the acres of wide, wooden aisles resplendent with clothes and notions, knickknacks and toys, sweets and soaps and ladies' wear. She bought almost nothing. For her it was, as the American embassy in Moscow had been, just a marvel to walk around in, like strolling through a museum, the very existence of which testified to the government's love for its people. She had quickly become an American, through and through. She loved it here. She said, repeatedly, to her husband, "Alka, do anything, but don't ever, ever make me go back [to Russia]."[1]

But Lee had not cooled since the crossing on the *Maasdam*. Initially, his anger was stilled in the new place, though their sex life slowed with his fatigue at the end of a hard day. He would plop down with a copy of the *Worker* or the *Militant* and read while she put supper on, but he pampered her however he could. He would take her to a delicatessen frequented by other émigrés, a bright and tidy little place where she could get herring and sauerkraut, sour cream and kidneys. He would buy her tiny jars of caviar at some small sacrifice of his own wants, just to watch her nibble it, her lips sucking the black roe off the tip of a spoon in the dusky light of the kitchen. Sometimes, after wandering through the air-conditioned aisles of the big store, she would put their dinner on a slow boil and carry Junie down the dry, hot road to meet Lee on his way home from work, and they would amble back to the house, hand in hand, trading little stories about the day, the baby cooing in her daddy's arms.[2] They were not unlike other young couples who would become commonplace a little later in the 1960s, living lean but somehow ennobling their lives with a vaguely socialist or bohemian sense that their struggle was an honest one, that young love made it easier, and that there were still pleasures to be found, however small.

If Marina ever thought back to the hazy promise she had been forced to make to the KGB, it must have made her ever more uneasy. She wanted never to return. Indeed, Lee would probably not be allowed to, having defected to Russia and then *un*-defected, but that did not mean that they wouldn't try to "switch her on" one day. It would only be for the sake of Uncle Ilya and Aunt Valya that she would comply, and she must have hoped that she would never be tested that way.

On August 16, 1962, the FBI came to their door, again in the form of agent John W. Fain. When Lee saw who it was, he shoved a copy of a Communist magazine under a cushion and then stood to greet the agent politely. Fain had not gone to Lee's workplace, not wanting to complicate his life, and he didn't want to come into the house, not wanting to worry Marina, so Lee went with him out to his car.

They were there for almost an hour. It seemed to Fain that Lee was considerably more relaxed this time, more compliant and at ease with himself, but he still wouldn't talk about why he had gone to Russia in the first place, parrying the question as he had before.

"It's nobody's business," he muttered to Fain. "It was something that I did. I went, and I came back."

He did allow, however, that the MVD arm of the KGB had given him both an entry and an exit interview, but he played it down, and agreed again to tell the Feds if the Soviets made any contact with him.

Apart from Lee's mention of the MVD, there was one other odd aside. Lee said that "he might have to return to the Soviet Union in about five years to take his wife back home to see her relatives,"[3] but Fain didn't pay it any mind, particularly, and it would probably have been a technical impossibility anyway. The agent, having made certain that the Oswalds were still steering clear of the local Communist Party, went back to his office and made an official recommendation that the agency close the file on Lee H. Oswald.

Marina had not been told of Lee's first meeting with Fain shortly after their return to the States. When he came inside and she asked him who the man was, he told her the fellow was from the FBI.

"And who are they?" she wanted to know.

"They're the security organs. In Russia it's the KGB. Here it's the FBI."

He sat down to a dinner that she had reheated too many times. She was upset, particularly at the mention of the KGB.

"They asked about Russia," he elaborated. "They wanted to know if Soviet agents had been here and asked me to work for them. I said no. They said, if anybody comes, please let the FBI know. I told them: 'I will not be an informer for you,'" he lied. "'Go ahead and do it if that's your job, but don't ask me to do it for you.' . . . Now it's begun . . . They'll never let me live in peace. They think anyone who's been there is a Russian spy. Let them think it . . ."

Unaware that the Feds were actually stepping *out* of his life, his depression returned.

And soon after that, the gorgon mother, Marguerite, found them again. She manipulated Marina without shame. She brought them a high chair for Junie and some new silverware, and then, on another night, a yellow parakeet in a cage that Lee had given her seven years before. Lee was so enraged at Marina's disobedience in letting "Mamochka" into the house that he took the cage outside and released the bird.[4]

The husband's beatings of his wife resumed and then increased. An explosion of rage, a punch in the face or multiple slaps, no particular attempt to aim the blows at body parts that would not be seen by others. And then, a few hours later, the contrition. The shrugging request for forgiveness. A walk over to Monkey Ward's, where he would buy her some trinket, buy the baby a toy, and then try, in all earnestness, to make gentle love to her as she closed her eyes.

On a gleaming September day that year, America's celebrated Yankee poet, Robert Frost, was sick in bed in a guesthouse in the Russian city of Sochi when in walked the Soviet premier, Nikita Khrushchev, himself, to check on the old man's recovery. Nikita was not a fan of all things American, nor did he care much for poets; but whatever his prejudices, the peasant-born Russian was capable of voluble, generous displays of affection and he happened to like this poet. That afternoon in Sochi, he pulled up a chair beside Frost's bed and scolded him that he must obey doctor's orders if he wanted to have any hope of living to be a hundred.

The poet was there at the request of the president, representing the U.S. in a cultural exchange. He had hoped to accompany the American secretary of the interior, Stewart Udall, to Pitsunda the day before, but as the American delegation was heading out to Khrushchev's vacation retreat on the Black Sea, Frost had found himself ailing and unsteady, so he was not asked along for the ride.

At Pitsunda, the chairman had told Udall that he wanted an accord in the ongoing Berlin problem, but then softened the rhetoric by extending an invitation for the First Couple to visit the Soviet Union and presenting the secretary with gifts for the president, including a case of wine and a Russian drinking horn. (When the wine was delivered back to Washington, the Secret Service would forbid the president to drink it.)

When Frost faltered, Nikita had sent his own doctor to Sochi, and then followed up with a visit of his own the next day. Frost was a Kennedy man, and as he and the chairman chatted, he implored Nikita to cast aside petty points of pride and reframe the East/West duality as something finer, more heroic: a "noble rivalry," perhaps. The Russian had admonished the poet about U.S. nuclear brinksmanship, and then took a swipe at Jack's unwillingness to buck the Republican tide and settle the German question. Nikita then smeared the collective manhood of America and Western Europe, citing Leo Tolstoy's maxim about men who have grown too old and sickly to make love even though desire still swelled in the mind. The old Yankee, laughing, said that America was too young for the metaphor to apply, and again encouraged the chairman to propose a simple fix for Berlin that the president could then enact.

"You have the soul of a poet," Nikita joked, patting the poet on the arm as he bade him farewell.

When Frost made it back to Moscow, he would misquote Khrushchev as having said that the Americans were "too liberal to fight." The Republicans had a field day.

When Jack heard about the misstep by America's "greatest living poet," he was forced to split some literary hairs. "You can't believe what Frost tells you," he said to friends. "He is not very reliable as a reporter."[5]

By early September, there were already ominous signs that the Soviets were at work in Cuba.

Khrushchev had come to feel that Kennedy was maligning Soviet military strength in his recent public pronouncements—and, worse, might even be entertaining a nuclear "first strike" as an option in the ongoing Berlin crisis. Khrushchev may have known that Robert McNamara, the secretary of defense, had a mandate to re-envision the American military: to bulk up the U.S. nuclear arsenal, create more nimble, clandestine military options, and do all he could to exert more civilian control over the armed services. Khrushchev, a man of combustible emotions, nursed fears that the American military establishment might try to seize back power from the interloping McNamara, who until recently had been an executive at the Ford Motor Company. Khrushchev imagined that the military might stage a coup that would reassert its power, wreak havoc in Berlin, and up the ante in other areas of confrontation. So, to the extent that his political dignity would allow it, the premier had been hinting that he wanted to get the German issues squared away and work toward an easier coexistence. At a farewell dinner for Llewellyn Thompson, the outgoing American ambassador to the Soviet Union, Khrushchev had approached Thompson on the lawn of his dacha to again pledge his desire to set Berlin right and urge Thompson to "Go home and tell President Kennedy what I said."[6]

But inside the White House, Jack's foreign policy leaders had fears of their own. The Americans had indeed been making a point of belittling Soviet military strength. That, in addition to the January meeting between Jack and Adzhubei in which Cuba felt threatened, had prompted the Soviet bear to crank up its defense spending, thus slowing the Russian economy. Would they embark on some military misadventure to reassert themselves somehow?

Fifteen months later, with Kennedy dead, Fidel would sit down for one last interview with French journalist Jean Daniel, with whom he had been speaking on the day of Jack's assassination. "It was this report [by Adzhubei] which triggered the whole [missile crisis] situation . . . Six months before these missiles were installed in Cuba, we had received an accumulation of information that a new invasion was being prepared under sponsorship of the CIA."[7]

Like the other plans out of Washington, Operation Mongoose may have come to the Castro brothers' attention just after its inception in late 1961; it was certainly known to them by May of 1962, when the operational activity began to increase. Indeed, given how deeply the Cubans had penetrated the CIA by then, someone, perhaps Antulio's "Professor," had specified that the attack was scheduled for October.

The resultant White House version of the missile crisis notes its origins in mid-October, but it begs the question of whether the crisis itself was precipitated as a direct result of the Mongoose endgame. The timing is simply too coincidental not to speculate on that question. Long before the crisis hit, the Kennedys were warned (by the Army coordinator for the Cuba Project[8]) that nukes might make their way to Cuba as a defense against invasion. Mongoose was hatching multiple schemes to "create incidents" around Guantánamo that would justify a U.S. attack, including one that would make it appear that a planeful of U.S. college students had been shot down by Cuba.[9] When the incidents came, U.S. troops amassed since October 6 in the Caribbean and elsewhere were poised to "defend" America.[10] The missile crisis was not deliberately staged as an inciting incident, but as it happened, when it came in the fall of 1962, America was loaded for bear. The country could not have been more primed for a showdown. As it happened, neither could Fidel.

Worse, the Kennedy White House now suspected that the Soviet leader might be looking for a way to boost his prestige at home and abroad with some sort of quick success.[11] If that took the form of defending little Cuba, then so be it.

As some of the New Frontiersmen analyzed the risks that the Soviets might take, other friends of the administration quietly expressed concerns about Jack's management of these rising stakes. Among them was Dean Acheson, who wrote to former president Harry Truman: "I have a curious and apprehensive feeling as I watch JFK that he is a sort of Indian snake charmer. He toots away on his pipe and our problems sway back and forth around him in a trancelike manner, never approaching but never withdrawing; all are in a state of suspended life, including the pipe player, who lives only in his dream. Someday one of these snakes will wake up, and no one will be able even to run."[12]

Khrushchev had sent a delegation to Havana, months earlier, to broach the possibility of deploying Soviet missiles on the Cuban mainland, ostensibly for the regime's defense but also for strategic purposes. The only person in Jack's intimate circle who is known to have had any advance warning of actual Soviet nukes in Cuba was Bobby Kennedy, who had received word of smaller rockets on the island from his Amigos de Roberto in New Orleans the summer before. It is not known whether he told Jack about the rockets at the time, but it cannot have come as any great surprise to Bobby when even darker suspicions began to arise in September. In all likelihood, the Amigos reports of more limited weapons gave the Kennedys pause and an added pretext for Mongoose. Then the discoveries of mid-October stopped them dead in their tracks.

The Russians first proffered the plan to Fidel and Raúl, who in turn took it to Che, to the figurehead Cuban president, Osvaldo Dorticós Torrado, to the grizzled Cuban Communist leader, Blas Roca, and to one of Fidel's closest advisers, Major Emilio Aragones. All of them ratified the proposal at once, and Fidel, not wishing to refuse such a Kremlin request, asked that when word of it got out, it be couched not as a reflection of Cuban weakness but as a gesture of international socialist solidarity.

Despite some Cuban concerns, Nikita was certain the missiles would not be discovered before they could be armed; and if by some chance they were, he assured Fidel that he would defend them in any case. The plan was for Khrushchev to travel to the UN once the missiles were armed, pay a visit to Kennedy, and then reveal the nukes in the form of a Cuban-Soviet military pact at a triumphal public event in Havana.[13]

But as the first shipment of missile components set out across the high seas, the chairman was jumpy. Thousands of his combat troops were aboard those ships. Twenty-four medium-range ballistic missiles, with a range between 200 and 1,200 miles, were snugly crated on the decks and beneath, along with sixteen launchers for intermediate-range ballistic missiles, each of which would be fitted with a nuclear warhead and two missiles with a range between 1,300 and 2,200 miles. The troops had been kept in the dark about their destination. To offset speculation, they had been issued winter gear, woollen underwear, heavy parkas, gloves, and even skis, but as they played cards and smoked and joked belowdecks, a few of them took out compasses; as hours ticked into days, it became apparent that they were headed past Gibraltar and cutting a path to the southwest. Finally, they were told. They were going to Cuba, news that, given the approach of the brutal Russian winter back home, must have been met with at least a few cheers.

In his haste, Khrushchev had made a gross miscalculation. Instead of sending out waves of half a dozen vessels here, or ten there, he had dispatched a virtual armada all at once. There was no way that such a fleet would not raise suspicions; and indeed, the CIA's flyovers, now a matter of global routine, had captured something unusual on film—the Soviet ships were carrying large cargos of some lightweight materiel.

At JM/WAVE headquarters in Florida, reports from the Cuban underground suggested that surface-to-air missiles were being installed as part of a new air defense system. One of their agents insisted that components consistent with medium-range missiles were being moved overland, but the reports were held, pending further reconnaissance. Rumors began to circulate in Washington, giving the Republicans fodder for further attacks on the Kennedy White House.[14] The 1962 congressional campaign was coming to a climax, and Nixon got into the act, along with senators Barry Goldwater, Kenneth Keating, Strom Thurmond, and John Tower. Once again, Jack Kennedy found himself the whipping boy for hard-liners. In September, he felt it necessary to warn the Russians that if the West ever discovered offensive missiles on the island, it would have "the gravest" consequences. He had drawn a line in the sand, committing himself to react in ways that might not be commensurate with the threat, much as he had during the campaign.

Meanwhile, through his representatives in Washington, Khrushchev kept up the ruse. On September 8, the first shipment arrived in Havana.

Cuba was not the only island front in the East/West war that was gathering that month. The other one was the island of Manhattan. In early October, a passenger plane arrived at New York City from Havana carrying Osvaldo Dorticós Torrado, there to attend the upcoming UN General Assembly. The Cuban ambassador to the UN, Carlos Lechuga, met the president's party when it arrived in the city. By this time, America was sending oblique warnings to Khrushchev via his factotums, Anatoly Dobrynin and Anastas Mikoyan. The chairman now suspected that his game had been discovered. But he was perplexed by the muffled response that had so far been coming from Washington; in the vacuum, he ordered his troops to accelerate the missile installations. The atmosphere was tense. When Soviet foreign minister Andrei Gromyko paid a visit to President Dorticós at his hotel suite in Manhattan, both men were so convinced that the Americans had bugged the rooms to detect any talk of missiles that they "spoke" to each other by writing back and forth on scraps of the hotel stationery.

Among those in the Dorticós entourage was another Cuban, one with a pressing and deadly agenda. Roberto Santiesteban Casanova, along with his allies already in New York (José and Elsa Gómez, members of the UN Cuban Mission, and Marino Suero and José García, Cuban members of the Fair Play for Cuba Committee), had come to the United States to plot the most daring and destructive terrorist attack the Castro brothers could devise.

Early on October 16, McGeorge Bundy was at the White House, staring at a raft of oversized aerial reconnaissance photographs. The photos seemed to prove that there were ground-to-ground missiles embedded in the landscape of Cuba. They had been taken on Sunday, just two days earlier—coincidentally, the same day that Bundy appeared on ABC's *Issues and Answers* to forswear any evidence that the Soviets had planted a "major offensive capability" in Castro's kingdom.

Just before 9:00 A.M., he punched the button on his intercom and asked the secretary to alert the president that he was on his way up to the family quarters on the second floor. There he found Jack half dressed, and showed him the packet of photos, pointing out the missile sites. By all accounts, Jack was floored. It was assumed that the missiles were more or less the equals of America's SS-4 weapons, with a range of just over a thousand miles, enough to hit anywhere inside the eastern half of the contiguous United States. The president, who knew of both Mongoose and the October invasion contingency plan, must have felt that he had been caught red-handed by Moscow; that they had checkmated him just as the October invasion plans should have been coming to fruition. For the second time in eighteen months, he had been trumped on Cuban soil.

A committee was quickly assembled, the group that would be dubbed the Executive Committee, or ExComm. When the president greeted them in the Cabinet Room a short time later, his four-year-old daughter, Caroline, was capering around the room, singing a nonsense song while he clapped along. It could not have been a more fitting tableau—an oblivious child dancing in a room quietly filling with grave men who had suddenly been tasked with trying to save the future.

The child skipped out, and Jack sat down at the long table with his brother, Bobby; Arthur Lundahl of the National Photographic Interpretation Center (NPIC); Dean Rusk, the secretary of state; George Ball, an undersecretary of state; Robert McNamara, the secretary of defense; Paul Nitze, an assistant secretary of defense; Roswell Gilpatric, a deputy secretary of defense; Lyndon Johnson, the vice president; Maxwell Taylor, the head of the Joint Chiefs; John McCone, the director of the CIA; Alexis Johnson, the deputy undersecretary of state for political affairs; Ambassador at Large Llewellyn Thompson; Douglas Dillon, the secretary of the treasury; presidential assistants Bundy, Ted Sorensen, and Kenny O'Donnell; and a few others, including Sidney Graybeal, a missile expert.

A military aide propped the photographic blowups on easels around the room. A secret tape recorder whirred somewhere out of sight, its microphones tucked in the curtains.*

"Okay," Jack began.

Lundahl was the first to address him. "This is the result of the photography taken Sunday, sir. There's a medium-range ballistic-missile launch site and two new military encampments on the southern edge of Sierra del Rosario . . ."

"Where would that be?"

"West-central, sir."

---

*What follows are audiotaped cameos of the conversations that occurred over the next fourteen days.

"How long have we got? We can't tell, can we, how long before it can be fired?"

"No, sir . . ."

McNamara said, "This is not defensed yet, I believe, at the moment?"

Lundahl confirmed it.

"This is important," McNamara went on. ". . . It seems almost impossible to me that they would be ready to fire with nuclear warheads on the site without even a fence around it . . . But at least . . . there is some reason to believe the warheads aren't present and hence, they are not ready to fire."

Members of Cuban intelligence would later be plagued by the same question—were these missiles actually armed and dangerous?

A short time later, the president asked for Rusk's opinion.

"Mr. President, this is, of course, a very serious development . . . I do think we have to set in motion a chain of events that will eliminate this base . . . So we have to think very hard about two major courses of action as alternatives. One is the quick strike . . . I don't think this in itself would require an invasion of Cuba . . . if we make it clear that what we're doing is eliminating this particular base or any other such base . . . We ourselves are not moved to general war. We're simply doing what we said we would do if they took certain action. Or we're going to decide that this is the time to eliminate the Cuban problem by actually eliminating the island . . . The time has come when Castro must . . . break clearly with the Soviet Union and prevent this missile base from becoming operational . . . [or] I think we'll be facing a situation that could well lead to general war. Now with that we have an obligation to do what has to be done, but to do it in a way that gives everybody a chance to pull away from it before it gets too hard . . ."

Later in the meeting, McNamara suggested that Jack take the counsel of General Taylor. Taylor spoke up. ". . . I'm thinking in terms of three phases. One, an initial pause . . . while we get completely ready . . . Then, virtually concurrently, an air strike against . . . missiles, airfields, and nuclear sites that we know of. At the same time, a naval blockade . . . Then the decision can be made as we're mobilizing, with the air strike, as to whether we invade or not . . ."

The conversation went on for a few more moments before McNamara reentered it. "The president ordered us to prepare an invasion of Cuba months ago," he said, referring to the Cuba Project, which had been worked to foment a coup that very month. ". . . We're as well prepared as we could possibly be, facing the situation we do . . . We've been moving already, on a very quiet basis, munitions [petroleum, oil, and lubricants] . . . So that kind of movement is beginning." An invasion was being readied.

Later still, Bobby spoke up. "Excuse me. I just wondered how . . . long would it take to take over the island?"

Taylor, a close friend of Bobby's, said it would be hard to estimate but might take five or six days, with a month for "cleaning that up."

"Five or seven days of air," said McNamara, "plus five days of invasion . . ."

The meeting went on all morning. When the session ended, the Pentagon was charged with working up scenarios for an air strike, closely followed by a full-scale invasion.[15]

Jack kept up his official schedule that afternoon. The Crown Prince of Libya had arrived for a formal luncheon, and among the guests was Jack's UN ambassador, Adlai Stevenson. Later, Jack took Adlai upstairs and showed him the U-2 reconnaissance.

"I suppose the alternatives are to go in by air and wipe them out," he told Adlai, "or to take other steps to render the weapons inoperable."

With typical caution, the ambassador argued against an air strike, urging a peaceful solution first.[16] That was no surprise to Jack, the man of action. He may even have felt his usual macho annoyance at the diplomatic reflex, but in ensuing days he would find himself taking exactly that approach against the advice of the Pentagon.

Meanwhile, Bobby was meeting in his office at Justice with the Operation Mongoose team, trying to factor the events of the day. Jack had been dissatisfied with the plans up until then, though reports differ as to why. In any case, Bobby now seemed receptive to the more aggressive sabotage ops that had recently been proposed by the CIA, suggesting that the president might be considering more direct U.S. military action for the first time. Talk then turned to the question of how many Cubans would rise to Fidel's defense if an uprising began, and even whether a band of Cuban exiles might be used to attack the missile sites. Bobby called Roberto San Roman, the brother of Pepe and one of the leaders of the anti-Castro exiles, and broached a "sinking of the *Maine*" scenario, as if the presence of missiles weren't provocation enough.[17] Finally, however, it was decided that such attacks by Cuban proxies weren't really viable under the circumstances.[18]

It seemed to take a while for the magnitude of the crisis to set in, but all the terms had changed. Singular acts of sabotage could be fuses leading straight to the horizon, to the edge of history itself. Neither of the Kennedy brothers was adept at self-criticism at this point, but as the situation worsened in the coming weeks it would provoke a new perspective in Bobby. He would veer from provocateur to peacemaker. He would duel with himself as never before, at least until the crisis passed, and it foreshadowed a capacity for growth. Here, he had a near-perfect justification to do to Castro what he had been plotting to do for eighteen months, but as the catastrophic consequences of this act unfolded in his imagination, there must have been a moment—whether standing in his children's nursery to watch them sleep, or riding from office to office through the rain-soaked, midnight streets of the capital—when he realized that he was, in effect, his brother's co-president, with all the attendant responsibilities. He could not simply enact Jack's secret agenda, leaving his brother to project virtue in public. That agenda had led them to this brink. They were playing with millions of lives now, even if he was not yet ready to confess it.

ExComm returned to the White House cabinet room at 6:30 P.M. A deeper probing of the photos seemed to indicate that each of the known launch sites had backup missiles. There were probably more missiles than first thought, and it was estimated that they'd be ready to fire within a few weeks. (Contrary to theories that would later emerge, there seemed to be no doubt that the missiles were real, not decoys.) Political questions of how to use the moment to sever Nikita from Fidel were discussed, as was the issue of Havana's intentions toward the rest of Latin America. After a concise laying-out of the military options, McNamara again addressed the moral elephant in the room.

"[Mr. President], I don't believe we have considered the consequences of any of these actions satisfactorily . . . I don't know quite what kind of a world we will live in after we've struck Cuba, and we've started it . . . Let's say . . . after we have launched fifty to sixty [air] sorties . . . How do we stop at that point? I don't know the answer to this . . . I don't believe they are entirely clear to any of us . . ."

But Bobby seemed intent on thinking of the Cuba problem within the small frame of the Western Hemisphere and the near future. "Mr. President," he cut in, "while we're considering this problem tonight, I think that we should also consider what Cuba's going to be a year from now, or two years from now. Assume that we go in and knock these sites out. I don't know what's gonna stop them from saying: 'We're gonna build the sites six months from now, bring them in again.' "

"Nothing permanent about it," Taylor seconded.

"Where are we six months from now?"

"You have to put a blockade in following any limited action," said Mc-Namara.

"Then we're gonna have to sink Russian ships," Bobby replied. "Then we're gonna have to sink Russian submarines. Now, [think] whether it wouldn't be the argument, if you're going to get into it at all, whether we should just get into it, and get it over with, and take our losses . . . Hell, if it's war that's gonna come on this thing, or if he sticks those kinds of missiles after the warning, then he's gonna get in a war six months from now, or a year from now. So. . . . ."

He was thinking out loud. Most of the other men there were more circumspect, since all were aware that they were under the president's microscope—and the lens of history as well. Bobby already had the president's full support and allegiance for life, so he was able to speak freely. Shrewd as he was, he appears in these records as utterly straight and transparent. At first, however, he remained focused on putting a stake through the heart of his enemy.

McNamara segued off of Bobby. "Mr. President, this is why I think tonight we ought to put on paper the alternative plans and the probable, possible consequences thereof . . . Because . . . these actions have not been thought through clearly. The one that the attorney general just mentioned is illustrative of that."

"Mr. Vice President," Jack said, "do you have any thoughts? Between [strike] options one and two?"

"I don't think I can add anything that is essential," Lyndon Johnson replied. (Bobby would later describe his contributions to these talks as "useless.")

McNamara pushed on to a closer elucidation of the options. He proposed that they carry out open surveillance, and then blockade any offensive weapons bound for Cuba.

"How do we do that?" Bundy wondered. The talks had a way of careening from the biggest philosophical questions to the most rudimentary points of tactics.

"We search every ship," the secretary of defense said.

"Yeah, well, it would be a search and removal, if found," Taylor specified.

"You have to make the guy stop to search him," said Bundy. "And if he won't stop, you have to shoot, right?"

"And you have to remove what you're looking for if you find it," Taylor said. You can almost see him shrug.

"That's right," said the president.

"Absolutely," McNamara replied, pressing on. "And then an ultimatum . . . a statement to the world, particularly to Khrushchev, that we have located these offensive weapons. If there is ever any indication that they're to be launched against this country, we will respond not only against Cuba, but we will respond directly against the Soviet Union with a full nuclear strike. Now, this alternative doesn't seem to be a very acceptable one. But wait until you work on the others."

October 18 was Lee Oswald's twenty-third birthday. He and Marina had been welcomed into a small group of people from Dallas and Fort Worth that included a number of Russian émigrés, all of them at least somewhat better off than the struggling Oswald family. The Oswalds were poorly dressed, their refrigerator almost empty. Marina's front teeth showed signs of rot. Lee, who had so often been the recipient of the small generosities of the Russians he met in Minsk, found himself just as well cared for by the Russians of central Texas.[19]

At the same time, he resented their munificence. Marina loved her new friends. His beatings, which had increased in response to Marina's tolerance of Marguerite, were now doled out as recompense for her social "betrayal" of him. Initially, they liked Lee and he took advantage. Once it was clear how devoted the Russians had become to Marina and June, he decided to quit his hated job at Leslie Welding and did so on October 8, telling Marina in vague terms that he had simply lost it. The work, he claimed, had been seasonal. He had expected to be laid off.[20]

But he still had to work at something, and she suggested that he might find a better job in Dallas, so he went there. Four days later, he landed a job at a graphics and photographic arts company, Jaggars-Chiles-Stovall, again through his new connections. But in contrast to his courtly manners in Minsk, he didn't bother to express thanks. Perhaps he believed that Americans could better afford to be generous. Soon enough, the canny Russians recognized that he was as slippery as an eel and just as much of a bottom-feeder, ingratiating himself, pretending to be a polite and sensitive husband, and accepting every thing from bus fare to hand-me-down clothes, even as he tormented Marina.

While Lee savored his brief autonomy in Dallas, Marina moved in with another friend, Lyolya Hall. It was to Lyolya that Marina unburdened herself, if not about Lee's abuse then at least about his premature ejaculation, which had returned to plague them again. She asked the older woman if it might be her fault, or if she knew of any remedies, or if they should see a doctor. Her silent suffering was starting to give way to the need for confidantes, an impulse that would both exacerbate the abuse and provide her only respite from it.

The day before Lee's birthday, she decided to defy him outright. She and Lyolya took the baby to St. Stephen's Eastern Orthodox church in Dallas to have June Lee Oswald baptized. Lee had told her he was living at the YMCA there, but Marina didn't want him to know what she had done, or that she was in Dallas. So she arranged for his meager birthday presents to be delivered to the Y by a friend, making up a fib to throw him off her scent.

It didn't work. He saw through her somehow, and the next time she saw him she had to admit what she had done with June. She was frightened, but he could be decent, placating—when he wanted to atone for his brutalities or cover his tracks. He reacted exactly as she hoped he might.

"Silly girl," he teased her. "Why didn't you tell me?"

"I thought you'd forbid it," she said.

"It's your right to do as you please," he assured her, in his most gallant tone of voice. She was relieved, for the moment, but she had fewer and fewer illusions about her "rights."

During these weeks in Dallas, Lee was unaccountably secretive about many seemingly insignificant things. He made a special effort to tell no one where he was living during his first weeks in Dallas. At one point, he told George Bouhe, one of the Russian friends, that he was staying at the Carlton Boarding House in the Oak Cliff neighborhood; in fact, he had never been there. No one knows exactly where he hung his hat from October 8 to 13, or from October 21 to November 2.[21] He was working the new job after October 12, but he did not always visit Marina in Fort Worth on the weekends.

What is known now, however, is that sometime in October or November—according to Oscar Marino and others whose independent knowledge would corroborate it—the Cuban regime made its first contact with Lee Harvey Oswald, exactly as the KGB had suggested they might the summer before.

The president was on the road by the late morning of October 18, still keeping to his published schedule while a subgroup of ExComm kept probing the depths back in Washington, meeting every few hours at the State Department. Bundy, Taylor, McCone, former secretary of state Dean Acheson,

McNamara, Dillon, Rusk, Sorensen, and Bobby were among those present that afternoon.

Bundy put the idea of a surprise attack against Cuba back on the table, though it had been set aside the day before.

"I'd like to reopen the question of a preemptive strike. I spoke with the president on his campaign swing this morning, and, speaking for myself, I favor decisive action, with its advantages of surprise and confronting the world with a fait accompli."

Acheson expressed his agreement. "Mr. Khrushchev has presented the United States with a direct challenge. It's a test of wills now and . . . we should clean out these missiles with a strike."

McCone was of the same opinion.

Bobby had become close to McCone, a Republican but a fellow Catholic whom Bobby had come to respect and to rely upon to shed light on the opposition's views. As the conversation continued, Bobby's gaze moved from man to man.

"I agree," said Taylor. "It is now or never. If we're going to do it Sunday morning, we'd have to decide it at once. If we do it Monday, we'll have to decide by tomorrow. We need forty-eight hours notice, and we're in."

Bobby had grown even closer to McNamara than to the new DCI, and must have been glad for his dissent.

"I will give orders for a standby," said the defense secretary, "but I do not advocate an air strike."

Sorensen felt that it was unfair to start reneging on the decisions they had made the day before, particularly while the president was away.

Bobby stood up, restless, his hands in his suit pockets, and moved to a window, staring out and at first speaking as if to himself. He looked almost fragile in the gray morning light.

"It sounds to me as if we're on the brink of a reversal of our decision to blockade," he murmured. He turned back to the group and grinned, subtly pulling rank. "But I too had a talk with the president this morning. We have all wrestled with this in nearly every possible way . . . I think it would be very, very difficult for the president of the United States to order [a surprise attack], with all the memory of Pearl Harbor and with all the implications this would have for us in whatever world there would be afterwards. For a hundred and seventy-five years we have not been that kind of country . . ."

He had been forced to someplace deeper in himself. Even though he would return to his vendetta against Castro soon enough, the realities he faced now were far more stark than the ones he had considered in the Mongoose planning, when it was only Castro's army they would be set against. Fully provoked, they held all of America's power in their hands, but with it came the full moral limits of that power in the post-Hiroshima world.

"A sneak attack is not in our traditions," Bobby continued. "Thousands of Cubans would be killed without warning, and a lot of Russians too. Now I favor action, to make known unmistakably the seriousness of our determination to get the missiles out of Cuba, but our action should allow the Soviets some room for maneuver to pull back from their overextended position in Cuba . . . We are fighting for something more than just survival. All our heritage and our ideals would be repugnant to such a sneak military attack . . ."[22]

He paused and took in the silent group. All eyes were on him.

Some members of ExComm would later recall a kind of sunset gaze that seemed to flicker in the president's eyes over the fourteen days of crisis; a look of the utmost dread, as quick and searing as sparks from a wood fire. He had said in his memoirs that he had always been hungry for great challenges, beyond the mere practice of the law, beyond even the protracted wrangling of legislation in the Senate.[23] The presidency had drawn him because it was the place where decisions had immediate weight, where years of legislative tap dancing could be swept offstage with one motion; but as the sheer complexity and danger settled upon him, he would wonder aloud how he and one other man on the other side of the planet could possibly find themselves at such obscene odds. It was insane. It was the terrifying amplification of conflict at its most stupid, territorial, and dogmatic. Why was Khrushchev upping the stakes in this way?

By Monday, October 22, the walls of secrecy were giving way. China had launched a surprise attack against India on the preceding weekend, and that was the headline above the fold on most of the nation's Sunday papers. But the *Washington Post* featured a piece on U.S. troop movements in Florida, attributing them to an incipient "Cuban crisis."[24]

As plans for air strikes were being dutifully made, Jack was still looking for another way out, listening intently to the objections of Bobby, McNamara, and McCone. Bobby insisted that a surprise attack was a Pandora's box—the possible Soviet responses were too unpredictable, with the worst case being the very worst of all, a full-tilt nuclear nightmare. They should institute a naval blockade and then "play for the breaks." McCone agreed, but wanted the air strike and invasion contingency to be near at hand.[25]

The Agency now estimated that eight to twelve of the missiles were fully operational, and could be unleashed with two and a half to four hours' notice.

In a meeting that morning with David Ormsby-Gore, the British ambassador to America, Jack remarked on how shrewdly Khrushchev was playing his hand. As the ambassador recounted it, the Russians had "offered this deliberate and provocative challenge to the United States in the knowledge that if the Americans reacted violently to it the Russians would be given an ideal opportunity to move against West Berlin," seizing the whole of that pivotal city and thus consolidating Moscow's control of Eastern Europe. "If, on the other hand, [Jack] did nothing, the Latin Americans and the United States' other Allies would feel that the Americans had no real will to resist the encroachments of Communism and would hedge their bets accordingly." The only road was the middle one, tough but flexible, with the moral onus being placed back on the Soviets.[26]

The president and Ormsby-Gore were close friends. They could be candid with each other, and Jack took the moment to express his disgust for the deluding effects of nuclear weapons.

But despite the threat of chaos, the loss of secrecy, the rumor mill grinding away on the right, and the unknowable schemes of the Marxist left, the Kennedys were gaining support where it counted most, politically, from America's closest allies and its former presidents. During the first few days, Jack had kept both Truman and Eisenhower fully informed by telephone. Until then, Ike's nickname for Jack was "Little Boy Blue," and Jack's for him "the old asshole," but Eisenhower had come around, making a trip to Washington for a briefing at McCone's home. The general's first instinct was to opt for the sneak attack, but he had come to agree that whatever the tactical advantages, such an attack would present a strategic backlash of monstrous proportions. He too soon came to favor the blockade, and would go so far as to say—on ABC television—that although there had been worthy criticism of Kennedy's recent policies, "the president's immediate handling of foreign affairs was not a legitimate topic" of criticism.[27]

As the ExComm meeting was coming to a close early that afternoon, the stresses in the room threatened to "go global." Given the complexity of a worldwide chain of command that had never been so tested, Jack was terrified that someone might jump the gun, that the system was not completely fail-safe. The forward line of U.S. nuclear weapons was in Turkey, and Jack ordered the Joint Chiefs to make doubly sure that the Americans manning the Jupiter missiles there adhered to the strict codes of presidential authorization. The brass insisted that their men had already been so instructed, but Jack and Bobby were taking no chances. They wanted them told again.

There was a moment of tension; it was another instance in which the New Frontiersmen felt it vital to keep the military subordinate.

Paul Nitze tried one last time to keep from ruffling the feathers of the bird colonels and admirals and generals over at the Pentagon. "I'm sure that these fellows are . . . Surely they're indoctrinated not to fire. This is what Secretary McNamara and I went over, looked into, and they really are—"

"Well, let's do it again, Paul," the president barked.

"I've got your point," Nitze capitulated.

There was a moment of nervous laughter around the table, the president obdurately pulling rank and Nitze well aware of it.

"Send me the documents," said Bundy, "and I will show them to a doubting master."

There was more laughter as the point was taken. What could possibly be the problem with double-checking the strength of your redoubts when all hell was about to break loose?

It was also decided that day that, lest the Soviets announce the presence of the missiles first and frame their installation as a vital act of defense, it was time for John Kennedy to tell the world what was happening.

At 7:00 P.M., all regularly scheduled programming was pulled from the airwaves.

As Jack sat there at his desk in front of the blacked-out windows of the Oval Office, surrounded by black baffles, black cameras, and black scrims, a handsome but gray man in the final years of the black-and-white era, his well-tanned and fine-cut glamour was gone. He was the man in the middle, the man who had asked for and been given all the glory and the difficulty that was inherent in the office. He sat motionless as the director counted down, five, four, three, two, one, and then he made his appeal to what was left of reason, in his friends, in his detractors the world over, and in his enemies.

"Good evening, my fellow citizens . . ."

As he laid out the details, the citizens of America were joined by the citizens of the world.

"All ships of any kind bound for Cuba from whatever nation or port will, if found to contain cargoes of offensive weapons, be turned back. . . ."

Khrushchev, Mikoyan, and Dobrynin were no doubt watching. Nixon, Goldwater, Ike, and Kenneth Keating were probably watching. Fidel and Raúl and Che would soon be watching.

"This quarantine will be extended, if needed, to other types of cargo and carriers."

Bill Harvey, Sergio Arcacha, David Ferrie, and Layton Martens were certainly watching.

"My fellow citizens, let no one doubt that this is a difficult and dangerous effort on which we have set out. No one can foresee precisely what course it will take or what cost or casualties will be incurred."

It is not known if Lee and Marina Oswald were watching. He had purchased a TV with a loan from one of her new Russian friends a few days earlier, then returned it to the store the next morning, lest they take offense at his lavish expenditure.

"But the greatest danger of all would be to do nothing . . ."

Whether Lee watched it or not, he must have heard about it—the entire world heard about it, later that night or early the next day.

"Our goal is not the victory of might but the vindication of right—not peace at the expense of freedom, but both peace and freedom, here in this hemisphere and, we hope, around the world. God willing, that goal will be achieved."

After the speech, as Bobby was leaving the White House, he came upon the Kennedys' friend and adviser Ed Guthman, slouched in a chair in the anteroom of the Oval Office. Jack was still working the phones into the wee hours. Ormsby-Gore had suggested that the president make the blockade zone smaller to give the Russians more time to come to their senses. The Navy was chafing against it, but Jack issued the order through McNamara anyway. The night watch would tell the tale, probably by dawn.

Guthman looked up at Bobby's rumpled and drawn form, the overcoat slung over his shoulder and the briefcase hanging from his arm like an anvil, and tried to broach the unspeakable.

There were plans being circulated to evacuate top officials to underground installations outside Washington, Guthman said. Even if the country was half eradicated, the other half radiated, it would still have its leaders.

Bobby looked off, pausing for a long moment, though his reply had formed instantly.

"I'm not going," he said. "If it comes to that, there'll be sixty million Americans killed and as many Russians, or more . . . I'll be at Hickory Hill."

He pulled his coat on, glanced down at the light still burning under the president's door, and bade Ed Guthman good night.[28]

Around the world, the hardware of mass extermination was wheeling into motion, klaxons sounding, pilots running to their jet bombers, troops in their nuclear bunkers deep in the earth readying the keys that would arm their warheads. In Times Square, electronic ribbons of news floated in the black sky, the headline going around and around and around. People stopped and stared up at it, murmuring questions to which there were no answers. Prayers came to those who had forgotten what they were. Had the people known what lay behind the headlines, there might have been more than prayers. A run on the banks, perhaps, or pitched battles to crowd into bomb shelters.

The presumption of an orderly world, held together in a balance of terror, was melting away before their eyes, but what could they do? Wait.

Inside the White House, nerves were frayed. Some time just after the blockade was instituted, there was a meeting at which the Cuba Project's "Task Force W" plans were being haggled over. Jack, Bobby, Richard Helms, Max Taylor, McCone, Bundy, and Bill Harvey were reportedly among those in attendance, and a fierce argument was brewing. In the grip of the stalemate, dangerous glitches had begun to occur, exactly as Jack had feared.

Bobby was in Bill Harvey's face. Bob had savaged Harvey in another, recent SGA meeting, before the crisis, in a personal attack that went on for almost ten minutes. Now Harvey was being blamed for the landing of a pair of two-man submarines on the Cuban shore, deployed for sabotage ops, even as the world was perched on a hair trigger. When it was learned that the operatives were out of radio contact and could not be recalled, Bobby went ballistic, charging Harvey with both dragging his feet and operating without proper permissions and oversight.

Harvey is said to have protested that he was operating alone because Bobby told him to. What's more, he said, the CIA did not have subs; he had sent the teams in at the behest of the Joint Chiefs. (Max Taylor does not appear to have come to his defense.) Harvey pressed his point, thundering that he had known that there were some sort of Soviet nukes in Cuba for a year and insisting that he had been trying to get through Bobby to the president to make his case, but had been stymied. Bobby tended to believe his Amigos and doubt the CIA. He had cast doubt on Harvey's intelligence even though it was basically in synch with Arcacha's from the summer of 1961. In order to prove his assertions, Harvey had sent nine men to their deaths. By his estimation, Bobby had either been holding that proof to justify an invasion when the timing was right, or been cruelly inept.

Jack said next to nothing as the joust went on, tapping a tooth with the tip of a pencil, the only sure sign that he was furious. When he did interject, Harvey made the fatal career error of turning directly on the president.

"We wouldn't be in such trouble now if you guys had had some balls in the Bay of Pigs!"[29]

A hailstorm of "liars" and "you sons-of-bitches" and other colorful invective then spewed, unrestrained, from the main combatants. Harvey had cooked his goose.

"You don't say that to the president in his own office," Sam Halpern would note years later, with some understatement. "But Harvey was the only guy who had the guts to do it."[30]

It was further reported that the spy and the attorney general promised to kick each other's ass. Finally, Bobby tossed Harvey's out of the president's office. Within days, their James Bond would be punted out of Task Force W, too.

Even still, Bobby continued sabotage talks with Roberto San Roman on the side. Rafael Quintero had entered the conversation as well, and the Cubans called him at Justice, now made fully aware of the stakes by Jack's speech. Bobby kept implying that if the current tactic failed, then invasion was imminent.

"This time it's for sure," he told Roberto, "and you Cubans, if you really want to help, what you have to do is get yourself a boat and try to sink one of those Russian ships trying to break the blockade . . . on your own."[31]

The reckless Bobby was forever reasserting himself. No sooner had he upbraided Harvey for courting chaos with CIA sabotage, than he was encouraging the Cubans to do the same thing, freelance.

On October 24, ExComm met again, now in anticipation of what the next wave of Russian ships to Cuba might do. McCone was receiving reports directly from the blockade zone, just minutes after the fact. The quarantine proclamation was now in full legal effect.

"Mr. President, I have a note just handed to me. It says that we've just received information through ONI [the Office of Navy Intelligence] that all six Soviet ships that are currently identified in Cuban waters—and I don't know what that means—have either stopped or reversed course."

These were craft bound for Cuba; but, beyond that, no one was quite sure what this report meant. McCone left the room to find out. The deployment of depth charges against Soviet submarines was discussed. McNamara said that there were practice depth charges that could be dropped without damaging the subs but would force the Soviets to surface at once.

These were the moments of utmost tension for Jack.

He ran a hand over his face, then covered his mouth with a closed fist, his eyes drained of their light, the irises gray. He stared at his brother across the table, the telepathic channels wide open between them, but clogged with a million questions.[32] Was the world at its end? Had they made some fateful error? The prospect of trying to raise a submarine, with all the attendant possibilities for miscommunication, had brought them to "the edge of a final decision."[33]

McCone returned a few minutes later.

"These ships are all westbound, all inbound for Cuba. 'Cuban waters' is considered west of 30 degrees [west longitude]. I just don't know what that is."

"Close to the barrier," McNamara ventured. Two of the ships, the *Kimovsk* and the *Gagarin*, were "roughly 500 to 550 miles from Cuba." Another of them, a tanker, might have been closer to the island. Still others were probably even closer.

McCone surmised that some might have either stopped or reversed direction, but it was terribly unclear. Reports dribbled in. The men talked over each other, at moments, but then Taylor had something more certain.

"Three ships are definitely turning back . . . certain others are showing indications that they may be turning back." American planes were heading out to confirm it. Jack wanted U.S. ships to restrain the impulse to investigate, however, fearing that a false report of attacks on a retreating vessel might reach Moscow.[34]

As the crisis wore on, with a storm of conflicting messages coming from Moscow, one critical choice after another was being made in Washington to forestall imminent disaster. Had the Americans known what kind of internecine power struggles were developing on the Communist side during this week, their hopes would have been even dimmer.

On October 26, as it appeared that the Kremlin was acting to de-escalate, Fidel became so enraged that—according to intercepted transmissions from one of the missile bases—he attempted to seize control of the Soviet missile arsenal on the ground, or at least at that site. These reports indicate that Fidel personally led a unit of the Cuban Army to attack and overrun a Soviet-manned surface-to-air missile base at Los Angeles, near Banes, in Oriente Province.

These would not have been the nuclear missiles; SAM rockets are defensive weapons for striking down incoming threats. Nevertheless, the site had been deemed important enough to be worth open combat to take it; Adrián Montoro, former director of Radio Havana Cuba, was among a number of stalwart Castroites who would confirm the battle, later on.[35] Some accounts would claim that as many as eighteen Soviets were killed in the skirmish.

Fidel was out to create an incident that would, in the words of a former comrade, tell him if "there was going to be a war or not."[36] More simply put, he was out to be sure there *would* be war.

Over the next two days, two other reckless confrontations almost did assure it.

On October 27, word was received that an American U-2 spy aircraft, taking routine atmospheric samples, had wandered off course over the North Pole and veered into Soviet airspace. When Soviet MiG fighters were scrambled to intercept it, American fighters were sent up as well and managed to escort the U-2 back out of harm's way. With that fearful scenario averted, another one took its place. Another U-2 failed to make its scheduled return, and in the middle of an afternoon ExComm meeting, word came that it had been shot down over Banes, killing the pilot, Air Force Major Rudolph Anderson Jr.

That was the same base that Fidel had putatively seized the day before. As Cuban revolutionary lore would have it, Fidel was present when the Soviets' radar picked up Anderson's incursion into Cuban airspace. The OK to fire on Anderson was given by the Soviet military commander in Cuba, Major General Igor Demyanovich Statsenko.

"How does one shoot down an attacking plane?" Fidel demanded of the Soviets manning the radar.

When a Russian officer showed him the button that would trigger one of the SAM-2 missiles, Fidel is said to have reached over and matter-of-factly pushed the button. The SAM screamed into the sky, gaining on Major Anderson's jet and then tearing it to shreds.[37]

Four days earlier, ExComm had discussed just such a shootdown scenario, taking it as a given that if a SAM were deployed, the launch site would be immediately bombed to cinders.[38] Whoever had taken out the U-2 gave the U.S. military the fodder it needed to push Jack and Bobby into the active use of force. The brass had hated the blockade idea, insisting that it was a passive, even weak, strategy; that the Soviets only understood aggressive, military means.

Bobby felt that "the noose was tightening" on all of the players.[39] Official Washington was nearly unanimous in its support for a direct reprisal. Every effort to buy time seemed only to make the Pentagon hungrier for action. The dogs of war were straining against their chains.

But Jack would not let the SAM site be attacked: "It isn't the first step that concerns me, but both sides escalating to the fourth and fifth step—and we can't go for a sixth because there is no one around to do so."[40]

The boys at the Pentagon were flabbergasted, but Jack held his ground. Had he known that Fidel might well have been the shooter, might still be at the site, and would probably be killed if Jack would only unchain his dogs, things probably would have been no different. The risks still would have been terrible. All it might have done was to hasten the understanding between him and Khrushchev that Fidel was unstable and not to be trusted.

According to an American intelligence officer, the idea that Fidel had shot down the U-2 was "intriguing," but such a clear shot could not have been taken unless the Russians had already locked on to the plane in preparation for a kill.[41] Under the circumstances, it was extremely unlikely that Khrushchev's troops would have risked such a lock unless the Russians had no choice; unless, as accounts from both the Cuban and the American side indicate, Fidel was effectively in control of that site and had someone lock on while themselves held at gunpoint.

The day after the U-2 incident, Sunday, October 28, at 10:00 in the morning, Khrushchev gathered his senior advisers at a guesthouse in Novo-Ogarevo, outside Moscow, hoping the more informal venue would send a signal that all was calm in the Soviet high command. Negotiations with the Americans now rotated around a quid pro quo in which the Russians would remove their nukes from Cuba if the Americans would take theirs out of Turkey and promise not to invade the Castro fiefdom.

Invasion was looming, however, in the wake of the U-2 shootdown. No options could be written off. Nikita's meeting was held in a formal dining room where he often feted other world leaders. On the huge table were folders—green, pink, blue-gray, and red ones—bulging with mail color-coded for the other sequestered officials who were bustling in.

As the squat and vigorous Khrushchev strode across the building's grand foyer, an aide loped along beside him, gesturing to a fat work folder clutched in his hand.

"There's a letter from Kennedy." The letter had been transmitted overnight, he told the chairman. "And there's something else—"

"Let's go in," Nikita said. "We'll look at everything there."

Khrushchev wanted Jack's letter read aloud, even though everyone had copies in front of them. Oleg Aleksandrovich Troyanovsky, the aide for international affairs, read the text in a monotone, a task which took nearly half an hour with translations.

The letter essentially agreed to lift the blockade with a promise not to invade Cuba, only if the Russians took out their missiles.

There was another report, this one from Ambassador Dobrynin, who had met with Bobby Kennedy the night before in Washington.

"Read it," Nikita ordered.

A wispy piece of onionskin paper fluttered in Troyanovsky's hands.

The U-2 incident had changed the landscape. The pressure on the president had been increased tenfold. Bobby had been blunt, telling Dobrynin, "We have to have a commitment by at least tomorrow that those bases would be removed," he said. It was not an ultimatum, but simply a statement of fact.[42] The Soviets, Bobby assumed, were as intent as the Americans were on avoiding a catastrophe.

But it might soon prove impossible, Bobby told Dobrynin. Some of the hard cases in the Pentagon, the military dead-enders, were spoiling for a fight, Bobby said. Dobrynin said that he had warned Khrushchev of "irreparable consequences," of a chain of events that could occur against the president's will. The implication seemed clear to the Russians: the American president was in danger of being overthrown if the stalemate continued much longer.[43]

Whether this was a gambit or not, whether Bobby actually said it or Dobrynin just interpreted it or Khrushchev himself misinterpreted it in the heat of the moment, it had the effect of throwing the stakes in Washington into sharp relief in that room.

"So? What do we think?" said Nikita when the memo had been read.

Silence, maybe the result of sheer exhaustion. Could their mortal enemies actually be exposing their throats like this? Was this an indication of weakness, or an example of the forces and counterforces sustained by democracies?

Khrushchev, as ever, discerned the subtext and the humanity therein. Kennedy was asking for help, he believed. They were being asked to come to terms before all terms became moot, and Khrushchev was inclined to back off his insistence on a joint missile removal, afraid that Kennedy might be losing his room to maneuver.

Nikita spoke for almost an hour, appealing to his circle to trust Jack now. Then came another message, related by courier, that the president was preparing to speak to the American people again that night. The clear assumption in the room outside Moscow was that, pressed to the wall, President Kennedy was about to announce an invasion of Cuba.

It was sometime on this same day of meetings at Novo-Ogarevo, probably as invasion began to seem imminent, that an even more astounding development was announced by Troyanovsky.

"Nikita Sergeyevich," he continued, scanning his hasty notes, "a very disturbing message has also come from Castro. [He] thinks that war will begin in the next few hours and that his source is reliable. They don't know exactly when, possibly in twenty-four hours, but in no more than seventy-two hours. In the opinion of the Cuban leadership, the people are ready to repel imperialist aggression and would rather die than surrender."

Troyanovsky sighed heavily, eyeing the chairman sidelong.

"Castro thinks that in [the] face of an inevitable clash with the United States, the imperialists must not be allowed to deliver a strike." The aide looked back at his notes, reprising his statement for clarity's sake. ". . . allowed to be the first to deliver a *nuclear* strike—"

"What?!" the chairman blurted.

"That is what I was told."

"What?" Nikita repeated, aghast. "Is he proposing that we start a nuclear war? That we launch missiles from Cuba?"

"Apparently. The text will be confirmed soon, and then it will be easier to tell what Castro really has in mind—"

"That is insane! We deployed missiles there to *prevent* an attack on the island, to save Cuba and defend socialism. But now not only is he ready to die himself, he wants to drag us with him." Without waiting for confirmation, Nikita decided then and there to put an end to the madness. "Remove them," he said of the missiles, "and as soon as possible. Before it is too late. Before something terrible happens."[44]

There were some 162 Russian missiles on Cuba at that moment, but that would have been a fraction of the total number that would have been launched if Fidel had gotten his way. Jack Kennedy had made clear, on October 22, that he would "regard any nuclear missile launched from Cuba against any nation in the Western Hemisphere as an attack by the Soviet Union on the United States, requiring a full retaliatory response upon the Soviet Union." America would launch against Cuba as well. Under NATO agreements and the Warsaw Pact charters, the nations of Europe would also enter the fray, immediately. By most estimates, hundreds of millions would die, maybe as many as a billion.[45]

As all reason seemed to be dissolving, a rumor was spreading through the ranks of Cuban intelligence; and, as Washington and Moscow were hammering out a solution, sidelining the furious Castro brothers, two of G2's top spies took a drive through the dark streets of Havana.

It was 4:00 A.M. when Juan Antonio "Coqui" Rodríguez Menier, a G2 senior officer at that time, climbed into the car of his friend and colleague, First Lieutenant Arturo Ángel Álvarez Lombardia, the chief of the Legal Section of Operations for G2 and a founder of the DSE. Menier gave voice to the rumors he had heard within MININT, rumors that—however outrageous—would explain why the tensions had risen to such a pitch between Castro and Khrushchev, even before Fidel's apocalyptic fit of pique. Could it be true that the Soviets had given some of the nukes over to Cuban troops?

When Menier broached it, Álvarez smiled ironically and tried to warn him off.

"Coqui . . . Coqui. Don't believe anything of what they say to you and only half of what you see for yourself. There is not a single Soviet—listen very well—a Soviet doesn't exist that does that. Do you think that they are crazy? It was another, different thing, but don't worry. In short, the rockets are not here and the Americans will not attack us for a while—"

"Okay, okay, but what happened?"

Álvarez smiled again. "Look, you know Fidel, don't you?"

Menier made a gesture indicating that he didn't, at least not well.

"You know that El Caballo, when he's angry, is a pain in the ass," Álvarez elaborated. "In the middle of this shit, he got inside the central bunker of the rockets. He wanted to have control of the buttons. There was a mess." Álvarez was laughing now, in a wheezy, gallows-tinged way. "Life is a bloody thing. After so much commotion and the danger of having a quarrel with the Soviets, the result was that the bunker [did not have] what he was looking for."

"What?"

"There were [no] nuclear missiles."

Menier was stunned. "I don't believe that."

"There was nothing. The Soviets are sons-of-bitches. They sent the rockets, but never the atomic warheads. If Fidel had shot the rockets, he would have made the most ridiculous action of the century. He would have killed only four cows in Kansas City."

"And the Yankees would make shit of us. That is great!"

"In spite of that, we won." How that calculation was made is not particularly clear, but Álvarez held to it. "Don't forget that. We won. Someday Fidel will accept that the cleverness of the Soviets made possible that the Americans didn't annihilate us."

The men drove on in silence, Menier struggling to decide whether this could really be the case. Years later, he would confirm Álvarez's claim in a talk with MININT Chief Pepe Abrantes, a personal associate of Fidel's. "They not only took the command post of the [missiles]," Menier would write of the Abrantes encounter, "but . . . in the shooting that took place [at the site], a Soviet colonel was dead and four other officers [were] hurt." So it was not the eighteen Soviets that others had reported dead, but there had still been bloodshed.

Abrantes also claimed to have been present when Fidel "convinced Nikita" to place the missiles in Cuba, Fidel reasoning that eventually there would be a battle with the United States and the closer the Soviet weapons were to America, the better the chances that they would not be intercepted before they struck.[46]

Given the exhaustive historical record of that time, claims like these deserve some skepticism, but Menier, Álvarez, and Abrantes were at the summit of Cuban intelligence when their conversations occurred. What is more, Menier—since his defection to the United States—has been considered a man of sterling devotion to the truth and is under the protection of the CIA.

Whatever game was being played between Nikita and Fidel of course paled in comparison to the one being contested between the USSR and the USA. As has often been reported, within thirteen days, the Soviets were persuaded to withdraw in exchange for a "no invasion" pledge by Kennedy. It is also now known that a secret "back-channel" agreement, one that would save face for Kennedy, was made whereby the U.S. would remove its nuclear-tipped missiles from Turkey.

However, it is now known that almost from the moment of the agreement, neither side meant to abide by it. And the fact that *both sides knew this* makes the entire flirtation with catastrophe even more insane—and meaningless—than could be known at the time. Only Castro emerged with a victory.

Within days, President Kennedy admitted to Secretary of Defense Dean Rusk, Undersecretary of State George Ball, and the entire National Security Council that he had no intention of being tied down to the "no invasion" pledge.[47] And although the United Nations had agreed to broker the formal written agreement, Kennedy ultimately refused to sign it, although Khrushchev kept writing him, urging him to do it. On January 7, 1963, both the U.S. and Soviet ambassadors asked the UN to just forget about it.[48]

Kennedy (through McGeorge Bundy) made another even more secret deal with the Soviets: not only was a full Soviet brigade allowed to stay behind,[49] but even more powerful Soviet nukes would be stationed in Cuba—in the form of Soviet subs with nuclear missiles. In the mid-sixties, the brigade would be transferred from Eastern Europe, where it had been configured to guard and handle tactical nuclear weapons. This implied that the unit's role in Cuba was to protect the storage of such weapons as well as other sensitive Soviet installations. These weapons would return to Cuba, but not until after President Kennedy's death. A groundbreaking 1982 study by Christopher Whalen of the Heritage Institute disclosed the following Soviet weaponry, all of which was superior to those that initiated the showdown, in Cuba *after* the crisis:

- a November-class nuclear attack submarine, and several support ships.
- TU-95D "Bear" bombers, capable of carrying nuclear bombs or launching nuclear missiles.
- Echo I-class nuclear-powered cruise missile submarine equipped to carry nuclear warheads. The Echo I could deliver four nuclear devices against targets in the United States.
- two squadrons of MIG 23/27, capable of carrying nuclear or conventional payloads up to 1,500 miles.[50]*

Thus, with all this new armament at his disposal, only Fidel Castro ultimately saw a gain from the crisis. The new nuclear arsenal, although positioned securely inside Soviet planes and ships, nonetheless gave the Castros some feeling of security against an all-out U.S. military invasion. But this was a few years off, and in the immediate wake of the crisis the brothers Castro were feeling as vulnerable as ever.

In the weeks that led up to the Cuban missile crisis, neither Marina nor any of Lee's "friends" or associates knew where he was living in Dallas. Apart

---

*And there was more, including: Kynda-class guided missile carriers, two guided missile destroyers, two Foxtrot-class attack submarines, a Kresta I-class guided missile cruiser, a Kanin-class guided missile destroyer, batteries of modified SA-2 antiaircraft missiles, and twenty-four AN-26 transport planes, capable of carrying troops anywhere in the Caribbean region.

from showing up at his new job at Jaggars-Chiles-Stovall, which he may or may not have done on a steady basis, his exact whereabouts were a mystery, as was the source of his money. Even if he was showing up at work, he was still often alone on weekends. Marina was living with various friends, ducking Lee or just letting him go on about his business in Dallas. The marriage was a war zone, more often than not.

Lee had paid back his brother, Robert, the $200 he had borrowed to bring the family to Texas from New York the summer before, and he may have borrowed further funds here and there, whether from Bouhe or another of their new acquaintances, George de Mohrenschildt. But even then, he would have been living on a shoestring, and yet he seemed uncharacteristically blithe about his funds at around that time.[51]

On November 4, Lee moved Marina and June into a house on Elsbeth Street in Dallas. Marina spent the evening cleaning the grime off the floors, the walls, the appliances and countertops. Lee made an effort to clean the icebox but then, at about 10:00 P.M., he told her that he was going out, saying that he had paid for the room at the YMCA and should just stay there. The fact was that he had not bunked at the Y since October 19, so it's not clear where he went that night. Marina, alternately defiant and resigned to her fate, kept working until almost dawn.

Antulio Ramírez Ortiz, the resident chef and mascot at G2 headquarters at that time, remembers well the climate in Havana just after the crisis ended. A Cuban mole inside the Kennedy apparatus, probably "The Professor," wired a dispatch to his handlers that the Kennedys—despite the agreement that ended the crisis—were still considering a Cuban invasion, if not soon, then eventually. Fidel was enraged. Stripped of his powerful weapons, albeit temporarily, he once again found himself working constantly to defend his regime against Washington. He had taken to referring to Khrushchev as "a cowardly queer," and Fidel swore that he would put a pox on both their houses.

As a result of the mole's report, hasty meetings were held in Havana's G2 headquarters in which the Cuban response was discussed. It happened that in November 1962, Antulio was having an affair with Olga, the wife of Dimitri Korchunov, an aide to the Soviet ambassador in Cuba. One day, in a state of near-hysteria, Dimitri rushed home and told Antulio that Castro had been given eighteen MIGs for self-defense against another U.S. invasion. However, Castro had lied to the Soviets about his intent: he wanted to bomb

New York with the Russian planes in order to start a war between the two superpowers. Dimitri was recalled to Russia during the emergency.*

In this atmosphere, Antulio scrawled these words in a notebook that would later become his memoir:

"All the boffins have been assembled to formulate plans for achieving the following objective: How can Cuba achieve dominance of South America, and, parallel to this, how can Kennedy be eliminated?"[52]

There were rumors about Lee Oswald's movements during that time. Frank Sturgis was a commander in Fidel's air force, then later, an anti-Castro fighter who would turn up as one of Nixon's Watergate "plumbers." Late in 1963, in the wake of the assassination, Sturgis claimed that Lee had been seen in Miami just after the missile crisis, trying to infiltrate the Anti-Communist Brigade that Sturgis headed. His claims showed up in an article by James Buchanan in Florida's *Pompano Beach Sun-Sentinel*, which asserted that Lee made contact with G2 agents there, and made a call to Cuban intelligence in Havana from a G2 safe house. Later, under FBI questioning, Sturgis admitted that his claims were speculative, based on second-hand accounts from associates.[53]

It would not be until 2005 that the truth of Lee's extracurricular activities in the fall of 1962 would finally be unfolded from the memory of Oscar Marino. The old Cuban would unburden himself in various venues, a few times in a dark corner of a Mexican hotel coffee shop, Oscar always nervous, proud, dignified, and refusing to accept even the cost of a cup of espresso. Though he had developed a strong trust with his interviewer and even still considered himself a Marxist, every moment of catharsis was still fraught with fear. G2 is omnipresent in the Cuban capital even to this day, and there were moments when it seemed that the old man was about to just get up and walk out.

"When did you first hear the name of 'Oswald'?" he was asked.

---

*Days later, Antulio stole microfilm from Dimitri, which Antulio claimed included plans for the attack. Official U.S. records corroborate that Antulio indeed at this time approached a Swiss embassy official, Alexis Kurth, with a packet of material, but Kurth refused to accept it. Antulio asserts that he later tried to reach the U.S. State Department with the information.

Whispering in the dim light of a cloudy afternoon, Oscar glanced toward the drowsy cashier and leaned in close, his elbows on the table.

"That was in the autumn of 1962, when Oswald was recruited. He was spoken of on the management level. I belonged to the strategic management level and was consulted for official reasons on the most important operations of the G2. Moreover, I had the documents on foreigners that we had recruited as fighters. Oswald was on a list of foreign colleagues and payees. He repeatedly received strategic money. No important sum, a couple of thousand dollars—only for strategic purposes. Money did not concern him—he wanted to perform something great for the revolution. He was in the USA, and was already a political activist who fought for the Cuban revolution."

Lee had not actually taken up arms when Oscar became aware of his name; his reference to Lee as a fighter was figurative. "He offered himself," Oscar elaborated. "He wanted to do something. He was an uprooted person and hated the social order in which he lived, a political fanatic. Oswald had some capacities that made him attractive to us."

It was, of course, G2's overwhelming preference, according to Menier, to use "true believers" as assets abroad, not agents who were doing it strictly for the money. They could be too easily wooed away.

"Wasn't he too unpredictable, too unstable?" Oscar was asked.

"There is always a risk, but we had no good choices in the USA," answered Marino. "We recruited him because we had no others. One takes what one gets. Do not forget what was happening in 1962. Cuba fought for its basic survival. Kennedy wanted to destroy us, but we had to export the revolution. It's the only way we would be able to survive. We needed fighters. And standing before us was an agent in the USA. We didn't choose him because he was the best. He was available. We needed people. We believed in the revolution and were determined to export it. And just imagine— someone in the USA."

How was Oswald contacted—where, and by whom?

Without a pause, Oscar said, "The first contact was made by Rolando Cubela. He encountered Oswald at least twice—to my knowledge in Mexico City."

The name Rolando Cubela struck the interviewer, Willi Huismann, with the force of a blow. In 2005, the elusive doctor was playing hard to get in Spain, where he was still alive and well and living in an upper-middle-class neighborhood of a major city. His story was legend. He had been both an intimate of the Castros and their mortal enemy. He had been the CIA's point man in the planned overthrow of the dictator. He had had personal contact with Robert Kennedy and been in a CIA safe house planning the murder of Fidel at precisely the moment that word came of the president's assassination in Dallas. He had served almost two decades in Fidel's prisons for a plot that was shattered in 1966, and he was thought to be, at the very least, a double agent of the Castro regime, even as he was thought—by the Agency— to have been plotting against that regime.

As the Cubela-Oswald connection sunk in, a battered taxi pulled up outside the smoke-stained plate-glass window. Oscar paused, sat back, and sipped his coffee as casually as a spymaster could. A plain-faced old woman got out of the cab, carrying a baby, and came into the coffee shop. She bought a flan to go, and a carton of milk, then shuffled back out to the cab, which drove on down the gloomy street.

The place was empty again, except for the drowsy proprietor, and talk returned to Cubela. "How could *this* man have signed up Oswald for the Cuban secret service?"

Oscar laughed.

"Life is not black and white . . . not at all in the world of the secret services. Cubela was a traitor and wanted to murder Fidel on behalf of the CIA. Correct. We did not know [that] when he was delegated to make the contact with Oswald. We trusted him at this time, fully and entirely. He was an important man in the revolution, a very capable commander. And he was able to travel without problems abroad, for he was at this time president of the Cuban student association. He made many contacts for the G2."

Oscar was asked if he himself was active in the recruitment of foreign agents.

He wasn't. "I was, at that time, in the headquarters in Havana, responsible for operations against the domestic counterrevolution. Strategically, I had nothing to do with Oswald. But my function in the G2 was so high that I had insight into all important operations." Among Oscar's key responsibilities was the monitoring of Rolando Cubela's travels and contacts.

Oswald lived in the enemy country, in the USA. "How could someone such as this be led and guided by Cuba?"

"Everything ran out of Mexico," Marino began to clarify. "Mexico was the key center for the export of the revolution. From there, the G2 was able to operate almost unfettered. Except for Mexico, the other Latin American countries had interrupted their relations with Cuba because of pressure from the USA. Cuban agents were equipped in Mexico with 'clean' Mexican passports, with which they were able to travel quietly into the USA, or into other countries of the continent. Mexico City became the espionage metropolis of the Cold War, an ideal place for double agents, traitors, and agent hunters. From there, both the Cuban secret service and the Soviet KGB initiated their operations against the USA." It was out of Mexico City that Cubela apparently initiated contact with Lee Oswald. "I know of two meetings with Cubela. In the autumn of 1962 and in the summer of 1963." There would be another trip to Mexico City in September of 1963 as well, and it would be the only one documented by later investigators, but Oscar knew only of these two encounters in the Mexican capital.

Oscar went on. "Cubela was able to begin his preparation of Oswald in his radical left-wing attitude—he worked with Oswald's own left-wing fanaticism. Oswald wanted to perform something, be a hero. Perhaps there would have been better fighters than him. Certainly we would have rather recruited an intellectual. But that was not so simple in the USA," he elaborated. "Oswald was available, and we used him."

"For what uses?"

With the lilt of irony, Oscar said, "That was not my department. I do not speak about operations that were led by others."

The old man was tired. Smiling wanly, he put some money on the table, a signal that this installment had come to an end. He struggled carefully to his feet, plucked his cane from the corner, expressed his thanks as if relieved of something, and then made his way to the street, the brass tip of his cane ticking across the linoleum.

When interviewed in 2005, Cubela denied even this benign contact with Oswald. But his denials must be weighed against other new evidence. FSB senior officer Nikolai, to his utter amazement, located evidence of the Oswald-Cubela liaison in the KGB archives, buried in a dossier labeled merely "Cubela." In it, Nikolai recounted, was a February 1, 1967, report from none other than Major General Igor Demyanovich Statsenko, the officer who—in 1962—had given the order to shoot down the U-2 spy plane at the height of the missile crisis. Statsenko was the commander of the Soviet military in Cuba in the sixties and an adviser to their "little Cuban brothers" in the Cuban military. His 1967 report was in reference to the charges that Cubela had conspired to shoot Fidel at the capital's May Day celebration in 1966. In the detailed file on Cubela's interrogation, made after his arrest, Statsenko mentioned that Cubela had talked about his meetings with Oswald. Statsenko appears to have been telling the KGB something that they had not known, or at least had never been able to confirm up to that point—that Castro's would-be murderer had also, by a serendipitously in-nocent coincidence, been Cuba's original contractor of Kennedy's future killer.

According to the KGB document that Nikolai had memorized, Cubela and Oswald met "repeatedly, several times," with the first rendezvous at the end of 1962—exactly when Oscar Marino said it had been.

Cuba's brief moment as a nuclear outpost, if not a nuclear power, had come to an ignominious end, at least momentarily. By all accounts from the Cuban side, Fidel, Raúl, and Che were so incensed by the outcome of the missile crisis that they declared covert war on the United States and the whole of Latin America, with or without the blessings of Moscow. On No-vember 28, Fidel ranted: "The North American millionaires . . . have orga-nized conspiracies, sent weapons and money to the counterrevolutionary gangs . . . , caused the death of over 80 workers . . . They have killed our teachers, workers, peasants, and militiamen . . . With a hypocrisy character-istic of Hitler, Kennedy ordered the invasion of the Bay of Pigs at the very moment when he was protesting that he had no aggressive intentions toward our country . . . Cuba is arming to defend itself against constant aggres-sions and threats of invasions on the part of the United States."

Six weeks later, his temper had not cooled. "Mr. Kennedy, between us and you and between those revolutionary soldiers and the Yankee empire there is much blood," Castro bellowed in Cuba, to deafening applause. And in a Cuban television speech on January 16, 1963, Castro virtually declared war against the hemisphere, telling viewers that their duty was to lead the whole South American continent in Cuba-style revolution.

A plan was soon put on the fast track. If the Cubans could not defeat the imperialists by conventional or nuclear means, they would revert to the guerrilla tactics that had served them so well against Batista. Two weeks af-ter the missile crisis, Che gave an interview to the *London Daily Worker*, saying, "If the missiles had remained, we would have used them against the very heart of the U.S., including New York. We must never establish peace-ful coexistence. In this struggle to the death between two systems we must gain the ultimate victory. We must walk the path of liberation even if it costs millions of atomic victims."[54] At the same time, he was party to the plan-ning of a smaller but no less vicious attack on New York.

At its inception, shortly after the Cuban revolution, the Fair Play for Cuba Committee drew the attention of both the FBI and the CIA. June Cobb was now a CIA informant, code-named LI/COOKY, living in Mexico

City; but before her return to the south, she had established contact with CBS News correspondent Richard Gibson, one of the FPCC's creators. It was Cobb who had determined that Gibson had traveled to Havana and met with Dorticós and Fidel, and that the organization had received money from the Cubans for the maintenance of its office in New York and other operating expenses.

Neither Cobb nor Gibson knew of Havana's more insidious intentions for the organization. Cobb had been south of the border for almost a year by the time of the missile crisis. Journalists/founders Robert Taber and Richard Gibson had moved on as well.

Had he known what was in store, Gibson might well have never created the organization. With Cuban terrorist/DGI agent Roberto Santiesteban in place under UN cover along with Elsa and José Gómez (under cover as switchboard operators for the Cuban mission) and FPCC members Marino Suero and José García, something big was being planned. Thankfully, it was this core group that the Feds began to track some time in late October or early November.

Sometime in the first week of November, the FBI began to receive information that explosives might be coming into the city under the watchful eye of that group. There were strong but worryingly vague indications that the target date was Thanksgiving weekend, possibly the day after the holiday, Friday, November 23. But what exactly was planned? As the date approached, it became apparent that at least twelve incendiary devices were in play, and by the beginning of the third week of the month, the FBI office in Manhattan was in full lockdown, now certain that the plot was probably aimed at civilian targets—department stores seemed likely, and there was evidence that Grand Central Station might also be included. November 23 looked increasingly certain to be the date.

The Feds could wait no longer. On November 17, as thousands of holiday travelers coursed through Grand Central and thousands more began their Christmas shopping, the FBI prepared to strike, staking out García's costume jewelry store on West Twenty-seventh Street. Late that night, the hammer came down. García was arrested, as were the Gómez couple and Suero. Inside the shop was a huge cache of explosives, some five hundred kilos of TNT,[55] along with detonators, grenades and incendiary devices, complete with instructions on how to connect them to detonators timed for a sixty- to seventy-five-minute ignition point. In a steel safe at the back of García's store, they found diagrams of the city's most vulnerable shipping docks and railroad freight yards.[56]

Santiesteban remained at large, but only briefly. At the climax of a police chase uptown, the suspect ditched his car and ran up Riverside Drive and into the park, shoving chemical formulas for explosives down his throat. He too was arrested, and once all five were in custody the full dimensions of the plot came out under questioning. It appeared that as many as twenty-five conspirators were part of it, operating out of a virtual "sabotage school" in midtown Manhattan. The plan was to wreak havoc at Macy's, Gimbel's, and Bloomingdale's department stores (on what was traditionally the busiest shopping day of the year), the Grand Central train hub, the Port Authority building, New Jersey's oil refineries, and the Statue of Liberty. Had the "Black Friday" plot succeeded, it would have probably have rendered 9/11 the *second* most devastating foreign attack on American shores in its history.[57]

In Havana, Castro would respond to the arrests with a rant against American police brutality and violations of Cuba's diplomatic immunity.

On November 21, Bobby Kennedy publicly praised J. Edgar Hoover and his agents for having "acted in continuation of a record that had saved the United States from a widespread Nazi espionage and sabotage network just prior to and during World War II."[58]

Five months after their arrest, the five plotters would be released from jail and returned to Cuba in exchange for CIA operatives who had been captured at the Bay of Pigs.

Exactly one year and one day later, another Cuban-bred terrorist plot against America would succeed. That one would kill only one man, but that crime would arguably be as traumatic to the American psyche as anything planned for the people of New York.

CHAPTER 8
Irresistible Targets

THERE ARE NO RECORDS AVAILABLE at the University of Buenos Aires to prove that Dr. Che Guevara was, in fact, a medical doctor. The Office of Academic Affairs says that his records have apparently been purloined by celebrity hounds, or otherwise mislaid.[1] If, in fact, Che did complete the studies required for medical certification, he must have been absent on the day when his class was sworn to the Hippocratic oath.

In the days immediately following the Bay of Pigs invasion, Dr. Guevara had appeared among the *brigadista* prisoners and promised them that they were about to die. When Che told you that you were about to die, this could usually be believed. Fidel, on the other hand, educated as a lawyer, was more judicious in his dispensation of ultimate penalties. Instead of killing the hapless invaders, he released them back to the United States in December 1962, for a controversial payment of $53 million in farm machinery, baby food, pharmaceuticals, and other basic goods that had stopped flowing to Cuba under the trade boycott.

The ransom fund was the result of Bobby Kennedy's tireless twenty months of arm-twisting U.S. corporations and affluent Catholics to donate the goods in return for tax deductions. The courage and selflessness shown by the exiles on that beach had struck a profound moral chord in him, and when Jack was told that Fidel was willing to ransom the brigade, he told Dick Goodwin, "Whatever it takes, let's do it . . . I put those men in there. They trusted me. I have to get them out."[2] Cardinal Cushing of Boston, who had helped to raise the materiel, noted that when he and the president spoke of the prisoners' plight, it was the first time he ever saw tears in Jack's eyes.[3]

Jack and Bobby would not relent in their efforts until all 1,113 survivors arrived in Miami. Enrique "Harry" Ruiz-Williams, the *brigadista* who had sustained seventy wounds and been sent back to the States shortly after his capture, had become a confidant to Bobby by then, and a helpmate in the process. On the day that the brigade was released, Harry and Bobby spoke by phone. "You got it, Enrique," Bob said. "This is it. The guy with the beard has accepted."[4]

Fidel had been ready to make the exchange in September. Bobby, however, knowing full well that the Republicans would accuse the Kennedys of selling out to the Castros, stalled the release until after the midterm elections in November. This condemned the prisoners to still more months of famished, degraded confinement, and the missile crisis further compounded the political problems, but virtually all survived in Fidel's dungeons.

But not all survived with goodwill toward the man in the White House. On December 29, 1962, as the men, their families, and supporters streamed into the Orange Bowl stadium to be welcomed home by President and Mrs. Kennedy, a faction of a hundred prisoners was boycotting. One of them, Enrique Llaca Jr., would soon make a public attack on Manuel Artime, Miró Cardona, and other leaders, charging them with "using the brigade for their personal benefit" and insulting the fighters with $250 handouts upon release.[5] In the wake of the October crisis, all counterrevolutionary planning was being reevaluated. Bobby was still driving the Agency to distraction, openly bringing exile leaders on ski trips to New England and visits to Hickory Hill, just as he had brought "roughnecks" home to the Kennedy mansion as a boy, but no one was promising another invasion attempt any time soon, at least officially. Jack had taken full responsibility for the Bay of Pigs disaster, though it had had many authors. But neither he nor Bobby had been able to defend the invasion publicly, and considerable bitterness had built up in the exile community. Jack had been warned that he might not want to subject himself to a public ceremony in Miami. His advisers feared that he might be booed.[6]

December 29 was hazy, with heavy tropical storm clouds wandering along the southern horizon as if cruising for a place to bomb. The First Lady stood anxiously in the wings of the Orange Bowl, gazing out at the patchwork of brightly clothed people in the stands. At last, Jack took her hand and they entered the stadium; as they strode to the fifty-yard line, forty thousand people stood up and cheered them and applauded. Even the ultracool Jack was filled with emotion. For a brief moment, there was forgiveness and contrition, however unspoken, and veterans of Brigade 2506 gave him the flag that had been kept hidden by one of the prisoners during their long incarceration. Kennedy swore a spontaneous oath that it would fly again one day over a free Havana.

That banner would remain in U.S. government custody for thirteen years until the Brigade vets repossessed it, but it was not for lack of effort by the Kennedy brothers. Jack was already in the process of creating a new entity, the Cuban Coordinating Committee (or CCC), ostensibly to help the *brigadistas* assimilate into American life but in fact to coordinate a new plan for a Cuban coup d'état. As the negotiations to free the Brigade were coming to fruition, Cuba specialists at the State Department, Defense, the Navy, the Army, and on the Joint Chiefs' staff had been devising a new, hemisphere-wide counterinsurgency strategy, plans for which would be sent to the National Security Council (and Bobby) for approval before the president took action. Secretary of the Army Cyrus Vance took charge of sifting through the intel reports from the field. Joseph Califano, who had worked under Vance at the Pentagon since one week before the Bay of Pigs invasion, was the Defense Department's point man on the committee. Alexander Haig, the CCC's deputy to Califano, claimed that they effectively comprised the "junction box" that enabled the Kennedys to circumvent the intelligence bureaucracy.[7]

In the wake of the missile crisis, the U.S. had promised Khrushchev that they would round up and arrest anti-Castro exiles, and the FBI, the U.S. Coast Guard, the Secret Service, and the British police in the Bahamas had already begun this work.[8] But the arrests were a ruse; in fact, the Agency was "reportedly recruiting particularly trusted and competent members of individual exile groups into its service."[9] It appeared that the administration was laying down its arms against Fidel. In fact, the Kennedys were simply trying to recentralize "the underground's control under the CIA and Robert Kennedy."

Within hours of Jack's speech at the Orange Bowl, he was in a swank house in a glade near Miami Beach's Fontainebleau Hotel, huddling with exiles to discuss this process: they would bust some anti-Castro cells and support others, while also pursuing an emerging strategy at CIA to recruit military leaders within Fidel's inner circle. Manuel Artime, Pepe and Roberto San Roman, Erneido Oliva, and Harry Williams were guests at the West Palm Beach compound that month. In January, their talks would continue at the White House.

In Lee Oswald's 1962 diaries, he once described himself as a "radical futur-ist,"[10] but by Thanksgiving of 1962 he had very little of the future left in him. He began the last year of his life trying to reconcile, yet again, with Marina. They were living in the two-story red brick slum on Elsbeth Street in Dallas's Oak Cliff, and their efforts at domesticity were halfhearted, if that. The only creature that either of them loved, without condition or complication, was their daughter Junie. The ground-floor apartment was a large, dank maze of tiny rooms, with too many doors and too many windows, which Lee always kept covered. He dotted the walls with decent enlargements he had done of the photos he had made in Russia, but it did little to lift the sense of gloomy entrapment. The building still stands, a horseshoe footprint, the ends thrust out to the street, the center set back around a cement courtyard, a low brick wall between it and the sidewalk, unadorned windows, dark, airless interiors, and a few tattered dusty trees.

They did get away from it at Thanksgiving that year, taking the bus to Fort Worth and spending the day with Lee's brother, Robert, and his wife. En route, Lee bought the soundtrack to *Exodus*, and they found some solace in that score in the coming months.[11] They were invited to a Russian post-Christmas party with the de Mohrenschildts, one at which the Oswalds were again the downscale couple, but where Lee had fun chatting up a young, rich, pretty Japanese woman named Yaeko Okui. He had spent time in Japan, of course, at Atsugi, and had told people that it was Japanese radicals who first gave him the idea to go to Russia, but he and Yaeko reportedly talked of nothing more than flower arranging. By the end of the evening Marina hated her, suspecting that Yaeko had designs on her husband.

Still, she was glad to be out, wherever they were invited. She expected that they might be asked somewhere for New Year's Eve. It was the most important holiday in all of Russia, one that she had always looked forward to and dressed up for and danced and drank through. But no invitation came, and Lee fell asleep early. She spent her first New Year's Eve in Texas drawing herself a bath and lying in it, imagining that the tub was full of champagne and the room aflutter with tinsel and crepe paper and hurtling corks. Furious and weeping, she eventually crawled out of the tepid water and sat down to write a letter to Anatoly, the bright, handsome, gentle man who reminded her so much of President Kennedy.

"Anatoly dear: Very late, I am writing the letter you asked me for. Late, I want to wish you a Happy New Year. It is not for this I am writing, however, but because I feel very much alone. My husband does not love me," she wrote. She was sad, she said, that there was an ocean between them, but she had no way back to Russia. "I regret that I did not appreciate the happy times we had together and your goodness to me," she wrote. "Why did you hold yourself back that time? You did it for me, I know, and now I regret that, too. Everything might have turned out differently." She wondered if Anatoly would ever have her back, given how she had hurt him, and then she closed by writing, "I kiss you as we kissed before." In a postscript, she added: "I remember the snow, the frost, the opera building—and your kisses. Isn't it funny that we never even felt the cold?"[12]

Marina finally got the courage to send off her letter on January 7, but she was still largely unfamiliar with how to conduct even the most routine bit of business in America, and she neglected to add enough postage to cover the weight.

Lee came home a few nights later, the letter in his hand, half-read. A battle erupted. He hit her twice.[13]

"You did it on purpose," he seethed. "You knew they changed the [price of] postage and that the letter would come back to me. You were trying to make me jealous! I know your woman's tricks . . . I'll never, ever trust you again."

She denied it all, but he couldn't be pacified. How could Lee Harvey Oswald, visionary and soldier, conceive of his wife's reaching for another man simply out of a devouring loneliness?

He forced her to get the letter and tear it up while he watched.[14]

On January 8, 1963, the CCC was officially established. Angelo Kennedy, an intimate of Artime's, was with him when a small group of exile leaders went to the Executive Mansion to learn of the CCC's grand scheme. Angelo waited in the reception area outside the Oval Office, but there was no doubt what was going on behind the closed door. When Artime emerged with his group, he was grinning; when they left the mansion, as Angelo recalled, "he gave me a huge hug, saying, 'We got it! We got everything!' " It was the beginning of a "very close" friendship between Jack and Artime.[15] While many of the exiles felt that the Kennedys were not trustworthy, Artime, a natural politician and himself a liberal, tried to bridge the antipathies of his compadres with the apparent sympathy and resolve at 1600 Pennsylvania Avenue. Jack and Manuel had met prior to Jack's nomination; the Cuban had been locked up on the Isle of Pines for most of the time since. The world had changed in the interim, but for all intents and purposes the secret war only changed its personnel and its frontline base of operations from Miami to New Orleans.

Bobby believed Jack wouldn't be reelected if Castro was still in power in November 1964, but by now there was more than the next election at stake. American fears had been cynically stirred by the 1960 campaign, which in turn had led to a real crisis. In making the paper tiger, Fidel, into a real one, the Kennedys had effectively forced themselves to keep going after him lest they lose the election for failing to "out-Nixon Nixon." It was the perfect self-fulfilling prophecy. Their provocations of Fidel had revealed a real and dangerous instability at the height of the missile crisis—reason enough to keep working toward his downfall.

But Washington had allowed Russian troops to stay in Cuba, though the nukes were gone, and—since the bad blood between Havana and Moscow had become obvious—the American press openly speculated that the Russians' goal might be as much to keep Castro on a short leash as to defend his regime. Nonetheless, their presence kept the option of a direct invasion off the table. If America attempted to invade, the thinking went, the Russians would have to preserve their standing in the emergent Communist world by hanging tough with Havana. But now, to further complicate matters, there was another opinion. Rumors would soon be circulating that a radical realignment might be in the works—an entirely different kind of "third way."

These speculations would not appear in print until later that spring, but in Bobby Kennedy's office there were apparently two tracks under discussion. One was the straight-out removal of Fidel by a new CIA putsch. The other was more pragmatic, but contingent on a daring new partnership. This was the so-called Laos solution.* It is not clear how long it was seriously on the table, but the *San Francisco Chronicle* would describe it as being "based on the idea of getting Russia's 'overt presence' out of Cuba in exchange for a negotiated 'neutral' regime including responsible advocates of a non-Communist Cuba." The idea—basically power-sharing under a new Cuban coalition—was reportedly gaining credence with militant Cuban exiles, presumably including Artime and some of his allies in the exile establishment, if not the entire former Cuban Revolutionary Council. The removal of Fidel was considered a requisite first step, and the exiles, it was said, would definitely support that.[16]

There were whispers of another solution, an even more remarkable one. In the years before the 1964 election, some held that Khrushchev feared a Kennedy loss. The Soviets still believed that a U.S. military coup against Jack had been imminent at the peak of the October crisis, one that would have been disastrous for Moscow. Caught between the dueling fears of Fidel

---

*The Laotian monarchy, which dates to the 1300s, shared power with the Communist Pathet Lao on and off through the 1960s and '70s. The Communists took complete control in 1975.

and the Pentagon, the Soviets themselves appear to have begun to consider the assassination of Fidel, and indeed were said to be planning one for the spring of 1963 until word of it leaked into the American press and the plan was scotched.[17] According to an account published just after Jack's assassination, it had been hoped that—under this "neutralist" solution, with Soviet troops on their soil and American hawks still circling low over their island—Fidel, Raúl, and Che would go quietly into exile, under the joint sponsorship of Washington and Moscow. "From the Soviet standpoint," this would be "a slight tactical retreat in Cuba to be offset by advances on other Latin American fronts, such as Brazil and Chile. From Castro's standpoint, however, it meant the end of his career as a world figure and [he] refused to go along with it."[18]

The exile factions were under their own internal strife, just as the Communist bloc was. The CRC would soon try to force Washington's hand against Fidel by undertaking sea raids, and a "bad faith" falling-out would result between the Kennedys and Miró Cardona. Under the "Laos solution," the Cuban Revolutionary Council would be mothballed.[19] In its stead would be a new "non-political anti-Communist Cuban war command," headquartered outside the U.S. The force would be made up of some former Brigade officers and some exiles in the U.S. Army. Thus, the Kennedy brothers started calling on Cuban exiles to join the American Army. An anti-Castro presence would embolden what was left of the Cuban underground. In one possible scenario, hard-line Communists inside Cuba would topple Fidel before announcing a nationalist regime that would negotiate with the U.S.-backed faction. If Castro clung to power for too long, the U.S. would then incite an incident, surround the island with troops to "prevent another Hungary," and intervene to oust him without resorting to a full-tilt invasion.[20] David Salvador, Manuel Ray, and Huber Matos would be the likely winners of a tightly controlled presidential election process.[21]

When the idea broke in the papers, the press was cautiously credulous. The *Los Angeles Times* wrote: "Under normal circumstances, this column would not report this fantastic story—except for the reliability of the source who in the past has furnished accurate information on Cuba and US-Soviet relations months before the events actuated."[22] The scenario gained traction in the American media in mid-1963, then faded, and then surged again just before and just after Jack's murder.

In that latest iteration, it was committed to paper in a CIA memo sent to the FBI's Latin specialist, Sam Papich. There it was presented as a ruse in which the U.S. would fabricate such a story and float it through a double agent to the notorious G2-infected Cuban delegation at the United Nations as an intimidation tactic. It was stressed, however, that the idea was still in the discussion phase and not yet consented to by Agency headquarters.[23] This suggests that the plan was never meant to be implemented, but was just a way to exploit the post-crisis rift between Fidel and Nikita. Still, if it had become possible, the Kennedys would have scored a foreign policy triumph, perhaps even a precursor to détente.

Whatever the case, the substance of these claims dovetails with a number of other strange developments in the Communist world that winter.

When Jack Kennedy and his wife left the Orange Bowl on September 29, 1962, the scent of forgiveness and restitution hung in the air, but it quickly began to dissipate. The common perception in South Florida soon became that the Democrats, and the Kennedys in particular, had sold out the counterrevolution. That misperception still predominates almost half a century later, even though no president since, whether Democrat or Republican, has moved to oust the Castro brothers; even with the fall of the Communist Soviet Union, and with the Republicans' dominance of the executive branch during that forty-six-year period. To this day, with the terms that ended the missile crisis never ratified, a tacit East/West pact to contain the Castro regime has clearly been in place, both in Moscow and Washington, ever since October 1962. Yet it's "the Kennedys" who remain the catchphrase for betrayal, ineptitude, and weakness among many in the Cuban community. It is one of those perceptual absurdities that tend to supplant facts in American life, and, indeed, the bigotry of many of those expatriates has accounted for Florida's key role in the victories of every Republican presidential candidate from Richard Nixon to George W. Bush.

Had it not been for Lee Harvey Oswald, however, the Kennedy brothers might still have ousted the Castro brothers, and the most virulently disgruntled exiles would be among those now running Cuba instead of forcing their "payback" on progressive American candidates at every opportunity. For all the weird, ongoing hope for proof that the mob or the CIA or the oil companies or even the Florida exiles killed Kennedy, the evidence is now overwhelming that a Cuban-style Communist, who had learned of the reinvasion (or "Laos" or "nationalist" plans), was the sole triggerman and that he did it with the aid and comfort of Fidel and Raúl Castro.

Jack died for the exiles' cause, and yet in many Cuban-American house-holds he is still considered a pariah.

No sooner had the *brigadistas* been welcomed back to America than Fidel and Raúl had a massive party of their own, on January 2, 1963, to celebrate the fourth anniversary of the revolution. Sitting on a reviewing stand in downtown Havana, under a huge banner picturing Fidel as a Venceremos freedom fighter, the men smoked cigars and waved to the throngs. Atten-dance was mandatory for the people of Havana, as it had been the year be-fore when Kennedy's mock casket was paraded through the streets. The people were more beleaguered now, however. There was more struggle and hardship in their faces. Cuba, once known as the "Pearl of the Antilles," was in a precipitous internal decline.

Nevertheless, along the boulevard thundered millions of dollars of weapons, up-to-the-minute antiaircraft missiles and coastal defense rockets strung like banderillas on the backs of trucks. Russian-built MiG jet fighters ripped across the sky. Helicopters, tanks, and heavy artillery rumbled past the dictator, followed by phalanxes of Cuban troops, arranged Roman style, twelve by twelve.[24] Four hundred foreign Communist leaders filled the re-viewing stand. It rivaled the displays in Red Square every May Day, and Fi-del was loaded for bear as he took to the microphone.

"For the first time in history, imperialism has paid war indemnification," he said of the prisoners' release. "They call it ransom. We don't care what they call it . . . They were defeated . . . At Giron Beach, they suffered their first defeat in Latin America . . . Kennedy, the intriguer, should stop dream-ing." He gripped the lectern, his voice rising to its hectoring, raspy tenor range. "Those militiamen and soldiers are the same ones who smashed, in 172 hours, the invasion of the pirates of Yankee imperialism. Proletariat mili-tia never would put itself at the service of Yankee imperialism." Kennedy had boasted that the Brigade flag would fly again over a "free Havana." "We are free, Mr. Kennedy," he railed, his voice cracking with passion. "We are a free territory of America!"[25]

The speech went on for ninety-two minutes, a veritable haiku compared to his usual three- and four-hour tirades. Kennedy had acted "like a vulgar pirate chief." Kennedy must have been drunk, he chided. There must be a bar in Miami called "free Havana." Every verbal attack was met with cheers.

As Fidel screeched to his conclusions and the crowds dissolved into the back streets, hunger and disaffection were loose in the land. Farm production was down 20 percent since the revolution. Land reform had been halted, the old, antebellum estates having been turned into vast collective farms, erasing any hope of even the smallest personal plots. The people had reacted to the mass farming plan with apathy and indifference. Most of the country's experienced agricultural managers had left the island.[26] Cuba's virtual monocrop, sugar, would fail that year, and there were growing shortages of all basic necessities. The building of housing and other such elements of the social infrastructure had been slowed, if not abandoned, in recent months, and the American embargo and naval quarantine had cut non-Communist shipping to Cuba to 25 percent of what it had been the preceding year.[27]

Fidel blamed the Americans, the "cretin" Kennedys; and after the New Year's celebration was over, the harangue continued on state radio, even as the people tried to forget their troubles and enjoy an evening of modest dinners and clandestine music devoted to nothing more "socialist" than desire, love, and loss.

And there was a new pattern of blame beneath the Castro brothers' usual vitriol—in the last weeks of 1962 and the earliest ones of '63, Fidel was almost as unstinting in his blasts at the Soviet Union. He was moving, tactically, even further to the left, a clear move to keep Khrushchev off balance. Now he had a host of new detractors within his ranks, from Communist hard-liners who resented his insolence toward Moscow, to military men disheartened by the loss of the Soviet missiles, and to more moderate supporters of the regime who thought Fidel's personal behavior to be increasingly extreme.[28] He had suddenly promoted a hundred officers, a stopgap to increasing unrest in his ranks,[29] but so paranoid had the Castros become at that point that they now kept their army on a 24-hour ration of ammunition, and their militiamen were required to return their weapons to the closest government arsenal after every training maneuver.[30] The Russians, for their part, had left seventeen thousand troops on the island to protect their defense installations.[31] Journalist Tad Szulc reported that most of the radar warning systems and air communications were still in the Russians' control and speculated openly that "this degree of control over the air force may be an assurance for the Soviets that the Cubans are *not tempted to take matters into their own hands when they spot a United States reconnaissance plane*" [emphasis added].[32]

The true extremes of Fidel's behavior back in October were not widely known for years to come, but Szulc's assertion, tucked into a story by a reporter trusted by both the Americans and the Cubans, confirms that not only did the Soviets and Cubans cross swords during the crisis, but that word of it had gotten back to the Kennedy White House.

At this point, Moscow and Beijing were bitter rivals for the fealty of international Communists. The USSR, now Cuba's economic lifeline, was demanding Havana's allegiance to their Communist "popular front" philosophy, a relatively moderate advance of Marxism through a wide variety of sociopolitical means. Beijing, on the other hand, was championing full-throated, violent revolution, worldwide, and it was to that corner that Fidel now moved, calling for a pervasive revolutionary upheaval across Latin America.

At a televised convocation of a hundred thousand people on January 16, Fidel essentially declared war on Latin America. It was the closing ceremony of a congress of hard-line female Communists from the region, and he spoke to them in Santiago, standing at the foot of a massive metal monument to Cuba's black independence hero Major General Antonio Maceo. As night was falling, he embarked on a speech about blood sacrifice and collective martyrdom.

He began with reasonable, scholarly words for the rendering of the poor into cannon fodder. "It is the masses who make history, and to make history it is necessary to bring the masses to battle. We don't deny the possibility of a peaceful transition, although we are still awaiting the first case . . . It is necessary to throw the masses into the struggle with correct methods and tactics." The Soviet deputy foreign minister, Vassily V. Kuznetsov, was in the audience, having been sent to Cuba to negotiate the withdrawal of Russian missiles and jet bombers. Without mentioning Khrushchev by name, Fidel slammed his American *and* Russian "critics," with their policies of "peaceful coexistence" and their "false interpretations of history." "The liberating movement is fighting . . . in Latin America, and this fight needs all the united forces of the Socialist Revolution," he seethed. He claimed that four political murders had occurred in Cuba since Jack's speech at the Orange Bowl.[33]

His eyes grew wilder. He seemed to pace, even though anchored to the microphone, as if he were in pain and starving and ready to be sprung from a trap. There were repeated references to death and blood. He was ready to die, he declared, and ready to take the Cuban people with him if the sacred revolution was to be taken down by Yankee imperialists. It became what the Cuban people still refer to as "Fidel's Ode to Death."

A tropical storm broke, dropping heavy, warm rain on the crowd.

He turned to the towering monument. "Thank you, Maceo, for giving us this opportunity! . . . We, who are pygmies beside you, we feel like giants, because with the blood of those like you who showed this country its path, a people of giants emerged . . . We never had such great expectations, but history and life imposed them on us, and we will know how to fulfill them."

As the vast crowd huddled in the deluge, he too was soaked and began to fling his hair back off his brow.

He stood tall, nostrils flaring. He raised his arms to evoke a cruciform, then pointed down with his index fingers.

"We're invincible!" he bellowed. "Because if all members of the Politburo have to die, we will die, and we will not be weaker for it! If all members of the Central Committee have to die, we will die, and we will not be weaker for it!" The litany went on to include the Congress, the party, and the members of the Young Communist Union. "And if, in order to crush the revolution, they have to kill all the people, the people, behind its leaders and its party, will be willing to die! And even then we will not be weaker, because after us they would have to kill billions of people in the world who are not willing to be slaves, who are not willing to continue being exploited, who are not willing to keep going hungry!"[34]

Fidel turned back to the towering sculpture of Maceo. "People die, but examples never die! People die, but ideas never die! And here we are ready to water our ideas with our blood!"

Fidel's motives were mixed that night. He was out to scare and provoke the Yankee enemy, of course, but he was also trying to outmaneuver the Soviets at a turning point in Marxist history. He was out to shame the Kremlin into giving him unconditional support, into bankrolling his failing state, lest Moscow lose the public relations war with the Chinese.

By U.S. estimates, the rolling inventory that paraded by Fidel that day was a fraction of what he now controlled, courtesy of Russian largess. He had a standing army of 75,000, a backup of reserves and militia totaling another 150,000. He had five hundred surface-to-air missiles at twenty-four antiaircraft sites, manned by the Russians. He had forty missiles at four or five coastal defense sites. His arsenal included twelve cruise missile boats, a hundred MiG fighters, ninety helicopters, a score of Soviet transports, and a variety of warplanes, among them seventeen American B-26s and ten British Sea Fury fighter-bombers. He had six submarine chasers, sixteen torpedo boats, 350 medium and heavy tanks, plus light amphibious tanks, scout cars, and armored personnel carriers, seventy-five assault guns, thirteen hundred pieces of field artillery, and seven hundred antiaircraft guns, nearly all of it supplied by Nikita Khrushchev.[35] And still Fidel defied him.

Jack's worst fears about the political fate of Latin America seemed about to be realized. While trying to put the carrot to work through Richard Goodwin and the Alliance for Progress, he had been forced to pick up the stick to send a message to the Russians and keep his home-front enemies at bay. The stick had brought him the Bay of Pigs fiasco and the missile crisis, and now, in its wake, a neo-Maoist hard-liner named Fidel who was either just manipulating Khrushchev or sincerely trying to rally the Chinese to help him wage violent revolution across the southwestern hemisphere. As if to guarantee that such a war would soon break out, a number of Republican Party honchos, like New York's Kenneth Keating and Arizona's Barry Goldwater, were continually trying to force Jack farther to the right, claiming that Kennedy had "lost the initiative [in Cuba],"[36] and otherwise charging him with weakness and inconsistency. As if partisan attacks weren't enough, accountants were getting into the act. According to the bean-counters, the "cost of Castro" was at about $21 billion, $20 billion of which was for the Alliance for Progress and the other billion said to be the sum of U.S. property seized by Fidel and Raúl, the cost of the Bay of Pigs operation, the military mobilization during the crisis, the "blackmail" money for the prisoners' release, and various "miscellaneous" expenses.[37]

So, with or without the tacit aid of Moscow, the plans to neutralize Fidel and Raúl had to continue, so far as the Kennedys were concerned.

As the secret war was redefining itself, the CIA's Desmond FitzGerald was about to replace the self-sabotaging Bill Harvey. A polished, socially agile veteran of Wall Street and the CIA, Des was a classic American patrician. Six months after the Orange Bowl ceremony, he'd related his sense of the warring Cuban exiles in a letter to his daughter: "I have dealt with a fairly rich assortment of exiles in the past, but none can compare with the Cuban group for genuine stupidity and militant childishness," he wrote. "At times I feel sorry for Castro—a sculptor in silly putty."[38]

This would have come as a surprise to some of the men whose cause he'd be taking up, learned, serious men like Artime, the San Romans, Arcacha, Bringuier, and Williams. Nonetheless, on January 25, 1963, Desmond FitzGerald was officially placed in charge of the Special Affairs Staff, the successor to Bill Harvey's "bang and boom" Task Force W. The housecleaning did not stop there. Operation Mongoose was no more. Ed Lansdale was shunted back to

FIDEL CASTRO RUZ

Fidel Alejandro Castro Ruz
in high school (l) and college (r).

Young revolutionaries Raúl Castro Ruz (l) and Ernesto "Che" Guevara (r).

Rolando Cubela, Guevara, and Ramiro Valdés.

Ramiro Valdés Menéndez.

Fabian Escalante Font
in the Sierra Maestra.

Fidel passes a warning to the Kennedys through reporter Daniel Harker.

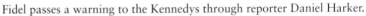

President John F. Kennedy signs Proclamation 3504 on October 23, 1962, authorizing the quarantine of Cuba during the missile crisis.

Rolando Cubela Secades circa 1959 (l, m) and in 2005 (r).

Cubela meets with America's last ambassador to Cuba, Philip Bonsal.

The July 20, 1963, suicide of Jack Dunlap, the KGB penetration agent inside NSA and CIA's "Staff D," which coordinated Cubela's murder plot against Castro.

LEE AND MARINA

Oswald with "Alfred from Cuba."

OSWALD IN MINSK

1961 rog.

With all my love

alek

Oswald with radio factory co-workers.

The Havana Headquarters
of the G2 Cuban spy agency.

G2 gofer Antulio Ramírez Ortiz in 2005.

CIA photo of Martin González Hernández,
the G2 agent identified by Ramírez as having advance
knowledge of Oswald's plan to kill Kennedy.

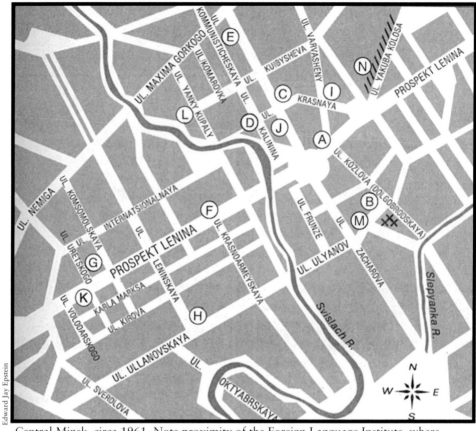

Central Minsk, circa 1961. Note proximity of the Foreign Language Institute, where Oswald socialized, and the KGB Training School, which trained Cuban spies.

Key to Map of Minsk

A. MVD training school
B. KGB training school
C. Belorussian Radio and Television Factory
D. Oswald's apartment
E. Prusakov's apartment
F. Palace of Culture
G. MVD-KGB headquarters
H. Hospital where Marina Oswald worked
I. Home of Alexander Ziger and family
J. Home of Erich Titovets
K. Home of Yuriy Merexhinsky
L. Home of Ella Germann
M. Foreign Language Institute
N. Apartments used by Cuban agents in training

KGB headquarters in Minsk.

KGB surveillance photos of
Lee and Marina.

Vladimir Alexandrovich Kryuchkov, of the KGB,
who forwarded the Oswald file to Havana.

Former JM/WAVE station, located
just south of Miami, in 1998.

Sam Halpern of the CIA's Cuba Desk in 2004.

THE SECRET WAR

President Kennedy at his Palm Beach home in December 1962 with Cuban
exiles who were key to the "secret war": (l-r) Álvaro Sánchez, Roberto
San Roman, Pepe San Roman, Kennedy, Manuel Artime, Erneido Oliva,
Enrique "Harry" Ruiz-Williams.

Ernest Hemingway's Cuban retreat, Finca
Vigia (Lookout Farm), the site of a hoped-
for assassination attempt on Fidel.

Hemingway and Fidel Castro exchange pleasantries at seaside after Castro won the
individual championship in the annual Hemingway Anglers Tournament on May 15, 1960.

Presidential advance man Marty Underwood shielding Senator Kennedy on the stump in Illinois, 1960.

photos Marty Underwood

Underwood greeting President Johnson and Secretary of State Dean Rusk as they arrive in Uruguay on April 11, 1967.

Underwood aboard Air Force One with LBJ and son Marty Underwood Jr.

Fabian Escalante.

Archive de Cuba

Wilfried Huismann

Escalante in his Havana office in 2005.

Cuban embassy employee Silvia Durán (left and above).

SILVIA, ELENA, AND ELENITA: *MEXICO CITY PARTIES AND POLITICS*

Elena Garro and Elenita Paz Garro.

Elena Garro.

Elena twisting with Mexican director Arturo Ripstein.

Oscar Contreras, 2005.

Win Scott

June Cobb, circa 1962.

Silvia Durán in custody,
November 23, 1963.

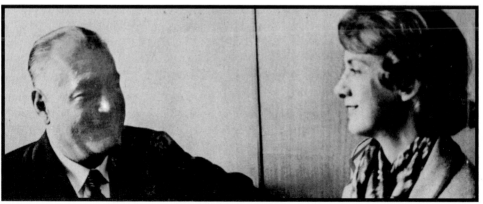

Dr. Juan José Arévalo with Cobb, who translated his book, *The Shark and the Sardines*, which Oswald was reading in the days before he killed Kennedy.

Top to bottom: Cuban consulate entrance; CIA surveillance outpost across from consulate; close-up of surveillance window; CIA surveillance technician caught in the act by Cuban intelligence camera; embassy entrance to Cuban compound photographed by CIA; close-up of gated entrance.

ESPIONAGE IN MEXICO CITY: THE CUBANS

Soviet embassy entrance.

CIA surveillance photo of unknown man entering the gates on October 2, 1963, initially misidentified as being Lee Oswald.

CIA overview of their photographic surveillance of the Soviet compound. Stars denote surveillance cameras.

ESPIONAGE IN MEXICO CITY: THE SOVIETS

KGB agents who confronted Oswald in the Soviet Consulate: (l-r) Valeriy Kostikov, Pavel Yatskov, Oleg Nechiporenko.

Raúl Castro (l) giving a
clenched-fist salute.

Lee Harvey Oswald making his statement
for the cameras shortly after his arrest.

Oscar Marino: "I only want to make my peace."

Senator Robert F. Kennedy
making his own kind of peace
in the Mississippi Delta in 1967.

the Pentagon, and Harvey was shipped off to the CIA station in Rome, where he could do little additional damage to the Kennedys' ongoing agenda.[39] He bade good-bye to his assassin-in-charge, Johnny Rosselli, at a booze-drenched dinner under the amazed surveillance of the mobster's FBI shadow detail, and then set sail for the old country.[40] From then on, the mob would no longer be gunning for Fidel, officially or otherwise.

Des bore no great enmity toward Fidel per se, though he was quickly informed that the Cuban leader was still target number one. He was driven by his belief that nuclear weapons were the scourge of the earth and should not be placed in the hands of apocalyptic types like Castro. To prevent this, he placed himself in service to a man he didn't much like at first, Bobby Kennedy.

In the new plotting, the goal was to find disaffected military brass within Castro's inner clique who would spearhead his "elimination" and takeover. At Bobby's directive, FitzGerald quickly generated a list of sabotage targets in Cuba, directed at infrastructure and set to commence in July at a rate of one target per month. In the course of that pursuit, twenty-five CIA agents, mostly Cuban exiles recruited as commandos, would end up being killed or captured in five raids on the island in the coming year.[41] Additionally, Des would be paying particular attention to the Fair Play for Cuba Committee, still in existence even after the New York plot had been thwarted the previous November. The secret war, both at home and abroad, had barely skipped a beat.

Working at the photo company Jaggars-Chiles-Stovall, Lee actually had a job he loved, for the first time ever. And at the end of January, he would be starting typing classes at a technical school, the better to write his great treatises. There were some fleeting moments of closeness between Lee and Marina, like the old days—the two of them against the world. One night, as they were talking about his former girlfriends, he asked her if she had been unfaithful to him since their marriage. She admitted to him—as if to make him appreciate her more—that she had had a lame sexual encounter with Leonid Gelfant when Lee flew off to Moscow to inquire at the U.S. embassy about returning to the States.

"You're putting me on," he kept saying. He didn't turn on her, but he didn't believe her, either. He merely accused her of trying to make him jealous again, and pulled even further away from her. It seemed that all he did now was work and read. He was burying himself ever deeper in the Communist periodicals he'd been ordering from back east, in the library books he'd bring home by the stack: books about Trotsky and Marx, books about American imperialism in South America, and particularly about the new Cuba.[42]

There were relatively quiet periods around the holidays, but as the new year rolled out his tension rose again. He had taken to punching her repeatedly in the face when she made him angry, no longer just slapping her once,[43] and he didn't bother to seduce her anymore when he was aroused: He simply forced sex on her. "Stop washing the dishes!" he would wail. "Lee's hot!"[44] As his fits got more bizarre and her ministrations failed to quiet him, the Elsbeth neighbors started talking. One tenant from an adjacent apartment took the super, Mahion F. Tobias, aside one afternoon.

"I'm afraid that man over there is going to kill that girl."

"I can't do a darn thing about it," Tobias said. "That's domestic troubles."

Tenants were forever complaining to him about the noise, the screaming baby, the sound of Mrs. Oswald hitting the floor. On another occasion, the tenant above them came to Tobias.

"I think he has made a new opening down there," she said. "I think he's put her right through there."

Lee had broken a window, perhaps with his fist or Marina's head, no one knew. Finally, Tobias had to warn him to "straighten up," or he would have to move out.[45]

Lee started badgering her to go back to the Soviet Union. The idea was anathema to her, even though there was precious little love left between them; she found ways to avoid the subject, though he forced her to write inquiries to the Soviet embassy in Washington from time to time. She discussed divorce with some of her émigré friends, but no one thought it was a good idea. He seemed to have a bit more money on hand than he was making, though he seldom shared any of it with her, as he used to. A year later, as his life was being dissected at the highest levels of government, his cash outlays for that period would exceed his known income: every three or four weeks, starting in August 1962, he'd send the State Department a money order (or cash) for about $10 toward repayment of a $396 loan he had made upon his return to the U.S. However, in the seven weeks between December 11, 1962 and January 29, 1963, he paid off the balance of the loan in three large amounts ($106, $100, and $190). Given that Oswald's known expenses from October to January, based on a laborious reconstruction by the Warren Commission, were $537, and his earnings were $892, paying the loan would have left him $101 in the red—making this a rather strange time to pay off a loan, unless he had a secret source of funds.[46]

Where the money came from was not determined then, and has been speculated on for nearly half a century. According to Oscar Marino, the money was provided by the Cubans, in modest amounts, either by Rolando

Cubela or some other G2 contact. It gave Lee some fiscal breathing room, and he did not spend conspicuously—just enough, on specific needs. Why would he have spent some of that money paying off a loan from the government he thought so little of? Because he would not be able to receive a new, updated passport before that debt was cleared, and apparently he might soon be doing some traveling.[47]

It was hard for Bobby to regain Jack's attention on the Fidel business. Other matters, such as Southeast Asia and Soviet nuclear might, distracted the president, and their history suggests that he was not as certain that Fidel had to be killed as Bobby was. It was only when Bob brought *New York Times* reporter Tad Szulc to see him that Jack's optimism about ousting Castro was reengaged. Szulc, who covered Cuba and knew the political terrain well, had received word that Fidel's revolutionary army was riddled with dissenters now. The notion that there was a real chance of a coup from within the military ranks, often touted by Cubela and the like but never verified, now became more than a notion. Over State Department objections, Jack signed off on the pitch made to him by Szulc and Bobby, and on February 9 a meeting was held at a CIA safe house in D.C. to set in motion the project code-named AM/TRUNK.

Other aspects of the Kennedy surge came quickly into focus. According to one of RFK's most trusted exile leaders, Erneido Oliva, both he and Artime met privately with Bobby at Hickory Hill in Virginia just weeks after their December 1962 return from prison in Cuba. Artime's close aide, Nilo Messer, said in 2003 that Bobby demanded that the camps for the invasion trainees be located outside of the U.S., where American laws would not apply. Messer added that "The organizer of this second plan against Castro was the Kennedy administration and mainly Robert Kennedy, who for us at that time was a hero. [The camps] were a Robert Kennedy plan, so he was involved all the time."

Soon the exile leaders were given an estimated $6 to $9 million budget to train their soldiers in Nicaragua and Costa Rica for the next invasion.[48] Eventually the counterrevolutionaries set up camp in Monkey Point and Puerto Cabezas, Nicaragua, and the Orlich farm in Sarapiqui, and Tortuguero, Costa Rica. The number of exiles there had reached about three hundred on the day President Kennedy arrived in Dallas later that year, the day that the plans began to crumble.

Interestingly, some of the exile leaders and their CIA overseers were pessimistic about the Kennedy plan, but, for the exiles, they felt they had no other choices. The CIA's JM/WAVE base boss, Ted Shackley, summed up the feelings of his colleagues. "We didn't see any evidence that the military revolt would be successful," Shackley said in 1997. "There was no proof of large numbers of Cuban officers interested." He was equally sober about the propects for training camps. "The whole operation was set up as a result of Artime's discussion with the Kennedys . . . it was an RFK operation, an exercise in futility."[49]

If Fidel's *Granma* revolutionaries were the first naval guerrillas, then this band would assume their own moniker for the operation: "Second Naval Guerrilla."

Back in Washington, however, not everyone was fully prepared for how blatant the talk of Fidel's assassination had become, especially since the appalling events of the past October. But at a CCC meeting that took place twelve days after its creation, on February 20, and attended by Jack's aide Ralph Dungan, Cyrus Vance, Richard Helms, Des FitzGerald, Bobby, the cautious Robert Hurwitch from State, and Califano, it was abundantly clear that murder was the first item on the CCC's agenda.

Califano, young, idealistic, and devoted to his boss, Cy Vance, was unnerved. He suddenly thought Bobby was obsessed with Castro. He had admired the way Bobby stuck it to southern segregationists like Mississippi's governor Ross Barnett, or Alabama's governor George Wallace, but that same pugnacity now struck Califano as merciless, even reckless with regard to Fidel. The subtext was obvious. No one tiptoed around it anymore, except with the thinnest euphemisms. When he left the meeting, Califano sensed that Castro was a walking dead man.

Vance shared the suspicion, and he was livid. The whole Cuba project had taken on this barbershop atmosphere, he said. "Too many people at the table, low-level aides sitting against the wall . . . when 'actions like this, however discreetly, are being discussed.' I took this comment to mean that he understood what I suspected: Bobby Kennedy and his brother wanted Castro assassinated."

Califano guessed that Des FitzGerald was caught up in the plots, maybe even the spearhead, "since he was the point man for covert raids and other dirty tricks to disrupt Cuba."[50]

Joe Califano's objections seem almost quaint now. Compunction about such things was still an integral part of the moral code of most of the people in high office back then. The line between the country's noble self-image and its "pragmatic" attraction to torture, invasion, occupation, execution, and/or assassination remained fairly well defended in Washington, even if it did harken back to a time of smaller dictators, less deadly weapons, and more overwhelming odds for victory. But Fidel and Raúl Castro's were not the only murders being contemplated in that brave new world, post-Hitler and -Stalin. Lumumba and Trujillo had been cut down. Mosaddeq and Árbenz would have been dispatched as well, if they hadn't known how to run. Fidel and Vietnam's Diêm would soon be next, if all went according to plan.

When Lee and Marina returned to America, he had applied for work as a Russian translator. He had worked hard to learn the language, but his Russian was only passable and that was part of his bitterness toward Russia: the effort he had expended had not been reciprocated by the country herself, he believed. Lee was not hired as a translator, but that episode did introduce the young couple to the circle of émigrés that now formed the core of their little social life.

At the center of that life was George de Mohrenschildt, a globe-trotting oil geologist, intellectual, dapper, handsome, and urbane. As with most international businesspeople of that time, George had been debriefed now and then by the CIA and even knew a few Agency people as social acquaintances, but they were not part of his tighter group of émigré friends. George appreciated Lee Oswald's rangy mind and his political intensity. Sometimes that intensity concerned him, and George wasn't impressed by the way Lee treated his wife, but he befriended both of them, at least in part to give them some relief from the home life George could sense was difficult at that time. The Oswalds were like the poor relatives at any de Mohrenschildt party, but the clique was largely made up of liberal bohemian types not given to snobbery.

George and his wife, Jeanne, threw a party on February 13 and invited Volkmar Schmidt to attend. Schmidt was a new friend, a German-born geologist who was doing research for Mobil Oil out in Duncanville and had met George through people at his lab because he was interested in studying Russian. Tall and blond, Schmidt had studied at Heidelberg and become close friends with the son of Dr. Wilhelm Kuetemeyer, a specialist in psychosomatic illness, an associate of Carl Jung, and an intimate of several of the people—Stauffenberg, Von Halen, and Von Trott—who had plotted with Dietrich Bonhoeffer to assassinate Adolf Hitler. Schmidt had been treated like a member of the Kuetemeyer family. He prided himself on having absorbed a good deal of secondhand knowledge about psychology, and George may have invited him that night expressly in the hope that he might be able to suss out and "help" his friend Lee.

According to Volkmar, as he expressed it thirty years later, "Lee saw in George . . . a man whom he would like to emulate. A man who was living a full life, who was a free spirit, who shared some of . . . Oswald's political beliefs. But what Lee didn't realize was that George was much more. That he was a very cultured man. Very sensitive. Had a much better education. So, Lee didn't have the means, literally, to emulate George."[51]

Nonetheless, George had been doing all he could to make Lee feel accepted, like an equal among equals, in solidarity. The little family was truly struggling, he'd been told, and the de Mohrenschildts had taken it upon themselves to help alleviate it a bit. The Oswalds still had no car. Lee held a very meager job. Marina still had no more than perhaps a hundred words of English, and George told Volkmar that he thought Lee to be "an interesting young fellow but a bit of a lost soul." It was Volkmar's impression that the young man had a lot of courage, energy, and determination; a lot of "good motives, but . . . no means to really achieve something."[52]

While the party spun around them that night, Lee and Volkmar found themselves sitting with beers at the kitchen table. At the outset, the German thought of Lee as a young revolutionary, a man who had invested himself in a great and perilous adventure but had come back disappointed. In conversation, after worrying the subject of Russia for a while, Lee suddenly turned to the USA and launched into an angry jag about Kennedy and the Bay of Pigs. His outrage was as pointed and outsized as if the invasion were still in progress. Volkmar tried to throttle the energy down, but it was clear that Lee was obsessed with Russia and America's corruption, Cuba's virtue, and Fidel Castro's heroic brilliance and victimization. He was even more obsessed with Kennedy, as perpetrator.

As the conversation stetched toward its third hour, Volkmar noticed that Lee paid absolutely no attention to his forlorn wife and child. They were sitting on a daybed in the next room, Marina sipping wine, sneaking cigarettes when Lee's back was turned, and trying vainly to find some way into the conversation. There were sad shadows around her ice-blue eyes, and a loose-limbed air of careless resignation in the way she moved.

Lee was still on about Kennedy. Volkmar sensed, strongly, that Lee was caught in a trap of his own making. "He could find nothing positive to fill this void in his life,"[53] so Volkmar tried to steer the conversation in a brighter direction.

"You know, the Bay of Pigs may have been one mistake, but there are many, many good things that Kennedy has done. He's still the best hope for the Western world, the world in general. The real problem in this country is the bigotry, the racism . . ."

Lee followed the lead. Hoping to refocus the young man's indignation, Volkmar seized on recent news stories about General Edwin Walker, a local army vet who had been relieved of his command for his extremist right-wing views. Walker had made speeches that so inflamed the September 1962 showdown over James Meredith's attempt to integrate the University of Mississippi that three journalists had been killed in the melee; Walker had been arrested on four federal charges, including insurrection. A month before the de Mohrenschildt party, a federal grand jury had dropped the charges, but Walker, a venomous leader of the Dallas John Birch Society, remained at large in the public imagination. The more Volkmar talked about Walker, the more Lee agreed with him. Volkmar had succeeded in deflecting his obvious rage away from Kennedy.

But as Lee kept talking, jabbing at this idiot, and that fascist, and those fools, Volkmar's sense of moral vertigo only increased. He began to see Lee as "spiritually totally empty." He became perturbed that Lee seemed to have no emotional relationship with Marina and the baby. He could see that Lee's "purpose in life was to achieve something politically. But he had no means . . ." This was the dilemma that he would see in a lot of his friends who later joined the archleftist Baader-Meinhof group in 1970s Germany. "I knew this was exceedingly dangerous," Volkmar would recount. "That he could explode. Not to—in my mind, not to be an assassin, but maybe beat up his wife or do something . . . Lee Harvey Oswald was a man in despair . . . in a desperate spiritual situation. He turned to politics because of, of lack of happiness, of achievement, of knowing what to fill his life with."

As their conversation wore on, Schmidt had an even more disturbing sensation. He found himself recalling Dostoyevsky's phrase "the logical suicide," and it kept reverberating. As Volkmar bade them good night, he made a special effort to connect with Marina. Their eyes met. He could see a secondary despair in her.

Nine months and a week later, when Lee appeared as the prime suspect in the murder of John Kennedy, Schmidt thought to himself that "Lee . . . would have found anybody, of any importance, to assassinate. He was looking for somebody important. To become history. To leave a mark in the history books, no matter what . . . A man who knows his powers but who has not . . . been given a good set of values to use his powers, will eventually commit suicide . . . He was just determined to have power. And this was probably his way of showing power."[54]

The first of his assassinations was attempted very soon after the de Mohrenschildts' party, and it may well have been Lee's conversation with an unsuspecting Volkmar Schmidt that determined the young revolutionary's target.

Edwin Walker was born in Texas, saw combat in both World War II and Korea, and, while commanding the Arkansas Military District in the late 1950s, was forced to implement the order handed down by President Eisenhower to forcibly desegregate Central High School in Little Rock, Arkansas. Sent to Germany to command the 24th Infantry in 1959, he took it upon himself to circulate literature from the John Birch Society to the troops under his command, and to publicly accuse such radical figures as Harry Truman, Eleanor Roosevelt, and Dean Acheson of being communist sympathizers. Under President Kennedy's watch, the general was relieved of his European command. He was hustled off to Hawaii while an investigation was carried out, but he chose to retire on November 2, 1961. He hated black people, brown, red, and yellow people, the Supreme Court, the majority of America's elected officials, all non-Christians (in which he included Catholics), and the Kennedys, to name a few. He was also a closeted homosexual.[55] After escaping indictment for his instigating role in a fifteen-hour white race riot at the campus of "Ole Miss," he soon joined another pestilent racist named Reverend Billy James Hargis, an evangelist who was leading an anti-communist campaign dubbed "Operation Midnight Ride," a nod to the murderous night rides of the Ku Klux Klan.[56]

Lee Oswald considered Walker to be a leader of a fascist organization,[57] and Lee now considered himself a hunter of fascists. It was coming time to take action.

On February 22, the Oswalds were invited to another party, this one at the home of Dr. Everett Glover, the same man who had introduced Volkmar Schmidt to the de Mohrenschildts.[58] There they met Ruth Paine, a Russian-language student amicably separated from her husband, Michael, a research engineer at Bell Helicopter, and Ruth would become a kind of godsend for Marina as the year stretched on. Marina was pregnant again.

Lee continued to beat her nonetheless. At the end of the month, the land-lady at the Elsbeth apartments had finally had enough and told the Oswalds to get out. On March 2, Lee found them a place on the top floor of a two-story white clapboard place just three blocks away, at 214 West Neely Street. It was not much better than the Elsbeth place, another warren of tiny rooms, but at least one floor higher and a bit sunnier, with a rickety little balcony out front and a scrap of yard in the back. It also had a tiny room, more of a closet, which Lee appropriated as his writer's office, installing some shelves and a lock.

"Look. This is my little nook. I've never had my own room before. I'll do all my work here, make a lab and do my photography," he told her. "I'll keep my things in here. But you're not to come in and clean. If I ever come in and find one single thing has been touched, I'll beat you."[59]

Lee was supposedly in his typing class five nights a week, but the class only met for three nights, and soon she suspected that he was exacting his revenge for the Anatoly episode by having an affair with Yaeko Okui, the Japanese woman they'd met at the end of December.

On March 8, Edwin Walker was at the Municipal Auditorium in Birmingham, Alabama, on a dais with Hargis. Hargis's Operation Midnight tour was burning its way through twenty-seven cities that spring, a "super-patriotic" paroxysm of song and hellfire meant to stop integration in its tracks. Walker, a celebrity since the riot at the University of Mississippi, was Hargis's "man on horseback," a hero who was being auditioned that evening as a potential front man, a speaker for the movement.

Tall and striking as Walker was, however, he had all the oratorical skill of a milksop, and that night's speech was a disjointed, mealy-mouthed mess. Hargis concluded that the former major general would prove more useful as a figurehead than as a man who could actually lead a charge.[60]

Lee, however, still considered him a demagogue with the power to rally millions to his cause. On March 9 and 10, he took a bus to Walker's home so he could take pictures of it and the area nearby. On March 12, the same day that Marina's new girlfriend Ruth Paine dropped by to see the house, Lee ordered a .38-caliber Smith & Wesson pistol from Seaport Traders in Los Angeles, and a $12.78 Mannlicher-Carcano 6.5-mm rifle from Klein's Sporting Goods in Chicago. On March 20, the guns were shipped. For these exchanges and others, Oswald had started using aliases; this time it was "A. J. Hidell." Marina would later explain: "Oh, he liked Fidel and thought Hidell rhymes with it."[61]

He had been checking at the post office nearly every day, and on March 25, Lee's weapons finally arrived there.

He brought them home and unwrapped them, and he would clean them, repeatedly, as if in some mantra state, arranging and rearranging the parts on newspapers in the living room.

Sometimes she would find him lying on the bed, hands behind his head, staring at the ceiling. When she'd ask him what he was thinking about, it was the new baby. "This time it's sure to be a boy," he would chortle. "Our David is going to be president!"[62] On another occasion, he insisted that they would name the new boy "Fidel." He would dote on her in brief moments, but mostly he just seemed ever more caught in his own centripetal thoughts. At night, he was now apt to call out in his sleep, blurting things in English that she wished she could understand, and then moaning fearfully.

On March 31, John Fain's successor in the regional FBI office, agent Jim Hosty, went to check in with the Oswalds at their old address in Fort Worth, only to learn that they had moved on. He tracked them to Dallas, to the Elsbeth location. He had been tipped off about Lee's subscription to the *Worker*, the American Communist Party's organ; he had learned of Lee's letters to the Fair Play for Cuba Committee; and on the same day that the "ready for anything" photos were made, the Elsbeth Street landlady informed him that Lee had been beating his wife. She had kicked them out, but she happened to know they had moved nearby, to a place on West Neely.

By the FBI's measure, these were all good reasons to get back in touch with him, but Hosty's only mission was to make a friendly contact, just to size Lee up and let them know that the Bureau was still keeping tabs. Hosty, though as savvy and expert as they come, was a big, friendly man by nature, ambling and easygoing, at least by all appearances. He would become something of a friend to Marina in the coming months; but on the day of that first visit, he did not find them home.

He must have missed them by just a few hours. Had he arrived while they were there, he would have done more than just keep tabs; he would have found a *tableau vivant* in the making, one that is now a photo icon of the era.*

---

*Lee Oswald may have been naive, but he was neither dumb nor a provocateur. He was a man who believed he was exceptional and would kill to prove it. His strangely blatant behavior, particularly in this period, has been contorted by conspiratorialists into a counternarrative in which he was deliberately misrepresenting himself. He could not have been that naive, or careless, or stupid, the theory goes. He had to have been a rightist trying to set up the left by posing as a revolutionary caricature. This, however, begs the question of whether any human being could really "act" so well, starting from the time he was fifteen years old until this year, when he was twenty-three. Could someone really put forth such a coherent and uninterrupted performance in defiance of his innermost self?

It was a Sunday. Lee waited until he heard the neighbors leave for church and then, as Maria was wrestling clean diapers onto the clotheslines in the back, he paraded down the back stairs dressed in black T-shirt, black pants, and black cowboy boots. He was wearing the holstered pistol and carrying two cameras, the new rifle, and copies of two of his radical periodicals, the *Worker* and the *Militant*.

She thought he looked ridiculous, and burst out laughing.

"Why are you rigged out like that?" she guffawed. "And where on earth did you get those guns? From Intourist?"[63]

He handed her the camera and told her to take his picture.

"Are you crazy?" she asked, as if she didn't already suspect. "I've never taken a picture in my life."

He persisted. The shadows were coming, he said. He didn't want to lose the light.

"I'm busy and I don't know how! Take it yourself . . . What a weird one you are! Who on earth needs a photograph like that?!"

Finally, she relented. There he stood, smiling vaguely, holding the two papers in one hand (one of them a publication of the American Communist Party) and the rifle in the other. Over the next forty years, it would become one of the most deconstructed images in the history of forensics, an example of the prodigious waste of time that most conspiracy theories encourage. It all amounted to nothing but the facts. He posed. She pressed the shutter release. When they were done and he was following her back up the stairs, she demanded to know why he wanted his picture taken with guns, of all stupid things.

He was sending the shots to the *Militant*, he said, ". . . to show I'm ready for anything."

He printed the shots, probably at work the next day, and gave a copy to Marina, inscribed to his child. "For Junie from Papa," he had written.

Why, Marina asked, would their child want a picture with guns?

"To remember Papa by sometime," he said.

He did as he had promised: he sent the photos to the offices of the *Militant*, care of the Socialist Workers' Party in New York City. He was announcing his importance, his resolve; but when Sylvia Weinstein opened the envelope and saw this grimly attired young gunman smiling back at her, she concluded that he was a kook. The party would have to take him much more seriously later that year, but initially she just thought that he would have to be "really dumb and totally naive."[64] Her colleague, the SWP's national secretary, Farrell

Dobbs, was a survivor of the McCarthy-era witch hunts, and he feared something worse, that this Texas nut was a provocateur trying to frame the party or otherwise entangle it in some dark web of intrigue. He made it plain that Weinstein should bring any further communications from this "weirdo" to his attention.

There is impressive evidence that Lee had already been in contact with Rolando Cubela by this time, either via correspondence, on the phone, in person, or through some G2 "cutout."

In preparing himself to kill Walker, Lee was auditioning for the Cubans. One of the books he had been reading that month was called *How to Be a Spy*.

Lee managed to stay one step ahead of Agent Hosty. On March 31, the same day Hosty came to Elsbeth Street, the FPCC received requests from Lee for forty to fifty pamphlets titled "The Crime Against Cuba," and Lee went off to picket with local FPCC members, hoisting a placard that read: HANDS OFF CASTRO, VIVA FIDEL!

The next day, April Fool's, Lee was let go from his job at Jaggars-Chiles-Stovall. It was apparently not for illicitly printing photos of himself, but because, according to his supervisor, Mr. Graef, business was slow, he hadn't been keeping up with the work there was, and he had been at odds with other employees. Lee had taken to reading his Communist literature on the job and—although Graef didn't mention it—that too might have contributed to his firing.[65] He was given a week's notice, but he did not tell Marina for days, and in that interim he kept up his reconnaissance on the Walker home at 4011 Turtle Creek Boulevard. Walker was out of town, but he was due back the following week.

Saturday, April 6, was Lee's last day at Jaggars-Chiles-Stovall.

On Sunday, April 7, as he had been doing in the preceding weeks, he left the house for most of the day, his rifle badly concealed under his olive-drab Marine raincoat. He was planning on doing some hunting, he told her. He had to go get some target practice, and do it where the noise wouldn't disturb people; she had seen him board a bus to Love Field, the airport where the big new jets would come and go. The rifle had been fitted with a telescopic sight, but that had no particular meaning for Marina. She loathed the thing. She could barely even bring herself to look at it.

And on Sunday evening, he returned home without it. She asked no questions. She was glad it was gone. And after supper he was gone again too, not returning home until late.[66]

On Monday, April 8, he dressed as he always did for work and went out for the day, still unable to tell her he'd been fired. He filed for unemployment and was gone for another long day and night.

As Lee Harvey Oswald sputtered and burned in Texas, the Kennedy administration faced massive daily problems on a thousand other fronts. Bobby was working around the clock at the Justice Department to stay abreast of the escalating battle between Martin Luther King's Southern Christian Leadership Conference and the city fathers of Birmingham, Alabama. Bobby had been slow to act in support of King's movement, seeing it conservatively, as more of a public-relations problem for the American government than a historical imperative. Even now, over two years into their administration, the Kennedys felt that King was too militant, was moving too fast. They felt he should give the newest Birmingham city administration time to atone for the racial sins of the outgoing one that spring, but the SCLC was refusing to stand down. Instead, Dr. King and his colleague Dr. Ralph Abernathy were about to get themselves arrested for the cause, and they would soon up the stakes further by calling forth a "children's crusade" of young black people whose collision with police dogs, truncheon-bearing cops, and water hoses was about to shock the world. The Birmingham jails were filling up fast. On April 10, "Bull" Connor, the commissioner of public safety, obtained an injunction from the courts barring any further protests and raising the bail-bond rate from $300 to $1,200, thereby presenting Dr. King and company with a fiscal crisis while Birmingham and the Kennedy brothers grappled with the moral one that the SCLC posed. Should they, or should they not, send in federal troops?

That same day, an American nuclear-powered attack submarine, the USS *Thresher*, disappeared at sea during deep-diving tests 220 miles east of Cape Cod. Aboard were 129 officers, crewmen, and military and civilian contractors, and when radio contact was lost with the boat, so close on the heels of the missile crisis, the Kennedy White House was presented with yet another ominous mystery. It would take months for the *Thresher* to be found, embedded in the ocean floor in six mammoth pieces, 8,400 feet underwater.

April 10 was also the day that Lee finally admitted to Marina that he had lost his job at the photo company. "I don't know why," he said to her, tears in his eyes. "I tried. I liked that work so much. But probably the FBI came and asked about me, and the boss just didn't want to keep someone the FBI was interested in. When will they leave me alone?"[67] It was not Agent Hosty's practice to compromise a man's job by questioning his employers;

but whether Graef had been straight with Lee or not, Lee was on the skids again. When he set out a few hours later, dressed in his best gray suit and a clean shirt, Marina assumed that he was going job-hunting.

He was gone all day, all evening. By ten o'clock that night, she was in a state of utter dread. She had been mulling over a thousand little signs of breakdown from recent weeks. She couldn't stand it anymore. She broke the sacrosanct rule and went into his tiny "office," and the moment she did, she knew that her instincts were correct. There, on a piece of paper, a key had been neatly placed, and a letter awaited her, written in Russian.

It was a list of instructions for what to do in his absence, almost a last testament. The key was to the mailbox at the post office on Ervay Street. He told her to get in touch with the Russian embassy—they would assist her. He had paid the rent, the water, and the gas bill. His last week's salary would be mailed by his former boss soon, "possibly." She could either throw out or give away his clothing, but he wanted her to keep his personal papers. "Certain of my documents are in the small blue valise," meaning perhaps his written plans for the murder of Walker, his diaries, and the story of his life. He told her where his address book was. He told her that the Red Cross would help her. He had left her $60, which could support them—Marina, now pregnant, and the young June—for "another 2 months using $10 per week." The last item, number 11, said, simply: "If I am alive and taken prisoner, the city jail is located at the end of the bridge through which we always passed on going to the city."[68]

Holding the letter, she began to shake all over.

Ninety minutes later, he staggered into the house, dazed, pale, sweating, weirdly exalted.

He told her, blankly, that he had just shot Walker. He took aim through a window while the man sat at his desk. She was apoplectic—she set upon him, haranguing him. He turned on the radio, anxious for the next jolt of adrenaline, of forward momentum through the mind-numbing grayness of his life. She kept pelting questions at him. Where was the rifle? Was the man dead? Why? Why?! He told her not to ask questions. He said something about how much better off the world would have been if someone had killed Hitler. She said that was absurd in peacetime. He repeated it. He stumbled through the rooms, shedding his wet clothes, and then collapsed facedown on the bed, dropping from the height of mania straight down into a dead sleep, like a man whose parachute hadn't opened.

Marina lay awake, a boundless pity spreading inside her, "almost physical in its closeness," and then a "fear of what the police would do to him."[69] Her first thought was that she should turn him in. Had she done so, Cuba might have fallen to the U.S. in the next few months. The Castros might have either followed Che to an early death or be living as country squires in dachas outside of Moscow, perhaps even sipping away their old age on South Beach, Miami. The phrase "the Kennedys" would not be a synonym for tragically misspent power, and the 1960s might not have carried the nation closer to civil war than it had been since Lincoln.

After all, the bullet Lee fired at Walker had clipped a wooden part of the window frame and passed through the general's hair instead of his brain. He would not have been tried for murder, but only for an attempt. Her "white Russian" friends would probably have taken care of her long enough for her to pull herself together, to raise her kids to adulthood and either wait for his parole or move on to another, saner marriage.

But she was a Russian, down to her marrow. She had been forced to agree to cooperate with her government at home; she believed that she held in her hands not just Lee and June's fate, but her aunt and uncle's fate as well. She was revolted at the prospect of returning to her homeland, and beyond that, she came from a world in which everyone was spying on everyone else; in which your only honor was never to become one of those people. If the state told her that it was her duty to inform, it was her duty *not* to do so.[70] It was bad enough that the KGB still held sway over her from half a world away. What would happen if she suddenly came under the scrutiny of the Americans?

And then, when she awoke the next day to the news that Walker was alive and had suffered only minor wounds, when the case began to go cold and there were no snarling police dogs and men muscling their way in and dragging Lee away, the questions faded. The abused party keeps trading up, taking the blows and the blame in some ever-dimmer hope that the cycle will end, that calm will come back, that they will no longer be the scapegoat for every injustice ever suffered by the one they once loved.

She extracted a promise from him that he would never do "it" again. She made him burn his precious documentation, the notebook he had kept of his reconnaissance on Walker. He convinced her that he was burning it all, piece by piece, over the toilet bowl, but even then he secreted enough away to use it later as proof to the Cubans that he was capable of killing and would do so one day. She stayed with him.

Eleven days after he took the shot at Walker, Lee heard that Richard Nixon was coming to town. He dressed in his gray slacks, a shirt and tie, then shoved his pistol into his belt and started out the door, leaving a newspaper spread on the coffee table with a headline that read "Nixon Calls for Decision to Force Reds Out of Cuba."

"Where are you going?" Marina demanded, eyeing the pistol.

"Nixon is coming. I want to go and have a look—"

"I know how you 'look,'" she said warily.[71]

Thinking fast, she came up with a ploy. She lured him into the bathroom, perhaps playing the coquette as she had at the beginning, but then slammed the door and held it closed long enough to remind him of his promise and browbeat him for endangering her pregnancy. He relinquished the gun. She forced him to take off his clothes. She drew a bath and put Junie in the water with him, and while he was there, talking with the child in quiet, sober tones, she bolted all the doors and locked the outside gates, and kept him well within her sight for the rest of the day and night.[72]

As it happened, it wasn't even Nixon who had been in town that day, but the current vice president, Lyndon Johnson. Apparently, it would not have mattered. Whoever was gunning for Cuba, Lee was gunning for them. He had found the hero of his life, the man who could be father and leader and saint all in one: Fidel. Author and espionage expert Edward J. Epstein, interviewed thirty years later, surmised what is now confirmed here: "If we take Oswald at the simplest level, what we see he's trying to do is enhance his credentials as a supporter of Castro. One of the ways he's trying to do this is actually work for Castro . . . trying to show that he can be a provocateur, an infiltrator, a demonstrator." He would soon position himself, in New Orleans, as a radio spokesman and debater for the cause, as well. "This is the simplest level; anything else becomes speculation of whether his true principles were not Castro but some other cause . . . A self-generated agent in intelligence parlance is a spy who has not yet made contact or is under the control of a foreign intelligence service. He's working on his own in the hope that his work will bring him to the attention and the reward of a foreign intelligence service . . . he was acting through the politics that had governed his life, he would have been very angry at Kennedy because President Kennedy . . . was opposing his hero, Fidel Castro . . ."[73]

Among those personal papers that Lee wanted Marina to keep in the event of his capture or death was his credo, printed painstakingly, by hand; much of it could have been a preamble to the Constitution of Woodstock Nation. In these papers, he lays out "an Atheian system, a system opposed to Communism, Socialism and capitalism." He called for "Democracy at a local level with no centralized State," and yet his anticapitalist manifesto insisted "That the right of free enterprise and collective enterprise be guaranteed." He demanded "That heavy graduated taxes of from 30% to 90% be leveled against surplus profit gains," but forbade the "nationalization or communizing of private enterprise or collective enterprise." At times, he seems just one recipe shy of an anarchists cookbook, demanding "That Fascism be abolished, That nationalism be excluded from every-day life, That racial segregation or discrimination be abolished by law," that all religious institutions be allowed to "freely function," that there be "Universal Suffrage for all persons over 18 years of age" (the voting age was lowered to eighteen during the Vietnam War), "that the dissemination of war propaganda be forbidden as well as the manufacture of weapons of mass destruction, that Free compulsory education be universal till 18," "that monopoly practices be considered as capitalistic," that individuals not be taxed and that the tax system be "subordinate to individual communities," and that "no taxes be levied against individuals."[74]

In another tract, he made it plain that the Communist Party USA must be severed from all Soviet influence because America's activists "have been weakened into a stale class of fifth columnists of the Russians." Again, there are images of collapse, particularly the implosion of capitalism, and a dream of "a special party" that "could safeguard an independent course of action after the debacle, an American course." He disavows violence against the state, believing the latter will fall of its own rot. Only "the intellectually fearless could even be remotely attracted to our doctrine, yet this doctrine requires the utmost restraint, a state of being in itself majestic in power."[75]

Even as his life dwindled down, he still clung to his idealism, to hope. His values were basically good ones, even then, and had he lived he would have seen some of the best of them realized. His was not an ideology of domination, of power abused. He stood firm against racism and any other form of ethnic supremacy. He was a champion of the weak, a foe of oppressors everywhere, and his dream was a generous dream of plenty, of bounty and goodwill.[76] Even as he was slipping deeper into lunacy, he was designing the great schemes of his "third way."

He had only a scattershot understanding of what sort of human community Fidel was creating, but he believed it might change the world for the better. This was just the beginning. Even as violence stunted his growth, he continued to think grandly, just like Fidel and Raúl and Che did. And at the end of his prescriptions for a new world of his design, there was the one note at the end, the one that reads years later like a kind of prayer that he'll be stopped before it's too late: "Sale of arms. Pistols should not be sold in any case, rifles only with police permission, shotguns free."[77]

Even as the black children of Birmingham were commanding Bobby's attention, he and Jack were cracking down on the renegade Cuban exiles and proceeding with whatever battle plan they could devise against Fidel that would not rekindle the conflict with Russia. While publicly disavowing any ongoing schemes to bring Castro down, the Kennedys pressed on quietly, still believing that their secrets were safe. "The White House had its own Cubans" now, said a CIA man of the time, "and its own plans for dealing with Castro. The rest of the exiles were told to 'stuff it,' but they weren't told why."[78] The ostrichlike confidence still held sway, even as Mongoose foundered.

On April 23, Bobby sat down yet again with the Special Group, this time to move the axis of the anti-Fidel efforts westward, out of Florida and over to New Orleans. It was at this meeting that he proposed a fresh study be made, designed to create "as much trouble as we can for Communist Cuba," trouble that would climax with the overthrow of "Castro in eighteen months," that was to say in October of 1964, a month before Jack was to stand for reelection. The study was also to explore "measures we should take following contingencies such as the death of Castro."[79] The Kennedys' "own Cubans" would be the ones based in New Orleans, where there was still an infrastructure of swampland training camps and hard-core activists—the Amigos were still anxious and waiting to serve.

But as Bobby was shifting his anti-Castro attention westward, Lee Oswald was being drawn eastward to the same place. It was there that he would confirm all his worst suspicions about the Kennedy plans and ready himself for war.

It was Marina who first suggested that Lee leave town for a while—maybe go back to New Orleans, where he still had some relatives and had lived as a boy. The police might yet show up at their door. If the case was going to go cold, it might happen faster if he was gone. After a few days of mulling it over, Lee came to agree with her. Besides, there were a whole lot of Cuban exiles down there to talk with.

So on April 24, Ruth Paine loaded up the Oswalds and her kids in her station wagon and drove Lee to the Dallas bus terminal. Even in their short acquaintance, Ruth had sensed just how tormented Marina's life was. She had even conspired to have Marina and June come to live with her, with the help of her soon-to-be-ex-husband, Michael. But that began to seem too risky. Lee was so possessive. He wouldn't even let her learn English. When it became clear that day that Lee was bound for Louisiana and would send for Marina later, it seemed like serendipity. Ruth casually offered to let Marina and child stay with her in Irving for a while, until Lee was prepared to have them come east. Much to Marina and Ruth's happy surprise, he accepted the offer immediately.[80]

In New Orleans, Sergio Arcacha, who had moved back to Miami, had been replaced by Luis Rabel Nuñes, but the Camp Street passions had never burned brighter. The new plan, now known as OPLAN-380-63, was embraced to the full by the exiles in New Orleans, from where volunteers were now being funneled to Central America for training. Mancuso's restaurant and Place Lafayette still teamed with refugees, night and day. There were at least six exile training camps and weapons caches tucked away around Lake Pontchartrain, one named McLaney Camp for the old Joe Kennedy pal who owned the land, Bill McLaney, and the other known as the MDC Camp (for the Movimiento Democrático Cristiano, the Christian Democratic Movement).

So active were the Pontchartrain sites that the FBI field office, acting on a tip, would bust the McLaney camp that summer. The Bureau had not been informed that it was part of a covert operation, and the Feds pulled a ton of TNT, twenty 100-pound bomb casings, napalm, fuses, and reams of other incendiary materiel from the place. Eleven exiles were taken in for questioning. The McLaney brothers, Bill and Mike, had had ties to the Nacional Hotel-Casino in Havana before the revolution, and Mike owned the Royal Haitian where Bobby and his brother-in-law, the movie star Peter Lawford, used to come to party, so the Justice Department intervened to prevent the eleven men from being charged.[81] The local Feds knew the rules, after that. Hands off Los Amigos de Roberto.

On the morning of April 25, 1963, Lee got on a pay phone and dialed one of those relatives of his who still lived in New Orleans. Mrs. Lillian Murret resided at 757 French Street, a longtime resident who loved her town and was generally proud of her heritage. She was stunned and not a little repulsed to hear Lee's voice.

"Hello, Aunt Lillian."

"Who is this?"

"Lee."

Lee. The one who had gone off to become a Commie over there in Russia.

Lee, who had made the headlines and shamed half the family with his shenanigans. She had thought he was still over there with those heathens.

"Well, I'm glad you got back," she hedged, as only a polite southern woman can.

The Murrets were forgiving folk. The family rallied to him, and Lee "stood on his pride" and claimed not to need their help, even as he took it. They were impressed with how much smarter he seemed, how much more worldly yet still kind of humble and pleasant enough.[82] They were a generous clan, and with the help of a Realtor friend of Lillian's, Myrtle Evans, they went about helping him find a cozy place where he and his little family could settle.

Lee found a job as a greaser for the grinding machines at the William B. Reilly Company, a distributor of Luzianne Coffee. The company's lofts were just a block from Arcacha's CRC headquarters, the Camp Street haven of the anti-Castro Cubans. Lee soon discovered Mancuso's and became one of those faces people started to recognize, though not necessarily to fraternize with.

On May 9, two weeks after his arrival and just short of a month since the Walker attack, Ms. Evans and he found a little "shotgun shack" sort of place at 4907 Magazine Street. That same day, Ruth Paine set out with Marina by car, and they drove the five hundred miles to New Orleans nonstop. It was a duplex, side-by-side, with a pitched roof, delicate French-style fretting and wooden filigree above the concrete porch and along its supporting columns. There was a dark, muddy, leafy-green garden on the Oswalds' side of the place; a hip-high iron fence, in the French manner, separated the house from the walk. A half century later, the place is still a charming but neglected little place in a neighborhood of neglected people, the same sort of home and district that Lee was always forced to choose.

Marina had to cope with her pregnancy in the stifling bayou heat, but the first month or so was among the best of their marriage, Lee seemingly calmer, the nightmare of April behind them. There was a little church thrift shop down the street that she would forage in, as much for the sweet idleness of the ladies who worked there as for the occasional find. There was a little corner store where they could buy sno-cones and Goo Goo Clusters and Pepsis. Sometimes he'd take her and the baby for longer walks, up around the library, or through one of the little vest-pocket parks.

Marina's reprieve did not last long. She was never quite sure where Lee was, whether at work or out "sniffing around," as she called it. Soon enough, though, his erratic behavior set in again, the crying dreams, the ugly outbursts and long silences, and with them her undermining despair. He would sit on that porch in the evening, while Marina cooked their supper, and dry-fire his rifle at passing cars.

She no longer spared him her disgust. "Is this the way you get to know the neighbors?! No one will speak to us," she would hound him.

"Castro needs defenders," he would sneer, sighting and pulling the trigger again.

"Oh, yes. Castro's big defender! Little Cuba needs you . . . Your dinner's getting cold."

On May 29, Lee received a letter at the Magazine Street address from Vincent "Ted" Lee of the Fair Play for Cuba Committee. Oswald had written to the New York office telling them that he wanted to form a New Orleans chapter of the organization. The head of the committee was encouraging, but he warned the Louisiana Communist against renting an office or otherwise drawing too much attention to himself. "You must realize," Ted Lee wrote back, "that you will come under tremendous pressures . . . We do have a serious and often violent opposition and this [gives rise to] many unnecessary incidents which frighten away prospective supporters. I definitely would not recommend an office, at least not one that will be easily identifiable to the lunatic fringe in your community . . . [We] have learned a great deal over the last three years through some bitter experiences . . ."[83]

Lee would ignore most of the advice he received from New York. He was not so much trying to start an organization as he was constructing a dossier that would impress the Cubans.

It was during the next few months that Lee, as avid a reader of newspapers as Jack Kennedy himself was, began to read between the lines and catch the drift of what was happening in the neighborhood around Reilly's. By this time, he was receiving regular shipments of FPCC material from their New York office; but initially he kept the stuff under wraps, still imagining that he could keep his true allegiances invisible. The material that "Ted" Lee started sending to him was full of linkages between the Kennedys and anti-Castro Cubans, some of it even referencing New Orleans, a clear signal that pro-Castro forces were alert to what was jelling there. Oswald would eventually bring his beliefs into the open; but in the meantime, he was skulking around on his self-appointed spy mission. At around this time, a man of his description inquired about renting an office at 544 Camp Street but then backed off. He was often seen around Mancuso's at the lunch hour or late in the afternoon, sipping Dr Pepper and trying to chat up any Cuban he could. He was pleasant enough, but no one could vouch for him, exactly.

It was definitely Lee who sidled into Casa Roca one day, a haberdashery owned by Carlos Bringuier, the local delegate to the exiles' Cuban Student Directorate (DRE), and tried to volunteer as a weapons expert. He told Carlos and two local teens that he had learned the techniques of guerrilla warfare in the Marine Corps, could make a homemade gun, could whip up a batch of gunpowder, could derail a train. Carlos was leery. There were a number of pro-Castro outfits trying to stir up trouble in town that spring and summer, and something about Oswald made Carlos decline his offer of help. The next day, however, Oswald returned, giving Carlos his Marine Corps manual as proof of his earnest intent. Carlos still has that manual. Lee had stamped his name on it, but he had also scrawled it in the lower left-hand corner when he was in the Corps, "Pvt. Lee H. Oswald." Carlos still would not admit him into the circle of the exiles.

Spurned, Lee sat down to write a ten-page "brief" with which he hoped to impress his handlers. "I infiltrated the Cuban Student Directorate (DRE)," he wrote, "and then harassed them with information I gained including have the N.O. City Attorney General call them in and put a restraining order pending a restraining order pending [sic] on some so-called bonds for invasion they were selling in the New Orleans area."[84]

He reiterated his master-spy claims to the FPCC. "I have infiltrated their plans for invading Cuba." His "infiltration" consisted of going up to a pair of youths selling war bonds, taking one to read, and then crumpling it up, laughing in their faces. He started distributing HANDS OFF CUBA! pamphlets in the street, and soon he had garnered the attention of the local TV outlets. He relished the attention, but was frustrated by it too because—as his crackpot celebrity grew—he had no television on which to watch himself. When his local grocer wouldn't even let him catch his face on the tube there one night, he tried to pull Marina over to Aunt Lillian's house to catch the report. She refused him.

"I see you all day at home in all forms," she sighed. "I don't want to see you on TV."[85]

And then Lee did something that had to have put a chill in Bobby Kennedy late that same year. As a parting shot to the exiles who had rejected him, Lee stamped Arcacha and Nunes's CRC address on the pamphlets. "It was a brilliant idea," Sergio Arcacha would say later. "Oswald was either trying to embarrass us or make us think we had a traitor in our organization." The more chilling probability was that Lee had himself become aware of Bobby's connection to the CRC—he was an obsessive reader of newspapers, and the *Times-Picayune* had made that connection fairly obvious.

By singling the CRC out among the raft of anti-Castro groups in town, he was sending that message. Whatever his specific motive, his street pamphleteering provoked such malice with Bringuier and other members of the DRE that a scuffle broke out one day between Lee and Carlos's posse of anti-Fidelistas. A crowd gathered, shouting, "Commie! Traitor! Why don't you go to Cuba!?"

"I say kill him!" someone else shouted.

"Yeah, *kill* the sumbitch!!" others let rip.

A cop tried to separate the combatants, but one of Carlos's people snatched Lee's fliers, made confetti out of them, and flung it into the air. When Carlos took off his glasses and got up in Lee's face, ready to duke it out, Lee put his arms up to protect his head.

"Okay, Carlos, if you want to hit me, hit me," he said calmly.

Two more cop cars pulled up and arrested Carlos and two companions, as well as Lee.[86] Lee couldn't post bail, spent the night in jail, and was questioned about his Marxist beliefs by a lieutenant of the Intelligence Division the next morning. He claimed that his "chapter" of the FPCC had thirty-five members, when it actually had a membership of one: himself.

The detective, Frank Martello, then asked Lee what he thought of Kennedy and Khrushchev.

"They seem to get along very well together," he replied in a calm, professorial tone.[87] His answer suggested a Moscow sellout.

As a form of recompense, Lee accepted a challenge to debate the Cuban issue on the radio. Opposing Lee would be Bringuier, an anti-Communist named Ed Butler, and reporter Bill Stuckey. When he arrived for the radio debate in the humid depths of summer, he looked like an undertaker in a worn, shiny tie and a black wool suit. During the preliminaries, Carlos told Lee that if he ever changed his mind and wanted to come over to the anti-Castro side, Carlos would try to help him. Bringuier was not alone among the exiles who considered Lee a wannabe agent for Fidel.

Lee said no, that Carlos was on the wrong side and that he was on the right. His gaze fell on his Marine Corps guidebook that Carlos had brought along.

"Carlos, please don't use that guidebook, because it's obsolete," Lee warned him. "You're going to get killed."[88]

Lee held his own on the air, at least initially. He could be impressive in his areas of knowledge, and he claimed to be a pure ideological Marxist, not a Soviet lackey. But as the debate stretched out, Butler revealed that Lee had lived in Russia, and Lee came undone. He felt "exposed." By this time, the

Russia vs. Marxism distinction was a critical one to him, like a Christian drawing a line between the pomp of High Church and gnosticism.

Later, he wrote to the Central Committee of the Communist Party to say that he "may have compromised the FPCC" and wondering if he should "go underground." The party's Elizabeth Gurley Flynn wrote back that she didn't think that was necessary, and advising him that the party might be in touch with him later.[89]

Lee, however, was sure that more action was required. He would go to Cuba, Marina would go back to Russia, and he would join her there if he didn't like Fidel's paradise. Since there was no direct travel from the U.S. to Cuba anymore, he would have to hijack a plane. Marina laughed him off when he told her he would need her help, but he went into training, building up his physique so he could subdue the pilot if necessary. He pulled maps, secured flight schedules, and developed a scenario in which Marina would assist him, hand in hand with Junie, keeping the passengers calm while he held a gun to the pilot's head.[90] She found that scenario hilarious.

The anti-Castro Cubans had seen through him, but Lee was undaunted. The Feds had lost his scent. He was invisible. As we shall see, he was making additional inroads with the Cuban G2. He had at least attempted to kill an anti-Castro racist, of that much he could be proud. He had suffered his "exposure" as a staunch "defender of little Cuba," and still had not been broken. Marina could still be trusted to keep his secrets, however disdainfully. He was ready to go to Mexico himself, if that's what it took to convince them of his sincerity, his true belief and deadly intent. Walker had been just a rehearsal.

In 2005, the first direct proof of the Oswald and Rolando Cubela connection was revealed, when Nikolai located a KGB folio on Cubela that contained CIA debriefing files of Cubela smuggled out of Langley by a KGB "penetration agent." In one of those files, it was noted that Cubela had named the shooter in the General Edwin Walker case as a Dallas resident named Lee Oswald. The file, said Nikolai, was from late spring or early summer 1963.

The source of this information, whether given directly to Cubela or conveyed to him through a cutout of some sort, could only have been Lee himself. He was never arrested or even suspected by the Dallas Police Department, and the only other person on earth who knew that he had taken the potshot was Marina, who wasn't talking. There were numerous ways that Oswald could have stayed in touch with Cubela et al. from New Orleans, since the area had a number of high-level Cuban agents, such as

Fernando Fernández, in place.[91] CIA counterintelligence senior officer Ray Rocca later testified that Fernández was sending New Orleans intelligence back to Havana via a mail drop in Mexico City.

The CIA's deputy chief of the Soviet Bloc Division, Tennent "Pete" Bagley, saw direct evidence that Soviet penetration agents were "feeding back" CIA operational plans to the KGB. At the time, at least five known Soviet spies were working within the NSA, while others, such as the notorious "Sasha" (identified in 1999 as former assassin Aleksandr Mikhailovich Korotkov), had penetrated deep into the heart of the CIA.* Consequently, during this period (1958–1963) the KGB succeeded in catching, and executing, the CIA's own prize moles in Moscow.

A likely candidate for stealing the CIA's Cubela file is Army sergeant Jack E. Dunlap, who was recruited by the Soviets while on assignment in Turkey in 1957 and soon reassigned to the National Security Agency (NSA) as liaison to the CIA. From 1961 to 1963, Dunlap sold NSA and CIA files to the Soviets. He came under suspicion in July 1963, and after failing a polygraph, he killed himself in his Cadillac by carbon monoxide poisoning. After his death, his widow found a stash of secret documents in his home. But what makes Dunlap most likely as a candidate is his access: he was assigned to courier CIA communications between the Cuba Desk that was running the Cubela operation and NSA.[92] So cocky was Dunlap that he would arrive at his pickups and joke, "Got anything for the KGB today?"

In the official report on the Dunlap incident, his modus operandi was laid out: General Garrison Coverdale, NSA chief of staff, had selected Dunlap to be his personal driver at NSA headquarters at Fort Meade, Maryland. Since the general's car had "no inspection" status, Dunlap could drive off the base with documents hidden in the car. Coverdale further arranged for Dunlap to receive top-secret clearance and a position in the NSA's traffic-analysis division, otherwise known as Staff D, which assisted the CIA in providing cover for the Cubela Castro plots.[93]

At the time of Dunlap's unconstrained pilfering, the CIA and NSA were redesigning the CIA's central computer system, and all the new passwords

---

*Confirmation of some of these KGB plants came from the KGB files themselves, with the 1996 defection of Vasili Mitrokhin. Some of the KGB sources cited, in addition to Dunlap, were NSA employees Bernon Mitchell, Norris Hamilton, Robert Lipska, Ronald Pelton, and William Martin.

and codes were easily within Dunlap's reach. CIA counterintelligence chief James Angleton worried that such a catastrophic breach, if it occurred, would be an unprecedented espionage coup for the Soviets, adding that Dunlap and his colleagues were "opening the window" for the KGB on virtually all American intelligence-gathering activities.[94] Colonel John "Jack" Frost, the NSA's deputy chief of staff, recalled that the Dunlap breach was "devastating." Codes were discontinued as U.S. intel went "in the clear," a costly procedure in which no codes could be used in transmissions, which were themselves drastically curtailed until the codes could be revamped.[95*]

Not long after the purloined CIA Cubela file—which named Oswald—was delivered to the KGB, and Marina simultaneously began petitioning to return home, Oswald's Minsk friends began hearing from the Soviet spy agency. After washing their hands of the unstable Oswald over a year earlier, the KGB suddenly contacted Oswald's former co-workers and friends. From Pavel Golovachev they demanded all correspondence he may have received from Lee. Pavel did has he was told, sitting in a smoke-clogged interrogation room while the items were meticulously examined and then handed back to him without explanation.

A few months later, when images of Lee's face had circled the planet in the wake of the assassination, Pavel was dragged back in. This time, everything pertaining to Lee was confiscated, and KGB agents grilled him ruthlessly. Once these artifacts were under their control, it wasn't Oswald who they wanted to talk about, but Marina. They browbeat Pavel with questions about whether he had ever slept with her. They squeezed him for the names of her lovers, if any. Pavel concluded that they were afraid she was about to become a security risk.[96]

In Havana, others joined the ranks of Oscar Marino and Antulio Ramírez in learning of the American malcontent and G2 wannabe Lee Oswald. When the G2 retirees spoke on the topic in 2005, among them was an eighty-year-old resident of Mexico who had been assigned to Havana's G2 archives in the early sixties. With no pension, Reynoso (his G2 cover name) still operates a small business repairing household electronics. Reynoso insisted on

---

*Frost could recall only three other such harmful NSA code breaches that mandated a "clear channel" response. However, none were by foreign intelligence, but instead by insecure actions of American political appointees.

not being identified, since, much like his CIA adversaries, he is still subject to a lifelong secrecy oath. He declared that he had put that part of his life behind him. On the other hand, he had little fear, since, as he said, he had nothing meaningful to contribute that could possibly incur the wrath of his former employer. As a lowly archivist with the rank of sergeant, he had had no contact with the operational side of things. Moreover, when he was coaxed into an interview for this book, he only had five minutes to spare—a customer was waiting urgently for a washing machine repair.

Asked about Oswald's trip to Mexico City in September 1963, Reynoso said, "I know absolutely nothing about it," and stood up to take his leave and attend to his customer. Before he could escape, Reynoso was quickly hit with another query: "So you never heard of him before the assassination?"

"I only heard of him once before that," Reynoso answered. "I saw his name on a document in the summer of 1963. It was my job to encrypt the files. I had the Lee Harvey Oswald file in my hand. Of course, I wasn't allowed to open or read it. So I can't say if Oswald was in Cuba or Mexico. I only know that he did meet with G2 officers. His file was kept in the section titled 'Foreign Collaborators in the Cuban Revolution.' "

How could he be so certain? Without hesitation, Reynoso explained: "I had the document in my hand. On it was written with thick pencil: Lee Harvey Oswald. I had to encode it and had to file it away under 'foreign colleagues' in the department archives. That was in the summer of 1963, the end of June. It could have been also the end of July. In any case, it was one of these months. It was rare that foreigners had a personal file, and when I read his name again in November in all newspapers, I was alarmed. The document was not especially extensive." With his thumb and index finger, Reynoso indicated a thickness of less than an inch.

When asked about the contents of the file, Reynoso reasserted that he had not been allowed to read the contents of any file, and that he had been watched scrupulously by his superiors. "I only observed it very fleetingly," Reynoso said, still trying to return to his business.

As he was turning away, one last question: "You must have seen something?"

"It was a report of a meeting with Oswald," Reynoso said. "G2 officers had met with him. I can say that, but I know no names and places."[97]

If the CIA knew who the Walker shooter might be, they were derelict in not tipping the Secret Service, the FBI, and the Dallas cops once Kennedy's

Dallas trip was set. But they have never admitted that they had this information, and indeed, the convoluted nature of the CIA filing system might have
prevented them from knowing for certain that they ever did "know" it. The
other possibility, in the era predating photocopiers, faxes, and E-mail, is
that Dunlap (or whoever) stole the only copy of the CIA's Cubela debriefing,
and that is what now lies in the KGB files in Russia.

In any case, the Agency did not pass the information on to the FBI. The
CIA had no right, at that time, to spy on American citizens unless they
could be proven to pose a national security threat. Oswald's case would have
been considered that of a pipsqueak leftist taking aim at a right-wing nut
who had declared himself a virtual enemy of the state, so that might have
been further disincentive for the politically liberal-leaning Agency to get involved. Most critical, however, was the fact that to tip off a local police department like that would have exposed a very valuable new asset, Dr.
Rolando Cubela. One can only imagine what the Agency thought of the
Walker-Oswald information when Cubela presented it, but it was probably
offered by the Cuban to prove that he had intimate knowledge of leftist "operations" inside the U.S. Cubela must have fed the information to the
Agency sometime before the Dallas assassination, when contact was cut.
And if he had fed it to them after Dallas, it would have strongly suggested
that Cubela was a double agent (as many CIA people suspected anyway)
with close ties to Cuba's "wet operations," thus someone who had played
the Agency and could not be trusted. If Cubela was ultimately working for
Fidel, even unwillingly, he would have exposed Havana even more as the
likely point of origin for the Dallas hit. If his allegiance had ultimately been
to Washington, then to tell them after Dallas would have demolished his last
remaining hopes for ousting Castro.

What's more, neither Cubela nor the Agency would have had any clue—
in April 1963—as to how the little-known ex-defector would soon be used
by America's Cuban enemy. To Cubela, he was still just another of his G2
contacts. To history, Nikolai's disclosures are yet more proofs of Lee's real
motive—he was already in close contact with the Cubans and had been
since late 1962. If only they would just let him show his true colors. To
Langley, he might have been considered just another nut from "nut country,"
who might get lucky and rid them of an even bigger nut one day, General Ed
Walker. If true, this would prove a monumental miscalculation.

Instead of pursuing the Oswald lead, the Feds were fixated on more pressing
Fidelista actions: Cuban assassins had targeted Boston's Richard Cardinal

Cushing, a Kennedy family intimate; other Cuban terrorists were plotting to kidnap the president's children; and the New York Police Department, working with the INS, had credible reports of four Cuban hit teams being dispatched to kill the president himself.[98]

All these plotters had something in common other than their heritage: they had entered the U.S. from the same city, using fake passports supplied by the local Cuban consulate. In just a few short years, Mexico City had quietly become one of the most dangerous flashpoints in the world. That's where the Feds wanted to focus their resources. And so, increasingly, did Lee Harvey Oswald.

CHAPTER 9
Spies Like Us

IN 1963, MEXICO CITY was not yet the desperate, slum-ridden megalopolis that it would become by the end of the century. Then, its population stood at about six million, less than a third of what it is today. Its middle class was still growing. The 1910 Revolution still chimed in the hearts of the people, living on as the all-powerful Partido Revolucionario Institucional, and—at least rhetorically—the country epitomized a "third way" between capitalism and Communism. The rich did not have the automatic indulgence of the Catholic Church, because the revolution had been hostile to the church since its victory; thus it was to the clergy's advantage to remain aloof from the oligarchs. The politicians mimicked the revolutionary rhetoric of Madero, Zapata, and Villa. Though the affluent still relied on the Defensa Federal de Seguridad (DFS) to make sure that the poetry of revolt did not inspire any actual revolting behavior, revolution was still in the air. The city was teeming with a new generation of young rebels, after all, arriving from points across South America. Some were Marxists, some priests.

The city was also the crossroads of the Cold War, where the United States, Cuba, the Soviet Union, and Mexico engaged in multilayered intrigue, double-dealing, and treachery that would make the Borgias giddy. Decades later, Oscar Marino and Reynoso would assert that Lee Oswald had first arrived there in the summer of 1963. There is no further evidence to confirm or deny the G2 men's claims; Lee's alleged recruiter, Cubela, denies any relationship with Kennedy's killer.* But there is no

---

*Efforts by the authors to persuade Cubela's CIA recruiter, Carlos Tepedino, to discuss these events have so far been frustrated as well.

doubt just what Mexico City meant at that time in the world of espionage.

"Everything ran out of Mexico," Marino would often repeat in interviews. "Mexico was the key center for the export of the [Cuban] revolution . . . The G2 was able to operate almost unfettered . . . From here the Cuban secret service, and also the Soviet KGB, initiated its operations against the territory of the USA." The Cubans' and the Soviets' international command posts were there; the most advanced, well-disciplined, and technologically sophisticated CIA station outside America was there as well.

Unfortunately for U.S. diplomacy, the first major CIA operator in Mexico was E. Howard Hunt. An archconservative, cocksure, racist, and nasty, Hunt offended nearly everyone he encountered, from the U.S. diplomats to the Mexican establishment, and he was not missed when he decamped to work with Operation Success in Guatemala in late 1953.[1]

Hunt's successor as the CIA point man was Station Chief Winston "Win" Mackinley Scott ("Willard C. Curtis" was his pseudonym for the CIA's written record). A native of Alabama, Win held a Ph.D. in mathematics from the University of Michigan by the time he was nineteen and had turned down a baseball contract with the major leagues to continue his academic pursuits. During World War II, he served as the first chief of the OSS in London and broke the German codes in the Caribbean. After the war, his thesis on algebraic matrices in cryptography garnered the attention of FBI recruiters, and the Bureau soon wooed him away from his teaching job. He served as a Fed in Havana, and as an agent in the Washington Office of Special Operations in the CIA when it toppled Árbenz in 1954. Two years later, he was reassigned to Mexico City. The man liked to work, and work smart. His files in Mexico were so capacious that the Agency estimated "it would take approximately six days and nights of steady burning to destroy the quantity of materials on hand." He was a staunch anticommunist, and he believed in a proactive CIA, not just one that mined data. His cover was as first secretary of the U.S. embassy. He was seldom without a suit and tie, complete with pocket handkerchief, but he was an easygoing southerner with a relaxed and confident air,[2] a white-haired but youthful man in his fifties who carried himself with as much warmth and equanimity as he did authority.

Working down the hall from Scott was Thomas Mann, the U.S. ambassador to Mexico at that time.*† The ground floor of the bland embassy building on Paseo de la Reforma was occupied by Sanborn's coffee shop, full of bright chrome and sun-kissed colors, a popular meeting place for modern diplomats, journalists, cops, spies, and technocrats. The Agency's office was in the midsection of the eighteen-story structure; but shortly after his arrival on the scene, Win insisted that his group be moved to the top floor. This became known as "the real embassy," not to mention the conning tower of the CIA's Latin American flagship. From there, the station chief oversaw a crew of dozens of full-time agents and operatives, and a matrix of surveillance systems unprecedented in the history of American spycraft. Win Scott was on top of the world.

His staff was topnotch as well. Win's second in command was Deputy Station Chief Alan P. White ("Arthur C. Plambeck"). His able assistant was Anne Goodpasture, a dignified, businesslike lady who had served in the OSS in Burma during World War II. She joined the CIA in 1951 and was first assigned to Western Europe, where she stayed until she was transferred to a decade-long stint in Mexico in 1957. She had also assisted in the Árbenz coup; her pseudonym was probably "Robert B. Riggs." The Cuban Division chiefs were Robert Shaw and David Atlee Phillips ("Orville Horsfall"), who was sent there by Des FitzGerald ("James Clark").‡ There was also an FBI presence in the embassy, anchored by legal attaché (LEGAT) Clark D. Anderson, deputy Eldon Rudd, and their assistants, George Munro and Michael DeGuire. These were the key players on the Mexican front of America's secret war against the Castro brothers, and in that pursuit Win's group produced some seven hundred documented reports a year.

In 1958, Win set up a tacit network around the office of the new Mexican president, Adolfo López Mateos, a web of agents and assets that would be

---

*No relation to the great German novelist.

†A diplomatic mission is the office of a country's diplomatic representatives in the capital city of another country. A diplomatic mission in any foreign (i.e., non-Commonwealth) country is called an embassy and the head of a mission is called an ambassador. A consulate undertakes a more restricted range of duties than a diplomatic mission. A consulate's prime task is to protect the interests of the nationals of its country.

‡ Other "Mexi" CIA officers of note included: Soviet Division chief Craig Ladillinger ("Douglas Feinglass"); Phillips's predecessor, Cuban Division chief Robert Shaw; technical chief Charles E. Flick ("Arnold F. Arehart"), and their colleagues Joseph Stephan Piccolo, Jr., Philip Agee, Joseph Burkholder Smith, Daniel Stanley Watson, Daniel Niesciur, Ernesto Rodríguez, and Boris and Anna Tarasoff, a husband-and-wife team of Russian translators.

known as LI TEMPO; Mateos would be LI TENSOR. The "LI" designated all Mexico-based operations designed to provide, as Anne Goodpasture described it, "an unofficial channel for the exchange of selected sensitive political information which each government wanted the other to receive but not through public protocol exchanges."[3] Mateos was a dashing, workaholic former minister of labor who believed in the one-party system. He would sing the praises of Fidelistas in public (the Mexican people had nearly as much affection for the Castros as for the Kennedys), and at the same time kept private eyes on them around the clock. He had annoyed Allen Dulles by giving an inaugural speech proclaiming himself a man of the "extreme left within the constitution,"[4] but what that really meant was that he was an ironfisted revolutionary of his own "third way," trying to ease the plight of the proletariat while preserving the gentry.

Mateos's backup man, while he was off on a series of well-publicized affairs, was Gustavo Díaz Ordaz, the minister of government. Díaz Ordaz, homely and dyspeptic, played the heavy, the Bobby to Mateos's Jack. "I'm ugly enough so that people can be afraid of me," he would say, and when radical unionists or students or peasants needed to be brought into line, down came his fist.[5] Win Scott would assign him the moniker LI TEMPO-2. Díaz Ordaz, as the new Mexican president in 1964, would be key in suppressing the Mexicans' probe of "the Cuban connection" at the request of his friend President Lyndon Johnson.

Win Scott's incredible matrix had two main reasons to exist—the Cuban embassy and the Soviet embassy, both located nearby. The tree-shrouded Cuban compound covered a city block bounded by Calle Francisco Márquez, Calle Zamora, and Calle Tacubaya. The embassy entrance was on the corner of Tacubaya and Márquez. The entrance to the garage, where Cuban intelligence agents could have meetings hidden from the CIA's surveillance, was on Márquez, and the consulate entrance was on the corner of Márquez and Zamora. Surveillance of that little compound was the CIA's highest priority in the world at that time, and it assigned fifty agents to work the sources who had knowledge of its secrets.[6]* Among them were eleven informants with access to the Cuban embassy (the LI TAMIL and LI RING projects). One of the known plants inside was a secretary (LI TAMIL-3). Another was identified

---

*Among these were agents with code names like LI RAVINE, LI COMET, AND LI RENO.

years later as Luis Alberu (LI RING-3), a colleague of two other key players in the Oswald connection, Maria Luisa Calderón and Silvia Durán.[7] Four consular employees and contactees had been turned as CIA doubles.

The Agency would go to any lengths to pierce the membrane of the place. By the time the Kennedys came to power, the place was smothered with photo and audio surveillance. Across the street, on the third floor of Calle Francisco Márquez 149-1 Colonia Condesa, the CIA conducted surveillance, attempting to photograph everyone entering and leaving the diplomatic office. The post was operated by Augusto César Rodríguez Gallegos, a Cuban posing as a Colombian, with Mexican nationals, American technicians, and former Cubans employed by the DFS (Mexican secret police) manning the equipment.

Thanks to a brilliant mother-and-son team of Cuban exiles who engineered much of the listening technology, and a sympathetic upholsterer, bugs were built into the arms of chairs in the Cuban ambassador's office and in the rest of the diplomatic suites. Tiny remote-controlled and self-charging radio receivers were embedded in the wood. The receivers could pick up conversation in the immediate area, could transmit via radio frequencies, and could be turned off and on by remote control to lengthen the life of their batteries. Each and every wall socket had a miniature microphone that could transmit to CIA listening posts nearby. Highly sensitized mini-amplifiers were installed behind all the telephone dials to eavesdrop on conversations within six meters of the desks and transmit them via the telephone lines to a distance of a kilometer or more, at full fidelity. When the phones were taken off the hook, the bug would stop working so the user wouldn't know that they were being checked on. That equipment could also be activated from a distance.[8]

It didn't stop there. The CIA had a concealed passport camera at the international airport, which allowed it to gain, with the assistance of Mexican passport authorities, advance notice of all passengers transiting to and from Cuba. Another airport operation (LI FIRE) provided complete manifests of all the incoming and outgoing flights by the forty-five international airlines that came through the Mexican capital. It had recently identified Vincent "Ted" Lee, who headed the American chapter of the FPCC (and who had communicated with Lee Oswald), as he went through Mexico City on his way to Havana. The "take," suitcases full of tapes and photographic film, was often trundled back to the station by Goodpasture.[9]

In the eyes of some, including the Kennedys, the civil rights crusade was pushing the river of change too fast, but Dr. Martin Luther King was trying to stem an even more radical tide within his ranks. At a recent Harlem appearance, young black radicals had thrown eggs at him. Their allegiance was turning toward firebrands like Malcolm X and Elijah Muhammad.

The bloody "Children's Crusade" in Birmingham in late April and early May had forced the Kennedy brothers to call in federal troops, and a tentative settlement was reached to try to restore something like normalcy to the city, if not the region. During the lull, black author James Baldwin hosted a summit between African-American cultural leaders and Bobby. The pow-wow took place in New York, at Joe Sr.'s apartment at 24 Central Park South.

Bobby and Baldwin, both men of passion, sensitivity, and caustic realism, had struck an unlikely chord in each other. Baldwin believed that whites intrinsically hated blacks, and that white liberals were the most heinous because they denied it. Nevertheless, a fledgling mutual trust developed between them. Both men felt that the next phase of the civil rights struggle was apt to be in the cities, where the teeming poverty and incipient black rage had been metastasizing for a century. Their thinking was prescient. By mid-decade, half the ghettos in America would be in flames. The meeting in Manhattan was meant to take the pulse of black leaders about the urban slums.

It would prove to be a minor disaster. Though attended by such members of the black cultural leadership as Lena Horne, Harry Belafonte, playwright Lorraine Hansberry, and the Urban League's Edwin Berry, it was a young black field secretary for CORE (the Congress of Racial Equality) named Jerome Smith who spoke the loudest. Smith had been jailed and beaten repeatedly by white southern cops, and he delivered a stark message to Bobby that introduced him to the youth of the 1960s at their most inconsolable.[10]

Bobby began nervously, expressing concern about the rise of Elijah Muhammad's Black Muslims.

Smith fired the first shot. It wasn't the Muslim crew that the white race should fear—the Muslims weren't risking anything but words. It was Gandhian pacifists like himself who they should fear, and whites would give up nothing unless they were afraid. It was immediately clear that the sparks coming off Smith would not be doused by any of the others.

The nonviolent revolution was falling apart, Smith insisted. He was right. The center would not hold. "When *I* pull the trigger," he snarled, "kiss it good-bye."[11]

He was the future. The violence of men who had tried to take the high ground would be the most brutal of all.

When Baldwin asked Smith if he would ever fight for his country, Smith screamed, "Never! Never! Never!"

Bobby was stunned. He said that this was nothing less than treason, and that raised a counterattack in Smith's defense.[12] The moderates largely fell silent, and to Bobby, the more radical ones seemed possessed. Smith's cry was coming straight from the streets.

The battle raged for three hours. When Bobby tried to reason by citing hopeful statistics, they threw them back in his face. When he spoke of the anti-Irish bigotry his ancestors had endured, only to put an Irish-Catholic in the White House; and when he predicted that a black man would be president in forty more years, Baldwin railed that his people had been in America far longer than any white Irishman. Jack was about to introduce a bill in Congress that would be the most sweeping civil rights act since emancipation, but even that seemed superfluous to the moment. Four hundred years' worth of black vitriol choked the room, and then devolved into hysterical laughter, as Clark would recount it, "the laughter of desperation."[13]

The sixties caught up with Bobby and blazed past him that day, right there in one of his father's lavish homes. It left him shaken and sobered and full of dread, much as the missile crisis had done just seven months earlier. Unlike that crisis, however, this was not an outright enemy one could afford to betray. This threat would not unify a country under siege from abroad. This threat, from a heartbroken American patriot, implied civil insurrection, a cancer that would eat all the white cells from within, and render unnecessary an attack from without. Bobby had been burned, but days later he finally began to understand Jerome Smith's rage. It was, he realized, even greater than his own righteous indignation, because Smith was not just fighting for the principle of equality, he was fighting to keep his people from being lynched. Once more, Bobby had seen, up close, the unraveling of his best intentions, the law of unintended consequences seething beneath all attempts to meet such anger halfway. One could be a warrior for the sake of power or a warrior in search of peace, but either way called for a full commitment. For Bobby, nothing less than a full embrace of the poor would suffice.

On June 24, Lee applied for a passport, now that he had paid off his loan from the State Department. His night convulsions had resumed, for the first time since just before the attack on General Walker. One night he had four seizures, his whole body shuddering at half-hour intervals even as he remained deeply asleep. To Marina, it looked as if he had been shot and was writhing in the aftershock, but she did not dare wake him.[14]

The next night, as she was watching him read in the flat, gray light of the parlor lamp, he looked up at her with a terrible hurt in his eyes. He turned away, got up, and went into the kitchen. She waited, the baby slumbering in her arms; but when Lee didn't come back, she put Junie down and went to the kitchen herself.

He was sitting in the dark, arms and legs hugging the back of a chair, his eyes peering down into a void that only he could see. She went to him, tried to soothe him, but he was weeping silently, his body convulsed with tears.

"Why are you crying?" He couldn't reply. The spasms just came harder. "Cry away," she said then. "It'll be better that way." Minutes went by, five and then ten. "Everything is going to be all right . . . I understand," she ventured, though she never would.

She held on tight, as if clinging to the neck of a bucking horse, and he wept and wept. But he was finally able to say, "I'm lost. I'm lost." He gagged. "I don't know what I'm supposed to do."[15]

The Cuban ambassador to Mexico was Joaquin Hernández Armas. The general consul was Eusebio Azcue López, a lean, coarse-complexioned, black-haired man with a taste for snazzy ties. He could force a smile, but it gave him the look of a handsome hyena. His more natural expression was one of cool remove, an air of continuous assessment that was a vital requirement of the job. (The CIA would profile Azcue as "part of a . . . select group of shock and confidential agents of Castro who are active in Mexico."[16]) In the summer of 1963, while the compound was closed to the public, he was training his replacement, Alfredo Mirabal y Díaz, the head of the consulate's DGI component, who in turn directed DGI senior operative Guillermo Ruiz Pérez, under cover as commercial attaché.

Azcue's secretary, Silvia Tirado de Durán, had replaced María Carmen Olavarri, a relative of Azcue's. Silvia, a Mexican citizen, came on board in August, not long before the consulate would reopen to the public. She was a brunette beauty of twenty-six with dark eyes, a ready smile, and a short bob haircut with long bangs that licked her eyebrows. An Agent Larson, one of the FBI men who kept tabs on such things, described her as "a 'Mexican Pepperpot,' a devout communist, and 'sexy.'"[17] The woman got around. She was married, with a four-year-old daughter, but she had friends in Texas who apparently came down to visit now and then. The CIA knew of a Richard J. Aranda, for example, and the two were spotted driving around in his 1950 Cadillac. They were thought to be lovers. There was also a man named C. J. Soles from Corpus Christi, who drove a '62 Fiat. They too had been seen on the streets of Mexico City the preceding winter, and were also considered to be sexual intimates. Silvia had had an affair with Cuba's UN ambassador, Carlos Lechuga (implicated in the November 1962 plot with the FPCC in New York City), and the tryst caused Mrs. Lechuga to divorce the ambassador. Silvia's husband, Horacio, wasn't too happy about all this, either. Their marriage wouldn't last. Silvia would also be connected to Lee Oswald in the coming months, in a variety of ways.

It was illegal for Mexican citizens to work for Communist bloc embassies without special permission, but Silvia was technically a temporary employee of the visa section of the consulate. She may have been a "devout" Communist, in Agent Larson's estimation, but she was not a member of the Mexican Communist Party. In fact, she disagreed with all its policies except for its support of Cuba. In that sense, she resembled Lee Oswald; to both, the Cuban experiment represented something different, less a product of Marxist late-Victorian Europe and Russia than a modern, populist form of regional socialism.[18] *

As a result of her ambivalent relationship with the party, Silvia didn't get her job through the usual Communist channels. In August of 1961, Silvia became a coordinator of the Mexican/Cuban Cultural Relations Institute, helping their fifty-five-year-old cultural attaché, María Teresa Proenza, by answering phones and doing secondary tasks. The job had come through Proenza's friendship with Silvia's brother-in-law. A few months after she was hired, she was invited to Havana as a guest of the Castro government.

As a young bohemian working in the city's art scene, she had made friends with María Carmen Olavarri, Azcue's secretary at the time. Olavarri was fired by the embassy in January 1963,[19] for unknown reasons, but she stayed in the job for months until someone could be sent from Cuba to replace her. In July she died in a car accident, and it was at the funeral that Silvia told Azcue that she would fill in for her dead friend. Azcue knew her husband, and liked and trusted Silvia enough to agree.

Most of the staffers doubled as spies, and another DGI agent, twenty-three-year-old María Luisa Calderón, had arrived from Cuba that January to start work there as well.[20] The place was crawling with spies, in fact. Manuel Vega Pérez and his assistant, Rogelio Rodríguez López, vetted the visa requests as their cover job. Vega had run assassination operations in

---

* The Warren Commission would doubt this characterization of her, but CIA wiretaps confirmed her position on these matters.

Nicaragua. Rodríguez had met with FPCC leader Vincent "Ted" Lee in Havana on numerous occasions.[21] According to the CIA, there were at least a dozen other Cuban intel agents on the premises at any given time.*

In addition to Proenza, there was another cultural attaché, Luis Alberu-Souto. Alberu, along with a still-unidentified female (believed to be one Consuelo Esperon), was spying for Win Scott, as part of his LI RING operation; it was Alberu who would report Silvia Durán's sexual adventures to the CIA. He was also charged with another task, one that had assumed new importance in 1963. At that time, America was intent on driving a wedge between Moscow and Havana by encouraging the mistrust that had raged during the missile crisis. Fidel was plagued now with a new kind of factionalism, not just from anticommunists within his ranks, but from heretofore loyal Cuban Communists who were tilting toward Moscow. Alberu planted documents on Teresa Proenza that falsely implicated a pro-Moscow Cuban vice minister of defense as a CIA spy. Moscow rose to the vice minister's defense (suggesting that they had vetted him thoroughly themselves). Havana responded by arresting the Cuban for treason, a measure of how paranoid the Castros had become about the Muscovites.

In 1978, the CIA was subpoenaed by the House Select Committee on Assassinations. The HSCA was interested in these operations, because Proenza was the first member of the embassy staff that Lee Oswald would have spoken to when he went there in September of 1963. But the Agency resisted going into detail. Whether or not Proenza was a witting part of Alberu's setup, to reveal her encounter with Lee would risk outing a much wider effort by Alberu and others to foment this division between Fidel and Moscow. When the Agency stonewalled the HSCA, it alluded to "a highly complex operations system" that should not be revealed to the public. It was "a Pandora's Box, the opening of which would not only expose the cryptonyms of other operations of this type, but . . . would expose hitherto secret techniques and assets [that] would make their employment in the future very difficult."[22]

Another "Mexi Station" tactic was the impersonation of enemy staff and the people who contacted them. The future director of the Assassination Records Review Board, Jeremy Gunn, who was given access to the CIA's HQ

---

*Other Cuban intel personnel included: Francisco Llagostera, Orestes Ruiz, Samuel Pérez, Raúl Aparicio, Rolando Estevea, Herberto Jorrin, Oscar Concepción, Antonio García, José Fernández Roa, Ernesto Andres Armona, Joaquin Hernández Armas, and Pereguina Alonso.

files, called these ruses "a standard operation."[23] The story of Elden Hensen, a cattleman from Athens, Texas, provides an example. In the second week of July 1963, Hensen, a Castro supporter, called the Cuban embassy in Mexico City twice from the Alameda Hotel. On July 19, he spoke with Luisa Calderón. Later that day, he received a call from someone who said he was from the Cuban embassy and who suggested that they meet at a restaurant. At the restaurant, Hensen offered to help the Castro government. The operative told Hensen he should never contact the Cuban embassy again; they would contact him. Unbeknownst to Hensen, the "embassy official" was actually a CIA operative who was attempting to pump Hensen for info about Cuban agents.[24] Other CIA documents perused by Gunn disclosed that the impersonations went both ways, with the CIA operatives assuming the identities of individuals who had recently called the target embassies. The CIA man would call the facility back, using the person's name in another effort to discern the enemy offices' inner workings.

Six adjacent buildings had surveillance posts around the compound, purchased by CIA cutouts. Their code names read like a spy ditty penned for the annual spoofs by Yale's Skull & Bones Club: LI ONION, LI MITED, LI CALLA, LI LYRIC, LI HABIT, LI TABBY. There were mobile service trucks (LI EMBRACE), and six mobile photo trucks (LI ENTRAP). The residences of dozens of Cuban diplomats and staff were tapped by the LI FEAT operation, using six base houses.*

The CIA Mexi Station had its hands full. The Cubans had stationed their best agents in Mexico City and were managing nearly all of their Western Hemisphere terrorist plots out of the compound. In her "History of the Mexico City Station," Anne Goodpasture noted: "The Cuban diplomats resorted to terrorist activities when it suited them."[25] Among cited examples was the kidnapping and drugging of a target who was then forcibly put on a Cubana Airlines flight to Havana. In addition to infiltrating local exile groups, the Cuban facility was a transit point for Castro's spies, who acquired forged travel documents at the consulate for transit throughout the hemisphere. Goodpasture added that "the Cuban consul in Mexico City was

---

*Among those were: Silvia Durán, Luisa Calderón, Alfredo Mirabal, Joaquin Hernández Armas, Ernesto Andres Armona, Francisco Llagostera, Orestes Ruíz, Samuel Pérez, Rogelio Rodríguez, Raúl Aparicio, Rolando Estevea, Herberto Jorrin, Oscar Concepción, Antonio García, José Fernández Roa, "Raúl," and Pereguina Alonso.

the coordinating point for arranging travel of a steady stream of pro-Castro revolutionaries to Cuba from throughout the Western Hemisphere."[26] Her boss, Win Scott, concurred: "We're completely infiltrated by Castro's agents. All they have to do is get into Mexico and walk across the border."

But the most threatening facet of the Cuban embassy was its oversight of assassinations. As recounted in many CIA and FBI documents, not only was the Cubans' Mexico outpost known to finance assassinations, but *all* Cuban ambassadors had to promise to oversee retribution murders if Fidel was ever assassinated.[27] Specific information about Cuban embassy–based DGI agents Vega and Rodríguez (who were soon to process Oswald's visa request) included the sobering fact that they had been among those who had masterminded successful assassinations.[28]

As later KGB foreign counterintelligence chief Oleg Kalugin noted, the Cubans, although tied to the USSR for support, utilized the Mexican consulate for activities not cleared with Mother Russia. "The Cuban Intelligence was dependent on Soviet support," Kalugin recalled in 2003. "Technical support, training—all sorts of gadgetry which we supplied to Cuban Intelligence. But in fact, Cubans were fairly independent. And they had their own targets."[29]*

The Cuban terrorists were aware of the CIA's remote surveillance posts, making a joke of it by photographing the technicians who were photographing them. The staff assumed the embassy was bugged, though the American-made devices themselves often went undetected for periods of time. The cat-and-mouse game was so intense that many secrets simply could not be kept, on both sides. It became a game of simple proliferation. Some of the plans were intercepted. Others weren't.

Late on the night that Marina had found Lee weeping in the kitchen, he returned to the theme he had been pressing on her for months. She was due to

---

*Kalugin related one specific example of Cuban embassy recklessness: "Some Americans, as a matter of fact, knew that it's better to contact Russians in Mexico, rather than in Washington. Or New York. Let me just cite a case which I handled later. A former officer of the CIA came to the Soviet embassy in Mexico City and offered his services to the USSR. The Soviets thought he was a mole and they just turned him away. He was so unhappy that he went to the *Cuban* embassy in Mexico City, and the Cubans say yeah, welcome aboard. So they took him to Havana, they called us in Moscow and said listen, I have a CIA guy, would you like to debrief him?"

give birth in October. He was "lost" and searching, daily, for a way to be found. Again, he urged her to write to the Russian embassy in Washington asking to be allowed to return to Minsk, but this time he told her that he might accompany her back to her homeland. This excited her. She had been increasingly concerned that America might just drive him crazy.

"You mean it?" she said. "You're not just joking?"

"I do," he assured her.

She twirled around the little living room and landed in his lap.

"I'll go with my girls," he went on. "We'll be together, you and me and Junie and the baby. There's nothing to hold me here. I'd rather have less, but not have to worry about the future . . ." He urged her to write a fresh letter to Nikolai Reznichenko, head of the consular section of the Soviet Embassy, immediately. She did so, happily this time. It was the first she had written of her own volition.[30]

But then he hedged. He wanted to visit Cuba first, he said, perhaps even China, and then join her back in the Soviet Union. Still, she was hopeful, and they wrote to their friends and relatives in Russia, among them Ernst Titovets, sounding certain and optimistic.[31] One of them wrote back, at the risk of being read by the KGB, to caution that Lee should be very sure he wanted to return, since it might be the last time that the Soviets would ever allow him to cross the Atlantic.[32] Lee shrugged it off. In his heart, it was still Cuba that lured him most forcefully.

He had glued a picture of "Uncle Fidel" on the wall of the Magazine Street place. He would wax poetic about the coming newborn, insisting that the child would be president one day, or that he himself would. He was devouring books from the Napoleon Branch of the New Orleans Public Library, particularly William Manchester's *Portrait of a President*, a biography of John Fitzgerald Kennedy. He openly compared himself to Kennedy, drawing parallels between their young children, their military experience in the Pacific. He read Jack's own *Profiles in Courage* and even checked out books he had learned that the president was reading. The Manchester book held references to Jack's fatalism and to his passing comments that he expected to have only one term in office. There was even a reference to the fact that Kennedy had not quite achieved the public devotion that Lincoln did, perhaps only because "he hasn't been shot."[33]

Lee was bounded on two sides by his emulation of Fidel and his absorption in Jack. He had become a sycophant of Vincent "Ted" Lee at the FPCC offices in New York; but with each letter extolling his courage and audacity as a spokesman and street hustler for the organization, Vincent Lee became more convinced that this Oswald was unstable. Ted stopped responding to him, certain that he would embarrass the organization, which was already under scrutiny from the Feds and CIA. Even still, Lee kept trumpeting his exploits to the FPCC, though he never again heard back from them.

The Russians had seen Oswald's instability and had warned the Cubans of it when they forwarded his dossier to Havana, even as they suggested that he might be useful. According to Oscar Marino, Cubela himself must have known that the man was unsound, even when contact was made with him in the fall of 1962. Oswald's shot at Walker could only have aggravated Cubela's uncertainties about Oswald—it proved that he was willing to back up his convictions, but it was also a wildly botched self-assignment that might explain why G2's contact with him had been so furtive.

Lee hated the Reilly job and was shirking it by early July, spending more and more time next door at the Crescent City Garage, owned by a fellow gun enthusiast named Adrian Alba. The garage man was very knowledge-able and had a rifle that Lee coveted. It was during these protracted lunch hours that Alba instructed Lee on what caliber bullets did the most damage to humans.[34]

Alba's lot was where the local members of the Secret Service, whose of-fice was just across the street, parked their cars, working their counterfeit and protection details. At this point, Jack Kennedy and Lee Oswald had just three months left to live, and after their deaths, Alba would become a prime witness to relevant comments made by John Rice, an agent who parked there. It was Rice, who supposedly had struck up a friendship with Alba, who would tell Alba that before the Amigos de Roberto had gotten a whiff that Lee was a rat, they had considered him for the assassination team against Fidel. He must have been peddling himself as such, and apparently his application went as far as Bobby Kennedy's desk at Justice before Lee was exiled from the exiles.

According to Rice and an unidentified New Orleans political writer known to Alba only as "Fitz," when Bobby first saw Oswald's name come up after Jack's death and traced it back to the CRC dossiers, he was heard to yell out in his office, "I've killed my own brother!"[35] Rice's comments cannot be confirmed, but they attest to the impression some had of Lee, that he was angling to learn more about the CRC's plans against Castro and did so by trying to be hired as an assassin. Thus he may have been known to Bobby (whether by name or not) well before Lee struck at the president. Alba's testimony also amounted to the first hint, shortly after the assassination, that Bobby considered himself complicit in his brother's death.

On July 19, Lee was fired from the Reilly Coffee Company. It was his third termination in less than a year, but it didn't matter. He was born for bigger things.

Two blocks away from the Cuban compound in Mexico City was the Soviet embassy and consulate, staffed by five consular officers and diplomatic personnel and housed in a single building at Calle Colzada, Tacubaya 204. A twenty-four-hour guard was posted at the entrance to the compound, which also housed sixteen Soviet families. Offices were not open to the public and could only be visited by appointment.

Nikolai Sergeyevich Leonov, who had befriended the Castros and Che in the mid-fifties, headed the KGB office, which consisted of Oleg Nechiporenko, Pavel Yatskov, and Valeriy Vladimirovich Kostikov, whose cover was senior consular officer handling the issuance of visas. He was believed by the CIA to oversee Western Hemisphere "wet operations" for the KGB's "Department 13," which also handled sabotage ops in the region.

Kostikov was a stocky, pale-faced man with a small mouth, a prominent brow and a thick nose upon which rested square tinted glasses. The CIA had first associated him with the KGB because of his freedom of movement around Mexico and his friendly relations with other known KGB spies, and because it was common practice for consuls to be active KGB officers. It was also known that Department 13's function was to interview all foreign defectors to the USSR and assess their usefulness as possible assets back in the country whence they came.

The CIA's Soviet Division deputy chief, Tennent Bagley, did an even more thorough workup on Mr. Kostikov's background: he "was born on March 17, 1933, in Moscow. In 1959, Kostikov applied for a visa to accompany Khrushchev's party to the United States, but we have no record of him having come to [America]. Kostikov served as an interpreter at international conferences in Madrid and Barcelona in 1958 and 1959. In late 1959 and early 1960 he attended Soviet exhibitions in Mexico City and Havana. He is known to have been in Cuba from January 6, 1960, to March 7, 1960. He was assigned to the Soviet Embassy, Mexico City, as Vice Consul on September 19, 1961. A fluent Spanish speaker, he had traveled abroad at least three times before his permanent assignment."[36]

Kostikov was also a contact of Rolando Cubela's, even as Cubela was doubling as the CIA's AM/LASH.[37] What is more, Cubela was an acquaintance of Teresa Proenza, the first person whom Lee Oswald would meet at the Cuban embassy when he arrived there a few months later.

The Agency maintained three surveillance sites around the Soviet compound on the Avenida de la Revolución, and they operated during business hours. Two sites covered the entrance. The third overlooked the garden area of the embassy. Win Scott had observed that there were four handsome town houses across the street from the gardens and had used a legal cutout, code-named LIMOUSINE, to buy them for the exclusive use of the U.S. government.[38] All surveillance photos and logs of the Cuban and Russian compounds were turned over to Win's CIA ace, Anne Goodpasture, two to three times a week. Between those two Communist outposts, the CIA had fifty phone lines wiretapped, monitored, and automatically tape-recorded. Tapes were removed daily and given to Boris Tarasoff, the CIA's resident Russian speaker, who translated them into English. Tarasoff's wife, Anna, prepared typewritten transcripts, which also went to Goodpasture. The original tape recordings were retained for approximately thirty days before reuse, but if an officer thought they were important or if they were "flagged," they could be held indefinitely. Goodpasture and Scott then sent copies to CIA headquarters.

Four of the most thorough and motivated clandestine services in history, located in the tight confines of Mexico City, were doing everything in their power to prevent each other's secrecy. Everyone was in everyone else's business. Win Scott had excellent relationships with the Mexican authorities, all the way up to the president's office, but the Russians and Cubans were nearly as well connected. As Jim Hosty, Oswald's FBI case officer in 1963, would later put it, "The Mexican people related more to Cuba because they were both Latinos. But there were dual loyalties, because they also liked the Kennedys, especially Jackie, who spoke to them in Spanish . . . These countries have to straddle a fence between the US and other considerations."[39] General Oleg Kalugin, head of KGB operations against the U.S. at the time of the Kennedy assassination, worked out of Washington and New York, but Mexico City was the third leg of the stool in the Western Hemisphere. "In Mexico City, Soviet intelligence felt much more comfortable than in the United States," he would reveal. "The local regime was fairly good to us. The Mexicans were friendly . . . we had sources inside the Mexican country—intelligence. So we were well-briefed by the Mexicans, they [told] us about what was going on. And that helped us to operate in that country more freely. So we could meet some individuals who would rather not meet in the United States."

Perhaps the best example of these dueling loyalties at work can be found in the behavior of the DFS, the Mexican secret police. Amazingly, at the same time, the DFS cooperated with the U.S., the Soviet, *and* the Cubans. It gave new meaning to the notion of a home-team advantage.

So it was not necessarily Win Scott who was the keeper of all secrets here. It was Fernando Gutiérrez Barrios, the same man who had intervened when the Castros and Che were busted by the Mexicans the summer before the *Granma* voyage in 1956. His cryptonym was LI TEMPO-4, his nickname El Pollo, the Chicken, in honor of his outsized beak. Now the number two man, within months Barrios would run the entire DFS; but he had power enough, even then, including his own death squad, the Brigada Blanca, which specialized in "disappearing" political opponents of all stripes, without a trace. One did not mess with Barrios. He had friends everywhere, Win Scott among them, and Fidel Castro too.

One night in early August, while Lee was shaving and June was playing at his feet, the toddler broke the mirror of her mother's makeup kit. Marina, seven months pregnant and superstitious by nature, was so disturbed that she cried, thinking it a bad omen for the unborn child.

She and Lee had been absorbed in the pregnancy of another woman as well, Jackie Kennedy. The wives of all three Kennedy brothers were pregnant that year, and Jackie's baby was due in the fall, as was Marina's. In Lee's mind, the coincidence was yet another indication that his family and the president's had much in common, and they speculated on the sex of Jackie's child almost as much as they did their own. Lee was hoping for a girl, but Marina wanted for Jackie what she wanted for herself, a boy.

When Patrick Bouvier Kennedy was born, prematurely, by cesarean section on August 7, 1963, it was Lee who broke the happy news to Marina. "Guess what, Mama?" He laughed. "Jackie's had her baby, and it's a boy." It gave him reason to believe she might be right about the sex of their child, since she had so adamantly predicted the sex of Jackie's.

Marina was so uneasy about her own pregnancy that Lee was cautious and considerate in telling her that little Patrick was not quite thriving.[40] The baby weighed just four pounds, ten ounces, and there were growing concerns.

Jack had not been present when Jackie miscarried in the summer of '56. He had been AWOL on a yacht full of femmes in the Mediterranean. His absence had nearly cost him his marriage. It gave rise to an emotional bond between Jackie and Bobby that changed the current of moral authority in the family, a bond that would become even stronger after Jack's death. Shortly after Caroline was born, Jack's sportin' life had taken him down to Cuba on another erotic tour. He had been flying to Florida when John Jr. made his debut in the fall of 1960. A month before Patrick's premature birth, it seems that Bobby had had to rescue Jack yet again, this time from one of his White House chippies, Ellen Rometsch, who the FBI suspected was an East German Stasi mole. Bobby had her deported back to the Old Country.

But the dynamic of the marriage was changing that year, perhaps partly because of the strains of office and the dangerous times they found themselves in. Jack had doted on Jackie during this pregnancy, and he barely missed Patrick's actual birth, only because the baby arrived so suddenly. The president did make it to the hospital at Otis Air Force Base soon after, and there it was he who first placed the newborn in Jacqueline's arms. This child's nativity seemed to have captured his attention in a way that the other births had not.

A longtime family friend, Betty Spalding, knew the First Couple well and would recall this time years later. "I think that Jack and Jackie both had their own particular problems. She had the same emotional blocks and limitations that Jack had, but they were both growing up emotionally. They were catching up. Their relationship was getting better and better."[41]

On August 8, Lee admitted to Marina that the Kennedy baby was not getting any better. He had given her updates as they became known, but it was clear that the doctors were at a loss. Marina took this as a very bad sign for her baby as well. Talk turned to what should be done if her life was threatened during childbirth. She hoped that Lee would opt for the baby to live, not her.

"Other babies we can have," he told her. "Junie has to have a mother."

Marina was entering her third trimester, but the Oswalds were so broke that she still hadn't been to see a doctor. If Jackie's baby could be at such risk, who would care about a lowly mother like her if *her* newborn had problems?

"No, no, you're not to worry," Lee insisted. "Once you're in the hospital, the doctors don't care whose baby it is. They do the same for everyone. I'll borrow money, I promise you, you'll never be thrown out of the hospital."[42]

Maybe the Cubans would help him again, he must have thought. Wherever he got it, there had to be another boost of cash soon. He was living far from Dallas now, and he had alienated most of the "white Russians" as it was. His local relatives weren't likely to loan him much, if anything. Unemployment benefits would only take them so far.

It was no wonder that Marina was in such a state. Lee had not let her learn English, but she had lived in America long enough to know one thing for certain: she was poor.

When asked that summer, in a moment of banter among male friends, how he'd like to die, Kennedy said he'd prefer to be shot, because he wouldn't feel a thing. On another occasion, he jokingly reminded the two men flanking him at a public ceremony that if he were shot at, the shooter might accidentally hit one of them. In more reflective moments, he seemed to be pondering not so much the means of death as the meaning of a life at it came to its end. The mortal struggle of his new son would presage his own, in but a few months' time.

Little Patrick was having respiratory problems when Jack first brought him to his mother. He was baptized, but when his breathing still seemed erratic, the obstetrician took caution and had the baby taken by ambulance to Boston. There, Patrick was diagnosed with idiopathic respiratory syndrome, and he was moved again to the Children's Medical Center at Harvard, to an experimental high-pressure room inside a room, a kind of bathyscaphe, thirty feet long, where his doctors might yet save him. Shuttling back and forth between Otis and Harvard, the president tried vainly to keep Jackie's hopes up and monitor Patrick's progress through a porthole on the side of the chamber. On the last night of his life, Patrick's condition was so unstable that the president slept in a patient room at the hospital.

He was awakened a few hours later and told that his son was foundering. They led him to an elevator, and while standing there, bleary-eyed and fearing the worst, he saw another child in a room across the hall who was severely burned. Despite his sense of urgency, he requested a piece of paper and penned a note to the child's mother, from one helpless parent to another.

Patrick lasted for two more hours, his body battling for each breath until he could fight no more. He was gone. When a doctor emerged from the chamber and told him the news, the president wandered away to a nearby boiler room, the only solitary place in the maze, and stayed there, weeping, for some time.

At the funeral, he was still in that no-man's-land of grief. Jackie was too frail to attend, but other family members at the Mass, a private ceremony held at the rectory that housed Cardinal Cushing, bolstered him. When the service was over and all but Cushing and the president had left the room, Jack picked up the casket and held it in his arms, rocking back and forth, so undone by this baby's awful struggle and death that the cardinal wept as well and had to struggle to pull him away.

"My dear Jack, let's go, let's go," he murmured. "Nothing more can be done."[43]

Word of Patrick's death came to Marina over the radio on the morning of August 9; when it did, she burst into tears. It might have been Lee's prattling on about the First Family that made their story so personal for her. Or it might have been Anatoly's resemblance to the president and her fixation on what might have been with him. It might have been the fear for their future that always began when Lee was out of work, and it was certainly her fear for herself, but it was, at its deepest, a reflection of how real Kennedy and his wife had become to her, through the images that accompanied them, through the sound of his voice, through the almost numinous optimism they seemed able to impart. It was one pregnant woman identifying with another. It was the escape from Marina's own life that they provided, and the shock of there suddenly being no escape. If Jackie could lose, then so could she.

Lee was moved as well, that morning. He pulled her close, trying to calm her down. He had heard that Jackie had a delicate constitution, he said. This was the third child she had lost. It was probably for the best, or Patrick would have spent his life as an invalid.

Even his own certainty had been shaken, but he kept up appearances. "We'll have an easier time. We haven't any money and maybe we can't get good doctors. But you're strong. We've got a baby already. Ours will be healthy." There in the kitchen, where she had said the same words to him six weeks before, he told her, "Everything will be all right."

He stared into her wet face, straining to believe it himself, and trying to smile in a way that wouldn't scare her more.

On Tuesday, August 27, hundreds of thousands of blacks and whites were arriving in the nation's capital for an unprecedented March on Washington on behalf of civil rights. They came even though it was not entirely clear that it would be peaceful. Dr. King and his lieutenants, Ralph Abernathy and Fred Shuttlesworth, had seen the edges of discipline fray in Alabama, the patience of their race giving way to cold, riotous fury at various points. Nevertheless, with the Associated Press and *Life* magazine photos of Birmingham still fresh in the mass mind, Bobby Kennedy called off the dogs, issuing Justice Department orders that the D.C. police leave their canines at home.[44] The District's fifty-nine hundred cops had been put on alert. There were four thousand Marines and soldiers standing by, and eventually nearly a quarter of a million marchers headed for the Washington Monument Mall. Downtown, the new hero of many black youth, Malcolm X, gave a press conference to demean the march, calling it the "Farce on Washington," and while singers Odetta, Bob Dylan, Joan Baez, and the trio of Peter, Paul, and Mary were greeting the sea of faces gathering around the reflecting pool at the Lincoln Memorial, Dr. King was backstage, narrowly averting a rhetorical showdown with younger black prophets who wanted to speak to the nation in much more heated terms about the increasingly confrontational struggle for equal rights.

Lee Oswald still didn't have a television, so he probably didn't see the coverage of the march, though he certainly would have supported it. He was saving his money. He had told Marina to prepare to go back to Russia as soon as she was approved. He had dropped his far-fetched plan to hijack a jet with a pregnant Russian woman and a child as his accomplices; his new notion was to get to Cuba legally, via the embassy in Mexico City.

According to the account of G2 archivist "Reynoso," Oswald had met with Cuban intelligence for two days that summer, either in Mexico or Cuba.[45] There is no way to confirm this, and his whereabouts that season were largely accounted for by Marina; but she would later report seeing him often in the company of Cubans in New Orleans. And of course, by mid-August he had become something of a local celebrity in support of Fidel.

A few doors down from Carlos Bringuier's Casa Roca clothing store was the Habana Bar, which Lee was known to have patronized, usually arriving in the company of Latinos. Evaristo Rodríguez was the bartender one night in August, and he would refer to Lee's companions as "Mexicanos,"[46] but the man he arrived with might have been either Mexican or Cuban. In any case, Rodríguez thought that Lee looked very drunk, and the other man was propping him up.[47] It was close to 3:00 A.M. Lee was dressed in black slacks, a short-sleeved white shirt, and a black tie, the uniform he usually wore when he was leafleting. The Spanish-speaking man ordered tequila and complained about the price, saying that the bar's owner must be a capitalist. Lee ordered a lemonade, but he soon became too sick to drink anything and retched on the table and the floor until the other man took him outside.

Orest Pena owned the cantina. He had come to the States well before the revolution, so he wasn't an exile per se, but he gave the superficial impression of being anti-Castro. He started showing up at some of the CRC meetings. He knew David Ferrie as "Captain Ferrie," had even taken some flying lessons from him, and when he became a familiar face, the local FBI man, Warren DeBrueys, started coming around to the bar and asking questions about the patrons. Pena made it a point to cooperate, telling DeBrueys who he thought was for Castro and who against, but it sounded a bit like an idle description of sports fans, not colored with any particular preference.[48]

But Pena's neighbor in the business district, Carlos Bringuier, who had a sharp eye for double agents and had pinpointed Oswald as such, came to regard Pena as at least a Castro sympathizer.[49] One known informant told DeBrueys he had once overheard Pena remark that "Castro should have been notified about that as soon as possible," a businesslike assertion that sounded routine. And at his bar, Pena was heard talking specifically about traveling to England, Europe, and Moscow. He had applied for a new passport on the same day that Lee had, June 24, and Lee had listed the same destinations as places he soon intended to visit.[50]

Whatever his ultimate affiliation, Pena ran afoul of DeBrueys. He told the FBI that DeBrueys was interfering in the CRC's operations, and that DeBrueys may have been compromising him at his place of business. It was an odd complaint, given that Robert Kennedy himself had warned the FBI off the CRC, and that the CRC now had a tacitly cooperative relationship with the Bureau. DeBrueys took umbrage and told Pena what he already knew, that he was FBI and could get him into "big trouble" if he talked about him anymore.[51] It's not known if Lee Oswald was among the men that Pena told DeBrueys about, but there is no doubt that Lee had Cuban associates that summer, and after his arrest on August 9 they probably weren't anti-Castro men.

On September 7, the Agency's officer, Nestor Sánchez, and his partner, Richard Maxwell Long, met with Cubela at a safe house in Pôrto Alegre, Brazil, to reassure him that the Agency had decided to utilize him in the next phase of their plan to overthrow Fidel. They discussed ways of approaching other Cuban military officers; once again, Cubela told Sánchez that he wanted assurances from a high U.S. government official, not someone from the CIA but a man at the top who could assure him of America's support for his actions, which included the decapitation of the Cuban regime. This was always the last word in any talks with Cubela—he wanted to hear it from the White House. Cubela was told that they would pass his request up the chain.

Within the Agency, however, there were a number of dissenting voices. The Cubela–AM/LASH gambit was rife with danger. Cubela's mistress and her brother were high-level G2 officers. He was thought to be as "change-able as the weather, . . . capable of rash, thoughtless, violent action under the strain of provocation, tense situations, or frustration." The year before, he had attempted suicide.

But the plot hurtled forward in hopes of success before the 1964 elections in the U.S. Joseph Califano, of the Pentagon's Cuban Coordinating Com-mittee, was being pressed by Des FitzGerald for all the Defense Department intel he could get on key Cuban military officers, scoping for a "mole" within the regime.[52] FitzGerald was about to brief the Joint Chiefs and, although Califano was excluded from the meeting on September 25, Des and the Agency were, according to memos later released, studying how Ger-man generals had plotted to kill Hitler, in order to develop a way to organize high-ranking Cuban officers to kill Castro.[53]

At the meeting that day, Des announced that they were having "great suc-cess" in finding such officers, and "that there were at least ten high-ranking military personnel who were talking to the CIA but as yet [were] not talking to each other, since that degree of confidence [had not] yet developed."[54]

Bobby had pushed for a secret base in Costa Rica, which was now carry-ing out raids in Cuba "with arms and transportation provided by the De-fense Department. [They] bombed railroads, bridges, piers, warehouses, power plants, and transformers" and "continued to infiltrate radio equip-ment, arms, and supplies to resistance forces on the island."[55] On September 6, Fidel publicly charged the U.S. with responsibility for an air attack on Santa Clara, Cuba.

For all of that boom and bang, however, and all of Bobby's surety that Cubela was the right man for the job, Cubela's detractors at CIA would prove to be correct: The Cubans were on to him. It was during that summer that Oscar Marino and others inside G2 became aware—either from the KGB Cubela file pilfered from CIA or from Cuban spies elsewhere in the U.S.—that Cubela was a "traitor," a double. And yet Cubela had not been arrested, not then. "His freedom made him useful to us," Marino would declare in 2005.[56] Two years after Kennedy's death, the CIA would interview Cubela's jeweler friend and co-conspirator, Carlos Tepedino (AM/WHIP), who confirmed the agency's nagging doubts: Cubela still "had strong connections with Cuban intelligence and *was probably cooperating* with it in various ways" [emphasis added].[57]

The same day that Cubela was having his meeting with the CIA in Brazil, Fidel was due at a reception at the Brazilian embassy in Havana.

There, he pulled aside AP correspondent Daniel Harker, within earshot of other journalists. Harker, a native of Colombia, spoke fluent Spanish and was preferred by Castro for American press interviews because of his accuracy in translating. "He often pulled me aside when he wanted to be certain his words were reported exactly as he said them."

"Hey, Colombian," said Fidel, "come over here, I want to talk to you." He started in about the recent attacks, the other reporters bending in to hear more.

"We are taking into account . . . the Caribbean situation," he growled, "which has been deteriorating in the last few days due to piratical attacks by the United States against the Cuban people . . . Kennedy is a cretin . . . the Batista of our times . . ." He never used the word "assassination," but his meaning was clear. "If US leaders are aiding terrorist plans to eliminate Cuban leaders, they themselves will not be safe. Let Kennedy and his brother Robert take care of themselves since they too can be the victims of an attempt which will cause *their* death."[58]

With that, Fidel strode on into the reception and began shaking hands, the lavish extrovert returning to his element. Could the information have come from Cubela, hoping to regain favor with the G2? It can't be known. What's certain is that the story hit the Associated Press and U.S. newspapers two days later, the *New Orleans Times-Picayune*—Lee Oswald's daily paper—among them.

In Washington, the Cuban Coordinating Committee took note and immediately ordered up a memo from its Cuban Subversion subcommittee on the prospects for Cuban retaliation against American officials and citizens.[59] Bobby had three reactions to Fidel's taunt: First, he ordered Rear Admiral John Bulkeley to take command at Guantánamo and "put a muzzle" on Fidel Castro. Bobby added, "The president wants you to go down there and show that bastard who's the boss in this part of the world!" Second, he instigated an investigation into how Raúl might react were Fidel to be killed. Third, he told the CIA's Cuba desk to speed up the AM/LASH plan, prompting Des FitzGerald to do what he—as the top man in an unprecedented covert action—should never have done: He was to schedule a trip to Paris to calm Cubela and assure him of Bobby's support.

Forty-two years later, Cubela was living in a metropolis in Spain. He had kept up the game until 1966, when Fidel finally arrested him for yet another plot; even then, Cubela did his time in such comfort that it begs the question of just how out of favor he really was with the Castros. He was eventually released, in 1978, and his soft time in Fidel's prison suggests that perhaps Dr. Cubela had just become so unpredictable that he was taken off the streets so that the Cubans could get him out of circulation and determine where his true allegiance lay. With his freedom returned to him, he would spend his days as a carefree bourgeois, wandering the old Spanish city, playing dominoes, eating well, and reminiscing with his trenchmates. One of them was Pablo Zepeda, a former bodyguard to Chilean president Salvador Allende who had witnessed the leader's suicide at the height of the Nixon-orchestrated coup. Zepeda was secretly reporting back to Havana, but the men became friends. Even though Cubela appeared to be active with militant anti-Castro exiles and radical right-wing groups in Europe, Zepeda concluded that he was—in the winter of his years—what he had always appeared to be, a mole for G2. It seemed that Zepeda was just keeping tabs on him for Fidel, and that Cubela may in turn have been keeping tabs on him.[60] To this day, Dr. Cubela is, in all likelihood, still on good terms with some in G2. Indeed, if that were not the case, there is little doubt that Cubela would have been killed long ago.

So just what were his allegiances in the Kennedy years? How was it that such a changeling reached the innermost sanctum of the Kennedys' trust? It can only be accounted for in the way that the Cuban's eventual reliance on Oswald can—he was the best that the Americans had on hand. When pressed, in 2005, on whether Bobby ever spoke of the murder plots, Cubela said, "He didn't want me to speak about it. The subject was avoided. But of course I told him: Castro is the main obstacle," he said. "He must be eliminated." The implication was that Cubela reported to Bobby directly, not just through Des FitzGerald's staff.[61]

In 2003, the CIA's Sam Halpern, who managed the Cubela affair with Des FitzGerald, was asked by ABC News if Bobby ever informed the Cuba Desk that he was aware of Cubela. Halpern replied, "No, but we knew he was." How? "Cubela told us so," Halpern replied without hesitation. "So we knew that Bobby was pushing him. We didn't know why or how or where or when, and maybe Cubela knew, but he never told us that. He was smart enough to keep some things to himself. But he was being used as a tool by Bobby . . . Cubela thought that Bobby was a great guy simply because he was using him and paying him well, using CIA money, of course.* I'm not sure that Cubela or Bobby knew precisely how much we knew about the activity. I mean, how much CIA knew."

Did Halpern ever doubt the hired assassin? "I always believed Cubela," Halpern said. "I don't think he ever lied to us at all. He had no reason to lie to us. And I believed him, and I know the case officers believed him. When he told us about Bobby's involvement, we all believed him. All the case officers involved and the people involved believed him, and had no reason to go questioning Bobby as to why he was doing it. You couldn't question him anyway. As the attorney general, he had a right to do what he wanted to do."[62]

There was absolutely no doubt in old Sam Halpern's mind that the man had at least a phone relationship with Bobby. It might have been one of the most tragic coincidences in history, if true: just months before Lee killed Jack, Bobby may have met with Lee's Cuban recruiter face-to-face, having hired him to do the same to Fidel.

To this day, Rolando Cubela Secades, who steadfastly denies what the KGB files, Oscar Marino, and others say about him, remains the greatest enigma of his time, the "Zelig" of the Cold War, assimilated by all, known by almost no one, and with none of that Everyman's redeeming traits.

The summer of 1963 was boiling hot and damp in New Orleans. The heat drenched your clothes, it filled your lungs, it grew mold everywhere, and it never left, making a liar of the night. The duplex on Magazine Street had no air-conditioning, just a fan, occasionally augmented with a block of ice set before it. Lee would lie on the couch naked for much of each day, reading on his stomach. When the sun went down, he would put on a pair of pants and go out to the screened porch on the side of the house and continue to read in

---

*The day after this 2003 interview, coauthor Russo, who participated in the interview and had known Sam Halpern for twelve years, decided to call him to be certain of his RFK-Cubela story. The suspicion was that he might have confused Cubela with Manuel Artime. By way of background, Sam, in addition to being a career CIA officer, was a trained historian who was a stickler for details and historical accuracy. (He had a degree in history from City College of New York and a master's from Columbia, and had pursued advanced studies in history at George Washington University.) In all the years Russo knew him, Sam would happily fact-check Russo's writings and reprimand him if a comma was out of place. This is not the sort of man who would exaggerate in the least, and he was completely uninterested in notoriety. In any event, Russo asked him: "Are you sure you weren't thinking of Artime?" "Absolutely not," Sam replied authoritatively. "Cubela. My memory is very clear on it."

the light of an old desk lamp he had put out there. Marina would take the baby out for a walk in the evening, searching for a briny breeze, and when she got home there he would be, to her relief, his solitary face floating in the dark. Sometimes he wouldn't even be reading, just staring at the street.[63] Marina believed that for all his obsession with politics, his true love was for his family; that his political self and the cold persona he couched it in were simply an expression of his need to be special. This was how she explained and accepted it. At least for now, he was trying to act it out peacefully. She could be grateful for that much.[64]

Marina knew, of course, that he was now deep into his political activity again. An exchange between them was typical of the clashes that kept repeating themselves that summer. She had caught him rubber-stamping FPCC handbills one night. Sheepishly, he started putting them away, but they both knew what it meant.

Why was he hiding the papers? she wanted to know.

"Do you like Cuba?" he said, in the babyish voice he thought could ingratiate him, could disarm her.

"Yes."

"Do you like Uncle Fidel?"

"Yes."

"Well, these papers will help people be on the side of Cuba. Do you want them attacking little Cuba?"

"No, and you don't have to hide them from me, either. Sit there and play your childish games."[65]

Resigned to it all by now, she would lose herself in magazines; more often than not, the first photos she would look for would be the ones of Jack and Jackie. She thought it remarkable that Americans would show their president kicking along a beach, barefoot, with his wet cuffs rolled up and a sweatshirt on, or tootling around in a little golf cart, or smoking a cigar at a candlelit party. She identified with Jackie. She wondered how Jack might be in bed, how his bad back might affect him. She particularly loved the shots of him grinning and windblown, because they were the ones that reminded her the most of her Anatoly. She admitted a few years later that she had been in love with JFK.

Lee was nearly as absorbed in the First Family as she was. When Jack spoke on the radio, Lee sat transfixed on the couch, sometimes translating for her but mostly not. On July 26, Jack made a speech to tell the world that a nuclear test-ban treaty had been signed with Moscow. That time, Lee carefully explained the speech's content to her, and then tucked back into his book.

When she foraged for pictures of them, it was one of the few activities that they shared. He seemed to have taken Jackie to heart, and he seldom spoke ill of Jack. Even when he mentioned that the president's dad had "bought him" the presidency, his tone was almost appreciative, as if Jack were at least making the most of it, as he was on behalf of the Negroes. It was only the Cuba policy that angered him, and even that seldom came up when they were simply admiring the Kennedys in the glossies. When Lee gave her a tiny allowance one day, Marina went out and bought herself a picture of the president.[66] Lee had his portrait of Fidel pasted to the living room wall. She had hers of Jack, and she hung it in the kitchen, erring on the side of caution by not placing him in view of the bed.

As August smoldered away, though, Lee's spooky energy was returning. He was nowhere near as abusive as he had been in Texas, but the prowling rest-lessness was encroaching again. After an entire spring and summer of trying to rally the people of New Orleans to Fidel's cause, he had pulled in not one member, not one follower for Lee Oswald's flock. He had papered half the town with leaflets, but the FPCC had been ignoring his communiqués. Only Cuban intelligence had paid him any money or any mind, and even they had been elusive.

Still, he was determined to get to Cuba by some means, and the legal ones he had found had the added advantage of keeping Marina off his back. Someone had told him that there was a Cuban embassy in Mexico City. That "someone" might have been a Cuban intelligence contact. According to one of the highest-ranking KGB officers ever to defect, Lieutenant General Ion Mihai Pacepa, "Mexico City [was] a favorite place for contacting our important agents living in the U.S."[67]

Oswald could go there to gain entry to Cuba; and since he had no intention of coming back, he wouldn't risk imprisonment or the fine levied on Ameri-cans who broke the embargo. He let up on his demands that Marina go back to Russia. He just wanted to be on his own for a while. Something in him could not rest easy. There was still something to prove.

Marina knew her husband well enough to see that he had become fixated again, and that once he was fixated, he wouldn't be talked out of it. He would have to see Cuba for himself.

All she could see in her mind's eye was a nation of poor people, like them but without the Kennedys, the Montgomery Wards, the magazines, and the delicatessens. But if that's where he decided he must go, she said, then "for heaven's sake take some American soap. It will be dirty there."

"I'll go there," he insisted, his excitement getting loose in him. "I'll show them my clippings, show them how much I've done for Cuba, and explain how hard it is to help in America. And how above all I want to help Cuba. Will you come to me if I send for you there?"[68]

"Hmm," she answered. "We'll see."

She would remain neutral, wanting nothing to do with Cuba nor with China, even if she did end up having to go wherever he ultimately settled. She could only hope that he'd wear himself out before that happened and just come home again, perhaps as a man who no longer needed politics in order to feel like a man.[69]

Marina had been writing to Ruth Paine, the tall Quaker lady from Dallas who had become such a friend and pen pal. Ruth's husband was leaving her. She and her kids had been traveling back east, but she was due south again soon and had promised to stop in to see them. By this time, Lee's plan to go to Mexico and Cuba was definite. Marina had written Ruth to gently plead for an invitation to stay with her, perhaps at least until the new baby was born. Marina did not tell her what Lee's real plan was, that he was unemployed and headed to Cuba. She could hardly bear to dwell on it for herself. It was dawning on both of them that they might never see each other again.

And then she came home one evening and found him dry-firing the rifle again, on the porch. He became so stingy by the end of the summer that she erupted one night over a penny-ante game of cards they were playing. He cut down on his eating, dwindling down to a stick-man, which she had seen him do just twice before: once while preparing to make his case to the American embassy in Moscow, and the second time when he was in training to assassinate Walker.

Ruth Paine agreed to take Marina in; and as Ruth's journey brought her closer, and Lee's departure was about to carry him away, Marina broke down and begged him to take her with him.

He seemed stunned at the plea, perhaps even shaken by the ferocity of her attachment. He seemed half detached, already.

"Where on earth can I take you?" he asked dumbly. "You're in the last stages of pregnancy."[70]

Ruth arrived with her kids. Lee put on a great show of ebullience and charm, thoroughly convincing to Ruth and perhaps sincere, on the eve of his liberation. He wouldn't let the women help him pack, and they went off for a housewives' tour of Bourbon Street, peering into the windows of the juke joints while their kids wriggled beside them to the sounds of the bump-and-grind bands. As he boxed the baby's clothes, scrubbed the place down, and bade good-bye to yet another shotgun shack, did this feel like the beginning of the adventure of a lifetime? Had he finally found himself?

The women came home, put the kids down, and settled on the porch with a pair of Coca-Colas, watching him pack Ruth's car. He told her that a particularly heavy bundle was full of camping equipment; in fact, it was his rifle.

On the morning of September 23, he busied himself in a dozen more little chores. The women fed their families, and the last few items were stuffed into the car. When the moment came, it was herky-jerky, beset with false starts and the squawking kids; and when he and Marina finally held each other, looked all the way into each other and allowed the truth of the moment, they both nearly broke into tears.

Once more, he made her promise that she wouldn't tell Ruth where he was headed. Had she known how soon he would be back, and then how soon after that he would truly be gone forever, she might have wished him a bright future in the land of Fidel. She might even have made that promise to join him there, the better to brighten his path.

CHAPTER 10
A Pawn in Their Game

PAMELA MUMFORD WAS EXCITED. It was the end of August 1963, and the heat of summer had melted down the glamour of New York City. The island felt like a kiln of baking metal, stone, and glass, and she and her roommate, Patricia Winston, were more than ready to get out of town. The two Australians, ages twenty-one and twenty-two, had just locked their apartment at 222 West Twenty-third Street and were headed uptown to the Port Authority terminal with all the anticipation of a pair of novitiates embarking for the Holy Land. They had worked hard and saved diligently so that they could finally see the rest of the country, and then some.

Over the course of the next several weeks, they hit Washington, D.C., and most of the eastern seaboard, southward to the Deco strands of Miami Beach. They saw New Orleans and much of the Old South. They saw half of Texas, it seemed, and finally landed on the streets of Laredo on Wednesday, September 25, their last American stop before they headed south of the border, bound for the Mexican capital.

The next leg of their journey, aboard a Flecha Roja bus, started at 10:00 A.M., took them across the border an hour later, and stopped in Monterrey at 6:00 P.M. There they got off and spent the night, planning when they awoke to investigate where they might stay in Mexico City.

During Lee and Marina's troubled summer in New Orleans, Lyndon Johnson and Texas governor John Connally had been subtly leaking the word to the press that President Kennedy would be visiting Texas in the fall.

There was no great love lost between the Boston Yankees and the Texas oil and cattle men, but the Democratic National Committee was $4 million in debt, and Vice President Johnson believed his home state would come to the rescue. Four fund-raisers were planned for the two-day whirlwind. The news of the trip finally spilled onto the front pages on September 26: the president would be paying a visit to a number of Texas cities on November 21 and 22. There were banner headlines in the *Dallas Morning News* and the state's other major dailies.

If Lee saw those headlines at the newsstand of the Houston Continental Trailways station, it would have to have been the first edition that arrived after midnight. He left Houston on bus #5133 at 2:35 A.M., killed time at the stop in Corpus Christi, and didn't get to Laredo until 1:20 in the afternoon. Wherever he read the news, it must have given him pause. By now, thanks to the Fair Play newsletter, he knew that the Kennedys were still plotting the overthrow of Fidel, even in the wake of the missile crisis. If he had told most people that, it would have been chalked up to leftist paranoia or right-wing wishful thinking. Yet it was true, and Lee was going south to offer his services in defense of the revolution.

Pamela and Patricia spent September 26 touring the city of Monterrey. That evening, they boarded another bus for Mexico City. There were some Brits up front, and a pale young American man, but the only open seats were in the back and that's where they settled. They would get some rest and be fresh for the capital when they arrived in the morning.

A little while later, the American ambled down the aisle and stopped by their seats. He wore a plain dark sweater and he could have used a shave, but he was just a bit older than they were, and they bantered back and forth for a while. He seemed excited, and he was definitely aiming to impress them, and he might have been a little bit lonely.

He had heard them speaking English, he said, and wondered where they came from.[1]

They told him. Australia. He said he was from Fort Worth, but he wanted them to know that he too was a world traveler, having served in the Marines in Japan and gone on a pilgrimage to Russia. He brandished his passport, not mentioning a wife even though his wedding ring was easily visible. He had been to Mexico before, of course; he looked out at the cactus whizzing by in the twilight, smiled contentedly, and gave a worldly little nod. Mexico. He never told them his name, but he seemed nice enough, quite chatty, actually, and when he sauntered back up to his seat they decided to call him Texas.

The people in the front had not heard him chatting up the Brits, but he had been quite loquacious with them as well, bragging that he was a Cubanophile—was headed to Cuba, in fact, hoping to see Fidel himself.[2] He was going by way of Mexico because U.S. law prevented him from taking a straight shot there.

The bus would pull in to some tiny town every few hours and jostle them all awake. It was during one of the stops that Texas, still trying to be cosmopolitan, recommended the Hotel Cuba as a good lodging in the capital. He wouldn't be staying there himself this time, mind you, but the Cuba was centrally located. It was clean, and it was affordable,[3] he said. Later, however, the ladies weren't so sure about his familiarity with native ways. At the next few stops, they noticed that he couldn't make sense of the Spanish menus and would order just by pointing at something on the list and making the most of it,[4] which often meant full meals instead of snacks. He was too thin anyway, they thought, so perhaps it was for the best, and he seemed to take it in stride, ever upbeat and good-humored, even in the middle of the night.

At midmorning, however, when their bus reached Mexico City, he suddenly became very businesslike, grabbing his one small bag and scurrying off into the crowd. They would not see him again until his face appeared in the world's newspapers.

There's no record that Lee ever stayed at the Hotel Cuba, and his penchant for using aliases makes that verification all but impossible. But the hotel he walked to that morning was well suited to his purposes. The Hotel del Commercio was just four blocks from the bus terminal. Gringos seldom visited, and the American ambassador at that time, Thomas Mann, considered it to be the city's "headquarters of pro-Castro activities." This was "not known generally at all . . . this information was current only in intelligence circles."[5] Somehow, Lee Oswald had walked straight into the lion's den.

The building, covered in tiles of candy-apple red, was a modest place with a cramped little check-in booth off a narrow entry hall. The rooms rented for 16 pesos ($1.28) per night, a good price for the parsimonious Oswald. He registered under "O. H. Lee," and was booked into number 18, a small, dark room with bath, paneled in a checkerboard pattern of brown and tan stained wood and bearing heavy velveteen drapes. He would spend very little time here during his brief stay in the city, and most members of the staff would have no recollection of him. A masonry contractor named Ernesto Lima would later testify that he saw Oswald socializing at the hotel with four Cubans, one of them a man with "dark hair, dark eyes, who appeared to be possibly Negro,"[6] but no one else, besides the clerk who checked him in and out, would recall seeing him during his stay. The maid would note only that he was gone each morning by the time she knocked at 9:00 A.M., his clothing hand-washed and hanging neatly on a towel rack. In the next year, the Warren Commission would make cursory inquiries of the Commercio staff, but they never accounted for the vast majority of the week Lee spent in the Mexican capital.[7] The commission's official finding would be that Lee "was seen with no other person either at his hotel or at the restaurant,"[8] a conclusion consistent with its political aims but an erroneous one.

After he checked in, he washed off two days of road grit, changed clothes, and put on a tie. He was very organized. Incomplete evidence suggests that he may have called the Soviet military attaché at 10:30 A.M. and phoned the Soviet consulate just after that, but he did not stay in the room for much longer.[9] He shouldered his small bag and, following the map on which he had marked his objectives, headed straight to the Cuban embassy two miles away.

When he rounded the corner onto Calle Francisco Márquez and Zamora around 11 A.M., it must have thrilled him to see it standing there. The consulate's whitewashed wall gleamed in the hazy morning sun, featureless at ground level apart from a few windows with wrought-iron bars. At some points, the wall was actually the outside of a two-story outbuilding, with a second-floor row of enigmatic windows. Oswald's timing was fortuitous: the consulate had been closed for over two years, due to harassment by locals, and had reopened just days before he rang the buzzer. The timing could not have been better for the CIA as well: on that very day, Friday, September 28, the agency had reinstalled its consulate surveillance camera, a "robot" camera that automatically shot a frame whenever someone worked the latch on the consulate gate.

By the time Lee found his way inside, past the guards, the thrill could only have given way to anxiety. He had bet a great deal on this moment, after all. The first staffer who greeted him was Teresa Proenza. She spoke only Spanish, so she relayed him to Silvia Durán, the secretary to the consul, Eusebio Azcue. She greeted him warmly in English and asked him to sit down at her desk and tell her the purpose of his visit.

Silvia liked this gringo immediately. Disarmed, he explained to her that he was a friend of the Cuban Revolution, that he was traveling to the Soviet Union and hoped to visit Cuba en route. Why he had chosen the Soviet ruse isn't known, but he urged her to issue him a transit visa as fast as possible because he wanted to leave on September 30. As a testament to his revolutionary fervor, he then started showing her the contents of his bag: proof that he had lived and worked in Russia; his marriage pact with a Russian woman; an eleven-page "résumé" that detailed his time in Minsk, his knowledge of Marxism, his abilities as a street agitator and public speaker, and his experience at Jaggars as a photo technician; his membership card in the FPCC; news clippings about his arrest in New Orleans, which featured Lee being hustled away by two policemen; and copies of his correspondence with hard-left organizations in the States.

As insurance, he also carried his reconnaissance photos of the Walker assassination attempt and assorted clippings from the aftermath,[10] the remains of the file that Marina had forced him to burn and flush less than six months before. This was his trump card, and he probably didn't play it with Silvia, but it's likely that he played it later that day.

Silvia was impressed. She wanted to help him. Much as he had found Rimma Shirakova to advocate for him in Moscow, he now lucked out with Silvia. She went directly to her boss, the consul, Azcue, and asked if he could expedite the visa-approval process. Azcue said he didn't have that power; Lee would have to fill out the application, and it would need to be approved in Havana. Lee balked, impatient with the bureaucracy, but he played along, since Silvia seemed undaunted and was helping him with the application. She told him where he could get a passport photo made nearby, and then she eased up close and told him, confidentially, that if he went to the Russian embassy and got permission to visit the USSR first, he might dodge the Cuban requirements.

While he was out getting his photos taken, she called the Soviets. They were blasé and said that his application to visit Russia could take months as well. When she told Lee the bad news upon his return, he blanched. She could see the anger flash in his eyes. He turned up the volume.

"That's impossible," he bellowed. "I have to go to Cuba right now, because I have permission of only three or four days in Mexico City. So I have to go quickly!"[11] The ruckus drew Azcue back out of his office; after discussion, it was decided that if the Russians gave him a visa, the Cubans could give him a fifteen-day visa to Cuba immediately, but otherwise it would take weeks.

By this point, Lee had become so rude and arrogant that Azcue wondered if the *Yanqui* was a plant, a provocateur.[12] Silvia was sympathetic, writing down her name and embassy number for him, but he was still obliged to go to the Soviet compound two blocks away.

He had no more luck with the Russians. Inside the Soviet consulate, he was immediately turned over to the KGB, its staff overseen by Raúl Castro's great friend, Nikolai Sergeyevich Leonov. He was shown in to Valeriy Kostikov, the KGB officer who issued visas (and oversaw the occasional assassination). He showed them his bona fides. He told them of his Russian life, his Russian wife, his status as a pro-Cuban activist. He claimed that the FBI was harassing him, constantly. Lee's command of Russian helped, but his air of desperation did not. Kostikov called his expert on foreign counterintelligence, Oleg Nechiporenko, for a second opinion. That opinion was that this Oswald was a man "in a state of physical and mental exhaustion."[13]

Lee had anticipated this release for so long. He had sacrificed everything to be there, down to his family and his health and pieces of his sanity. Told that the process would take four months, he came apart.

"This won't do for me! . . . For me, it's all going to end in tragedy," he screamed.

Lee left. The Russians decided to contact KGB headquarters in Moscow, on the off chance that they had reason to grant him the instant visa. He went back to the Cubans and found them closed for siesta, but Lee was allowed to wait. When Silvia returned, he lied, telling her that the Soviets had given him the visa, then amending that when a call to the Soviets failed to confirm it. A scene erupted. He seemed both furious and very, very sad. She went back to get Azcue again.

"I think he's becoming crazy," she told the consul.

Azcue came out, perplexed now, since even a provocateur wouldn't go off like this.

"If you are a friend of the Cuban revolution, you don't have to be like that—you *harm* the revolution, you don't help with this attitude—"

"I have to, to, I need that visa, I have to go to Cuba—"

"Look," Azcue snapped, "I already explained it to you: . . . [as] soon as you get the visa from the Soviet Union, you will have your Cuban [visa] without any problem."

But Lee only grew more furious and insistent, till Azcue's temper ran short.

"Listen, if you continue like this, I'm going to kick you out!"[14]

Lee took himself out.

At some point in all this, Silvia hinted to Lee that it might help his situation if he could get a letter of recommendation from some Mexican held in good stead with upper-echelon revolutionary Cubans.[15]

Thus, one late afternoon in late September 1963, Oscar Contreras, a law student at National Autonomous University, was sitting with three friends in a cafeteria in the philosophy department when an American man at a nearby table struck up a conversation with them. That particular part of the cafeteria was designated as the Bloque Revolucionario, and Contreras belonged to a left-wing student group that supported the Castro Revolution and had contacts in the Cuban embassy. The American told them that he was a revolutionary and the chairman of a Cuba solidarity group in New Orleans. Someone had recommended Contreras to him, he said, because the Mexican might help him get to Cuba.[16] (That "someone" may have been Silvia Durán's close friend Ricardo Guerra, the chairman of the school's philosophy department.)

The American introduced himself curiously, spelling out his entire name "Lee Harvey Oswald," as would befit someone anxious to be remembered.

Contreras and his pals chuckled at the name; "Oswald" was the handle of a well-known cartoon character in a show about rabbits. Once again, his "Ozzie the Rabbit" moniker from the Marines had arisen with a new set of potential friends, but Lee must have shrugged it off. Anything that made his name stick with them was all right with him. He seized the cheerful moment to tell them his story.

He said he was a painter who had just left Texas because the FBI was bothering him. Life in the U.S. was not for him. He wanted to devote himself to the revolution. Cuba was where he belonged, but for some reason the Cuban consulate was refusing him a visa.

Could the students help him, through their friends in the embassy? Contreras, who would later become paranoid about this encounter and tell slight variations of it in coming years, was initially sympathetic. The American, with his broken Spanish and his intelligent manner and his humble ditty bag, seemed unerringly sincere. He shared their political beliefs, and Contreras soon took a liking to the guy. He told him that they would do what they could for him.

The American kicked around with them for the rest of the evening and, although Contreras would later vow to his friends that he would never reveal it, he eventually admitted that Oswald spent the entire night with them in the group's communal apartment in the city center. His politics were considered very radical, an added inducement to feed him, share some *cervezas* and some rum, and talk into the wee hours. They then gave him a mattress to stretch out on, side by side with the rest of the comrades.

Contreras would be a bit fuzzy on whether it was that night or the next morning that they sent the oldest member of their group, a Peruvian anarchist, to the Cuban embassy to speak up for Oswald. The Peruvian knew Azcue personally and could get to the truth of what was happening. But when he returned not long afterward, he took Contreras and a few of the others aside and told them that the embassy had encountered the American and suspected that he might be a provocateur trying to infiltrate left-wing groups; maybe even a CIA agent and a dangerous man. They commanded the students to break off contact with him at once. Local G2 and DGI (and perhaps Mexican) operatives had him under surveillance.

Contreras, who sat on his story for four years, broke the news mildly, in passing, telling Oswald only that they could not help him. Apparently, Lee said nothing. He just zipped up his bag, brushed himself off, and left, once again the misunderstood rabbit in a barracks full of real men.

At 9:30 A.M on Saturday, September 28, unshaven and unkempt, Lee was rattling the gate of the Soviet compound again. Kostikov thought he looked haunted, "hounded," but he let him in, and they were soon joined by another KGB officer, Captain Pavel Yatskov. When the American sat down, he started waxing eloquent about his wife and child, the simple beauties of Russian life, and how he wanted to go to Cuba to "help the Cubans build a new life."[17] But then he returned to the subject of the FBI, and his tone shifted again, edging toward hysteria. Suddenly he was begging, weeping.

"I am afraid . . . they'll kill me," he wailed. "Let me in!"

He launched into a rant, at times bordering on gibberish. He was being followed everywhere, he claimed, even there in the city. He imagined it was the FBI; but if he had actually noticed anyone, they were probably G2 agents, not the American Feds. Nechiporenko bounded in, all suited up for a volleyball match with his colleagues, just as Lee was reaching into his Eisenhower jacket and pulling out a .38 revolver. The American started waving it over his head.

"See?! This is what I must now carry to protect my life!"[18]

He set the gun down on the desk. The other men disarmed it, one of them putting the bullets in a drawer, but they were at a loss about what to do with the man. Finally, his sobs subsided. When the anguish settled back down to maundering, they gave his gun back to him, bullets and all, and escorted him to the door.

"If they don't leave me alone," he slurred, "I'm going to defend myself."[19]

He raised his collar to shield himself from the surveillance outside and went off into the searing daylight. It was about 10:30 A.M.

One hour later, according to CIA phone-tap transcripts, Silvia Durán, with Oswald by her side, called the Soviets from the Cuban consulate. She then gave the phone to Oswald, who, in what she later characterized as "hardly recognizable Russian," told the Soviets he had come there to get his address from Durán, and would bring it back to the Russians after they hung up.

None of this makes any sense, of course, but what is more perplexing is that the Cuban consulate was closed on Saturday, and Durán has sworn under oath that she only saw Oswald on Friday. Likewise, the Soviets say they never received the Saturday call from Durán.

Since the transcript exists, and the CIA translators have sworn to its authenticity, someone must have been dissembling.

What was going on?

KGB and Cuban sources make it clear that Lee arrived in Mexico that September having had some sort of contact with the Cubans in the past eleven months. Through Cubela, the CIA, the KGB, and almost certainly G2 all knew by then that a "foreign collaborator" named Oswald, from Texas, had tried to take down the reactionary general Edwin Walker. But one gets the sense that Lee was discovered by G2 to be every bit as unstable and unnerving as the Soviets suggested when General Kryuchkov first tipped the Cubans about him after Lee's return to America. Had the contact with G2 been sustained, he would have known better than to go to Mexico City and pursue a trip to Cuba that way; indeed, they would probably have discouraged it. Not only did his mental state make him unsuitable for any mission requiring the appearance of normality, but to bring him to Cuba would have blown his cover, rendering him ineffective for any stealthy use inside American borders. So it's likely that he went to Mexico without the prior knowledge of his Cuban contact in the U.S., and thus no familiarity among officials at either the Cuban or Russian embassies, especially the secretaries who would first greet him.

Nonetheless, the FBI has known since 1964—from Fidel's own mouth—that during one of Lee's emotional seizures during his second trip to the Cuban embassy, he said the words "I'm going to kill that bastard! I'm going to kill Kennedy!"

Fidel told this to the American Communist Party officials (and FBI informants for thirty years) Jack and Morris Childs,[20] and stressed that he had learned of it immediately after it was said, from his Cuban embassy officials in Mexico,[21] but considered it to be the frothing of a lunatic. In July 1967, Fidel reprised the story to the British writer Comer Clark: "I was told he [Oswald] wanted to work for us. He was asked to explain, but he wouldn't. The second time [Oswald came to the embassy], he said he wanted to 'free Cuba from American imperialism.' Then he said something like, 'Somebody ought to shoot that President Kennedy. Maybe I'll try to do it.'"[22] Fidel has admitted that he had advance warning of a crazed Texan on the hunt for Kennedy, but has insisted that there was no more to it. The worst Castro could be accused of was failing to intercede in a plot against the U.S. president while that president was busily plotting Castro's own death.

But there was much more to it than that.

CIA headquarters would go so far as to assert that it did not even know of Oswald's appearance at the Cuban embassy until it had had a chance to review the wiretaps after the assassination. This would stand as the official summary of events, as related by Langley to the Warren Commission. But CIA translators Boris and Anna Tarasoff had caught Oswald on the Saturday phone call with Durán to the Soviets. Anna would insist that the CIA's alert on Oswald "was marked urgent,"[23] and all reports were shot to headquarters, nearly in real time. It was Lee's trundling back and forth between the compounds that seized their attention. Win Scott likewise knew the truth all along. As he wrote in his unpublished autobiography, *Foul Foe*:

> Lee Harvey Oswald became a person of great interest to us during the 27 September to 2 October, 1963 period . . . [In] the Warren Commission Report [p. 777] the erroneous statement was made that it was not known until after the assassination that Oswald had visited the Cuban Embassy! . . . Every piece of information concerning Oswald was reported immediately after it was received . . . These reports were made on all his contacts with both the Cuban Consulate and the Soviets . . . Persons watching these embassies photographed Oswald as he entered and left; and clocked the time he spent on each visit.[24]

Anne Goodpasture, Win's assistant assigned to the surveillance operations,[25] was, according to the station's head of Cuban ops David Atlee Phillips, the case officer who ID'd Lee Oswald in Mexico City,[26] but she would deny any knowledge of Oswald taps or photographs for decades. Win Scott may have had one view of how Oswald was being handled at headquarters, while Goodpasture was purveying quite another. Then, out of nowhere, Goodpasture would suddenly improve her memory.

When pressed as to why they did not admit their knowledge of Oswald's Cuban embassy contacts, former CIA director Richard Helms claimed that "they didn't want to blow their source,"[27] meaning the wiretaps and their human assets.

The cameras were all in place. So were all the taps and the informants. Dave Phillips and the Tarasoffs remembered other transcripts of Lee's visits to the

Soviets, including a long discussion in which he spoke of wanting money in exchange for information.[28]

Win Scott's deputy chief, Alan P. White, would play tapes from Mexico of Oswald for Warren Commission staffers in April 1964.[29]

FBI agent Michael DeGuire, stationed in Mexico City at the time, remembered that Oswald was photographed with the KGB's Kostikov at an undisclosed restaurant, near a water fountain.[30]

Scott apparently had an Oswald photo, but it would never be delivered to future government investigators, though many agents confirmed having seen or heard of the picture.[31] Among them was Joseph Stephan Piccolo Jr., a CIA Latin specialist and anti-Cuban agent who was in Mexico City from 1957 to 1968, although not in 1963. He would tell the HSCA investigators that he was shown two Mexican surveillance photos of Oswald outside the Cuban embassy that were apparently found by headquarters' Charlotte Bustos.[32]

At least two of the FBI's Mexican contingent, Eldon Rudd and his assistant, Michael DeGuire, knew there was much more to it. Someone had headquarters make an official decision to keep this advance knowledge out of the public record. The trouble with that strategy, however, was that headquarters was completely at odds with most of its senior officers who were actually on site at the Mexico City station.

And there was one more reason for concern. The CIA, for all its advanced technology and patriotic intentions and sheer human talent, could not penetrate the Cuban spy apparatus.[33]

All that the Agency had were tapes and photos of a lost man, but they had no presence inside the deepest reaches of Cuban intelligence. From their vantage, watching Oswald be pulled in by the Cubans was like seeing Jonah fall into the belly of the whale: no sooner did they "find" him—and likely impersonate him, à la Elden Hensen two months earlier—than he was lost to them again.

Boris and Anna Tarasoff, the Russian couple charged with translating wiretaps for the CIA's Mexico station, were adamant that they transcribed at least three more calls involving Oswald, the Soviets, and the Cubans. The longest of those transcripts, which has never surfaced, was from Monday, September 30. On that same day, a credit examiner named Pedro Gutiérrez Valencia paid a visit to the Cuban embassy to review a credit report for an embassy employee, Luisa Calderón. Pedro worked for a local department store, Palacio de Hierro, and he was fairly familiar with the layout of the embassy, since the Cubans did a lot of business at the store. His frequent visits there, as well as to the Soviet embassy, had also made him a valued informant for the CIA.*

He found Luisa's office quickly and sat down with her. He had some bad news.

Her credit application was fraudulent. The Mexican Foreign Office had no record of her employment at the embassy. He had tried to validate the information she gave through the Department of Motor Vehicles and had looked wherever else he could, but for all intents and purposes there was no "Luisa Calderón" on the public record. It's not known how the prospective shopper, Luisa, took the news, but it had to have annoyed her. She was a spy and G2 was generally better at covering their people than that. It was a simple credit line, after all.

Pedro left. As he was making his way across the courtyard of the compound, he paused to light a cigarette near the corner of a building. Suddenly, a stocky, light-skinned Latino with what Pedro described as "negroid" hair came around the corner and bumped into him.

"*Está bien, chico*," the man said, the use of the nickname marking him as a Cuban.

Pedro shrugged it off and kept walking. He was now just ahead and to the side of the Cuban, who was walking with another man, a white American. The Latino was perhaps thirty-three, stood about five feet, four inches, and wore a crisp black suit, a white shirt, and no tie. The American could have been a tradesman, pale, a bit rumpled and wearing an Eisenhower-type windbreaker.

As Pedro walked along, he heard the American refer to the Cuban as "Ernie" a few times, and he realized that they were having an argument. The words "Castro" and "Cuba" and "Kennedy" were spat back and forth, and when they passed Pedro and were approaching the gate that fed onto Calle Francisco Márquez, the Cuban was counting out money, which he then passed to the American. They left the compound, got into a beige, late-model Dina-Renault, and drove away.

---

*According to CIA surveillance records, Gutiérrez had also done business at the Soviet compound on Friday the twenty-seventh, the very day of Oswald's first visit there. What is most bothersome is that the CIA had surveillance photos of Gutiérrez entering the compound on that day, yet somehow they missed Oswald. Anne Goodpasture herself ID'd the Gutiérrez photo, adding that "he was known to the station." (HSCA Mexico City Report, pp. 138–39)

Two months later, after the assassination, Pedro would identify the American as Oswald. He would report this encounter directly to the new American president by letter, and would tell his tale, repeatedly, to FBI agents. The car would show up again on surveillance on February 25, 1964, and would be traced by the CIA Mexico City station. The owner would be identified as Arturo Goana Elias; when his name came up, every Mexican police and regulatory agency ran his name through every imaginable data sieve. Goana was never found. He had dropped off the face of the earth in 1957. Someone had stolen his identity.[34]

Silvia Durán would suffer for her brief association with Lee Oswald, one that would become a love affair as well. She would be beaten and threatened by the Mexican authorities, hounded and humiliated. Even now, in her old age, there are knocks on her door in the night—journalists, historians, freaks. Given her ongoing fear, there must also be clandestine operatives keeping watch, still warning her away from the reality of that time lest it mar the smug face of history. Through the crack in the door, she would contend for many years that she never saw Lee Oswald again after he left the Cuban embassy in a fit of pique. But Luis Alberu, the undercover CIA agent in the Cuban embassy, would know better, and there are many other sightings of them from Lee's long "lost weekend."

According to a couple of Cuban newspapermen, one a former head of intelligence under Cuban president Carlos Prío, Lee was seen with Silvia Durán going to a place called Caballo Blanco, a popular restaurant on the city's outskirts, in Chapultepec Park. There, the newspaperman said, they met with Joaquin Hernández Armas, the Cuban ambassador to Mexico, for a long conversation, after which Armas and Oswald left to continue talking in a secure automobile. The FBI got wind of this from a source inside the Johnson White House.[35]

Oscar Contreras, the law student who befriended Lee at the university and was then warned off him by Consul Azcue, would see the gringo again at a party in Mexico City a few nights later. Oswald seemed to have "many contacts, with revolutionaries and with revolutionary snobs." Asked in 2005 if Silvia Durán was at that party, Contreras said, "I can't say with certainty. She was usually at such parties there."

Did she have a relationship with Oswald?

"Their private lives have nothing to do with politics," Contreras replied, as if the murder of a U.S. president shouldn't encroach on the sex life of the perpetrator. But then another name occurred to him. "Elena Garro was there at the party with Oswald. She was at all the parties back then."[36]

Helena "Elenita" Paz, the daughter of Octavio Paz and Elena Garro, was a teenager in 1963. As a privileged bohemian girl, she had lived all over the world, moving among the likes of Jorge Luis Borges and André Breton, not to mention Che Guevara. Her mother's marriage to Paz was ending in 1963, but Garro was still a whip-smart and daring scene maker, and it was common for her to bring Elenita to parties of the city's leftist intelligentsia.

Forty-two years later, Elenita's parents were dead and she was living in a bungalow in Cuernavaca with a dog and thirty-five cats. Though apparently not an advocate of violent revolution, she considers herself a Communist and she spent most of her adulthood estranged from her famous father. The rift was great enough that he let her fall into poverty, and she has never quite found her way out. She would dismiss him, ultimately, as "a reactionary. Fidel Castro's enemy number one, one of the bourgeoisie." Once a beautiful woman, she now is now marked by illness and grief, but on the day she sat down in her patio to recall those wild nights so long ago, dignity required that she put on a flowing floral dress. She chain-smoked, her lipstick clotting the filters of her cigarettes.

When she was asked about Lee Oswald, there was no ripple of panic on her face, just a sharp nod and the flick of her ash. It was the end of September, she said, around the time of the visit of the Russian cosmonaut, Yuri Gagarin, to Mexico. That was another event her mother had taken her to, and the fifteen-year-old had thought "Gagarin was a picture pretty fellow."

The party where she encountered Lee took place at the home of Silvia Durán's brother-in-law, Ruben Durán. There were some forty partygoers there, many of them Cuban embassy employees, including Consul Azcue.[37] Silvia and her husband, Horacio, were in attendance, as was General José Jesús Clark Flores. In the blur of partying that year, it was uncertain to Elenita whether it was the same party at which Azcue, Communist writer Emilio Carballido, and a "Latin American Negro man with red hair" argued about President Kennedy.[38]

People were dancing to the Twist, and everyone was drinking with gusto. Silvia has admitted having many such "twist parties" in 1963, and that the Paz-Garroses attended at least one at Ruben's home.[39] Elenita and her mother were the only non-Communists on the dance floor.

"Lee Harvey Oswald was with two other gringos at the party. They sat that evening in a corner, drank beer, and conversed in English. Oswald spoke arrogantly and aggressively. I asked Horacio who had brought along this strange fellow, and he said, 'Silvia invited him.' "

Elenita knew Silvia and Horacio from the Cuban social scene that swirled around the embassy. "My aunt Deba instigated me dancing with Oswald." The bold teenager "went over to him and asked him, but he rejected me with a rough 'No.' He was very cold."

By this time, Silvia had stepped in to head off any further discussion between them. At the time, Elenita assumed that Silvia might have designs on the man.*

Elenita pulled on her cigarette. "He was the most attractive. The others were the usual boring gringos. Oswald had made me somewhat curious. I wanted to learn more about him. He fascinated me."

Over the din of the music, conversation rose and fell. Some of it was flirty and frivolous, some more serious. Some of it was devolving into drunken political invective. At one point, she believes, Azcue and Carballido were ranting in harmony about Kennedy, finally reaching the same conclusion—that the only way to deal with the American president was to kill him.[40]

The day after the party, Elenita saw Oswald again. "I met with Silvia's husband Horacio for a coffee in Sanborn's Restaurant. It was on Insurgentes Sur Street. We spoke over his impending separation from Silvia. There, I see suddenly this Oswald on the sidewalk, accompanied by the same men who were at the party. I say, 'Horacio, there is that strange gringo again. What do you really know about him?' Horacio answers, 'Don't ask. He's a dangerous man.' "

Asked if Silvia had a relationship with Oswald, Elenita said only, "In any case, they were friendly."[41†]

In 1965, her mother Elena Garro had been more forthcoming. Durán and Oswald were lovers, she said. This was corroborated two years later, with-

---

*Silvia's name and phone number would later be found in Lee's address book.
†Oswald may have left in his belongings tiny clues regarding all of his extra-official doings. After Oswald's arrest for the assassination, authorities would confiscate his Mexico City tourist guidebook, *Esta Semana* ("This Week"), September 28–October 4, 1963. The brochure contains Oswald's marginal notes that display his interest in attending the Sunday 4:30 P.M. bullfights, the Palace of Fine Arts, and various movie houses. According to the KGB, these were also the favored sites for "iron meetings," quick emergency meetings made in order to arrange a longer one at a later time. It may be portentous that Oswald noted next to the bullfight ad, "buy tickets"—in plural. (Int. with KGB defector Lt. Gen Ion Mihai Pacepa by Jamie Glazon in *Frontpage* magazine, 10/03/2007, "Programmed to Kill: Lee Harvey Oswald, the Soviet KGB and the Kennedy Assassination.")

out Garro's knowledge, by the CIA's informant (and Durán's close friend) in the Cuban embassy, Luis Alberu.*

Anne Goodpasture would one day be forced to concede that the CIA's tapes of Oswald at the embassies had indeed survived the assassination. As the Agency reported, the master tapes had been destroyed after they were transcribed, but the best bits were dubbed to another reel that Win Scott kept in his office.

At a deposition in 1995, Goodpasture went on record to say: "They made a copy at the tap center . . . There would have been two copies of the conversation; one the master tape, the other one with a segment of a single conversation on it . . . I'm sure they would have sent it to Washington. What happened from there, I don't know."[42]

Melbourne Paul Hartman knew. Hartman, a member of the CIA headquarters' Office of Research and Analysis, received them (and many more cartons of material) at Langley. He testified that they arrived from Mexico City soon after Win's death in 1971, and the shipment contained a four-inch bundle of reel-to-reel tapes marked "Oswald Case." "Someone had cleaned out a safe and sent them to me to put in a file," Hartman went on. (It is established that John Horton, Scott's successor at the station, cleaned out Scott's home safe after he died, and shipped the trove back to HQ.[43]) Without opening them, he placed them in the CIA's "Oswald 201 file."† They have since disappeared.

Among the myriad possible motives for removing an Oswald recording is that its discovery could jeopardize ongoing CIA operations. The Tarasoffs recalled an Oswald phone call on October 3, when he was known to be on the bus back to Dallas by 8:30 A.M., before the embassies even opened. Unless Oswald managed to make a call from a pay phone en route, he was being impersonated. In fact, the files of another impersonation victim, Elden Hensen, were merged into Oswald's CIA 201 file after the Mexican trip but *before* the assassination, as Russell Holmes, the custodian of Oswald's CIA 201 file,

---

*Elenita's mother first told the story to the CIA eleven months after the assassination; she had wanted to relay it immediately, but was dissuaded by a family friend who warned her that the local Communists would kill her.
†According to the CIA's Clandestine Services Handbook, a 201 file is opened on "subjects of extensive reporting and CI [counterintelligence] investigation, prospective agents and sources, and members of groups and organizations of continuing interest." Oswald's 201 was opened in December 1960, fourteen months after his landing in Moscow.

admitted over three decades later. This was done, Holmes explained, because both men had been contacts of Luisa Calderón. It may also have been done because both men were dupes in a CIA impersonation ploy. If so, the airing of the Oswald tape might have revealed the CIA's work in Mexico City.

And then there is the man who preferred to allow only his first name, Antonio, to be used. When first discovered in 2005, he was running a small taxi business in Mexico City, a small, portly, nervous man who agreed to be interviewed in a park, at a noisy street café, the better to be unnoticed. He was too twitchy to be entirely nondescript, though, shifting back and forth on his chair, the sunlight through the trees mottling his face. Antonio was not happy to be speaking of Oswald forty-two years later, nor did he feel that he'd have much to add.

"Very simply, I have anxiety. I erased my past as a G2 officer, put it successfully out of my life, discarded even my Cuban accent . . . and now you come and ask me about Oswald."

Antonio enlisted in the Cuban secret service in 1960, as an eighteen-year-old boy, and it seemed like a great career opportunity in the first blush of the revolution. He never rose to a very high service rank, but he was sent to Mexico to work security at the Cuban embassy. It was his job to help stave off hostile bugging operations, and to monitor and photograph suspicious visitors.

"Oswald came into the embassy because he wanted a visa. I saw him when he went in through the main entrance."

Did he see him again?

"Yes, yes, twice, and to be sure, in the garage of the embassy. That was a sort of ramp that is no longer there today. I saw him because I was responsible, among other things, for the security of the garage. In those days, one was able to arrive on foot from the offices into the parking garage, or with the car through an underground entrance."

The garage entrance was hidden from CIA surveillance. The Agency admitted later that it wasn't until October that it set up a camera that covered the consulate gate.

"In the garage he conversed with a G2 officer, a half hour or so," Antonio explained. "On two different days. I do not know the officer's name. He wasn't stationed in the embassy, very elite. It had been said previously to us: No questions—he can go where he wants; he's an elite officer. His cover name read 'Carlos.' Nothing more was said to us."

How did they know he was an "elite" officer?

"We—that is, all the colleagues of G2 at the embassy—received previous instructions. One said to us: he has free access to all rooms. That meant he was on a secret mission. So he can move freely, and he is a man of confidence."

"What did he look like?"

Antonio shifted on the chair, head not moving much but eyes darting about.

"He was a tall, slim black with reddish hair.[44] I never saw him again after [those meetings]. They were supposed to meet there, so I had to allow Oswald access—because he was meeting the black man there. They knew each other. Both times [the conversations lasted] approximately a half hour. They took leave with a handshake. 'Carlos' went away in his vehicle and Oswald left on foot, just like he came."

Antonio was pressed as to whether the encounter between Lee and the red-haired black man could have been just a matter of chance. Was it possible that Lee was waiting for an appointment in the consulate and was killing time on the embassy grounds?

Antonio shook his head violently.

"That's impossible. Oswald had no access authorization to the garage. He simply could not have gone there. I had to let him through because it was arranged with 'Carlos.' 'Carlos' was with his car, a dark Chevrolet; he came and was already waiting for him in the garage. Oswald came after him, on foot. They welcomed each other with a handshake. They knew each other. That was clear. Of the conversation itself, I got nothing; it was held in English. When I saw Oswald's photo later in the newspaper, after the attack, I got a terrible fright; I was so near Kennedy's murderer without suspecting it!"

Why did the meeting with Oswald occur in such an unusual place as a garage?

"That I do not know. Probably, one assumes, because there were no microphones of a hostile service."

What was happening in the embassy after the shooting of Kennedy?

"There were many trips in and out, to and from Havana. The Soviet embassy stopped all contact with us for almost two weeks, even though they're only a couple of streets away from us. That was very noticeable, because there were normally many contacts between us."

What became of Silvia Durán?

"After her interrogation by the Mexican police, she no longer worked at our embassy. She never came again, but she obtained money. One of my

tasks was to serve as a courier for the G2. I had to deliver, repeatedly, envelopes with money for Silvia Durán at her mother's."[45]

Oscar Marino confirmed what Antonio said. Asked about a redheaded
black man who went by the name "Carlos" and might also have used the
nom de guerre "Ernesto," or "Ernie," he said, "Yes, he was in Mexico as a
Cuban spy . . . Based on your description, I have no doubt. He's the one . . .
In 1963, there were only two red-haired blacks in the entire G2. One of them
was in Cuba. That can't have been him. The other was actually in Mexico.
He comes from the vicinity of Santiago. His correct name is César Morales
Mesa. He was active in Mexico as a Cuban spy, sent there to work with
Mexican secret service (DFS) in counterespionage. He was the link between
DFS and us. I can confirm [that he dealt] directly with Oswald—and also
handled the strategic money for Oswald. I knew him."[46]

By the summer of 1963, as Bobby Kennedy kept pushing for a new invasion
of Cuba, he was once again losing patience with the CIA, this time on the
Vietnam front. When they wouldn't get off the dime, Jack told the Pentagon
to take on the task, and Defense Secretary Robert McNamara, who was
charming the Kennedys socially as much as he was dazzling them with his
management skills, was happy to oblige. With Bobby's approval, he hired a
marine named Victor "Brute" Krulak, an old war buddy of Jack's, to start
creating a master plan to do to Hanoi what the U.S. government had so far
failed to do to Havana.[47]

By September, however, while Lee Oswald was about to volunteer for
duty in Mexico, the North Vietnamese army was threatening to take advantage of an escalating crisis in Saigon, where Buddhist protests were swelling.[48]
Bobby Kennedy was losing faith in the repressive Diêm regime, and he took
to grilling McNamara about whether Diêm and Nhu could win the war, in
addition to managing the spiraling conflict erupting outside the windows of
the presidential palace.

It wouldn't matter by November 1. Diêm and his brother would be overthrown. Madame Nhu, stylishly stranded in Beverly Hills, would claim that the
American troubles in Vietnam had just begun—adding, with a flourish, that
"whoever has the United States as allies does not need enemies."

On Wednesday, October 2, Bobby Kennedy met with the SGA, and together
they approved nine more missions against Cuba, among them a number of
sabotage operations.[49] That was also the day that José Alemán, a Cuban exile

living in Miami and a valued source for local intelligence, informed his FBI contacts that three known Cuban G2 agents had recently shown up in Miami and then proceeded on to Texas. Alemán had a bad feeling about the three. "I advised the FBI in long conversations that I thought something was going to happen," Alemán would testify years later. "I was telling them to be careful."[50]

And on that same day, Lee Oswald paid his hotel bill and boarded a Transportes del Norte bus at 8:30 A.M., headed back to America. The bus approached the Texas border at 1:30 A.M. on October 3; but before it could cross over, Lee was taken off the transport by Mexican authorities. They thought he had exceeded his fifteen-day tourist visa. But when they realized their mistake, he was allowed to reboard. Other passengers heard him griping about "bureaucrats" as the bus proceeded.[51] The bus crossed the U.S. border at 1:35 A.M. and pulled into the Laredo terminal at 3:00 A.M. Lee transferred to a Greyhound carrier and proceeded on to Dallas, arriving at 2:20 that afternoon. Young Lee Oswald, world traveler and revolutionary without portfolio, had made his last long journey in search of fame and glory. He would find it only by returning home.

Forty-four years later, after months of conversations with Mexican investigator Mauricio Laguna Berber, Silvia Durán let down her guard, if only for a moment. During a private meeting with Mauricio in the presence of some local Communists, Silvia whispered, "There was a *complot*," a conspiracy. Durán said she would think about the possibility of revealing the truth, but it would be very dangerous. Later, when a film crew arrived with camera equipment in tow, she spoke only by phone, saying that she had been "advised" by friends not to do it.

However, as will be seen, some details of that *complot* had been divulged to senior U.S. officials decades earlier, and when those facts would be woven with revelations yet to come from the likes of Oscar Marino, the need for a cover-up by *all* parties would be abundantly clear.

CHAPTER 11
Runaway Train

A NOTHER POLITICAL STORM is about to make landfall, a collision of various high-pressure systems from the east and the south and from inside the White House itself. Despite the greatness that is in him, John Kennedy is caught in a constant dance of compulsion and deniability, and as his days are coming to an end he is on the brink of destroying his administration from within. At the same time, even as he and Bobby still plot to overthrow Fidel, they are at odds over whether to dump Vietnam's president Diêm overboard, or lash him to the mast and ride out the gale blowing in from Vietnam.

Bobby Baker, a Carolina playboy and secretary of the U.S. Senate, once "supplied" the possible East German spy, Ellen Rometsch, for the the president's pleasure, but Baker is now up to his neck in an influence-peddling scandal. As Baker's follies threaten to expose Jack, the FBI's racist chief, J. Edgar Hoover, has newfound leverage to get Bobby's approval for more wiretaps on Martin Luther King. Bobby, who approved and then disapproved it in times past, is forced to approve it once more, lest Hoover foment a political *coup* against the Kennedys.

Jack will stand for reelection in just over a year, and in the fall of 1963 Bobby is like the sorcerer's apprentice, knee-deep in a deluge and without enough buckets. He is monitoring the Cuban intrigue closely. Since the Pôrto Alegre meeting with the CIA, Rolando Cubela has been training in France as D-day for the Cuban coup approaches. From October 3 to 24, Bobby and the CCC escalate attacks on Cuban infrastructure, twenty-one sorties in all. On another southern front, Bobby is battling southern Dixiecrats over ever more chaotic civil rights issues, exacerbated by the grotesque murders of four young black girls in a September bomb blast at a church in Birmingham. He is tending to the far eastern front, Vietnam, and is in close contact with Los Amigos, especially Harry Williams and Manuel Artime, whose training camps are in high gear in Guatemala, Costa Rica, and Nicaragua, preparing the AM/TRUNK and OPLAN-380-63 phases of the new Cuban invasion.

But the secret war against the Castros is no secret to anyone at this point. The G2's Juan Felaifel is even more aware of the Kennedys' new plots against Cuba than he had been of the Bay of Pigs attack. Cuban intelligence has Cubela's number, first and foremost, and all that extends from it. Cubela's assassination of Fidel is to occur in two phases. If Fidel is killed but there is no quick coup, an uprising is to begin in the Escambray with the support of approximately a thousand mercenaries from Artime's camps, coming in through Punta Icacos and creating a government approved by the Organization of American States. Several Central American governments stand ready to lend their support.[1]

At the center of this typhoon of change sits Lee Oswald, on a sagging bed in the Dallas YMCA. He has arrived back in Texas, the last place he thought he'd ever be again, and taken a room there without even telling Marina that he has returned. In his first days there, he files for unemployment, and then applies for a job at the Padgett Printing Corporation. When Padgett turns him down, it is then that he calls his wife.

She is overjoyed that he has not gone to Cuba. When he finally hitchhikes a ride from a black man who takes him over to Fort Worth, she welcomes him with desperate love, savors his rants about Communist "bureaucrats," and lets herself believe that he has abandoned his plans to go fight for Fidel's Revolution. He pads around behind her at Ruth's house, in his childlike mode, kissing her, fawning over her and baby June, and fussing over her diet for the sake of the baby that is about to be born. They sit on the kids' swings in the backyard that evening, Lee telling her about his trip. It seems to her that once he accepted the trauma of not being allowed into Cuba, he had a good time there, going to a bullfight and taking in a few of the sights.[2]

Marina's first blush of relief and joy soon starts draining away, however. His dark eyes get darker—behind the smile is the old brooding. She tries to chalk it up to his being jobless again, failing to realize that he is actually worse off than when he left.[3] He spends weekends with his family at Ruth's, but he has taken a place on Marsalis Street in Dallas, and five nights a week he is there, alone.

In Mexico City and Havana, Castro's agents—and perhaps Fidel himself—hold their collective breath, wondering if their disturbed, newfound wunderkind will actually make the attempt on "that bastard" Kennedy. According to the new G2 sources, if he succeeded in murdering the president, he too would be murdered. The Cubans have been wise enough to minimize any links with Lee, while convincing him that he could commit the political crime of the century and get away with it. All he has to do, up to the point of exfiltration, is to proceed with his plan, as a solo act. At most, G2 will have to do little more than encourage him from the wings, in a stage whisper heard only by him.

Early in October, Agent James Hosty is visiting the Dallas Immigration and Naturalization office on another matter when his buddy behind the counter hits him broadside with a question.

"What do you think about Oswald being in touch with the Russians in Mexico City?" As a matter of routine, the CIA has notified the FBI and State Department about Oswald's visit to the Soviet embassy (though not his discussions with the Cubans).

"Whoa!" says Hosty. "That's news to me."

It is news he can do nothing about, in fact. The "third agency rule" forbids information from passing easily between investigative bodies. In fact, privacy and civil rights regulations under Title 18 U.S. Code, Section 781 prevent agencies from reporting a person to the Secret Service without a specific threat having been made against the president. It prevents pooling of information, as well. What's more, if a person has been in touch with an embassy, he can't be interviewed unless it's cleared with the agency developing this information.[4] If Hosty goes to Lee's place and pops the question of what he was doing at the Russian embassy, it will blow the massive, top-secret CIA penetration of Soviet operations in Mexico City.

But Hosty is undeterred. He has been trying to track Lee for months. He knows that the squirrelly young Communist ducked out to Louisiana the preceding summer. Then in September, the New Orleans bureau informed him that Lee had had his mail forwarded to a home in Irving, Texas, outside Dallas, the home of Ruth Paine.

There has to be some way to put this guy on notice.

In these final days, Lee is casing high-rise buildings in downtown Dallas, looking for a suitable shooting perch, while, on weekends, Ruth Paine is teaching him how to drive. That, in itself, snaps a portrait of his ambivalence.

He's kicked out of Marsalis Street and takes a room on Beckley Street under his alias, O. H. Lee. He holes up in his room there, listening to a shortwave radio, to scalding tirades on Radio Havana.[5] To his housemates, he's a sneering loner. To Ruth Paine, he's an overgrown adolescent trying hard to be a man. To a car salesman he banters with at a lot one day, he's a happy-go-lucky customer who says he's about to come into some money. To one of Ruth's neighbors, he's just a hard-luck guy who needs a job and Linnie Mae Randle has this teenage brother, Buell Frazier, who's working at the Texas School Book Depository. Maybe Buell can help him.

Ruth calls the superintendent there, puts in a good word. Lee comports himself well, telling the man that he's fresh out of the Marine Corps.[6] Ancient history, of course. If the man only knew. On October 16, Lee starts work, filling textbook orders.

Lee spends his twenty-fourth birthday, October 18, at Ruth Paine's house with his pregnant wife and child. He is sweet-tempered this evening, massaging Marina's feet, caressing her head as she dozes in front of the tube. The TV is still a luxury for them, and Lee is captivated by two movies that night.

The first one, *Suddenly*, stars Frank Sinatra as an assassin who attempts to shoot an American president from a window perch, using a rifle. In the second, *We Were Strangers*, John Garfield plays an American who aims to kill a vicious Cuban dictator and his cabinet with a bomb. The plot is thwarted and the hero dies, but the attempt sparks a revolt and fulfills its purpose, anyway. The dictator is ousted, and when Marina wakes up to a scene of ecstatic crowds cheering their liberation, Lee reminds her that that is just what happened in Cuba not so long ago. It's the first time she has heard him wax enthusiastic about Cuba since his return from Mexico.[7]

Lee hasn't told her that he received a special birthday gift that day: his visa has been miraculously approved by the Cuban foreign ministry, even without the prior receipt of a Soviet visa. The approval should have taken three months, but his visa will be waiting for him in Mexico City in a matter of days. There is no evidence that the Cubans contacted him about this, as if it was agreed during his September trip that it would be there when he next came through.[8]

Later, Marina admits to him that, although she doesn't think about Anatoly any more, she dreamt about him the night before. She teases him about how well Anatoly used to kiss her, but he asks her, with unusual grace, not to speak of "the others" anymore. He wants only to kiss her himself tonight, and they make love. It is the last time they ever will.[9]

On October 20, Ruth rushes Marina to the hospital in Fort Worth, where she gives birth to little Rachel Oswald.

On October 23, Lee writes a letter to Arnold Johnson of the Communist Party, USA, saying that he has just crashed a meeting headed by General Edwin Walker.[10] He does not mention that he had been Walker's would-be assassin six months earlier, but Lee is practicing his marksmanship once more. According to local gun aficionados, he's a regular at neighborhood rifle ranges. At one, he is seen firing at three targets in succession, simulating a moving target.

On October 25, he attends an ACLU meeting with Ruth's husband Michael,[11] perhaps still searching for what he had almost found in New Orleans—his own third way, a place between invisibility and infamy where he might yet live out his life.

In 1963, Dallas, Texas, has become to right-wing, paranoid politics what Birmingham is to racial hatred.

In Garland, just outside Dallas, someone informs the FBI that their Cuban neighbor has just put a bumper sticker on his car reading "Kill the Kennedy Klan." The wording suggests that the Ku Klux Klan produced the sticker, but hate is a big tent under which many are welcome. Coincidentally, the Cuban hater's name is Raúl Castro Baille.[12]

On October 24, United Nations Day, Adlai Stevenson, the U.S. ambassador to the UN, is roughed up and spat on by anti-Kennedy demonstrators in Dallas. Later, Adlai will be tempted to warn Jack away from Dallas, but the premium placed on courage by the Kennedy family dissuades the ambassador. Even Texas politicians, Democratic National Committeeman Byron Skelton and Governor Connally among them, are now warning the president's advisers against bringing him to Dallas, suggesting that they drop it from the itinerary. In other cities, too, plots to kill Jack are unearthed and thwarted, including a Cuban exile hit squad rumored planning to attack him in Chicago, at the Army-Navy football game.

Harry Williams, one of Los Amigos, is asked to help scotch a plot in Miami. He's given a list by the Secret Service with the names of five people from the Bay of Pigs Brigade who want to kill Jack. Harry doesn't know the guys personally, but he manages to waylay them in a motel in Key West and hold them there until Jack has left Miami.[13]

As the Vietnamese coup is ratcheting up, under the direction of General Duong Van Minh ("Big Minh"), the White House must give some hint as to where its loyalties now lie. Minh knows not to ask for overt support, just an assurance that the U.S. will not thwart the plot now coalescing against

Diêm. One contingency includes assassination. The White House expressly says it won't condone that, but in all other matters it chooses the language of misdirection.

The Unseen Hand, the White House cables instructions to its Ambassador Lodge: he is not "to give any active covert encouragement to a coup. Urgent covert effort to identify and build contacts with possible alternative leadership as and when it appears. We repeat that this is not repeat not to be aimed at active promotion of [a] coup but only at surveillance and readiness . . . This effort must be totally secure and fully deniable."[14]

Bobby, as he eventually had during the missile crisis, is trying to turn down the temperature on Diêm. At a meeting of the Vietnam group at the White House on October 30, the president is struggling to find some truth amid the flurry of teletyped cryptograms between his staff and Saigon.

Rusk is worried. ". . . If we support Diêm, then we will disrupt the war effort because we will be acting against those generals who are now fighting . . . against the Viet Cong. If we support the rebel generals, then we will have to guarantee that they are successful in overthrowing the Diêm government."[15]

Bobby is opposed to a coup at this point. He doesn't trust the competence of the usurpers, the same men who had backed out months before. Washington could be placing Vietnam and even all of Southeast Asia in the hands of a man they barely know. In earlier meetings, he even posed the question of whether they should just get out of Vietnam altogether, while they still could, but the idea has no traction now.[16]

"This risks so much. If it fails, Diêm throws us out," he warns.

Again, he's in the minority, even if McCone and Max Taylor agree with him.

Vice President Johnson concurs as well, though his influence on foreign affairs has all but dried up.

Months earlier, at an NSC meeting, Lyndon had rebuked the president for "playing cops and robbers," and demanded that he deal "straight" with Diêm and "go about winning the war."[17] He believes in limiting America to an advisory and financial role in 'Nam, no more, and this is not the first time he and Jack have tangled on Indochina.

Two years earlier, in 1961, the president had asked Johnson to go to Southeast Asia on a fact-finding mission. Lyndon, perhaps already sensing the pugnacity of the new administration, had told him point-blank that he wasn't going and that "no one else would go to Vietnam," but Jack sent him on a five-nation grand tour anyway, along with his military aide and fellow Texan Colonel Howard Burris.

Among their stops was India. The two big Texans strode into a welcoming banquet in the presidential palace in New Delhi, an exquisite room lit by five hundred candles in golden candlesticks, and were seated at the table of honor with Prime Minister Jawaharlal "Panditji" Nehru. They had not yet had their substantive talks with Panditji, but he well knew the reason for their tour and had quickly laced into Lyndon about the so-called domino theory, the fear of successive Communist takeovers across the region. Nehru insisted that Russia and China did "not want a billion more Asian mouths to feed" and were not interested in propelling a domino effect, even if Ho Chi Minh's Communist/nationalists happened to take over South Vietnam.

"If *we* are willing to risk that they won't expand across Southeast Asia, then why won't *you?*" Nehru asked Johnson. He was not the first leader on the veep's tour who had asked it.[18]

More drinks arrived.[19] There would be no more talk of Vietnam that night, but in all their subsequent discussions, Nehru kept reiterating the same point, as did other heads of state whom they met with in the region—the United States of America did not want to take on Vietnam for the sake of forestalling some wider war that would never be. Lyndon had embraced the logic of that and had forcefully delivered those opinions to the president. It had not sat well.

Sometime during this latest crisis, Bobby conveys that message to Lyndon, yet again, through Burris.

"Tell him to lay off on the Vietnam stuff," Bobby growls. "He served his purpose when he delivered Texas in '60, and that's all he was needed for."[20]

But Lyndon is right, and Bobby might be coming to realize that.

Bob's dissent on the 'Nam question marks a rare divergence of opinion between the brothers, and—given Bob's persistent and well-spoken doubts—the president is not so certain himself by nightfall. He decides to take a reactive approach, hoping to hide his presence as much as possible. Rather than give the plotters advance assurances, Jack places the onus on them to convince the U.S. that they can succeed.[21]

"If we miscalculate," Jack tells his advisers, echoing Bobby, "we could lose our entire position in Southeast Asia overnight."

Another cable is fired around the world to Lodge. The White House will not accept that it cannot control events, it says, and so it is redefining the terms yet again. Jack's appointment of the overconfident Lodge to the morass of Vietnam had shocked his staff. Lodge was competent but not gifted, by any means. For Jack, it had seemed a bit perverse, a sink-or-swim challenge placed on a longstanding Massachusetts rival whom he could send to Vietnam so he wouldn't make political mischief in the States. Some saw it as almost an Irish joke on a pompous, Protestant Brahmin, played as payback.

Now the joke is on Jack. In his reply, the ambassador dares to condescend to the president himself.

"Thanks for your sagacious instruction," his cabled reply ends. "Will carry out to the best of my ability."

A short time later, when the brothers catch a few moments alone in the Oval Office, Bobby slams Lodge.

"He sounds amused," Bob says. "I told you he was going to be trouble—"

"You know what's terrific about you," Jack shoots back, "you always remember when you're right."[22]

Neither man will accept that they're losing control of events by the hour, but they can neither discourage nor postpone what's happening. Lodge is the man on the ground, with an outsized influence on how things play out.

On October 31, Jack gives a press conference in which he opines about gradual U.S. troop withdrawals, with the hope that the Vietnamese will eventually be able to do battle against the Viet Cong on their own.[23] But late that night, just after noon on November 1 in Saigon, Big Minh clambers to his feet at a friendly officers' club luncheon with the joint general staff of the Vietnamese Army and declares that a coup is under way. MPs pour into the banquet room, secure the exits, and take aim at the lunch crowd, Minh demanding pledges of support from them all, regardless of their sympathies.[24]

It is All Saints' Day, and monstrously hot and humid. President Diêm and his brother, Nhu, are taking siestas in their rooms at Gia Long Palace, even as the rebel army is busy seizing the airport, the navy's headquarters on the Saigon River, the city's police station, and the government's radio station.[25] As the siege of the palace begins that evening, Diêm is firing frantic cables to the White House, demanding to know the U.S. position and pitifully offering eleventh-hour concessions to the Americans' demands of recent months.

The Cabinet Room has become a war room, heaped with maps and printouts of incoming cables. Jack advises Rusk to postpone recognition of the new Vietnamese government should the coup succeed, and then leaves to attend the All Saints' mass at Holy Trinity Church in Georgetown.

Diêm is now offering to surrender, begging only for safe passage out of the country for himself and his brother. The American embassy thinks it can secure a plane for that purpose, but it could take twenty-four hours. Big Minh replies, to the American military's point man, "I can't hold them that long."[26]

Early on the morning of November 2, a white flag appears from a first-floor window of the palace after a night of shelling by mortar and artillery, but Diêm and Nhu are nowhere to be found. They have fled through secret tunnels to a clubhouse of Nhu's in a suburb of Cholon. While the army's search fans out from the crumbling palace, the hunted brothers leave their hideout and take refuge in a Catholic church. They are not given the satisfaction of being martyred there. When they're captured, they're removed to an army personnel carrier.

At 9:00 A.M. in the White House, the president convenes the morning's crisis meeting. Bobby and McCone, Taylor and McNamara, Rusk and Averell Harriman all wait at the ready, but just as they're beginning, Michael Forrestal enters, a cable in hand, from Lodge: Diêm and Nhu are dead, either murdered or suicides.

The president reads it, his face going slack. He lurches to his feet and leaves the room, ashen and distraught. No one has ever seen him lose himself that way, not even Bobby. Someone picks up the cable and speaks the words, all eyes still on the door.

"What did he expect?" Taylor mutters.

It will be as it was with Lumumba's murder just after Jack assumed the presidency, a sickening blow, a thing one doesn't get used to, a thing one must not get used to, but a thing that happens.

In another barrage of cables, the new regime upholds the suicide claim, but Jack, who knows what a devout Catholic Diêm was, will not believe it. Suicide was not an option for a believer like Diêm; Jack is right. The bodies were "discovered" with bullets lodged in the back of their heads, and multiple bayonet wounds. They might have been saved, Jack learns. The Americans might have gotten them out had the brothers not lost themselves in the maze of Cholon, or had the U.S. embassy been able to summon a plane, or had Diêm himself been another kind of man.

There are official words of condolence and honor for Diêm's efforts to serve, but Madam Nhu snarls, from what is now her exile, that it is Kennedy's fault and that from then on, Vietnam will soon be a nightmare for America, on a monstrous scale. The United States has just taken over a country and become its sole protector, as if by accident.

On Saturday evening, November 2, with just twenty days left to live, John Kennedy is carried out of Washington by helicopter to the family's new home on nearby Rattlesnake Mountain. He needs the solace of an evening with the kids and Jackie; but at dinner an old friend, Mary Gimbel, breaks the gaiety with talk of the week's events, pronouncing judgment on Diêm and Nhu.

"They were just tyrants," she says.

"No," Jack says, gazing off, "they were in a difficult position. They did the best they could for their country."[27]

In the Sunday papers, alongside the news photos of Diêm and Nhu's mutilated corpses are the pictures of the new regime, a puppet dictatorship reliant on the White House to determine its every move. The deposed leaders are buried in unmarked plots in a graveyard adjacent to Lodge's ambassadorial residence in Saigon. For all the American attempts to float above the fray and delay quick recognition of their new dependents, the bodies of Diêm and Nhu are effectively dumped at their feet, for all the world to see.

On the same day that Ngo Dinh Diêm is overtaken by his military, FBI agent Jim Hosty decides to pay a visit to Marina Oswald at Ruth Paine's house in Irving, Texas. It's a deliberate scheme—made against regulations—to gather information on Lee without seeing him directly.

At the Paine home, all the kids are down for their naps and Marina is primping, since Lee will be there in a few hours. Ruth is puttering when Hosty knocks. Ever gracious, and well aware of Lee's history, Ruth is neither surprised nor intimidated to find a Fed at her door. She lets him in, and the two banter a bit before he eases into the subject of Lee.

No, says Ruth, he's not living with them. No, she's not sure where in Dallas he's residing right now, maybe Oak Cliff. She balks when Hosty asks her where he's working. Lee has claimed to have lost a few jobs because of FBI men butting into his work life, but Hosty repeats the company line: they don't compromise people with their employers. Reassured, Ruth tells him that he's working at the job she helped find for him, through friends, at the Texas School Book Depository.

Jim Hosty, a stocky, handsome, dark-haired man with an easy manner and fastidious habits, is hardly an imposing presence, much less a threatening one. Nonetheless, Marina's afraid of him at first, even repulsed, associating police of all sorts with the KGB and knowing that Lee fears them too. But with Ruth translating, Hosty woos her, establishing such a rapport that he feels secure in venturing into the realm of secrets—if KGB agents try to recruit her by using threats against her or her family, he tells her, then she should come to the FBI. Hosty will protect her.

He takes it one step further, into Lee's Cuban shenanigans. Marina, a socialist bred in the bone, quibbles with him over U.S. press reports that Fidel is a threat. She thinks they're exaggerated. When Hosty tells her he knows about Lee's activist period for the FPCC in New Orleans, she brushes it off. "Oh, don't worry about *him*," she says. "He's just young. He doesn't know what he's doing. He won't do anything like that *here*."[28]

The next day, at the FBI field office in Dallas, a man hand-delivers an unsigned note for Hosty, who is out of the office. To the best of Hosty's recollection, years later, it reads: "If you have anything you want to learn about me, come talk to me directly. If you don't cease bothering my wife, I will take appropriate action and report this to the proper authorities."[29] Hosty assumed one of his "right-wing nuts" had written it.

Early that month, behind the Spanish arches and porticoes of the G2 building in Havana, Antulio Ramírez Ortiz is talking, in passing, with an agent he knows only as "Martín."

In the minds of most of the agents at headquarters, there is no question that the Kennedys have not yet relented in their pursuit of Fidel and Raúl. Look what they just did to Diêm! And he was one of their anti-Communist compadres! Antulio, ever the eager mascot devouring news from the front, bugs Martín for more details of the presumed next invasion from the Kennedys. Martín casts the possibility aside. It's going to end before it begins, he says, with utter certitude.

But how? Antulio thinks it's one thing to repeat the success they had at Bahia de Cochinos, but this invasion could only be larger and it will be quite another thing to nip it in the bud. How?

"We're going to knock them out in a matter of seconds," Martín insists, ". . . by eliminating their own president. The donkey Kennedy."

Antulio rears back, an incredulous smirk on his face, but Martin stares at him, tough, cold, certain.

"Do you want to make a bet? During this month of November."

By the way he says it, Antulio can tell that Martín is not joking, that some plan is afoot, one more adept than any that has gone before. The older man turns sharply and strides down the hall before the mascot can find out more.[30]

In early November, Lee writes a letter to the Soviet embassy in Washington, informing them of the details of his Mexican trip. He notes that he could only stay in Mexico for fifteen days because of his visa restrictions. "I could not take a chance on requesting a new visa unless I used my real name," Oswald writes, "so I retured [*sic*] to the United States." He adds cryptically, "Had I been able to reach the Soviet Embassy in Havana as planned, the embassy there would have had time to complete our business." What the "business" was can only be guessed. He also makes reference to the departure of Azcue as consul, which he could not have known of unless he was in some sort of interim contact with the Cuban embassy.

On November 6, Lee the bibliophile checked out a critique of the Kennedys' Latin American policy from his local library. *The Shark and the Sardines*, by Juan José Arévalo, was translated by none other than June Cobb.

Sometime about 10:00 on Saturday night, November 16, at the Alright Parking Garage in downtown Dallas, a pale, nervous man startles Hubert Morrow, the night manager, suddenly sauntering into the lot. This garage is adjacent to FBI headquarters, but here is Lee Oswald with a parcel under his arm. It's completely wrapped up, but Morrow thinks, even then, that it looks a lot like a gun muzzle.

Lee wants to know if he could see Main Street from the top of the roof.

"You probably can, but you're not allowed up on that roof."

Lee asks him about the president's motorcade, whether it will be going down Elm Street or Main. Morrow thinks it's supposed to go down Main.

Can you see Main from the roof? Lee asks it, straight out.

You could, yes.

Lee wanders off, figuring that Morrow's not going to let him up there.[31]

He's living out in Oak Cliff, but he has come to know downtown Dallas well in recent weeks; which nightclubs have the best shows; what buildings have which sight lines. He has the job at the depository, but he has applied for various other ones in the area, including one as a bellhop at the famous Adolphus Hotel on Commerce Street.[32] They don't hire him, but by mid-November he's becoming one of the nighttime regulars of the neighborhood.

Within a few days of his first encounter at the Alright, he goes back. This time he talks to Mrs. Viola Sapp, a cashier at the garage.

"Hello," he says to her, "my name is Mr. Oswald. I'm new in town and I'd like to see about a job here."

"Have you had any experience [as a garage attendant]?"

"No," he admits.

"I'm sorry, we're full up. However," says Viola, "we have some openings at our other garages if you're interested."

"No, I've been walking around here at night, and I really love this building and location. I like how all the floors are open to the street and you can see the people on the street below. Tell me, does the top floor have a roof?"

Viola is feeling something strange wafting off this man. He's shining her on, maybe.

"No," she replies.

"Do you think I could go up? I just love Dallas, and I'd like to see the sights—"

"Absolutely not," she tells him. "No one is allowed up there."

"But I sure would like to—"

"No!"[33]

He says nothing more: just puts on an understanding little smile, then strolls away with a nonchalance that seems practiced.

On Wednesday, November 20, Antulio and the G2 agent he knows as Martin are having lunch in the dining room of Havana's Hotel Saratoga when Martin shows him a postcard sent from the town of Los Palacios, and signed by a "C. J. Fortes." Antulio, trusted gofer that he is, knows the real names and war names of many agents, only the war names of some others. In this case, he knows that C. J. Fortes is actually Juan Valverde, aka Captain Carlos Enríquez Valverde Rodríguez. It bears Martin's address at the embassy.

"Well, fancy that," says Antulio, looking at the little scene of entertainers on a beach, "Captain Juanito is out for some fun with the mariachis and the local girls." He glances at the date. "How did you get hold of the postcard so quickly?"

Martin takes the card back with a serious look.

"It came from the diplomatic pouch. And he isn't looking to have a good time—he's there on official business." Martin leans in. He's not trying to impress Antulio. He's impressed himself by what he's going to tell him. "His mission is connected to what I told you about before."

Antulio remembers. He has been thinking about this scenario since Martin mentioned it at G2 headquarters.

"The attempt to assassinate Kennedy? But that's ridiculous." Antulio, the young man brazen enough to be the first in history to hijack an American commercial jet, is neither shy about his opinions nor terribly impressed by his hierarchies, even inside G2. Martin's about to contradict him, but Antulio hurtles along. "You don't have the slightest chance of succeeding.

Besides, the risks for Cuba would be too great; it would be counterproductive in every respect. Impossible . . . *Suicidal*—"

"And that is exactly why it will work. No one will believe it. There is a crazy Johnny [American] who claims he is willing to do it . . . *if* he is promised safe refuge and money when he gets to Mexico afterward. We only made promises [to the killer], and words . . . float away in the wind. We only promise."

(That same usage—Martin's allusion to words disappearing in the wind, and the prediction that it would succeed because no one would believe it—would, as will be seen, be echoed almost exactly by Oscar Marino in Mexico forty years later.)

Antulio is silent now, rapt. Again, Martin's eyes say that this is absolutely real, and the younger man recalls that it has been set for that month.

"Whether he does it or not—that is his affair. And there is nothing on record. We only promised that—"

"Why? What were your motives?" Antulio presses. It still seems a bit *loco* to shoot so high, but then again, Raúl and Fidel are nothing if not a bit *loco*.

Martin replies with alarming simplicity. "Revenge!" he says, as if talking to a fool. "How many assassination attempts on Fidel Castro has this guy approved already? Answer me that!"

Antulio remains dubious. There may even be the slightest part of him that doesn't want to see Kennedy killed.

"As far as I know, it's the CIA that plans and orders such operations—"

"It's the same thing! Kennedy authorized these thugs. Who issued the orders for the massacre in the Bay of Pigs?! How many Cubans were murdered on our own beaches? What do you think? Including women and children, army and police officers . . . When such an opportunity offers itself, then someone is going to pay. Understood?!"

It seemed that the fix was in.

"And you think that this opportunity came knocking in Mexico?" he asked, to be sure he was getting it all.

"It didn't just '*come knocking*,'" Martin fumed, "*it smashed its way inside and disappeared through the door again!*"

Just a few days later, while the Cubans' "crazy Johnny" is being held at the Dallas police headquarters, Martin will order Antulio to never, under any circumstances, bring up the subject again.[34]

Twelve years after that, while Antulio Ramírez Ortiz is serving time in a U.S. prison for the 1961 airline hijacking, the CIA will assess his memoir,

Castro's Red Hot Hell, in which he not only describes the Oswald/Kennedy file that he saw in 1962, but the "war names" of the G2 agents he worked with at their headquarters on Havana's Fifth Avenue. The Agency's summary reads, in part: "Much of the information in his manuscript concerning his background and activities has been confirmed by data in his [CIA] file . . . There is no indication that Ramirez is a fabricator." A memo from the 1978 House Select Committee on Assassinations (HSCA) added, "The significance of this [knowledge of war names] is that agents never allow outsiders to know their war names, and knowledge of these names indicates some degree of access." The Agency checked out many dozens of assertions in the manuscript, verified many, and found no errors of fact, although some points were impossible to vet. Despite the foregoing, the HSCA, which showed relatively little interest in the Cuban allegations, dismissed the Ramírez story as "incredible."

It should also be noted that in Ramírez's 564-page memoir/manuscript, the scattered mentions of Oswald, when added together, amount to less than three pages, indicating that the author was not trying to capitalize on what was obviously a microscopic part of his overall experience.

The CIA will also show Antulio fifteen uncaptioned mug shots of known G2 agents, only six of them showing men known to the CIA as Martin. He will identify the specific man he knew as Martin, as his G2 contact/source. The CIA knows that his full name was Martin González Hernández.

In 1968, Ramírez was arrested in Cuba, on false charges of spying for the U.S. After his release in 1972, he was caught trying to escape Cuba and sentenced to three more years in prison. In 1975, Antulio Ramírez Ortiz would be allowed to defect to the U.S., where he served ten years in prison for the 1961 hijacking, living out the remainder of his life in the U.S.

That afternoon, Ethel Kennedy is bustling around helping Bobby's secretary, Angie Novello, pull together a surprise party at the Justice Department for Bobby's thirty-eighth birthday.

It's a busy day for Bobby. The day before, November 19, Cuban exile leader Tony Varona, attending the Cuban Officer Training Program at Fort Holabird, Maryland, got a call from fellow RFK confidant Erneido Oliva summoning him straight to Washington for a special secret meeting with the attorney general.[35]

Bobby probably speaks with Des FitzGerald on the nineteenth or twentieth as well. Des reports that AM/TRUNK infiltrators in Cuba have been told to monitor coded messages on Voice of America broadcasts that will "inspire the rebel army to unite and rise [up] in a coup against Fidel." Embedded in the texts are "two major guarantees from the US government."[36] With Des's help, monies are moved around from various federal pots to keep Williams's and Artime's troops fed and clothed and primed, while Bobby keeps close tabs on the head of the ouster, Cubela, and the preparations of his AM/LASH plot going on in Paris.

Late in Bobby's workday, Ethel barrels in and pulls him away from the desk. Corks are popped. Seals on scotch bottles are broken. Somebody tosses a handful of confetti. Bobby's in a mordant mood, and while his staff pours and parties around him, he steps up onto a chair and makes a lacerating, self-mocking speech about all the administration's great accomplishments and what a towering asset he will be to the president's reelection bid in the coming year. He cites the disastrous results of their civil rights policies, their unsuccessful pursuit of Jimmy Hoffa, and the invasive application of wiretaps in the pursuit of justice. Kennedy kids careen through the crowd. The family's massive dog, Brumus, barks and slobbers. Bobby's staffers laugh and tipple and toast him, but when John Douglas and Ramsey Clark leave the festivities, they can't help but be concerned about the depth of his melancholy.[37] He looks too lean, almost stringy, and chronically fatigued. His wife and doctor have been advising ways to help him keep the weight on, but no one can keep the pressure off, Jack least of all. Up at the White House, the president often tells people that he wishes he had two Bobbys, but he knows too well that the one he's got is way overdrawn.

Somebody takes a jangling phone off the hook, but shoptalk seeps back into all attempts at jollier conversation. When that party finally breaks up, he and Ethel have to go get ready for another one that night.

That evening of November 20, within an hour of Bobby and Ethel's arrival at the annual White House reception for the judiciary, Lee Oswald is home from work and stuffed away in his airless little space in the rooming house at 1026 Beckley Street, just off the living room. A few of the other tenants are waiting for the evening news to come on TV, Hugh Slough among them. They rarely see the man they know as "Mr. Lee." It's a little peculiar, but after a month or so they don't think that much of it anymore.

Jerry Duncan, who works at the service station across the street, has come over to say hi to Hugh. Jerry has met "Mr. Lee," he says, and he'll introduce him to Hugh if and when he ever comes out of his hole.

The news comes on. The top story, of course, is the presidential visit in two days. The anchorman says he's about to announce the exact motorcade route so that folks can see their president, live and in person, and enjoy the festivities; and in that split second, Mr. Lee comes busting out of his bedroom, his eyes riveted on the TV screen. Jerry's trying to introduce Hugh to him, trying to get his attention, but Lee is glued. They're showing all the exact turns that the parade will take.

The president and First Lady will land at Love Field shortly before noon, their motorcade taking them to Main Street; from there they'll turn onto Houston, then to Elm Street, and onto the Stemmons Freeway for the final leg to the Dallas Trade Mart. There he will make a speech on international relations.

Jerry tries again to jump-start a little side conversation so he can introduce his pal Hugh to the guy. After all, they do live in the same household together. But the story is over in less than five minutes, and before Jerry can get a word in, Lee turns on a dime, goes back to his room, and shuts the door.

It's the only time Hugh ever sees Lee "live and in person." The next time he sees him, Lee will be *on* the TV, and Slough's and Duncan's names will be footnotes to history.[38]

The White House reception is packed that evening. The judiciary soiree has traditionally been reserved for judges and their spouses and the top dogs at Justice, but Bobby has thrown the doors open wider, inviting the whole Justice Department family, secretaries, elevator men, phone operators, clerks, all of whom are thrilled to actually be inside the Executive Mansion after so many years of government service.

The First Couple stay for most of the reception, but they take a break upstairs in the family quarters before it ends, Bobby wandering up there too, a short time later, and settling in for a chat with Jackie. Though she has never been a gung-ho political wife, she is almost fully recovered from baby Patrick's death and is actually looking forward to some time on the road with Jack.

The president joins them. In a way, he says, the current feuds between the Texas pols will make the trip that much more engaging, what with all the fur flying between populist Democrats like Ralph Yarborough and the oil Dems of Governor Connally's faction. Jack likes both Yarborough and Connally, and he seems optimistic that, between fund-raisers, he'll be able to forge a peace. It won't be due to any special effort on Lyndon's part, however. Jack's peeved at his vice president, calling him a son-of-a-bitch for not working harder for the campaign in his own state.[39]

The relationship has never been particularly easygoing. The smooth, cosmopolitan Jack and the crude, backslappin' Lyndon have shown a certain wily respect for each other's skills, both political and otherwise. It has even been said that they both make use of the same secure suite in a hotel near the White House, one trysting there when the other one isn't, and they've even haggled over its availability from time to time,[40] but the brothers, particularly Bobby, have never treated Lyndon all that well. There are rumors around town that they plan to dump him from the ticket in '64, given Lyndon's ties to the besieged Bobby Baker and other issues, but others have denied the idea. The Kennedys need to keep Texas in their column, and it will be easier to keep the Senate Rules Committee's corruption investigation off Lyndon's hide if he's still in the vice president's mansion.

The weightier and more acute problems between them may lie in the wake of the Diêm matter. Two nights hence, after the Dallas appearance, Lyndon plans to host the Kennedys overnight at his ranch in Johnson City, Texas, and there he intends to confront Jack on the "adventurism" of Cuba and Vietnam. He has never liked the Kennedys' counterinsurgency game, and he will once again tell Jack that he should poll the Asian leaders he sent Lyndon to speak with in 1961; see what *they* think about this Vietnam escapade.[41] According to one of Johnson's closest friends, he will take his dissatisfaction one step further—he will inform the president that he is removing himself from the 1964 ticket.[42]

But on that Wednesday evening, the brothers don't dwell much longer on Lyndon. Ethel comes up from the reception and reminds Bobby that there's one more party for him that night, at home with the kids at Hickory Hill. The four are in a teasing mood, enjoying each other's company for another few minutes, Jack and Jackie unusually affectionate, Bobby savoring a moment's peace with his wife. Finally, though, Jackie steadies herself on Jack's arm and slips into her high heels again, as if to make one more appearance downstairs. Jack kisses Ethel on the cheek. Jackie takes Bobby's hand and squeezes it, one of the little signals of her long appreciation. A moment that might otherwise have been unmemorable in the full spectrum of Robert Kennedy's life is about to become unforgettable.

The next day, Thursday, November 21, advance man Marty Underwood is worrying even more than is his habit. While scouting the Texas trip two weeks earlier, he was alarmed by the local hostility toward President Kennedy. In fact, it had been so palpable that he had even called Washington to make sure the Secret Service would be bringing the limousine's protective "bubble top" along on the coming trip. The president would probably refuse to use it, but some of his White House staffers wanted to have it just in case.

Once they're down there, John Connally, the Texas governor, recommends using it. Jackie's also inclined to put it on, but Jack tells Marty, "This is Jackie's first trip [to Texas], and the people love her, and I'm going to keep it down." Presidential assistant Bill Moyers, a Texan who knows the political stakes here, tells the Dallas protective services people to "get that goddamned bubble top off unless it's pouring rain."

This president does not make Marty Underwood's job easy. Intensely conscious of political theater, he's the one who wanted a motorcade through Dallas, even when the local Democrats tried to nix it. He has come to Texas to mend fences, and how is he supposed to do that if he is kept under glass like a pheasant and surrounded by men with guns? He says no to Secret Service men hugging the running boards, no to motorcycles rumbling alongside the limo. The people need to be able to see their leader and his wife; that's why his staff has insisted on publishing the motorcade route in the newspapers.

There have been some twenty-five thousand threats to Jack since he took office. When Marty's CIA buddy Win Scott heard about the Texas trip, he cautioned him that any presidential visit along the U.S./Mexican border makes a tantalizing target for Cuban agents, and that they can cross that border at will.[45]

From Marty's perspective, it's good to have the First Lady on the trip. She seems to have some new influence over Kennedy since the death of the baby. Jack had never been a particularly sensitive man, especially in public, but Marty has heard that Patrick's death has really changed him, and he has noticed an unprecedented flow of affection between Jack and Jackie. At the San Antonio stop, during the dedication of the Air Force School of Aerospace Medicine, the president asks a scientist if their work there might improve oxygen chambers for premature infants.

"They were all over each other . . . crazy about each other," Marty will put it in 2003. The advance man had seen the president's extramarital antics firsthand. He knew how cavalier Jack was about fidelity, and Marty will go one step further: "It was the first time Kennedy knew love."

In any case, in the fall of 1963, Jackie has signed on to go anywhere Jack goes that year, and he's going to great lengths to please her.

San Antonio is more liberal than the rest of Texas, and the city's Latin poor have caught the same spirit that the Alliance for Progress has inspired south of the border. They are bursting with Catholic pride and affection, an exuberance that turns into something beyond Marty's expectations, or the president's. At one rope line, Jackie feels a scary surge of energy moving toward them at one point, the sum total of a kind of glad delirium, but she and Jack emerge from the crowds unscathed and exhilarated.

Before they reboard the plane, however, Colonel John "Jack" Frost, the NSA's deputy chief of staff assigned to the Air Force Security Agency, also meets with Kennedy on this leg of the journey. Frost is stationed at Lackland Air Force Base in San Antonio, and has been monitoring the situation in advance of Jack's trip.

"Mr. President, NSA has collected over a thousand threats in recent weeks," says Frost, "mostly right-wing types. But we think you should be safe and put the bubble top up tomorrow."

Surprisingly, Jack doesn't say anything for a moment, appearing to actually consider the question for a change. But then Jackie jumps into the rare silence surrounding the president.

"We'll do no such thing," she said. "We'll show these Texas sons-of-bitches they can't scare us."[44]

The reception at the Houston airport is a little more sedate than in San Antonio, but by the time Jackie is addressing a ballroom of Hispanic citizens in the Rice Hotel's ballroom late that afternoon, deploying her loveliest Spanish, she is beating Jack at his own game. The crowd goes wild.

"What did you say?" he asks her afterward.

"I'll never tell you," she teases him.

Later that night, as Marty dines with them in the hotel room, Jack congratulates him on another tremendous piece of advance work.

"It wasn't because of me," says Marty, "it's because Mrs. Kennedy was there."

"Great," Jack quips, "I'll never live this down."

The First Couple is so flirtatious with each other that Marty makes himself scarce for a while until it's time to get back to the airport for the evening jump from Houston to Fort Worth. At the airport, before boarding the plane, Jack wants to wade into the crowds once more, in tight close-up, but Marty has heard of more threats. He tells the president that he's worried about the next day and, by implication, the moment at hand, but Jack ignores him and, against every effort of his Secret Service guys, he charges into the dark to work the line, going hand over hand into the waiting crowd.

It's pandemonium, but they wrangle him back to Air Force One; when he's at the top of the jet-stairs, he turns back and grins, waves, and says to whoever's listening, "Where's Marty? . . . Marty worries too much . . ."[45]

Also on the night of November 21, Jack Ruby, the owner of the Carousel Club, a Dallas strip joint and cop hangout, goes onstage to demonstrate the new invention that's going to make him rich. Jack is always coming up with ways to get rich. He's had five previous nightclubs—the Singapore, the Silver Spur, Bob Wills' Ranch House, the Vegas Club, and the Sovereign—and all of them were supposed to have made him rich. None of them did. In fact, more than one of them has gone bankrupt, but Jack keeps trying.

His beginnings stacked the deck against success. He grew up an Orthodox Jew in Chicago with a father who was so brutal that his mother divorced him, taking young Jack and his sister, Eva, away when Jack was ten.

Now he and Eva are partners in these "show-bars." They're not exactly getting rich on this latest venture, but Jack's happy: he's a creature of the night, and he loves law-enforcement people and they love him, or at least they patronize his place because they know Jack Ruby will treat them right. He loves the law, loves law*makers*. He especially loves U.S. presidents, a fascination that began with Pearl Harbor. He has sold busts of Franklin Roosevelt for a living. He punched a guy out on Roosevelt's behalf once, and even took a whack at a guy for insulting Eisenhower.[46]

He really likes Kennedy, too. He certainly loves his family, that beautiful wife, those beautiful kids. They're so young and fresh and bright that it even inspired Jack to try to get into physical fitness, all that stuff that JFK got the country on about. Ruby has decided that his resident comedian and master of ceremonies, Wally Weston, is going to be the first guy in Dallas to get in shape the Kennedy way. Jack bounces into Wally's apartment and wakes him up one day, tells him to get dressed, and then drives him fifty miles out of town, whereupon he shares his publicity brainstorm with Wally, and then tells him to get out of the car. He'll see him back at the club. Wally does his act with his feet in a bucket of ice that evening.[47]

Jack Ruby loves the Kennedys. Eva would say so later: "One of things [her brother] loved about this president, he didn't care what you were, you were a human being and Jack [Ruby] felt that this was one time in history that Jews are getting the break. He [Kennedy] put great Jewish men in office."[48]

He loves his religion, and his sister, and his hometown. He's a patriot, a law-abiding citizen. That does not mean, however, that Jack Ruby will not take whacks at people when they cross him. Usually they're creating some sort of disturbance in his club. His cop friends know that when there's a radio call about trouble at the Carousel, all they've got to do is go over there and stand at the bottom of the stairs and wait for the offending party to roll down to them and out the door. Slap the cuffs on him, he's gone. Jack Ruby is his own bouncer.[49]

He carries a gun, too. He has to carry a lot of money around late nights on the weekends, sometimes two or three thousand dollars. He would have bought a safe but it was too expensive, so his friend Joe Cody, a Dallas cop, suggests he get a gun instead. A lot cheaper. So they go to Ray Brantly's hardware store and Jack, who's a bit at a loss with guns, asks Cody what to do. Cody says buy the Colt Cobra there. Jack buys the Colt Cobra, and that's that.

So Jack, at any given moment, is packing heat just as a business necessity.

And he has had some dust-ups about President Kennedy, too, not just FDR and Ike. Jack Ruby is as anti-Communist as the next guy, probably more so, but one night some acquaintance of his comes in and he's got this hate literature, all this right-wing stuff, and Jack just snatches it out of the guy's hands and says, "I'm going to send this stuff to Kennedy! Nobody has the right to talk like this about our government."[50] Jack confiscates it and shoves it in a trunk of his somewhere. Some investigator finds it after history gets made, and thinks that *Jack Ruby* is the right-wing nut. Crazy.

He's even had to set Wally Weston straight on Kennedy, too, now and then. Even Wally buys into this stuff from time to time.

On Thursday night, November 21, Ruby bounds on stage with his "twist board," his new invention that emulates the latest dance craze and also takes the weight off. At least that's the idea. Jack's demonstrating how it works. He's up there in his gassed-back hair and his Aqua Velva and his pinkie ring and his suit and tie, ever immaculate, and he's just twisting away.

And he says, "Even President Kennedy tells us to get more exercise."

And some heckler yells out, "That bum!"

And Jack Ruby is off the stage. He comes flying down into the crowd and he is in this guy's face.

"Don't *ever* talk that way about the president!" he screams.[51]

Sometime earlier that day, the twenty-first, Lee Oswald comes to a decision. Motive, means, and opportunity have appeared before him in a near-perfect triangulation. There is a kind of precision to it all now; he just enacts the role he has created. But his means, his rifle, is tucked away behind Ruth's house. She has had it in her possession since Lee packed up her car with their possessions and she took Marina and Junie out of New Orleans. For the triangulation to be perfect, he has to go over to Ruth's.

He goes to find Buell Frazier, the kid who helped Lee get this job, and asks if he can get a ride back to Irving with him that night. He's got to pick up some curtain rods in Ruth's garage, he explains, and he'll stay the night out there, maybe. He usually just goes out on weekends, never on a Thursday, so it will be a surprise for Marina and Junie and Rachel.

Buell says, sure, why not. He's used to driving Lee when he needs a lift, since his home is just a few doors down from Ruth's. Some suspect that he's been driving Lee to the shooting range now and then. So after work, they get in Buell's old black Ford hardtop and head out there, the sun lying low, the daylight dwindling down to embers, neither man saying much.

Buell parks the car in his driveway and agrees to wait there for Lee the next morning and give him a lift back to work. Lee heads up the walkway toward the house where his wife and two young daughters, one just weeks old, are staying. He is not a religious man, and yet it's as if he's a supplicant tonight, as if he is there to ask Marina or God or someone to let this cup pass from him. Lee has arrived at the end of his life still seeking a sign that he is loved well and truly enough by someone that no one else's attention or adoration matters. The one adult person in the world who has some meager power to reach into him and warm his heart and stay his trigger hand, even for just a moment, is Marina Prusakova Oswald.

But she's angry at him this evening. She didn't expect him, and now here he is. She can't even bring herself to go out and greet him, and when he finds her in the bedroom, he can tell that she's mad, but not that the anger masks a deep fear. He goes over to the bassinet to gaze on his new baby, and then he tries to kiss Marina. She turns away, folds the laundry. She has found out that he's using one of his aliases again, this time at the rooming house in Oak Cliff. He has too many names.

The night is one of missed cues, false starts, those small but awful domestic disconnections. The vengeful coquette, tired of the husband's erratic behavior, his secrecy, his rages, his sexual stinginess, his lies, makes him doubt himself all night. He asks her to move into a better place in Dallas with him. He is asking for another chance.

Ruth comes in with groceries and interrupts them, telling them that the next day "Our president is coming to town."

"Ah, yes," Lee says, putting on that air of worldliness, as if he has considered this fact already from every conceivable and disinterested point of view.

He's helping Marina fold diapers when she says, "Lee, Kennedy is coming tomorrow. I'd like to see him in person. Do you know where and when I could go?'

"No," he says. There's the slightest moment of hesitation. How would he not know that?

And how could he do the deed if she were there watching?

As the twilight fills the rooms with a last rosy sheen, Lee goes out and puts Junie on his shoulders, and the two of them try to pluck a butterfly from the air. When it won't be caught, he tries to capture falling oak wings for her, father and daughter lurching together, their four hands grasping at the dusk as the little pods spin out of reach.

He tells Marina he has warned the FBI to stay away from her. She doubts it, calls him "a brave rabbit." Her anger about the alias has faded, but the unease has not. It always seems to portend something scary.

Three times he asks her to come into Dallas with him. "I'll get us an apartment and we'll all live peacefully at home," he declares. Marina nurses the newborn. Lee puts Junie to bed, cradles Rachel in his arms while they watch a war movie until the baby falls asleep. Three times she refuses to try again with him in Dallas. For once, she is in a position of control, a position from which she might get him to stop his nonsense and really come home to her, without bringing such nightmares with him. Three times he tries to kiss her, and each time she refuses.

"I was like a stubborn little mule," she'll recall when he's dead. "I was maintaining my inaccessibility, trying to show Lee that I wasn't easy to persuade. If he had come again the next day and asked, of course I would have agreed. I just wanted to hold out one day at least."[52]

She can tell he's sad. She cannot know what conclusions he has drawn. He is barely twelve hours away from changing the world. Something in the banal frustration of the evening threads a thousand other nights together, a thousand nights that ended with the same tentative conclusion—that he was great but would never get his due, that he was lovable but would never quite be loved, that he must destroy what cannot be reformed and start from scratch.

November 22 dawns blue on the Kremlin in Moscow, the candy-colored onion domes of St. Basil's Cathedral and the stout brick walls of Spasskaya Tower throwing shadows across Red Square. Bundled and befurred bureaucrats march into the white and gilt office buildings of the government, and inside one of them, down one of those halls, is the office that processes visa and citizenship applications.

The apparatchiks there have been discussing a most bizarre series of application letters that have been funneling to them through the Soviet embassy in Washington; letters from the odd, mousy defector Lee Harvey Oswald and his wife, Marina, the niece of the MVD officer in Minsk, Ilya Prusakov. There has been a good deal of internal discussion about these people. Each letter smells of something fishy. First, she wants to return with her two children. Then they all want to come. Then perhaps he will and perhaps he won't. The KGB men certainly have received word from their colleagues Kostikov and Nechiporenko that Oswald has been knocking on embassy doors in Mexico City.

On this day, the chief of the KGB's department of foreign intelligence composes the letter to them that will—without explanation—make it official: Oswald is not to return.[53] Perhaps he has heard that the Cubans have allowed him to visit there, but neither he nor his wife will be allowed back inside the USSR. She may yet prove valuable there in the States. He has no value anywhere, at least not to the Russians.

Marina sleeps fitfully. At one point she opens her eyes and sees that he is awake, staring at the ceiling. She rolls close to him, lets her foot touch his, but he kicks her away violently. She rolls back, eyes fixed on the darkness herself until she's able to doze off for a little more rest.

As he lies there, the battle must be raging. He's a poor man thinking about a rich man, or a plain man thinking about a handsome man, or an everyman thinking about the most famous man in the world, the better to purge himself and cleanse and start anew. He is thinking about a simple masterpiece of nihilism: a kill in the name of class warfare; or in the name of his poor white masculine dignity; or in the name of all his unfinished books and unpublished manifestos; or perhaps only in the name of his loveless heart, and his locked and screaming mind. It exhausts him, but eventually he makes his choice and falls asleep.

When the alarm clock rings a while later, he doesn't turn it off. He's usually awake in time to do so before it rouses the babies, but this morning he sleeps through it. She pokes the button and lies there a while, reaching for the tail of a dream.

She drifts for ten more minutes, then tells him it's time to get up.

"Okay," he whispers from the fog.

He gropes his way to the bathroom in the half-light, cleans himself, and then comes back to the bedside.

Tenderly, he asks if she has purchased some shoes she was going to get.

She hasn't had time yet. "You must get those shoes, Mama. And, Mama, don't get up," he says. "I'll get breakfast myself." He kisses the sleeping children but not his wife, as he usually does.

"I've left some money on the bureau. Take it and buy everything you and Junie and Rachel need. Bye-bye," he says, tiptoeing out the door. He has left her $170, and in a small dish on the dresser he has left his wedding ring.[54]

In Washington, Bobby is scheduled to sit down with some of his most closely held Amigos that day, Manuel Artime, Roberto San Roman, and Harry Williams. But the exiles meet first without him, in a safe house in northwest Washington with the Agency's Richard Helms, Howard Hunt, and a few other agents. Harry Williams will later recall it as "the most important meeting I have ever had on the problem of Cuba." Afterward, the Amigos are ebullient. Plans for Harry's group to launch their attack from the Dominican Republic are beginning to jell. Artime seems ready to roll out of Central America, and he and Williams are planning a unified front on a third flank.[55]

If Marty Underwood had been a superstitious man, he might have paused when Secret Service agent Ron Pontius handed him the Saint Jude and Saint Christopher medals the president had left on the showerhead in his suite in Fort Worth's Hotel Texas. And if he had seen the right-wing attack ad that ran in the *Dallas Morning News* that morning, he would probably have insisted on putting the bubble top on, himself.

The ad's wide black border alone would have chilled him. A group from the John Birch Society had paid to excoriate the president in print, accusing him of everything from contributing to the Communist slavery of Cuba, to scrapping the Monroe Doctrine "in favor of the 'Spirit of Moscow.' " Had they known how relentlessly the Kennedys were pursuing the Castros, they might have retracted that charge, but the rest of the accusations were just as unfounded. The ad has been financed by right-wing WASPs, including Nelson Bunker Hunt, the son of millionaire H. L. Hunt, but strangely, it is signed—in a club of Catholic-bashers, racists, and anti-Semites—by a Bernard Weissman.

If Marty had heard the president speculate to his wife that morning about how easy it would be to assassinate him; if he had known of Jack's other premonitions, or had heard him warn Jackie that they were "heading into nut country now," he might have taken them all as omens that could not be ignored.

But Marty serves at the president's pleasure. He's got a job to do. He cannot endow each little coincidence with prophetic meaning and still continue to function. For the moment, he's too busy herding the presidential party into the limousine for the airport and the hop to Dallas.

As Buell Frazier comes out of his sister's house and meets Lee for the ride in to work, he notices a package on the backseat of his car, a little over two feet long and wrapped in brown paper.[56] Lee tells him that it's those curtain rods he came out for, and that may be true: the evidence is conflicting as to whether his Italian rifle was in the package or already waiting for him in the building. In any case, it would be in his hands in four hours.*

"Oh, yeah," says Buell. "You said you were going to get some yesterday . . ."

They drive into Dallas, neither of them particularly quiet or talkative. It's just like any other day. If all ends well, Lee will take his bow in Mexico that night, or perhaps even Havana itself. He is both inside his life and outside it as he rides, playing the role of Lee on a normal day.

They arrive at the place where Buell usually parks, in a lot near the book depository. It's their custom to walk together up to the building, but today Lee's out of the car in a flash, hoisting the package out of the backseat and hustling on ahead.

He reaches the building well before his 8:00 A.M. starting time, and Lee Harvey Oswald disappears inside.

---

*Numerous reports described Oswald as having the rifle in his possession the weekend *before* that last trip to the Paine house. Frazier himself has always conjectured that Oswald took the gun to the depository in pieces over several days.

CHAPTER 12
Desolation Row .

WHEN THE THIRD AND LAST bullet has been fired, what ricochets away from the impact is chaos, spinning in fragments around the world. House painters are working on the old mansion at Hickory Hill, and, beside the pool, Bobby is having a working lunch with two of his federal anti-mob attorneys, Silvio Mollo and Bob Morgenthau. The phone rings. Ethel gets up from a chaise to answer it, and at that moment one of the guests notices that a painter is lurching down his ladder and running toward them, a transistor radio in his hand. Ethel answers the call, pauses, turns to her husband.

"Bobby . . . J. Edgar Hoover is calling," she says quizzically. Hoover never calls there.

The words "the president" trail toward them across the lawn, and the house painter has stopped in his tracks, his brush hanging slack at his side, dripping green paint on the lawn. Ethel turns toward the man, takes a few steps as if magnetized, then turns back to the two guests, now on their feet.

Bobby is listening to Hoover on the line. A moment passes, and then he hangs up and lurches away from the pool, his hand over his mouth, his face a rictus of shock.

"Jack's been shot," he gags. "It may be fatal."

Ethel moans, sags against him, clutches at him. They turn and move instinctively toward the house, the painter watching them pass, the enormity of it hitting them all.

At nearly the same moment, CIA director McCone is having lunch with Richard Helms at Langley when an aide bursts in with news of the shooting. McCone, assuming that it's part of a larger plot, orders the emergency Watch Committee into action. Within minutes, the entire Agency is clambering to battle stations. Khrushchev's location cannot be determined. The teams that keep tabs on the Soviet leader have lost him. Every scenario presents itself at once, a hydra-headed monster of their worst imaginings. Have the Chinese hit both the American and Soviet leaders? Or have the Russians lashed out, moving Khrushchev away from Moscow in preparation for a U.S. nuclear retaliation? As all the implications hit him, McCone is also recalling how Bobby and Ethel reached out to him when his first wife died. He calls for his car and driver and is soon speeding to Hickory Hill.[1]

In the book depository, Oswald stashes his murder weapon between stacks of boxes diagonally across from his sixth-floor perch, then starts descending the old wooden stairway. When he is confronted on the second floor by a Dallas cop, Oswald is momentarily cool, but the brief encounter must have shaken him, because he exits the building leaving his dark blue windbreaker behind in the first-floor domino room—it will not be discovered by authorities for almost four weeks.[2] The oversight will prove to be momentous.

Bobby sits on the edge of a bed, a phone to his ear. He is waiting to speak with Clint Hill, one of Jack's Secret Service men who is at the hospital in Dallas. Hill has seen it all at its worst, and Bobby needs to talk to him. Assigned to Jackie, Hill ran to Jack's limo from the car behind as soon as he saw the first shot strike. It was Clint who was trying to reach the car, who had just toed the bumper when the limo driver made the disastrous mistake of slowing down and turning to look at the wounded president just before the second shot hit him. It was Clint who had been pulled in by the First Lady as the president's brain exploded, and Clint who had laid on top of the First Couple and shielded them.

Hill takes the phone in Dallas.

"Hello, Clint," Bobby murmurs.

"Hello, General."

"It's serious, then?"

"It is, yes," Clint tells him.

"Is he conscious?"

"No. No, he's not."

"Has a priest been called?"

"Yes."

". . . Will you call me back?"

"I will, sir."[3]

Bobby hangs up. Ethel is pressed up against a wall of the bedroom, absorbed in her husband's every move. He looks up at her, a terrible sorrow passing between them.

As the last of John Kennedy's life ebbs away on a chrome table in the Parkland Hospital ICU, Vice President Johnson is secreted in a small room a few yards off, and he is terrified. His Secret Service agents tell him that this could be a global plot to eliminate the whole American government. A casket is ordered to the hospital, and the agents decide they must move the deceased president and his successor back to the presidential jet and get airborne as quickly as possible. In their haste, however, the presidential "bag man" who carries all the codes for the country's nuclear arsenal is separated from Johnson's security detail. If a nuclear attack is unleashed on the U.S., the president-to-be will not be able to order a response for thirty minutes, a potentially catastrophic interval. The officer manning the traveling White House switchboard, nestled inside Air Force One, calls the Pentagon to tell the secretary of defense and the Joint Chiefs that they "are now the president" until Lyndon Johnson can be sworn in.[4]

In Paris, the man who first vetted Lee Oswald for G2 is now about to be sent forth to kill Fidel Castro, as least so far as his CIA handlers here in the safe house are concerned. Rolando Cubela has just been given the Paper Mate pen syringe. He has not said so, but he considers it to be an amateur's device. Only guns and ammo will take the Castros down. He slips the pen into an inside pocket, weighing his reply.

But before he can give it, a telephone rings across the room. His CIA wrangler, Tepedino, answers, then passes the phone to Nestor Sánchez, whose cover name is Nicholas Sanson. The call is urgent, he says.

Sanson listens briefly and then hangs up, pausing for a long moment.

President Kennedy has just been shot, he says, in Texas.

It's not yet certain whether the president has lived through the attack, but Sanson ends the meeting then and there. The pen is suddenly forgotten. America's second Cuban coup attempt in two and a half years is over before it begins.

The men stand to put on their coats.

"Why do such things happen to good people?" Cubela says, the question hanging there.

Tepedino breaks the silence.

Does Rolando want to be taken back to his hotel, or someplace else? Cubela declines both options and leaves on his own, walking into a cold drizzle. It is dark by this time in the City of Light. He wanders in a half trance and finds himself on a bridge, staring into the swirling River Seine. On impulse, he reaches into his pocket, removes the tube, and lets it drop into the slithering current. Already, people are yelling the news from their windows to passersby along the riverbank.

Kennedy, the American president, is dead.

Rolando Cubela walks on into the city's embrace, ever ambivalent, ever mysterious.

A short time later, the French president, Charles de Gaulle, makes a statement: "I am stunned. They are crying all over France. It is as though he were a Frenchman, a member of their own family."

In West Berlin, people are already flowing into the dark streets, torches afire, in mourning.[5] Similar fires are being lit in most of the capitals of the world. En route to Tokyo when the news comes, Secretary of State Rusk orders the jet to reverse course, and as he and five other cabinet members are winging back to Washington, grown men are losing their composure and all on board are bracing themselves for a larger attack. As the news orbits the earth, millions grieve; but in Peking, schoolchildren break into laughter and applause at the news. From her exile, Diêm's widow, Madame Nhu, sneers that "the chickens have come home to roost." When she sends a letter to Jackie Kennedy a few days later, she takes another bitter stab at the dead president. "Extreme graciousness with communism does not protect from its tortuous blows," she writes.[6]

Lee Oswald has the world in his hands. He does not yet know that the president is dead, but he knows that he hit him; and he's in the house on Beckley Street, fumbling for his pistol and a replacement jacket, having hopped a bus and then a cab to get there from the book depository. He pauses, breathes deeply, collects himself, and leaves the house, racing past his landlady, Earlene Roberts, who is transfixed by the reports on TV.

In coming years, it will be alleged that Quinton Pino Machado, a former strongarm in Castro's diplomatic corps, is among those waiting that day to escort the killer to Redbird Field, four miles from Lee's Beckley Street address. Oswald is supposed to be dressed in specific clothes, likely the blue jacket left back at the depository, so that he can easily be picked up on the street upon exiting the building. Other sources will assert that the Cubans were not there to rescue Oswald. Far from it. Under the pretext of rescuing him, they intended to fly him over the Gulf of Mexico and throw him out of the plane.

Four years after the assassination, following an arduous secret reinvestigation of Oswald in Mexico, Win Scott will finally offer his educated guess as to who else was there to greet Oswald and take him to Redbird.

It's just after 1:00 P.M., but the streets of Oak Cliff are deserted. The killer's still at large, according to the TV and radio reports. Having botched his rendezvous, Oswald is now frantic, improvising his next moves. Perhaps he picked up the light gray Eisenhower windbreaker, the closest thing he had to what he was supposed to wear, in hopes that his "rescuers" would still locate him. But all it did, as he sweated under it on this 68-degree day, was make him stand out to any citizen, or cop, who might encounter him as he worked on Plan B.

At the Cuban embassy in Mexico City, Luisa Calderón is at her desk. At 2:00 P.M., her phone rings, a giddy friend on the line.

"Luisa, Kennedy has been killed! Assassinated in Texas."

"No, really?! When?"

"At one o'clock—"

"Fantastic! Wonderful." Luisa laughs, her thoughts racing ahead.

"Apparently, his wife and brother were also wounded—"

Their laughter overwhelms them for a moment.

"Wonderful," Luisa gushes. "What good news!"

"The consequences? Only good ones," the caller sings, succumbing to hysteria once again. Luisa tries to compose herself.

"He was a family man, yes," Luisa says, "but also a degenerate aggressor—"

"Three shots in the face!"

"Perfect . . ."[7]

The call ends.

Luisa dials a number on her phone. An embassy colleague picks up, someone named Nico. They too have a laugh at Kennedy's expense, and then Nico asks her this:

"Okay. What time will the plane arrive?"

"At four, and at four-thirty they must be at the airport."[8]

He acknowledges it and signs off with her.

Momentarily, the atmosphere inside the embassy becomes harried. Silvia Durán will concede fifteen years later that "all was confusion," but will hold that the Cubans "were all really sorry." It's her birthday. She goes home for lunch and to help prepare a party for that night.[9]

In the coming days and weeks, many agents will be packing their bags to go back to Havana, Luisa Calderón among them. Vega and Rodríguez-Lopez, the DGI agents who vetted visa requests and forwarded Oswald's to Havana, are also packing up.[10]

In Havana at the hour of Kennedy's murder, Teresa Proenza's brother, Álvaro Proenza, is at work in Che Guevara's office. Top Cuban officials are parading in and out, with Che holding court, and Álvaro quickly concludes, from their attitudes, that "they knew it was going to happen." Based on the atmosphere he observed in the official Cuban circles, Álvaro will further conclude that Fidel has to have played "some role in the Kennedy assassination." As to Teresa herself, a newly defected and highly regarded DGI senior officer will soon tell the CIA that because of Teresa's recent improper encounters and/or communications ("a moral situation") in Mexico City in September and early October, she is immediately recalled to Havana and placed under house arrest, which will continue for three years.[11] Cuban cultural attaché Raúl Aparicio Nogales will describe Proenza's new occupation in Cuba as "unemployed." Asked why, he'll say, "What you might imagine, but do not say it." During a conversation between Raúl Aparicio and María Teresa Proenza, Proenza herself will mention the reason: "Osvaldo." It will never be ascertained if she means Cuban president Osvaldo Dorticós or Lee Harvey "Oswaldo." Alvaro Proenza will later state that it was a chance contact between Teresa and an "acquaintance" of Lee Oswald's in the Cuban embassy that caused all of her problems, including her house arrest.[12]

John McCone has arrived at Bobby's house. It's all unimaginable at this point. When the DCI is led upstairs to the second-floor library, Bobby is hypnotically going through the motions of knotting a tie and affixing one of his brother's commemorative Navy clasps to it.

With barely a greeting, Bobby looks at McCone, his eyes red-rimmed.

"He had the most wonderful life," he says of his brother.

Bobby intends to go to Andrews Air Force Base to catch a jet to Dallas, he says, but the plan will change almost as soon as it's made. There is so much to deal with here, and Jack's body will soon be coming back to Washington. He has already ordered the Secret Service to collect all the president's Oval Office Dictabelt recordings and deliver them to Hickory Hill, and now there's another phone call from the White House. Bobby picks up. It's Bundy, calling him back.

Already, the attorney general is fixed on who might have done this, and he has been sending out feelers nationwide. Before he leaves the house, Bobby will call his trusted associate Jules Draznin, a member of the National Labor Relations Board, living in Chicago. Bobby suspects that "the Outfit," the city's mob fiefdom run by Tony Accardo, with Giancana, Murray Humphreys, and their Vegas underboss Johnny Rosselli, might have killed Jack. Or it might have been their man running the Teamsters, Jimmy Hoffa. Bobby had always thought it would have been himself who might be killed, not the president; but if anyone can penetrate the formidable web around the Accardo crew, Draznin can.

Hoffa is currently under DOJ investigation. He would have motive. Walter Sheridan will check into that. A call goes out to Harry Ruiz Williams, Bobby's close Amigo. Was it a plot by anti-Castro Cubans, estranged after the missile crisis? Williams pledges to check it out, but he doubts it.

And while Bobby seeks his revenge, he moves also to protect Jack's legacy. Presuming that Jack's "personal" letters and papers now belong to his estate, Bobby instructs Bundy to get a locksmith into the White House and change the combinations on the president's safes and files. He also commands that anything dated after November 8 of this year be moved straight to the national security staff offices and kept under twenty-four-hour guard. This raw grist of history will be spirited out of Washington in the next few days and weeks, much of it never to be seen again.[13]

As Bobby takes action, the facts of this murder are already being managed by American officials and countermanaged by their enemies. The first obfuscations have begun, on both sides of the Iron Curtain.

Nikita Khrushchev had been corresponding with Kennedy, in secret. Together, the two men had come to realize that within their relationship would be established whatever political center might exist in the postwar world. It was they who must filter out the extreme voices around each of them, and they who might yet control Fidel and Raúl Castro.

Nikita's foreign minister, Andrei Gromyko, calls him in Kiev in the middle of the night to tell him the news. The Soviet leader breaks down and weeps, appalled to learn that Kennedy has been destroyed with his wife at his side, that she has been so traumatized. But bereft as he is, he too is wondering if this is a Chinese plot to kill both the Soviet and American leaders. He has described Mao Tse-tung as "a lunatic on a throne" and has defied the Chinese leader by making rapprochement with the West on nuclear issues, including a Limited Test Ban Treaty with Kennedy. Mao believes that a world war with the West is inevitable. Khrushchev has rejected that idea, hoping for an accommodating duality, perhaps a slower, less violent demise of capitalism, or even an agreeable balance of territories. Mao, and now perhaps the Castro brothers, think otherwise. Could this be a preemptive bid for Chinese global dominance?

He cannot ponder it for long. He puts all Soviet troops on worldwide alert. He is well aware that his absence from the Soviet capital could invite American suspicions that he has gone to ground, braced for their nuclear reprisal. It's decided that he must immediately board a night train that will return him to Moscow.[14]

In all but the official sense, Lyndon Johnson is the president now, though he has not yet been sworn in. While the nation exists without a leader, the most pressing concern is getting the presidential party out of Dallas, into the air and out of danger. Lyndon refuses to leave Texas without Mrs. Kennedy, and Jackie won't depart without Jack's body, so—after a bitter jurisdictional squabble between federal and state authorities—John Kennedy's remains are driven at high speed through the streets of Dallas, in violation of a Texas law requiring local autopsies in homicide cases.

The press corps, the flight crew, and much of John Kennedy's White House staff sit dumbstruck on the sweltering plane, or stand in the aisles, barely speaking, rudderless. The new president's belongings are being moved from Air Force Two to One, and when Jack's casket is finally taken aboard and positioned in the rear of the plane, Jackie takes the seat beside it, where she will remain for most of the flight back to Washington.

All await Lyndon Johnson's approval for the convoy's departure.

But no one can find Lyndon on Air Force Two. Brigadier General Godfrey McHugh tries to maintain decorum, but he boards One and keeps coming up short there as well. Lyndon is nowhere in sight in the main cabin. He's not in the presidential bedroom, either. In desperation, McHugh shoves open the door of the bathroom and discovers Lyndon there, muttering about "Conspiracy, conspiracy, they're after all of us!"

McHugh has to spend a few minutes quietly talking Lyndon down,[15] but eventually the new commander in chief gets his bearings. No amount of preparation can ready a person to suddenly assume the responsibilities of this office. He had awoken that morning with the intention of telling Jack that he was planning to leave the ticket in 1964. He had been all but gone from the Kennedy administration when he got to Texas two days earlier. But now, as he's leaving it, he is about to be sworn in as the thirty-sixth president of the United States.

By the time McHugh talks him through the moment, Lyndon is fully in control of himself again, a onetime "master of the Senate" who is now the commanding leader of a nation in agony and terror. By phone, Bobby has advised Marty Underwood that any judge can administer the oath of office. Marty has scribbled the oath on a pair of five-by-seven-inch index cards, and Judge Sarah Hughes has come aboard to conduct the ceremony.

Fidel is in a lunch conference with French journalist Jean Daniel at one of the official residences at Varadero, an aide-de-camp, Major Vallejo, across the room monitoring radio broadcasts from Miami.[16] Daniel has recently met with the American president, and he has come to Castro with a message from Kennedy, one that analyzes their violent history and makes an overture of peace.

But now the word comes that this president is dead. Fidel stands, walks to the window, and takes in the sea.

"Everything is going to change," he says. "At least Kennedy was an enemy to whom we had become accustomed."[17]

Oswald, of whose existence and intention he had been informed seven weeks before, has struck, and he has succeeded. Fidel knows that this was possible, that it was in fact likely, but he too needs plausible deniability. He takes a long, portentous moment, then looks sharply at Daniel.

"This is an end to your mission of peace," Fidel says.

The conversation labors on, both men no doubt mired in their own thoughts, and as it draws to a close, Fidel returns to the day's earth-shaking implications.

"Now they will have to find the assassin quickly, very quickly. Otherwise, you watch and see, I know them, they will try to put the blame on us for this thing."

Lee is scuttling down a suburban street near the intersection of Tenth and Patton. Of all the places he could be at that moment, he is stranded and exposed in a pretty, middle-class neighborhood, like a day laborer waiting for a lift back to Skid Row.

What can he be thinking? Does he hitchhike to Redbird, now that his rendezvous has been blown? Is there a moment when he thinks he has been left in the lurch intentionally? Does he know that there is a bus that stops nearby that could get him to the Mexican border, and he has just enough money to buy a ticket?

Lee doesn't know it yet, but there is now a description of the prime suspect, a composite drawn from witnesses near where the shots were fired and depository co-workers, and an all-points bulletin goes out from police head-quarters.

The suspect in the shooting at Elm and Houston is reported to be an un-known white male, approximately thirty, slender build, height five feet, ten inches, weight one hundred and sixty-five pounds, reported to be armed with what is thought to be a .30-caliber rifle . . . No further description is given at this time, 12:45 P.M.

Officer J. D. Tippit has heard the dispatch, and he is approaching the in-tersection of Tenth Street and Patton at about 1:14, when he sees a young man in a light-gray jacket, roughly fitting the description. Tippit decides to stop the man, who was likely disheveled and dripping perspiration. The moment he does, Lee's backup plan, if he had devised one yet, unravels. It takes only seconds.

A medical photographer from Baylor University, Jack Tatum, is about to turn onto Tenth when he sees a squad car pull up next to a walking man, who then bends over and talks to the officer through the passenger window. The pedestrian's hands are stuffed in his pockets; but as Tatum drives past Tippit's car and through the intersection, he hears four or five gunshots. He stops, looks back, and sees the cop lying in the street.

Lee walks around the front of the car and shoots Tippit point-blank in the head, where he lies already mortally wounded.

Lee looks up from the corpse to see Tatum's car stopped up the street. Lee starts loping toward him, gun raised. Tatum puts his car in gear and pulls out with Lee still advancing on him, just fifteen yards or so away. Tatum accelerates, keeping an eye on the rearview until Lee turns and runs down Patton Street, while onlookers hear him mumble to himself, "Poor dumb cop."

Tatum doubles back to see if he can help Tippit, but it's too late.[18]

Now it all comes crashing down on Lee. He's a man without a plan. All he can do is find a place to hide, a place where he can collect his thoughts.

As police race to the scene of their fallen brother, Oswald lies low, most likely hiding in alleys, behind Dumpsters, and in stairwells. About twenty minutes after the slaying, a shoe-store manager named Johnny Brewer looks up from his work in a shop on Jefferson Boulevard, six blocks from the Tip-pit murder scene, to see cop cars screaming by and a man's face pressed close to his recessed window. His hair is disheveled. He looks out of breath, flushed and frightened, sneaking quick looks over his shoulder as the cop cars hurtle past. Moments later, Brewer sees him duck into the Texas

Theatre a few doors down. He doesn't pay. The titles up on the marquee are *Cry of Battle*, starring Van Heflin, and *War Is Hell*, and this is what Lee will be watching during the last moments of his freedom. It will take seven cops to subdue him. Lee bites and punches. He tries to get off a shot with his pistol, but as he's disarmed he screams, "I am not resisting arrest!" and when they drag him out of the movies, a crowd has gathered. In the hysteria that now chokes the city, they assume that this is the assassin. They want to kill him.

In Mexico City, Luisa Calderón receives another call at the embassy, a breathless female voice.

"Luisa, have you heard about Kennedy yet?!"

"Yes," she replies. "I knew almost before Kennedy did."

"They've arrested the guy. He's president of a Fair Play for Cuba Committee."

"I already knew that. A gringo, right?"

"It seems he lived for a time in Russia, but they wouldn't grant him citizenship—"

"Damn it! How do they know that already?! Did they say his name?"

"Oswald—something like that. He hasn't confessed to anything . . ."[19]

Calderón hangs up the phone, her mind reeling, the fact hitting her with perfect finality. The revolution has struck a lightning blow for the oppressed masses the world over,[20] and she may have played a small part.

Twelve years later, when the CIA reviews this conversation in light of all it has learned in the interim, it concludes that "Luisa Calderón, as a member of the DGI unit in Mexico City, could very well have known something that would make what she said to her unidentified caller less a matter of boastful self-indulgence than was assumed at the time."[21]

Daylight is waning in the nation's capital, shadows climbing the great dome. The red and yellow trees around the White House thrash about in the autumn winds, bright leaves blowing free from their boughs and racing away along the empty paths.

At Hickory Hill, Bobby and McCone wander outside, stepping into the evening glow of Indian summer. Various Kennedy children are poised on the lawn, shocked into uncommon stillness. Bobby comforts them as he can, pulling one close, tousling another's hair, urging them to pray, to write letters to their beloved fallen uncle. As the kids move off, their small voices trailing after them, he turns back to McCone.

He must ask his friend a question, one that might have been unthinkable before the missile crisis; before the specter of a domestic coup was briefly raised by the Soviets and even alluded to by the Kennedys.

"You know," Bobby would say later about that moment on the lawn, "at the time I asked McCone . . . if [the CIA] had killed my brother, and I asked him in a way that he couldn't lie to me, and they hadn't."[22]

Robert Kennedy takes his word for it, and in all the years since, for all the Agency's clear failures around Jack's death, for all their deliberate obfuscations in the aftermath, there has yet to be any credible evidence that the CIA ever opted to kill its own master.

Two hours after Lee is booked at Dallas Police headquarters, he is being led down a crowded hallway toward a police lineup when he first catches sight of network television cameras. Though handcuffed, he raises his right hand in the traditional "clenched fist" salute that has been provenance of Marxists and Communists since the 1930s. It is also a favorite greeting of Che and the Castros.* Oswald's victory salute, which was often on display in the *Militant* and the *Worker* newsletters[23] he received, is lost on most people in the moment, but the initial investigation quickly reveals his political obsessions.

With an apparent Communist sympathizer now in custody in Dallas, the State Department is quickly spinning with its own speculation. The nation's leadership orders up a dossier on the former defector and finds that it's a large one. Had the assassination been ordered by Moscow? Llewellyn Thompson doubts it. The Russians don't operate that way, he insists in the first meeting, not by killing heads of state. Such a precedent could wreak havoc in world affairs, he says, and Averell Harriman concurs. Still, it seems clear that Oswald's professed Marxism could, at the very least, undermine the administration's work toward détente with Khrushchev.[24]

Nikita himself will soon hear from the new president, who will promise that there will be no attack from the United States. But while Khrushchev does his private best to maintain some sort of diplomatic equipoise with Washington, there is good reason to fear the arrest of Lee Oswald. When the American first defected to Russia in 1959, his case was brought to the attention of Gromyko himself, along with Deputy Premier Mikhal Porfirovich

---

*Lee's friend George de Mohrenschildt, in his unpublished manuscript *I Am a Patsy!* (National Archives and Records Administration), says Lee admired Che even more than he admired Fidel.

and KGB chief Aleksandr Nikolaevich Shelepin.[25] That alone could raise unwanted interest at this terrifyingly delicate moment.

Dobrynin has just sent Khrushchev a coded message from Washington. It mentions the frequent recent correspondence to the Soviet embassy from Lee and his wife: "The last letter from Oswald was dated November 9. It is possible that the US authorities may ask us to familiarize them with the correspondence in our possession. [They] are aware of the existence of this final correspondence since it was conducted through official mail. Inasmuch as there is nothing that compromises us in this correspondence, we might agree to do this as a last resort (after removing our internal correspondence with the MFA)."[26] The MFA was the Soviet Ministry of Foreign Affairs, and that internal correspondence would certainly have been as interesting to the Americans as the rest of it, but the Russians quickly ascertained that the Americans wanted to know very little.

But it is the Soviets who first alerted the Cubans to Oswald's very existence, a fact that they would cover up for over forty years.

The Soviet press reacts swiftly, both to shield the Soviets from suspicion and to weaken the American right's capacity to undo the new détente. It starts turning Lee into a "patsy" of the American right, a faux Commie, a steward of the Birchers and Klansmen, the oil magnates and "super-patriots" of apocalyptic reactivity.

The first salvo from TASS, within hours of Jack's death, read: "From the moment of Kennedy's arrival in Dallas, small groups of ultra-right-wing elements had demonstrated in different sections of the city under Confederate flags and slogans hostile to Kennedy . . . In the speech President Kennedy was scheduled to deliver at luncheon, the text of which was found in his pocket, he denounced his ultra-conservative opponents."

Pravda emblazons its front page with a memorial photo of Jack, praises his "steps toward cleansing the international situation," and denounces the sharp attacks upon him "from American 'madmen.'" Slavic funeral songs issue from Soviet radio stations nationwide, and Kennedy's inaugural speech and his American University speech on disarmament are played and replayed on Soviet television in ensuing days. This is but the first of the attempts to insulate the USSR from blame for Jack's death.[27]

When Khrushchev's deputy Mikoyan arrives a few days later for Kennedy's funeral, Llewellyn Thompson will tell him that the Soviet campaign to blame the American right is bringing counterassertions of "communist and Cuban connections." Mikoyan protests that he doesn't "want to make complications," but says that he resents Llewellyn's insinuation while the case is still awaiting investigation.[28] Llewellyn may simply be asking the Russians not to inflame the American right, rather than expressly warning them of U.S. suspicions about Moscow and Havana.

Sitting in the dim rear compartment of the jet, her pink wool suit caked with Jack's blood, Jackie Kennedy is approached by someone who suggests that she come away from the casket and change her clothes before landing.

No, she says. "I want them to see what they did to him."

Who "they" exactly are will not become clear for years to come, but Jack Kennedy has died because, first, the right demanded a murderous and relentless response to Fidel Castro, and second, the Kennedys were themselves caught up in the hysteria of the times; they knew the Castros were ruthless killers who coveted the Bomb. Who knows what might happen if they prospered? Their humiliation over the Bay of Pigs only fueled the fire. The Kennedys chose a scalpel over a cudgel. A gun had undone them both.

Early that afternoon, an air traffic controller at Redbird, Louis D. Gaudin, is observing a two-toned green-and-white Comanche-type airplane over at the Texair hangar, where it's being serviced. At one point, his curiosity aroused, he strikes up a conversation with the three well-dressed passengers, and they indicate that they're "headed southbound." Sometime between 2:30 and 3:00 P.M., an hour or so after Lee's arrest, the plane taxis and takes off.

Forty minutes later, the same aircraft returns with only two men aboard. This time, it is met by a part-time Texair employee who is thought to also be working a second part-time job at the Dallas Police Department. The plane takes off again a short time later.[29] The owner of Texair, Merritt Gobel, will be too frightened to discuss the incident in coming years, saying only that the flight "was common knowledge. That's all I can say."[30]

Late that night, a twin-engine plane sets down at the Mexico City airport with two Cuban men aboard. They have traveled from Dallas, by way of Tijuana, and are met by diplomatic personnel from the Cuban embassy. One of the passengers is Miguel Casas Sayez, a gangster-revolutionary of the G2 and a fierce proponent of Raúl Castro. Casas Sayez is allowed to avoid customs and immediately boards a Revolutionary Armed Forces jet bound for Cuba.[31]

Jim Hosty will become aware of allegations of mysterious flights that day. He will be told by another FBI officer "that the CIA agents in Mexico City were investigating the possibility of Castro's involvement. They picked up information about a mysterious person flying in from the United States, and then departing under mysterious circumstances on an airplane for Cuba, when all of a sudden they received orders to cease and desist their investigation."[32]

The exact nature of the Oswald "rescue" plan will remain murky, but at one of his clandestine talks forty-two years later, Oscar Marino says, "There was no plan to save him. The assurances he was given [in Mexico City] were carried off by the wind." On another occasion, when asked if there was an offer to get Lee out of Dallas, Oscar replies, "Yes . . . Our people did not strategically support him . . . We used Oswald, but for security reasons the connections to him were loose. No officer of the G2 was, to my knowledge, on the spot in Dallas, strategically. I do not know whether an observer went." Marino readily admits that the Oswald operation was not his; he was only familiar with bits of the story, especially Oswald's recruitment. But his seemingly paradoxical statement that there was an offer to spirit Oswald out of town, *but not save him*, strongly suggest that the plan was to get him out of the country and then out of this world, either by killing and burying him somewhere in rural Mexico, or simply shoving him from a plane over the ocean. (This scenario was actually voiced by retired G2 agents in 2005, but they refused to go public.)

In any case, on November 22, 1963, there is no value in keeping him alive, nor will it make sense to keep him under house arrest somewhere for decades. Leaving him in the lifelong care of the Castro brothers is far too dangerous. But now his keepers have failed to exfiltrate him, and he has been caught. He is therefore at the mercy of his questioners, and his relationship with Havana could soon bring down a hard rain on the Cuban people.

It is not known exactly when or where Jack Ruby hears the news of the president's murder, but by all accounts he is devastated in its wake. Friends find him sobbing. He's incoherent at times, agonizing as much for Jackie and the children as for the man himself. Even as the most cursory evidence against Oswald is coming in, he tells his attorney, Phil Burleson, "Oswald didn't just kill the president, he killed the father of the First Family!"[33]

He has seen the Birch Society ad from the newspaper the day before, and he's particularly aggrieved that it's signed by a Jew. In fact, the signature has provoked rumors, in a city now infected with them, that the murder was a Jewish conspiracy, as if old Joe Kennedy's appeasements of Hitler in the 1940s might have come back as a sacrifice of his son today.

He's shattered. He's indignant on behalf of the Jews. Joe Cavagnaro, one of his employees at the Vegas Club, watches as he grieves "like you would if it were your own cousin or brother." On the phone to his old Chicago pal, Larry Meyers, he moans, "Those poor people, I've gotta *do* somethin' about it!"

Ruby tells his sister Eva, "I never felt so bad in my life, even when Ma and Pa died . . . Someone tore my heart out." Before sundown on Friday, he's already thinking about heading down to the Hall of Justice and blowing Lee Oswald to kingdom come.

At the Dallas Police headquarters, Lee is now being questioned in a hot, smoky interrogation room. He has killed two men that day. He has either been left high and dry by his Cuban angels, or has—more likely—simply failed to meet up with them on time. He sits at a table with a black eye and other minor injuries, a sallow, oily-haired little man in a sweaty T-shirt. There are fourteen cops, agents, and detectives seated around him, but his manner is unperturbed, self-satisfied, impenetrable. He must know by now that he will never be free again, that he will not live out his life as an exile hero, re-voicing the future of socialism under some faroff banana tree. And yet there he sits at the center of them, seemingly calm and self-possessed.

As his inquisitors pepper him with questions, he lies, smirks, obfuscates, dodges. He lies about owning any guns. He lies about aliases, about the photos that show him armed and "ready for anything." He lies about where he lives. He's giving them nothing.

But Jim Hosty is there, and Hosty has been pursuing him since his return to Dallas. He goes out on a limb, already knowing the answer to his next question.

"Have you ever been to Mexico?" he asks Lee.

"Yes," he shoots back, "I've been to Tijuana when I was in the Marine Corps."

"Have you been to Mexico City?"

Suddenly, the insouciance drains away. Lee is startled. "How did you know? I—I—I didn't—I've never been there!" He starts to admit it. Then he back-tracks. "No, I've never been there. How'd you know about that . . . ?"[34]

Within days, on November 28, Marina will be on the grill too. Speaking through Russian translators to the FBI's Wally Heitman, she will also lie about the Mexico trip. In the midst of questioning about something else entirely, she blurts, "By the way, Lee has never been to Mexico City." Heitman is stunned. He hasn't asked her about Mexico.

"Why did you say that?" he asks.

"I heard about it on television," Marina fumbles.

Weeks after that, Heitman will ask her why she lied about Lee's trip. "I wanted to save something for the Warren Commission," she'll say. Another lie. At the time of her first interrogation, there was no Warren Commission yet. The executive order was signed on November 29.[35]

At 5:30 on the evening of his brother's murder, Bobby arrives by helicopter at Andrews Air Force Base, the secretary of defense at his side. It's dark by now, and when they disembark, Bobby takes one look at the sea of Washington officials and media people gathered to greet Air Force One and just wants to hide. He wants only to prepare himself for Jackie, to be there when she lands.

There's an empty Air Force truck near where the jet will park, and Bobby vaults inside. There, sitting on the side bench amid the smells of old canvas and machine grease, he prays and waits until the faroff sound of an approaching aircraft engine and the bite of tires on tarmac grows to a screaming din. The plane has arrived, and with it his shattered sister-in-law and the thirty-fifth and thirty-sixth presidents of the country he loves. He stays in the darkened truck until the aircraft's door opens, and then leaps out and up the jetway and inside.

Faces part for him, dozens of tear-streaked faces of friends and colleagues, loved ones and rivals, all blurring around him as he shoves his way past Lyndon to the back of the plane—the terribly peaceful tableau of Jack's bare box and his beautiful, shattered wife poised on a chair beside it, dressed in red-stained pink. She stands for him. They embrace, Bobby gazing over her shoulder at the mute container that holds his once dashing brother.

The vice president's residence is under heavy guard by Secret Service agents, resolute and somber, scanning the front gate, the trees, the skies. A black limousine enters the compound, carrying the director of Central Intelligence.

Inside, as he waits, the new president chain-smokes and sips an orange soda, the blue light of the TV playing across his features, along with the amber glow of a fire on the hearth. John McCone is shown in. The DCI has brought a file with him, and as Lyndon leafs through it, he strokes his brow slowly, trying to absorb it all thoroughly and quickly. McCone himself may have just been briefed about the deadly details. Lyndon has been kept in the dark about a lot of things, particularly the nature of the plots against the Castros. This briefing amounts to a crash course, and the conversation moves intently, by harrowing degrees.

Apparently, McCone informs him, we were meeting with AM/LASH in Paris at about the same moment as President Kennedy was hit; meeting to plan a new attempt on Castro. The variables and possibilities are immense. Lyndon keeps referring to the astonishing details of the file spread across his lap.

The new president assumes that this AM/LASH person has since been called off and asks who the man is. When it's explained that he is Rolando Cubela Secades, one of Castro's inner circle, Lyndon insists that his case officer call him to break off contact, immediately. He also wants these plans for an "imminent" invasion of Cuba put on hold.

So McCone feels that the assassination did not come from the Russians?

The director feels it probably did not, as do the men at State. All the NSA intercepts show that the Soviets are clearly surprised and alarmed. Khrushchev seems almost to be suffering a personal loss. But the Cubans are another story. All first indications are that Havana is in a panic. There's been a flurry of phone calls from Osvaldo Dorticós and the Cuban consulate in Mexico City about this employee there, Silvia Durán, who has been detained by the Mexican police and is about to be arrested. Dorticós has been worrying all day about whether the police might threaten her to get testimony that the Cubans gave money to Oswald.

This would be explosive, and the Agency doesn't know the facts yet, but Dorticós is obviously frantic about it. Lyndon probes more deeply. The men speculate on whether the Cubans are capable of this on their own. McCone believes that they are.

Castro publicly threatened both John and Robert not two months ago. In that interim, Diêm has been assassinated, thus increasing Havana's cause for alarm, and it's known that Fidel's Mexico City embassy has ordered assassinations throughout the hemisphere. If the Castros have gotten wind of the ongoing plot to overthrow them, there would be added motive.

Talk turns back to the subject of Silvia Durán. She knew Oswald. It appears that they met when he was there in September. As soon as the Agency heard that the Mexican police were moving on her, they told the station chief to try to head off the arrest, but it was too late. If the Cubans are involved, then the U.S. government wants to know it before the Mexican police do. If she had remained at large for a while, the intercepts might have told the U.S. much more of the story. Now, however, the Cubans are alerted.

Johnson must wonder why Oswald wasn't waylaid when he was in Mexico, or shortly thereafter. That passage of the conversation can only be sticky. However it played out, McCone is by now convinced—and tells the president, according to LBJ speechwriter Leo Janos—that "It was the Castro connection."[36]

Lyndon then calls to stop the Dallas district attorney's plan to formally charge Lee Oswald with committing the crime "in the furtherance of a communist conspiracy." That language cannot be permitted. The charge shall be confined to "murder of the President." He then calls his old Senate colleague, the powerful southern Democrat Richard Russell, asking his advice on what to do with the Oswald/Cuba evidence.

"Don't let it out!" Russell worries. "If you do, it's World War III."

Johnson soon convenes a meeting in McNamara's office, attended by the Cuban Coordinating Committee. Here, he makes it clear that they must not allow the American people to believe that Fidel Castro could have killed their president. The reason, according to CCC aide Alexander Haig, is that there will be such a conservative groundswell in America that it will run the Democratic Party out of power for two generations.

Haig, echoing the Janos report, will further recall, "During that meeting I received a message from the CIA. In it is described a visit not only to Mexico but to Cuba under the auspices of the Mexican embassy—by Lee Harvey Oswald. I brought this message to the meeting immediately, because they were dealing with the subject of the Cuban Coordinating Committee and covered program." Haig handed it to the person whose job it was to share it with those in the meeting, and waited outside for any response. "I received a message back from that meeting: 'It's a non-message. You have not seen it,' " came the reply from inside.[37]

In Washington, Bobby and Jackie spend half the night in a suite at the Bethesda Naval Hospital, Jack's autopsy proceeding a few floors below them. Jackie smokes. Someone puts on Gershwin, softly, in the background. Later, she is given a sedative that does nothing for her. Periodically Bobby goes downstairs[38] to hurry the investigators, virtually guaranteeing an incomplete procedure—the truth about Jack's health must never become public. Complicated medical-legal autopsies can take days, and they have already scaled back to a simple pathological autopsy at Bobby's insistence, but he still wants it done faster, warning that Jackie is on the verge of collapse. Without even the time to shave the head, the autopsists remove the president's brain for later sectioning, but then Bobby orders them to stop. At his insistence, they will deliver Jack's brain to Bobby, who will oversee its storage for the next three and a half years.

He chooses a better casket than the one in which they brought Jack home from Dallas. When the body is taken to the White House early on the twenty-third, when it's set on the same catafalque that bore Lincoln's body, Bobby asks that the East Room be cleared of all but the three priests kneeling in prayer. The casket is opened. He has brought McNamara in with him, and when the two of them gaze upon Jack, Bobby decides then and there that he doesn't want an open-casket ceremony. Even in the candlelight, the face looks too waxen, not as Bobby wanted him to be remembered.

Bobby is led from Lincoln's bier to Lincoln's bedroom, keeping control of himself until the door closes and he is alone. Then, from outside, his friend Charles Spalding hears him cry out, weeping and demanding, "Why, God? Why?!"[39]

CHAPTER 13

Cannons in the Rain

AT 10:01 A.M. ON NOVEMBER 23, less than twenty-four hours after the assassination, while Oswald is still alive in Dallas, Lyndon Johnson takes a call from FBI director Hoover, who updates him on the arrest and the evidence. Johnson asks about Mexico City. In summarizing the CIA's data from Mexico, Hoover informs the new president that "the picture and the tape do not correspond to this man's voice, nor to his appearance." It will be learned later that a photo mismatch of Oswald was due to the CIA's hasty submission of an irrelevant surveillance shot. Hoover's reference to the voice recording will provide the original evidence that the Oswald tapes had not been routinely erased seven weeks before the assassination. The rest of the fourteen minutes of the Johnson-Hoover conversation will be erased from Johnson's taped record sometime afterward.[1]

When Elena Garro and her daughter, Elenita, see the photo of Lee Harvey Oswald on the front pages that morning, the two are faced with a terrible choice. They have met the man, right there in Mexico City not two months ago—Elenita even asked him to dance—and now he is charged with the murder of the American president. It's an unbearable thing to know, but to tell it is to incite or even expose the Cubans, some of whom are Elena's friends, others of whom might harm her and her daughter.

But Elena lives by her instincts and believes in justice, so she snatches her daughter's hand, drags her down to their car, and goes speeding up Zamora Street until she slams to a halt at the gates of the Cuban embassy. She flings herself from her car, Elenita right behind her, and marches up to the gate, grabbing the cold iron curves of it with both hands.

"Murderers! Killers! Assassins!" she screams, and her daughter picks it up.

"You had President Kennedy murdered!" Elena says, again and again.

"Killers! Murderers! *Assassins!*" Their voices echo through the streets.

Faces appear at the doors and windows of the embassy, some of them laughing, others making careful note. Finally, when the women are screamed out, Elena spits through the black metal latticework, gives it one last kick, turns, and stomps back to the car, Elenita breathless in her wake.[2]

Whether their friend Silvia Durán saw their harangue or not, Silvia goes home for lunch on this day, and when she does, everyone there is astonished to see her. Her brothers-in-law come running, and when her maid sees her, she bursts into tears.

"You're alive!?"

Of course she is. "Why?" wonders Silvia. What makes her say that?

Because some man came to the house that morning, the maid bawls, and he said that Silvia had an accident, that she was dead; and then they took her brother-in-law, Ruben, away to identify her remains. Silvia goes straight to Ruben's house, the same place where the party was that Lee attended two months before. When she arrives there, Ruben's wife is just as shocked to see her.

"Silvia, you're okay!" Tears fill her eyes. She is flanked by two men who won't let the women embrace. Silvia, as if to challenge them, stalks back to the bedroom looking for Ruben and finds him sitting on the bed, surrounded by photographs. There are men hovering over him, and he too is shocked that she's alive.

"What happened?" he asks.

"I can't remember," she says, dodging the question on impulse. It has been a nightmarish twenty-four hours. Since she doesn't know who these men are, she's not going to give up anything. She reaches for the bedside phone to call the police or a lawyer, but one of them grabs her hand.

"You can't call," he tells her. "You're under arrest."

She thinks she hears one murmur to another that she "is the accomplice of Kennedy." He must mean Oswald. Or does he? Which side are these men on?

Again, they tell her that she's under arrest, she and Rubén, her husband, Horacio, and the rest of their family. She eases down onto the bed.

"You have to show me an order signed by a judge that I'm under arrest."

They try to cuff her. She kicks at them, catching one straight in the groin, but they cart her off anyway.

As they take her out of the house, she's screeching to anyone who will listen, "Call the police, call the police!"

One of them claps a hand over her mouth, smelling of nicotine and sweat. They drag her to a station wagon parked at the corner. There is a man there, but she doesn't know him, so she goes quiet for a moment, weighing her options.

"Don't cry," he says, as if to soothe her, but then he adds, "you scandalous woman. Scandalous old woman, *shut up!* Where we are going, we will *see* what's going to happen to *you.*"

She falls silent, tries to hold it together. As it happens, they *are* the police—the worst of them, the DFS. They're taking her to the office of State Security.[3]

They will keep her all night, but all she will tell them is the party line: she met Lee Oswald, she and the other staff members tried to process his various unreasonable requests, he had a tantrum, and then he left, and that's the last they ever saw him.

It had snowed, gloriously, for Jack's inauguration, but today it's pouring rain, the capital sodden, except for the wet red and gold leaves still clinging to autumn. The president's casket lies in state in the East Room of the White House. It has been decided that Kennedy is to be the first chief executive to be buried at Arlington National Cemetery, and it falls to Bobby to go there and pick the piece of ground where he'll be interred. Joe Califano, Cy Vance's man on the Cuban committee, has been assigned to go with him.

Bobby looks to Califano like a man who has had every bone in his body broken. "I have never seen a sadder man or woman," Califano will say later. "Walking like a zombie, eyes hollowed from lack of sleep." The place they find is on a rise overlooking the District, situated just down a slope from a gracious white mansion, Arlington House, built by George Washington's step-grandson. Even under the thick drape of clouds, the majesty of the city is clear from here. It's the right resting place.

"This is where we'll bury the president," Bobby says, almost in a whisper.

He turns up his collar and walks back down the slope, gets in his car, and leaves. Four and half years later, this will become his own resting place.

Califano had observed Bobby closely on the CCC, and would continue to do so for those remaining years. In hindsight, after struggling to process those memories, he will conclude "that the paroxysms of grief that tormented Robert Kennedy for years after his brother's death arose, at least in part, from a sense that his efforts to eliminate Castro led to his brother's assassination."[4]

On Sunday, November 24, Win Scott cables headquarters that one of Kostikov's contacts at the Soviet embassy was none other than the slippery Rolando Cubela. The American ambassador, Thomas Mann, follows that cable with another reaffirming what McCone told Lyndon on the twenty-second—he believes the Soviets were smart enough not to get involved, but not the Cubans. He is looking into it further.

In Mexico City and Havana, knowledgeable G2 contacts are being reined in. Orders are sent to Cuban embassies from Fidel's inner sanctum, commanding all to keep quiet and, above all, to "quit laughing in public" about Kennedy's death. Fidel's local enforcers become the Mexican secret police, a brutal ally of G2. Havana prefers to leave no mark on the investigation, especially on Mexican nationals, but people with any knowledge of Oswald in Mexico are potential targets, particularly those who try to pass their knowledge to the authorities. They are being systematically threatened or beaten until they change their stories.

But a friend of the Garro family gets to them before the secret police or the Cubans do. A Mexican government functionary named Manolo Calvillo comes to pay a visit to Elena and Elenita, and the moment he arrives he puts a record on the turntable and cranks up the amp to full volume. Their display at the Cuban embassy has angered the wrong people. Drawing the mother and teen close to him, he says, "Your house is being watched. There are a couple of gangsters outside, hired by the Communists to kill you." They are both to go and pack clothing for an indefinite stay. Somehow, he is able to sneak them out of the house a few minutes later, undetected, and takes them to another part of the vast city, to the Hotel Vermont, where they will be hidden until further notice. In the coming January, two Communists will find mother and daughter and warn them again never to reveal that they saw Oswald at the party at Ruben Durán's.[5]

Perhaps only in a place as politically overwrought as Dallas could rumors of a Jewish plot against Kennedy have spread so quickly. The conspiracy, supposedly keyed by Bernard Weissman's signature in the reactionary newspaper ad of the twenty-second, had made its way back to Jack Ruby (né Rubenstein), and it only increased his anguish at the president's murder. Jack spends half the day wailing his heart out at his synagogue. His brother, Hyman, would recall that the other mourners there "didn't believe a guy like Jack would ever cry. Jack never cried in his life. He is not that kind of guy to cry," but he wept with loud abandon.[6]

Though nearly bankrupt, Ruby decides to honor the fallen president by closing the Carousel Club for a respectful interval. He tells Eva, "Listen, we are broke anyway, so I will be a broken millionaire. I'm going to close for three days."[7] He spends the rest of Saturday at police headquarters, looking for the object of his hatred. At one point in the Hall of Justice, he considers shooting Oswald as he is being led from room to room during questioning, but there are too many reporters in his way. He doesn't want to accidentally hit one of his friends in the press.[8]

By Sunday, he has almost talked himself out of it. Ruby has some business to take care of near the police station; when he gets downtown, he parks, leaving his beloved dog in a hot, closed car for the moments it will take him to wire some money from the Western Union station. He's always got his gun on him now, especially when he's got to do any sort of transaction. When he walks past the entrance to the garage beneath headquarters, he sees the big TV lights glowing down there and hears the ruckus, but he walks on. He's got a life. He's got his dog in the car. He's got to pull himself together.

Meanwhile, after over an hour of delays from last-minute interrogations and transportation snafus, Lee Oswald is finally taken downstairs for the transfer. As Jack Ruby exits Western Union, he can't help but wonder what happened with "that commie rat" Oswald. He decides to walk the city block, where the police station exit ramp is buzzing with activity. It must not have happened yet. Oswald must still be down there.

He decides to walk down the ramp and take a look, and yes, the killer of his president is just about to come out, and it's like a red cape in front of a bull. Moments later, at 12:21 P.M. as a smirking, self-satisfied Lee appears between a pair of tough-eyed Dallas detectives—one of whom, big Jim Leavelle, has known Ruby for thirteen years—Jack just loses it. He sees his moment. He reaches into his coat. He pulls out the Cobra and blows Lee Oswald out the back door of history. The bullet tears through him like a corkscrew, hitting nearly every major organ; Leavelle will later be amazed that it didn't pass clean through the suspect and on into him. Indeed, the bullet passes from the left side of Oswald's diaphragm, through his abdomen, intestinal artery, aorta, spleen, and right kidney, and lodges just under the skin of his right side. Any further and it would've hit Leavelle as well.

As Lee lies bleeding on the pavement in a blur of flashcubes and stunned faces, Dallas Police detective Billy Combest drops to his hands and knees and asks him if he has anything to say. Lee shakes his head "definitively," according to Combest, but at the same moment he raises his clenched fist one more time in the Marxist salute. It would be his last statement to the world.[9]

Officially, Lee will be said to have died in the same Parkland Hospital where Kennedy did two days before, but Jim Leavelle will remain certain that he died in the ambulance, en route. He gave a sigh, Jim said, that sound of dying.

They wheel him into Parkland, where doctors work feverishly for over an hour to restore life. But he is officially pronounced dead at 1:07. While he's awaiting autopsy, Jim watches as a nurse carefully incises Lee's flesh and pops the bullet from his body. The detective takes out his penknife and hands it to the nurse.

"Now, I want you to scratch your initials on the butt of that bullet," he tells her, "and I'll scratch mine, because we're gonna be talking about this thing for the rest of our lives."[10]

Ruby's act has done far more than just take the heat off the Jews in Texas. In still one more dramatic display of the Law of Unintended Consequences, Ruby has forever removed the Cubans' and Soviets' worst nightmare: an Oswald who might crack under confinement and point the accusing finger in their direction.

Still, this most simple of violent, emotional acts—regardless of the extraordinary consequences, or perhaps because of them—has since been endowed with a nonexistent complexity. Ruby's bullet silenced Lee, but Lee might well have remained silent anyway. That bullet followed logically from Ruby's mean life. It flowed from the purest kind of human motive, heartbreak and the resulting vengeance. Texas law was still more like frontier justice at that time. Murderers tended to do two to ten years in jail and that was that.

Even as Ruby is booked for the murder of Lee Oswald, he expects to do soft time, as a hero. After the fact, he will tell one of his cop friends, "I just wanted to show that the Jews didn't kill Kennedy. We avenged him." He'll tell a Dallas reporter that he did it in order to prove that "Jews have balls."[11] He will spend the rest of his life in jail, but—as if to explain it all to himself—he keeps a picture of President Kennedy in his cell. He kisses that photo of the dead president every day.

On November 25, after both President Kennedy and his assassin have been buried and Jack Ruby is locked up in the Dallas city jail, Win Scott is at the Mexico City Station poring over the transcript of Dorticós's frantic call to Armas about "the money," combing it for every nuance. Downstairs in the U.S. embassy offices, Ambassador Mann is still burrowing into the Oswald-Cuban links himself. He cables the State Department with his opinion that the Cubans are definitely involved.

As one of the few in leadership old enough to remember how the horrors of World War I were initiated by an assassination, Lyndon Johnson is working around the clock to prevent a nuclear showdown with the Soviets. In a dramatic meeting at the White House, he cancels the Cuban invasion plans that he has just learned of from the CIA, calling them "hogwash."

On separate fronts, he and Robert Kennedy are moving to limit what emerges. Deputy Attorney General Nicholas Katzenbach is the Justice Department's point man on Bob's investigation, and he has to have been keeping the attorney general apprised of the Mexico connections at every step, even as Bob keeps pushing Draznin and Sheridan to investigate Hoffa and the mob.

But for all the attempts to stanch the flow of evidence, more witnesses keep coming through the U.S. embassy door. At around noon, a young man named Gilberto Nolasco Alvarado Ugarte shows up and says he wants to talk with an American official. He needs to tell them about something he knows, something very disturbing that he does not want to keep within himself.

The next day, Win Scott's deputy station chief, Alan White (field pseudonym "Arthur C. Plambeck"), picks Alvarado up and drives him far out of his neighborhood to a spot on the south side of the city, where the man feels it's safe to tell his story. Alvarado is a democratic leftist working as a penetration agent for the anti-Castro Somoza regime in Nicaragua. The Cubans, assuming that he's one of theirs, have helped him to obtain Mexican citizenship with false IDs supplied by the Cuban embassy. He expects to go to Cuba, momentarily, to be trained in sabotage. Although White is not aware of it, Alvarado has been a reliable source for the CIA during the preceding spring.

In the course of developing his Cuban cover, Alvarado says, he has been inside the embassy repeatedly in recent months, and during one of those visits, he too saw Oswald. It was near a patio by the bathroom door on the embassy's ground floor, about noon on a day in late September. Alvarado says there were three men standing there, talking: a black man with reddish hair, prominent cheekbones, and a scar; a Canadian with a blond pompadour; and Oswald, who was wearing a black jacket, buttoned white shirt, dark gray pants, and eyeglasses. He carried a green passport, and he had a pistol in a shoulder holster.

A tall, mixed-race Cuban in his late thirties came from Consul Azcue's office and joined them, giving money to the black man. Alvarado, a trusted saboteur-in-training as far as the G2 people were concerned, tells White that he heard the following fragments of conversation:

The black man said, in English, "I want to kill the man," or words to that effect.

Oswald replied, "You're not man enough. I can do it."

A few moments later, the black man said to the gringo, in Spanish, "I can't go with you. I have a lot to do."

Oswald replied, "The people are waiting for me back there," as if to say he was already covered.

The black man turned the Azcue money over to Oswald, a few thousand U.S. dollars, according to Alvarado's estimate. He also counted out what appeared to be about two hundred pesos.

Within moments, a pretty Cuban embassy employee who had the sensual ease of a prostitute joined them and gave Oswald an *abrazo*, a hug. Alvarado memorized the address she gave him in case he wished to find her—Calle Juarez #407. The address would turn out to be that of Luisa Calderón.[12] As Alvarado was leaving the embassy, so were the three men, through the gate near the corner of Tacubaya. Just outside the compound, they got into a black car and drove off.

Alvarado tells White that he tried to pass this information to the U.S. embassy when he first witnessed it in September, but they said he was wasting their time and hung up on him.

It's late afternoon by the time White drops the Nicaraguan off in a neutral neighborhood, and when he returns to the station and tells Scott and Mann that Alvarado had a story of money changing hands, it dovetails tidily with the intercepts. At 2:00 A.M. on November 27, they send David Atlee Phillips to follow up with Alvarado at a safe house. Phillips is "impressed" by his "wealth of detail," and when he reports back to Scott and the ambassador, he describes the young penetration agent as "completely cooperative," and "showing some signs of fearing for his safety."[13]

While the Agency and the embassy people in Mexico are still operating in good faith to get all they can on the Cuban connection, Washington is moving to quash those lines of inquiry. For his part, Fernando Gutiérrez Barrios of the Mexican DFS is feeding the Americans information while reporting as well to the Mexican president, Adolfo López Mateos, and to Fidel—all to maintain the "lone nut" narrative that is already taking shape. When Luis Echeverría (Win Scott's informant, known as LI TEMPO-8), the secretary to Minister of Government Gustavo Díaz Ordaz (LI TEMPO-2), receives a report that Silvia Durán is among those about to embark for Havana, he decides to take her back into custody, delivering her to Barrios. If there was a conspiracy, the Mexicans want to know so they can manage it, and Durán might just be intimidated enough to reveal the plot. Plus, there's another advantage: she's far enough down the food chain from Azcue and Mirabel that they won't be compromised.

So on the morning of Wednesday, November 27, Silvia Durán is picked up yet again, just as she's sitting down to her breakfast. This time the DFS starts out a bit more politely. They send two agents, and they *ask* her if she'd like to go with them to answer a few more questions. She doesn't even need to take her car, because they are going to bring her home themselves.

She might be wishing she was already in Cuba, but she has to play along, so she calls the consulate to tell them she's going back to the police station and will be coming in late. The DFS keeps her for two and a half days, telling her it's for her own protection.

"They were very rough this time," she will recall fifteen years later. "They were very angry with me, the man that . . . I kicked him in his balls. He was very angry, and they repeat the same questions but they were more . . . [unintelligible]."

The assembled officers harangue her from midmorning until 6:00 that night, Barrios among them. His goal is as much to determine if she is a true believer in Fidel as it is to find out how far and wide the apparent Oswald plot extends.

"I had the feeling that I was going to die," she'll recall, "and I said okay, if I'm going to die, I'm going to die with pride, my child will not be ashamed. I remember I do anything that—I was very dramatic in those moments. So, sometimes I lost my temper. I never say no bad words or nothing. I cry sometimes, I shout and things like that but then I sat down again."[14]

She is beaten, but Silvia Durán gives up only one more piece of information, and it's the same line she'll give to one of Scott's best informants four years later. According to Mexican sources, she will admit only that she had an affair with Lee Oswald. Given her ultimate allegiance to Fidel, had the DFS men beaten her to death, she would have died proud that night.*

It's not known whether she knew that her embassy colleague Luis Alberu was an undercover CIA asset; but when they spoke in 1967, she admitted to him that she had "liked Lee Oswald from the start" and thought nothing of bedding him. But this was no ordinary affair. When news of Oswald's identity came out, it sent her long-suffering husband, Horacio, into a rage. He forbade her to work for the Cubans anymore, or even to see any of them, and the couple went into a kind of self-imposed internal exile. She told Alberu that she believed her phone was tapped, either by the Mexican authorities, or

---

*Photos of Silvia Durán in custody show her face pummeled and puffy. She did not work for the Cuban embassy again.

more probably the CIA, since "tapping was [an] expensive proposition and the Mexicans wouldn't be able to afford it for so long a period."[15]

The saga of Silvia Durán was far from over. When Antonio, the Cuban embassy security guard, was persuaded to speak at a small Mexican café in 2005, he dwelled on the aftermath at the Cuban outpost and its implications for Silvia.

"There were many trips in and out, to and from Havana," Antonio recalled. "The Soviet embassy stopped all contact with us for almost two weeks, even though they're only a couple of streets away from us. That was very noticeable, because there were normally many contacts between us. After [Durán's] interrogation by the Mexican police, she no longer worked at our embassy. She never came again, but she obtained money. I know it because one of my tasks was to serve as a courier for the G2. I had to deliver, repeatedly, envelopes with money for Silvia Durán at her mother's."

With that, Antonio said his good-byes and bolted out of the café, fading into the crowds milling through the park.[16]

Durán surfaces again in 1978, before the House Select Committee, and then disappears once more. Her last comment on the subject will be the fleeting admission in 2005 that there was a *complot*, a conspiracy; and when investigators seek her out today, she is still so terrified that she'll do little more than whisper through the door.

As for her friend Teresa Proenza, the Cuban Communist Party member and alleged lesbian press attaché who helped to get Silvia hired at the embassy in the first place, the last Alberu hears of her, she is "in a Cuban jail as a result of a conviction for espionage on behalf of [deleted] CIA."[17] It is not known if she is still alive, but if so, she'd be approximately ninety-three years old today.

By November 27, Ambassador Mann is lobbying hard for the arrests of Calderón, Azcue, and Mirabal, but it's made abundantly clear that President Johnson, Hoover, Richard Helms at CIA, and Nick Katzenbach are opposed. If the Mexican government, at the directive of the United States, arrests the outgoing consul and his replacement at Cuba's most important embassy, there will be no turning back. It won't take long for the American press, and then the American people, to recognize that the government thinks there was a link between Oswald and the Cubans.

The CIA doesn't want to deal with Alvarado, either, and neither does the FBI, so Hoover decides to fob him off on the Mexicans. While the Americans assume that Barrios is working on their behalf to manage these witnesses, he is doing the same for Fidel; he's taking everyone's measure and deciding who will and will not become a problem. A story is taking shape about what happened in Dallas, and for at least a time it will be Barrios who determines what that story is.

Hoover, at Johnson's command, decides to send one of his few Spanish-speaking agents, Laurence Keenan, down to Mexico to put a cork in this bottle. Keenan thinks he's going to help Mann's maverick investigation, but he's about to find out otherwise.

From Langley, the CIA has cabled Nestor Sánchez, Cubela's case officer in Paris, to order him return to Washington immediately. The FBI sends an international Teletype. The Bureau is rescinding its earlier instruction to its agents, worldwide, reversing the order to make contact with all informants in the field for any information on the Kennedy assassination. Agent Laurence Keenan has arrived in Mexico City.

At this point, the DFS is the presidential police force headed by Gustavo Díaz Ordaz (LI TEMPO-2), the Mexican government's second in command and a CIA asset who will himself become president of Mexico in a matter of months and serve until the end of the decade. As it happens, he is also a personal friend of the new American president, and they begin to actively coordinate on the incipient cover-up.

Under Lyndon's direction, U.S. authorities in Mexico have been forbidden from interviewing any more Cubans, especially the ones who have been flooding the U.S. embassy's phone lines with local tales of Oswald and G2.

By the afternoon of November 28, Win has aligned himself with his superiors: nothing good, he now believes, can come from proving a Cuban connection.[18] Scott calls Luis Echeverría, the head of the Mexican Ministry of the Interior, and says he'd like for him to do the interrogation of Alvarado. But Echeverría says that Barrios will do the honors. The Mexicans will follow the Johnson administration's lead, but they'll do it on their own terms.

By transferring the interrogation over to the DFS, the Ministry of the Interior will now subject a deep-penetration Nicaraguan agent to questioning in order to silence him, a bizarre confusion of roles that will compromise Alvarado horribly, just for trying to help the American government. His cover will be blown; Barrios will know that he has been spying on the Cubans. The investigation is going badly awry.

FBI agent Laurence Keenan has arrived in Mexico City.

A meeting is held between Keenan, Scott, Mann, and Phillips, and it's here that Mann is ordered to stop investigating the rapidly accruing evidence against the Cubans.

"I received this instruction to drop the investigation," Mann will recall thirty years later. ". . . It was the only time in my career that I was ever told to stop investigating. I still think it was strange . . . I had this suspicion that our intelligence community, which included Win Scott, knew much more about it [the assassination]."

Mann will have a hard time letting it go, even as he gets "death threats, quite often in envelopes slipped under the embassy gates."[19]

By 11:30 that evening, Alvarado has undergone four hours with Barrios, who emerges and reports to Scott. At first, he says, he thought Alvarado was telling "a fantastic lie," but even after this second go-round he has not been able to shake the Nicaraguan off it. Alvarado "is telling the truth, essentially," reported Barrios, "or is the best liar I have talked to in my many years, and I have talked to some of the biggest."[20]

Alvarado's Nicaraguan handler arrives, apparently not knowing that his man is being harried, and vouches for Alvarado, saying that he usually provides good information on Communists. Barrios promises Scott that he will go back in and get even tougher. Whatever Win Scott thought that meant, we can only guess. In any case, Scott informs Washington.

In the dark chaos of these Mexican nights, it is no exaggeration to say that the fate of the world lies briefly in the hands of Fernando Gutiérrez Barrios. Whatever is going on in these interrogation rooms in the dank secret chambers of the DFS, he makes certain that Havana's knowledge of these events is not even implied on the record. This is where the dirty work of cover-up begins. This is another of the crucibles in which the grand illusions of the sixties are about to be formed, all for the sake of keeping the peace—or protecting an old friend named Fidel.

By 10:30 the next morning, November 29, Gilberto Alvarado Ugarte has signed a statement recanting everything. He will tell his handler that he recanted because Barrios threatened to hang him by his testicles, and he now resents the U.S. for handing him over to the Mexicans. CIA headquarters is relieved, and Helms asks Scott to thank Barrios on behalf of President Johnson.[21] Barrios has come up with a deft way to please both masters. As the FBI's Jim Hosty will express it, "both Cuba *and* the CIA wanted the witnesses to change their testimony. Neither Cuba nor the U.S. wanted this story to come out."[22]

*   *   *

On November 29, Lyndon has decided to establish a commission to investigate the assassination. It must be headed by someone whom the American people can put their full trust in, and so Bobby's aides meet with Chief Justice Earl Warren, a Kennedy family friend, and ask him to head up the inquiry. Warren, however, fears that his appointment as head of the judiciary could compromise what is essentially an executive branch investigation, thus violating constitutional provisions for the separation of powers. He turns them down flat.[23]

But Johnson won't hear of it. In one week, he has grown from a snubbed and sidelined vice president to a battle-minded chief executive trying to stave off a catastrophe. He sits Warren down in the Oval Office, eyeball to eyeball, confiding his fear that he's facing the same situation that initiated the First World War.

He cajoles him, "You'd go and fight if you thought you could save one American life . . . Why, if Khrushchev moved on us, he could kill 39 million *in an hour* . . . I'm asking you something and you're saying no to everybody when you could be speaking for 39 million people."

Lyndon then shares with him the report on the questioning of Alvarado, and alludes to other evidence. The implication is clear. This could involve Cuba, which means it will soon involve Russia. Tears come into Warren's eyes.

"I just can't say no," he finally concedes.

The next nine months of Warren's life will age him tremendously. His children will fear for his life, but he agrees to head up what will be known as the Warren Commission.

On December 2, back in Mexico City, in the shadow of a sixty-thousand-seat bullfight arena on Florida Street, Pedro Gutiérrez Valencia sits at his Formica kitchen table and stares at a ten-day-old newspaper. He can hear some kids fighting in the street, a *guitarra* pulsing from someone's balcony. He's a little hungry and he can smell the fresh tortillas his wife has rolled out on the counter, but nothing can distract him from the faces of the two dead men on the front page. One face is the president's, the other the face of his killer, the face of the man he saw at the Cuban embassy, either on September 30 or October 1 when he went there to give Luisa Calderón her credit report. He does not know that another man has already been roughed up and threatened by the DFS for trying to tell virtually the same story that he is about to tell. Even if he did know, it would probably not stop him from spooling the blank page into his Corona typewriter and popping his knuckles, and then starting to type the address he has gotten from the library.

To: "President Lyndon B. Johnson, The White House, 1600 Pennsylvania Avenue . . ." He does not exactly feel better as he types, but he knows it's the right thing to do.

"Dear President Johnson . . ."

Perhaps it takes him a few tries to get it right. Perhaps his wife brings dinner and sets it at his elbow and he has a pile of crumpled pages before he gets it just so, but Gutiérrez's letter will find its mark. It will reach the president. It will be passed to the FBI, and—for reasons he will never know—it will also attract the attention of the Cuban G2, exactly the people he did not want to attract.

In 1964, after the FBI comes and interviews Gutiérrez, the Cubans come in their wake and threaten to kill him if he doesn't recant his letter. The stress nearly kills him. He will decide that the only way he'll survive is to flee Mexico, change his name, and move to a secret location in the United States. Even then, he fears that the Cubans might still try to get him, so when he has the chance, when he is called to testify by the HSCA in 1978, he will recant his letter to the president of the United States. As an old man, he'll want to have nothing to do with what he saw when he was young.

Alvarado will go silent, too; he'll die in Nicaragua in 2000, having said nothing more about Lee Harvey Oswald.

In December, Vincent T. Lee shuts down the Fair Play for Cuba Committee when its landlord evicts the group from its national office in Manhattan. After Oswald's connection to the FPCC becomes known, public opinion has solidified harshly against the committee, making it impossible to continue its work.

Exhausted as he is in those first few weeks after Dallas, Lyndon Johnson works the phones, continuing to coordinate with Gustavo Díaz Ordaz. Translating for him now is Thomas Mann. "Lyndon Johnson had lines into Mexico that I knew nothing about," Mann will one day recall. "He was an amazing man," and all the more so because he was risking permanent damage to history in defense of a peaceful present. Their meetings will continue long after Ordaz assumes the Mexican presidency, sometimes at the Johnson ranch in Texas. Thomas Mann will continue as translator, the better to keep the secrets tightly held between them.[24]

Barrios's massive classified Oswald file will eventually be entrusted to his protégé Vicente Capello. Only in 2005 will Capello allow Huismann and

Mauricio Berber a sneak peak into those files, and included along with the arrest photos of Silvia Durán are additional shots of a Cuban.

"Who is he?" one of the investigators asks.

"I don't know," says Capello, hastily locking the carton.

Weeks later, Mauricio persuades him to open his treasure trunk once again. In the second sighting of the files, Mauricio gets a longer look at one of the photos: the portrait of a slim Cuban, swarthy, with curly hair and Negroid features. The hair color is not apparent—the photo is in black and white. But along the bottom edge, it carries the memo: "*Pelirrojo*, agent of the G2." *Pelirrojo* means red-haired.

Capello closes his file carton once more, but not before Mauricio and Willi have noticed an index card cross-referencing a letter dated December 1963, from the office of the Mexican president, addressed to the head of the Mexican secret service, with the order: "The new American President L.B. Johnson has asked for them to immediately stop all investigations regarding Lee Harvey Oswald." According to the index card, this letter is signed by Díaz Ordaz.

"So where is his original letter to the head of the secret service?" Huismann wants to know.

Capello shrugs his shoulders and says, "If it is here, we'll find it."

After two days of searching, Capello comes back to report that there is no such letter. The investigators insist. If there's an index card, then there has to be a document that the card refers to.

"What index card?" Capello replies. The card is no longer where it was in the cross-file, either.

There will be no transcripts or recordings of the most sensitive communications that weekend: between Johnson and Bobby, Johnson and Ordaz, Scott and Johnson, Barrios and Scott and the rest. Nearly half a century later, the wry former CIA staffer from Operation Mongoose, Sam Halpern, will say, simply, "The good stuff isn't written down, and it certainly isn't recorded." All CIA station chiefs could reach the president directly, at least in Halpern's time, without even going through the CIA communications center.

The FBI had the same resource. Ray Wannall, the Bureau's longtime chief of worldwide counterintelligence, said, "All of the pertinent information that we got that was of possible value or known value to the White House or the secretary of state was given to them, and the way it was given is what we call *blind memorandum*, just a piece of paper with no letterhead on it. An agent would just take it in his hand, carry it to the White House or the State

Department, show it to the appropriate official there, and take it back. We never left it there for it to rattle around in somebody's files and compromise the operation."[25]

By mid-December, all the major players, the U.S., the USSR, Cuba, and Mexico, are coming together to create a global cover-up. The Cubans have called many of their Mexico City embassy staffers home and intimidated others. The Soviets have distanced themselves from both Cuba and Oswald, and paid elaborate tribute to Kennedy. The Mexicans have acted as the silencer for Washington, Havana, and Moscow. Lyndon has micromanaged the U.S. investigation, strong-armed prosecutions in Dallas and Mexico, and put an official end to the secret war against Cuba, including all attempts on the lives of Fidel and Raúl Castro: Lee Oswald has procured for them a stay of execution and a reprieve for their tormented regime.[26]

In the Central America training camps, Los Amigos de Roberto are inconsolable. Not only have they lost their greatest ally in Jack Kennedy, but their hopes for reclaiming the homeland now rest with a man they barely know. And in the first few weeks of his presidency, Lyndon Johnson has become a vortex into which all the shards of evidence, rumor, and half-truth will disappear until he can determine how to reframe them.

On December 19, Joe Califano is given the task of informing the Cuban exiles that the program of embedding the new invasion force in a "training program" within the Army will be ended. Califano will recount it as a "wrenching meeting" with exile leader Lieutenant Erneido Oliva at Sheppard Air Force Base in Wichita Falls, Texas.

"Tears came to [Oliva's] eyes as he heard our decision against such a plan. He made one last plea to use the Brigade to invade Cuba. Then, as he came to realize there was no room for discussion, he slumped into a wooden chair."[27]

Three days later, Oliva and three other top exile leaders resign from the Army.

Oliva will recall it differently. In mid-January of 1964, he is undergoing artillery training at Fort Sill, Oklahoma, when he's summoned to Washington by Bobby Kennedy. Once he's there and settled in his hotel, Bob sends a car for him and meets Oliva outside the Executive Mansion, whereupon he tells him that Lyndon has decided to end the Special Presidential Program for BOP veterans in the U.S. military, the euphemism for the Cuban reinvasion plans set to happen before the November elections. Bobby has tried to dissuade Johnson, to no avail.

"A few minutes later we went to the library," Oliva will recount, "not the Oval Office, and Johnson came in and flatly told me my program with the Cubans had to be terminated. Bobby didn't say anything . . . He didn't want to try and persuade the president in front of me. So he was only listening, his head bowed. Pretty sad."

The meeting lasts sixteen minutes and, as it ends, the president asks Oliva to go directly over to the Pentagon. There, Robert McNamara, Cyrus Vance, Joe Califano, and Al Haig inform him that he will have to go to all the military bases and tell his fellows the news. It is not known whether this includes the Central American bases where the re-invasion maneuvers had begun; but four months later, Oliva resigns from active duty.[28] He will live out his days believing that if Jack Kennedy had survived his first term, the invasion would have proceeded as planned.[29]

On the last day of 1963, Ralph A. Dungan, a New Frontiersman and a close aide of Jack's since his days in the Senate, sat down and wrote a memo about the assassination to Bobby's deputy, Nick Katzenbach. He attached a twenty-page study of Oswald by José I. Lasaga, a Harvard-trained clinical psychologist, and former head of Havana's Villanueva University Department of Psychology.

Attached to the memo, Dungan included a photograph from *Bohemia* magazine that depicted the aforementioned "casket" of JFK being paraded before the Castros and Che in 1962. In the attached study, Lasaga came to a number of remarkably accurate conclusions. First, he said, Castro was, at minimum, the "intellectual author" of the crime, who, "knowing that Oswald had conceived the idea of killing the President, gave his plan the necessary push that would make it a reality, by approving the idea and offering to protect him after the crime had been perpetrated." The only possible remaining question is, was Castro also the "originator of the crime"? Without the benefit of the past forty-five years of evidence, Lasaga, nevertheless, saw a great deal in the speech Fidel gave the day after the assassination, on November 23, 1963. The key, Lasaga claimed, was in a paragraph wherein Castro starts to ramble about how "the revolutionaries are forced to defend themselves." The speech becomes disjointed, "just as when a person is touching a point liable to excite in him great anxiety. In psychoanalysis that paragraph would have been said to correspond to one of those moments in which things that are desired to be kept in silence, struggle to come out." In other words, Castro's ego desperately wanted to justify his crime, but he had caught himself just in time. "Perceiving the perilous ground on which he began to tread, his words reflect the fear which seizes him at the possibility of saying something that might jeopardize him."

Lasaga, and likely Dungan too, was convinced that Castro's motive was to "interrupt the rapprochement between Washington and Moscow, thereby ruining the possibility of an agreement between the Russians and the Americans whereby it would have been possible to eliminate Fidel's outfit from Cuba." The matter-of-fact inclusion of this argument, which must certainly have made it to the desk of Bobby Kennedy, implies that rumors of a "Laos Solution" to Cuba, a U.S./USSR collaboration to squeeze the Castros out of power, was more than a rumor but quite likely an intended by-product of détente: in effect, it suggests that the process of "policing the world" would become a joint one with the Soviets. And the added incentive for Fidel to "oust" Kennedy was probably unknown to Dungan and Lasaga, that being the other provocations of the AM/LASH/Cubela plot, and OP-PLANS.

They knew nothing of the events reported by Elena and Elenita Garro yet, but they did know of Lee Oswald's meeting in a Mexico City restaurant with Cuban diplomats, information obtained from a "very reliable source." They cited that as also key to understanding the crime.

Dungan and Lasaga also believed that Oswald did not confess "because he was not a fanatic, as Booth [Lincoln's killer], Guiteau [Garfield's], or Czolosz [McKinley's], all of whom sought fame for their crime." Instead, Oswald was "a disciplined Communist, who knew that he was doing his duty for his party, and was afraid that he might let slip out the most important of secrets: the existence of a great accomplice."[30]

This may not have been strictly true. The Cuban promises made to Lee Oswald must have included references to what would be his heroic place in the Communist pantheon. But it's accurate insofar as Lee was disciplined enough to stand by the terms of his recruitment, maintain his secrets to the end, and do his part to cover the unseen hand of "Uncle Fidel."

According to all credible forensic evidence, John Fitzgerald Kennedy was shot by one man from one perch. But in the wake of the unimaginable complication that Lee Oswald created, Lyndon Johnson, Nikita Khrushchev, Gustavo Díaz Ordaz, and the Castro brothers became Bobby's de facto conspirators in a cover-up that would extend from the Kennedy Library to the KGB archives, from the G2 files to the vaults of the Mexican DFS, from the CIA tombs to the most intimately held secrets of Bobby himself. The Warren Commission, charged with solving the case, was forcibly misled in a deliberate campaign orchestrated by Bobby and Lyndon, Bobby acting largely in the interests of his family's legacy, Lyndon in the interests of the nation's security. The more that Bobby worked to curate the facts that the commission would see, the more the real truth forced a horrible reckoning upon him. During the last weeks of 1963 and throughout most of 1964, these two men, who disliked and would soon come to hate each other, were forced to collude in the most intimate way. It may have been an act of self-defense on Bobby's part, but it was an act of national defense on Lyndon's. Indeed, for all the cultural damage that would result from the commission's half-truths, all the weakening of the bond between the American people and their government, Johnson could not have predicted those alienating, perhaps even revolutionary effects in the cold winter days of December 1963. All he could see was the limits of military power in such a vacuum. All he could do was opt to "manage the truth" in hopes of keeping America's national pride, grief, and rage from dragging the world to extinction.

It may have been Lyndon Johnson's finest hour.

CHAPTER 14
The Games People Play

LYNDON JOHNSON WAS A RESTLESS soul. His wife, Lady Bird, said that he "acts as if there is never going to be a tomorrow,"[1] and for the first few hours after the assassination, he had believed it. The next day, back in Washington, Jack's predecessor, Dwight Eisenhower, was on hand to give the new president his support.

"I'd known him for a long time. He was, as he always is, nervous—walking around and telephoning everyone . . . I would mention someone in the conversation and he would snatch up the receiver and call the person. He asked my advice about many matters . . . As far as I could see at that time, [his] only intention was to find out what was going on and carry policy through. He suggested nothing new or different."[2]

This statement would prove prescient. By and large, Lyndon's presidency would become a thankless exercise in what might have been. He would see great legislative success, harvesting bushels of bills that had failed to thrive under Jack's care, but he would mostly be a stand-in for a dead man, never quite getting credit for the successes but serving as a ready scapegoat for the failures.

Johnson was a prodigious smoker, a very capable drinker, a teller of tall and ribald tales. He was also, for all his bravado and achievement, a very insecure person. He was brilliant and he was decisive, but he knew that the New Frontiersmen disliked him. Bobby Kennedy had practically forbidden him to move into the Oval Office. But when it came to covering Jack's tracks over Cuba, he was cunning as hell.

While Lyndon was assuming power, Bobby was nearly catatonic with grief and guilt. For all those who were trying to round up any conspirators in Jack's murder, no one wanted to know more than his little brother. However, he knew that some knowledge could never be acted upon: proof of a mob hit, if any were found, would disgorge too much ugly Kennedy family history, and, worse still, a Cuban angle would expose the White House's own murder plotting, marring Jack's name for all time.

Bobby was so devastated after Jack's death that he left the Justice Department to Nick Katzenbach's care for months. When he did finally return, he was a morass of pain, his eyes perpetually red, his concentration shattered. He could barely bring himself to speak, even to Ethel. His old *amigo* Sergio Arcacha called with condolences, and the conversation lasted only a minute or two. When he could steel himself to ask Harry Williams, point-blank, what he thought about Dallas, Harry told him that he thought Castro did it. Bobby didn't reply, but his face told Harry that he was beginning to accept it. He created a small shrine to his brother in a dim, hidden corner of the office, an altar of remembrance that no one knew about except his closest intimates. There he would put photos, rosaries and statuettes, books and little artifacts, touchstones that would draw him away from his desk repeatedly in the course of a day, until the altar became his focus, the place where he mourned.

The Warren Commission was beginning its work, but Bobby would never really cooperate with it. It's likely that he simply could not decide whether to tell them about Cuba. In the end, he would choose to stonewall; and throughout, he had a mole inside the process to keep tabs on where Warren's people were going. A senior official from Justice had been assigned to the staff but he was really working for Bobby, reading everything that went through the commission's hands. At least half a dozen of the DOJ man's fellow staffers knew why he was there, including Warren himself.

Bobby was also pressing on with his own investigation. By the end of 1963, Jules Draznin, acting on his orders, had dogged down every Mafia angle he could think of, from one end of the country to the other. It was probably sometime just before the end of 1963 that he came to report to Bobby, either at Hickory Hill or in the big, high-ceilinged office at Justice, now somehow funereal and grim.

Bobby's suspicions about the mob had seemed impractical from the outset. American organized crime was reaching the absolute height of its power, and it had not got there by overreaching. The worst-case scenario for the gangsters would be that they had killed the president while his brother remained in office as the attorney general. It simply made no sense for them to assassinate Jack.

Mooney Giancana certainly didn't need to kill Jack Kennedy. He and Rosselli had long since abandoned the crusade to kill Fidel, but he was still effectively immunized from Justice Department prosecution by his part in the fixed election of 1960, in Bobby's inherited plots, and in Jack's infidelities. If Mooney had ever taken the stand in his own defense, he could have spilled the truth of it all over the attorney general. Al Capone's young guns were not like the out-of-control East Coast mob families. They thought of the syndicates as just that, the criminal shadows of the corporate world, well dressed, well defended, and far too powerful to get mixed up in killing a president—or even a local official, for that matter. Mooney Giancana already had Kennedy politically dead to rights, and might very well have played that card before the 1964 election. He had also exacted a slice of revenge by withdrawing his hit men at the time of the Bay of Pigs, effectively helping to cripple Kennedy's presidency.

Jules also quashed the notion that Ruby had mob associates who wanted Oswald killed. As an adult, the closest Ruby ever got to the mob was going through Carlos Marcello, the old, avuncular crime boss of New Orleans, to hire strippers for his clubs in Dallas. "Ruby was intent on taking care of the guy who killed his beloved president," Jules said, years later. "I believe it to this day. I told that to Bobby face-to-face in a private meeting."[3] As for a connection between Ruby and Oswald, Dallas detective Jim Leavelle and his partner had questioned scores and scores of people in Dallas who said they had seen the two men together. Oh, one said, he spied them in this bowling alley. Another said, yeah, it was in a cocktail lounge. Still another claimed that she saw them in a deli, eating bagels and cream cheese. But they all sounded sketchy to Jim, and when it came down to it, not one of them would ever agree to take a lie detector test.[4]

When Draznin had finished laying out the evidence against the mob's involvement, Bob stared at him for a long moment, and then looked off at the naked trees through the window, slowly nodding his head. Jules's case was ironclad, and no Oswald-Ruby link has ever been proved.

The other angles weren't panning out either. Had the CIA (or even a rogue element within it) been proven to have unseated a president, Bobby, or someone near him with less to lose, would not have hesitated to tell the world about it. And had anti-Castro Cuban elements been responsible, they too would have been charged, but there was no evidence of this either. Oswald's knowledge of the Camp Street CRC had by now been documented—he had stamped their address on his pro-Castro pamphlets.

Still, Bob kept up the search, despite his borderline catatonia. He was sneaking in and out of Dallas that winter, following his own leads. One night at the Adolphus Hotel, Al Maddox, the deputy sheriff of Dallas County, arrived for drinks with Sheriff Bill Decker, and when they walked in the front door, they saw Bobby Kennedy standing there in the lobby.

Decker turned to Maddox and said, "'You didn't see anything,'" Maddox recalled, "and I *didn't* see anything."[5]

The FBI agent who ferried Bobby to and from the airport, Vincent Drain, used to drop him a mile from the Love Field terminal so he could jog the last bit before flying back to Washington.[6] Not once did the Dallas press report on Bobby's visits, and the Kennedy inner circle never went on the record to speak of them either.

The fury that he had first aimed at God, he now seemed to be aiming at himself. Though his Catholic beliefs were essential to him both before and after, they helped him less now than other texts did. Jackie tried to help him by guiding him to books: Camus, the Greeks, Edith Hamilton. From *The Greek Way*, he copied out a number of hard lessons: "The gods who hated beyond all else the arrogance of power, had passed judgment upon them. The time had come when the great Empire should be broken and humbled. Insolent assurance will surely, soon or late, be brought low." Herodotus and Aeschylus spoke to him: "All arrogance will reap a harvest rich in tears. God calls men to a heavy reckoning for overweening pride . . ." From Camus, he copied: "I feel rather like Augustine did before becoming a Christian when he said, 'I tried to find the source of evil and got nowhere.' . . . Perhaps we cannot prevent this world from being a world in which children are tortured. But we can reduce the number of tortured children. And if you believers don't help us, who else in the world can help us do this?"

He was drinking medicinally for a time, driving around the capital at night in the family's Ford Galaxie convertible. He plowed through rainstorms and snowstorms with the top down, his red, gloveless hands and head exposed to the slashing wind. He would get a few drinks in him and guide the car through the icy, empty streets to Arlington Cemetery and scale the fence, stumbling among the headstones and prostrating himself on Jack's grave.[7] He had memorized this from Aeschylus, and it must have rained down upon him on these nights: "God, whose law it is that he who learns must suffer. And even in our sleep pain that cannot forget, falls drop by drop upon the heart, and in our own despite, against our will, comes wisdom to us by the awful grace of God."

He could not bear this loss. He would live on the edge of the forest of grief for the rest of his life, as if being called to walk into it and never come back.

On February 14, 1964, CIA Soviet specialist Tennent "Pete" Bagley Jr. was being driven to the airport in Geneva, Switzerland. Sitting at his side was the chief of the KGB's Seventh Directorate, Yuriy Ivanovich Nosenko. Nosenko, age forty-seven, had been stationed in the Soviets' Geneva consulate. It had been his job to recruit foreign spies there. He had also headed the Second Chief Directorate's "Tourist Department," which controlled the files of foreign tourist defectors, Marxist romantics, and would-be intellectuals like Lee Harvey Oswald. But Yuriy Nosenko's own militancy and romanticism had worn off long ago. He was ready to leave the KGB. He was ready to pass through the Iron Curtain, to see what was on the other side. They boarded a direct flight to Washington, first class all the way.

Upon his arrival, Nosenko was given the code name AE FOXTROT. He was the first KGB man of any stature to defect since Jack Kennedy had been killed, and he was immediately sealed in the pressure cooker of a CIA debriefing from which he would not be released for three and a half years. He had told Bagley that he held two pieces of information that were invaluable to the United States, and he expected to be treated accordingly; but as the Agency chauffeur drove them to the first of his North American safe houses late that night, Nosenko had entered a very deep well of CIA suspicion and misgiving. Had he known just how deep that well was in the wake of Dallas, he might have taken a weekend ski trip to Zermatt on the Matterhorn, instead.

He took the men at Langley to be reasonable men. In their first debriefing, Nosenko told them, in no uncertain terms, that a deep mole had *not* penetrated the CIA, as had been claimed three years earlier by a previous KGB defector. Major Anatoliy Mikhaylovich Golitsyn (AE LADLE), from the Soviets' Helsinki embassy staff, had come over at age forty-four, and had told his interrogators that he knew only that the mole's last name began with a "K," and that his nickname was Sasha. Bolstering Golitsyn's credibility was the fact that he had provided critical information that led to the exposure of many Western agents who were doubling for the Soviets, including such turncoats as Kim Philby, Donald Duart Maclean, Guy Burgess, John Vassall, Aleksandr Kopatzky, and others.

But by far the most important Nosenko disclosure was that he had personally handled the Oswald KGB file, and could say categorically that the Soviets believed Oswald was unstable when he lived there and therefore he was of absolutely no interest to the KGB. As comforting as the Oswald claim would have been to most of official Washington, the CIA's counterintelligence chief, James Jesus Angleton (who had personally escorted Golitsyn to the U.S.), could not let Nosenko's other claim stand. He was so certain that moles had compromised the Agency that he spearheaded an internal movement to check Nosenko's bona fides.

Indeed, under scrutiny, many mistakes and inconsistencies arose during Nosenko's interrogations. Further complicating the issue was the recent defection to the FBI of Aleksandr Kulak (FEDORA), a KGB officer working at the United Nations New York secretariat, who confirmed Nosenko's story about Oswald but was soon unmasked as a fake defector, which tainted Nosenko by association. On the other side, those who doubted Golitsyn were quick to point out that the super mole he predicted, Sasha, was never found.

All this played out against the long history of sophisticated, and mind-numbing, Russian disinformation, which had been a cornerstone of its spycraft for a century. As former NSA deputy chief Colonel Jack Frost explained, "By its very nature, the Soviet culture was much better suited to secrecy and disinformation than we were."[8] As the initial danger of a nuclear showdown began to ease, the political dis-interpretation of Dallas in the Russian press was now being adapted to an exportable form. Khrushchev had eased restrictions on Russian literature, allowing the publication of Solzhenitsyn's *One Day in the Life of Ivan Denisovich* and bringing a small measure of self-criticism to Soviet culture; but Nikita would soon be driven from power, and new forms of historical fiction were about to be deployed for the new youth market in America.

Meanwhile, the dueling defectors at the CIA had virtually split the Agency down the middle over whom to believe.

It was decided that Nosenko should be kept in solitary confinement indefinitely to see if he would spill the truth of why he had defected. He had spilled it already, in fact, but not enough CIA guys believed him. If he had been sent as an apologist for the KGB, a psychological operative, a disinformer, then he would be psychologically operated on, as well.

Yuriy Nosenko was placed in his own private gulag and kept in solitary for 1,277 days, from 1964 to '67, in windowless, ten-foot-square CIA rooms in Clinton, Maryland, and Camp Peary, Virginia. A sixty-watt bulb was left burning in his unheated cell for twenty-four hours a day. He was under round-the-clock visual surveillance through a barred door, and wasn't allowed to lie down between 6 A.M. and 10 P.M. When he made a sanity-preserving chess set out of dust and threads, it was confiscated. For nearly the entire length of Lyndon Johnson's presidency, no one spoke to him except interrogators, who questioned him on 292 different days; but when he made a calendar out of lint, it was swept away. He was allowed no books, no newspapers, no television or radio. Until a doctor improved his diet, slightly, it consisted of weak tea, watery soup, porridge, and either bread or macaroni.

He became like a lobster under a lid, clamoring daily to get out of hot water. They tried to boil him down in countless inhuman ways, and it went on and on, through what was left of John McCone's run as DCI (1961–65), then under William Raborn's term (1965–66), and well into the reign of Richard Helms (1966–73). During this period, he failed three polygraphs; but even under this extraordinary duress Nosenko held firm—Lee Harvey Oswald was not an agent of the KGB.

After almost four years, the man was released, and was later acknowledged as a hero by new management at CIA under DCI William Colby (1973–76). He was given a house in the southeastern United States and a yearly pension. Amazingly, Golitsyn, who contradicted much of what Nosenko said, was also set up with a pension and a free home in the Northeast.[9]

Still, the divisions caused by the Nosenko-Golitsyn debate within the CIA were disastrous, deadlocking its Soviet Division for a decade, and bringing about the downfall of Angleton. When a massive amount of data (twenty-five thousand pages) from KGB files was smuggled to England in 1992, it was learned that both defectors were in fact authentic; their presence in America had caused so much anguish in the Kremlin that Golitsyn (code-named GORBATY, "Hunchback," by the Sovs) and Nosenko (IDOL) were placed on a list for assassination by the KGB, which had largely been out of the "liquidation" business since 1962.[10]*

Golitsyin's "Sasha" error was later explained, as well: SASHA was not the agent's nickname, but his code name. His full name was revealed in 1999 as Aleksandr Mikhailovich Korotkov.[11] Other errors by both defectors were

---

*In his seminal 1999 book *The Sword and the Shield*, Cambridge intelligence scholar Christopher Andrew details the story of KGB officer Vasili Mitrokhin, who, over a twelve-year period, made copious daily notes of every KGB memo he could observe. He accomplished this while overseeing the sealing and checking of 300,000 KGB files when they were in transit to a new storage facility. When he defected to England in 1992, he brought the trove, totaling some 25,000 pages in six cases. The unprecedented treasure included countless revelations about KGB methods, defectors, and disinformation campaigns.

attributed to their incomplete access to information and a desperate desire to be accepted in the West; they were saying what they *thought* the U.S. wanted to hear. According to high-ranking KGB defector Lieutenant General Ion Mihai Pacepa: "I know for a fact that Nosenko was a bona fide defector. But he belonged to a KGB domestic department and knew nothing about PGU foreign sources—just as a middle level FBI agent would know nothing about CIA sources abroad."[12] Neither of the defectors was a dissembler, after all, but there was a Communist culture war against America in the works, post-Dallas, and it was about to get under way.

The *real* Soviet disinformation that was launched that spring went totally undetected for years. It was then that the KGB, following on the first response of the Soviet press to the assassination, developed a more episodic and methodical approach to its "theorizing" about the American right wing. The objective was to create the illusion of "blowback" against the CIA—to make it appear that an Agency plot against Jack had been exposed by objective investigators. This propaganda campaign, meant initially to shield Moscow from suspicion and Cuba from retaliation, had the added benefit of turning the New Left in the U.S. and other Western democracies against the CIA, against the government—against a system they had already begun to reject. The Kennedy assassination would be a turning point.

By 1964, the people born during or after World War II were reaching the age of awareness and, for some, of noncompliance in the "perpetual war." Kennedy had presented himself as a new kind of modernist leader, a young man of aggressive goodness, extending the New Deal to the whole Western Hemisphere. He was tough but optimistic and ready to do battle to spread world peace. The American public educational system was in its golden age; these kids were smart, and the New Frontier was nearly as fresh and engaging for them as it was for their young parents. Television sets brought space launches into the classrooms. There were little kids living in the White House, and they rode ponies around the lawn. The sense of triumph and promise was so effervescent that pundits took to calling it the American Century.

But then came Dallas. For tens of millions of children, the public execution of JFK was the first time they had ever imagined their parents' deaths; with Jack's death, with the slaying of the new Modern Hero, the afterglow of the victorious 1950s suddenly did a quick fade, like the lights going down in a theater.

With the First Family's exit, a whole other array of images rushed into the vacuum. The comfortable sense of control and order that marked the 1950s was gone in a few seconds, replaced by the unprocessed lessons of the recent past. Just as the Japanese had awakened "the sleeping giant" of America in the 1940s, Lee Oswald awoke the giant of the 1960s, and the camera had brought it straight home in that bloody weekend of November 1963. The camera was changing everything.

World War I had cost nearly twenty million lives and left twenty-one million wounded. World War II had gobbled up seventy million human beings, forty-seven million civilians, and twenty-five million combatants. The Second World War was brought home in living color, and, when it ended, it seemed that every veteran had, high on his bookshelf, books of photographs from the death camps and the radiation fields. Movies brought real war to your local theater. During the Eisenhower and Kennedy years, children enacted "duck and cover" drills in their classrooms, rehearsing for the apocalypse as if it might be no more than a passing tornado or hurricane; but when Kennedy died, no one believed that anymore.

Small wonder that a revolt was in the making. World War I had caused the revulsion of Dada and the Surrealists. The ghastly pietàs of Hiroshima and Auschwitz brought an even wider revulsion, the disdain of the Beats and then the disgust of the hippies. Once the nationalistic fervor had worn off, the new enemy was not so much the Commies as the ugly absurdity of war itself. Just as it had been their parents' moral task to stand up to Hitler and Stalin, it soon became their children's self-determination to try to dissemble the war machine itself, worldwide, a "never again" agenda taken to its logical extreme. When the camera soon brought them a fresh hell, Vietnam, on a daily basis, and the government started drafting the males into service, many in that generation snapped. It seemed that they too were about to be fed into the meat grinder of history's favorite pastime, unless they stood together and refused.

Those who did refuse took the consequences. Some were isolationists. Others were pacifists, and still others were just cowards. But for many resisters, a perpetual war against Communism had come to seem like an absurd way to win the hearts and minds of the globe's poor people. The resisters simply didn't want to police the world. They refused to fight those who sought communal solace in a dictatorship of sharing, even if it meant a sharing that had to be enforced by the relinquishment of one's individual rights and aspirations. Perhaps, for the enemy, survival came first; personal liberty came later, if ever. Perhaps it was enough for the enemy to *have* just enough. They would learn about their hopes and desires later, and who were we to try to impose their selfhood now? Why should Americans kill them to bring them to the Enlightenment?

Careless as the reasoning was in some ways, after two world wars and a missile crisis, it seemed quite sane. It defined, in effect, the first post-apocalyptic generation, a phoenixlike cohort, born to prevent the end of the world that seemed so close at hand.

Soviet propagandists stepped straight into this incipient Western culture clash, as if they had torn a page straight out of Turgenev or Dostoyevsky and knew exactly how to turn father against son.

Enter Carl Aldo Marzani, an American publisher born in Italy, and a Communist who had been recruited as a Soviet agent, perhaps before World War II, when it might still be chalked up to youthful exuberance. His code name was NORD, and by the 1960s he was based in New York City. His Manhattan apartment, bedecked with posters and tracts and newspapers, was a salon of sorts for Red spies, rogue writers, and tipsy anarchists. While they debated the future over cheap vodka and old cheese, Marzani was pressing their ideas into print, cranking out hundreds of titles on progressive subjects, all under the rubric of the Liberty Book Club. That club had become so boldly pro-Soviet that the KGB decided to keep the doors open with generous infusions of cash. In fact, they were generous enough to have given Marzani some $70,000 between May 1960 and September of 1961, plus another ten grand a year for advertising. It was all part of the KGB's new concept of "active measures," a wedding of the old propaganda and disinformation techniques with the new psychological warfare.

It was Marzani who, in 1964, published the first book about the assassination in the U.S., *Oswald: Assassin or Fall-Guy*, written by a German Communist named Joachim Joesten. It was Joachim's thesis that H. L. Hunt and Bunker Hunt, two ultraconservative Texas oilmen, had rigged the Kennedy assassination for fear that Jack was dragging the nation toward Communism.[13]

Then came Mark Lane, a lefty New York lawyer who was soon developing his own evening promenade, at a small theater near his even smaller office on lower Fifth Avenue. It was there that Lane extolled his version of events in what became known as The Speech. The New Left, leery of Old Left Communism but regrouping for the next phase of the progressive fight, was looking for a populist hook when Lane came along. The shocking spectacle and bizarre aftermath of Kennedy's death had transformed his image from that of a centrist Cold Warrior into one of a liberal martyr. For the new youth culture, the death soon became a rallying point, and when the Warren Commission Report hit the shelves, Lane was among the first to see its gaps and flaws in logic as an opportunity.

Lane's little theater became a counterculture hot spot. He updated The Speech weekly, but it was all to prove the same thesis—that the CIA had killed John Kennedy. Lane was also being subsidized, though perhaps unwittingly and on a much smaller scale than Marzani, by KGB-connected journalists, among them Genrikh Borovik, who encouraged his efforts.[14] At one point, while on a tour of Europe in 1964, Lane tried to finagle a side trip to the USSR to share some of his new "discoveries" with his mentors, but the Russians decided that it would be politically safer to keep him at arm's length.

When Lane's *Rush to Judgment*, a surgical reconstruction of the evidence, came out in 1966, the hardback edition went straight to the top of the bestseller list, as did the 1967 paperback edition. The Speech rolled out of his funky little theater, hit the street like a new pop record, and then took to the road, carrying him to financial gain and national fame. By 1971, the Communist Party USA was telling Moscow that Lane was no more than a self-promoter, but by then his message was out and a major publishing phenomenon had developed. For a time, his campus tours were rivaled in popularity perhaps only by those of the Grateful Dead.[15]

The conspiracy fever dropped a bit as the decade wore on, but when the Watergate scandal broke in 1972, the KGB saw an opportunity for another active measure. One of the principal Nixon conspirators, E. Howard Hunt (who had worked in the Mexico City station prior to Win Scott's arrival there), had been whispered to have been on the scene in Dallas. He wasn't, but he was certainly knee-deep in Watergate, thus a convenient CIA target for the KGB. Perhaps their most daring and cynical bit of mischief was in the forging of a handwritten note that Lee Oswald supposedly sent to Hunt before he shot Jack.

"Dear Mr. Hunt," the note began, "I would like information concerning my position. I am only asking for information. I am suggesting that we discuss the matter fully before any steps are taken by me or anyone else. Thank you, Lee Harvey Oswald."

Using Oswald's handwriting samples acquired during his time in Minsk, the KGB worked on the note for months. It was shared with three of the most prominent conspiracy theorists, along with a cover letter that claimed it had also been sent to the new FBI chief, Clarence Kelley, who was clearly trying to bury it. Strangely, it was several years before it hit the mainstream press. Perfect as it looked, there was a glitch. Its dissemination may have been slowed by confusion over whether "Mr. Hunt" was E. Howard, the Watergate stooge, or H.L., the Texas oil magnate originally charged in Joesten's book, a man of means who could afford to use the libel laws with frightening effect, if he so chose. When the forgery finally did hit the mass media, the *New York Times* compromised itself by validating the handwriting as Oswald's, and Marina herself confirmed it,[16] but the "Mr. Hunt" confusion continued.

Nonetheless, the KGB had gotten very good at the craft of political fiction, and they continued to take active measures to discredit the CIA throughout the Cold War. The books they directly sponsored enabled others from more independent sources, and those etched the myth ever deeper: *The Second Oswald* by Richard H. Popkin, *Accessories After the Fact* by Sylvia Meagher, and *Six Seconds in Dallas* by Josiah Thompson all sold well, and a spate of movies like *Executive Action* and *The Parallax View* brought Hollywood into the act.

Then, in 1975, a photo technician named Robert Groden acquired the one piece of 8mm movie footage of Kennedy's actual murder from *Life* magazine and unspooled it for the world on Geraldo Rivera's 1975 television show, *Goodnight America*. But by showing the multiple-generation print of "the Zapruder film" in real time, Groden failed to reveal that a frame-by-frame examination shows the forward movement of the president's head as he was hit from the rear, where Oswald had perched. Not until the film was properly slowed and analyzed by the millisecond was it clear that the fatal bullet had come from behind, causing Jack's head to buck forward, briefly, and *then* snap back as the round exited. Those facts did not stop Groden from turning this personal coup into "the smoking gun" that proved "the grassy knoll theory."*

So it was that by the mid-1970s, 80 percent of the American people believed that John F. Kennedy had been the victim of some sort of conspiracy; they just weren't sure which one. The numbers have not changed much since then. "It was ironic," as James Piereson wrote, "that the idealism encouraged

---

*Years later, Groden would also purloin the JFK autopsy photos from the National Archives, helping himself to another piece of history in the name of open, honest government, and to a nice profit.

by Kennedy's leadership was killed off by the cynicism arising from his assassination."[17]

For all the self-evisceration that the CIA was going through, a number of critical questions were never asked of Nosenko and Golitsyn. Neither defector was ever asked about the alleged ease with which the KGB allowed Marina to emigrate to the U.S., or about the possibility that the KGB shared its "Oswald file" with Cuba, an ally with whom it shared so much of its intelligence. Twelve years later (1976), a retired James Angleton composed thirteen questions he would have liked to have posed to Nosenko. The majority of those questions were concerned with one topic: the extent of cooperation and intelligence-sharing between the Soviets and the Cubans.[18] As one might infer from the list, Angleton, who conducted his own investigation of the Kennedy assassination, was certain that the man who had green-lighted the hit was the bloodthirsty RFK alter ego, Raúl Castro.[19] Was the CIA's lapse on the queries a case of "don't ask, don't tell"?

Over the years, the Nosenko-Golitsyn affair has been widely publicized. Both of the key players have been trotted out by a penitent CIA and allowed to tell their stories to selected writers, who concocted books and movies about them. But within weeks of Nosenko's journey to the U.S., a foreign spy with much more meaningful contributions to make regarding the Kennedy assassination was also packing his bags for America. His secrets—about Oswald in Mexico City—were gleaned from firsthand participants, and they threatened to catapult the official investigation to a whole new level of magnitude. In stark contrast to the Nosenko rebus, the CIA agreed unanimously that this man, a Cuban agent, was telling the truth. However, his story was not only eclipsed by the Nosenko-Golitsyn affair, but his name and most of his details were classified until 2003.

His CIA handlers, who became his lifelong friends and supporters, gave him the nickname "Laddie."

One afternoon in Havana during the Nosenko-Golitsyn winter, a remarkable group of senior DGI officers had just sat down to lunch at G2 headquarters. As they settled into a meal of paella, *plátanos*, yellow rice, and flan, one of them brought up the subject of Oswald in Mexico City.

Among the dozen or so master spies dining that rainy afternoon were: Roberto Santiesteban, who a year earlier had traveled to New York with Silvia Durán's lover Carlos Lechuga to attempt to immolate New York City with two members of the Fair Play for Cuba Committee; Ernesto Andrés Armona, a redheaded black agent who worked under cover of the Mexico City consulate; Manuel Vega Pérez, a known assassin who handled Oswald's visa request in Mexico and alerted Havana to his presence there; and Norberto Hernández Curbelo, who investigated Luisa Calderón's romantic correspondence with an American just before Kennedy's death. Most of these diners had one thing in common besides their place of work: they had all been recalled back from Mexico City to Havana soon after the Kennedy assassination.

Although they spoke with the discretion that's typical of old spies, it was clear that the subject of Oswald was much more than idle parlor chat; many of these men had experienced something so profound that the DGI had spared no effort to stem the flow of their information from the Cuban consulate in Mexico City. Had it not been for one of these executives, Vladimir Rodríguez Lahera, who had already decided to defect to the U.S., the truth of the DGI's post-assassination terror might never have surfaced. The lunch fortified Rodríguez Lahera in more ways than one—it gave him the final impetus to leave Cuba forever.

Not long afterward, in April 1964, as the Warren Commission Report was fast approaching its deadline for the printer, Rodríguez Lahera kissed his wife and their two children good-bye in Havana and set off on the road to defection. Vladimir had priceless information about Castro, which he hoped he could trade for a better life for his family. For the men who would soon greet him from the CIA, that knowledge would be both a blessing and a curse: he would be their most prized Cuban turncoat, but also the sum of all their worst fears. There would not be one of comparable value—for better *and* for worse—until 1971, with the defection of another senior Cuban spy named Gerardo Peraza.

Vladimir was twenty-seven when he defected, and at five foot two and 130 pounds, he was not exactly one of Fidel's mangy proletarian *barbudos*, nor was he some Cold War icon like that year's James Bond in *From Russia with Love*. When he arrived in Ottawa on or about April 21, he appeared to be your average unprepossessing family man with the keen, direct manner of a kindly professor. One would never suspect that he was an officer in Raúl Castro's DGI; but within hours of his arrival, Vladimir presented himself to Canadian authorities, announced that he was defecting from Cuba, and asked for asylum in America.

Des FitzGerald, then head of the CIA's Special Affairs Staff, was the first to receive the news in his office at Langley. He put his best officer, "Staff D" veteran Harold Swenson (aka "Joseph Langosch") on the case. Swenson, forty-eight, was an ex-Marine who had been mustered into the Agency in 1955. For the last year he had been Des's main man on Cuban intel; he had been the one who had tried to warn the SAS boss off the Paris meeting with Rolando Cubela the previous autumn. That rendezvous had violated all rules of deniability, even by the cocksure standards of the era. Des had come to regret having done it, and Swenson's credibility had been bolstered as a result.

Rodríguez Lahera had already let it be known that he had knowledge of the workings of the Mexico City embassy, among other matters. As Swenson prepared to fly to Ottawa, the Cuba desk gave Vladimir the code name AM/MUG-1 and devised a detailed list of questions for Swenson to put to him. At the top of the list was: Did Castro have any connection to Lee Oswald?

Swenson and Vladimir finally sat down together in a sunny safe house outside Ottawa on the fifth of May. It would be the first of a number of sessions the men would hold together. There were formal introductions, starting with the Cuban's background information, which Swenson scribbled down in a notebook:

The man grew up in the Santiago region. He studied civil engineering at the Institute of Havana. At twenty he was already a father of two, but upon graduation in 1957 he joined the July 26th Movement. Batista's agents picked him off almost immediately, however, and he spent a year in prison. Released in 1958, Vladimir remained a true believer. He went straight back to the mountains of the Sierra Maestra, found the Castro boys, and took up arms alongside them, winning their respect and trust. When Batista finally fell, the young soldier accepted an assignment to the New Cuba's fledgling intel service, the IS. By the summer of 1963, Vladimir was an agent of the DGI and, once inside Raúl Castro's clique, was assigned to "M Section," where he was responsible for recruiting agents in El Salvador.

To prove his bona fides, the small Cuban produced a big ream of classified Cuban documents. Swenson suppressed his excitement and gave Vladimir the next test, shoving the CIA's "mug book" across the table and asking him to ID as many faces in it as he could. Within minutes, Vladimir had identified more than three dozen Cuban agents, their war names, and their respective intel responsibilities.

This was already a mother lode. The CIA still harbored the illusion that it knew far more about the Cuban DGI than the Cubans knew about the CIA, but even in 1964 an intelligence bonanza like this was a considerable rarity.

Swenson's most crucial question was answered without hesitation.

Did the Cubans have any connection to Lee Oswald?

Yes. Vladimir stated that, from what he had been told around the DGI lunch table by their Mexico City staff, Lee had had contacts with Cuban intelligence *before* his Mexico trip, had at least met with Cuban agents in Mexico in September 1963 (if not before), and had maintained contact with them after he returned to the U.S. Among those Cuban agents who had dealt with Lee in Mexico were Manuel Vega Pérez (whom Lee may have known by his alias "Marcos") and Rogelio Rodríguez López (who went by three aliases: "Eduardo," "Casimiro," and "José Antonio"), both of them DGI staff officers assigned to the Mexico City Cuban embassy, and Maria Luisa Calderón. Pérez and López, who handled Lee's visa request and forwarded it to Havana, had their DGI credentials later verified by Swenson and the CIA, and López was also determined to be in regular contact with the Fair Play for Cuba Committee's V. T. Lee.

Rodríguez Lahera also remembered the red-haired mulatto who worked in the Commercial Attaché Office at the Cuban embassy in Mexico City, but was actually a G2 agent with an "ultra serious demeanor." He had been one of the diners who just regaled Vladimir with tales of Mexico City. Ernesto Andrés Armona Ramos was born in 1918 and attended university with his friend Fidel, staying a key contact while Fidel was in Mexico in 1956. An expert in guerrilla training, Armona was assigned to Mexico in August 1962. He was known to have stopped at the Mexico City embassy only at the time of Oswald's visit. Five months after the Kennedy assassination, he was recalled to Cuba and demoted "for keeping poor financial records."[20]*

Lastly, after the assassination, according to Vladimir, all DGI travel and pouch transmittals were suspended worldwide.

Vladimir's disclosures provided the first clear confirmation that Lee Oswald had probably been considered at least some sort of Cuban asset before he made his embassy threats against JFK in September. What's more, Vladimir concluded that Lee's contact was none other than Luisa Calderón, the DGI agent on the secretarial staff at the Cuban embassy and the same woman whose exclamations of delight had been secretly recorded by the CIA when she heard about the murder in Dallas. Vladimir added that a DGI colleague, Norberto Hernández Curbelo, had told him that he had intercepted a

---

*Note: the obvious confusion about the myriad names proffered for the "red-haired Negro"—Carlos, Ernest, Cesar—might be explained by the fact that Cuban intelligence agents often utilized three or more aliases.

"love letter" sent between Calderón and an American who signed his name as, according to Rodríguez Lahera's memory, something sounding like "Ower." It was this colleague who also concluded that Luisa's relationship with Lee "went beyond her capacity as secretary in the Mexico City [Cuban] Consulate." Perhaps Silvia Durán was not Lee's only lover in Mexico.

By this time, the U.S. investigators had written evidence from Lee that he had been in touch with someone inside the Cuban embassy in the weeks between his September visit and the day he killed Kennedy. As noted earlier, on November 12, a week before the Cuban consul, Azcue, was to be replaced, Lee already had knowledge of Azcue's impending departure from the Mexico City embassy, and either Silvia Durán or Calderón were now suspected to have been Lee's correspondents. In any case, Calderón was now, Vladimir confirmed, safely beyond reach. She had been recalled to Havana immediately after Jack Kennedy's death, and was now resettled in the luxurious Vedado district, kept in the style befitting a heroine of the revolution. (Years later, in the mid-1970s, Fidel himself refused to let the chief counsel of the House Select Committee on Assassinations speak with her, telling G. Robert Blakey that she couldn't meet with him while he was in Havana because of "illness.") Vladimir made it plain that the DGI had gone to extraordinary lengths to cover its tracks in the aftermath of the murder in Dallas.

It was the first springtime since that murder, a time that should have been one of hope and renewal. A young rock 'n' roll band out of England was doing its best to cheer up the Western world. Its second UK album had come out on the very day that Jack Kennedy was killed, but when the Beatles arrived on American soil for the first time on February 7, 1964, it was as if the Kennedy wake might finally be over. In fact, however, it would last for at least two more generations.

A week after Swenson and Vladimir finished their sessions in the safe house outside Ottawa, Fidel Castro sat down to what he thought would be a confidential meeting with two trusted American Communists, and confirmed a version of what Vladimir had just told U.S. intelligence. Morris Childs, treasurer of the American Communist Party, and his brother, Jack, editor of the party organ, the *Daily Worker*, were meeting with Fidel when suddenly the premier let out an extraordinary admission: Lee Oswald had offered to kill President Kennedy because the Kennedys were threatening the Castros. Fidel said his people told him "immediately" that a gringo had come to the Cuban embassy in Mexico, ranting that he would "kill that bastard, Kennedy," but Fidel was quick to add that his regime had turned the offer down as the ravings of a madman.[21]

Fidel's monologue about Oswald's rejection would later prove to be a cover story. The accounts of Lee's "ravings" were calculated, too, on the part of the Cuban diplomats who had greeted him in the embassy the previous September. The Cubans' response to his hysteria had been a performance for the benefit of CIA surveillance bugs inside the Cuban embassy. It wasn't until they got Lee out to the parking garage that they talked with him candidly, and Fidel was probably reading from the same two-tiered script when he planted his cover with Childs, allowing that he knew of Oswald but had no link to him. However he was gauging his comments on June 12, it does not seem that he knew that Jack Childs and his brother Morris were the greatest Communist party informants (as SOLO SOURCE) the FBI ever had. The Fed's head of counterintelligence, Ray Wannall, said that "if Childs said Castro said that, you can take it to the bank." In the still-precarious world six and a half months after the assassination, it would have been nearly suicidal for Fidel to tell the Childs brothers this if he'd thought it would go straight back to Washington. Even if Vladimir hadn't just made it clear that the Cubans had ongoing contacts with Kennedy's killer, Fidel would at least be guilty of having had passive inside knowledge of a plot on Kennedy's life and done nothing to stop it. That alone could have earned him more trouble from Washington.

In 2005, Oscar Marino, without knowing he was corroborating SOLO, detailed what he had learned secondhand about what had really transpired in the Cuban embassy that week in September 1963.

"Oswald volunteered to kill Kennedy," Marino explained, much as Castro told Childs. "He was so full of hatred that it gave him the idea. He wanted it himself [because] he hated his country. He was already prepared to do it. He was soldier of the revolution and offered his services to us in order to kill Kennedy."

What Marino said next flies in the face of what Castro would like the world to believe. "Let's just say we used him," Marino said. "He adopted our plans as his own—his idea was a natural projection of our wish." Marino wanted to be clear, stating, "That doesn't mean he was brainwashed—that wasn't necessary. Is it so important, whether or not he acted on his own initiative? He was an instrument of the G2. It makes no difference whether he volunteered or was used. It ends up the same."

So in short order, Vladimir had given the CIA chilling details of Fidel's intelligence apparatus's advance knowledge of Oswald, Childs had confirmed

Castro's own prior awareness of Oswald's threat to the FBI, and it was all coming just as the Warren Commission was completing its report to the American people. Why then did it take generations for them to learn these critical details? How is it that a semi-fictional version of these events quickly supplanted the stark truth and then proceeded to sour the American public's relationship with its government for so many years afterward?

Beyond Johnson's fear of a world war, the CIA knew that it had fumbled, terribly, and did not want to reveal its failures. And, in the wake of Jack Childs's report to FBI headquarters, Hoover did not want to blow Childs's cover by revealing what Fidel had said. Hoover also knew that his Bureau had not adequately kept tabs on Oswald, particularly after he went to Mexico City; thus they withheld most of the fine points of the Childs/Castro conversation from the Warren Commission and quietly demoted seventeen of their agents, Jim Hosty among them.

Not until twenty-nine years later, in 1995, not until its other records had been opened, did the commission release an appended document (CD 1359) containing Fidel's admission of Oswald's Mexico City offer.

Vladimir "Laddie" Rodríguez Lahera's debriefing with Agency men Swenson, Barney Hidalgo, and Joseph Piccolo Jr. continued well into the summer of 1964. Des FitzGerald, who had been promoted to CIA Western Hemisphere chief, monitored the process closely from Washington, and when Laddie was deemed ready, he was put on the CIA payroll temporarily, admitted into the United States from Canada, and ensconced in a comfortable safe house in Silver Spring, Maryland, the leafy suburban lap of his former enemy. It would be a monumental stretch to imagine that Des did not inform his friend Bobby of the latest Rodríguez Lahera developments.

Everything Laddie told his new sponsors about Fidel and Raúl and their dictatorship was vetted, and proved true. In 1965, his family was sent for in Mexico City, still the favored way station for Cubans coming and going at that time, and his wife and children were all reunited with him in America.

As the family remade itself after months of worry and fear, Laddie continued to divulge Cuba's deepest intel secrets to its greatest enemy. Two years later, when he would apply for permanent U.S. residence, the CIA's newest Western Hemisphere chief, William Broe, wrote the CIA director: "Lahera has provided voluminous, accurate, and valuable information on the organization of the Cuban intelligence services, their operations, staff members, and agents . . . His value to us will continue to be considerable as a fluent spokesman for the anti-Castro cause." Like so many other Cuban exiles, the Rodríguez Lahera family eventually settled in the Miami area. Vladimir suffered an untimely death (cause unknown to authors) in September 1986, at age forty-nine. Harold Swenson retired from the CIA in 1968 and died in 2000, in Mercer, New Jersey.[22]

In April 1964, Warren Commission staff attorneys William Coleman and David Slawson, under the direction of commission counsel Lee Rankin, went to Mexico City and met with CIA and embassy officials. The commissioners' later conclusion about the trip? "Mr. Rankin, Mr. Slawson, and Mr. Coleman, all expressed concern over the inability of the Commission or of any of the governmental agencies to fill in the very large gaps still existing in Oswald's visit to Mexico," they wrote in their report to the full commission. "We pointed out there were many days during which we knew nothing of his whereabouts and that the evenings of this entire trip were unaccounted for. Furthermore, the testimony of the clerk at the Hotel Commercio seemed to us highly unsatisfactory. The clerk admitted that the hotel registry showed Oswald's name, but he completely denies any other memory whatever of Oswald being at the hotel, and all the subordinate personnel, such as cleaning ladies, etc., likewise deny any memory of Oswald." Three decades later, Coleman and Slawson would recall the Oswald wiretap recordings being played for them by Win Scott and Alan White in April 1964, seven months after they had allegedly been destroyed.

Slawson and Coleman had been sent on a fool's errand. As fast as Earl Warren's group was writing its history in Washington, it was being unwritten in Mexico City.

On the second day of July, 1964, President Johnson signed the Civil Rights Act in an East Room ceremony, Dr. King standing just behind him, along with a small army of the bill's champions and fixers. It was a great and good moment for the nation, but a testy one between the president and his attorney general. Bob had been pushing for its passage for over a year, but Lyndon still managed to slight him at the ceremony.

By the summer, Bobby was seriously weighing a departure from the Justice Department. It was a job he had never really wanted, and there were several options that interested him: going back to Massachusetts as a college president or governor, or making a run for the Senate in the state of New York. He had given some thought to the vice presidency, should Lyndon offer it, but most of the party bosses weren't blessing the idea and Bob could not imagine that "Colonel Cornpone" would really have him as the veep, anyway. That became official on July 29.

When Lyndon and Bobby sat down at 1:09 P.M. in the Oval Office, Barry Goldwater, the horn-rimmed cowboy from Arizona, had just won the Republican nomination in San Francisco. Lyndon was riding a 75 percent approval rating and seemed to be a sure bet to win. He began that afternoon with a list of talking points, drawn up by his adviser Clark Clifford.

"I have asked you to come over to discuss a subject that is an important one to you and me," the president began, like an actor doing a cold reading at an audition. Johnson continued for a few paragraphs, speaking no doubt of how well Bobby was serving the country with forbearance and decency, and of his gratitude, et cetera; but his first verse ended with: "I have concluded that it would inadvisable for you to be the Democratic candidate for Vice President this year."

There must have been a moment's grudging relief for Bobby. He was free. As Lyndon larded on his admiration and spoke of Bobby's inevitable run for the White House himself one day, the attorney general looked down and saw that the "record" light on the president's speakerphone was on. It would be best to keep his responses circumspect.

Toward the end of the conversation, Johnson dangled an ambassadorship, mentioning the USSR, Great Britain, France, and the United Nations. Bobby told him that he preferred to remain at Justice. Lyndon allowed that he would probably do the same, in his position, and then started complimenting Bobby's "unusually competent" staff at the DOJ while disparaging his own appointees at the White House. When Lyndon asked him to run his campaign against Goldwater, Bobby told him that he felt it would be a conflict of interest for the AG to do that, and if he quit Justice to run it free and clear, he would be out of a job in November.

When the meeting broke up after an hour, Bobby stood and said, either sadly or ironically, depending on the source, "I could have helped you, Mr. President."[23]

A few days later, back at Justice, Bobby dictated his long-delayed letter of reply to the inquiries sent by the Warren Commission. His secretary, Angie Novello, took it down in the condensed light of a hazy, subtropical afternoon.

". . . I would like to state definitely that I know of no credible evidence to support the allegations that the assassination of President Kennedy was caused by a conspiracy . . . I have no suggestions to make at this time regarding any additional investigation which should be undertaken by the Commission prior to the publication of its report . . ."

Less than a month later, he would announce his bid for the U.S. Senate seat held by Jack's old Cuba detractor, the silver-toned, white-haired, and well-heeled Republican Kenneth Keating.

The next night, on the eve of his party's convention, Lyndon started making noises to his press secretary, George Reedy, about declining the Democratic Party's nomination. It was a sticky night, the ozone hanging heavy in the air, and Lyndon padded out of the White House and started ranting about quitting the presidency. As he lumbered around the dark grounds, huffing down one cigarette after another, Reedy dogged along just behind him. The accounts are messy, but they amounted to this:

I'm gonna quit the presidency, Lyndon kept threatening. He had always hated the White House and had drafted his withdrawal speech.

The long-suffering Reedy had to have reminded him that he was about to be nominated by acclamation, but Johnson felt that the major elements of the party were all against him. He was a southerner, so the North was against him. The Negroes didn't like him. The unions didn't like him. The Ivy League intellectuals hated him.

Poor Reedy. Now he reminded the most powerful man on earth that if he quit, it would throw the whole convention into disarray. It would give the White House to Goldwater, a nice enough hombre who was, however, by any intellectual measure, "all hat and no cattle."

But Lyndon thought that Bobby was already looking to "disarray" things; that Dr. King was looking to "disarray" things. There were rumors that they were all huddling in Hyannis Port that very night, he said, plotting a stampede straight to Bobby! There were rumors that "the runt" had even turned Jackie against him. That's why he had intervened to keep the convention from playing the memorial movie about his brother until LBJ's running mate, Hubert Humphrey, was justly nominated. That's why he had put J. Edgar Hoover on the case, to pepper his men throughout the ranks of every delegation, keep their ears to the ground, and steer any such stampede straight over a cliff before it started.

Those were wise moves, Reedy demurred, finally letting Lyndon stomp off into the night ahead of him, still muttering about all the enemies lurking in the bushes of his mind.

Lyndon's fifty-sixth birthday, August 27, would find him sitting in the presidential suite of his hotel in Atlantic City, watching on TV as a sea of white straw hats and "All the Way with LBJ" posters bobbed about the convention floor a few miles away. Reedy was with him again, watching him chug soda and stare at the screen with the volume turned down.

At the convention site itself, Bobby and his old friend John Seigenthaler were being led along the dark walls to a moldy little dressing room stuck deep under the stands. Bobby was wearing a black tie, a white shirt, and a form-fitting black pin-striped suit, a picture of elegance that night, however mournful. As the celebration for Humphrey thundered above them, Bobby joked that Lyndon had probably put them down there "with orders to forget us. They'll probably let us out day after tomorrow."

But there was no forgetting him, any more than they would forget his brother. When Bobby was finally led up to the podium to introduce the film about Jack, the convention stood as one, a cascade of applause rising and rising, along with the tears of the party and the nation. He stood at the center of it, tears in his eyes but not quite falling, his buoyancy intact. For anyone who watched, whether they loved him or hated him, it was a singular moment of connection by one man to a nation, and to a planet beyond.

As the outpouring continued, Senator Henry Jackson, presiding at the convention, just leaned close to Bobby's ear and said, "Let it go on . . . Just let 'em do it, Bob . . . Let them get it out of their system."[24]

Back at the Presidential Suite, Reedy watched Lyndon's profile as he watched the glowing face of Bobby. Bobby would nod, blink back the feelings, raise a hand as if to quiet them, but then gaze out across the crowd, at the goodwill he must certainly have needed.

"Thank you," Bobby kept saying toward the microphone. "Thank you . . . Please, please . . ."

The pandemonium continued for twenty-two full minutes. Lyndon watched along with the rest of his fellow citizens, and when it was over, and Bobby's speech was over, he offered a benediction from Shakespeare, the words that Jackie had chosen for him, from *Romeo and Juliet*.

> *When he shall die*
> *Take him and cut him out in little stars*
> *And he will make the face of heaven so fine*
> *That all the world will be in love with night,*
> *And pay no worship to the garish sun.*

* * *

On August 22, two days before the Atlantic City convention began, Bobby had announced that he would seek nomination as the Democratic Party's senatorial candidate in the state of New York. If he won it, he'd be running against a Republican incumbent, one of Jack's detractors, Kenneth Keating, in the general election. His brother Teddy had been injured in a plane crash two months earlier, a brush with death that had almost driven Bob out of politics, but Jack's legacy still weighed upon him, and he could no longer serve Lyndon Johnson as AG. When other potential candidates shrank from the challenge, New York City's powerful Democratic mayor, Robert Wagner, was forced to endorse him.

Still undermined by his melancholy, he struggled for easy rapport and good humor with the voters. Referring to Johnson's archconservative Republican opponent, Goldwater of Arizona, he joked with crowds in the mountains of upstate New York.

"The Catskills were immortalized by Washington Irving. He wrote of a man who fell asleep and awoke in another era. The only other area that can boast such a man is Phoenix, Arizona."[25]

But he was still a fitful speaker, given to stilted delivery and only brief moments of inspiration. At one appearance, he was so choked up when he referred to his dead brother that he was rendered speechless, tears streaming down his face for a full minute or two until he could collect himself. As the one-year anniversary of Dallas approached, some of his advisers felt it necessary to try to jolt him out of his brooding interludes. He believed that the crowds were only there because of Jack, and he would reinforce the differences between them by becoming distant and awkward on the stump, the antithesis of the extroverted politician. Bobby's friend Chuck Spalding went skiing with him after Jack's death and saw a man whose grief was becoming a sanctum he didn't want to leave. " 'You almost prolong the pain not to lose the person,' Spalding thought. 'It just hurts so bad. Then you figure, if it doesn't hurt I'll be further away from what I've lost. So it just seemed that those nights would go on forever.' "[26] Still, he treaded on for the sake of the family name.

Five and a half years earlier, just after the Castro brothers overthrew Batista, June Cobb had gone to Havana to seek help from Cuban doctors in her mission to rid the Indians of Colombia, Ecuador, and Bolivia of their rampant coca addiction. She had been touched and inspired by Fidel's defense of the poor and had made the pilgrimage to meet with his new minister of health in hopes of receiving some financial and professional aid.

It had been a heady leap from there to the role of translator, adviser, and friend to Fidel, but then came his jailing of a close friend of hers, and then came more violence against his people, and by the summer of 1964 June had become so disgusted that she was working as a CIA contract agent in Mexico City. She was looking for a new place to rent when a writer pal of hers named Eunice Odio suggested she call one of her friends—none other than Elena Garro.

June had heard of Elena; and when they met, the two women hit it off immediately. In August, with much fun and fanfare, June moved in with the extended female family of the Garro/Paz household: Elena, Elenita, and Elena's sister, Deba.

Garro had been divorced from Octavio Paz since 1959, but she was well known as an archprotector of the Indian peoples of Mexico, a blistering "defender of the weak against the strong," as Cobb would express it years later. Even without the glow of celebrity, Elena and Elenita Paz still brought their unique feminine flair to the city's literary scene: two scintillating Spanish-Mexican blondes in contrasting paisley and pearls. In 1964, Elena had just published the first of what would be thirteen novels and had captured the Award Xavier Villaurutia. Her canon would eventually include seventeen plays, a number of short stories, and a biography, and she was well on her way to being considered a major Mexican writer.

It's not known if Elena ever discerned June's relationship with the CIA, but she knew that June had connections at the U.S. embassy, and the women came to trust each other as friends. Occasionally, when all were sitting up at night, sipping on the patio and smoking, the three of them, Elena, her sister Deba, and Elenita would return to the haunted "twist party" where they had met the assassin. They'd describe it all again, with a recall of specific detail that impressed June, and they told essentially the same tale that Elenita would tell the WDR film team forty-one years later in Cuernavaca. In a recent interview, one CIA Mexico City contract agent who befriended the Garros recalled their demeanor after the assassination. "I was in the room with them when Elena, Elenita, and Deba were all talking excitedly about having seen Oswald at the Durán party," the agent said in 2008. "Although Elena was prone to having a persecution complex at times, she was not a fabricator. There is no doubt that the three of them believed Oswald was at that party."[27]

By this time, Garro, like Luis Alberu, had also learned independently that Silvia Durán and Oswald had been lovers. The party at Ruben's apartment was a hot scene, typical of the Cuban embassy crowd. Elena was convinced that it had been set up by the Cuban and Mexican underground to validate Lee as a member of the inner circle, so that he'd have allies who would recognize him and help enable his escape.[28]

On October 5, June committed the report to paper and took it to the CIA station. In hindsight, the women had tried to identify or at least render a word portrait of every face at last fall's twist parties. Included in the account was the description of a "red-haired Negro" among the guests. Some have argued that Elena could have borrowed her sketch of the *pelirrojo* Negro after reading of the Alvarado story in the recently published Warren Report. However, the report was not published in the U.S. until October 5, the same day of the Cobb memo—and June Cobb is certain Garro had told her the story in September.[29] Additionally, Win Scott wrote on October 5 (the very day he received the Cobb summary) that the "Garros [Elena and her daughter] have been talking about this for a long time."[30] Beyond that, Elena Garro was already famous. She already had enough troubles as a friend to leftists and as an agitator for the indigenous people of her country. She wasn't doing it for the attention; and in any case, June's memo did not seem to stir up much of it.

Alongside Lyndon's landslide victory over Goldwater, Bobby Kennedy had won the race against Keating in New York, and in early November the Garro/Paz household was heartened to hear that the senator-elect was coming to Mexico City to dedicate a housing project in his brother's name. What should they do? They asked June. It seemed like a golden chance to tell the president's brother himself what they had seen. June agreed. It could only help matters, and she suggested that they use Elena's clout to get close, carry a huge bouquet of yellow roses, and see if they could catch his attention. June said she would go with them. But when the day came, on November 14, she was very sick with bronchitis and told the other women that they would have to go on without her.

They did, but they were prevented from getting close enough to Bobby's entourage. As he slipped from sight, there were already men attaching themselves to him. He would be followed everywhere he went by the Mexican DFS.[31] According to an unsourced report cited by author David Talbot, Bobby did manage to make some inquiries about Oswald's sojourn there a year earlier, but Win Scott's available records give no indication that Bobby met with him.[32]

When the women got home from the airport, Elenita discovered that their cat's back legs were broken. She accused June of having done it, an absurd notion, particularly since the patient hadn't been out of her room since they left for the airport. A screaming match ensued and June soon moved out, but she did send another entreaty to the Agency, nudging the U.S. government to take a proper statement directly from Elena Garro and her relatives.[33]

On November 24, a year and two days after Dallas, Elena Garro finally sat down and told her incredible tale to the FBI Mexico City legal attaché (LEGAT), Clark Anderson.[34] Her words were dutifully transcribed, then the report was filed and forgotten. On December 25, 1965, she told it to yet another American official, the U.S. embassy's political action officer, Charles Ashman. But her charges, her careful rendering of a party that now scarred her memory, would be ignored for fourteen more years, when it would be given only cursory consideration in the CIA-mob-exiles-did-it zeitgeist of the seventies.

On September 24, 1964, the official Warren Commission Report was delivered to the Oval Office. Its conclusions were, in hindsight, as accurate as possible, given the commission's absurdly short investigative calender and its utter lack of foreign intelligence. It named, correctly, Oswald as the lone shooter, lashing out for reasons only he knew. Additionally, the report said that it found "no evidence of a conspiracy." A far cry from saying there *was* no conspiracy. The commissioners and their staff may have suspected that there was more to it, but couldn't make the case in their constrained pressure cooker. Indeed, over the decades, some surviving senior staff have stated that had they known about the Castro plotting by the Kennedys— first disclosed a decade after their work—they would have looked at the entire event differently and perhaps directed a much different, and longer, investigation.

In handpicking most of the commission's personnel and directing its focus, Lyndon had fended off world war and saved Bobby Kennedy's secrets. There is no particular evidence that Bobby appreciated it, but he surely knew it, even if he couched Johnson's actions only in terms of national security.

Ten months earlier, as he sat locked inside the bathroom of Air Force One before its takeoff from Dallas, Lyndon's very first intuition was that a conspiracy had befallen the American government. That hunch followed from his feeling that America was misguided in its Cuba policy, and he was right on both counts. His whole first year in office was an attempt to cauterize the wound of Dallas, and he was preoccupied with it nearly every waking hour, even as he was defining his presidency. He launched a personal campaign for

Medicare. He dreamed aloud of a "Great Society." He declared a "War on Poverty." He got his Republican opponent to stand down on the race issue during their presidential campaign, giving the country time to adapt to the Civil Rights Act. He continued Jack's peace overtures to the Russians by offering them a mutual reduction in bombers and atomic materials. All of this was done with one eye on the bottom line—his ubiquity and popularity. He too had learned that the presidency was an epic play with him as the star, and he was minutely aware of each act of fealty and every single slight. After one of his speeches to a joint session of Congress, he told an effusive senator that he had gotten eighty choruses of applause, and damned if he wasn't dead right. The one-time Master of the Senate had been standing at the center of his old forum, keeping score even as he spoke to the nation.[35]

When he wasn't wrangling with Congress, nose to nose, the long arm of LBJ was reaching for the telephone, his lifeline, his form of remote control, and his consolation in moments of melancholy reflection. During the last week of September, he was splayed out behind his desk and working the phones more than usual. On the horn with Senate Majority Leader Mike Mansfield, he admitted what few in the Congress had been briefed about.

"There's a good deal of feeling that maybe the Cuba thing . . ." His voice trailed off for a moment. He was always careful not to be too definite about it. "Oswald was messing around in Mexico with the Cubans."[36]

Later, he was on with Senator Richard Russell, the old Dixiecrat whom he had pressured to be on the investigating panel.

"I don't believe it," Russell admitted of the report.

"I don't either," said Lyndon.

He never would believe the commission report. His staunch contention would always be that "Oswald was a Communist agent." A year before his death, in 1971, he would finally start revealing his secret to people outside his close circle, telling the publisher of his autobiography that he would prove the Oswald-Castro connection one day.[37] But there weren't enough days left at that point.

For all the ways in which Lyndon served the legacy of President Kennedy, there was one glaring way in which he didn't. Not long after he took office, he hired a new Latin American adviser straight out of Mexico City: Thomas Mann, the former U.S. ambassador, the same man who translated Lyndon's friendly talks with Ordaz and thereby helped eclipse the Cuban Connection. The moment Lyndon appointed him, the Kennedy men knew that the

Alliance for Progress was in trouble, that Mann was there to gut the human principles of it and make it just a new form of colonialism.

Bending Richard Russell's ear yet again, Lyndon whined about the Kennedy Court's reaction to the coming Mann Doctrine. "They're tryin' to run him off," he squawked to the senator, " 'cause he believes in free enterprise."

It was a bit of hyperbole. The Alliance had not been anticapitalist. What Bobby, Dick Goodwin, and their allies were objecting to was the flat-out demolition of its Progress. Mann wanted to upend the whole idea. He wanted to re-emphasize military order over messy constitutional self-government, and push private investment ahead of social justice. Arthur Schlesinger saw Mann's appointment as a retread of the old "Tex-Mex policy of condescension and manipulation" of the Latin American continent, and as LBJ's "declaration of independence" from the Kennedys.[38] Johnson had easily won the election, and once he was in, he didn't need to kowtow to "the Harvards" anymore. As the Johnson era began, Hickory Hill became "the other White House," the gathering place for a government in internal exile.

The Alliance for Progress had promised a new day for the whole Catholic continent of Latin America, one in synch with the spirit of Vatican II and the anti-Communism of reform, even radical reform if that was necessary. The Alliance had promised a rapid increase of per capita income and pledged itself to more democratic government. It swore to wipe out adult illiteracy by the end of the 1960s. It would impose price stabilizations to prevent inflation or deflation, and it insisted on a more equal distribution of income, on deliberate economic and social planning, and on land reform. Toward that end, U.S. economic assistance jumped by nearly 300 percent in the first year of the Kennedy era.

But Lyndon made it plain that the Alliance was going to lie fallow. By the time his successor, Dick Nixon, came in, it would become a dust bowl. The two of them would assure that there would be no net gain of resources or development for the southern continent. They would demand that whatever aid was granted be paid back to America and its other First World creditors. Whatever profit was made with the new investments usually flowed back to the States, and that profit would exceed any new investments. The American armaments industry was one of the most apparent beneficiaries; the flow of weapons increased, even as political pressure for reform dwindled. Underfunded and quickly co-opted, the Alliance was fast becoming a fiasco. Instead of American business sucking up the bounty of Latin America one company at a time, the Alliance became an American meta-company and did what the north had always done to its southern neighbors—it took the best and left the rest.

One year later, in the fall of 1965, Senator Robert Kennedy and a group of colleagues were headed on a fact-finding tour to South America. Had Jack not died, it might have been Bobby who was guiding policy in the region; instead, he and Johnson were in a backstreet brawl, partly over the dying Alliance and partly over the drift into Vietnam. Had Jack lived, it could almost as easily have been the Kennedys who were making these mistakes, but the excruciating lessons of the assassination had changed Bobby profoundly. He was no longer willing to live by the sword alone.

The overthrow of President Diêm in Vietnam had created an unexpected domino effect, in-country, one avaricious and violent bunch falling before another. Ambassador Lodge had proposed rallying the demoralized and leaderless South by dropping some bombs on the North. Lyndon had rejected that idea, but Jack's hawks—Rusk, McNamara, Rostow, and Bundy—were increasingly prone to such new measures themselves, and foreign affairs was not Lyndon's strong suit. Kennedy's brain trust would tell Johnson what choices Kennedy would have made, and Johnson would generally follow their lead.[39] By February of 1965, he *was* bombing the North. By the summer, he had sent in fifty thousand U.S. troops, still convinced that he was playing it straight up the middle, between full withdrawal and dangerous escalation.

Lyndon and Bobby had been maintaining the appearance of a truce, but now Bobby was edging into more public dissent. "The essence of successful counterinsurgency is not to kill," he said in a speech at the International Police Academy, "but to bring the insurgent back to national life . . ." Further, as his brilliant young aide and speechwriter Adam Walinsky insisted, American politics was misjudging the world situation at its own peril. Not every homegrown revolution was a Communist conspiracy, Bobby now believed.[40] "Our approach to revolutionary war must be political—political first, political last, political always. Where the needs and grievances of the people begin to be met by the political process, insurgency loses its popular character and becomes a police problem." It could not have been more informed by the tragedy of Cuba, nor more infused with the new Catholic agenda of nonviolent change.

Bobby's third way in Vietnam was not a storm of American B-52s raining shrapnel on the North Vietnamese, it was aggressive negotiations toward a democratic spectrum of social ideas—a war of words.

His third way in Latin America, once he made it plain that the gloves were off with Lyndon, was to go down and revive the Alliance for Progress by appealing directly to the people of the region. Some in Lyndon's State Department saw it coming and hit him head-on. They implied that Bobby had no right to object, given his brother's ugly history of failure in Cuba.

It was hard to argue against the very men he had been in such harmony with for three years, but it was not enough for Robert Kennedy to undergo a conversion; he had to talk it and walk it, through action. Under the guiding hand of "the Harvards," the new president had authorized an invasion force in the Dominican Republic; had recognized a military junta in Brazil just twelve hours after it toppled a freely elected constitutional government; and was withholding aid to Peru because of a dispute over U.S. oil-drilling rights.[41]

In a political slugfest on Latin American policy at the State Department, Bobby went fifteen rounds with Jack Hood Vaughn, Mann's fresh replacement as LBJ's Latinist. It was Vaughn and a whole table full of minions versus Bobby and his moral bodyguard, Walinsky.

"Well, Mr. Vaughn," Bobby said, "let me get this straight. You're saying that what the Alliance for Progress has come down to is that you can lock up your political opposition and outlaw political parties and dissolve the congress, and you'll get all the American aid you want. But if you mess around with an American oil company, we'll cut you off without a penny. Is that right? Is that what the Alliance for Progress has come down to?"

Vaughn sat there at the long table, all the players waiting to see if he would hedge; instead, he simply admitted that the southwestern hemisphere was headed back in time.

"Well, that's about the size of it, Senator," he said.

By the time Bobby boarded a jet in Miami on November 10, bound for Lima, Peru, his junket bore the first signs of becoming a crusade. Along for the ride were Ethel, his amanuensis Angie Novello, and a self-contained complement of friends, advisers, journalists, filmmakers, and photographers, all of them swirling around the senator like fireflies in a jar. In Lima, they rendezvoused with more friends, a veritable goodwill tour taking shape.

The U.S. embassy in the Peruvian capital had a kid-gloves itinerary in mind—American factory tours, a nice bullfight. But Bobby had come to call forth the bulls himself. He and his people were there to document the real conditions of the country. It was a pilgrimage: a first foray into what Robert Kennedy was really looking for by that time, a third way. Unspoken as it was, he was posing a direct challenge to the ideologues Fidel, Raúl, and Che, who he suspected had killed his brother. He was also posing one to Lyndon Johnson, who he suspected was abandoning the Latin American people.

He shook off his embassy wranglers and descended into the *barriadas* of Lima. At his first meeting with university students, he said it, straight out: "The responsibility of our time is nothing less than a revolution," one that could be "peaceful if we are wise enough; humane if we care enough; successful if we are fortunate enough. But a revolution will come whether we will it or not. We can affect its character; we cannot alter its inevitability."[42]

In the same breath, he defended America's attempt to maintain its balance in a violent world. When students spewed venom about American imperialism, Bobby pointed out that the U.S. had given aid to right-wing and left-wing governments alike, and his message of regional accountability was constant.

Surrounded by glowering young faces, faces gnarled by poverty and nursing the grudges that Fidel had planted, he said, "You are the Peruvian leaders of the future. If you think the Alliance for Progress is imperialistic, then don't join . . . If you object to American aid, have the courage to say so. But you are not going to solve your problems by blaming the United States and avoiding your own personal responsibility to do something about them."[43]

Back and forth he kept traveling. At a soirée of Peruvian intellectuals, he heard the Latin version of the liberal cant that he hated. The neglect they showed toward their own people was repeatedly justified by their certainty that Big Oil and "the Rockefellers" ran the world and would never set them free. Bobby scoffed at that and challenged them as well.

They went on to Cuzco, the ancient capital in the Sacred Valley of the Incas. There were welcoming ceremonies, and the entourage was swept up in the bold colors of the dancers, the soaring, reedy call of the flutes, and the bright black eyes of the children surrounding them. The people were poor. There was hunger in their cheeks. Their children's stomachs were distended and their legs gaunt with rickets, but when Bobby hauled himself up onto the back of a green panel truck and let it carry him deeper into the heart of the city, they were clinging to every balcony and lamppost yelling, "Viva Kennedy!" just as they had for Jack and Jackie, years before. "Viva Kennedy! . . . Viva!"

At one point, a crowd of two thousand surged through a barbed-wire barricade. Bobby's face was cut, his suit ripped, but there was something revelatory in such exuberant melees, the crowd reaching for some touchstone of hope, change, freedom, relief.

Then it was on to Chile, where he huddled with President Eduardo Frei, a tough leftist democrat of the new breed. There were more students who wanted a piece of him in Concepción, a Communist stronghold. Mass protests might greet him, and local tradition forbade police on campuses, so he'd have no cordon of protection. A delegation of Marxist students came to his hotel, and a debate about blood and money ensued. His advisers warned him away.

Two student members of Frei's Christian Democratic Party came to see him, however. "If you don't come," they told him, "it will be a great victory for the Communists."

That was that. When night fell, Bobby and his circle of roughneck friends entered the campus like a flying wedge barreling down a football field. They deposited the senator in the center of a screaming gymnasium full of students.

This time it was not "Viva!" It was "Kennedy, *paredon*!" Kennedy, to the wall! They showered his contingent with eggs and garbage, but Bob put his head down and walked through it, unstained.

"If these kids are going to be young revolutionaries, they're gonna have to improve their aim," he said to Seigenthaler.[44]

He stood his ground, challenging them to a civil debate. They stood theirs, the chant building and building; but even as it did, some of the students were reaching out to shake his hand. There was the opening, the third path. He walked down it and clasped their hands, looked them in the eye, greeted them as Catholic brethren, as children of God. When he saw one of the Marxist leaders who had been at his hotel, he reached out for him too; as he did, another student spat in his face and the leader pulled that kid away. Finally, when everyone realized that the scene was beyond words, he waved and left, but there was applause in his wake. There were some who saw that he was just a man, a brave, conscientious one.

A few nights later, he insisted on being taken to a coal mine that descended diagonally from the shore, some two miles beneath the sea. There, at the end of the hellish shaft, he was greeted with wide smiles and open hearts by Communist miners who couldn't believe their eyes.

"If I worked in this mine, I'd be a Communist too," he told a journalist.[45]

The phrase became a litany. A hundred thousand people came to greet him in Natal. In Recife, Brazil, his group spent the night in another hell on earth, eating with the people and falling asleep to their mournful music. The next day, Bobby excoriated a sugarcane overlord who wouldn't pay what Brazilian law required.

"You're breeding your own destruction," he told the man, "if you don't pay people a decent wage."[46]

After vaulting over another open sewer in another ghastly slum; after slipping through the foul runoff from an entire hillside of tarpaper shacks so he could kick a soccer ball around with a gaggle of little ghosts, he said it again to Dick Goodwin.

"These people are living like animals," he said as they drove away, "and the children—the children don't have a chance. What happened to all our A.I.D. money? Where's it going?" American aid was still tied up, he was told, because of the oil dispute. In disgust, he leaned back and gazed out at a line of thin men leading thinner donkeys up the road they were descending.

"Wouldn't you be a Communist if you had to live there?" he murmured. "I think I would."[47]

In that, there was an admission. Perhaps only a rich man could imagine a third way in such a desperate land. But then perhaps only a rich man could convey a believable hope when there was so little time left.

The trip seemed reckless, even to some of Bobby's entourage. His empathy had always compelled action. Now, with the eyes of his father and older brother no longer upon him, he was free to feel again. But there was an edge of self-righteousness to it all. Perhaps it was only the ardor of the recently converted. Perhaps it was the overcompensation of a man who felt his guilt so intensely that he had to embrace its opposite. Perhaps it was the fervor of someone who was returning to himself and wished, with all his heart, that he had never wandered so far off course. More likely, it was all of those sensations at once.

Whatever the reasons, in his own attempt to heal and to atone and to get back to the work at hand, Bobby had served notice on the president he had been trying to avoid confronting; the president to whom he owed his political future. But despite the debt of well-kept secrets he owed to Lyndon Johnson, there were too many ways in which they had begun to differ. They were trading places, the hard young warrior finally seeking some peace, the cautious old politician being led into war.

The American center was in crisis now. The unspoken pact that he had made with Lyndon was about to come apart, and the chances for real reform, for a real synthesis of America's best traits, might come apart with it.

The students and the poor were the canaries in this particular coal mine. They were the ones who were warning of the collapse to come. Bobby had seen it in 1963 when confronted by James Baldwin and Jerome Smith. Now the impatience and intemperance of American youth was sweeping the nation, and it had been exacerbated, terribly, by the secret disinformation campaigns of foreign intelligence services, unscrupulous authors, a rabid southern district attorney, and the secrecy surrounding the Warren Commission's proceedings. The government's initial refusal to show the public the eighteen-second film of their president's murder didn't help either.

The very young reformers that democracy needed most to keep in its fold were being radicalized by suspicions planted by their own government and by its mortal enemies. On some level, Bobby must have known that the steel-edged neoliberalism he was trying to hammer out might be too little, too late. If the right kept advancing toward him and the left kept marching away, he would be trying, in vain, to hold on to a fast-dissolving center.

CHAPTER 15
Sympathy for the Devil

ONE NIGHT IN HAVANA, late in 1964, a group of dancers took to the floor of a faded nightclub and were soon in the thrall of a beautiful, complex Cuban dance called *la rueda*, the Wheel, a kaleidoscopic circle of multiple couples, ever folding and unfolding, always turning as a whole even as the shifting pairs turned and spun and caressed within. It opened and closed like the flowers in the women's hair, the lantana and gazania and plumeria, and to watch it was to become entranced by sensual coherence in motion.

It was to catch a glimpse of Cuba without the sharp edges, without the pain, in perfect, human harmony.

And in the middle of it danced Dr. Rolando Cubela, fitting in perfectly with the flow, or seemingly so. In fact, he was now known by Cuban intelligence to be politically ambidextrous and probably, in effect, a double agent one day, a triple agent the next; a wheel within a wheel within a wheel, reporting on the U.S. and exile plans against Fidel, even as he remained obsessed with removing *el loco* himself.

He was a conflicted but tenacious man. He was also a man who liked to indulge himself. Every night, he was seen gliding through a different Havana cabaret, from the Tropicana to the Capri, and always with the same group of chattering associates. They drank and smoked and danced; money rolled off them like beads of sweat, and where it came from, the G2 could only guess. There was plenty of gossip about Cubela, including claims that he was as ambidextrous sexually as he was politically; that he might even be Raúl's lover, the "husband" in a long-standing relationship. Those rumors notwithstanding, Raúl's men were tired of guessing at the source of his assets or the endpoint of his allegiance. They were going to force his hand this time. "We knew he was capable of [assassination]," the chief of Cuban counterintelligence, Israel Behar, would claim in 1992, "so we infiltrated his group" and short-circuited his plans, "again, and again, and again."[1] Still, Cubela continued to confound the spooks on all sides. His charisma and audacity had a way of attracting and emboldening Fidel's internal enemies that must have made him useful to the regime.

But Fidel may have discerned that the threat to his rule was very close by now, and pervasive. His Havana nights had been increasingly paranoid, and perhaps even more so after Dallas. In 1963, he had launched a second purge of his bodyguards, members of the People's Socialist Party (PSP) who had replaced his original 26th of July protectors. The Castros had come to conclude that their PSP body-men were members of the party's first "Microfaction," insiders who had been incited by Moscow to overthrow the brothers.[2] By '64, he had scraped out that internal rot, only to sense that the Yanks were eating away at him again. It was then that he showed signs of wanting to talk directly with Lyndon Johnson about a rapprochement. He hinted at it to the *New York Times*. There was talk of Che meeting with the Americans, through a British intermediary, when he went to the UN in December. Whatever it was that prompted him to try again, it was the first such entreaty since Che's appeal to Richard Goodwin in August of 1961. But Lyndon ignored these signs.[3]

To the exiles, Rolando Cubela still seemed hell-bent on unseating Fidel from within. And he wasn't alone. Johnson had ended CIA sabotage operations against Cuba, but that did nothing to slow "autonomous groups" from continuing—and there was no way the CIA was going to cut them off cold once again, as they had at the Bay of Pigs. The CIA's AMTRUNK operation remained in business, if only in the form of Agency supervisors from afar, and Manuel Artime's Movement for Revolutionary Recovery (or MRR) was still preparing an insurrection from its camps in Costa Rica and Nicaragua. JM/WAVE continued to supply Cubela, Artime, and others with weapons and support, as long as they weren't for the direct murder of Fidel. As the U.S. election had approached in 1964, it was as if the old Kennedy White House still hoped it might use proxies to topple the Castros, whether or not Lyndon Johnson went along. Johnson, of course, wanted nothing to blow up on him before Election Day, and it seems that the Agency kept him in the dark.

And from the Agency's perspective, Cubela's coup now had potential conspirators from Cuba's military elite, men like Efigenio Ameijeiras Delgado, Faustino Pérez, and Juan Almeida who had been with the Castro brothers all the way back to the *Granma* landing. They were so far inside the circle that, as far as Des FitzGerald was concerned, it was too good an opportunity to pass up and would be too terrible a betrayal to leave them hanging.

There must also have been a measure of vengefulness in the CIA's quiet support for these efforts, given their humiliation after Dallas and suspicions that Fidel was involved. It was in no one's interest to accuse Fidel publicly of being an assassin, but the CIA quietly continued to encourage his removal.

However, the Agency could never be certain that these alleged Judases in Castro's military really would revolt. Perhaps they were just toying with their American contacts, another in a long line of sophisticated Cuban spy-ops. There was also a certain anxiety about the volatile anti-Castro exiles that already considered themselves "betrayed" after the missile crisis. At very least, it seemed prudent that any shutdown of anti-Castro operations be gradual. Perhaps they should marry Artime's gutsy insurrection with Cubela's internal cabal and hope for the best. It might be the last best hope they had of bring the Castro boys down.

So, according to an Agency inspector general's report of the time, agents "contrived to put Artime and Cubela together in such a way that neither knew that the contact had been engineered by CIA." On December 10, 1964, Nestor Sánchez filed a memo with the Paris station: "Artime does not know and we do not plan to tell him that we are in direct contact with Cubela, nor does Cubela know and we do not desire he know that we are in direct contact with Artime."

Seventeen days later, it was arranged. On December 27, Artime and Cubela met for the first time in Madrid. They met again on December 30, the CIA kept apprised because significant money was being spent, even if the Agency wasn't giving official approval to any such plan.[4]

Cubela and Artime got down to business. Cubela wanted a silencer for the 7.62 mm FAL rifle he had chosen; he'd asked the Americans to provide him one, but they had refused. Artime told him that he'd get him one, or some other rifle with a silencer. The plan was for Cubela to carry the silencer back with him to Cuba, or for Artime to cache another properly fitted rifle for him somewhere in Cuba, for pickup. If procuring the right one didn't happen, the ultimate solution was for Artime's group to make an FAL silencer themselves and then send it off to a site in Europe, where Cubela could secure it.[5] What neither man knew was that—yet again—their cover had been blown; the man who helped Artime construct the silencer was the brother of Cuban G2 agent Juan Felaifel, who was still Artime's intelligence chief. There were simply no secrets from Raúl, it seemed, no matter how hard one tried.

They agreed that they would strike at the beach resort of Varadero in Matanzas, on the north coast of Cuba. Appropriately, there would be a 26th of July commemoration there that day, and Fidel was set to give one of his extravagant speeches, his entire cabinet in attendance. As he waxed patriotic, Cubela would take him down where he stood, with the rifle. Artime and a horde of MRR henchmen would land, seize the single road that led to the site, and—with the help of dissident commander Calixto García—take the cabinet hostage. With Fidel cut down, this would trigger their coconspirators in the Central Army Command to topple the regime, secure the airwaves, and round up the Castro brothers' government, one *barbudo* at a time. Cubelo would lead the Directorio Revolucionario (DR) group. Efigenio Ameijeiras Delgado, from the 26th of July Movement, would lead some of the armed forces from the Special Affairs section; and a third Movement group from the Western Army, headed by Commandante Guillermo García Frías, would provide the third flank. The Western Army, whose turf included Havana, comprised half of the Cuban Army. Artime had even gone so far as to commission the construction of some elegant little helicopters to help complete the seizure of Varadero from the air.[6] Cubela had not been very compliant on the day of the Cuban revolution, five years earlier. Upon seizing the presidential palace, he and Che had reached a standoff, Cubela and his unit tempted to keep it for themselves. Now, however, Cubela promised not to oppose Artime—the most popular leader among the exiles and the Cuban people—as the junta's president-apparent.

Despite Johnson's disassembly of the 1964 invasion plan, including the murder plots, the Agency recommended that the administration back this particular scenario, and they asked that the money pipeline stay open until at least the end of February 1965. The White House, however, was not comfortable with Artime anymore, and the State Department was downright dubious of the whole thing. The money slowed down to a trickle, and then the presidents of Costa Rica and Nicaragua were discreetly asked to shut down the base camps.

While the Johnson White House worked to suffocate the new plot, Artime tried to hold on with his cash reserves, even as attrition began to set in, and the exiles' rumor mill had begun to rev up once again. The end of Fidel was nigh! But as soon as the plot seemed like it might continue without Washington, Raúl's extraordinary intelligence machine revved up to meet it at the other end. So sophisticated was his operation by now that he was tapping phones of exile leaders inside the United States and monitoring their mail.[7]

His G2 had placed tabs on Cubela's assistants and his backups; one of Cubela's mistresses was thought to be a G2 asset, and her brother was certainly an agent,[8] yet still he polished his weapon, kept up his nightlife, and threw money around like confetti.

Meanwhile, Fidel was making one last attempt to talk directly to President Johnson, probably expecting the worst. In April, Fidel's mistress Celia Sánchez called New York attorney James Donovan (who had had a good rapport with Castro since the Bay of Pigs prisoner negotiations) and asked him to intervene. Fidel himself asked Donovan to come to Havana immediately, but the State Department derailed the idea, and the lawyer wasn't about to defy them.

By June 1965, the demoralized and furious MRR commandos began to drift home to Miami and New Orleans, and the stories of Artime's wobbly coup plan were so pervasive that the CIA knew it couldn't succeed, whether autonomous or not. Word got back to the Agency that Cubela had been bragging about the putsch during one of his bacchanalian trips to Rome, another example of his strange tendency, whether deliberate or unconscious, toward self-sabotage. They warned Artime that Cubela was untrustworthy.[9] His lack of discipline was a risk the MRR could not afford.

On June 23, the CIA sent out cables to all its agents to terminate all contact with Rolando Cubela Secades. Just as Johnson's signing of civil rights legislation would give the segregationist South to the Republicans for generations to come, this last attempt at a coup would deliver the Cuban exiles in South Florida to the party of Nixon. The Democratic Party's presidential candidates have suffered for it ever since.

On March 1, 1966, Reuters reported from Havana that Dr. Cubela had finally been arrested, along with Major Ramón Guin Díaz, José Luis González Gallarreta, Alberto Blanco Romariz, and Juan Alsina Navarro, all for alleged "counterrevolutionary activities involving the Central Intelligence Agency." The men were caught planning still another strike against Fidel at the upcoming May Day celebration. Had Cubela finally declared himself, for real? Had he actually been ready to bring down Fidel, after so many years of proposing it and preening as the revolution's moderate heir apparent?

La Cabaña fortress is a museum now, but it was once a slaughterhouse. Built in the eighteenth century by King Carlos III of Spain, its cornerstone was laid in 1763 on the high ground that is the eastern shore of Havana's harbor entrance, and it was erected, at great expense to the Spanish crown, to replace crumbling fortifications beside the old El Morro fortress. By the time it was completed in 1774, it stood as the most formidable military compound in the New World. For the next two centuries it served as a fortress and prison for the Spanish occupiers, and then as Batista's military prison during his two terms as the Cuban president.

At dawn, its beige and pink stone walls glow softly until the sun crawls higher and fills its avenues with tropical daylight. Wind-tattered greenery sprouts from its turrets, bringing a bit of unearned life. Its terraces are topped with grass, and in its short minarets the guard towers have small windows and gun portals from which to sight the sea or the prisoners within.

It was "liberated" in January 1959 by Che Guevara's squadron, and with that he became the latest lord of the manor. He ruled his citadel from a fine Baroque office overlooking the killing ground, with black and white checked marble floors, dark wainscoting, slanting, beamed ceilings, and virgin-white stucco walls. From here, Che directed the work of the Purging Commission, which had the task of trying and executing the low-level soldiers, the decadent journalists, and the unlucky friends of friends who were dragged before it in the thirsty, early days of the victory.

Executions were held from Monday through Saturday. It was a busy time, as many as seven firing squads per day; the executioners took fifteen pesos per elimination, their officers ten pesos more. The accused, early on, were former Batista officials, members of the "Bureau for Repression of Communists," journalists, upstart priests, and those who were simply out of favor. Their relatives were forced to serve as jurors, but the verdict was universal. Che pronounced judgment in a slow, frigid Argentine drawl, to the cheers of the spectators in the gallery, and then the prisoners would be taken to the "good-bye rooms," where those same relatives would whisper pleas for forgiveness and bid their loved ones farewell. The condemned were then escorted to a wall below, where Che could watch them bargain or beg or scream their innocence. One stouthearted *capitán* gave the order for his own eradication, and once the bullets had chopped him up he hung from the wall with the rest of that day's kill until the birds had eaten his soft parts.[10]

It was here that they brought Rolando Cubela, and it must have given him pause. Some six hundred people had been murdered there within the first five months of Che's tenure. Rolando was a special case, or so he hoped. He had served with distinction. He had killed for these friends of his and had scouted the ultimate assassin for them. But he had also defied Che, briefly, on the very day that the revolution was won, and now here he was, staring into his eyes and knowing full well that this was payback time. The doctor would now have to bargain for his life.

We know little of his interrogation or his trial, but there is evidence, brought to German filmmaker Willi Huismann by "Nikolai," that during his questioning Cubela reminded his captors of his relationship with Lee Oswald. According to a report of Cubela's interrogation made by the KGB's Major General Igor Demyanovich Statsenko, the commander of the Soviet military in Cuba, the would-be assassin, in a attempt to have his punishment mitigated, reminded his prosecutors that it was his initial meetings with Oswald that led to the ultimate removal of Castro's archenemy, Jack Kennedy. According to Statsenko's notes of the February 1967 questioning, Cubela said that he met Oswald "repeatedly, several times," the first time at the end of 1962. The very mention of this in Statsenko's report suggests that it amounted to evidence of Cuban involvement with Oswald that had been previously kept from the Russians.

On March 7, 1966, at La Cabaña, Dr. Cubela and his collaborators were put on trial. All confessed their guilt. In the ordinary conduct of Cuban justice, Cubela, and at least Guin and Romariz, would have been sentenced to death by firing squad; but a letter arrived for the prosecutor on March 9, a letter from Fidel Castro, requesting "that the court not ask the death sentence for any of the accused." The lead investigator for the prosecution was none other than Fabian Escalante.*

---

*Escalante was appointed head of the Department of State Security (DSE) in 1976. Two years later, members of the HSCA visited Cuba and requested help with investigating the assassination of John F. Kennedy. Escalante was asked to oversee this investigation. As a result, HSCA counsel Blakey and his staff were denied access to key witnesses, such as Luisa Calderón. In 1982 Escalante became a senior official in the Interior Ministry. By this time he was considered to be Cuba's leading authority on the history of CIA activities against his country. He became head of the Cuban Security Studies Center in 1993. This allowed him to become Cuba's chief propagandist regarding the assassination of John F. Kennedy. As he points out, along with "Colonel Arturo Rodríguez Mendoza (now deceased), I studied all the available material and publications, consulted with former agents and operatives, and investigated all the accessible documentation." In 1995, Escalante hosted a Kennedy assassination conference in Nassau for U.S. conspiracy theorists, wherein he pointed them toward the CIA, Cuban exiles, and the mob as Kennedy's killers—anyone but the Castros. He reiterated that party line in 2005, when confronted by Willi Huismann's cameras.

The verdict came on March 10, 1966: Cubela and Ramón Guin were sentenced to twenty-five years imprisonment; Jose Luis Gonzáles Gallarreta and Alberto Blanco Romariz to twenty years; and Juan Hilario Alsina Navarro to ten years. The CIA's 1967 *Inspector General's Report on Plots to Assassinate Fidel Castro* points out that "None of Cubela's dealings with the CIA from March 1961 until November 1964 were mentioned in the trial." It further states that "the trial evidence was confined to Cubela's counterrevolutionary activities growing out of those meetings with Artime in December 1964 and February 1965."

What's more, Cubela "was given a relatively light sentence, considering the seriousness of the charge. Upon incarceration, he reportedly functioned as a prison physician and drove around in a jeep unescorted. Such treatment by the government of Cuba is quite unusual and, if true, is an indication that he was trusted."[11] That is an understatement. Cubela had conspired with the CIA, repeatedly, on one of the most delicate and dangerous of Cold War missions, and yet undocumented reports tell of a man who was well housed and well fed in an airy, rural reformatory; who read at his leisure, drank good wine, and consorted with whomever he wished.

Still, he was locked up, however gently, and this man who had shared the dais with the Castros and Che on many occasions would not be seen again in public for twelve years. By that time, Cuba's own cult of conspiracy was under way. Countless new films and screeds, including books by Claudia Furiati and Fabian Escalante, would advance still more blind theories about Dallas, all of which came back to pinning the murder on the CIA.

In 1978, fifteen years after Dallas and ten years after Bobby's murder, the Kennedy brothers' photos still hung—in memoriam—in millions of poor homes throughout Latin America. Sometimes they even hung alongside a memento mori of Che, who by then had been executed by CIA-backed Bolivians. In August of that year, as if to join what they couldn't beat, the Castro brothers convened a "Cuban Youth Tribunal," a major point of which was to announce that the CIA had killed Kennedy. It was an odd piece of revisionism. After nearly twenty years of denouncing the Kennedys as capitalist homunculi, less than men, they chose an international conference of idolatrous youth to present "evidence" that John Kennedy was a victim of his evil government, thus transforming him from antagonist to fellow victim.

And who was brought forth as a "witness" in one of the sultry afternoon sessions, but Rolando Cubela, the recruiter of Jack's assassin.[12] We do not know exactly what the doctor told the crowd, but very soon after the tribunal,

Cubela was sprung. With the help of friends in G2, he was able to purchase a home in Spain, where he moved after his release. He had served less than half of his sentence.

Long before that, however, back in January 1967 while Cubela was still in prison and Bobby was still very much alive, the long-festering enmity between Bobby and President Johnson broke into full view. It had been aggravated by the Kennedy family's feud with historian William Manchester, their handpicked chronicler, over passages in his upcoming book *The Death of a President*. A settlement was reached in which Manchester excised some portions, and what remained was largely a Kennedy hagiography with LBJ as the boorish antagonist. Johnson was incensed. Even a handwritten note of apology from Mrs. Kennedy could not assuage his feeling that he had been portrayed as a power-mad rube.

Jack Newfield, a radical reporter who had once demonstrated against Bobby, had considered him to be a cold Irish enforcer who dawdled on civil rights and conducted himself with a merciless sense of entitlement. Since a tête-à-tête on Vietnam, however, Newfield had changed his opinion. "I was not fully prepared for the changes," he wrote of their meeting. "Instead of the military crew cut, his graying, ginger hair now lapped over his earlobes in the shaggy style of the alienated young. His blue eyes were now sad rather than cold, haunted rather than hostile."[13] The two men called a cease-fire and discovered, to their shock, that they related to each other enormously. Bobby was hungry to know what Newfield had experienced as a veteran of the civil rights era, what the outsider knew about power. Newfield strove to understand Bobby's view from within, the awful ambiguities of trying to lead.

The Vietnam War was escalating, furiously now, and Bobby was among many of Jack's former staffers who had become uneasy about whether it could be won and whether it was right in the first place.

You've got to speak out against it, Newfield pressed him as 1966 was coming to an end. If Bobby's mind was made up, if he was certain that the whole thing was a hell-ride and bound to get worse, then he had to say so before it *got* worse.

Bobby wasn't sure that another speech would do any good.

If it would, he said, "I would make it tomorrow. But the last time I spoke, I didn't have any influence on policy, and I was hurt politically. I'm afraid that by speaking out I just make Lyndon do the opposite. He hates me so much that if I asked for snow, he would make rain, just because it was me. But maybe I will have to say something. The bombing is getting worse all the time now."

Newfield would not let up, nor would Bobby's young aides, speechwriter Adam Walinsky and Peter Edelman, his low-key legislative craftsman. These three brought the 1960s in from beyond the Beltway. They were his guides to the underworld of radical youth, and they continued to goad him, knowing that his moral instincts were goading him from within.

When Senator Kennedy made a journey to Europe, it became a kind of traveling pageant in Jack's memory, but it was also fraught with domestic politics. Bobby twice crossed swords with Johnson. First he went to Oxford University and expressed deep-seated doubts about Lyndon's recent resumption of the bombing of North Vietnam. Then, in Paris, as official peace talks were about to begin, he met quietly with the North Vietnamese delegation, offering to convey their terms of disengagement to the U.S. president. The meeting didn't stay quiet for long. When it hit the international papers, Lyndon was enraged.

And as of February 6, shortly after Bobby's return to the States, the relationship went into free fall.

The two men met in the Oval Office, Johnson opening with an attack about Bobby's apparent leaks to the press in Paris. Bobby denied it, claiming that it was "your State Department" that leaked, to which Lyndon replied, "It's not my State Department, goddamnit. It's *your* State Department!"[14] He was offended by Bobby's public call for negotiations, insisting that the United States military would have the war won by midsummer. In his eyes, Bobby, his shaggy young staff, and the old Frontiersmen who had left the executive branch along with Kennedy were leading an antiwar movement to unseat him. It validated every suspicion he had had before the 1964 convention. Bobby Kennedy was comin' after him.

"I'll destroy you and every one of your dove friends in six months," the president railed. "You'll be dead politically in six months!" He swore that all Bobby was doing was protracting the conflict. "The blood of American boys will be on your hands," Lyndon snarled. A group of young Chilean Marxists had said his hands were bloody just eighteen months earlier, red with the blood of American imperialism. "I never want to hear your views on Vietnam again," Lyndon was screaming. "I never want to *see* you again!"

The harangue went on for eighty minutes.

"I don't have to sit here and take that shit," Bobby bellowed before calling the president a "son-of-a-bitch," and finally exiting the room.

And so their collusive partnership ended.

At the time of this clash, Johnson had already gotten wind of a story that would soon appear in Jack Anderson and Drew Pearson's syndicated news column, Washington Merry-Go-Round. It was the story that Bobby Kennedy had hoped would never appear, the first one that would tell the world what he had worked so hard for over three years to suppress: the story of the Castro plots, with Bobby front and center. Lyndon's reaction suggests that his knowledge of the plots had been sketchy since taking office. It came as a minor revelation—or, perhaps more, a confirmation—of all that had been going on beyond his sight while he was vice president.

And he would use it if he had to, or so he thought.

At the same time that the press was getting wind of the Kennedy-versus-Castro blood feud, the district attorney of New Orleans was fomenting some theories of his own about what had happened in Dallas. They would prove to be among the most harebrained notions, enabled by the most amoral abuse of power, that even New Orleans could cook up. Remarkably, the popularity of these notions would be enhanced by yet another piece of fiction from the Soviet KGB. Their "active measures" campaign was shaping up as an astonishingly effective act of psychological warfare, and DA Jim Garrison was about to become another of the KGB's puppets.

It wasn't surprising that the first legal eruption of the conspiracy trends should come in New Orleans. Lee Oswald had no public profile anywhere else. In Dallas, he was just another shambling white boy trying to scrape by. But here he had achieved a small measure of notoriety, even fame. He had gotten himself onto the tube, on the radio, and into the papers. He had made himself a "somebody" to prove his mettle to the Cubans, and there is evidence that he met a fair number of them in his few months there. It wasn't a big town, after all. Beyond that, the Big Easy was still a product of the Napoleonic Code, its history of French and Spanish parlor intrigue coalescing with the Creole realms of miscegenation, Afro-Cuban magic, and the necessity of keeping secrets from an untrustworthy white society. New Orleans cooked up plots as well as it cooked up gumbo, and some of its great chefs were lawyers.

And in 1967, Jim Garrison *was* the Big Easy, tall as a lamppost, corruptible as Judas, and loud as a ragtime band. A family man, he was quietly rumored to have pedophilic leanings, to be friendly with local crime boss Carlos Marcello, and to have the whole local judiciary in the palm of his hand. He was not above giving or taking a bribe, and "Big Jim" was as ambitious as a pirate in a brothel. Nonetheless, he was excellent at playing the role of reformist White Knight, and he was popular with the masses, if only for his entertainment value.

In the early sixties, he had developed a hatred for David Ferrie, who—along with local detective Guy Banister—had been keeping a dossier on his misdeeds for years, hoping one day to drop the bomb on the DA and run him out of office. This became the first link in a chain that would eventually lead Garrison to pursue half of Bobby Kennedy's New Orleans Amigos, but it started as a vendetta against Ferrie alone. And with his bizarre appearance and frequently questioned sexuality, Ferrie was an easy target.

No sooner had Lee Oswald been arrested in 1963 and his time in New Orleans been revealed than Garrison started fishing around for his local connections. A local loudmouth named Jack Martin, with a reputation as a drunk and blowhard, planted the notion that Ferrie and Oswald were acquainted, though their only association had been when Lee briefly joined the Civil Air Patrol as a teenager in the fifties. During Oswald's fleeting CAP career, he is known to have attended only one campout "bivouac" near Alexandria Airport,* where Ferrie was the guest instructor. They had had no other contact since, but one more coincidence inflamed Big Jim's ambition—Ferrie had made a trip to Houston during the week of the assassination. Small matter that Ferrie had been devastated by Kennedy's murder; to Big Jim's way of thinking, there was a conspiracy afoot.

On the night of November 25, 1963, the day that JFK had been laid to rest, Garrison sent one of his men to Ferrie's apartment without a search warrant. Ferrie's friend Layton Martens would later claim that the real reason for the raid was that Garrison wanted to seize David's incriminating files; but whatever the motive, there was no case to be made, and the matter was dropped until late 1966.

Louisiana senator Russell Long is said to have been the first to plant doubts in Big Jim's mind about the Warren Commission Report, and on the eve of the Anderson-Pearson revelations, Jim saw the controversial report as a way in to gain national prominence. He was particularly curious about 544 Camp Street, about the Feds' apparent disinterest in it as a piece of the Oswald puzzle. Garrison threw caution to the wind and went back to Ferrie, a convenient and vulnerable target. This would lead him to the rest of the CRC crowd, even though they had actually been secret employees of Jack Kennedy, not his killer.

A district attorney in Louisiana has extraordinary power. His signature on a bill of information is all that is needed to formally charge someone with a

---

* Approximately 200 miles northwest of New Orleans.

crime, and Garrison used it with abandon. When he went after Ferrie for a second time, however, he started with a subpoena. He did so with the full knowledge that Jack Martin had long since recanted his claim about Ferrie knowing Lee.

Ferrie went straight to the FBI office in town. As Ramsey Clark, the new attorney general, put it to LBJ, "Ferrie wanted to know what the Bureau could do to help him with this nut [Garrison]."[15]

On a wet, sloppy day in mid-December 1966, Ferrie loped into the city courthouse to answer the subpoena in Garrison's office. He cut a strange figure, as always, tall and clownlike with his beady eyes, flushed cheeks, and sketched-in eyebrows. His alopecia had rendered him nearly bald, so he wore a "monkey fur" toupee.* Jim immediately set to questioning him again about the assassination.

Ferrie repeated exactly what he had told him in 1963—he had no knowledge of Lee Oswald (his CAP bivouac with Oswald in attendance had failed to even register). As for any other association, Ferrie did not have the faintest idea what Garrison was talking about. Two months later, in late February 1967, Ferrie died of a brain aneurysm. There were a couple of notes left behind that seemed to foretell his death, and Garrison immediately leaped to the judgment of murder. Bobby Kennedy called the coroner, asking for details of the death. It wasn't murder. Although he had been a pilot for most of his adult life, Ferrie had a blood pressure that exceeded 200, spontaneous nosebleeds, and other complications.

In the wee hours of March 2, Bobby, with the help of Goodwin and Frank Mankiewicz, completed work on the speech that would finally deliver what Newfield had begged for. There were now four hundred thousand American troops in Vietnam. The killing was being visited upon every home, televised by satellite, and each night brought a new tableau of dead and dying Americans and Vietnamese. The senator crawled into bed vexed by his own stark images, slept for a few hours, and then hit the floor again at dawn.

Ethel knew how important the day would be. It might be the first step in a run for the White House.

"Hail, Caesar!" she cried, the kids all looking up at their tired father.

Smiling wanly, he accepted a cup of coffee, glancing at the table full of

---

*Ferrie endured a few accusations that he had made overtures to young boys, but the supposed victims denied it and he was never charged.

newspapers, cereal boxes, and sticky jelly knives. He yawned, tousled a few little heads of Kennedy hair.

He had talked to his brother, the senator from Massachusetts.

"I spoke to Teddy last night. He said to make sure that they announce it's the Kennedy from *New York*." It was a joke, but no one was kidding themselves. There would be no political cover for Bobby's speech, and no turning back.

Their oldest, Bobby Jr., walked in with his pet coatimundi, which proceeded to chomp onto his mother's leg. Never a dull moment at Hickory Hill.

"He's biting me," Ethel screamed. Bobby Jr. took note. "Oh, God, he's *biting* me!"

Father and son set about unsnapping the jaws of the little coon from Mom's leg. Ethel went off to see a doctor.

While breakfast flew by him, Bobby poured more coffee and went over the speech one last time. Ethel hobbled back in a while later, her leg plastered with bandages.

"Well, if these are all the scars the Kennedys end up with by five o'clock, it'll be all right," she sighed.[16]

Bobby chuckled, kissed them all good-bye, and headed up to Capitol Hill.

The president, it turned out, had booked himself a full day, hoping to lead the press away from Bobby's groundbreaking speech, but in the end Bobby would get all the ink. Reporters tailed him everywhere that day.

Lyndon had accused Bobby of undermining the troops. Hunched and haggard in the center of a circle of microphones, he replied.

"You have to balance that against what you think does the greatest amount of good. I don't think we're going to end the war by military action."

"Are the American people more hawkish than doveish?" a reporter asked. "Yes," Bobby ceded.[17]

Nevertheless, he turned and headed to the Senate chamber to say what he believed. As the truth of his warring past and his brother's murder was worming its way to the surface, he was about to stand up, make at least a partial confession of his sins, and declare himself a man of peace. In some sense, the final chapter of his life began on this day, at 3:40 P.M., and the speech would be just the overture of an extraordinary outpouring of concern for the nation and the world.

He opened it by saying, in deference to custom and in keeping with his belief, that the United States should stay in Southeast Asia until its commitments had been fully discharged. But then he moved to the crux of the matter.

"Ten thousand miles from this chamber we are engaged in a violent conflict that has engulfed the land of Vietnam. I discuss this war knowing that its tangled and resistant complexities make judgment difficult and uncertain; and knowing, therefore, of the grave and painful responsibility borne by the president of the United States. As he must make the ultimate decisions, he is also entitled to our hopeful sympathy, our understanding, and our support in the search for peace . . . We are not here to curse the past or to praise it. Three presidents have taken action in Vietnam . . . As one who was involved in many of those decisions, I can testify that if fault is to be found or responsibility assessed, there is enough to go around for all—including myself . . . The issue, therefore, is how we can serve at once the interest of our country and the most compassionate cause of humanity—the common cause of peace . . . The most powerful country the world has known now turns its strength and will upon a small and primitive land. And still there is no peace."

The war abroad would gradually spread into a war over what America was becoming, and that speech would continue to amplify itself for the next fifteen months, the last months of his life.

A year later, he would say, "Every night, we watch horror on the evening news. Violence spreads inexorably across the nation, filling our streets and crippling our lives. [This administration has no answer to the war], none but the ever-expanding use of military force . . . Can we ordain ourselves to the awful majesty of God—to decide what cities and villages are to be destroyed, who will live and who will die, and who will join the refugees wandering in a desert of our own creation?"

Bobby grabbed all the headlines that night, but the next day, March 3, a week after David Ferrie's death, the Washington Merry-Go-Round piece hit the stands. In it was the first unconfirmed report of the Kennedy brothers' plots on Fidel and their possible relation to Dallas. Garrison was mentioned, with caveats, but RFK's secret was leaking out, and long-standing rumors of a relationship between Bobby and the local CRC did nothing to deter the DA from going after those exiles. At this moment of Bobby's antiwar declaration, he suddenly found himself in a crossfire of a kind he hadn't anticipated. Lyndon put the full-court press of the presidency on him, his vindictiveness fully engaged. Bobby shored up his cover as best he could, sending his "eyes" down to keep watch on Garrison. The CIA director, Richard Helms, kept a curtain up between Lyndon's avid new curiosity about the Castro plots and Bobby's place within them, but Johnson was no fool and the two caretakers of the assassination's secrets were now fully at war with each other. The immediate danger of a nuclear holocaust had passed. Now it was just good old-fashioned bare-knuckled American politics, pure and simple.

But there was a brief truce called, at the grave of the fallen president.

On the cool evening of March 14, as Lyndon was still wincing from Bobby's Senate speech, he ordered the U.S. Army to block the Arlington Memorial Bridge, establish a cemetery command post, and take control of the grounds with three hundred military personnel and fifty more on reserve. A canvas was to be erected to screen the resting place of John F. Kennedy, and federal troops would move into position around it.

Bobby had become all too familiar with the site at Arlington. The Parks Service had completed the landscaping of a permanent burial site twenty feet from Lot 45, Section 30, where Jack's body had been interred forty-four months earlier, and now a crew of only two men moved a tractor and a crane into place. It was time to rebury the martyred president, along with the bodies of the two children he and Jackie had lost. There would be an official ceremony in the morning, with Lyndon Johnson and the Kennedy family present.

As the crewmen prepared themselves, two surprising observers came on site. Bobby and Secretary of Defense Robert McNamara arrived, and the crew was told to begin, the backhoe operator's shovel biting into the ground to a depth just an inch from the vault. A short time later, Bobby's brother and fellow senator, Teddy, arrived, along with Richard Cardinal Cushing, the highest-ranking prelate of Boston. One of the four men had brought along a small wooden box, which was placed on the ground beside the Cardinal. The remaining soil was brushed back. At one point, Bobby himself manned a shovel, and as he balanced atop a pile of dirt, staring down into Jack's grave, a workman carefully wrapped the vault in steel cables. Slowly, with a heave of the crane's engine, the tomb was raised; for a moment, it hung suspended before the brothers and friend, the pastor and crew and soldiers. Then, as it glided over the ground and settled with a soft, stony thud into the fresh grave, Bob took out a Kennedy half-dollar, scraped a bit of soil from the vault, and tossed the coin into the new grave in some private ritual of continuity.

Conspiracy theorists had already developed an obsession with the whereabouts of JFK's brain, imagining that it had been spirited away to prevent confirmation of "the second gunman theory," but the remains had been in Bobby's near-continuous control since he foreshortened the autopsy in 1963. And years later, witnesses would attest that on this night, the brain was finally interred where it belonged. "The president's brain is in the grave," Bobby's press aide Frank Mankiewicz would later report. "LBJ, Ted, Bobby and maybe McNamara buried it when the body was transferred."

The vigil would rotate until well past midnight, Ethel, Ted, Warren Billings, and Jackie taking their turns among the mourners, along with Bobby. Always Bobby.

Bobby would put Garrison under his microscope in the coming months, hoping to keep him from his Amigos. He called on Walter Sheridan, his former ace at the DOJ who had investigated Bobby's nemesis, Jimmy Hoffa. Now, Walter was to burrow into the Garrison pile, and he did so under the cover of making a documentary about the inquiry for NBC News. Big Jim knew full well what Sheridan's former job had been, though. When the newsman tried to talk with one of the DA's witnesses, Garrison punched back with a bribery charge against Sheridan. Bobby intervened with a public statement. The charges were dropped, but Garrison went on the record to claim that Bobby was obstructing justice, and even threatened to subpoena the senator himself. That too was derailed, and Bobby kept burrowing in, through Walter, Mankiewicz, and a Garrison insider named William Gurvich. By this time, all were convinced that the DA was just a grandstander grabbing for headlines, but Bobby met with Gurvich in New York to cap his suspicions.

Gurvich told Bobby flatly, "Senator, Mr. Garrison will never shed any light on your brother's death."

"Then why is he doing this?" Bobby said. It made no sense. Gurvich could hear the anguish in his tone.

"I don't know," Gurvich admitted, ". . . I wish I did."[18]

There would be rumors, after the DA's case fell apart, that he was receiving encouragement from Richard Nixon, who still wanted to be president. He still had his own moles and—since the Kennedys had inherited the Castro plans from him, after all—he knew better than anyone the veracity of the Merry-Go-Round claims. By this logic, Nixon thought he might be running against Bobby as the '68 Democratic standard-bearer, not Johnson, so why not start digging the dirt early. It was equally plausible that Johnson was tacitly encouraging Bobby's "outing" too. And then again, it may simply have been what it appeared to be, Big Jim's particular brand of blind justice.

The DA's next scenario was that David Ferrie and the head of the city's CRC branch, Sergio Arcacha Smith, had set up Oswald, who was actually *anti*-Castro. According to this bent logic, that was why Lee had stamped the

Camp Street address on his leaflets, because he thought himself a supporter
of the CRC and decided to affiliate himself with them. Wildly far-fetched as
this theory was, Garrison adopted it with the same poker-faced fervor he
always used to sell his notions. According to this script, Lee was an innocent, a patsy, and with Ferrie now dead, it must have been Sergio Arcacha
who set him up to kill Kennedy as recompense for abandoning the anti-
Castro movement. It was an extraordinary bit of theater. The New Orleans
DA was concocting a case against Arcacha now, one of the very few Cubans
who knew, for certain, that John Kennedy had been their last, best hope for
their country's liberation.

On April 3, 1967, Sergio was placed under arrest in his Texas home, with his
wife and children standing by. He was charged on two counts: burglarizing
the Houma weapons depot, and withholding evidence of a plot to kill the
president.

The Houma incident had actually been a transfer of arms being cached
at one of the CIA's camps along Lake Pontchartrain, one authorized by the
Kennedy bureaucracy. In essence, Bobby, or someone in Justice, had given
permission to the transfer that Garrison was now claiming was a theft, and
it further begs the question of the DA's political motives. In fact, as his angle
of attack seemed ever more directed at Bobby than at Jack's murder, the
absurdity forced an ABC News man to put it straight in Big Jim's face.

"What you are saying, then," said the newsie, "is that Senator Kennedy,
by not cooperating, is, in effect, letting the murderers of his brother walk
the streets!?"

"Well, yes," said Jim, "that's a fair statement."[19]

When Garrison's boys took Arcacha into custody, they tried to strongarm him into talking without his lawyer present. Sergio resisted. They had
to release him on $1,500 bail,[20] and for the next five months Big Jim tried to
extradite him from the Lone Star State. When Arcacha begged Attorney
General Ramsey Clark for help against Garrison, Johnson's DOJ declined.
Layton Martens got the same hands-off attitude when he tried to get the
FBI's support. Both of these rebuffs suggest a coordinated effort between
the White House and the Bureau to create maximum discomfort for Bobby,
and his fear of exposure also kept him from doing anything overt. But as the
extradition effort was bearing down harder and harder, John Connally, the
governor of Texas who had been wounded by the same bullets that killed
Jack, stepped in to block Garrison's path.

Sergio underwent a polygraph test, admitting that he had known Ferrie and was the head of the New Orleans chapter of the CRC, but insisting that he had no knowledge of any plot to kill JFK. Nobody asked him about Bobby; had they done so, he might have failed the test in order to cover his amigo, but as it was, he passed with a 100 percent truthful score.* Nonetheless, he was fired from his executive job at an air-conditioning company in Dallas. There were death threats. He and his wife had to set up special protocols for their kids' security at school, and the police started patrolling their house on the quarter hour.

Bobby asked Sergio to come to Washington during this travail. Bob was solicitous in the extreme, but by the end of their visit it was clear that he would not do anything directly to save Sergio. In effect, Sergio had been declared merely an "asset," which meant that now that he was in danger of exposure, the government would not be able to claim him.

It was only when Sergio got back to Texas that some relief did come.

He and his lawyer, Frank Hernandez, were summoned to Governor Connally's office in Austin. Upon arrival, they found the reception area filling up with reporters. The men eased their way through to the inner sanctum and were greeted by the governor, a handsome man of Texan proportions with white, wavy hair, a lopsided smile, and a sharp nose for political bull. He ushered them to some sizable leather furniture, and they settled in, Sergio impeccable and unassuming. Surrounded by western paintings and Remington reproductions, the courtly Cuban told his story, asking, of course, that it be kept private. The flame of Sergio's youth had dwindled in recent years, and he had, of course, heard that Artime and the rest of their allies had been scattered to the trade winds. It was now every man for himself. Apparently left in the lurch by Bobby, he could only entrust himself to the governor's care. It was his last chance to avoid Garrison.

So he told his melancholy tale of Cubans playing war games in Louisiana swamps; of shipping them out for heavier maneuvers in Central America; of monies and moral support from Washington; of the bygone day when there was still hope of ousting Fidel. Kennedy's tacit approval was understood, if not directly expressed.

Connally seemed to have known some of this information in advance. When Sergio's story was complete, the governor paused thoughtfully for a long moment, stroking his chin. He was impressed by the Cuban's forthright manner. Finally, he tipped his hand.

---

*Layton Martens also passed the polygraph with flying colors.

"Why did you bring your lawyer?" he asked Sergio.

Sergio smiled and shrugged. "I'm under indictment."

Connally stood. Arcacha was not under indictment in Texas, he said, and this state was his home. He told Arcacha that he would not approve his extradition to Louisiana, and then led the two men to the outer office where some fifteen journalists now waited. Guiding Sergio up to the microphones and cameras, he made the same statement there: Sergio Arcacha was an innocent man being harassed by the district attorney of New Orleans, and Connally was not about to let him be hijacked to Louisiana. He was staying there in Texas, where he belonged.

For Sergio, it was as if a suit of mail had been lifted from him. It wasn't a full acquittal, but he was safe in Texas and might yet regain some normalcy for his family. Failing a public declaration from Bobby, there could have been no better testament of faith than that from the man who had almost died with Jack.

Garrison eventually gave up on trying to destroy Sergio. Until the day he died, the Cuban patriot believed that what he had experienced in Texas had been Bobby's sidelong way of protecting him, and shielding himself, through the good graces of John Bowden Connally Jr.[21]

But Garrison was simultaneously playing another hand. The story was huge now, and Big Jim was not about to be bested. The international press was hungry for it, sucking what few facts they could from the bare bones Big Jim offered. Layton Martens would later insist that by this time the DA was offering bribes to the witnesses and players,[22] in exchange for "cooperation." Some took those bribes, some didn't, but none of the Cuban Revolutionary Council men did. So where to go next? Who could be the next whipping boy?

The answer was Clay Shaw. On specious leads from a ne'er-do-well insurance salesman/cabdriver, Garrison would indict the head of the New Orleans Trade Mart, a self-educated man who succeeded in nearly everything he did, despite his quiet sexual preference for other men and the prejudice that followed it. A tall man with a continental ease and a white crown of curly hair that he wore primed back, Clay cut a regal figure around town and was very well known. He bought real estate, investing smartly, and he had plotted his retirement well so that he could relax into the shadows of his town house in the Quarter and indulge his passion for writing plays. But in March, he was indicted for the murder of the president.

Shaw was a lifelong liberal. He had worked and voted for Kennedy in the 1960 election, as had David Ferrie. "If there was one person in New Orleans who believed in John F. Kennedy," a friend later commented, "it was Clay Shaw." Garrison, however, had come across the name "Clay Bertrand" in the Warren Commission Report and then found himself an attorney named Dean Andrews who would testify (along with a cab driver) that "Clay Bertrand" was Clay Shaw. Garrison went further, claiming that Shaw used the "Bertrand" name in the city's homosexual nightlife, even though aliases would have been absurd in such a small subculture in such a laissez-faire town. Shaw was a VIP in New Orleans. Nonetheless, the prosecutor fabricated a whole series of forced linkages from "Bertrand" to Shaw, from Shaw to Ferrie, and from Shaw to the CIA. This daisy chain was the one that invited the KGB back into the mix. Soon they had joined in the character assassination.

During the Cold War, the Soviet Union became expert at the art of *desinformatsiya*, the use of the pen as well as the sword in the furtherance of strategic goals against its adversaries. It was expressly intended "to manipulate and control the adversary's interpretation of its own intelligence," following Vladimir Lenin's answer to "his first intelligence chief, Felix Dzerzhinsky," when he asked Lenin "what sort of disinformation should be fed to the West . . . Lenin replied, 'Tell them what they want to believe.' "[23]

In the early sixties, they used it to fool the CIA into believing the Soviets had a greater capacity to build nuclear weapons than actually existed. They used it to create the impression that their missile guidance system was inaccurate.[24] From the mid-sixties to the mid-seventies, they would use it to feed erroneous material to JFK conspiracy theorists, and they would use it to railroad Clay Shaw. It didn't even stop there. In April 1977, Yuri Andropov, chairman of the KGB, would announce to the Soviet Politburo that it was releasing yet another wave of disinformation "to further implicate 'American special services' in the Kennedy assassination."[25]

Clay had enlisted in the Army and risen to the rank of major.[26] He was a centrist patriot with a deep streak of mistrust toward Communism. Clay's two "crimes" would turn out to be his membership on the board of a trade promotion group based in Rome, and his routine participation in the CIA's Domestic Contact Service whereby the Agency got tidbits of usually mundane information from U.S. businessmen who traveled abroad. He was one of 150,000 such men, products of the World War II era who became "assets"-in-passing at a time when the country felt deeply threatened by totalitarianism. Their reports might include updates on a highway project proposed for Nicaragua, or what the street effects were of such-and-such a devalued currency.[27]

Garrison arrested him on March 1, charging him with conspiracy to murder the president. When Chief Justice Warren delivered his report to President Johnson in 1964, it was so full of holes that members of the commission, including Hale Boggs, were loath to sign the thing. Now, nearly two and a half years later, the Soviets had been looking for every way to exploit and further taint that document. On March 4, Department A of the First Chief Directorate launched a new disinformation operation, with Shaw as its fresh target. Its mouthpiece would be *Il Paese Sera*, one of two house organs of the Italian Communist Party.

The first article alleged that Clay served as one of the directors of the Rome World Trade Centre (Centro Mondiale Commerciale, or CMC). He was actually just a rotating member of the board, as the head of a trade mart in a major American port city. It would go on to claim "that CMC was used as a conduit by the CIA for subsidies to anti-Communist groups; that CMC had links with the Italian Fascists; that CMC was affiliated with Permindex (Permanent Industrial Exhibitions); that Permindex had been expelled from Switzerland because of (undisclosed) criminal activities."[28] The conflation, from Clay's place on the board to his place in a plot to kill the president, was unsubstantiated, but within a day the story had spread worldwide and Big Jim Garrison's phone was lighting up with calls from Moscow to Mexico, from Tokyo to Rio. Follow-up stories appeared, in which Clay became ever more central to an expanding ring of evildoers. Even Garrison himself began to feed on the KGB's "revelations," becoming convinced of his own fabrications.

Pravda whipped up a piece, extracted from the Roman newspaper. The Montreal paper *Le Devoir* translated the *Pravda* article, and then their New York correspondent expounded on it. The magazine *Canadian Dimension* pushed it further, deep into 1968, and that same year the American New Left's glossiest mag, *Ramparts*, made Shaw's involvement an article of faith, nationwide. Books like *The Kennedy Conspiracy: An Uncommissioned Report on the Garrison Inquiry* and monographs like *The Torbitt Memorandum* ratified the story.[29]

But there was no evidence beneath it.

On March 1, 1969, two years after his arrest, Clay Shaw's six-week trial would come to an end. The jury's deliberations lasted less than an hour; the verdict, not guilty. One of the jurors would later say that they could have come to it in half the time if a number of jurors hadn't needed to use the bathroom.

Jim Garrison's witch hunt was over, but in the course of it Clay Shaw had been forced to sell everything he owned. His lawyers were generous in waiving the bulk of their fees, but the investigation and court costs were astronomical. Clay was stripped of $200,000, his life savings.[30] His health declined. Clay Shaw spent the rest of his days as a ghost of the Quarter, still living and breathing but dispirited and emotionally violated. The question of "why?" kept coming back to him. Some of the local courthouse sages who knew about the recurrent claims against Jim believed that it was a simple matter of a powerful man in the closet of pedophilia deciding to destroy a powerful man who was out of the closet as a homosexual. Clay Shaw was not so sure. It sounded a bit too psychologically oblique to him, perhaps. He attributed it, rather, to a night years before when the two men had been seated across from each other at the fine, palm-tasseled French Quarter restaurant known as Brennan's.

Clay was relaxing at a table with Ella, the owner, chatting over aperitifs in the candlelight. Garrison and his beautiful wife, Liz, were seated across from them when the district attorney's tone started to rise. He started heckling Liz, belittling her, his big face flushed with Brandy Alexanders. Clay and Ella's conversation had been arrested by now, and others had taken pause as well. Abruptly, Garrison raised his hand and slapped Liz and she lurched away, and as Garrison reached to grab her, unsettling the table, Clay stood up and put a stop to it. He was six-four, as tall as the DA, and when he loomed beside him and told him to control himself, Garrison looked up, shocked, slack-jawed and damp with rage, then cursed him, took his wife's wrist, and left. To Shaw, that seemed to be the only thing that would explain Garrison's relentless zeal in trying to turn him into Oswald's mentor. It certainly wasn't the evidence.

Astonishingly, thirty-six hours after Shaw's acquittal, Garrison charged him with perjury. But Shaw was not going to take this madman's persecutions anymore: He and his attorneys hit back immediately, filing a tough but unsuccessful civil rights complaint against Garrison and, in state court, an equally unsuccessful motion to quash the perjury charges. In 1970, Shaw filed a $5 million damage suit in Federal District Court, naming Garrison, his financial backers, and "star witness" Perry Russo. It was Shaw's attempt to exact some measure of justice by winning back some of what had been stolen from him. One year later, he filed another suit against Garrison to prevent him from ever charging him again in this case. On May 27, 1971, federal judge Herbert W. Christenberry enjoined Garrison from prosecuting the perjury charges and, for that matter, ever hauling Shaw into a court-room again in connection with the Kennedy assassination. The ruling broke new ground in the area of "equitable estoppel"* and is now taught in law schools. Christenberry concluded that Garrison had never had any "factual basis for questioning Shaw about the assassination" in the first place, adding that Garrison "resorted to the use of drugs and hypnosis on Russo, purportedly to 'corroborate' but more likely to concoct his story." He called Garrison's treatment of Shaw "outrageous and inexcusable."

Shaw's biographer, Patricia Lambert, summarized, "By placing the legal equivalent of a roadway spike strip in Jim Garrison's path, Judge Christenberry's decision finally extended the rule of law in New Orleans to include Clay Shaw; and by exposing in his opinion the DA's outrageous tactics, Christenberry ripped away Garrison's crusading seeker-of-truth public mask. In short, Judge Christenberry convicted Jim Garrison and vindicated Clay Shaw."[31]

Shaw was ruined financially by the witch hunt and trials, and the broken man died in 1974 of lung cancer before his civil damage suit against Garrison could be concluded. It is now known that, sadly, Garrison and his co-defendants were close to agreeing to a six-figure settlement when Shaw passed away. It is perhaps worth noting that Shaw's terminal illness, which was public knowledge, was no inducement to quick action on the part of those on the other side.

But before his death, Shaw finally completed a first draft of that play he had started before Garrison destroyed him. *The Rings of Ulloa* is ostensibly about the first Spanish governor of Louisiana, Antonio de Ulloa. But as Shaw told friends, it was actually about historical abuses of official power, especially those of Jim Garrison.

Shaw's many friends took up a collection and installed a plaque on one of the many French Quarter buildings he had restored. Their loving attempt to set history straight reads: "Clay Shaw was a patron of the humanities and lived his life with the utmost grace; an invaluable citizen, he was respected, admired, and loved by many." His defense attorney, Irvin Dymond, was similarly honored after his death in 1998 with a plaque above the door to the courtroom where he defended Shaw, the room now called the "F. Irvin Dymond Courtroom."

---

*A legal principle that prevents a person (such as DA Garrison) from asserting or denying something in court that contradicts what has already been established as the truth.

Though a misguided movie once featured him as its hero, no plaques are known to have been erected to honor Jim Garrison in New Orleans, the city that knew him for who he really was.

In April 1967, President Johnson was headed to another of the Punta del Este conferences in Uruguay. The man who had gelded the Alliance for Progress was hoping to avoid too much flak from the progressives.

Jack Kennedy and advance man Marty Underwood had been friendly colleagues since the 1960 election push in Chicago; but since Kennedy's assassination, Marty had become virtually indispensable to the new president. It was common for him and Johnson to share drinks in the residence and talk shop deep into the night; Johnson had Underwood placed on the Department of Commerce payroll to keep his employ off the White House books. In the aftermath of Johnson's administration and even into the years following his death, few people knew of Marty's presence on the scene, much less his tight friendship with Lyndon. His current obscurity is a measure of how trustworthy he was in his day; and, decades later, the American people would reap the reward of his discretion.

A year later, Lyndon would send his crack advance man on the most delicate errand of his presidency; but in the spring of 1967, Marty's tasks remained more routine. Still, the advance reports out of Uruguay were very disturbing. Perhaps because of Fidel's renewed sense that he was a target of the Yankees, Latin America's most militant Marxists were reputedly once again gunning for the American president. The CIA had already sent Joe Then down to assist Win Scott in securing the path. Sam Papich, the FBI's Latin American expert and liaison to the CIA, had joined them in the pinch, and rumors of assassination plots were rampant. A Buenos Aires weekly, *Correo de la Tarde*, had reported that Raúl Castro and General Fabian Escalante had been seen coming in and out of the airports at Montevideo and Punta del Este.[32] Escalante was believed to be operating out of the provinces of Salta and Jujuy, and the Castros' plots were not limited to Lyndon; intelligence indicated that they had designs on other leaders as well. "The Castro Communists will try to assassinate Presidents Johnson, [Brazilian president] Costa e Silva and [Argentinian president Juan Carlos] Onganía . . . The order to finish off Johnson, Costa e Silva and Onganía has been given and is attributed to the most reliable information," the article continued. "The intelligence services of Argentina are on the lookout for deposits of arms and food supplies located in the provinces of Salta and Jujuy."[33] One report predicted the use of a pilotless "drone plane" which would be crashed into the house President Johnson would be staying in. Another indicated that Molotov cocktail bombs would rain down on the presidential limousine.[34]

No sooner did Lyndon and his entourage arrive than leftist militants threw firebombs at the U.S. embassy and set fire to one of the station wagons in the president's security detail. Marty's hotel room window was shattered by a rock tied to a picture of President Johnson.[35] But extraordinary new security measures had been put in place, and that was as far as the radicals got in laying siege to the conference.

Marty's notes made no mention of any arrests of would-be assassins, and Lyndon quashed all other reports made by his friends and colleagues Scott, Then, and Papich. They have never been made public, and the sole remaining accounts are those contained in Marty's files and those from Argentine news services. It is not known why President Johnson hid the Uruguay stories, but it seems consistent with the entire way he managed the Cuban connection throughout his presidency. If it became known that Havana was again trying to kill the American head of state, then the wound might be horribly reopened. In 1967, there might yet have been calls for nuclear vengeance. For the rest of his life, Lyndon's probings of the Castros' network would be tentative, extremely secretive, and tinged with ambivalence. It wasn't until eleven months later, when he himself was accused in print of being a party to Jack Kennedy's murder, that he would send Marty back to Mexico.

In June, the State Department finally heard the Oscar Contreras story, which sighted Oswald with Communists at Mexico City's National University, and recounted Contreras's evening with him. State forwarded it to the CIA, which called the report "the first piece of substantive information about Oswald's sojourn in Mexico since the assassination." Thus, on June 14, 1967, CIA director Richard Helms and Western Hemisphere chief Des FitzGerald instructed Win Scott to reopen the Oswald case. Such was the sensitivity of the communication that Helms used his pseudonym, "Thomas W. Lund," and addressed Scott by *his* pseudo, "Willard Curtis." Helms directed Scott to begin the investigation after his own review of the just-obtained Oscar Contreras story, noting that it represented "the first solid investigative lead we have had on Oswald's activities in Mexico . . . the matter warrants your personal attention with the possible resources at your command."[36] Helms further warned Win that "it is essential that all of us be particularly careful to avoid making any kind of statement or giving any indication of opinion or fact to unauthorized persons."

The president, politically besieged as he was, had been having a recurring dream. He was a boy, back in Texas, and lassoed head-to-toe to a straight-backed chair, a thousand Texas longhorns stampeding toward him from all sides.[37]

He might have to do something drastic to save his political hide, but first he would have to answer the question that had plagued him since the darkest days of 1963—had Bobby, indeed, gotten his brother killed? And if so, what were the risks of using that fact, both to himself and the world at large?

CHAPTER 16

Ain't No Man Righteous, No Not One

WHEN JACK KENNEDY DIED, there were 16,732 American troops in Vietnam. By January 1968, there were 525,000, and they were dying at a rate of more than twenty per day.* The American government itself was being ripped apart. Bob McNamara was so distraught about the disposition of the war that when a crowd of protesters burned him in effigy outside his Pentagon window—when one man actually set *himself* on fire—the secretary had to agree with their position.

And McNamara was about to get himself fired.

"Every day," Lyndon Johnson would say later, "Bobby would call up McNamara, telling how the war was terrible and immoral and that he had to leave. Two months before he left he felt he was a murderer and didn't know how to extricate himself. I never felt like a murderer, that's the difference."[1]

The summer before, as the formerly integrated civil rights movement began its *dis*-integration, a string of cities were engulfed in riots, starting in the South and burning northward until Newark, Harlem, and Detroit were in flames. Lyndon sent in troops, his speeches less and less attuned to the causes of such revolt than simply to judging the effects. The campuses were not on fire, nor were people being killed there yet, but they too were in turmoil as the war's appetite for men increased.

Given all this, the pressure was building for someone to take the presidency away from Lyndon Johnson; but for all of Bobby's aggressive outrage, he was resisting the call. Another antiwar candidate had already entered the fray, Eugene McCarthy, the senator from Minnesota. Bobby thought he'd be

---

*The least disputed death toll by war's end would be 1 million Vietnamese combatants; 4 million Vietnamese civilians; and 58,226 Americans. Casualties continue to mount, even today, from unexploded ordnance buried in the land, mostly cluster bomblets.

easy to beat; he was a Catholic, and they had that in common, but Mc-Carthy was an intellectual, a professorial type, and Bobby didn't think he could handle the rigors of a campaign, let alone the Oval Office. Teddy was against Bobby's jumping into the race, though. There must have been deep-seated concerns within Bobby, too.

One night at the Caravelle, a restaurant on the East Side of Manhattan, Bobby and Ethel were having dinner with the Schlesingers and Mr. and Mrs. Benno Schmidt. Benno had clerked for Earl Warren and worked in the DOJ, and he and Arthur were debating the prospects of an RFK campaign. Ethel wanted her husband to go for it. Benno wasn't so certain. Bobby, after a career as a heavy, didn't think anyone besides New Yorkers would be able to tolerate him, much less relate to him.

"I think if I run I will go a long way toward proving everything that every-body doesn't like me has said about me . . . that I'm just a selfish, ambi-tious, little SOB that can't wait to get his hands on the White House."

Ethel rolled her eyes, leaned in close to scold him. "Bobby, you've got to get that idea out of your head; you're always talking as though people don't like you. People do like you, and you've got to realize that."

He goaded her with a smirk. "I don't know, Ethel, sometimes in moments of depression, I get the idea that there are those around who don't like me." She had rescued him, repeatedly, from the depths of despair, and yet she was one of the biggest supporters of a presidential bid.

As Benno drove them back to their apartment at United Nations Plaza, her belief in his prospects had begun to sway him a bit. Perhaps he was more personally appealing than he thought,[2] and in any case he couldn't be less appealing than Lyndon, could he? As the Schmidts and Ethel bantered on, he savored the warmth of her beside him and gazed out at the ruckus of Manhattan. He had been groomed for power. Jack's work had been left un-finished and the country had declined since his death. The promises he had made might never be kept under Johnson, and the more Johnson faltered, the more certain it was that the pendulum would swing to the right, the prom-ises would be dashed for another generation.

But the stakes attached to power were now so terribly high, perhaps too high for any one leader to set right. Conflict was the order of the day, and Bobby seemed to provoke more of it. Ethel's sunny side notwithstanding, he had been the flak-catcher for a family that created flak. He had real enemies, worse ones than Jack had ever had. And he had ten children by then, a wife he loved, and a decent old age to look forward to.

*   *   *

It would cost him half of his treasured staff, but he decided not to run.

He would lose Walinsky and, at least temporarily, Dolan and Edelman too. His young hotshot, Allard Lowenstein, came around after two dispiriting months of stumping for Gene McCarthy; he knew McCarthy didn't have the muscle and Bobby did. Al was a New York Jew who—at not quite thirty—had gone undercover in South-West Africa to build a case against the South African government. What other men talked about, he went out and did, and when he made this last appeal to Bobby he was a man in despair for his country. He made at least a dozen arguments, all of them good ones and all of them patiently deboned by Bobby, until Lowenstein was trembling with desperate sadness. He could not listen anymore, and Bobby could see it.

He tied it up, saying simply, "It can't be put together—"

"I don't give a damn whether you think it can be put together or not! We're going to do it without you, and that's too bad because you could have been president!"

Al stomped out, but Bobby wouldn't let him leave like that. He came after him, touching his shoulder.

"I hope you understand I want to do it, and that I know what you're doing *should* be done; but I just can't . . ."

Al couldn't even bring himself to speak. He nodded, acknowledging Bobby's attempt to comfort him, but all he could do was walk on, leaving the senator slouched at his office door.[3]*

On January 30, as Bobby was giving reporters an off-the-record notice of his decision, the Tet Offensive struck. All of the Johnson administration's assurances of victory, in Vietnam and at home, were struck down with it. When the North Vietnamese and the Viet Cong attacked thirty provincial capitals in South Vietnam and were able to breach the American embassy compound in Saigon itself, Bobby Kennedy was forced to reconsider his choice.

By March of 1968, Lyndon Johnson was in the throes of a profound depression. He had taken to having his evening meal upstairs at the White House and then returning to the situation room late at night, much as Lincoln had done at Stanton's War Department office during the Civil War, to monitor reports from the battlefield in Vietnam. Unlike Truman, who claimed not to

---

*Allard Lowenstein would serve in the 91st Congress and on various commissions of the UN before being assassinated in March 1980.

have lost a wink of sleep after deciding to drop a nuclear bomb on Hiroshima, Johnson was haunted by the destruction his choices had wrought, much as he kept his torment hidden.

And he was haunted by the unanswered questions surrounding Dallas, too, sometimes making references out of the blue to those unsolved mysteries. One day, when Marty Underwood had brought his son, Marty Jr., around to meet the president of the United States, the subject of his predecessor came up and Lyndon blurted out, "Well, Slim, your dad and I will never live to see the truth come out, but that truth will come out someday."

On another of the nights that the two spent together, sipping highballs in the residence, Lyndon told him, "Marty, I've got two cancers: Vietnam and the Kennedy assassination."

Late that winter, America seemed to be on the eve of a cultural war between the states, fueled by alienated youth, a press caught in a blizzard of disinformation, and a presidency more and more given to secrecy and paranoia.

As the tide of blood rose in Vietnam and in the streets of America's ghettos, the homely, the awkward, brutish, bellicose, and lonesome aspects of Lyndon's persona made him the national scapegoat. The Warren Commission Report, unknowingly with the help of the KGB, had foisted a poisonous list of conspiracy theories upon the people. Now, President Kennedy's brother seemed on the brink of declaring his candidacy, and what was worse, the *Christian Science Monitor* had run a piece that described one particularly nasty rumor: Lyndon was the ultimate monster, a man who was capable of conspiring to kill his own predecessor.

"Did you see that fuckin' paper that came out today?" Lyndon railed at Marty. "It says *I* was behind his death!"

Marty had never seen him in such a state. The president paused, eyes downcast, and then he asked a stunning favor of him. "I'd like to know what your friend down south knows. But I can't send you officially, it wouldn't look right."

Marty knew what friend he was referring to: Win Scott, still the CIA station chief in Mexico City. It was a difficult task. If anyone got wind that he was going down to meet with Scott, it would give the appearance of undermining the Warren Commission.[4] Win, after all, had never been interviewed under oath by the commission (although he conducted a hollow session with staff attorneys in April 1964), and Lyndon himself had put the clamps on a wider investigation in Mexico.

But the timing for such a trip could not have been better. Just one month earlier, Scott and his assistant Anne Goodpasture had completed an exhaustive nine-month review of Oswald's Mexico City stay, as ordered by the CIA director, Richard Helms, and seconded by Des FitzGerald, the previous June. Goodpasture's report candidly admitted the obvious: critical leads were not followed up at the time, and many key questions were never even asked. For Scott, she noted in the margin, "It is hard to believe the Commission served the public well," and she added, if only to cover their sins of omission, that, "The Warren Commission did not do an adequate investigative job."[5] Given Bobby's relationship with Helms and especially with Des, he too must have been apprised of this report.

Marty Underwood did not say another word about Lyndon's tacit request, but he knew he could not refuse. He had come to care deeply about Lyndon Johnson. He was also aware that the relationship between the president and Bobby Kennedy could only get worse. Bobby was doubtless looking for more dirt on Lyndon. Dispatching Marty to Mexico was not only a way for Lyndon to gain knowledge that would defend his honor against the press; it was also a way to arm himself in case the New York senator tried to expose Lyndon's own secrets.

Marty had made his decision. On a dolorous March day, he bought his own ticket to Mexico City. It was a matter of loyalty. Besides, he could use a bit of sun.

Win Scott met his good friend at the Mexico City airport, and they made their way out of town to a safe house. Win, however, was resistant when he heard why Marty had come. On his own volition, Win had learned more about Jack Kennedy's murder than even a spymaster wanted to know.

"Aw, Marty, stay out of it," he groaned. "You've got a little son to raise."

But it was a done deal. Within an hour they reached a safe house in Milpa Alta, in the mountains south of the city. After drinks and a simple meal, they sat down by a piñón fire.

Scott had dropped his guard completely. He began by telling Marty that in the years after Kennedy was killed, Win had determined that a well-known Cuban assassin had been in Mexico City precisely when Lee Oswald was there in September 1963. Then, on November 22, the same man had mysteriously slipped through Mexican customs from Texas. Win had no proof of a direct role in the murder in Dealey Plaza, but he believed his sources completely.

"Marty, we fucked up with this guy," Win said.

Underwood was scribbling away on a stash of White House stationery as Win laid out all he had learned. The contents would be conveyed to President Johnson in a dossier and then squirreled away in Marty's sister's house for years thereafter, but what he wrote that evening confirmed and went beyond what Vladimir Rodríguez Lahera had told Des FitzGerald's staff in the spring of 1964. It confirmed the worst that Lyndon and Bobby had imagined during the months of the Warren Commission's investigations.

On the White House paper, Underwood wrote: "Early on the morning of November 22nd, 1963, a small Cuban airplane landed at the Mexico City airport. The single occupant transferred to another plane that was waiting at the far end of the airport. It immediately took off for Dallas, Texas. Later that evening the same plane returned from Dallas and the occupant transferred back to the Cuban airplane. After many months of checking, we are confident that the occupant was Fabian Escalante, one of the top aides to Fidel Castro. Escalante definitely had been identified in a flight from Havana to Mexico City in September, 1963."[6] Escalante was functioning at the time as one of Raúl's most trusted senior intelligence operatives, often rumored to be involved in the business of assassination.*

"It is our belief he was sent by Castro as an observer. We were aware that several Castro henchmen had infiltrated the United States via Mexico City and Florida [in] the first six to seven months of 1963." Escalante, the same man who had attended spy school in Minsk when Oswald was there, who infiltrated the Bay of Pigs training camps, and who worked in Raúl's "Attacks Bureau" monitoring plots against the Castro brothers, now worked closely with Raúl in espionage in South and Central America. At the time of the assassination, Escalante's official assignment had been to penetrate a CIA operation called "Sentinels of Liberty," aimed at recruiting Cubans for the anticipated 1964 coup.[7]

Win Scott's account demonstrates that he never forgot about those reports of mysterious Cubans traveling between Texas, Mexico City, and Havana on the day of Kennedy's death. And some trusted source had delivered up the name Escalante.

Marty and Scott talked late into the night and finally finished up at about 4:00 A.M. Marty never revealed what else they spoke of, but the bombshell was Escalante, the agent believed to be responsible for responding to threats against his president. It mirrored other information from former Cuban diplomat Rafael Nuñez that Escalante had also been in Mexico City when Oswald was there in September 1963.

"I have the information," Nuñez had said in 2005, "and I also remember,

---

*See Underwood's notes at http://cuban-exile.com/brothersinarms.html.

that in 1963 Fabian Escalante was in Mexico on a covert mission, in the guise of vice-consul. He was the one who received Oswald when he turned up at the Cuban embassy in Mexico. That opens a dangerous door—because when Fabian Escalante appears on the scene, you're dealing with a G2 operation of the highest order."[8] To attach Escalante's name to any aspect of Dallas was tantamount to naming one of the Castro brothers themselves. Of course, none of this holds the weight of certain proof, but it exemplifies the powerful Cuban leads that were allowed to fall through the cracks.

There was yet another Cuban who recalled Escalante's presence in Mexico City. Antonio, the security guard who provided cover for Oswald's garage meeting with the black, red-haired agent, remembered Escalante being on the premises of the Cuban embassy in 1963.

"Yes, naturally I knew of Escalante," Antonio said without hesitation in 2005. "I only saw him a single time at the embassy. He was present when Oswald was here. Exactly when I cannot say, but it was August or September 1963."

The next morning, Marty packed his bags. He had gotten what he came for. As Win drove him back to the airport, the men settled in to proud talk of their spouses and kids. At the terminal, Win turned to Marty and said, "I'll probably never see you again."[*]

Marty didn't ask Win why that was; whether he was ill or was just off to another trouble spot. One didn't ask a CIA man such things. The men just made a four-handed clasp, eye to eye, and Marty climbed out. He doffed his scuffed fedora one last time in Win's direction and then stepped into the terminal.

When Marty got back to Washington, there were other details he had scribbled down, but he would share them only with Johnson.

"Lyndon went all to pieces when I told him," Marty remembered.[9]

When Marty next revealed his handwritten memo in 1994, there were many sections that had been blacked out. Pressed to reveal what had been redacted, Marty Underwood said simply, "There are some things I'll take to my grave."

Although the Underwood trip to Mexico had confirmed the worst-case scenario of the secret war against Castro, Lyndon Johnson never publicly used

---

[*] Scott's prediction proved accurate: he died in Mexico City in 1971, two years after his retirement, having never seen Underwood again.

what he had learned against Bobby Kennedy. He had threatened to use the Castro death plots, ever since Bobby's presumptive peace overture in Paris in February 1967, vowing to destroy "the little runt." But four and a half years after Dallas, he must still have feared an East/West confrontation and damage to the Democrats. The party was his religion, after all. Bobby's men had discovered evidence of illegitimate Johnson children, at least one rigged Texas election, and LBJ ties to a Mafia bagman. Lyndon may simply have let Bobby's people know that they had each other checkmated with secrets. He could have stopped Bobby's presidential bid in a minute. He could then have halted McCarthy by declaring a cease-fire and opening peace talks with Hanoi.

But Johnson was weary. Some time later, he would sit down with Doris Kearns at his ranch in Texas, his silver hair lapping over his collar, hippie-style, and recall:

"I was being forced over the edge by rioting blacks, demonstrating students, marching welfare mothers, squawking professors, and hysterical reporters. And then the final straw. The thing I feared most from the first day of my presidency was actually coming true. Robert Kennedy had openly announced his intention to reclaim the throne in the memory of his brother. And the American people, swayed by the magic of the name, were dancing in the streets. The whole situation was unbearable for me."

In the Red Room of the mansion hung a portrait of Woodrow Wilson, and Lyndon became obsessed with the twenty-eighth president "stretched out upstairs at the White House, powerless to move, with the machinery of the American government in disarray around him."[10] Lyndon was having a recurring nightmare by this time, one of lying on a bed in the residence with his own head but the shrunken, inert body of Wilson. Startled awake, drenched and shaken, he would grope for a flashlight and descend to the Red Room to touch Wilson's portrait, as if to assure himself that they were separate men, and that one of them was dead. Only then could he get back to sleep.[11]

By March 9, at around the same time that President Johnson was getting ready to send Underwood to Mexico City, Bobby was struggling night and day with whether to make a run for the presidency. The Tet Offensive had given McCarthy's bid all the more urgency, and young people, the ones who would have to keep up the fighting, were leaping to his side in droves. The New Hampshire primary was just days away.

Finally, with the quiet support of some Midwest Democratic governors he had met with en route to California, Bobby made his final choice. He was going to do it, after all. He was going to run. But before he announced it, there was one more trip he had to complete.

César Chávez, the leader of California's migrant farm labor force, had been on a hunger strike—he was doing penance for violence that had broken out in pursuit of a National Farm Workers Association. On March 10, Bobby arrived in Delano, California, to be with Chávez as he broke the fast in a Mass of Thanksgiving.

On the way from the airport to César's side, another throng of jubilant faces greeted him. He jumped on top of another car, punching the air with a fist and shouting "*Viva! Viva la huelga!*" Long live the strike! Men grabbed him in bear hugs. Children clung to his arms and ladies kissed him. He was one of theirs. They swept him up, hoisting him along and shaking his hands until they bled. When he reached Chávez, practically borne hand-over-hand to the stage, the union leader grinned and greeted him as a prodigal brother. After twenty-five days on his strike, César had lost thirty-five pounds and was so weak that Bob had to break his bread for him at the communion service, and someone else had to read his speech.[12]

Bobby sat next to Chávez on the makeshift little stage, among thousands of poor celebrants solemnly reenacting the Last Supper, and listened to what Chávez had written:

"When we are really honest with ourselves, we must admit that our lives are all that really belong to us. So it is how we use our lives that determines what kind of men we are. It is my deepest belief that only by giving our lives do we find life. I am convinced that the truest act of courage, the strongest act of manliness, is to sacrifice ourselves for others in a totally nonviolent struggle for justice. To be a man is to suffer for others. God help us to be men."[13]

A few days later, on March 17, Bobby made his announcement in the Old Senate Office Building, from the same caucus room where Jack had begun his bid for the presidency eight years before, then the same age as Bobby was now. Most of the people within his circle were relieved and energized that Bobby was in. Despite McCarthy's strong numbers coming out of the New Hampshire primary, they feared that "Clean Gene" was too genteel to really take the fight to Lyndon.

But initially, in the rest of the country, Bobby's announcement only seemed to cause more division. He was splitting the antiwar vote. He was muscling in after McCarthy had done the dirty work. He was exploiting the country's civil chaos in order to play savior. He was his old ruthless self.

In the years after his brother's death, Bobby had flung himself around the world. He had walked the infamous slums of Brooklyn's Bedford-Stuyvesant, the desperate hollows of white poverty in West Virginia, and the harrowing black shantytowns of Mississippi. He had gone to South Africa, had stood before a crowd at the University of Cape Town, preaching hope while apartheid enforcers looked on in disgust. Gradually, he had understood that he was Jack's equal, as a thinker, as a speaker, and perhaps even as a leader. He had begun to find his way out of the forest of grief and had been able to draw strength from those who needed him most.

He was still capable of irascibility and impatience, however. He was still conscious of his life as a political passion play, but he had gained self-awareness of a kind he might never have achieved if Jack had lived. Bill Moyers found him in a reflective mood the last time he would see him, that spring in New York. As they were walking to dinner in midtown, Moyers looked back on his youth.

"When I arrived in Washington, I had far more energy than wisdom," he said.

"Same here," Bobby admitted.

When they had reached the Caravelle and settled in to Bob's favorite booth, talk turned briefly to what Moyers would do now that he had left his spot as White House press secretary. He was glad to be out of the bunker, heady though it was. No longer the apologist in chief, the former Baptist minister was weighing various options. As the table was cleared and coffee arrived, Bobby looked up at Moyers, a long, blank stare in his eyes.

"I have myself wondered at times if we did not pay a very great price for being more energetic than wise about a lot of things, especially Cuba."[14] The words hung there. Bobby stirred his coffee. They both understood what he was talking about.

All he could do at that point was to keep striving to redeem himself in the exercise of power, the only way he knew how.

But the political landscape of America was about to shift beneath him once again.

On March 30, Lyndon Johnson looked unusually relaxed as he polished up the televised speech he would deliver to the nation the next evening. There had been some suggestions that he take a swipe at Bobby in the text, something like "This is not statesmanship. This is rank opportunism. And the American people know the difference between those who ask what they can do for their country, and those who ask what their country can do for them."[15] It was a lame gambit, and Lyndon wasn't going to link his domestic political problem with a speech about the all-consuming war in Vietnam. He took questions in the Rose Garden at noon, affable and expansive amid the budding trees.

"I think you will get from the speech generally the government's position and the course that we intend to take," Lyndon drawled.

A reporter wondered, "Sir, will it be painful?"

A smile creased the president's face. "You call me and tell me after you hear it."

The next night, even when he handed his speech to the U.S. Army Signal Corps man who would feed it into the TelePrompTer, he was still not sure how it would end. It wasn't until thirty-five minutes into it that he raised his right hand slightly, an intimate signal to his wife, and said:

"With American sons in the fields far away, with America's future under challenge right here at home, with our hopes and the world's hopes for peace in the balance every day, I do not believe that I should devote an hour, or a day, of my time to any personal partisan causes. Or to any duties other than the awesome duties of this office—the presidency of your country. Accordingly, I shall not seek, and I will not accept, the nomination of my party for another term as your president."

Minutes later, Bobby's American Airlines flight from Phoenix arrived at John F. Kennedy Airport in New York. He had been in flight during the speech and had no idea what had transpired until a young campaign worker and John Burns, the state Democratic chair, managed to come aboard before Bobby and Ethel got off.

The young campaigner cried, "The president withdrew, the president withdrew!"

"Johnson isn't running," Burns echoed.

Bobby was so stunned that he dropped back into his seat, trying to fathom it. As he waded through a few hundred delirious supporters inside the terminal, he barely uttered a reaction to a startled covey of journalists. He said nothing for most of the forty-minute ride back to the apartment. It wasn't until they were headed down the East River Drive that he finally spoke.

"I wonder if he would have done it if I hadn't come in . . ."

Ethel squeezed his hand, and they rode on in silence, the campaign looming before them. When they reached apartment 14F UN Plaza, the household was already crammed with beaming friends. But Bobby thought the joy was premature. Ethel, ebullient as ever, ignored him and broke out some

Scotch. The mood soon became so dizzy that Bobby asked his friend Bill vanden Heuvel to take a few of them aside and ask them to calm down. There were already reporters taking positions outside the building. It would not do for loose lips to make too much of the Kennedy reaction.[16]

And besides, Robert Kennedy was now a man for whom grief was never far removed. It was he who had tripped into offering Johnson the VP slot in 1960. In some sense, he had brought him to the presidency and had then made him pay for the sin of not being his brother. He had decided to mount a challenge that would remove the Texan from office, and had then proceeded to remove him without a fight. The two of them had created an immense power vacuum that someone would have to fill at an extremely volatile moment in the nation's history.

In the next few months, as the nomination came closer to his reach, it became clear that he would probably be running against Nixon, the very man whom Jack had defeated for the presidency, and the original spearhead of the secret war against Castro.

Four days after Lyndon's abdication, Dr. Martin Luther King was gunned down on a concrete balcony of a cheap motel in Memphis.

Bobby was campaigning in Muncie, Indiana, that afternoon, and was scheduled to speak in the poorest heart of the Indianapolis ghetto that night. In Muncie, a black kid had asked Bobby if he truly had faith in white America's willingness to mature on matters of race. Bobby had sworn that he did believe it and then, moments later, had learned that the kid's spiritual leader had been shot. On the plane to Indianapolis, when word came that King was dead, Bobby recoiled, clapped his hands to his face.

"Oh, God!" he moaned. "When is this violence going to stop?"[17] He stole away, weeping, and then fairly staggered off the plane.

It was cold, the trees thrashing in a hard wind from the northwest. The crowds in the city's poor black neighborhood had been waiting for an hour, but they were festive that night, a few cozy barrel fires warming them. Obviously, they had not heard the news. The candidate's car pulled up at the end of a parking lot where a great stand of budding oak trees made a canopy over an impromptu stage, a flatbed truck. Spotlights were trained on it, the blowing smoke and dust caught in their beams. Pulling his black overcoat tight, he gave a small acknowledgment to the cheers and then stepped up to the microphone, hunched against the wind, his face a white plank of sorrow, and began an impromptu speech.

"I have bad news for you, for all of our fellow citizens and people who love peace all over the world, and that is that Martin Luther King was shot and killed tonight." From the crowd came cries and gasps and the gagging of disbelief.

The speech he gave that night was not the kind of speech he would have given five years earlier. Now he knew what murder really was, what assassination really meant, and the speech would live on as testament to that knowledge.

He would speak of Jack's murder at the hands of a white man. He would remember his own lacerating grief on the hillside at Arlington, and offer a drink from the cup from his own solace, quoting Aeschylus. " 'In our sleep, pain which cannot forget falls drop by drop upon the heart until, in our own despair, against our will, comes wisdom through the awful grace of God.' What we need in the United States is not division; what we need in the United States is not hatred; what we need in the United States is not violence or lawlessness, but love and wisdom, and compassion toward one another, and a feeling of justice towards those who still suffer within our country, whether they be white or they be black . . . Let us dedicate ourselves to what the Greeks wrote so many years ago: to tame the savageness of man and to make gentle the life of this world.

"Let us dedicate ourselves to that, and say a prayer for our country and for our people."[18]

A combustion raged through the nation's ghettos that night and in the ensuing days, but the tormented black neighborhood of Indianapolis was not one of them—a small measure of what the confluence of words and spirit and the speaker of those words can mean, and of what is lost when they are silenced.

Bobby would be silenced soon himself, assassinated in Los Angeles by another angry twenty-four-year-old man, this one of Palestinian descent. In yet another whiplash move of the wrenching sixties, Lyndon Johnson would soon stand beside Bobby's coffin, would watch his beloved Democratic Party go down in defeat, and find himself on Inauguration Day sitting not behind Bobby or Hubert Humphrey, as he had expected, but behind Richard M. Nixon.

Johnson himself would die in 1973, a lonely, haunted figure whose finest hour, when he labored in secret to prevent World War III, would be largely forgotten.

In 1976, Fabian "Roberto" Escalante Font was named the head of the Department of State Security (DSE). It was in that position that he denied the House

Select Committee on Assassinations access to key witnesses including Luisa Calderón. In 1982, he became a senior official of the Interior Ministry under his mentor Raúl, and was considered to be Cuba's leading authority on CIA activities against Cuba. In 1993, he was named head of the Cuban Security Studies Center, giving him full access to all agents, operatives, and materials germane to the murder of John Kennedy. In 1995, he hosted the Nassau conference on the Kennedy assassination, becoming one of the most adamant prevaricators on the subject.

Escalante still serves in the Cuban government. He is a big, clean-shaven, open-faced person, and with his gray hair combed over in a boyish forelock, it's hard to picture him as the young G2 man who trained in the USSR, possibly even Minsk, when Lee Oswald was there and then returned to Cuba to run the spy operations against the Bay of Pigs training camps in Central America. It's harder still to see him as the stealth operator who ran Cuba's "wet" operations throughout the region, as some believed, and, along with Raúl, was still gunning for John Kennedy's successor (in Uruguay) even while positioning himself as Cuba's official CIA basher. But that is Fabian Escalante, a garrulous, bright-eyed man with a very dark past. His face is fleshier now, his charm a bit practiced, but he remains a hero of the Revolution and he enjoys his position immensely.

On a stormy day in 2005, he was waiting in his Havana office for the arrival of Willi Huismann, who had booked him for an interview. Finally, Raúl's top soldier in the secret wars of Latin America would answer a few questions about Dallas and the events leading up to it. Escalante, immaculate in a white guayabera, was neatly arranged in a modern, blond-wood-paneled office, white Venetian blinds closed behind him, a Cuban flag furled in the corner, and a portrait of Fidel staring down from above.

Fabian treated Willi and his cameraman to espresso while the lights were being set, the three men bantering in Spanish and stirring their coffee with little stalks of raw sugarcane. Questions had been submitted in advance.

Escalante had been told of Marty Underwood's secret dossier to LBJ, the one scribbled out in Mexico in March 1968. On the basis of Marty's meeting with Win Scott, Willi put the first question to him, point-blank.

"What business might have brought you to Dallas back then, on the very day that Kennedy was shot?"

"Who says this document is genuine?" was Escalante's first reply. "We live in a world where today something is no longer true that only yesterday seemed certain. There are intelligent people who doubt the authenticity of the pictures of the American moon landing." His right hand reached heavenward and dawdled there. "Were they really on the moon? Apparently yes, but I'm not so sure." He smiled sweetly and shrugged, his hand coming to rest over his heart. "So much is forged and falsified. What is true, what's a lie?" He raised his right hand as if under oath. "One day we will know whether or not the Americans really did land on the moon—and if Oswald shot Kennedy or not."

"What do you think?"

"There were several snipers. Whether they were North Americans, Japanese, Chinese, or Germans I don't know, because I wasn't there."

"Or your people?" Willi shot back.

"Out of the question, we had no reason to be—"

"Kennedy was your archenemy, after all—"

"That's not enough. We have the ethics and morals of our revolution. We've only survived—we have been victorious over the world's largest empire for over forty years—because the strongest weapons of our socialist revolution are its solid, fundamental moral and ethical principles."

Willi then pressed him on the KGB document about Oswald in the old Soviet archives, the one sent by Kryuchkov to Ramiro Valdés, chief of G2, on July 18, 1962. It alerted the Cubans to Oswald's departure from the USSR, and suggested they take up surveillance of him in the States, though, as "Nikolai" reported it to Willi, Lee was considered "ideologically unsound and psychologically unstable."

Escalante brushed it off. "Completely false. A forgery. I venture to state that quite clearly. You can also ask Commandant Ramiro Valdés. He is— now as then—one of the leaders of our country. That telegram is a fake; the simple fact that I would have seen it otherwise is proof enough." (Valdés, in fact, refused to meet with Willi.)

"What is doing the misleading, the telegram or the KGB itself?"

"That's what I'd like to know. Do you know if the Americans really did land on the moon?"

"We're not talking about the CIA here, but about the KGB archives."

"Very well. But the KGB was only master of its own archives up to a certain point of time, my good friend," said Escalante. "I was in Moscow in 1994 at a conference on the missile crisis. I spoke there with the head of the Soviet Communist Party archives. He told me that a group of American researchers worked in the archives of the Communist Party and the KGB. How many documents might they have planted there? I don't know, but I know what the American Secret Service is capable of."

The fear that "Nikolai" felt each time he traveled to Austria was still vivid in Willi's mind and made it clear how sacrosanct those KGB files still were. He moved in tighter on Escalante.

"The CIA smuggled that telegram from 1962 into the KGB archives thirty years later?"

"Is there any other explanation?" said Fabian, still smiling.

Willi pivoted out of the clinch and pressed him on the identity of the red-haired black man, the high-ranking G2 operative who went by the name Carlos Morales Mesa, and who was seen with Oswald by "Antonio" and others on site.

The old spymaster was growing tired, his smile beginning to sag.

"Black people don't have red hair," he said.

"Some do."

"Blacks are black. Whites can be redheaded. I had a good laugh when I read your question. Maybe a black person can dye his hair red, but that would be very conspicuous. I wouldn't use someone like that as an agent."

It didn't really matter that Escalante had not identified the red-haired Afro-Cuban. Oscar Marino, still loyal to the revolution, had done so in Mexico City. And Escalante's dismissal of the very idea of redheaded black Cubans was so lame that he could barely deliver it with a straight face (see page 504, note 44).

As for Oswald's time in New Orleans, Escalante insisted that Lee's confrontation with Carlos Bringuier was too penny-ante to result in a radio debate. Bringuier, the progressive Catholic lawyer turned haberdasher, could only have been a CIA agent who got Oswald on the radio in order to set him up as a lunatic follower of Marx and Engels, the better to blame Communists for the impending assassination. It was the old party line—the Americans had killed their own president using a dummied-up Communist who was actually a fascist or a dupe. Again, Escalante made this claim with his hand raised to protest his sincerity.

It was clear that Escalante, the man who had approved hits throughout the region from the 1960s to perhaps even the present day, was not going to give Willi anything. He leaned back in his chair and put a hand to his chest once more.

"I can't tell you how often I've dreamed of traveling to Mexico—a country so rich in tradition. Unfortunately, it never worked out. You can do all the research you like. You won't find any witnesses."

There was one last wan smile, in parting, and the reporters were shown to the door.

As of 2005, the year of that interview, sixty-seven foreign nationals had been reported killed or "disappeared" by the Castro regime, twenty-five of them specifically by assassination, and fourteen of those American citizens killed inside the United States. Since the regime came to power, some forty-one American citizens have been killed in total, whether by assassination or firing squad, or by other unknown means resulting in their disappearance. Cuban intelligence has been credited with the murder of citizens from Argentina, the Bahamas, Bolivia, Chile, Denmark, France, Haiti, Honduras, Mexico, Portugal, Spain, and the United Kingdom, in addition to the U.S. They range from Rogelio González Corzo, a Spanish citizen and Catholic youth leader executed at La Cabaña fortress, to Honorato Rojas, a Bolivian guide to Che's guerrilla band in 1967, shot to avenge an ambush at Vado del Yeso. In some cases they were comrades in arms deemed too ill to be kept as soldiers. In others, they were democratic leftists campaigning for non-Communist reforms. In nearly every other case, they were leaders or other influential people working for just causes considered counter to the interests of the Cuban state.[19]

And at the dark heart of G2 where those decisions were made, in the name of what was left of his revolutionary ideals, Fabian Escalante played a vital role from beginning to end, even as he smiled and swore his innocence.

Fidel Castro would lead Cuba—and, intermittently, the rest of the Third World—for fifty years. He began to fade only in mid-2006, struck with a still-undisclosed serious illness, and even then clung to his presidency for a year and a half while the world waited to see whether the Castros would finally fall.

On February 24, 2008, Raúl Castro Ruz took his brother's place before the National Assembly of People's Power at the Convention Center in Havana, and became president of Cuba. Fidel, from his sickbed, could see the transfer of power only on television. Atop his pile of pillows, a cigar still smoldering at his fingertips, the once black-bearded hero of Marxism was now a frail vestige of the young and legendary Fidel. As he watched his younger brother take power, it must have occurred to him that it was Raúl to whom he owed his long life, Raúl and the tight gun laws of Cuba. It was Raúl who had enabled him to lie here and grow old, and now it was Raúl who would defend Cuba in its transitional time.

"Fidel is Fidel," Raúl was reminding the People's Assembly, "we all know it very well. Fidel is irreplaceable, and the people shall continue his work when he is no longer physically with us." Raúl hastened to add that he *was* still with them, and that "his ideas will always be with us, the same ideas that have made it possible to build the beacon of dignity and justice our country represents." He quoted Raúl Roa: "Fidel hears the grass growing and sees what is happening around the corner."

The new president thanked the people on behalf of the Revolution's leadership, citing their "serenity, maturity, self-assurance, and combination of genuine sadness [at Fidel's resignation] and revolutionary determination."[20] Cubans on the street were apt to characterize it more as resignation, suspicion, and apathy.

But in the coming weeks, Raúl announced twenty startling reforms. Four days after his acceptance speech, he signed two United Nations human rights treaties. The next day, wearing a black business suit and tie, he met with the Vatican Secretary of State, Cardinal Tarcisio Bertone, who promised to help Cuba soften, if not eliminate, the U.S. and European Union embargoes that had stood against them for fifty years. Raúl promised to consider the release of political prisoners in return for five Cuban prisoners in U.S. jails. On March 13, he lifted the ban on computer ownership. On the fifteenth, he allowed farmers to purchase their own equipment; and in ensuing days, he launched an emigration Web site for Cubans living abroad, and encouraged letters to the editor of *Granma*. Letters both for and against the reforms began streaming in to the party organ like migrating birds returning home. He released a frank and fairly comprehensive economic report on the health of the nation; acted to decentralize Cuban agriculture; decided to permit the Cuban people to own their own cell phones; and allowed citizens to stay in tourist hotels.

Yoani Sánchez, age thirty-two, is a slender, pretty brunette with bushy bangs and a prominent nose, a child of the revolution who learned German in school and speaks it like a native. She dresses up like a tourist when she wants to update her blog, "Generación Y," and then sneaks into one of the big hotels where only tourists are allowed to use the Internet. She quickly takes a seat at the cyber-kiosk and starts typing as fast as she can. An hour on the Net costs $6.00, a fortnight's pay, so she takes twenty minutes for $2.00 and fills her allotted time with reports about daily life, a chronicle she has been keeping up since some time in 2007.

On this day in the fall of '07, five months before Raúl's speech, she writes about the police on the streets of Havana, the way they make random checks of people's bags and bundles, searching for black-market merchandise.

"We are taking advantage of an unregulated area." She smiles to a reporter. "They can't control cyberspace."

She has built her site on servers outside the country, and most of her audience consists of Cubans living abroad. Access to the World Wide Web is still forbidden, but others in Yoani's group post on blogs like "My Island at Midday," a sporadic Internet diary, and "Havanacity," where an outrider named "Tension Lia" documents the slow disintegration of the island's architectural treasures.

Only two hundred thousand citizens in a nation of eleven million can access the Internet, but even some among them have started to aim their words in a new and provocative public way. Luis Sexto writes a column for *Juventad Rebelde*, the Communist Youth newspaper. In the fall of 2007, he wrote, "Without public criticism, mistakes will continue to hurt our country." It was a brief but soaring flight into the twenty-first century.[21]

By May 2008, President Raúl Castro Ruz had commissioned a new foreign TV channel. He had removed limits from farmers' salaries, and allowed renters to gain title of ownership for their apartments. And, in what might be a manifestation of the guilt that once caused him to exhume and dump hundreds of his victims' caskets into the Caribbean, he had commuted the death sentences of a number of prisoners, political and otherwise.

When a Cuban television documentary aired in late 2007 to uphold the virtues of the early 1970s censorship crackdown, an extraordinary backlash ensued.[22] The seventies in Cuba were marked by a new assertion of Soviet-style media policies in which artists, writers, homosexuals, and other renegade types were rounded up, jailed, and in some cases tortured or executed. The program defending this purge unleashed such a wave of protest from those who could access the World Wide Web, the academics and intellectuals emboldened since Fidel's illness, that Raúl's people were forced to meet with their representatives and issue a public apology for the TV show.

Raúl, the awkward, runty kid brother of the Revolution, the sensitive one who his family thought would come to nothing, is now the president of Cuba, as his counterpart, Bobby, might have once been in America. Raúl is the last man standing. He alone may yet live long enough to come to terms with the politics of murder; with the slow diminution of his once-vital brother; with their promise of plenty that devolved into poverty and inequity. Perhaps, in the time he has left, Raúl will join the radical center, the global quest to finally synthesize the best of both dreams and find the unifying human principle that was just becoming clear when assassins nearly killed it in '63 and '68.

It would only be right for Raúl to carry on such a quest, and for America to join him in mutual atonement. Together, perhaps, they might yet lay down their weary burden and find that third way, a renewed plan of freedom for the hemisphere to share.

A new Camelot, in memory of all those who died trying.

Raúl could take a lesson from Robert Francis Kennedy. In observing Bobby in the last years of his life, his friend Jack Newfield would often recall Pascal's line "A man does not show his greatness by being at one extremity, but rather by touching both at once."

Bobby Kennedy struggled, in thought and deed, to reconcile the need for communal care and the aims of individual achievement, striving at the end of his life toward a synthesis that he had once resisted.

Taking time out of the campaign, during that portentous spring of '68, Bobby went back to his city, New York, and into the tough neighborhood of Spanish Harlem. His friendships were as all-embracing as his politics at that point, and the friend who went with him that day was José Torres, the former light-heavyweight champ from Puerto Rico who had come of age on these streets. It was a broiling day, and they toured the neighborhood for five hours, Bobby, like his brother Jack, preferring direct observation to the ministrations of experts.

They talked at length with the men on the street corners and the women on the stoops, learning what they needed to know to propose alternatives to the welfare state. They laughed and tussled with kids who had opened a hydrant and flooded a side street. They watched an inning of a manic stickball game, played to the accompaniment of merengue and salsa and mambo from the open windows. Everywhere they went, the senator and the prizefighter were suggesting a better life just by their presence on old, familiar streets. Kids clamored to be with them, to walk the streets beside them, like they too might one day lead a throng of new kids with bright hopes shining from their eyes. Mary McGrory had once said that Bobby needed children as much as children needed him. For all the heat and the grit and the struggle, these days gave him much more than they took.

As the sun went down and the sweat cooled on their backs and they turned to trudge back home, the two men crossed Park Avenue, not the grand promenade of midtown, but the whittled-down, dark and decaying end of town. They had been gabbing all day, and they were quiet as they walked down to the car, the elevated trains moaning and groaning overhead. Torres had been wondering something. Bobby was a politician, sure, a consummate one. But nevertheless, José had been wondering why a rich man's son from the cool, crisp, clean coast of New England came uptown to the slums in search of human connection. And what was it, he wondered, that drove him for sixteen, eighteen hours a day to stand firmly planted in the ghetto and gaze at the pinnacle of the White House, in the same all-encompassing moment, day in and day out? How did one hold those two ideas in their head at once?

As they were coming to José's car, the boxer asked him, "Why are you doing this? Why are you running?"

Bobby slowed, hands in his pockets, and mumbled so softly that Jose had to lean in close to hear him.

"Because I found out something I never knew," he said. "I found out that my world was not the real world."[23]

If it is more possible for a camel to pass through the eye of a needle than for a rich man—or a rich nation—to enter the kingdom of heaven, then perhaps all that was left for Robert Kennedy was to seek a heaven here on earth, and call it some new kind of America.

Afterword

THE PLAYWRIGHT ARTHUR MILLER maintained that all dramatic writing is essentially a voyage into history, an attempt to understand "what just happened." Nearly half a century after the murder of John F. Kennedy, we are still groping for understanding of what just happened—not only in the event itself, but in its terrible ricochet through our body politic.

Assassination has seldom been effective as a tool for quieting political stress. At minimum, it tends to exacerbate international tensions; at its most extreme, it has started a world war. In the wake of Kennedy's murder, the swift actions of many players averted what might have otherwise been an international crisis. But in the years to come—and this is the central irony of Kennedy's death—the need for vengeance would turn inward, against America itself. The impact of that killing is still felt.

Political charisma may be defined as much by the inspirational power of the spoken word as by any other trait. People follow a political poet, a voice that articulates their yearnings, their outrage, and their hope. But the same voice that can turn belief into action seems also to be the kind of incantatory voice most likely to incur the wrath of the political killer. The presumption of the assassin is that he (or she) knows best what the people need—they just need to be freed of their leader. The killer proves his power by showing he can silence that voice.

One of the more outspoken Cuban exiles tried to head off the Bay of Pigs invasion, insisting that it was "anti-historical," a complete failure to understand what Castro had done and what could not be undone by murdering or overthrowing him. The administration didn't listen to him, any more than Lee listened to Marina after he tried to shoot Walker; he went on to impose himself on history by murdering Kennedy instead. He carried out that assassination in order to prevent another one, that of Fidel Castro, and the simple moral logic of Lyndon Johnson's decision to cancel further murder attempts against Fidel was almost Solomon-like. An eye for an eye, a tooth for a tooth. We were even, in Johnson's mind. Too many others would have died for our revenge if we had taken it.

And besides, the Cubans' hand in it was so nearly invisible that for the new president, continuing the cycle would have been the most harrowing of judgment calls. Johnson arrived at the presidency as a man with limited foreign policy experience, skeptical about the political uses of violence. He would soon overcome those doubts, to his everlasting regret, but his first few days in office speak volumes about the limits of power and the wisdom of restraint. His first exercise of power was the power of inaction, of turning the other cheek.

The effects of assassination are simply too unpredictable to be used by a nation as an instrument of change. John Kennedy's murder illustrates it, terribly. As with Lincoln's death, it was followed by an initial rush of disbelief and anguish. Then—when Kennedy's assassin was killed—came pure incredulity. The public could not accept that such a death was simply the culmination of a dark, circular logic of force and counterforce. It must have been something more labyrinthine, more insidious; something more in keeping with his extraordinary iconic power.

But in a way, Jack Kennedy was just a victim of the new post-atomic theories of war. After World War II, the first coups d'état engineered by America relied heavily on psychological operations for their success. America's military reputation was so well established that the mere threat of U.S. action was enough to scare certain foes into submission. Augmented with some fake radio broadcasts, some well-timed explosions, and some smoke and mirrors, these early putsches could be arranged on a low budget, and carried out leaving few if any Yankee fingerprints.

But if that didn't work, the next step up was assassination and—with the murder of Patrice Lumumba—it was just becoming a possibility as Eisenhower left office. Political murder was a way to achieve big results with narrowly applied pressure; to alter the perception of security in one stroke, and thereby ensure an eventual social collapse, a tabula rasa on which to impose a new paradigm.

The effect of Lee Oswald's crime is paradoxical. On one hand, Lee achieved his political goal; he ended the secret war against the Castro brothers. Since that small, proxy war had provoked a nuclear confrontation thirteen months earlier, it could be said that he reduced the chances of a big, hot war by ending the little one. On the other hand, he raised such fear in the minds of international leaders that it very nearly provoked a *new* nuclear showdown. Johnson was essentially forced to do in November of '63 what Khrushchev had done in October of '62: he backed away from the endgame. In a way, it was a fitting reflection of Lee's inner tensions: between the peacenik idealist and the gunslinger. In the screed he wrote on the *Maasdam*, during his return voyage to America, he debated the relative merits and injustices of the world's two dominant systems, and then ended with a prediction of an imminent nuclear war. Between the lines was a prediction that he would help it along.

But the effects of his crime within the country would be decisive. The murder triggered a cover-up, meant to prevent a catastrophe. The cover-up created a sense of something hidden. That unease was exploited by two decades of Soviet disinformation, streamed into the American media. It set off a political chain reaction that ended in the presidential candidacy of RFK five years later, whose own assassination created yet another blowback, the victory of Richard Nixon. Nixon's hubris in office exacerbated the growing political alienation of the American people, and ended, a decade after Dallas, in the Watergate scandal. That scandal threw open the doors of Washington's secrets and revealed that the White House, the CIA, and the FBI were all capable of murder abroad, thus reinforcing the fear that they were capable of murder at home—even the murder of a president.

The repercussions seem unending: When Watergate hit, Nixon tried to use his knowledge of the Kennedy-CIA plots to blackmail the CIA. Nixon's own election, like those of many Republican candidates to follow, had been greatly aided by the politically powerful Cuban exile community in Florida. Ironically, these voters might have had a different party allegiance if Kennedy had lived to redeem his failure at the Bay of Pigs with a more successful conclusion to the war he had fought on Cuba's behalf.

And arguably, it was Florida's Cuban hard-liners who prevented Al Gore from capturing the White House, which may have made possible the war in Iraq and the lamentable mishandling of the relief efforts in the Gulf Coast after Hurricane Katrina.

Robert Kennedy was a transitional figure, a man who remade his life as a reformer of the real world, the new, nuclear world. From his furious debate with himself, he emerged as a progressive politician of a new kind—part

Puritan, part Victorian, part Greek tragedian, part Boston bruiser, and part Catholic liberation theologian. He was lost to America before he had fully found this new self, but his virtue, as a political penitent, is part of why we still ponder his loss. Until RFK, democratic leaders were required to project absolute, paternal certainty on the public stage or risk the loss of their power. But by the end of his life, Bobby's appeal was fraternal, less that of the self-possessed father than of the evolving son. That alone marked him as a truly democratic man, morally charged but wary of his own self-righteousness; perhaps seeing the enemy as the shadow side of himself, and thus still capable, if not of friendship, at least of truce.

Bobby and Lyndon, with the help of the Russians, the Cubans, and the Mexicans, all helped to push the country to the right when it was in none of their interests to do so.

The impact of Dallas on the American left has not been so thoroughly explored, but it suffered not only JFK's death, but the subsequent murders of other progressive and radical leaders, both political and "countercultural." Oswald set something terrible loose in the country; in the coming years, his successors would count among their victims Malcolm X, Dr. Martin Luther King Jr., Robert Kennedy, Fred Hampton, George Jackson, Allard Lowenstein, John Lennon, Harvey Milk, and George Moscone.

JFK died for his anti-Communism, and yet for decades he was seen by the American right as a quasi-Communist, particularly in the conservative bastion of Dallas, Texas. When Oswald's true links to Havana and Moscow were suppressed, the mysterious assassin was assumed to be tied to the right wing; this was partly because Oswald—apart from his rabid *Fidelismo*—was in most other ways an ideological kin of the man he killed. When his links to Havana were suppressed, his crime made even less sense, and was even more open to interpretation. No Communist in his right mind would kill Kennedy for his civil rights policies, or his brother's attempts to clean up corrupt labor unions, or his quest for nuclear disarmament. Thus, Lee could not have been a Communist. He must have been posing as one.

James Piereson suggests that Lee Oswald was so enigmatic that he had to be recast as a John Wilkes Booth, an emissary of the right, as a means of "restoring moral cohesion to the situation." He observes that Jack's murder at the hands of a radical leftist would have been akin to Lincoln being assassinated by an abolitionist. "Such an act would have been nearly impossible for Northerners to assimilate within the cultural framework of the Civil War era . . . it would have rendered somewhat illogical the assertion of martyrdom on the slain president . . . Southern rebels . . . would have been held blameless . . . the outpouring of grief following the president's assassination would have been mixed with confusion as to the moral meaning of the event."[1]

So it was that Jack became a martyr for civil rights, as Lincoln was for abolition. In the either/or Cold War world, Oswald had come to see Kennedy as a rightist. The American right saw JFK as a leftist, and therefore, at least when he died, the New Left embraced him as one of their own, though he was a somewhat fitful liberal. It was simply too mind-boggling to think he had been killed by a leftist.

The Warren Commission's findings and the Lyndon-Bobby cover-up allowed the left to disown Oswald, and gave some of them license to take more radical—even violent—action, thereby alienating the center. Rather than taking Lee as a cautionary example and continuing to renounce violence, as King had urged them to do, the left was increasingly factionalized, the violent ones smearing the nonviolent. Bobby entered the presidential fray, in part, to try to drag the left back into the political mainstream, to bank their energy and put it to good, populist use. But when he and King and the others were gunned down, progressives were so grief-stricken and demoralized that they threw up their hands. The death of any one messenger shouldn't be enough to silence the voice of change, but six, eight, ten poets killed was enough to at least induce resigned cynicism. Lest more of their leaders be killed, the left counted up what victories they could and allowed themselves to be shunted to the sidelines.

Among the least understood results of the Dallas blowback was how the Soviet and Cuban disinformation programs changed public perception of the assassination. There were reasons to doubt the Warren Commission findings, as we have described, but the way in which its holes were filled with phony, Communist-made counternarratives should have been another cautionary tale for America. But the mutual demonization of the left and the right gradually admitted to the most inane conspiratorial thinking, and allowed the conceit that "perception becomes reality" to worm its way into the highest levels of our political culture.

Just before the 2004 presidential election, *New York Times* reporter Ron Suskind documented a conversation with a top presidential adviser who described the president's critics as living in the bygone "reality-based community" of people who believe that problems are solved through "judicious study of discernible reality." Empires like ours, the adviser said, create their own reality, acting upon history as if drawing shape from a total void, and leaving historians and citizens to adjust to the new world their leaders have unilaterally made. Such are the dangers of being the world's sole superpower. It begins to think it truly is super.

The hokum dreamed up by the Soviets and Cubans after Dallas set a new standard for the diabolical, the corrosive, and the preposterous in public discourse. Given America's occasional gullibility, its relative insularity, and its taste for the lurid, the nation is far more vulnerable to disinformation attacks, both from without and within, than it was in the 1960s. Propaganda too easily supplants reality, and the age-old agreements on cause and effect become just another story line, to be adjusted at will by the most clever political "actor."

The only players who benefited from the shooting in Dealey Plaza were the Castro brothers. They have been able to remain in power for five decades, under three Democratic and five Republican presidents, since Kennedy.

All courtesy of one twenty-four-year-old with a $13 rifle, and a handful of Cuba's shadow warriors who gave him encouragement.

With *Brothers in Arms* we have tried to present the assassination of President John F. Kennedy as much as possible as a human event. What emerges, after years of sitting down and talking with those who were there, is not some vast labyrinth of ongoing deceit, but a series of personal and political choices made in the heat of battle. It is our hope that this chronicle will reduce the heat that still burns after Dallas, and add some light to its retelling. This is not a work aimed at assessing blame at the Castros, or the Kennedys, or even Oswald, but to explain how all were caught up in the hysteria of the moment, and how the misguided appeal of the politics of murder skewed their moral compasses. We can only hope that it will caution its readers; that it will better enable this work in progress called America to see the realities around it and act accordingly, from left, right, and center, to restore our good name. Perhaps it will bring some peace, if only some peace of mind.

Acknowledgments

Brothers in Arms builds on the work of a generation of writers and investigators who have, through relentless use of the Freedom of Information Act and other methods, waged a nonstop campaign to uncover the secrets of the Kennedy era. James Lesar, the late Bernard "Bud" Fensterwald, Harold Weisberg, and Mary Ferrell were among the trailblazers, followed in recent years by Mark Zaid. Sadly, the Kennedy family has been a major stumbling block in this effort, steadfastly refusing to release to historians the vast trove of government papers (many of them concerning the secret war with Castro) that were deeded to Robert Kennedy after President Kennedy's death.

For their invaluable assistance with this book, special thanks go to Dale Myers, Todd Vaughn, W. Scott Malone, and Jack Clarke for reading early drafts and making important suggestions. Countless former government officials have shared their insights over the years, especially the FBI's James Hosty and the CIA's Sam Halpern and Ned Dolan. Archival guidance came from Jim Gillespie of the Eisenhower Library at Johns Hopkins University and Regina Greenwell and Barbara Cline of the LBJ Library at the University of Texas. Gary Johnson, at the Library of Congress Photo Section, gave timely and informative responses to our photo queries. At the National Archives in College Park, Maryland, Steve Tilley, Martha Murphy, Marty McGann, and Joseph Scanlon were, as always, at the ready with answers to our questions, in addition to being outstanding guides through the labyrinth of historical material in their custody.

Gus Russo would additionally like to thank for their sundry important contributions: Gordon Winslow and Suzie Winslow, Noah Lukeman, Mark Allen, Linda Woolley of Alphabet Bookshop, Mark Obenhaus, Peter Wronski, Ed Gray, Courtney Atkins, Tony and Paula Russo, Ellen and John Bollinger, John Stewart, Jay Greer, Sally Rosenthal, the Singing Montgomerys (Claire and Monte), Bob Harris, Janet and Steve Nugent, Steve Parke, Susan Mangan,

Karen Rinaldi, and Kevin Perkins and the gang at Allied Advertising. Subliminal aural contributions were rendered by Django Reinhardt, Shelby Lynne, Tom Jobim, the Pizzarellis, Basia Trzetrzelewska, Danny White, and Mark Reilly.

Steve Molton would like to thank Pamela Galvin-Molton for her gentle sacrifice, streetwise faith, wise input, and unbridled devotion to this book's completion. For the foundation they provided, special thanks are also due to Mary Dian Molton, Dr. Warren Molton, my boon companions Jennifer and David Molton, Helen Geroux, and their four great families. For his unstinting friendship and for sharing his insight during this process, added thanks go to Richard Dean Rosen. The generous support and effort of friends Joan Boorstein, Melanie Fleishman, Jon Karas, and Maggie Soboil provided the impetus, early on, to pursue this story. Mojave Desert amigos Chuck Heiss and Werner Summer made countless contributions to our well-being during the course of this work, and Joshua Tree National Park gave us a constantly renewable vision of the American promise that still exists.

Both Russo and Molton are most indebted to the courageous, tireless work of documentary filmmaker extraordinaire Wilfried Huismann, who has arguably spent more time investigating the foreign implications of the Kennedy assassination than anyone. It is always a privilege to work alongside him. At the German television network WDR, Heribert Blondiau, Mina Darbale, Reinhard Grossmann, Gabriella Spierer, and many others were instrumental in bringing the truths to the surface. Our dear FSB friend "Nikolai" was perhaps the bravest of all, and cannot be praised enough for his contributions. In Mexico, Mauricio Laguna Berber put in many months securing interviews with retired Cuban intelligence officials, a key part of bringing the story, finally, into focus.

Our West Coast Team, Jeff Silberman, Yvette Perkins, Jerry Offsay, and Jeff Ross, have always given wise counsel, even before they became our great friends. To our literary agent, Deborah Grosvenor, we owe special thanks for her original conception of the project and her tireless creative commitment both to the book proposal and its ultimate placement at Bloomsbury. At Bloomsbury, Nick Trautwein executed a brilliant line edit, and the deft touch of copy editor Phil Gaskill and proofreader Nancy Inglis are likewise felt on every page. Judith Hancock contributed the masterful index. Lastly, Bloomsbury managing editor Greg Villepique coordinated the transformation of the initial bloated manuscript into a finished book when almost no one believed it could be done.

Appendix: The Marty Underwood Story
by Gus Russo

I met Marty Underwood in 1993 through a mutual friend, the late Robert White, a well-known JFK memorabilia collector. I had been friends with Bob since high school, and when I returned to Maryland after many years in New York, we were again neighbors in Catonsville. I had visited Bob's collection (more than one hundred thousand pieces, which he started amassing as a high-schooler, and which he kept in his mother's basement) countless times. Much of the collection had come from Kennedy staffers, Kennedy's secretary Evelyn Lincoln, Secret Service agents, butlers— anywhere Bob could find it. But the most prized artifact, an Oval Office rocker that bore the imprints of Kennedy's back brace, had come from an odd source, a White House insider named Marty Underwood. This came as a bit of a shock; I had spent years studying the Kennedy administration, but I had never heard of Underwood.

Bob told me that Underwood had been a close confidant of Johnson, and through that connection had ended up with many White House collectibles, including the rocker and one of the pens used to sign the Nuclear Test Ban Treaty. I was fascinated, but Bob warned me that Marty was very private about his White House years and almost never gave interviews. He had sold the rocker only because he wanted to give the money to a fund for his new grandson.

Nonetheless, I called Marty, introduced myself as Bob's friend, and met with him in Parkville, Maryland, for what would be the first of dozens of lunches. Having just come off of twenty months of research on the *Frontline* documentary "Who Was Lee Harvey Oswald?," I had a first question ready for Marty: "How is it I never heard of you?"

"I did everything I could to stay out of the press," he said. "My job performance depended on it. I was the ultimate fly on the wall." Marty had been an advance man for Mayor Richard Daley in Chicago when he was discovered by Joe Kennedy in 1960 and conscripted into JFK's electoral army. After the election, Marty occasionally went to Washington when an extra advance man was needed on presidential trips. After the assassination, Johnson brought Marty to D.C. full time, where he worked under the cover of the Commerce Department. Marty advanced hundreds of LBJ trips, working closely on security details with the FBI's terrorism expert Sam Papich and various CIA station chiefs. During our lunches, Marty told me stories of LBJ and Hoover, JFK with Monroe and Judy Exner, the November 1963 JFK trip to Houston, the 1960 election rigging in Chicago, and many others.

At one lunch in 1994, Marty mentioned his friendship with the late CIA Mexico City station chief Win Scott. This got my attention, of course; Scott had played a critical role in the investigation into Oswald's time in Mexico City. Scott, Marty said, was "probably the best friend I had." The two had first worked together when Marty advanced JFK's 1962 trip to Mexico City, from June 29 through July 2. While he was there, Win Scott's Mexico City station uncovered a Cuban plot to assassinate the president: A Cuban with a concealed weapon was arrested and released, but little else has been revealed of the incident. When I asked Marty if Scott ever spoke to him about the Kennedy assassination, Marty answered, "I don't talk about those things."

However, after much prodding over many months, Underwood finally told me that at one time LBJ had asked him to talk to Scott about possible Cuban blowback on JFK. This was in 1968, when Johnson and Bobby Kennedy were procuring dirt on each other after Bobby had infuriated Lyndon by meeting with the North Vietnamese delegation in Paris.

Marty said that he went to Mexico City and met with Scott in a safe house thirty minutes outside of town.* Scott told him that he had determined after the assassination that a known Castro henchman had been in Mexico City when Oswald was there two months before the murder, and that he had mysteriously slipped from Texas through Mexican customs and on to Havana on November 22. Although Scott had no specific evidence, he believed the Cuban had been involved in the killing in Dallas. "Marty, we fucked up with this guy," he said at the safe house. Underwood told me that Scott gave him the Cuban's name but that he couldn't remember it all these years later. He then said that he took notes at the Scott meeting and he was certain that the Cuban's name would be on the notes, which were in storage

---

* This is the encounter described in chapter 16.

at his sister Rose's home in Iowa. He said when he next visited her he would try to retrieve them.

Some months later I received a postcard from Dubuque, which said simply, "The man's name was Fabian Escalante." At the time I had never heard that name, despite being familiar with many of the Cuban notables. In 1968, Underwood had also mentioned Escalante in his report to LBJ; Johnson, Marty said, "turned white." LBJ knew that Escalante was a dangerous Cuban intel officer, an intimate of Raúl Castro who was at the top of the list of potential presidential threats.

Next, Marty gave me photocopies of his notes from Mexico City, written on White House stationery and dated March 1968.* The two pages he offered, not the entire document, included Escalante's name as part of a larger report, blacked out in places. When I asked Marty about the rest of the report and the blacked-out sections, he said, "There are some things I'll take to my grave." He also gave me a report from Sam Papich at the FBI, who had warned of a Raúl Castro–Escalante attempt on Johnson a year earlier in South America.

By 1996 I had begun investigating the Escalante material in earnest. I also checked up on Marty, who was vouched for by numerous White House senior staff.† I called Sam Papich, who also vouched for him, and verified that they had both been concerned that Escalante would try to kill Johnson. Numerous Cuban defectors I spoke with in Miami and elsewhere spoke of Escalante as a dangerous man, accustomed to overseeing "wet operations." Eventually I pounded out a rough draft of Marty's story. Much to my disappointment, when I showed it to Marty, he said he never intended for the episode to be made public. He said he thought we were only having lunch chatter, and he was right. He asked me to not use the material until after his death, and I reluctantly agreed.

However, I shared my research with the Assassination Records Review Board (ARRB), which had been impaneled by Congress to locate every scrap of paper, public or private, that related to Kennedy's death. I insisted to David Maxwell, then the ARRB's executive director, that what I was giving him was on deep background, and only for the purpose of having him determine what, if anything, the CIA files had on Escalante. When I told Marty I had passed the information along, he said that if they made his name public, he would deny everything. I told him that I understood that

---

* See Underwood's notes at http://cuban-exile.com/brothersinarms.html.
† See chapter 6 for more details.

they would work on this angle very secretly and only release what they might find on Escalante. However, the ARRB tried to interview Marty, who consistently dodged their calls. They threatened a subpoena. Marty called me and told me that if they persisted he would have to lie to them and say I had completely misunderstood him. A subpoena followed, and Marty eventually met with senior staff and told them exactly that.

Despite the fact that I had given the board copies of Marty's 1968 notes, Underwood told them that those notes never existed, and that I had misinterpreted musings Marty had written in 1993 and given to me. He suggested that I had confused these notes with writings from other trips he had taken to Mexico in 1962 and 1966. Marty even gave the board a copy of his notes of the 1966 trip, which, of course, made no mention of the assassination. But this does not explain why the papers Marty gave me, the ones that did discuss Escalante's role, were dated March 1968 *by him*. Marty's new version also failed to explain the large portions of material he redacted before giving me the papers, or the other reports on Escalante he gave me, which he had obtained from the FBI in 1968. However, while this was ongoing, ARRB senior intelligence analyst Jeremy Gunn was at the CIA asking about its Escalante file, and seeing things that startled him.

In 1997, while the ARRB drama was playing out behind the scenes, I began working for Sy Hersh and ABC TV on the documentary adaptation of Hersh's book *The Dark Side of Camelot*. When Sy hit a wall in trying to corroborate the story of JFK's mistress Judith Exner, I told him I knew someone who knew all about it, Marty Underwood. Sy became anxious to sit down with Underwood, and I called a number of times on his behalf, but Underwood repeatedly put him off. I eventually succeeded in persuading Marty to meet for lunch with Hersh, myself, and the program's executive producer. At the meeting, Marty said that RFK's people had asked him to follow alleged courier Exner from D.C. to Chicago to make sure a document delivery from Kennedy to Outfit boss Sam Giancana at Union Station was successful. My perception was that Marty was speaking on background, not agreeing to have his name or story used. Sy disagreed, maintaining that Marty had no problem with having the story used in his book or film.

But in a phone call, Marty said he had informed Hersh not to use the story. His sister Rose had told him, "JFK was nothing but nice to you, so why do this to him?" and he couldn't help but agree. When Marty found that his tale was in the book, he became incensed, blamed me, and never took my calls again. Hersh's book came out in 1997, with Underwood included. However, as I had promised Underwood, I did not publish his Mexico City revelations.

When the ARRB's final report was released in September 1998, it confused Underwood's 1966 Mexico City trip with the 1968 trip—exactly as Underwood hoped it would. But what Kennedy assassination buffs should have noted was the fact that Jeremy Gunn, the ARRB's chief intelligence analyst (and later executive director), who had handled the Underwood-Escalante story and had already seen powerful material about Escalante at CIA, was no longer on the panel when the report was written. There the story sat.

After Underwood died in March 2003, I gave the Escalante research material to Willi Huismann, who took it from there. In our 2006 documentary, Willi confronted Escalante on film in his Havana office. With a dismissive smile on his face, he denied any link to Oswald or the assassination; what's more, he denied ever traveling to Mexico, a contention soundly rebutted by a number of his former colleagues. In the research process, we were given access to secret KGB and Mexican police files that had never been seen before (including by the board); these files corroborated much of the Mexico City story in chapter 10.

I also had a chance that year to speak with Jeremy Gunn about how he had followed up the Underwood-Escalante story before he left the board. In a recorded conversation, he said:

> The single most interesting part of the story is Mexico City, and the single most tantalizing lead we received was your report on Escalante, which we followed up aggressively. I went to CIA and saw their file on him [Escalante], which I can't discuss because it's classified. All I will say is that I saw some things there that made my jaw drop. Bottom line, follow Escalante, especially where he was before the assassination [that is, in Minsk and Mexico City] . . . After we asked for the file, the CIA perked up and took an interest in it. I don't know what they did about it, but it was clear they hadn't looked at it in years . . . I didn't trust Underwood when he spoke to us and tried to water down what he told you about his meeting with Scott regarding Escalante. Underwood tried his best to put us off until we finally subpoenaed him.

After my film with Willi, *Rendezvous with Death*, played on television in sixteen countries (though not in the U.S.), I was asked to show the film separately to the National Archives JFK staff, the CIA declassification staff, and U.S. archivist Alan Weinstein and his staff. In all, some sixty government officials watched the film, most taking extensive notes. As a result, there was a swell of interest in declassifying the files on Escalante and other Cuban agents. Using back channels, official new demands have been sent to foreign governments to come clean with what they know. I have been informed that, during this process, Jeremy Gunn was brought in to give his version of the story, and he repeated almost word for word what he had told me in 2003. Other senior members of the ARRB have recently expressed their frustration at not being able to obtain the KGB's encrypted file on Oswald, which they were offered for a price, before the offer was withdrawn. At this writing, they continue to lobby Washington officials to press for the material. The National Archives has been negotiating behind the scenes with the CIA since 2006 to fulfill their pledge to release files relevant to the Cubans mentioned in the film, as well as the material Jeremy Gunn perused in the 1990s.

Notes

Abbreviations

CCIR—Church Committee Interim Report.

CCR—Church Committee Final Report.

CD—Warren Commission Document.

CE—Warren Commission Exhibit.

FL: WWLHO—*Frontline*, "Who Was Lee Harvey Oswald?," PBS, airdate November 16, 1993.

HSCA—House Select Committee on Assassinations.

NARA—National Archives and Records Administration, College Park, Maryland.

RWD—*Rendezvous with Death*, WDR (Germany) documentary, airdate January 2006.

WC—Warren Commission Report.

Note: Unless otherwise indicated, all interviews are by the authors.

Chapter 1: Living Through Another Cuba

1. CIA intercept transcript, November 22, 1963; CIA "blind memo," May 7, 1964.
2. CIA intercept transcript, November 22, 1963; CIA "blind memo," May 7, 1964.
3. CIA intercept transcript, November 22, 1963; CIA "blind memo," May 7, 1964.
4. Geyelin, p. 4.
5. Latell, p. 13.
6. Cox, p. 110.
7. Brian Latell, interview of Jaime Costa, Miami, February 25, 1986.
8. Latell, pp. 124–125.
9. Szulc, p. 335.
10. Ibid.
11. Geyer, p. 144.
12. Szulc, p. 337.
13. Ibid., p. 323.
14. Geyer, p. 274.
15. Fidel Castro speech, Havana, March 8, 2003.
16. Barrios obituary, Philip Gunson, *Guardian*, November 2, 2000.

17. *Los Angeles Times*, "Conducting an Overt Operation," June 30, 1999.

18. Latell, p. 129.

19. Leonov, p. 29. Translations by Alexei Porfirenko.

20. Reeves, p. 15.

21. Ibid., p. 16.

22. Hamilton, p. 781.

23. Latell, p. 82.

24. *Psychiatric Personality Study of Fidel Castro*, CIA Report, December 1, 1961.

25. The Soviet KGB did such a workup on Jack as he was coming to power. The profile stressed that "the relaxed and predictable days of the Eisenhower regime were at an end," and when the Cuban Dirección de Inteligencia (DGI) did a similar workup, they concluded that a Kennedy-backed invasion of Cuba was at hand (Corson and Crowley, p. 271).

26. Hersh, p. 33.

27. Latell, p. 32.

28. Fidel Castro speech, Tuxpan, Cuba, December 4, 1988.

29. Courtois.

30. Brian Latell, interview of Norberto Fuentes, Coral Gables, Florida, November 12, 2004.

31. Brian Latell, interview of Manuel Romeu, Hato Rey, Puerto Rico, February 27, 1986.

32. Ibid.

33. Interview of Mike Howard of the Secret Service, December 7, 1993. Howard learned this when he was assigned to debrief the Oswalds after the assassination.

34. WC, testimony of John Pic Oswald, Vol. XI, pp. 38–39.

35. WC, testimony of New York juvenile court psychiatrist Dr. Renatus Hartogs, Vol. VIII, p. 205; Clarke, pp. 107–108.

36. FBI Affidavit of Palmer McBride, November 26, 1963 (CD 75).

Chapter 2: Revolution

1. Leamer, pp. 405–406.

2. Ibid., pp. 402–403.

3. Ibid., p. 404.

4. Hoffa, pp. 93–94.

5. Thomas, *Robert Kennedy*, p. 91.

6. W. Johnson, pp. 24–25.

7. Murray Kempton, "The Uncommitted," *Progressive* magazine, September 1960.

8. Plimpton, pp. 194–195.

9. Latell, p. 12.

10. Szulc, p. 490.

11. Jeffrey J. Safford, "The Nixon-Castro Meeting of 19 April 1959," *Diplomatic History*, Vol. 4 (Fall 1980).

12. Franklin, p. 20.

13. Interview of June Cobb, April 9, 2008.

14. Gosse, p. 130.

15. Interview of June Cobb, April 9, 2008.

16. Brian Latell, interview of Ernesto Betancourt.

17. Draper, p. 63.

18. WC, Folsom Exhibit One, Vol. XIX, p. 3.

19. Ibid., p. 111.

20. WC, letter from Lee Oswald to Robert Oswald, November 26, 1959, CE 295, Vol. XVI, p. 816.

21. Posner, p. 21.

22. Epstein, *Legend*, p. 81.

23. WC, affidavit of James Botelho, Vol. VIII, p. 315.

24. Hemming was not the only witness who would later attest to seeing an American in civil-ian clothes at the Monterey Park house during the first half of 1959. In January, the cops were called there to break up an argument at the Velásquez home, possibly a symptom of the factional disputes erupting in Cuba at the time. Thirty-five Cubans were present that night, and nine of them were taken into custody. After the Kennedy assassination, the edi-tor of the *Los Angeles Times* would investigate rumors that Lee had been among those photographed by the cops, but the reporter he assigned to the story was told by police that the CIA had removed some of those photos and the ones remaining did not show Oswald.

25. Interview of Gerry Hemming, June 5, 1992.

26. Epstein, *Legend*, p. 89.

27. Warren Commission interview of Nelson Delgado, extracted in Epstein, *Legend*, p. 89.

28. CIA, "Review of Allegations of Castro Cuban Involvement in the John F. Kennedy Assas-sination," 4-15-75 (#104-10088-10035; NARA).

29. WC, testimony of Sgt. James A. Zahm, Vol. XI, p. 308.

30. McMillan, p. 69.

31. Mailer, pp. 43–44 (his account of Rimma Shirakova's perceptions of Oswald).

32. Ibid., p. 45.

33. Ibid., p. 48 (Simchenko's account).

34. Ibid., p. 49 (Shirakova's account).

35. Draper, p. 65.

36. CE 1385, Vol. XXII, pp. 702, 706.

37. McMillan, p. 5.

38. Ibid.

39. FL: WWLHO: interview of Vladimir Semichasty, April 6, 1993.

40. Clarke. Note: Clarke claims that tendons were cut, but other accounts suggest that the wound was more superficial.

41. Mailer, p. 50 (Shirakova's account).

42. FL: WWLHO: interview of Dr. Lydia Mikhailina, January 1993.

43. Interview of Allen Campbell, February 2, 1993.

44. FL: WWLHO: interview of Vasili Petrov's son (name withheld by request), January 10, 1993.

45. Franklin, p. 24.

46. Schlesinger, *JFK*, p. 4.

47. Collier and Horowitz, p. 199.

48. Wills, p. 217.

49. Interview of Ted Sorensen, New York, April 15, 2008.

50. CE 943, Vol. XVIII, p. 157.

51. McMillan, p. 84.

52. Edward Jay Epstein, "Who Was Lee Harvey Oswald?," *Wall Street Journal*, November 22, 1983.

53. WC, Lee Oswald, in his "Ship Diary," traveling back from Minsk, 1962 (CE 25).

54. Interview of former Dallas FBI agent Ferris Rookstool, June 10, 1993. Rookstool was a close family friend of the Mohrenschildts. He not only recognized Jeanne de Mohrenschildt's handwriting, but remembered "Ha-Ha-Ha" as being one of her favorite derisive expressions.

Chapter 3: The Patriot Game

1. See Wronski's Russian research at: http://www.russianbooks.org/oswald/project.htm.

2. Ibid.

3. Referred to in Mailer as "Igor Ivanovich Guzmin."

4. Wronski, op. cit.

5. Referred to in Mailer as "Stepan Vasilyevich Gregorieff."

6. Posner, p. 58.

7. See note 1 (chapter 3) about Wronski's research.

8. Mailer, p. 120.

9. Draper, pp. 60–61.

10. De Mohrenschildt manuscript, "I AM A PATSY!," p. 93. Noted in HSCA, Vol. XII.

11. Ibid.

12. Ibid.

13. CE 3140, p. 822.

14. CE 1824, Heitman interview of Marina, January 31, 1964.

15. Alan Sagner, "How the Fair Play for Cuba Committee Was Formed," *Fair Play Newsletter*, Vol. 1, No. 2, May 6, 1960.

16. CIA Telex from Mexi COS to White House and McGeorge Bundy, November 28, 1963.

17. Summers, p. 193.

18. Interview of June Cobb, New York, April 9, 2008.

19. Szulc, p. 56.

20. For more on the Morgan story, see Shetterly.

21. Interview of June Cobb, New York, April 9, 2008.

22. June Cobb testimony before Senate Judiciary Committee, March 30, 1962.

23. Interview of Aureliano Sanchez Arango Jr., May 7, 1998; Prouty, p. 50.

24. Andy Postal Memorandum for the Record Re: Chronology of Events As We Now Know Them, September 12, 1975, Assassination Archives.

25. Copeland, p. 202.

26. CCIR, pp. 72–73.

27. CCIR, especially testimonies of Bissell and Esterline, Edward Hinkle; also JFK Records, Bissell phone conversation with Joe DeGenova, June 5, 1975.

28. Interview of Sergio Arcacha Smith, June 3, 1999.

29. J. Kennedy, pp. 132–133.

30. R. Martin, *Hero for Our Time*, pp. 509–510.

31. Garwood, p. 158.

32. Interview with Sergio Arcacha Smith, Miami, June 4, 1999.

33. Hersh, pp. 170–171, 176–177.

34. Goodwin, p. 108.

35. Oswald diary as cited in Mailer, p. 117.

36. Extra page not included in Oswald diary, as cited in Mailer, p. 119.

37. Jack Pfeiffer, official CIA historian.

38. Center for the Study of Intelligence, "CIA Briefings of Presidential Candidates," p. 56.

39. CIA Pfeiffer Report, quoting from a memorandum from the meeting written by Henry Holland, a former assistant secretary of state for inter-American affairs.

40. Davis, p. 331.

41. Robin Erb, "Kennedy Presidency Almost Ended Before He Was Inaugurated," *Toledo Blade*, November 21, 2003; "Confesses Plan to Kill Kennedy," *Chicago Daily Tribune*, December 17, 1960, p. A2.

42. RFK Oral History, p. 21.

43. Schlesinger, *RFK*, p. 247.

44. Seigenthaler Oral History, JFK Library, pp. 183–201.

45. Thomas, *Robert Kennedy*, p. 111.

46. June Cobb testimony before Senate Judiciary Committee, March 30, 1962, p. 31.

47. Oswald's "Historic Diary"; CE 24, entry for January 2, 1961.

48. WC, Vol. 1, pp. 205–206.

49. Ibid.

50. Interview of Rafael Nuñez, April 12, 1995.

51. Kirkpatrick, p. 197.

Chapter 4: On the Beach

1. Goodwin, pp. 146–148.

2. Schlesinger, *JFK*, pp. 176–184.

3. Bravo, p. 97.

4. Escalante, *Executive Action*, p. 77.

5. University of Miami "Escalante" profile.

6. Interview of Nuñez, April 12, 1995.

7. "ZR RIFLE" television documentary transcript, Havana Cubavision Network, November 27, 1993.

8. Unclassified telegram from U.S. embassy, Managua, to U.S. secretary of state, July 16, 1973.

9. Interview of Domingo Amuchastegui, August 20, 2007.

10. Hersh, p. 187.

11. Ibid., p. 207.

12. Inspector General's Report on Plots to Assassinate Fidel Castro, p. 79.

13. McMillan, pp. 73–74.

14. Ibid., p. 75.

15. FL: WWLHO: interview of Oleg Pavlovich Tarusin, January 21, 1993.

16. Russo, pp. 408–409, citing: interviews with Jeanne Humphreys and Robert McDonnell (Giancana's lawyer); Rosselli quotes in *The Last Mafioso,* by Bill Roemer, in *Man Against the Mob;* Trafficante quotes in *Mob Lawyer,* by Frank Ragano.

17. *Memorandum on Castro's Statements and Notes on Cuban Trip,* from John E. Nolan Jr., April 5–9, 1963, p. 24 (JFK Library).

18. Ibid., p. 21.

19. Ibid., pp. 17–18.

20. Ibid., pp. 21–22.

21. Ibid., p. 2.

22. Menier, *The Way It Happened,* p. 192.

23. *New Orleans Times-Picayune,* January 5, 1961, section 1, p. 2.

24. HSCA Report, Vol. X, p. 127.

25. *New Orleans Times-Picayune,* April 11, 1961, section 3, p. 4.

26. Associated Press, "CIA Said to Know of Bay of Pigs Leak," April 29, 2000.

27. Hersh, p. 208.

28. Ibid., p. 212.

29. Ibid.

30. Schaap, pp. 256–257.

31. Nolan to Kennedy (see note 17 above).

32. Wofford, p. 350.

33. Fontova, *Exposing Real Che,* p. 55.

34. Nolan to Kennedy (see note 17 above), p. 14.

35. Ibid., p. 15.

36. Beschloss, *Crisis Years,* pp. 122–123. *See also* David and David, p. 157.

37. Wyden, pp. 290–291.

38. Ibid., p. 291.

39. Reeves, pp. 94–95.

40. Fontova, *Exposing Real Che,* p. 58.

41. CIA Special National Intelligence Estimate, December 8, 1960.

42. Collier and Horowitz, p. 340.

43. Wyden, p. 290.

44. Don Bohning, "Cuban Army Seen as Key to Ouster of Castro; Bay of Pigs vet speaks up." *Miami Herald,* April 16, 2000.

45. H. Johnson, p. 171.

46. Ibid., pp. 202–203.

47. McMillan, p. 95.

48. Ibid., pp. 97, 100–107.

49. FL: WWLHO: interview of Vacheslav Nokonov, April 12, 1993.

Chapter 5: Meet the Boys on the Battlefront

1. Reeves, pp. 97–99.

2. McGehee, Conclusion.

3. RWD: interview of Antulio Ramírez, 2005.

4. Reeves, pp. 150–151.

5. Reeves, p. 152.

6. McMillan, pp. 110–111.

7. Menier, *Protecting and Promoting Fidel,* p. 34.

8. Fernández, p. 42.

9. Hans de Salas-del Valle, *Fidel Castro.*

10. Testimony of Juanita Castro, House Un-American Activities Committee, June 11, 1965.

11. Testimony of Pedro Diaz Lanz before Senate Internal Security Subcommittee, July 14, 1959.

12. Fontova, *Favorite Tyrant,* p. 3.

13. RWD: interview, June 2005.

14. Testimony of Gerardo Peraza before U.S. Senate, Subcommittee on Security and Terrorism, Committee on the Judiciary, "Hearing on the Role of Cuba in International Terrorism and Subversion; Intelligence Activities of the DGI," February 26, 1982.

15. McMillan, pp. 127–128.

16. Ibid., pp. 129–130.

17. Ibid., p. 131.

18. Interview of Morris Brownlee, November 29, 1993.

19. Interview of Layton Martens, New Orleans, June 6, 1999.

20. Interview of Sergio Arcacha Smith, May 14, 1994.

21. Interview of Layton Martens, New Orleans, June 6, 1999.

22. Interview of Sergio Arcacha Smith, Miami, June 3, 1999.

23. Ibid.

24. Interviews and research for the Hemingway story were conducted in 2001 by Gus Russo and David Corn for their article "The Old Man and the CIA," in the March 26, 2001, issue

of the *Nation*. The Lansdale memo was originally brought to Russo's attention by Prof. Larry Haapanen and David Lifton. Russo and Corn conducted over fifty background interviews with aides to Lansdale, Hemingway, Richard Helms, and the Kennedys; and referenced works such as: Mary Hemingway's Oral History at the JFK Library; *How It Was*, by Mary Hemingway; *Hemingway in Cuba*, by Norberto Fuentes; Clifton Daniel's memoir, *Lords, Ladies, and Gentlemen*; and *Edward R. Murrow*, by Joseph Persico.

25. KGB transcript from surveillance of Oswald home, July 26, 1961, as cited in Mailer, pp. 216–218.
26. Goodwin, p. 191.
27. Schlesinger, *JFK*, p. 762.
28. Ibid., p. 763.
29. Goodwin, p. 192.
30. Ibid., p. 196.
31. Ibid., pp. 198–202.
32. Speech by New York congressman Steven Derounian, quoted by Goodwin.
33. Reeves, pp. 175–176.
34. McMillan, pp. 156–157.
35. Ibid., p. 157.
36. Kalugin was interviewed for the 2003 ABC Peter Jennings Special "Beyond Conspiracy," for which coauthor Russo was the lead investigative reporter.
37. Menier, *Protecting and Promoting Fidel*, p. 51.
38. Interview for television documentary "638 Ways to Kill Castro," Freemantle Home Entertainment, 2006.
39. Reeves, p. 267.
40. FL: WWLHO.
41. Nechiporenko, p. 63.
42. Mailer, p. 252. Varying accounts suggest greater and lesser threat levels of these experiments. Nonetheless, they were an early indication of his interest in explosives.
43. Ibid., p. 252.
44. Ibid., p. 260.
45. Ibid., pp. 273–274.
46. RWD: interview, 2005.
47. Hosty, p. 113.
48. CE 986; Epstein, *Assassination Chronicles*, p. 447.

Chapter 6: Both Sides Now

1. *Bohemia* magazine, January 1962.
2. Beschloss, *Crisis Years*, p. 361.
3. Fursenko and Naftali, pp. 152–154.
4. Beschloss, *Crisis Years*, p. 362.

5. Fursenko and Naftali, p. 150.

6. Lansdale, Memo for the Record, March 16, 1962.

7. Interviews and research for the Hemingway story were conducted in 2001 by Gus Russo and David Corn for their article "The Old Man and the CIA," in the March 26, 2001, issue of the *Nation*. The Lansdale memo was originally brought to Russo's attention by Prof. Larry Haapanen and David Lifton. (See chapter 4, note 26 for more detail.)

8. Thomas, *Robert Kennedy*, p. 272.

9. *Harper's*, August 1975.

10. Bohning, p. 184.

11. Bissell, p. 201.

12. 1967 CIA Inspector General's Report, by Jake Earman.

13. Interview for television documentary, "638 Ways to Kill Castro," Freemantle Home Entertainment, 2006.

14. David Martin, "The CIA's Loaded Gun," *Washington Post*, September 10, 1976, p. C1.

15. Transcript of Halpern interview for ABC News, February 21, 1997, Peter Jennings Reports: *Dangerous World, The Kennedy Years*.

16. Sources for CIA in Miami: *Cold War in South Florida: Historic Resource Study*, by Steven Hach (ed. Jennifer Dickey), National Park Service Southeast Regional Office, U.S. Department of the Interior, October 2004; "Twilight of the Assassins," Ann Louise Bardach, *Atlantic Monthly*, November 2006; South Campus history page, University of Miami Libraries, accessed January 24, 2007. The first photograph on the page apparently shows Building 25 in 1946; "South Campus site formerly home to spies, surveillance," Walyce Almeida, *The Hurricane* (University of Miami student newspaper), December 1, 2006; *Spymaster: My Life in the CIA*, Theodore G. Shackley, 2005, Brassey's; *The Castro Obsession: U.S. Covert Operations in Cuba, 1959–1965*, Don Bohning, Potomac Books, 2005.

17. Powers, p. 142.

18. Demaris, p. 238.

19. Mailer, pp. 221–222.

20. Ibid., p. 224.

21. WC, Lee Oswald's *Historic Diary*, entry for October 21, 1959, CE 24, Vol. 16, pp. 94–105.

22. Ibid.

23. Blakey and Billings, p. 147.

24. FBI report of affidavit from Palmer McBride, November 26, 1963.

25. WC, Exhibit 94, p. 1.

26. Mailer, p. 223.

27. McMillan, pp. 186–187.

28. Ibid., p. 190.

29. Ibid., p. 191.

30. Ibid., pp. 195–196 (Lee Oswald writings quoted).

31. WC, Lee Oswald's *Historic Diary*, entry for October 21, 1959, CE 24, Vol. 16, pp. 94–105.

32. McMillan, pp. 215–216.

33. Casasin, HSCA Staff interview, August 17, 1978, and Walter P. Haltigan, HSCA Staff interview, June 13, 1978, in HSCA Staff Notes section of the JFK Collection, NARA. The HSCA verified that Haltigan's assistant, Robert G. Lamprell, in fact delivered the memo to CIA headquarters.

34. FL: WWLHO: interview of Deneselya, May 10, 1993.

35. FL: WWLHO.

36. Mailer, p. 352.

37. WC: report of FBI Special Agents John W. Fain and B. Tom Carter, dictated July 2, 1962 (Exhibit No. 823, Vol. 17, pp. 728–731); testimony of John W. Fain, Vol. 4, pp. 403–418.

38. WC, testimony of Robert Oswald, Vol. 1, pp. 315, 389.

39. Underwood background: Jim Arpy, "My Friend (and Boss), the President," *Dubuque Tri-City Times*, November 17, 1968; Valenti, *A Very Human President*, pp. 29–30; "One Step Ahead," by F. de Sales Meyers, *Baltimore Sun Magazine*, July 22, 1979.

40. Schlesinger, *JFK*, p. 768.

41. *Oklahoma Tribune*, May 18, 1976.

42. *Human Events* magazine, recalled in an article by John Martino, January 1964.

43. RWD: interview, 2005.

44. Christopher Andrew, "KGB Foreign Intelligence from Brezhnev to the Coup," *Intelligence and National Security*, Vol. 8, No. 3 (July 1993); more details on Kryuchkov from Andrew and Mitrokhin, *The Sword and the Shield*, and various November 2007 newspaper obits of Kryuchkov.

45. RWD: interview, 2005.

46. Ibid.

47. Ibid.

48. Ibid.

49. Ramirez, *Castro's Red Hot Hell*, p. 226; JFK Collection, NARA; FBI, 124-10063-10135, file #89-43-A-1A383. (Note: the English translation is over 800 pages; the page citation is to that translation.)

50. CIA's *Inspector General's Report on Plots to Assassinate Fidel Castro*, p. 83.

51. CIA AMLASH File; JFK Collection, NARA.

52. RWD: interview, 2005.

53. Cable from John Whitten, CIA, to the White House, Department of State, and the FBI, titled "Cable Concerning the Lee Harvey Oswald Case," December 18, 1963.

Chapter 7: Talking Cuba Crisis

1. McMillan, pp. 227–231.

2. Ibid., p. 232.

3. Ibid., p. 233.

4. Ibid., pp. 235–237.

5. Beschloss, *Crisis Years,* pp. 421–422.

6. Ibid., p. 409.

7. Jean Daniel, interview of Fidel Castro, *New Republic,* December 1963.

8. "Memo for Lansdale from Brigadier General W. H. Craig, 17 Jan. 1962," JCS Papers in Kennedy Collection.

9. JFK to Lansdale memo, "Justification for U.S. Military Intervention in Cuba," Memorandum, March 13, 1962, and other JCS documents in the JFK Assassination Collection at the National Archives, College Park, Maryland.

10. For details of the troop placement, see Report of the Dept. of Defense and the Joint Chiefs of Staff on the Caribbean Survey Group, "Justification for U.S. Intervention in Cuba," March 9, 1962, available at NARA; the report of Admiral Robert Dennison, commander in chief of the North Atlantic Fleet (CINCLANT), obtained under FOIA by WGBH-TV, on file at the National Security Archive in Washington; and Reeves, p. 367.

11. Walt Rostow quoted in Beschloss, *Crisis Years,* p. 410.

12. Acheson letter to Truman quoted by Beschloss, *Crisis Years,* p. 410.

13. Beschloss, *Crisis Years,* pp. 398–399.

14. Ibid., pp. 413, 424.

15. Excerpted from May and Zelikow, pp. 47–77.

16. May and Zelikow, p. 77.

17. Thomas, *Robert Kennedy,* p. 234.

18. May and Zelikow, p. 77.

19. McMillan, pp. 246–247.

20. Ibid., p. 252.

21. Ibid., p. 258.

22. Schlesinger, *RFK,* pp. 508–509, based on the record made by Leonard C. Meeker, the State Department legal adviser.

23. Kennedy White House Dictabelt recordings given to Gus Russo by Kennedy's secretary Evelyn Lincoln.

24. May and Zelikow, p. 204.

25. Ibid., p. 207.

26. David Ormsby-Gore (aka Lord Harlech) interviewed by Richard Neustadt, transcript approved March 12, 1965, John F. Kennedy Library Oral History Project, p. 15.

27. *New York Times,* October 22, 1962, p. 1.

28. Schlesinger, *RFK,* p. 514.

29. Hersh, p. 375.

30. Ibid.

31. Bohning, p. 124.

32. Schlesinger, *RFK,* p. 514.

33. Ibid.

34. Excerpted from May and Zelikow, pp. 355–361.

35. Sources: "Was Castro Out of Control in 1962?," by Seymour Hersh, *Washington Post,* October 11, 1987; "The Day Castro Almost Started World War III," by Daniel Ellsberg, *New York Times,* October 31, 1987; "Cuba: Even Dicier Than We Knew," by Raymond Garthoff, *Newsweek,* October 26, 1987.

36. Carlos Franqui, *Family Portrait,* summarized in "Did Fidel Push the Button?," *Time,* March 16, 1981. Franqui, a Cuban émigré living in Italy and an old Castro comrade, left Cuba in anger over Moscow's increasing influence.

37. Franqui placed the incident at a base in Pinar del Río, southwest of Havana, but the SAM-2 was known by U.S. intel to have been fired from Banes, as confirmed by Hersh in "Was Castro Out of Control in 1962?," *Washington Post,* October 11, 1987.

38. Executive Committee of the National Security Council minutes, October 23, 1962, RFK papers.

39. R. Kennedy, pp. 75–76.

40. Ibid.

41. "Did Fidel Push the Button?" *Time,* March 16, 1981.

42. Robert Kennedy to Dean Rusk, October 30, 1962, as quoted from RFK papers by Schlesinger, p. 521.

43. Khrushchev, p. 498.

44. Sergei Khrushchev, "How My Father and President Kennedy Saved the World," *American Heritage,* October 2002.

45. Paul Kengor in PBS documentary "The Castro Experience," January 2005.

46. Menier, *The Way It Happened,* pp. 249–251; authors' interviews of Menier, October 2007.

47. Kennedy to McNamara, memo (FRUS, 1961–1963, Vol. XI, pp. 379, 381); "Cuban Missile Crisis and Its Aftermath," State Department Release, 1997—summarized in Associated Press, "Papers: Kennedy Broke Pledge," April 6, 1997.

48. Dean Rusk admitted the impasse to the Senate Foreign Relations Committee. See National Security Archive briefing paper, *Cuban Missile Crisis, 1962: The Making of US Policy,* especially Rusk memo: "Briefing of the World Situation," January 11, 1963.

49. On October 23, 1979, McGeorge Bundy submitted an op-ed titled "The Brigade's My Fault," in which he absolved the Carter administration of the brigade, and confirmed the existence of the secret shared agreement about existent troops. Attributing the brigade's re-discovery to his "being lax on intelligence," Bundy wrote, "most of them [troops] did leave *but we neither required nor got a pledge that all would go*" (Bundy, "The Brigade's My Fault," *New York Times,* October 23, 1979). Dobrynin cites Bundy's op-ed as indicative of the fact that President Kennedy himself had been aware of the detachment's existence.

50. Christopher Whalen, "The Soviet Military Buildup in Cuba," June 11, 1982, Heritage Foundation; "Second Unit of MiG-23s Identified in Cuban Hands," *Aviation Week and Space Technology,* February 8, 1982.

51. Mailer, p. 453.

52. Ramírez, p. 151; JFK Collection, NARA; FBI, 124-10063-10135, file #89-43-A-1A383. (Note: the English translation is over 800 pages; the page citation is to that translation.)

53. For example, see: November 26, 1963, *Pompano Beach Sun-Sentinel*; FBI records: February 27, 1964, memorandum from William Branigan to William C. Sullivan 1993.08.04.18:45: 23:780037; 105-82555-2464; Branigan to Sullivan 2.27.64; 124-10035-10367, 62-109090-63, 124-10035-10367, Report of James O'Conner 4.4.64; Hede Massing Debriefing 2.7.64—all at NARA JFK Collection.

54. *London Daily Worker*, November 1962.

55. Forty-two years later, the ten blasts that al Qaeda operatives set off in the Madrid subway system would kill or maim nearly two thousand people using only a hundred kilos of TNT.

56. Breuer, p. 3.

57. Ibid. Military historian William Breuer researched the plot most thoroughly, and interviewed FBI assistant director Ray Wannall. Secondary sources include: *New York Times* (November 19 and 20, 1962); declassified FBI documents; and coauthor Russo's interview of Wannall, June 18, 2003.

58. *Baltimore Sun,* November 21, 1962.

Chapter 8: Irresistible Targets

1. Fontova, *Exposing Real Che,* p. 24.

2. Reeves, p. 445.

3. O'Donnell and Powers, pp. 275–276.

4. Roberts, p. 99.

5. *Washington Post and Times Herald*, January 6, 1963, p. A15.

6. Reeves, p. 445.

7. Haig, pp. 109–110.

8. See HSCA Report, Vol. X, pp. 12–14 for details.

9. Dan Kurzman, "U.S. Builds Up Underground Support in Cuba," *Washington Post*, August 13, 1963, p. A1.

10. CE 97, pp. 426–427.

11. CE 994, Vol. XVIII, p. 625.

12. McMillan, p. 307.

13. Ibid., pp. 306–308.

14. Ibid., p. 308.

15. Interview of Angelo Kennedy, April 24, 1997.

16. "Plan for Neutral Cuba Is Reported," *San Francisco Chronicle*, April 20, 1963.

17. Ibid.

18. John Martino, "Cuba and the Kennedy Assassination," *Human Events,* January 1964.

19. "Plan for Neutral Cuba Is Reported," *San Francisco Chronicle*, April 20, 1963.

20. Ibid.

21. Kluckhohn, p. 138.

22. George Weller, "Exiles Suspect Move to Retire Castro," *Los Angeles Times*, September 27, 1963.

23. CIA Record Number: 104-10419-10021, Record Series: JFK, Agency File Number: Russ Holmes Work File, Comments: JFK-RH10:F189, Memorandum from Mr. D. J. Brennan, Jr. to Mr. S. J. Papich, Subject: Anti-Castro Activities Internal Security—Cuba, May 24, 1965.

24. *Chicago Daily Tribune*, January 3, 1963, p. 1.

25. Ibid.

26. "Growing Food Shortages Said to Plague Cuba," *Washington Post and Times Herald*, January 9, 1963, p. A14.

27. "Castro Derides U.S. on Captives," *New York Times*, January 3, 1963, p. 1.

28. Tad Szulc, "Castro, Despite Missile Affair, Still Defiant," *New York Times*, January 7, 1963, p. 11.

29. "Castro Promotes 100 Officers," *New York Times*, January 5, 1963, p. 3.

30. "Castro's Blast," *Washington Post and Times Herald*, January 3, 1963, p. A16.

31. Tad Szulc, "Castro's Island Fort," *New York Times*, February 4, 1963.

32. Ibid.

33. "Castro Asks War on Imperialism," *Washington Post and Times Herald*, January 17, 1963, p. 1.

34. Oppenheimer, pp. 399–400.

35. "Cuban Arms Estimated," *Christian Science Monitor*, January 5, 1963, p. 3.

36. "U.S. Loses Initiative in Cuba: Keating," *Chicago Daily Tribune*, January 14, 1963, p. 9.

37. "The Cost of Castro," *Chicago Daily Tribune*, January 21, 1963, p. 20.

38. Interviews by Thomas of Sam Halpern, Albert Francke, Joan Denny, letter from Des FitzGerald to Frances FitzGerald, June 25, 1963, in the Frances FitzGerald papers at Boston University, cited in endnote for Ch. 20, note 25 in Thomas, *Very Best Men.*

39. Thomas, *Very Best Men*, p. 291.

40. *Alleged Assassination Plots*, pp. 84–85, fn. 4; D. Martin, pp. 145–146; "Report on Plots," pp. 53–54; Schlesinger, *RFK*, p. 484.

41. Thomas, p. 293.

42. Epstein, *Legend*, p. 482.

43. Ibid., p. 317.

44. Ibid., p. 318.

45. WC, testimony of Mr. and Mrs. Tobias, Volume X, p. 256.

46. WC, Appendix XIV, Study of Oswald's Finances; Mailer, pp. 484–485.

47. Mailer, p. 485.

48. Bohning, p. 188; Don Bohning, "Cuban Army Seen as Key to Ouster of Castro; Bay of Pigs vet speaks up." *Miami Herald,* April 16, 2000.

49. Interviews of Quintero, November 6, 1997, Shackley, December 10, 1997, Messer, June 10, 1999, and Angelo Murgado, January 8, 1998; interviews supplied by Judith Artime that she conducted with many of her father's associates for her college thesis, *The Golden Boy* (1996); Bohning, pp. 190–192.

50. Califano, p. 121.

51. FL: WWLHO: interview of Volkmar Schmidt, June 17, 1993.

52. Ibid.

53. Ibid.

54. Ibid.

55. "General Walker Faces Sex Charge: Right-Wing Figure Accused in Dallas of Lewdness," *New York Times*, United Press International, July 9, 1976, p. 84; "Police Arrest Retired General for Lewdness," *Dallas Morning News*, March 17, 1977, p. B18; "Judge Convicts, Fines Walker," *Dallas Morning News*, May 23, 1977, p. 8.

56. "Hargis Says Walker Will Join in Tour," *Dallas Morning News*, February 14, 1963, section 1, p. 16; "Walker Preparing for Crusade," *Dallas Morning News*, February 17, 1963, section 1, p. 16.

57. WC, testimony of Marina Oswald, Vol. 1, p. 16.

58. William E. Kelly telephone interview of Volkmar Schmidt, January 1995.

59. McMillan, p. 332.

60. McWhorter, p. 316.

61. WC, testimony of Marina Oswald, Vol.V, p. 401; HSCA testimony of Warren DeBrueys, May 13, 1978, p. 26.

62. McMillan, p. 334.

63. Ibid., pp. 340–341.

64. Interview of Sylvia Weinstein, June 12, 1993.

65. Mailer, p. 502.

66. McMillan, pp. 348–350.

67. Ibid., p. 351.

68. Ibid., pp. 352–353.

69. Ibid., p. 353.

70. Ibid., p. 354.

71. Posner, p. 119.

72. McMillan, pp. 368–370.

73. FL: WWLHO: interview of Edward J. Epstein, June 30, 1993.

74. CE 98, Vol. XVI, p. 433.

75. CE 97, Vol. XVI, pp. 426–427.

76. McMillan, p. 378.

77. CE 98, Vol. XVI, p. 434.

78. Hinckle and Turner, p. 176.

79. CCR, p. 171; FRUS, 1961–1963, Vol. XI, pp. 781–782.

80. McMillan, p. 382.

81. Interview of William McLaney, April 10, 1994.

82. McMillan, pp. 383–385.

83. WC, Lee (Vincent T.) Exhibit No. 3, Vol. XX, pp. 514–516.

84. CE 93, Vol. XVI, p. 341.

85. McMillan, p. 351.

86. Interview of Carlos Bringuier, New Orleans, June 7, 1999.

87. McMillan, p. 431.

88. Interview of Carlos Bringuier, May 5, 1993.

89. WC, Johnson exhibit #4A, Vol. XX, p. 265.

90. McMillan, p. 444.

91. Weisberg, pp. 154–155; Adolfo Merino, "The Charge," UPI, September 2, 1964; Rocca testimony before Church Committee, February 15, 1976.

92. A good bio of Dunlap and his Staff D association is located at the Web site for Arlington National Cemetery: http://www.arlingtoncemetery.net/jedunlap.htm; interview of Edward Jay Epstein, March 12, 2008.

93. Confirmation of Dunlap's role came from the KGB archives pilfered by Vasili Mitrokhin in 1996 (see Andrew, p. 344); also Epstein, *Deception*, pp. 173–175.

94. Edward Jay Epstein interview of Angleton, Epstein's Web site: edwardjayepstein.com.

95. Interview of Col. John "Jack" Frost, March 27, 2008.

96. Peter Wronski interview of Golovachev in the journal *The Third Decade*, Vol. 8, No. 4, May 1992.

97. RWD: interview of Reynoso, August 2005.

98. *Boston Herald American*, March 31, 1963; McCarthy, pp. 9–19.

Chapter 9: Spies Like Us

1. Morley, p. 85.

2. Ibid.

3. Ibid.

4. Ibid.

5. Ibid., p. 94.

6. Newman, p. 360.

7. Ibid.

8. "The Cuban Youth Tribunal Accuses the U.S. in JFK Killing," from a supplement to the state newspaper *Granma*, August 20, 1978.

9. David Atlee Phillips, HSCA testimony, March 25, 1978.

10. Schlesinger, *RFK*, p. 331.

11. McWhorter, p. 454.

12. Schlesinger, *RFK*, p. 332.

13. McWhorter, p. 454.

14. McMillan, p. 417.

15. Ibid., p. 418.

16. CI Staff, CIA FOIA HH9013.

17. WC, Slawson Memo, April 22, 1964.

18. CIA 559-243, 844-888, 385, 807-828, 643-273; WC, p. 305.

19. CIA 201-291531, FOIA 10679.

20. CIA Report on Calderón; April 25, 1965, NARA #104-10408-10144.

21. Ray Rocca, Church Committee interview, March 15, 1976; CIA review of Oswald file, May 23, 1975, p. 19.

22. Gaeton Fonzi to G. Robert Blakey, memo (telephone interview of Álvaro Proenza), April 14, 1978; Elizabeth Mora, testimony, in "FBI LEGAT Mexico City to Director," January 24, 1964.

23. Interview of Jeremy Gunn, September 8, 2003.

24. CIA Memo: Mexico City to HQ, #5448, July 20, 1963.

25. Anne Goodpasture, "History of the Mexico City Station," internal CIA document, November 16, 1978, p. 234.

26. Ibid., p. 225.

27. For example, see: interview of Cuban ambassador to Morocco, Walterio Carbonell, *Miami Herald*, October 23, 1975; CIA cable, JM WAVE to Director, November 30, 1963; FBI Report of William Stevens, File #105-655, October 24, 1962.

28. CIA Counterintelligence Chief Ray Rocca's Church Committee interview of Dan Dwyer and Ed Greissing, March 15, 1976; CIA review of Oswald file, May 23, 1975.

29. Interview of Kalugin by ABC News for Peter Jennings, *Beyond Conspiracy*, July 28, 2003.

30. McMillan, pp. 418–419.

31. Ibid.

32. Unpublished Warren Commission Document No. 928, May 6, 1964, memorandum from Richard Helms, deputy director of plans of the CIA, titled "Contacts Between the Oswalds and the Soviet Citizens, June 13, 1962, to November 22, 1963."

33. McMillan, pp. 420–427.

34. Posner, pp. 130–131.

35. M. Scott Malone, PBS *Frontline* interview of Adrian Alba, February 27, 1993, repeated by Alba to coauthor Russo in July 1993 and Gerald Posner in 1994.

36. Baron, *KGB Today,* p. 307.

37. CCR, Book V, p. 78.

38. Morley, pp. 88–89.

39. Interview of James Hosty, September 18, 2007.

40. McMillan, p. 435.

41. As quoted in Leamer, p. 698.

42. McMillan, p. 436.

43. Leamer, pp. 696–698.

44. McWhorter, p. 488.
45. RWD: Reynoso interview, 2005.
46. CD 1203, 21; Rodriguez WC testimony, April 4, 1964.
47. CD 1203, 21; Rodriguez WC testimony, April 4, 1964.
48. WC testimony, Vol. XI, pp. 341–342.
49. Interview of Carlos Bringuier, July 10, 1994.
50. CE 950, 278, 285–286; Hoover to Lee Rankin [Warren Commission attorney], letter regarding Pena passport, July 1, 1964.
51. WC testimony, Vol. XI, pp. 361–362.
52. Califano, p. 124.
53. Califano citing: JCS Memo for the Record, Walter Higgins; "Briefing by Mr. Desmond FitzGerald on CIA Cuban Operations and Planning," JFK Collection, JCS Papers, J-3, #29, 202-10001-10028; NARA.
54. Walter Higgins, Memo for the Record: "Briefing by Mr. Desmond FitzGerald on CIA Cuban Operations and Planning," JFK Collection, JCS Papers, J-3, #29, 202-10001-10028; NARA.
55. Califano, p. 124.
56. RWD: interview of "Oscar Marino," August 21, 2005.
57. CCR, Book V, p. 79.
58. AP and *New Orleans Times-Picayune*, September 9, 1963; Schorr, p. 165.
59. Coordinator of Cuban Affairs to the Interdepartmental Coordinating Committee of Cuban Affairs, Memorandum, September 27, 1963, Subject: Contingency Paper Assignments re Possible Retaliatory Actions by Castro Government, *in* CCR, Book V, p. 16.
60. RWD: interview of Pablo Zepeda, 2005.
61. RWD: interview of Rolando Cubela, 2005.
62. Interview of Sam Halpern, August 25, 2003.
63. McMillan, pp. 451–452.
64. Ibid., p. 411.
65. Ibid., pp. 409–411.
66. Ibid., pp. 412–415.
67. Jamie Glazov, "Programmed to Kill," *Front Page* magazine interview of Ion Mihai Pacepa, October 2, 2007.
68. McMillan, p. 447.
69. Ibid., pp. 447–448.
70. Ibid., pp. 460–461.

Chapter 10: A Pawn in Their Game

1. WC, testimony of Pamela Mumford, Vol. XI, p. 217.
2. WC, affidavit of passengers John Bryan and Meryl McFarland, Vol. XI, p. 214.
3. FBI interview of Patricia Winston, December 18, 1963.

4. WC, testimony of Pamela Mumford, Vol. XI, p. 218.

5. WC, Coleman-Slawson Report of Mexico City Trip, April 22, 1964.

6. CD 1256; CE 2450; CE 3074; CD 1243; CIA 538-801A; FBI 105-82555-4809, 4450, 4478, 4405, 4640 (NARA).

7. WC, Coleman-Slawson Report of Mexico City Trip, April 22, 1964.

8. WC, p. 735.

9. WC, Coleman-Slawson Report of Mexico City Trip, April 22, 1964.

10. Epstein, *Assassination Chronicles*, p. 594; author interview of Epstein, March 11, 2008. Although Epstein could not recall the source of the Walker photo information, he is certain of its accuracy, since every line of the book was sourced for his publisher. He believes that Marina mentioned it in one of her numerous FBI or Secret Service interviews.

11. FL: WWLHO: interview of Silvia Durán, May 8, 1993.

12. FL: WWLHO: interview of Mrs. Eusebio Azcue, May 8, 1993.

13. Nechiporenko, p. 70.

14. FL: WWLHO: interview of Silvia Durán, May 8, 1993.

15. HSCA, Vol. III, pp. 106–107; JFK Document 014975, interview of employees of the Cuban consulate in Mexico City, p. 421.

16. RWD: Contreras interviews in August 2005.

17. Nechiporenko, p. 78.

18. Ibid., p. 77.

19. Ibid., p. 80.

20. SAC New York to Director, FBI AirTel, June 12, 1964 (released on March 30, 1995).

21. Schorr, p. 177. (The Clark story was ghostwritten by Nina Gadd.)

22. Ibid.

23. HSCA testimony of Boris Tarasoff, April 12, 1978.

24. HSCA Mexico City Report, p. 125; Winston Scott, *Foul Foe,* unpublished manuscript, p. 273 (NARA).

25. HSCA Mexico City Report, p. 125.

26. David Atlee Phillips to deputy director of operations, recommendation, June 21, 1973.

27. Newman, p. 418.

28. Morley, p. 184.

29. Interviews of Coleman and Slawson, 2003.

30. Interview of Jim Hosty, October 12, 2007. Hosty was told of it by DeGuire in 1976.

31. Ed Lopez to Fonzi. Other CIA personnel who have claimed to have seen or heard of that photo are: Phillip Agee, Daniel Stanley Watson, Joseph Piccolo, Joseph B. Smith, and Daniel Niescuir.

32. Morley, p. 181.

33. Miami Station Chief Ted Shackley, Outside Contact Report with HSCA Counsel Blakey and Fonzi [undated], *in* Fonzi, p. 360.

34. CE 2121; RWD: interview of Gutiérrez's granddaughter, 2005.

35. MIAMI SAC to Director, FBI Teletype, January 4, 1964. The first source was the exiled Cuban newspaperman Dr. Eduardo Borrell Navarros.

36. RWD: interview of Contreras, 2005.

37. Police officer Charles Thomas, memo, December 10, 1965.

38. HSCA Mexico City Report, pp. 217–218.

39. Ibid., p. 252.

40. Police officer Charles Thomas, memo, December 10, 1965.

41. RWD: interview of Paz, 2005.

42. Gunn ARRB deposition of Anne Goodpasture, December 15, 1995 (NARA).

43. Hartman HSCA Security classified testimony, October 10, 1978; also Horton memo to Michelle Seguin, Assassination Records Review Board, May 16, 1996 (NARA).

44. Some, such as Fabian Escalante and, most recently, author Vincent Bugliosi, derisively dismiss the very concept of a "red-haired black." But Escalante knows better, and Bugliosi should. Cuba is a genetic melting pot where the Creole-Irish-African mix occasionally produces a recessive trait of dark skin and red hair in some individuals referred to colloquially as "high yellows." (A quick Google search locates numerous references to redheaded blacks from the Caribbean.) When Cuban-born CIA agent Barney Hidalgo was interviewed by the HSCA, he said, "Of course there are redheaded Cubans." (HSCA Security classified testimony, August 10, 1978, p. 28.) CIA contractor Gerry Hemming saw many high yellows as well when he soldiered in Cuba in the late fifties. (Hemming interview, January 31, 2006.) In 1961, gangster Johnny Rosselli passed poison pills, intended to be slipped to Fidel, to a reddish-haired Afro-Cuban by the name of Rafael "Macho" Gener in the Boom Boom Room of Miami Beach's Fountainebleau Hotel.

On page 732 of his 2007 *Reclaiming History* CD-ROM, Bugliosi, as only he can, takes a sarcastic swipe at *Rendezvous with Death* filmmaker Willi Huismann, saying, "Huismann also isn't troubled by the fact that black men don't have red hair." Although one could explain Bugliosi's ignorance by assuming that the above references had eluded his prodigious research skills, how does one explain his seeming ignorance of one Malcolm Little, aka "Malcolm X," a well-known naturally red-haired black, who grew up with the nickname "Detroit Red"?

As for Escalante's denials, the reader can draw his own conclusion about why he might make a statement that has elicited laughs from every Cuban who has heard it.

45. RWD: interview of Antonio, 2005.

46. RWD: interview of Oscar Marino, 2005.

47. Thomas, p. 269.

48. Beschloss, *Crisis Years,* p. 654.

49. CCIR, p. 173.

50. José Alemán, Church Committee interview by Andy Purdy, March 10, 1977; Alemán, HSCA testimony, September 27, 1978.

51. Letter from the FBI to the Warren Commission, dated June 29, 1964, with attached report of interviews of Mr. and Mrs. Juan M. de Cuba (CD 1187), CE 2459, WC Vol. XXV, pp. 2–3, CE 2460, WC Vol. XXV, p. 6; FBI report, June 11, 1964, of interview of Eulalio Rodríguez-Chávez (CD 1166), CE 2456, WC Vol. XXV, p. 3; CE 2532, re: Oswald's Mexico City trip, p. 9; CE 2121, pp. 61, 76.

Chapter 11: Runaway Train

1. Juan Felaifel, interview on "ZR/RIFLE," November 19, 1993.
2. McMillan, pp. 470–471.
3. Ibid., pp. 473–474.
4. FL: WWLHO: interview of Jim Hosty, June 22, 1993.
5. Bugliosi, p. 770.
6. McMillan, p. 474.
7. Ibid., p. 476.
8. CE 2120, 2445, 2564.
9. Ibid., McMillan, p. 476.
10. Ibid., p. 485.
11. Ibid.
12. FBI report of Heitman to Secret Service (Dallas), April 29, 1964 (NARA).
13. Interview of Harry Williams, December 22, 1993.
14. White House communiqué to Ambassador Lodge at American embassy, Saigon, as quoted in Reeves, p. 617.
15. Reeves, p. 641.
16. Thomas, p. 270.
17. Beschloss, *Crisis Years,* p. 654.
18. Interview of Col. Howard Burris, June 2, 1999.
19. Ibid.
20. Ibid.
21. Reeves, p. 641.
22. Ibid., p. 642.
23. Ibid., pp. 642–643.
24. Ibid., pp. 643–644.
25. Manchester, p. 1216.
26. Reeves, p. 650.
27. Ibid., p. 651.
28. McMillan, pp. 494–495; author interviews with Jim Hosty, June 1993.
29. Senate Intelligence Committee, Performance of Intelligence Agencies, "Appendix B: Hearings on FBI Oversight before House Subcommittee on Civil and Constitutional Rights," Sec. 2, Pt. 3, October 21 and December 11–12, 1975.

30. Ramírez Ortiz, as quoted and translated by Willi Huismann, 2005.

31. FL: WWLHO: interview of Hubert Anderson Morrow, June 11, 1993.

32. FBI interview of Cristobal Espinosa Landivar, December 2, 1963; WC W.D. Tyra interview, CD 206, p. 484.

33. FL: WWLHO: interview of Viola Sapp, July 15, 1993.

34. Ramirez Ortiz, as quoted and translated by Willi Huismann, 2005.

35. "Robert G. O'Connor, Memo for the Record," U.S. Army file, National Archives.

36. From the CIA's AM/TRUNK file, summarized in "AM/TRUNK Chronology dispatch."

37. Schlesinger, *RFK*, pp. 606–607.

38. FL: WWLHO: interview of Hugh Slough, June 6, 1993; interview of Jerry Duncan, July 2, 1993.

39. Schlesinger, *RFK*, p. 607.

40. Interview of Col. Howard Burris, June 2, 1999.

41. Ibid.

42. Interview of Horace Busby, October 7, 1993.

43. Interview of Marty Underwood, May 10, 1993.

44. Interview of Col. John "Jack" Frost, March 27, 2008.

45. Interviews of Marty Underwood, 1994.

46. Barry Boesch, "Jack Ruby: Obsessions and Contradictions," *Dallas Morning News*, JFK Memorial edition, 1983.

47. Interview of Wally Weston, June 12, 1993.

48. WC, Eva Grant testimony, Vol. XIV, pp. 469, 484.

49. Interview of Joe Cody, June 12, 1993.

50. Garry Wills and Ovid Demaris, "You All Know Me! I'm Jack Ruby!" *Esquire*, May 1967.

51. Ibid.

52. McMillan, pp. 521–523.

53. Nechiporenko, p. 99.

54. McMillan, pp. 521–526.

55. Hinckle and Turner, 251.

56. Interview of Buell Frazier, February 16, 1987.

Chapter 12: Desolation Row

1. Beschloss, *Crisis Years*, p. 672.

2. CD 205, FBI interview of Roy Truly, December 18, 1963; after this interview, hairs on the jacket were matched to Oswald. Marina also recalled Oswald's blue jacket. *See* Myers, pp. 278–281.

3. Schlesinger, *RFK*, p. 655.

4. Beschloss, *Crisis Years*, p. 673.

5. Ibid., p. 674.

6. Ibid., p. 676.

7. CIA intercept transcript, November 22, 1963; CIA "blind memo," May 7, 1964.

8. CIA intercept transcript, November 22, 1963; CIA "blind memo," May 7, 1964.

9. HSCA interview of Silvia Durán de Tirado, June 6, 1978.

10. CIA debrief of AM/MUG-1 (LAHERA), May 7, 1964.

11. Ibid.

12. HSCA memo from Fonzi to Blakey, April 14, 1978.

13. Interview of Church Committee investigator James Johnston, December 27, 1993; *Boston Globe*, March 31, 1993; Burke, pp. 44–45, 61, 128; Russo and Hersh interview of Ted Kennedy aide Rick Burke, January 29, 1997.

14. Beschloss, *Crisis Years*, pp. 676–677.

15. HSCA interview of Brigadier General Godfrey McHugh, May 11, 1978.

16. Beschloss, *Crisis Years*, p. 678.

17. Jean Daniel, "When Castro Heard the News," *New Republic*, December 7, 1963, pp. 7–9.

18. Interview with Jack Tatum, June 21, 1993.

19. CIA intercept transcript, November 22, 1963; CIA "blind memo," May 7, 1964.

20. CIA wiretap of Calderón, in NARA audiovisual department.

21. CIA "Review of Allegations of Castro Cuban Involvement in the John F. Kennedy Assassination," April 15, 1975 (#104-10088-10035; NARA).

22. Roberta Greene, recorded interview of Walter Sheridan, June 12, 1970, RFK Oral History program, as quoted in Schlesinger, *RFK*, p. 616.

23. David Emerson Gumaer, "Clenched Fist," *American Opinion*, January 22, 1971, p. 15.

24. Beschloss, *Crisis Years*, p. 674.

25. Michael Dorman, "Conspiracy Revisited," *Newsday*, August 17, 1999.

26. Ibid.

27. Beschloss, *Crisis Years*, pp. 677–678.

28. Michael Dorman, "Conspiracy Revisited," *Newsday*, August 17, 1999.

29. Interview with Louis Gaudin, January 20, 1994; FBI Dallas Field Office File #62-109060, 4755, March 10, 1967.

30. Interview with Merritt Gobel, January 19, 1994.

31. CIA Headquarters to Mexico Station, cable, December 1, 1963; cited in CCR, Book V, pp. 60–61, and fn. 68. Also, CIA Dispatch (routing classified), January 31, 1964.

32. Interview with Jim Hosty, June 22, 1993 (*Frontline*).

33. Barry Boesch, "Jack Ruby: Obsessions and Contradictions," *Dallas Morning News*, JFK Memorial edition, 1983.

34. Interview with Jim Hosty, June 22, 1993 (*Frontline*).

35. Heitman, pp. 19–20.

36. Janos testimony to Church Committee, October 14, 1975; Senate Select Committee on Intelligence, Box 337, Folder 2 (NARA).

37. RWD; author interview of Alexander Haig, 2005.

38. HSCA Outside Contact Reports with Capt. John Stover, November 28, 1978, May 11, 1978.

39. Schlesinger, *RFK,* pp. 610–611.

Chapter 13: Cannons in the Rain

1. What makes this erasure suspicious is that all the other recordings that surround this call on the cassette are intact and clear. The government contractor who duplicates tapes for the public, The Cutting Corp., concluded that the erasure was intentional (NARA RIF #180-10110-10484). LBJ archivists Regina Greenwell and Claudia Anderson tried to dissuade researcher Rex Bradford from acquiring the tape. When he did, he discovered the gap.

2. RWD: interview of Elenita Paz, Mexico City, 2005; HSCA, "Mexico City Report," p. 213.

3. HSCA Cornwell interview of Silvia Durán de Tirado, June 6, 1979 (NARA).

4. RWD: interview of Joseph Califano; Califano, p. 126.

5. CIA Mexico City Report, pp. 219–220.

6. Posner, pp. 374–375.

7. Ibid., p. 374.

8. Interview of Lonnie Hudkins, June 19, 1993.

9. Summers, p. 547, n. 35; Davison, p. 254.

10. Molton and Russo interview with Jim Leavelle, Dallas, June 9, 1999.

11. Wills and Demaris, p. 72.

12. NARA #124-10230-10457, FBI, November 28, 1963.

13. According to CIA document #104-10015-10244 (NARA), a 7-page report on Alvarado went from Winston M. Scott to Director McCone at CIA, dated November 29, 1963.

14. HSCA interview of Silvia Durán de Tirado, June 6, 1978.

15. CIA Report, May 26, 1967, "The Report of [Deleted]."

16. RWD: interview of Antonio, 2005.

17. Ibid.

18. Win Scott measured his words when questioned by a Warren Commission staff lawyer who came to Mexi five months later: "In my professional opinion, there was probably not a foreign conspiracy connected with Mexico." He actually went beyond the potential for Castro involvement, but also to the possibility that the Soviets may have had a connection to it.

19. FL: WWLHO. Interview with Thomas Mann, May 12, 1993.

20. CIA Mexico City Chronology, 38, citing MEXI 7156 (NARA).

21. Morley, pp. 229–230.

22. Interview of James Hosty, September 18, 2007.

23. *Washington Post*, November 14, 1993.

24. Russell, p. 454.

25. Interview of Wannall, June 18, 2003.

26. Memo for the Record by Earle Wheeler, "Meeting with the President on Cuba, Dec. 19, 1963"; NARA JFK Collection, JCS Papers, #22-10002-10010.

27. Califano, p. 126.

28. Don Bohning, "Cuban army seen as key to ouster of Castro; Bay of Pigs vet speaks up," *Miami Herald*, April 16, 2000; Bohning, pp. 244–245.

29. Bohning, p. 197.

30. White House Memo, Dungan to Katzenbach, December 31, 1963 (NARA).

Chapter 14: The Games People Play

1. Manchester, *Glory and the Dream*, p. 1237.

2. Ibid.

3. Seymour Hersh interview of Jules Draznin, April 17, 1994.

4. Interview of Jim Leavelle, June 9, 1999.

5. Interview of Al Maddox, June 12, 1993 (*Frontline*).

6. Interview of Vincent Drain, October 18, 1993.

7. David and David, p. 215.

8. Interview of Col. Jack Frost, March 27, 2008.

9. Nosenko-Angleton-Golitsyn background from: David Wise, *Molehunt*; Edward Epstein, *Deception*; Tennent Bagley, *Spy Wars*; Tom Mangold, *Cold Warrior*; and Joseph Trento, *The Secret History of the CIA*.

10. Andrew and Mitrokhin, p. 397.

11. Ibid., pp. 91, 177.

12. Interview of Lt. Gen. Ion Mihai Pacepa in Jamie Glazov, "Programmed to Kill (Lee Harvey Oswald, the Soviet KGB and the Kennedy Assassination)," *Front Page*, October 3, 2007.

13. Andrew and Mitrokhin, pp. 226–227.

14. Ibid., p. 228.

15. Ibid.

16. Ibid., pp. 228–229.

17. Piereson, p. 126.

18. The list was given to author Ed Epstein in 1976. It is included in his book *Deception*, pp. 280–290.

19. Trento, p. 267.

20. CIA interviews of Lahera, August 18, 1964; February 5, 1965 (NARA).

21. SAC New York to Director, FBI AirTel, June 12, 1964; (released March 30, 1995).

22. Lahera material condensed from HSCA's massive AMMUG file at NARA; see especially the debriefs of May 1964.

23. Shesol, pp. 204–205.

24. Ibid., p. 220.

25. Schlesinger, *RFK*, pp. 666–670.

26. Ibid., p. 614.

27. Confidential interview, April 4, 2008.

28. John Newman, interview of June Cobb Sharp, March 4 and March 17, 1995, cited in Newman, p. 380.

29. Newman, p. 380.

30. NARA document #104-10016-10031; PS#72-109.

31. Memo, Direccion Federal de Seguridad, November 16, 1964, cited in Morley, p. 337.

32. Talbot, p. 301.

33. Newman, p. 382.

34. "Willard Curtis," Memo for files, November 25, 1964.

35. Manchester, *Glory and the Dream*, p. 1238.

36. Lyndon Johnson to Mike Mansfield, phone conversation, September 28, 1964, LBJ Library; Beschloss, *Taking Charge*, p. 561.

37. Weidenfield, p. 350.

38. Shesol, p. 156.

39. Ibid., p. 260.

40. Ibid., pp. 275–276.

41. Ibid., p. 279.

42. Schlesinger, *RFK*, p. 749, citing William vanden Heuvel, "Notes on RFK South American Trip (2)," 8–12, vanden Heuvel Papers; *New York Times*, November 14, 1965.

43. vanden Heuvel and Gwirtzman, pp. 166–167.

44. Jean Stein, recorded interview of John Seigenthaler, May 15, 1970, in Plimpton, p. 27.

45. Schlesinger, *RFK*, pp. 694–698.

46. vanden Heuvel and Gwirtzman, p. 175.

47. Shesol, p. 280.

Chapter 15: Sympathy for the Devil

1. *Time Machine: The CIA*, Israel Behar interview for this BBC/US film production, broadcast in U.S. on November 13, 1992.

2. Menier, *Protecting and Promoting Fidel*, p. 49.

3. Bohning, pp. 174–175.

4. Ibid., p. 227.

5. Ibid.

6. Ibid., pp. 227–228.

7. Interview of CIA's Ted Shackley, December 12, 1997.

8. Noted in Church Committee review of AM/LASH file at CIA: Johnston to Senator Hart, Memorandum, January 27, 1976.

9. Bohning, p. 235; and Powers, p. 152.

10. From an account by Jose Vilasuso, La Cabaña lawyer under Che Guevara.

11. From CIA document RIF 104-10102-10221 (NARA).

12. "The Cuban Youth Tribunal Accuses the U.S. in JFK Killing," supplement to the state newspaper *Granma*, August 20, 1978.

13. Newfield, p. 23.

14. Shesol, p. 366.

15. Ramsey Clark to LBJ, phone conversation, February 22, 1967, LBJ Library.

16. Schaap, pp. 17–24.

17. Schlesinger, *RFK*, pp. 771–772.

18. Kirkwood, pp. 540–541.

19. Phelan, pp. 168–169.

20. *Dallas Times-Herald*, April 4, 1967.

21. Interview of Sergio Arcacha Smith, Miami, June 3, 1999.

22. Interview of Layton Martens, February 6, 1994; Brener, p. 138.

23. Edward J. Epstein, "Disinformation," *Commentary*, July 1982.

24. Ibid.

25. Jamie Glazov, interview of Lt. Gen. Ion Mihai Pacepa in "Programmed to Kill Lee Harvey Oswald, the Soviet KGB and the Kennedy Assassination," *Front Page*, October 3, 2007.

26. Interview of former *New Orleans Times-Picayune* reporter Rosemary James, June 8, 1999.

27. Steve Dorrill, "Accepting Communist Propaganda at Face Value / Permindex: The International Trade in Disinformation," *Lobster: The Journal of Parapolitics, Intelligence and State Research*, #3, 1983.

28. Ibid.

29. Ibid.

30. Interview of former *New Orleans Times-Picayune* reporter Rosemary James, June 8, 1999.

31. E-mail from Patricia Lambert, April 27, 2008. Lambert authored the seminal book on the Garrison charade, *False Witness* (1998), and is currently working on a biography of Clay Shaw.

32. News release from weekly *Correo de la Tarde*, Buenos Aires 4 (AFP), pp. 13–14.

33. Ibid.

34. Reports of FBI's Sam Papich to Martin Underwood, who gave them to the authors.

35. Martin Underwood, Uruguay notes, April 11, 1967, p. 5.

36. Helms letter first noted in HSCA Mexico City Report, p. 237; see fns. 1032 and 1033 for identification of Helms ("Director"). The "Lund" letter obtained under FOIA by Scott's son, Michael. Discussed in detail in Morley, p. 245.

37. Kearns, p. 32.

Chapter 16: Ain't No Man Righteous, No Not One

1. Kearns, pp. 320–321.

2. Schlesinger, *RFK*, p. 840.

3. Plimpton, pp. 223–224; Arthur Schlesinger interview of Lowenstein, February 26, 1973; Newfield, p. 204.

4. Interview of Marty Underwood, June 29, 1994.

5. Morley, p. 246.

6. Notes of conversation between Marty Underwood and Win Scott, Mexico City, Mexico, March 1968, p. 3, paragraph 3.

7. Ibid., p. 4, paragraph 4.

8. RWD: interview, 2005.

9. Interviews with Marty Underwood, June 10, 1993, and June 29, 1994.

10. L. Johnson, p. 425.

11. Kearns, p. 342.

12. Thomas, pp. 358–359; Schlesinger, *RFK*, pp. 846–847.

13. Matthiessen, p. 176.

14. Wofford, p. 426.

15. Shesol, p. 435.

16. Ibid., pp. 435–436.

17. Schlesinger, *RFK*, pp. 873–875.

18. Remarks by Senator Robert F. Kennedy on the death of the Reverend Martin Luther King, rally in Indianapolis, Indiana, April 4, 1968.

19. *See* Truth Recovery Archive on Cuba, www.CubaArchive.org.

20. Remarks by President Raúl Castro Ruz before the National Assembly of People's Power, February 24, 2008.

21. Esteban Israel, "Blogging from Havana, Secretly," Reuters, October 10, 2007.

22. Ibid.

23. David and David, p. 3.

Afterword

1. Piereson, p. 84.

Bibliography

Books and Unpublished Research Papers

Agee, Philip. *Dirty Work: The CIA in Western Europe*. Secaucus, N.J.: Lyle Stuart, 1978.

Andrew, Christopher, and Vasili Mitrokhin. *The Sword and the Shield: The Mitrokhin Archive and the Secret History of the KGB*. New York: Basic Books, 1999.

Argote-Freyre, Frank. *Fulgencio Batista: From Revolutionary to Strongman*. Rutgers: Rutgers University Press, 2006.

Bagley, Tennent H. *Spy Wars: Moles, Mysteries, and Deadly Games*. New Haven: Yale University Press, 2007.

Barron, John. *The KGB Today: The Hidden Hand*. New York: Reader's Digest Press, 1983.

———. *KGB: The Secret Work of Soviet Secret Agents*. New York: Bantam Books, 1974.

Bennett, Richard M. *Espionage: An Encyclopedia of Spies and Secrets*. London: Virgin Books, 2002.

Beschloss, Michael. *The Crisis Years: Kennedy and Khrushchev, 1960–1963*. New York: HarperCollins, 1991.

———. *Taking Charge: The Johnson White House Tapes 1963–1964*. New York: Simon & Schuster, 1997.

Bissell, Richard M. *Reflections of a Cold Warrior*. New Haven: Yale University Press, 1996.

Blakey, G. Robert, and Richard Billings. *The Plot to Kill the President*. New York: Times Books, 1981.

Bohning, Don. *The Castro Obsession: U.S. Covert Operations Against Cuba, 1959–1965*. Washington: Potomac Books, 2005.

Bonachea, Ramon L., and Marta San Martin. *The Cuban Insurrection, 1952–1959*. New Brunswick: Transaction Books, 1974.

Bourne, Peter G. *Fidel: A Biography of Fidel Castro*. New York: Dodd, Mead, 1986.

Bravo, Marcos. *La Orta Cara del Che*. Bogotá: Editorial Solar, 2004.

Brener, Milton E. *The Garrison Case: A Study in the Abuse of Power*. New York: Potter, 1969.

Breuer, William B. *Vendetta!: Castro and the Kennedy Brothers*. New York: John Wiley, 1997.

Bugliosi, Vincent. *Reclaiming History: The Assassination of President John F. Kennedy*. New York: Norton, 2007.

Burke, Richard E. *The Senator: My Twelve Years with Ted Kennedy*. New York: St. Martin's Press, 1992.

Califano, Joseph A. *Inside: A Public and Private Life*. New York: Public Affairs, 2004.

Castañeda, Jorge G. *Compañero: The Life and Death of Che Guevara*. New York: Knopf Publishing Group, 1997.

Clarke, James W. *American Assassins: The Darker Side of Politics*. Princeton: Princeton University Press, 1982.

Collier, Peter, and David Horowitz. *The Kennedys: An American Drama*. New York: Warner Books, 1985.

Copeland, Miles. *The Game of Nations: The Amorality of Power Politics*. New York: Simon & Schuster, 1970.

Cornwell, John. *Hitler's Pope: The Secret History of Pius XII*. New York: Viking, 1999.

Corson, William R., and Robert T. Crowley. *The New KGB, Engine of Soviet Power*. New York: Quill, 1986.

Courtois, Stéphane, et al. *The Black Book of Communism: Crimes, Terror, Repression*. Cambridge: Harvard University Press, 1999.

Cox, Harvey. *Fidel and Religion: Castro Talks on Revolution and Religion with Frei Betto*. New York: Simon & Schuster, 1987.

Daniel, Clifton. *Lords, Ladies, and Gentlemen: A Memoir*. New York: Arbor House, 1984.

David, Lester, and Irene David. *Bobby Kennedy: The Making of a Folk Hero*. New York: Dodd, Mead, 1986.

Davis, Mike. *Planet of Slums*. New York: Verso, 2006.

Davison, Jean. *Oswald's Game*. New York: W.W. Norton, 1983.

Demaris, Ovid. *The Last Mafioso: The Treacherous World of Jimmy Fratianno*. New York: Times Books, 1981.

Draper, Theodore. *Castro's Revolution: Myths and Realities*. New York: Praeger, 1962.

Epstein, Edward Jay. *Deception: The Invisible War Between the KGB and the CIA*. New York: Simon & Schuster, 1989.

———. *Legend: The Secret World of Lee Harvey Oswald*. New York: Reader's Digest Press, 1978.

———. *The Assassination Chronicles*. New York: Carroll & Graf, 1992.

Escalante, Fabian. *Executive Action: 634 Ways to Kill Fidel Castro*. New York: Ocean Press, 2006.

———. *JFK: The Cuba Files*. New York: Ocean Press, 2006.

Falk, Pamela S. *Cuban Foreign Policy: Caribbean Tempest*. Lexington, Mass.: Lexington Books, 1986.

Famerée, Joseph. *Vatican II*, Vol. 3, "Bishops and Dioceses." Maryknoll, NY: Orbis, 2000.

Fernández, Alina. *Castro's Daughter: An Exile's Memoir of Cuba*. New York: St. Martin's Press, 1998.

Fontova, Humberto E. *Fidel: Hollywood's Favorite Tyrant*. Washington: Regnery, 2005.

————. *Exposing the Real Che Guevara*. New York: Sentinel, 2007.

Franklin, Jane. *Cuba and the United States: A Chronological History*. New York: Ocean Press, 1997.

Franqui, Carlos. *Diary of the Cuban Revolution*. New York: Viking Press, 1980.

————. *Family Portrait with Fidel*. New York: Random House, 1984.

Fuentes, Norberto. *Hemingway in Cuba*. New York: Lyle Stuart, 1984.

Furiati, Claudia. *ZR Rifle:The Plot to Kill Kennedy and Castro*. Melbourne: Ocean Press, 1994.

Fursenko, Aleksandr, and Timothy Naftali. *One Hell of a Gamble: The Secret History of the Cuban Missile Crisis, Khrushchev & Kennedy, 1958–1964*. New York: W. W. Norton, 1997.

Garwood, Darrell. *Under Cover: Thirty-Five Years of CIA Deception*. Stafford, Va.: Dan River Press, 1980.

Geyelin, Philip L. *Lyndon Johnson and the World*. New York: Praeger, 1966.

Geyer, Georgie Anne. *Guerrilla Prince: The Untold Story of Fidel Castro*. Boston: Little, Brown, 1991.

Goodwin, Richard N. *Remembering America: A Voice from the Sixties*. Boston: Little, Brown, 1988.

Gosse, Van. *Where the Boys Are: Cuba, Cold War America and the Making of a New Left*. New York: Verso, 1993.

Hach, Steve (ed. Jennifer Dickey). *Cold War in South Florida: Historic Resource Study*. Atlanta: U.S. Department of the Interior, National Park Service, 2004.

Haig, Alexander M. Jr. *Inner Circles: How America Changed the World*. New York: Warner Books, 1992.

Halperin, Maurice. *The Taming of Fidel Castro*. Berkeley: University of California Press, 1981.

Hamilton, Nigel. *JFK: Reckless Youth*. New York: Random House, 1992.

Hebblethwaite, Peter. *Paul VI, The First Modern Pope*. New York: Paulist Press, 1993.

Heitman, Wallace. *Wife of the Accused Assassin*. Victoria, B.C.: Trafford, 2006.

Hemingway, Mary. *How It Was*. New York: Knopf, 1976.

Hersh, Seymour. *The Dark Side of Camelot*. New York: Little, Brown, 1997.

Hinckle, Warren, and William Turner. *Deadly Secrets: The CIA-Mafia War Against Castro and the Assassination of JFK*. New York: Thunder's Mouth Press, 1992.

Hoffa, James. *Hoffa, The Real Story*. New York: Stein and Day, 1975.

Hosty, James P. *Assignment Oswald*. New York: Arcade, 1996.

Huismann, Wilfried. *Rendezvous Mit Dem Tod*. Zurich: Pendo, 2007.

Jennings, Phillip. *Goodbye Mexico*. New York: Forge Books, 2007.

Johnson, Haynes. *The Bay of Pigs*. New York: Dell, 1964.

Johnson, Lyndon B. *The Vantage Point: Perspectives of the President, 1963–1969*. New York: Holt, Rinehart & Winston, 1971.

Johnson, William O. *Robert Kennedy at Forty: A Biography of the New York Senator*. New York: Norton, 1965.

Kasarda, John D., and Allan M. Parnell (eds.). *Third World Cities: Problems, Policies, and Prospects*. Newbury Park, Calif.: Sage, 1993.

Kearns, Doris. *Lyndon Johnson and the American Dream*. New York: Harper & Row, 1976.

Kennedy, John F. *The Strategy of Peace*. New York: Harper & Bros., 1960.

Kennedy, Robert F. *Thirteen Days: A Memoir of the Cuban Missile Crisis*. New York: New American Library, 1969.

Kessler, Ronald. *The Sins of the Father: Joseph P. Kennedy and the Dynasty He Founded*. New York: Warner Books, 1996.

———. *Inside the CIA*. New York: Pocket Books, 1992.

Khrushchev, Nikita S. *Khrushchev Remembers: The Last Testament*. Boston: Little, Brown, 1974.

Kirkpatrick, Lyman B. *The Real CIA*. New York: Macmillan, 1968.

Kirkwood, James. *American Grotesque: An Account of the Clay Shaw–Jim Garrison Kennedy Assassination Trial in New Orleans*. New York: Harper Perennial, 1992.

Kluckhohn, Frank L. *Lyndon's Legacy: A Candid Look at the President's Policy-Makers*. New York: Devon-Adair, 1964.

Kotz, Nick. *Let Them Eat Promises: The Politics of Hunger in America*. Englewood Cliffs, N.J.: Prentice-Hall, 1969.

Latell, Brian. *After Fidel: Raul Castro and the Future of Cuba's Revolution*. New York: Palgrave Macmillan, 2005.

Leamer, Laurence. *The Kennedy Men*. New York: William Morrow, 2001.

Lennon, John. *The Compleat Beatles, Volume One*. London: Delilah Communications/ATV Music Publications, 1981.

Leonov, Nikolai. *Likholete*. Moscow: Mezhdunar, 1994.

Livingstone, Harrison Edward. *High Treason II*. New York: Carroll & Graf, 1992.

Mailer, Norman. *Oswald's Tale: An American Mystery*. New York: Random House, 1995.

Manchester, William. *The Glory and the Dream: A Narrative History of America, 1932–1972*. Boston: Little, Brown, 1974.

———. *The Death of a President*. New York: Harper & Row, 1967.

Mangold, Tom. *Cold Warrior: James Jesus Angleton*. New York: Simon & Schuster, 1991.

Martin, David. *Wilderness of Mirrors*. New York: Harper & Row, 1980.

Martin, Ralph G. *Seeds of Destruction: Joe Kennedy and His Sons*. New York: G.P. Putnam's Sons, 1995.

———. *A Hero for Our Time: An Intimate Story of the Kennedy Years*. New York: Macmillan, 1983.

Matthiessen, Peter. *Sal Si Puedes: Cesar Chavez and the New American Revolution*. New York: Random House, 1969.

May, Ernest R., and Phillip D. Zelikow. *The Kennedy Tapes: Inside the White House During the Cuban Missile Crisis*. New York: Norton, 2002.

McCarthy, Edward V. *Working Press*. New York: Vantage, 1992.

McGehee, Ralph. *Deadly Deceits: My 25 Years in the CIA*. New York: Ocean Press, 1999.

McMillan, Priscilla Johnson. *Marina and Lee*. New York: Harper & Row, 1977.

McWhorter, Diane. *Carry Me Home: Birmingham, Alabama, the Climactic Battle of the Civil Rights Revolution*. New York: Simon & Schuster, 2002.

Meier, August, and Elliot Rudwick. *CORE: A Study in the Civil Rights Movement, 1942–1968*. Urbana: University of Illinois Press, 1975.

Menier, Juan Antonio Rodríguez. *The Way It Happened*. Bloomington: Author House, 2006.

———. Unpublished manuscript, *Protecting and Promoting Fidel: Inside Cuba's Interior Ministry*.

Morley, Jefferson. *Our Man in Mexico: Winston Scott and the Hidden History of the CIA*. Lawrence: University of Kansas Press, 2008.

Myers, Dale K. *With Malice: Lee Harvey Oswald and the Murder of Officer J.D. Tippit*. Milford, Mich.: Oak Cliff Press, 1998.

Nechiporenko, Oleg. *Passport to Assassination*. New York: Birch Lane Press, 1993.

Newfield, Jack. *Robert Kennedy: A Memoir*. New York: Dutton, 1969.

Newman, John. *Oswald and the CIA*. New York: Carroll & Graf, 1995.

Nietzsche, Friedrich. *On the Genealogy of Morals*. New York: Vintage Books, 1967.

O'Donnell, Kenneth T., and David F. Powers. *Johnny, We Hardly Knew Ye*. Boston: Little, Brown, 1972.

Oppenheimer, Andres. *Castro's Final Hour: An Eyewitness Account of the Disintegration of Castro's Cuba*. New York: Simon & Schuster, 1992.

Persico, Joseph. *Edward R. Murrow: An American Original*. New York: McGraw-Hill, 1988.

Phelan, James. *Scandals, Scamps, and Scoundrels*. New York: Random House, 1982.

Piereson, James. *Camelot and the Cultural Revolution: How the Assassination of John F. Kennedy Shattered American Liberalism*. New York: Encounter Books, 2007.

Plimpton, George (ed.). *American Journey: The Times of Robert Kennedy. (Interviews by Jean Stein.)* New York: Harcourt Brace Jovanovich, 1970.

Polmar, Norman. *Spy Book: The Encyclopedia of Espionage*. New York: Random House, 1998.

Posner, Gerald. *Case Closed: Lee Harvey Oswald and the Assassination of JFK*. New York: Random House, 1993.

Powers, Thomas. *The Man Who Kept the Secrets*. New York: Knopf, 1979.

Prouty, L. Fletcher. *The Secret Team: The CIA and Its Allies in Control of the United States and the World*. Englewood Cliffs, N.J.: Prentice-Hall, 1973.

Ragano, Frank. *Mob Lawyer*. New York: Random House, 1996.

Ramírez Ortiz, Antulio. *Castro's Red Hot Hell*, unpublished (NARA).

Ray, Ellen (ed.). *Dirty Work 2: The CIA in Africa*. Secaucus, N.J.: Lyle Stuart, 1979.

Reeve, Simon. *One Day in September: The Full Story of the 1972 Munich Olympics Massacre*. New York: Arcade, 2000.

Reeves, Richard. *President Kennedy: Profile of Power*. New York: Simon & Schuster, 1993.

Robbins, Carla Anne. *The Cuban Threat*. Philadelphia: ISHI Publications, 1985.

Roberts, Allen. *Robert Francis Kennedy: Biography of a Compulsive Politician*. Brookline Village, Mass.: Branden Press, 1984.

Roemer, William F. *Man Against the Mob*. New York: D.I. Fine, 1989.

Russell, Dick. *The Man Who Knew Too Much*. New York: Carroll & Graf, 1992.

Russo, Gus. *The Outfit: The Role of Chicago's Underworld in the Shaping of Modern America*. New York: Bloomsbury USA, 2002.

Rynne, Xavier (F.X. Murphy). *Vatican Council II*. Orbis, 1968.

Schaap, Dick. *RFK*. New York: New American Library, 1967.

Schlesinger, Arthur. *A Thousand Days: John F. Kennedy in the White House*. Boston: Houghton Mifflin, 1965.

———. *Robert F. Kennedy and His Times*. Boston: Houghton Mifflin, 1978.

Schorr, Daniel. *Clearing the Air*. Boston: Houghton Mifflin, 1977.

Scott, Peter Dale. *Deep Politics and the Death of JFK*. Los Angeles: University of California Press, 1993.

Shackley, Theodore G. (with Richard A. Finney). *Spymaster: My Life in the CIA*. Dulles, Va.: Potomac Books, 2005.

Shesol, Jeff. *Mutual Contempt: Lyndon Johnson, Robert Kennedy, and the Feud That Defined a Decade*. New York: W.W. Norton, 1997.

Shetterly, Aran. *The Americano: Fighting with Castro for Cuba's Freedom*. Chapel Hill, N.C.: Algonquin Books of Chapel Hill, 2007.

Steinfels, Peter. *A People Adrift: The Crisis of the Roman Catholic Church in America*. New York: Simon & Schuster, 2004.

Sterling, Claire. *The Terror Network: The Secret War on International Terrorism*. New York: Reader's Digest Press, 1981.

Stockton, Bayard. *Flawed Patriot: The Rise and Fall of CIA Legend Bill Harvey*. Washington: Potomac Books, 2006.

Suchlicki, Jaime. *Cuba: From Columbus to Castro and Beyond*. Dulles, Virginia: Brassey's, 2002.

Summers, Anthony. *Conspiracy*. New York: Paragon House, 1989.

Szulc, Tad. *Fidel: A Critical Portrait*. London: Hutchinson, 1986.

Talbot, David. *Brothers: The Hidden History of the Kennedy Years*. New York: Free Press, 2007.

Thomas, Evan. *Robert Kennedy: His Life*. New York: Simon & Schuster, 2000.

———. *The Very Best Men*. New York: Simon & Schuster, 1995.

Trento, Joseph. *The Secret History of the CIA*. Roseville, Cal.: Prima, 2001.

Valenti, Jack. *A Very Human President*. New York: W.W. Norton, 1975.

vanden Heuvel, William, and Milton Gwirtzman. *On His Own: Robert Kennedy, 1964–1968*. Garden City: Doubleday, 1970.

Weidenfeld, George. *Remembering My Good Friends*. London: HarperCollins, 1995.

Weisberg, Harold. *Oswald in New Orleans*. New York: Canyon Books, 1967.

White, Theodore. *The Making of the President 1960*. New York: Atheneum, 1961.

Wills, Garry. *Why I Am a Catholic*. Boston: Houghton Mifflin, 2002.

Wills, Garry, and Ovid Demaris. *Jack Ruby*. New York: New American Library, 1967.

Wise, David. *Molehunt*. New York: Random House, 1992.

Wofford, Harris. *Of Kennedys and Kings: Making Sense of the Sixties*. New York: Farrar, Straus & Giroux, 1980.

Wyden, Peter. *Bay of Pigs: The Untold Story*. New York: Simon & Schuster, 1979.

Miscellaneous Reports

Artime, Judith. *The Golden Boy*. Thesis, September 1996.

Blazquez, Agustin, and James Sutton. *Castro and International Terrorism,* September 16, 2001, ABIP.

de la Cova, Antonio. "Academic Espionage: US Taxpayer Funding of a Pro-Castro Study." The Selous Foundation's Institute for US–Cuba Relations, February 1, 1993.

de Salas-del Valle, Hans. *Fidel Castro on the United States; Selected Statements, 1958–2003*. Institute for Cuban and Cuban-American Studies, Occasional Paper Series, February 2003.

Gumaer, David Emerson. "Clenched Fist: A History of the Communist Salute," reprint from *American Opinion* magazine, January 22, 1971.

Hudson, Rex A. "Coordinating Cuba's Support for Marxist-Leninist Violence in the Americas." The Cuban American National Foundation, 1988.

Lago, Armando. "Cuba: The Human Cost of Social Revolution."

———. *Cuba: Raúl Castro Directly Responsible for 550 Executions* (preliminary draft). Lago's work can be accessed at Maria Werlau's Free Society Project, Inc., at http://www.cubaarchive.org.

Mora, Frank O. "Cuba's Ministry of Interior: The FAR's Fifth Army." *Bulletin of Latin American Research*, Vol. 26, No. 2, pp. 222–237, 2007. National War College, National Defense University, Washington, D.C.

Peraza, Gerardo. Testimony before U.S. Senate, Subcommittee on Security and Terrorism, Committee on the Judiciary: "Hearing on the Role of Cuba in International Terrorism and Subversion; Intelligence Activities of the DGI." February 26, 1982.

Pons, Eugene. *Castro and Terrorism: A Chronology 1959–1967*. Institute for Cuban & Cuban-American Studies, Occasional Paper Series, September 2001.

Valenta, Jiri, and Virginia Valenta. "Soviet Strategies and Policies in the Caribbean Basin." In Howard J. Wiarda and Mark Falcoff (eds.), *The Communist Challenge in the Caribbean and Central America* (Washington: American Enterprise Institute, 1987), p. 79.

Radio Martí Program's interview with Major Florentino Aspillaga Lombard, August 1987.

Hearings before the Senate Judiciary Committee, Subcommittee to Investigate the Administration of the Internal Security Act; 89th Congress, 2nd Session. Especially testimonies of Viola June Cobb, Juan Orta, and executives of the Fair Play for Cuba Committee. U.S. Government Printing Office, 1962.

Investigation of the Assassination of President John F. Kennedy: Performance of the Intelligence Agencies, Final report, Books I-V, Select Committee to Study Government Operations with Respect to Intelligence Activities, 94th Congress, 2nd Session, U.S. Senate. U.S. Government Printing Office, 1976.

Investigation of the Assassination of President John F. Kennedy, Final Report, and Appendix to Hearings Before the Select Committee on Assassinations, U.S. House, 95th Congress, Vols. I–XII. U.S. Government Printing Office, 1979.

Report of the President's Commission on the Assassination of President John F. Kennedy [Warren Commission Report] and 26 volumes of hearings and exhibits. U.S. Government Printing Office, 1964.

United States Information Agency. Radio Martí Program, "The Defection of A MININT Official," Cuba—Quarterly Situation Report, Third Quarter 1987, p. V-13.

U.S. Senate Interim Report of the Select Committee to Study Government Operations with Respect to Intelligence Activities; Alleged Assassination Plots Involving Foreign Leaders. U.S. Government Printing Office, 1975.

U.S. Congress, Senate, Committee on the Judiciary, Internal Security Subcommittee, Hearings, Part 20, Communist Threat to the United States through the Caribbean, October 16, 1969, citing the testimony of DGI defector Orlando Castro Hidalgo.

U.S. Department of State, Bureau of Public Affairs. Cuba's Renewed Support for Violence in Latin America, Special Report No. 90, December 14, 1981.

U.S. Department of State, Foreign Relations of the United States (FRUS), especially 1961–1963.

U.S. Department of the Army. 57-page "Notes on the DGI," March 25, 1973; released under FOIA, March 22, 2002.

U.S. Department of State. Patterns of Global Terrorism: 1985, 1986.

U.S. Department of State. Patterns of Global Terrorism: 1986, October 1987, pp. 1, 3, 24–25.

U.S. Departments of State and Defense. The Soviet-Cuban Connection in Central America and the Caribbean, March 1985.

U.S. Congress, Senate, Committee on the Judiciary, Internal Security Subcommittee. The Tricontinental Conference of African, Asian, and Latin American Peoples, 1966.

U.S. State Department, Patterns of Global Terrorism—2000. Released April 30, 2001. This is an annual report sent to Congress that has been listing Cuba since 1993. See US-Cuba Policy Report, April 30, 2001.

Index

A Note on the Authors

Gus Russo is the author of *Supermob*, *The Outfit*, and *Live by the Sword*. He has worked as an investigative reporter for PBS's *Frontline*, ABC News Special Reports, and Dan Rather's *CBS Reports*, and as a consultant for programs such as *60 Minutes*, *60 Minutes II*, and *Eye to Eye with Connie Chung*. He lives in Baltimore.

Stephen Molton is a novelist, screenwriter, filmmaker, and professor. He adapted Gus Russo's *Live by the Sword* as a miniseries for cable television, and has written screenplays for New Line Cinema and Paramount Pictures, among other companies. For twenty years he served as a creative executive for such networks as Home Box Office, MTV, and Showtime, and since 2007 he has taught in the graduate film program at Columbia University. He and wife, Pamela Galvin, divide their time between New York City and Pioneertown, California.